Lecture Notes in Artificial Intel

Edited by J. G. Carbonell and J. Siekmann

Subseries of Lecture Notes in Computer Science

Boris Konev Frank Wolter (Eds.)

Frontiers of Combining Systems

6th International Symposium, FroCoS 2007
Liverpool, UK, September 10-12, 2007
Proceedings

 Springer

Series Editors

Jaime G. Carbonell, Carnegie Mellon University, Pittsburgh, PA, USA
Jörg Siekmann, University of Saarland, Saarbrücken, Germany

Volume Editors

Boris Konev
Frank Wolter
University of Liverpool
Department of Computer Science
Ashton Building, Liverpool L69 3BX, UK
E-mail: {B.Konev; F.Wolter}@csc.liv.ac.uk

Library of Congress Control Number: 2007933812

CR Subject Classification (1998): I.2.3, F.4.1, F.4

LNCS Sublibrary: SL 7 – Artificial Intelligence

ISSN   0302-9743
ISBN-10   3-540-74620-X Springer Berlin Heidelberg New York
ISBN-13   978-3-540-74620-1 Springer Berlin Heidelberg New York

Springer is a part of Springer Science+Business Media

springer.com

© Springer-Verlag Berlin Heidelberg 2007
Printed in Germany

Typesetting: Camera-ready by author, data conversion by Scientific Publishing Services, Chennai, India
Printed on acid-free paper   SPIN: 12115235   06/3180   5 4 3 2 1 0

Preface

This volume contains the proceedings of the Sixth International Symposium on Frontiers of Combining Systems (FroCoS 2007) held September 10-12, 2007 in Liverpool, UK. Previously, FroCoS was organized in Munich (1996), Amsterdam (1998), Nancy (2000), Santa Margeritha Ligure near Genoa (2002), and Vienna (2005). In 2004 and 2006, FroCoS joined IJCAR, the International Joint Conference on Automated Reasoning. Like its predecessors, FroCoS 2007 offered a forum for the presentation and discussion of research activities on the combination, integration, analysis, modularization and interaction of formally defined systems, with an emphasis on logic-based ones. These issues are important in many areas of computer science, such as logic, computation, program development and verification, artificial intelligence, automated reasoning, constraint solving, declarative programming, and symbolic computation.

There were 31 submissions to FroCoS 2007. Each submission was reviewed by at least three Programme Committee members. After extensive discussion within the Programme Committee, 14 papers were accepted for presentation and publication in this volume. In addition to technical papers, the volume also includes four invited contributions by Sava Krstic (Intel Corporation, USA), Roberto Sebastiani (University of Trento, Italy), Viorica Sofronie-Stokkermans (Max-Planck-Institut für Informatik, Germany), and Michael Zakharyaschev (Birkbeck College London, UK).

Many people and institutions contributed to making FroCoS 2007 a success. We are indebted to the members of the Programme Committee and the additional refereees for the thorough reviewing work; the members of the FroCoS Steering Committee for their support, to Andrei Voronkov for free use of the EasyChair conference management system, to sponsorship from EPSRC, and to Dave Shield and Thelma Williams for their invaluable assistance in hosting this conference.

June 2007

Boris Konev
Frank Wolter

Conference Organization

Conference Chair

Boris Konev

Programme Chair

Frank Wolter

Programme Committee

Alessandro Armando
Franz Baader
Jacques Calmet
Silvio Ghilardi
Bernhard Gramlich
Deepak Kapur
Till Mossakowski
Joachim Niehren
Albert Oliveras
Dirk Pattinson
Silvio Ranise
Mark Reynolds
Christophe Ringeissen
Ulrike Sattler
Amilcar Sernadas
Cesare Tinelli
Luca Viganò

External Reviewers

Pedro Adao
Daniel Bond
Torben Braüner
Sylvain Conchon
Giovanna D'Agostino
F. Miguel Dionisio
Tim French
Olivier Gauwin
Isabelle Gnaedig
Guillem Godoy

Florent Jacquemard
Oliver Kutz
Giacomo Lenzi
Denis Lugiez
Christopher Lynch
Jacopo Mantovani
Paulo Mateus
Aart Middeldorp
Sara Negri
Andrei Popescu
Albert Rubio
Peter Schneider-Kamp
Lutz Schröder
Aaron Stump
Guido Tack
Rene Thiemann
Kumar Neeraj Verma
Dirk Walther

Table of Contents

Section 1. Invited Contributions

Section 2. Technical Papers

Architecting Solvers for SAT Modulo Theories: Nelson-Oppen with DPLL

Sava Krstić and Amit Goel

Strategic CAD Labs, Intel Corporation

Abstract. We offer a transition system representing a high-level but detailed architecture for SMT solvers that combine a propositional SAT engine with solvers for multiple disjoint theories. The system captures succintly and accurately all the major aspects of the solver's global operation: boolean search with across-the-board backjumping, communication of theory-specific facts and equalities between shared variables, and cooperative conflict analysis. Provably correct and prudently underspecified, our system is a usable ground for high-quality implementations of comprehensive SMT solvers.

1 Introduction

SMT solvers are fully automated theorem provers based on decision procedures. The acronym is for *Satisfiability Modulo Theories*, indicating that an SMT solver works as a satisfiability checker, with its decision procedures targeting queries from one or more logical theories. These proof engines have become vital in verification practice and hold an even greater promise, but they are still a challenge to design and implement. From the seminal *Simplify* [9] to the current state-of-the-art *Yices* [10], with notable exceptions such as *UCLID* [6], the prevailing wisdom has been that an SMT solver should contain a SAT solver for managing the boolean complexity of the input formula and several specialized solvers—linear arithmetic and "theory of uninterpreted functions" obbligato—that communicate by exchanging equalities between variables ("the Nelson-Oppen style"[15]). This much granted, there is a host of remaining design issues at various levels of abstraction, the response to which distinguishes one solver from another.

Our goal is to define the top-level architecture of an SMT solver as a mathematical object that can be grasped as a whole and fruitfully reasoned about. We want an abstract model that faithfully captures the intricacies of the solver's global operation—what is going on between the architectural components and what is going on inside the components that is essential for interaction. We achieve this goal by presenting the SMT solver as a non-deterministic transition system. The ten rules of our system (Figure 5) provide a rather detailed rational reconstruction of the mainstream SMT solvers, covering the mechanisms for boolean search, communication of theory-specific facts and equalities between shared variables, and global conflict analysis. The system provides a solid theoretical basis for implementations, which can explore various execution

B. Konev and F. Wolter (Eds.): FroCos 2007, LNAI 4720, pp. 1–27, 2007.
© Springer-Verlag Berlin Heidelberg 2007

strategies, refinements and optimizations, assured of fundamental correctness as long as they "play by the rules".

Following the precursor [12] to this paper, we adopt a logic with parametric polymorphism as the natural choice for SMT solvers, emphasizing *cardinality constraints*—not the traditional *stable-infinity condition*—as an accurate expression of what matters for completeness of the Nelson-Oppen method in practice.[1] Our main results are the termination, soundness, and completeness theorems for our transition system.

Related Work. We were inspired mainly by the work of Nieuwenhuis, Oliveras, and Tinelli [16] on *abstract DPLL* and *abstract DPLL modulo theories*—transition systems that model a DPLL-style SAT solver [8] and an SMT solver that extends it with a solver for *one* theory. In the follow-up paper [3], the same authors with Barrett extend their system with features for "splitting on demand" and derive from it the $DPLL(T_1, \ldots, T_n)$ architecture. This architecture is closely related to our system NODPLL (Section 5), but is significantly less detailed and transparent. It refines DPLL *modulo a single (composite) theory* with appropriate purity requirements on some, but not all rules. In contrast, NODPLL is explicitly *modulo multiple theories*, with rules specifying actions of specific theory solvers and the solvers' interaction made vivid. For example, equality propagation is spelled out in NODPLL, but which solver in $DPLL(T_1, \ldots, T_n)$ derives $x = z$ from $x = y$ and $y = z$ is not clear. Another important difference is in the modeling of conflict analysis and it shows even if our systems are compared at the propositional (SAT solver) level. While [16] and [3] view confict analysis abstractly, tucking it in a general rule for backjumping, NODPLL has rules that directly cover its key steps: conflict detection, the subsequent sequence of "explanations", generation of the "backjump clause", and the actual backjump. In an SMT solver, in particular with multiple theories, conflict analysis is even more subtle than in a SAT solver, and the authors of [16] are the first to point out its pitfalls ("too new explanations") and identify a condition for its correct behavior. NODPLL neatly captures this condition as a guard of a rule.

Our work also builds on [7], which has a transition system modeling a Nelson-Oppen solver for multiple theories, but does not address the cooperation with the SAT solver. Formal models of SMT solvers that do handle a SAT solver together with more than one theory are given only in the paper [3] discussed above and earlier works [2], [5]. Barrett's architecture of *CVC Lite* as described in [2] is complex and too low-level for convenient analysis and application. The system $SMT(T_1 \cup T_2)$ of Bozzano et al. [5] describes in pseudo-code a particular approach for equality propagation taken by the *MathSAT* solver, which can be modeled in NODPLL; see Section 5.6.

Outline. Section 2 contains (termino)logical background as developed in [12], but divorcing the solver's polymorphic language from *HOL*, to emphasize that

---

[1] The justification for the presence of non-stably-infinite theories in the Nelson-Oppen framework is studied in recent papers [20,17,4]; in [12], it is shown that the concept of stable-infinity can be dismissed altogether.

$\Sigma_{\mathsf{Eq}} = \langle \mathsf{Bool} \mid =^{\alpha^2 \to \mathsf{Bool}}, \mathsf{ite}^{[\mathsf{Bool}, \alpha, \alpha] \to \alpha}, \mathsf{true}^{\mathsf{Bool}}, \mathsf{false}^{\mathsf{Bool}}, \neg^{\mathsf{Bool} \to \mathsf{Bool}}, \wedge^{\mathsf{Bool}^2 \to \mathsf{Bool}}, \ldots \rangle$

$\Sigma_{\mathsf{UF}} = \langle \Rightarrow \mid @^{[\alpha \Rightarrow \beta, \alpha] \to \beta} \rangle$

$\Sigma_{\mathsf{Int}} = \langle \mathsf{Int} \mid 0^{\mathsf{Int}}, 1^{\mathsf{Int}}, (-1)^{\mathsf{Int}}, \ldots, +^{\mathsf{Int}^2 \to \mathsf{Int}}, -^{\mathsf{Int}^2 \to \mathsf{Int}}, \times^{\mathsf{Int}^2 \to \mathsf{Int}}, \leq^{\mathsf{Int}^2 \to \mathsf{Bool}}, \ldots \rangle$

$\Sigma_{\times} = \langle \times \mid \langle -, - \rangle^{[\alpha, \beta] \to \alpha \times \beta}, \mathsf{fst}^{\alpha \times \beta \to \alpha}, \mathsf{snd}^{\alpha \times \beta \to \beta} \rangle$

$\Sigma_{\mathsf{Array}} = \langle \mathsf{Array} \mid \mathsf{mk\_arr}^{\beta \to \mathsf{Array}(\alpha, \beta)}, \mathsf{read}^{[\mathsf{Array}(\alpha, \beta), \alpha] \to \beta}, \mathsf{write}^{[\mathsf{Array}(\alpha, \beta), \alpha, \beta] \to \mathsf{Array}(\alpha, \beta)} \rangle$

$\Sigma_{\mathsf{List}} = \langle \mathsf{List} \mid \mathsf{cons}^{[\alpha, \mathsf{List}(\alpha)] \to \mathsf{List}(\alpha)}, \mathsf{nil}^{\mathsf{List}(\alpha)}, \mathsf{head}^{[\mathsf{List}(\alpha), \alpha] \to \mathsf{Bool}}, \mathsf{tail}^{[\mathsf{List}(\alpha), \mathsf{List}(\alpha)] \to \mathsf{Bool}} \rangle$

Fig. 1. Signatures for theories of some familiar datatypes. For space efficiency, the constants' arities are shown as superscripts. Σ_{Eq} contains the type operator Bool and standard LOGICAL CONSTANTS. All other signatures by definition contain Σ_{Eq}, but to avoid clutter we leave their Σ_{Eq}-part implicit. In Σ_{UF}, the symbol UF is for *uninterpreted functions* and the intended meaning of @ is the function application. The list functions head and tail are partial, so are represented as predicates in Σ_{List}.

parametricity is not tied to higher-order logic, even though it is most conveniently expressed there. In Section 3, we overview purification—a somewhat involved procedure in the context of parametric theories—and give a suitable form of the non-deterministic Nelson-Oppen combination theorem of [12]. Section 4 is a quick rendition of the core DPLL algorithm as a transition system covering the essential features of modern SAT solvers. Section 5 contains the description of our main transition system for modeling combined SMT solvers, the basic correctness results for it, and some discussion. All proofs are given in the appendix.

2   Preliminaries

We are interested in logical theories of common datatypes and their combinations (Figure 1). A datatype has its syntax and semantics; both are needed to define the theory of the datatype. We give a brief overview of the syntax and an informal sketch of semantics, referring to [12] for technical details.

Types. A set O of symbols called TYPE OPERATORS, each with an associated non-negative arity, and an infinite set of TYPE VARIABLES define the set Tp_O of TYPES over O. It is the smallest set that contains type variables and expressions $F(\sigma_1, \ldots, \sigma_n)$, where $F \in O$ has arity n and $\sigma_i \in \mathsf{Tp}_O$.

A TYPE INSTANTIATION is a finite map from type variables to types. For any type σ and type instantiation $\theta = [\sigma_1/\alpha_1, \ldots, \sigma_n/\alpha_n]$, $\theta(\sigma)$ denotes the simultaneous substitution of every occurrence of α_i in σ with σ_i. We say that τ is an INSTANCE of σ if there is some θ such that $\tau = \theta(\sigma)$.

Signatures. A SIGNATURE is a pair $\langle O \mid K \rangle$, where O is a set of type operators and K is a set of CONSTANTS typed over O. By this we mean that every element of K has an ARITY, which is a tuple of types $(\sigma_0, \ldots, \sigma_n)$. Here, $\sigma_1, \ldots, \sigma_n$ are the argument types of k, and σ_0 is its range type. Constants whose range type is Bool will be called PREDICATES.

We will use the more intuitive notation $k :: [\sigma_1, \ldots, \sigma_n] \to \sigma_0$ to indicate the arity of a constant. Moreover, we will write $k : [\tau_1, \ldots, \tau_n] \to \tau_0$ if there is a type instantiation that maps $\sigma_0, \ldots, \sigma_n$ to $\tau_0, \ldots, \tau_n$ respectively. Note the use of :: and : for the "principal type" and "type instance" of k respectively. Also note that arities are not types—the symbol $\to$ is not a type operator.[2]

Terms. For a given signature $\Sigma = \langle O \mid K \rangle$ and every $\sigma \in \mathsf{Tp}_O$, we assume there is an infinite set of *variables of type* σ; we write them in the (name,type)-form v^σ. The sets Tm_σ of Σ-TERMS OF TYPE σ are defined inductively by these rules:

(1) every variable v^σ is in Tm_σ
(2) if $t_1 \in \mathsf{Tm}_{\tau_1}, \ldots, t_n \in \mathsf{Tm}_{\tau_n}$ and $k : [\tau_1, \ldots, \tau_n] \to \tau_0$, then $k\, t_1 \ldots t_n \in \mathsf{Tm}_{\tau_0}$

Type instantiations act on terms: define $\theta(t)$ to be the term obtained by replacing every variable x^σ in t with $x^{\theta(\sigma)}$. If $t \in \mathsf{Tm}_\sigma$, then $\theta(t) \in \mathsf{Tm}_{\theta(\sigma)}$. We define $t' \sqsubseteq t$ to mean that $t' = \theta(t)$ for some θ, and we then say that t' is a TYPE INSTANCE of t and t is a TYPE ABSTRACTION of t'.

For every term t, there exists the MOST GENERAL ABSTRACTION t^{abs} characterized by: (1) $t \sqsubseteq t^{\mathrm{abs}}$; and (2) $t' \sqsubseteq t^{\mathrm{abs}}$ for every t' such that $t \sqsubseteq t'$. The term t^{abs} is unique up to renaming of type variables and can be obtained by erasing all type information from t and then applying a type inference algorithm. For type inference, see, e.g., [13].

Semantics. The type operators List and Array have arities one and two respectively. The meaning of List is a function of arity one (by abuse of notation, also denoted List) that given a set E as an argument produces the set $\mathsf{List}(E)$ of all lists with elements in E. The meaning of Array is a function that given two sets I and E as arguments produces the set $\mathsf{Array}(I, E)$ of arrays indexed by I with elements in E.

The meaning of polymorphic types is defined once we know the meaning of type operators. For example, the meaning of the type $\mathsf{Array}(\alpha, \mathsf{Array}(\alpha, \beta))$ is a function that given any two sets I and E (as interpretations of type variables α, β) produces the set $\mathsf{Array}(I, \mathsf{Array}(I, E))$. If there are no occurrences of type variables in a type (e.g., $\mathsf{List}(\mathsf{Bool} \times \mathsf{Int})$), then the meaning of that type is always the same set; if the set is finite, we call the type FINITE.

The meaning of a constant is an indexed family of functions. For example, the meaning of cons is the family $\{\mathsf{cons}_E \mid E \text{ is a set}\}$, where cons_E is a function that takes an argument in E and an argument in $\mathsf{List}(E)$ and produces a result in $\mathsf{List}(E)$.

The meanings of type operators and constants of a signature together determine a STRUCTURE for that signature. The structure gives meaning to all terms.

---

[2] In [12], the type and term languages asssociated with a signature were defined as subsets of the higher-order logic, where the function space type operator is primitive and so arities could be seen as types.

Consider $t = \mathsf{read}(\mathsf{write}(a^{\mathsf{Array}(\alpha,\beta)}, i^\alpha, x^\beta), j^\alpha)$. Once α and β are interpreted as concrete sets (I and E, say) and interpretations for the variables a, i, x, j (elements of $\mathsf{Array}(I, E), I, E, I$ respectively) are given, the polymorphic term t becomes a well-defined element of E. In [12], which should be consulted for more details, this element is denoted $[\![t]\!]\langle \iota, \rho \rangle$, where ι and ρ together define an *environment* for t: ι maps the type variables α, β to sets I, E respectively, and ρ maps the variables a, i, x, j to elements of $\mathsf{Array}(I, E), I, E, I$ respectively.

As a boring exercise, the reader may furnish the signatures in Figure 1 with meanings of their type operators and constants, thus obtaining definitions of structures $\mathcal{T}_{\mathsf{Eq}}, \mathcal{T}_{\mathsf{UF}}, \mathcal{T}_{\mathsf{Int}}, \mathcal{T}_\times, \mathcal{T}_{\mathsf{Array}}, \mathcal{T}_{\mathsf{List}}$.

Satisfiability. A Σ-FORMULA is an element of $\mathsf{Tm}_{\mathsf{Bool}}$. If ϕ is a Σ-formula and $\mathcal{T}$ is a Σ-structure, we say that ϕ is SATISFIABLE in $\mathcal{T}$ if $[\![\phi]\!]\langle \iota, \rho \rangle = \mathsf{true}$ for some environment $\langle \iota, \rho \rangle$; this environment then is called a MODEL of ϕ. We also say that ϕ is VALID if $\neg\phi$ is unsatisfiable. Validity is denoted $\models_\mathcal{T} \phi$, and $\phi_1, \ldots, \phi_n \models_\mathcal{T} \phi$ is an abbreviation for $\models_\mathcal{T} \phi_1 \wedge \cdots \wedge \phi_n \supset \phi$. The THEORY of a structure is the set of formulas that are valid in it.

An ATOMIC Σ-FORMULA is either a propositional variable or a term of the form $k\, t_1 \ldots t_n$, where k is a predicate. A Σ-LITERAL is an atomic formula or its negation. A CLAUSE is a disjunction of literals. A QUERY is a conjunction of formulas. Clauses containing the same literals in different order are considered equal. (We think of clauses and queries as sets of literals and formulas respectively.) A CONVEX THEORY is defined by the property that if a set of literals implies a disjunction of equalities, then one of the disjuncts must be implied.

A CARDINALITY CONSTRAINT is an "equality" of the form $\alpha \doteq n$, where α is a type variable and n is a positive integer; an enviroment $\langle \iota, \rho \rangle$ satisfies this constraint if α is in the domain of ι and the cardinality of the set $\iota(\alpha)$ is n.

Combining Structures. Two signatures are DISJOINT if the only type operators and constants they share are those of Σ_{Eq}. If $\mathcal{T}_1, \ldots, \mathcal{T}_n$ are structures with pairwise disjoint signatures, then there is a well-defined *sum structure* $\mathcal{T} = \mathcal{T}_1 + \cdots + \mathcal{T}_n$; the semantics of its type operators and constants is defined by the structures they come from. The types and terms of each $\mathcal{T}_i$ are types and terms of $\mathcal{T}$ too. We will call them PURE, or i-PURE when we need to be specific. The attribute MIXED will be used for arbitrary terms and types of a sum structure.

Solvers. A SOLVER for a fragment of a theory is a sound and complete satisfiability checker for sets of formulas (QUERIES) in the fragment. A STRONG SOLVER checks satisfiability of queries that contain formulas and cardinality constraints.

In practice, theory solvers are built for queries consisting of literals only. The well-known argument that this is sufficient in general begins with the observation that every query Φ is equisatisfiable with one of the form $Q = \Phi_0 \cup \{p_1 \Leftrightarrow \phi_1, \ldots, p_n \Leftrightarrow \phi_n\}$, where the p_i are propositional variables, the ϕ_i are literals, and Φ_0 is a propositional query, the boolean skeleton of Φ. A truth assignment M to propositional variables that satisfies Φ_0 can be extended to a model for Φ if and only if the query of literals $Q_M = \{\phi_1', \ldots, \phi_n'\}$ is $\mathcal{T}$-satisfiable, where ϕ_i' is either ϕ_i or $\neg\phi_i$, depending on whether $M(p_i)$ is true or false. Thus, satisfiability of Φ is decided by checking if Q_M is satisfiable for some model M of Φ_0. This, of course, calls for a SAT solver to efficiently enumerate the models M.

Parametricity. There is uniformity in the way "polymorphic" functions like cons compute their results—a consequence of the fact that the definition of cons_E takes the set E as a parameter, making no assumptions about it. Precisely pinning down this uniformity concept is somewhat tricky and we content ourselves with definitions of *parametric type operators* and *parametric constants* that are most convenient for our purposes. They are needed for proper understanding of Theorem 1 below, but not for much else in this paper. Thus, the reader may safely proceed with only a cursory reading of the rest of this section.

Recall first that a relation between two sets A and B is a PARTIAL BIJECTION if it can be seen as a bijection between a subset of A and a subset of B. Define an n-ary set function F to be PARAMETRIC if it is functorial on partial bijections. This means that given any partial bijections $f_i\colon A_i \leftrightarrow B_i$, where $i = 1,\ldots,n$, there exists a partial bijection $F(f_1,\ldots,f_n)\colon F(A_1,\ldots,A_n) \leftrightarrow F(B_1,\ldots,B_n)$; moreover, there is a requirement that the identity and composition be preserved. That is, $F(id_{A_1},\ldots,id_{A_n}) = id_{F(A_1,\ldots,A_n)}$ and $F(g_1 \circ f_1,\ldots,g_n \circ f_n) = F(g_1,\ldots,g_n) \circ F(f_1,\ldots,f_n)$, where $A_i \overset{f_i}{\leftrightarrow} B_i \overset{g_i}{\leftrightarrow} C_i$.

Consider a structure whose type operators are all parametric in the above sense and let $k :: [\sigma_1,\ldots,\sigma_n] \to \sigma_0$ be a constant of this structure. Observe that if $\alpha_1,\ldots,\alpha_m$ are all type variables that occur in the types σ_i, then any interpretation ι of type variables (that is, an assignment, for each i, of a set A_i to α_i) interprets each type σ_j as a set, say S_j, and interprets k as a function $k_\iota\colon S_1 \times \cdots \times S_n \to S_0$. Suppose now we have two interpretations ι, ι' for type variables, the first just as above, and the second with A_i' and S_j' in place of A_i and S_j. Suppose also that $f_i : A_i \leftrightarrow A_i'$ are partial bijections. Since the type operators of our structure are assumed parametric, there are induced partial bijections $g_j\colon S_j \leftrightarrow S_j'$, for $j = 0,\ldots,n$. We say that the constant k is PARAMETRIC if in this situation we have $g_0(k_\iota(x_1,\ldots,x_n)) = k_{\iota'}(g_1(x_1),\ldots,g_n(x_n))$ for every $x_1 \in \mathsf{dom}(f_1),\ldots,x_n \in \mathsf{dom}(f_n)$.

Finally, a PARAMETRIC STRUCTURE is required to have all type operators and all constants parametric. Our example structures $\mathcal{T}_{\mathsf{Eq}}, \mathcal{T}_{\mathsf{UF}}, \mathcal{T}_{\mathsf{Int}}, \mathcal{T}_\times, \mathcal{T}_{\mathsf{Array}}, \mathcal{T}_{\mathsf{List}}$, with the notable exception of $\mathcal{T}_{\mathsf{UF}}$, are all parametric; so are the structures describing sets, multisets, and arbitrary algebraic datatypes [12].

We should note that the well-known concept of REYNOLDS PARAMETRICITY in programming languages [18] is neither weaker nor stronger than the concept we are using. In particular, $\mathcal{T}_{\mathsf{UF}}$ is Reynolds parametric. See [12].

3   Purification and Non-deterministic Nelson-Oppen

In the untyped setting, to *purify* a query consisting of mixed formulas is to transform it into an equisatisfiable query consisting of pure formulas. The transformation iteratively replaces a pure subterm t in a mixed formula with a fresh *proxy variable* x, and adds the pure *definitional equality* $x = t$ to the query. For example, purifying the one-formula query $\{1 + f(x) = f(1 + f(x))\}$ results in the query $\{y = f(x), z = 1 + y, u = f(z), z = u\}$ that contains two pure *UF*-equalities, one pure arithmetical equality, and one equality between variables, which is a pure formula in any theory. (For Σ_{UF}-terms, we use the familiar notations $f(x)$ or $f\,x$ instead of the syntactically correct $f@x$.) The essence of Nelson-Oppen cooperation is in giving each theory solver the part of the purified query that it understands and then proceed with the solvers deducing in turn new equalities between variables and letting the other solvers know about them.

Types complicate purification, exposing the pertinence of *cardinality constraints*. The typed version of the example above would have $\{y^{\mathsf{Int}} = f^{\mathsf{Int}\Rightarrow\mathsf{Int}}\,x^{\mathsf{Int}},$ $u^{\mathsf{Int}} = f^{\mathsf{Int}\Rightarrow\mathsf{Int}}\,z^{\mathsf{Int}}\}$ as a pure query to pass to the solver for uninterpreted functions. But this query is not pure since the type Int is foreign to the theory $\mathcal{T}_{\mathsf{UF}}$. As a way out, we can create the 'type-abstracted modification $\{y^{\alpha} = f^{\alpha\Rightarrow\alpha}\,x^{\alpha}, u^{\alpha} = f^{\alpha\Rightarrow\alpha}\,z^{\alpha}\}$, which *is* a pure $\mathcal{T}_{\mathsf{UF}}$-query; however, while being sound, this transformation may compromise completeness. Take the example

$$
\begin{aligned}
\Phi_1 &:\ \mathsf{distinct}(\mathsf{fst}\,x^{\mathsf{Int}\times\mathsf{Int}}, \mathsf{snd}\,y^{\mathsf{Int}\times\mathsf{Int}}, \mathsf{fst}\,z^{\mathsf{Int}\times\mathsf{Int}}) \\
\Phi_2 &:\ \mathsf{distinct}(\mathsf{fst}\,x^{\mathsf{Bit}\times\mathsf{Bit}}, \mathsf{snd}\,y^{\mathsf{Bit}\times\mathsf{Bit}}, \mathsf{fst}\,z^{\mathsf{Bit}\times\mathsf{Bit}}) \\
\Phi\ &:\ \mathsf{distinct}(\mathsf{fst}\,x^{\alpha\times\beta_1}, \mathsf{snd}\,y^{\beta_2\times\alpha}, \mathsf{fst}\,z^{\alpha\times\beta_3})
\end{aligned}
\tag{1}
$$

where $\mathsf{distinct}(x_1, \ldots, x_n)$ denotes the query consisting of all disequalities $x_i \neq x_j$ and Bit is a two-element type belonging to some bitvector structure $\mathcal{T}_{\mathsf{BV}}$. The $\mathcal{T}_{\times}$-query Φ is the best pure approximation for both Φ_1 and Φ_2. It is satisfiable, and so is the $(\mathcal{T}_{\times} + \mathcal{T}_{\mathsf{Int}})$-query Φ_1, but the $(\mathcal{T}_{\times} + \mathcal{T}_{\mathsf{BV}})$-query Φ_2 is *not* satisfiable. Thus, to make a $\mathcal{T}_{\times}$-solver properly deal with Φ_2, we should give it the abstraction Φ together with the cardinality constraint $\alpha \doteq 2$.

3.1   Solving Semipure Queries

Let us now repeat the above in general terms. Suppose $\Sigma = \Sigma_1 + \cdots + \Sigma_n$ is a sum of pairwise disjoint signatures $\Sigma_i = \langle O_i \mid K_i \rangle$ and $\mathcal{T} = \mathcal{T}_1 + \cdots + \mathcal{T}_n$ is the corresponding sum of theories. Recall that a Σ-term is i-PURE if it is a Σ_i-term. Ignoring "impurity" at the type level, define a Σ-term to be i-SEMIPURE if it can be generated using only constants from K_i. Also, let STRICTLY i-SEMIPURE terms be those that are i-semipure and have no occurrences of logical constants. For example, the queries Φ_1 and Φ_2 above are semipure, while Φ is pure.

Every i-semipure term t has the best PURE ABSTRACTION t^{pure} defined to be the most general abstraction of t with respect to the signature Σ_i. Thus, for every semipure query Φ there exists an essentially unique pure abstraction Φ^{pure}. For example, $\Phi_1^{\mathrm{pure}} = \Phi_2^{\mathrm{pure}} = \Phi$, where the queries are from (1).

Note that Σ-terms without occurrences of non-logical constants are i-semipure for every i. For such a term t, we define t^{pure} to be the $\mathcal{T}_{\mathsf{Eq}}$-pure abstraction of t. For example, $(x^{\mathsf{Int}} = y^{\mathsf{Int}} \wedge u^{\mathsf{Int}\times\mathsf{Int}} \neq v^{\mathsf{Int}\times\mathsf{Int}})^{\mathrm{pure}} = (x^{\alpha} = y^{\alpha} \wedge u^{\beta} \neq v^{\beta})$.

If the query Φ is semipure and θ is a type instantiation such that $\theta(\Phi^{\mathrm{pure}}) = \Phi$, denote by Φ^{card} the set of cardinality constraints $\alpha \doteq n$, where $\alpha \in \mathsf{dom}(\theta)$ and

$\theta(\alpha)$ is a finite type of cardinality n. One can show that *an i-semipure query Φ is $\mathcal{T}$-satisfiable if and only if $\Phi^{\text{pure}} \cup \Phi^{\text{card}}$ is $\mathcal{T}_i$-satisfiable* [12]. Hence, a strong solver for i-pure queries suffices to solve i-semipure queries.

3.2   Purification

Let $\mathcal{T}$ and $\mathcal{T}_1, \ldots, \mathcal{T}_n$ be as above. Given any input $\mathcal{T}$-query, we can purify it by introducing proxy variables and definitional equalities and so obtain an equisatisfiable $\mathcal{T}$-query, say Φ, that contains only semipure formulas. In fact, we can obtain Φ such that every formula in it is either a propositional clause or has one of the following DEFINITIONAL FORMS:

$$(A)\ \ p \Leftrightarrow (x = y) \qquad (B)\ \ p \Leftrightarrow \phi \qquad (C)\ \ x = t$$

where (i) p, x, y are variables, ϕ is a strictly semipure literal, and t is a strictly semipure term; (ii) every variable occurs as the left-hand side in at most one definitional form; (iii) no (propositional) variable that occurs in propositional clauses of Φ can occur in the right-hand side of any definitional form. This is proved in [12] under the assumption that non-logical constants do not take arguments of boolean type.[3]

Partition now Φ into subsets $\Phi_{\mathbb{B}}, \Phi_{\mathbb{E}}, \Phi_1, \ldots, \Phi_n$, where $\Phi_{\mathbb{B}}$ contains the propositional clauses in Φ, $\Phi_{\mathbb{E}}$ contains definitional forms (A), and each Φ_i contains the definitional forms (B) and (C) whose right-hand sides ϕ, t are strictly i-semipure. Note that $\Phi_{\mathbb{B}}$ is i-pure for every i, and $\Phi_{\mathbb{E}}$ is i-semipure for every i.

Example 1. Purifying the formula $f(x) = x \wedge f(2x - f(x)) > x$ produces $\Phi_{\mathbb{B}} = \{p, q\}$, $\Phi_{\mathbb{E}} = \{p \Leftrightarrow y = x\}$, $\Phi_{\mathsf{UF}} = \{y = f(x), u = f(z)\}$, $\Phi_{\mathsf{Int}} = \{z = 2x - y, q \Leftrightarrow u > x\}$. For readability we omit type superscripts on variables, but see Figure 4 below where this example can be seen in its full typed glory.

3.3   Nelson-Oppen

Let $\Phi = \Phi_{\mathbb{B}} \cup \Phi_{\mathbb{E}} \cup \Phi_1 \cup \cdots \cup \Phi_n$ be as above and let us call a variable SHARED if it occurs in at least two of the queries $\Phi_{\mathbb{B}}, \Phi_{\mathbb{E}}, \Phi_1, \ldots, \Phi_n$. For a set V of variables, define an ARRANGEMENT on V to be a consistent query that for every two variables $x, y \in V$ of the same type contains either $x = y$ or $x \neq y$. Partitioning V into subsets V^σ according to the types of variables, we see that an arrangement determines and is determined by a set of equivalence relations on each class V^σ.

The following result is a slightly more general version of (and easily derived from) Theorem 1 of [12]. It is the basis of the non-deterministic Nelson-Oppen procedure in the style of Tinelli-Harandi [19], but for parametric theories.

---

[3] This assumption is hardly a restriction since we have the polymorphic if-then-else constant ite handy in Σ_{Eq}. Bringing the input query to the desired equisatisfiable form Φ also requires that all occurrences of ite be compiled away by replacing $z = \text{ite}(p, x, y)$ with the equivalent $(p \supset z = x) \wedge (\bar{p} \supset z = y)$.

Theorem 1. *Suppose each of the theories* $T_1, \ldots, T_n$ *is either* T_{UF} *or is parametric. Let M be an assignment[4] to shared propositional variables and let Δ be an arrangement of all remaining shared variables. Then:* $\Phi \cup \Delta \cup M$ *is T-satisfiable if and only if (with the convention that $T_{\mathbb{E}}$ stands for T_{Eq})*

- $\Phi_{\mathbb{B}} \cup M$ *is satisfiable;*
- $(\Phi_i \cup \Delta)^{\text{pure}} \cup \Phi_i^{\text{card}} \cup M$ *is T_i-satisfiable, for every* $i \in \{\mathbb{E}, 1, \ldots, n\}$.

4   DPLL with Conflict Analysis

We define a transition system DPLL that models the operation of a DPLL-style SAT solver, including conflict analysis. In Section 5 it will be extended with rules for Nelson-Oppen cooperation of multiple theories.

The only parameter of DPLL is a finite set of propositional literals L, closed under negation. A DPLL *state* is a triple $\langle \Psi, M, C \rangle$, where: (1) Ψ is a set of clauses over L (2) M is a *checkpointed sequence* of literals in L, meaning that each element of M is either a literal or a special checkpoint symbol $\square$, (3) C is either a subset of L or a special symbol no_cflct.

The "input" to DPLL is an arbitrary set of clauses Ψ_{init}, modeled as an initial state in which $\Psi = \Psi_{\text{init}}$, $M = [\,]$, and $C = $ no_cflct. The rules describing the state-to-state transitions are given in Figure 2. The rules have the guarded assignment form: above the line is the condition that enables the rule, below the line is the update to system variables Ψ, M, C.

The notation used in the rules is defined as follows. The negation of a literal l is $\bar{l}$. The relation $l \prec l'$ means that an occurrence of l precedes an occurrence of l' in M. Note that M can be written uniquely in the form $M = M^{\langle 0 \rangle} + \square + M^{\langle 1 \rangle} + \square + \cdots + \square + M^{\langle d \rangle}$, where $+$ denotes sequence concatenation and $\square$ does not occur in any $M^{\langle i \rangle}$. The superscripts indicate "decision levels" and $M^{[m]} = M^{\langle 0 \rangle} + \square + \cdots + \square + M^{\langle m \rangle}$ is the prefix of M up to decision level m. A literal can occur at most once in M; we write level $l = i$ if l occurs in $M^{\langle i \rangle}$. Finally, the number k occurring in the rules is an arbitrary non-negative integer.

An example run of DPLL is given in Figure 3. The correctness of the system is expressed by the following theorem, proved in the appendix.

Theorem 2 (Correctness). *All runs of* DPLL *are finite. If, initialized with the set of clauses Ψ_{init},* DPLL *terminates in the state $\langle \Psi, M, C \rangle$, then: (a) $C = $ no_cflct or $C = \varnothing$; (b) If $C = \varnothing$ then Ψ_{init} is unsatisfiable; (c) If $C = $ no_cflct, then M is a model for Ψ_{init}.*

By restricting the set of behaviors of NODPLL, we can obtain more accurate models of modern SAT solvers. Let Explain_uip be the rule obtained by strengthening the guard of Explain with the conditions $\forall l' \in C.\ l' \preceq l$ and $\exists l' \in C.$ level $l' = $ level l that force the explanation sequence to find the first "unique implication point" [14] and stop when it is has been found. Consider the strategy

---

[4] We view assignments as sets of literals; e.g. $\{\bar{p}, q, \bar{r}\}$ is the assignment that maps p, r to false and q to true.

Decide	$\dfrac{l \in L \quad l, \bar{l} \notin M}{M := M + \square + l}$
UnitPropag	$\dfrac{l \vee l_1 \vee \cdots \vee l_k \in \Psi \quad \bar{l}_1, \ldots, \bar{l}_k \in M \quad l, \bar{l} \notin M}{M := M + l}$
Conflict	$\dfrac{C = \mathsf{no\_cflct} \quad \bar{l}_1 \vee \cdots \vee \bar{l}_k \in \Psi \quad l_1, \ldots, l_k \in M}{C := \{l_1, \ldots, l_k\}}$
Explain	$\dfrac{l \in C \quad l \vee \bar{l}_1 \vee \cdots \vee \bar{l}_k \in \Psi \quad l_1, \ldots, l_k \prec l}{C := C \cup \{l_1, \ldots, l_k\} \smallsetminus \{l\}}$
Learn	$\dfrac{C = \{l_1, \ldots, l_k\} \quad \bar{l}_1 \vee \cdots \vee \bar{l}_k \notin \Psi}{\Psi := \Psi \cup \{\bar{l}_1 \vee \cdots \vee \bar{l}_k\}}$
BackJump	$\dfrac{C = \{l, l_1, \ldots, l_k\} \quad \bar{l} \vee \bar{l}_1 \vee \cdots \vee \bar{l}_k \in \Psi \quad \begin{array}{c} \mathsf{level}\ l > m \ge \mathsf{level}\ l_i \\ (i = 1, \ldots, k) \end{array}}{C := \mathsf{no\_cflct} \quad M := M^{[m]} + \bar{l}}$

Fig. 2. Rules of DPLL

$$(((\mathsf{Conflict}\,;\,\mathsf{Explain\_uip}^*\,;\,[\mathsf{Learn}\,;\,\mathsf{BackJump}]) \parallel \mathsf{UnitPropag})^*\,;\,[\mathsf{Decide}])^* \quad (2)$$

where $\parallel$ denotes the non-deterministic choice, α^* means "apply α as long as possible", and $[\alpha]$ means "apply α once if possible". Note that the rule Conflict is triggered by a clause all of whose literals are asserted false in M, and UnitPropag is triggered by a clause in which all but one literal is asserted false in M. To turn (2) into a deterministic algorithm, one must specify the search for the trigger clause. This is what the "two-watched-literals" scheme is for; it ensures that trigger clauses are quickly found after each Decide step. When Decide is to be applied, the choice of the decision literal is based on some heuristics, the most popular being VSIDS of [14]. As for the "non-chronological backtracking" in BackJump, the backjump level m is normally taken to be the minimum possible, i.e., the largest of the numbers level l_i ($i = 1, \ldots, k$). With the exception of restarts and clause forgetting (easily modeled, harder to tune; see Figure 6), the above gives a rather complete top-level picture of *Chaff* [14]. One can also prove that for the strategy (2) the guard of Learn is automatically satisfied, justifying the fact that the implementations do not perform this expensive check.

The top-level *MiniSAT* [11] looks almost the same; we only need to replace Explain_uip* in (2) with the sequence Explain_uip* ; Explain_min*, where the conflict clause-minimizing rule Explain_min is obtained by strengthening the guard of Explain with the condition $l_1, \ldots, l_m \in C$.

$$\langle \Psi, [\,], \text{no\_cflct} \rangle \xrightarrow{\text{Decide}} \langle \Psi, \square 1, \text{no\_cflct} \rangle \xrightarrow{\text{UnitPropag}}$$

$$\langle \Psi, \square 12, \text{no\_cflct} \rangle \xrightarrow{\text{Decide}} \langle \Psi, \square 12\square 3, \text{no\_cflct} \rangle \xrightarrow{\text{UnitPropag}}$$

$$\langle \Psi, \square 12\square 34, \text{no\_cflct} \rangle \xrightarrow{\text{Decide}} \langle \Psi, \square 12\square 34\square 5, \text{no\_cflct} \rangle \xrightarrow{\text{UnitPropag}}$$

$$\langle \Psi, \square 12\square 34\square 56, \text{no\_cflct} \rangle \xrightarrow{\text{Conflict}} \langle \Psi, \square 12\square 34\square 56, \{2,5,6\} \rangle \xrightarrow{\text{Explain}}$$

$$\langle \Psi, \square 12\square 34\square 56, \{2,5\} \rangle \xrightarrow{\text{Learn}} \langle \Psi', \square 12\square 34\square 56, \{2,5\} \rangle \xrightarrow{\text{BackJump}}$$

$$\langle \Psi', \square 12\bar{5}, \text{no\_cflct} \rangle \xrightarrow{\text{Decide}} \langle \Psi', \square 12\bar{5}\square 3, \text{no\_cflct} \rangle \xrightarrow{\text{UnitPropag}}$$

$$\langle \Psi', \square 12\bar{5}\square 34, \text{no\_cflct} \rangle \xrightarrow{\text{Decide}} \langle \Psi', \square 12\bar{5}\square 34\square \bar{6}, \text{no\_cflct} \rangle$$

Fig. 3. A run of DPLL. The initial set of clauses $\Psi = \{\bar{1} \vee 2, \bar{3} \vee 4, \bar{5} \vee 6, \bar{2} \vee \bar{5} \vee \bar{6}\}$ is taken from [16]. The Learn move changes Ψ into $\Psi' = \Psi \cup \{\bar{2} \vee \bar{5}\}$. The BackJump move goes from decision level 3 to decision level 1. The final assignment satisfies Ψ.

5   The Combined Solver

In this section, we define of our Nelson-Oppen-with-DPLL transition system NODPLL, state its correctness results, and discuss some features and extensions. The system can adequately express important design decisions and allows a great deal of freedom for implementation.

The parameters of NODPLL are pairwise disjoint theories $\mathcal{T}_1, \ldots, \mathcal{T}_n$. The "input" to NODPLL is a $(\mathcal{T}_1 + \cdots + \mathcal{T}_n)$-query Φ, purified into $\Phi_{\mathbb{B}} \cup \Phi_{\mathbb{E}} \cup \Phi_1 \cup \cdots \cup \Phi_n$ as in Section 3. Assume that all variables occurring in these formulas have distinct names and let $\text{vars}(\Theta)$ denote the set of names of variables in Θ.

5.1   State, Rules, and Initialization

Let $I = \{\mathbb{B}, \mathbb{E}, 1, \ldots, n\}$. The state variables of NODPLL are the following:

- SHARED VARIABLE SETS V_i for $i \in I$. These are sets of variable names, not necessarily disjoint. For every $i \in I$ define (paraphrasing [5]) the set L_i of INTERFACE LITERALS to consist of variables in $V_i \cap V_{\mathbb{B}}$ and their negations, and also equalities of the form $x = y$, where $x, y \in V_i \setminus V_{\mathbb{B}}$.
- LOCAL CONSTRAINTS Ψ_i for $i \in I$. Here, $\Psi_{\mathbb{B}}$ is a set of propositional clauses and Ψ_i for $i \in \{\mathbb{E}, 1, \ldots, n\}$ is a set of (pure) $\mathcal{T}_i$-formulas and cardinality constraints. We require that $\text{vars}(\Psi_{\mathbb{B}}) \subseteq V_{\mathbb{B}}$ and that $\text{vars}(\Psi_i) \cap \text{vars}(\Psi_j) \subseteq V_i \cap V_j \cap V_{\mathbb{E}}$ for distinct $i, j \neq \mathbb{B}$.
- LOCAL STACKS (checkpointed sequences) M_i for $i \in I$. Any element of M_i is either $\square$ or a LABELED LITERAL—a pair $\langle l, j \rangle$, where $l \in L_i$ and $j \in I$.
- The CONFLICT C—either a set of labeled literals or a special symbol no_cflct.

The input query Φ defines the INITIAL STATE s_{init}^{Φ}, in which: $\Psi_{\mathbb{B}} = \Phi_{\mathbb{B}}$; $\Psi_i = \Phi_i^{\text{pure}} \cup \Phi_i^{\text{card}}$ for $i \neq \mathbb{B}$; $M_i = [\,]$ for every i; $C = \text{no\_cflct}$; $V_{\mathbb{B}} = \text{vars}(\Phi_{\mathbb{B}})$; $V_i = \bigcup_{j \neq i} \text{vars}(\Phi_i) \cap \text{vars}(\Phi_j)$ for $i \neq \mathbb{B}, \mathbb{E}$; and $V_{\mathbb{E}} = (\text{vars}(\Phi_{\mathbb{E}}) \cap \text{vars}(\Phi_{\mathbb{B}})) \cup \bigcup_{i \neq \mathbb{B}} (V_i \setminus V_{\mathbb{B}})$. An example is given in Figure 4.

The transitions of NODPLL are defined by the rules in Figure 5. The following two paragraphs explain the additional notation used in these rules.

(a) $\Phi = \{f^{\mathsf{Int} \Rightarrow \mathsf{Int}}(x^{\mathsf{Int}}) = x^{\mathsf{Int}}, f^{\mathsf{Int} \Rightarrow \mathsf{Int}}(2x^{\mathsf{Int}} - f^{\mathsf{Int} \Rightarrow \mathsf{Int}}(x^{\mathsf{Int}})) > x^{\mathsf{Int}}\}$

(b)
$\Phi_{\mathbb{B}} = \{p^{\mathsf{Bool}}, q^{\mathsf{Bool}}\}$ $\Phi_{\mathsf{Int}} = \{z^{\mathsf{Int}} = 2x^{\mathsf{Int}} - y^{\mathsf{Int}}, q^{\mathsf{Bool}} \Leftrightarrow u^{\mathsf{Int}} > x^{\mathsf{Int}}\}$
$\Phi_{\mathbb{E}} = \{p^{\mathsf{Bool}} \Leftrightarrow (y^{\mathsf{Int}} = x^{\mathsf{Int}})\}$ $\Phi_{\mathsf{UF}} = \{y^{\mathsf{Int}} = f^{\mathsf{Int} \Rightarrow \mathsf{Int}}(x^{\mathsf{Int}}), u^{\mathsf{Int}} = f^{\mathsf{Int} \Rightarrow \mathsf{Int}}(z^{\mathsf{Int}})\}$

(c)
$\Psi_{\mathbb{B}} = \{p^{\mathsf{Bool}}, q^{\mathsf{Bool}}\}$ $\Psi_{\mathsf{Int}} = \{z^{\mathsf{Int}} = 2x^{\mathsf{Int}} - y^{\mathsf{Int}}, q^{\mathsf{Bool}} \Leftrightarrow u^{\mathsf{Int}} > x^{\mathsf{Int}}\}$
$\Psi_{\mathbb{E}} = \{p^{\mathsf{Bool}} \Leftrightarrow (y^{\alpha} = x^{\alpha})\}$ $\Psi_{\mathsf{UF}} = \{y^{\beta} = f^{\beta \Rightarrow \beta}(x^{\beta}), u^{\beta} = f^{\beta \Rightarrow \beta}(z^{\beta})\}$

Fig. 4. Initialization of NODPLL. *(a)* the input query Φ from Example 1, *(b)* the result of purifying Φ, *(c)* generated local constraints for NODPLL. The shared variable sets are $V_{\mathbb{B}} = \{p, q\}$, $V_{\mathsf{UF}} = \{x, y, z, u\}$, and $V_{\mathsf{Int}} = \{x, y, z, u, q\}$. Note that a variable of Φ, say x^{Int}, has different "identities" in the pure queries Ψ_i: x^{α} in $\Phi_{\mathbb{E}}$, x^{β} in Ψ_{UF}, and x^{Int} in Ψ_{Int}. They all have the same name, but different types.

We write $C^{\flat}$ for the set of (unlabeled) literals occurring in C. We write $l \in M_i$ to mean that $\langle l, j \rangle \in M_i$ holds for some j. For $i \neq \mathbb{B}, \mathbb{E}$, the symbol $\models_i$ denotes entailment modulo $\mathcal{T}_i$; $\models_{\mathbb{B}}$ is propositional entailment, and $\models_{\mathbb{E}}$ is entailment modulo $\mathcal{T}_{\mathsf{Eq}}$. Note that all literals occurring in the rules contain untyped (shared) variables and so there is an abuse of notation when we write $\Psi_i, l_1, \ldots, l_k \models_i l$ in the rule Explain$_i$. Of course, this entailment should be understood as $\Psi_i, l'_1, \ldots, l'_k \models_i l'$ where each primed literal is obtained by replacing the untyped variables occurring in it with the equally named typed variable of Ψ_i. (Recall that the variables of Ψ_i have the same names as variables of Φ_i, but possibly more general types.) The same convention is used in the rules Infer$_i$ and Conflict$_i$.

It is easy to see that *all local stacks have the same number of occurrences of* $\square$. Thus, each M_i can be written as $M_i = M_i^{\langle 0 \rangle} + \square + M_i^{\langle 1 \rangle} + \square + \cdots + \square + M_i^{\langle d \rangle}$, where d is the CURRENT DECISION LEVEL and $\square$ does not occur in any $M_i^{\langle k \rangle}$. Note that some of the sequences $M_i^{\langle k \rangle}$ may be empty; however, $M_{\mathsf{Bool}}^{\langle k \rangle}$ is non-empty for $1 \leq k \leq d$ and its first element is called the kth DECISION LITERAL. The rule Explain uses the notation $\langle l, j \rangle \prec_{M_i} \langle l', j' \rangle$; by definition, this means that both labeled literals occur in M_i and that the occurrence of $\langle l, j \rangle$ precedes the occurrence of $\langle l', j' \rangle$. For correctness of this definition, we need to know that *in any local stack, any literal can occur at most once*. This invariant is proved in the appendix. Finally, the function level used in the BackJump rule is defined only for literals that occur in $M_{\mathbb{B}}$; we have level $l = k$ if l occurs in $M_{\mathbb{B}}^{\langle k \rangle}$.

This completes the definition of the system NODPLL. As with DPLL, to check the satisfiability of a formula Φ, we can start with the state s_{init}^{Φ} and apply the rules of NODPLL in arbitrary order; if we end up with a final state in which $C = \mathsf{no\_cflct}$, then Φ is satisfiable; otherwise, the final state will have $C = \varnothing$ and Φ is unsatisfiable.

Example 2. If NODPLL is initialized with $\Psi_{\mathbb{B}}, \Psi_{\mathbb{E}}, \Psi_{\mathsf{UF}}, \Psi_{\mathsf{Int}}$ from Figure 4, the first 13 steps could be (1) Infer$_{\mathbb{B}}$, (2) Infer$_{\mathbb{B}}$, (3) LitDispatch$_{\mathbb{E}}$, (4) LitDispatch$_{\mathsf{Int}}$,

$$
\begin{array}{ll}
\text{Decide} & \dfrac{l \in L_\mathbb{B} \qquad l, \bar{l} \notin M_\mathbb{B}}{M_\mathbb{B} := M_\mathbb{B} + \square + \langle l, \mathbb{B} \rangle \qquad M_i := M_i + \square \ \ (\text{all } i \neq \mathbb{B})}
\end{array}
$$

$$
\text{Infer}_i \qquad \dfrac{l \in L_i \qquad l, \bar{l} \notin M_i \qquad \Psi_i, M_i \models_i l}{M_i := M_i + \langle l, i \rangle}
$$

$$
\begin{array}{l}
\text{LitDispatch}_i \\
(i \neq \mathbb{B})
\end{array}
\qquad
\dfrac{l \in L_i \qquad \langle l, j \rangle \in M_\mathbb{B} \qquad l \notin M_i}{M_i := M_i + \langle l, j \rangle}
$$

$$
\begin{array}{l}
\text{EqDispatch}_i \\
(i \neq \mathbb{E}, \mathbb{B})
\end{array}
\qquad
\dfrac{x, y \in V_i \qquad \langle x = y, j \rangle \in M_\mathbb{E} \qquad x = y \notin M_i}{M_i := M_i + \langle x = y, j \rangle}
$$

$$
\begin{array}{l}
\text{LitPropag}_i \\
(i \neq \mathbb{B})
\end{array}
\qquad
\dfrac{l \in L_\mathbb{B} \qquad \langle l, i \rangle \in M_i \qquad l, \bar{l} \notin M_\mathbb{B}}{M_\mathbb{B} := M_\mathbb{B} + \langle l, i \rangle}
$$

$$
\begin{array}{l}
\text{EqPropag}_i \\
(i \neq \mathbb{E}, \mathbb{B})
\end{array}
\qquad
\dfrac{x, y \in V_\mathbb{E} \qquad \langle x = y, i \rangle \in M_i \qquad x = y \notin M_\mathbb{E}}{M_\mathbb{E} := M_\mathbb{E} + \langle x = y, i \rangle}
$$

$$
\text{Conflict}_i \qquad \dfrac{C = \text{no\_cflct} \qquad \langle l_1, i_1 \rangle, \ldots, \langle l_k, i_k \rangle \in M_i \qquad \Psi_i, l_1, \ldots, l_k \models_i \text{false}}{C := \{\langle l_1, i_1 \rangle, \ldots, \langle l_k, i_k \rangle\}}
$$

$$
\text{Explain}_i \qquad \dfrac{\langle l, i \rangle \in C \qquad \langle l_1, i_1 \rangle, \ldots, \langle l_k, i_k \rangle \prec_{M_i} \langle l, i \rangle \qquad \Psi_i, l_1, \ldots, l_k \models_i l}{C := C \cup \{\langle l_1, i_1 \rangle, \ldots, \langle l_k, i_k \rangle\} \setminus \{\langle l, i \rangle\}}
$$

$$
\text{Learn} \qquad \dfrac{C^b = \{l_1, \ldots, l_k\} \qquad C^b \subseteq L_\mathbb{B} \qquad \bar{l}_1 \vee \cdots \vee \bar{l}_k \notin \Psi_\mathbb{B}}{\Psi_\mathbb{B} := \Psi_\mathbb{B} \cup \{\bar{l}_1 \vee \cdots \vee \bar{l}_k\}}
$$

$$
\text{BackJump} \qquad \dfrac{C^b = \{l, l_1, \ldots, l_k\} \qquad \bar{l} \vee \bar{l}_1 \vee \cdots \vee \bar{l}_k \in \Psi_\mathbb{B} \qquad \begin{array}{c}\text{level } l > m \geq \text{level } l_i \\ (i = 1, \ldots, k)\end{array}}{C := \text{no\_cflct} \qquad M_\mathbb{B} := M_\mathbb{B}^{[m]} + \langle \bar{l}, \mathbb{B} \rangle \qquad M_i := M_i^{[m]} \ \ (\text{all } i \neq \mathbb{B})}
$$

Fig. 5. Rules of NODPLL

(5) $\text{Infer}_\mathbb{E}$, (6) $\text{EqDispatch}_{\text{Int}}$, (7) $\text{Infer}_{\text{Int}}$, (8) $\text{EqPropag}_{\text{Int}}$, (9) $\text{EqDispatch}_{\text{UF}}$, (10) $\text{EqDispatch}_{\text{UF}}$, (11) Infer_{UF}, (12) $\text{EqPropag}_{\text{UF}}$, (13) $\text{EqDispatch}_{\text{Int}}$, with these rules modifying the local stacks as follows:

$$
M_\mathbb{B} : [] \xrightarrow{(1)} [\,\boxed{p}\,] \xrightarrow{(2)} [p, \boxed{q}\,]
$$

$$
M_\mathbb{E} : [] \xrightarrow{(3)} [p] \xrightarrow{(5)} [p, \boxed{y = x}\,] \xrightarrow{(8)} [p, y = x, z = x] \xrightarrow{(12)} [p, y = x, z = x, u = y]
$$

$$
M_\text{UF} : [] \xrightarrow{(9)} [y = x] \xrightarrow{(10)} [y = x, z = x] \xrightarrow{(11)} [y = x, z = x, \boxed{u = y}\,]
$$

$$
M_\text{Int} : [] \xrightarrow{(4)} [q] \xrightarrow{(6)} [q, y = x] \xrightarrow{(7)} [q, y = x, \boxed{z = x}\,] \xrightarrow{(13)} [q, y = x, z = x, u = y]
$$

We omit the labels in labeled literals; the highlighted occurrence of each literal indicates its label in *all* stacks. The execution terminates in 6 more steps

$$
\begin{array}{l|c}
\text{Forget} & \dfrac{C = \text{no\_cflct} \qquad \phi \in \Psi_{\mathbb{B}} \qquad \Psi_{\mathbb{B}} \smallsetminus \{\phi\} \models \phi}{\Psi_{\mathbb{B}} := \Psi_{\mathbb{B}} - \{\phi\}} \\[2ex]
\text{Restart} & \dfrac{C = \text{no\_cflct}}{M_i := M_i^{[0]} \ (\text{all } i)} \\[2ex]
\text{ThLearn}_i & \dfrac{l_1, \ldots, l_k \in L_{\mathbb{B}} \qquad \Psi_i \models_i l_1 \vee \cdots \vee l_k}{\Psi_{\mathbb{B}} = \Psi_{\mathbb{B}} \cup \{l_1 \vee \cdots \vee l_k\}}
\end{array}
$$

Fig. 6. Additional rules for NODPLL

$\text{Conflict}_{\text{Int}}, \text{Explain}_{\text{UF}}, \text{Explain}_{\text{Int}}, \text{Explain}_{\mathbb{E}}, \text{Explain}_{\mathbb{B}}, \text{Explain}_{\mathbb{B}}$ that transform C as follows: $\text{no\_cflct} \to \{q, y = u\} \to \{q, z = x\} \to \{q, y = x\} \to \{q, p\} \to \{q\} \to \varnothing$.

An imlementation of NODPLL would require theory solvers $\mathbf{S}_{\mathbb{B}}, \mathbf{S}_{\mathbb{E}}, \mathbf{S}_1, \ldots, \mathbf{S}_n$. Each solver $\mathbf{S}_i$ would be responsible for maintaining its local stack M_i, local constraint set Ψ_i, and for the implementation of the rules $\text{Infer}_i, \text{LitPropag}_i, \text{EqPropag}_i,$ $\text{Conflict}_i, \text{Explain}_i, \text{BackJump}$. The SAT solver $\mathbf{S}_{\mathbb{B}}$ would additionally implement the rules $\text{Decide}, \text{LitDispatch}_i, \text{Learn}$; and the pure equality solver $\mathbf{S}_{\mathbb{E}}$ would additionally implement the rules EqDispatch_i. In addition, a central controller $\mathbf{C}$ would be needed to manage the global conflict set C. With a little effort to ensure that explanations from theory solvers are expressed in terms of SAT literals, the conflict set could alternatively be handled by the SAT solver.

5.2 Correctness

A labeled literal may occur in more than one local stack. As local stacks grow and shrink during a run of NODPLL, the same labeled literal may become created (by rules Decide, Infer, or BackJump), multiply its presence in local stacks (the dispatch and propagation rules), then partially or entirely disappear from the stacks (rule BackJump), then become created again etc. This intricate dynamics makes NODPLL significantly more complex than DPLL, but the basic correctness properties still hold.

Theorem 3 (Termination). *Every run of NODPLL is finite and ends in a state where $C = \text{no\_cflct}$ or $C = \varnothing$.*

Theorem 4 (Soundness). *If a final state with $C = \varnothing$ is reachable, then the input query is $\mathcal{T}$-unsatisfiable.*

Completeness results for NODPLL are derived from Theorem 1. Note that Theorem 1 immediately implies a complete decision procedure: enumerate all assignments M to shared propositional variables and all arrangements Δ for other shared variables and see if there is a pair M, Δ that is consistent with all local constraints Ψ_i. Instead of this inefficient blind search, NODPLL progressively builds M as $M_{\mathbb{B}}$ and Δ as the set of all equalities implied by $\Psi_{\mathbb{E}} \cup M_{\mathbb{E}}$. Thus, when an execution of NODPLL started at s_{init}^{Φ} reaches a final state where $C = \mathsf{no\_cflct}$, if we can prove that the accumulated M and Δ are consistent with the local constraints, it would follow that Φ is satisfiable. However, if a participating theory $\mathcal{T}_i$ is not convex, it may happen that Ψ_i implies $x = y \vee u = v$, while neither $x = y$ nor $u = v$ is implied by any local constraints; thus, Δ contains $x \neq y$ and $u \neq v$ and so is not consistent with Ψ_i. It is well known that convexity guarantees completeness for the original basic Nelson-Oppen cooperation algorithm [15], and case (i) of Theorem 5 is the analogous result for NODPLL. Completeness can also be achieved by proxying all equalities between shared variables with fresh propositional variables ([5], see Section 5.6 below), leaving it to the SAT solver to find the arrangement of shared variables by purely boolean search. This result is covered by case (ii) of Theorem 5.

Theorem 5 (Completeness). *Suppose each of the theories $\mathcal{T}_1, \ldots, \mathcal{T}_n$ is either $\mathcal{T}_{\mathsf{UF}}$ or is parametric. Suppose a final state with $C = \mathsf{no\_cflct}$ is reachable from the initial state generated by the input query $\Phi = \Phi_{\mathbb{B}} \cup \Phi_{\mathbb{E}} \cup \Phi_1 \cup \cdots \cup \Phi_n$. Suppose also that one of the following conditions holds:*

(i) $\mathcal{T}_i$ is convex and $\Phi_i^{card} = \varnothing$, for all $i \in \{1, \ldots, n\}$;
(ii) for every pair x, y of shared variables of the same type, $\Phi_{\mathbb{E}}$ contains a definitional form $p \Leftrightarrow (x = y)$.

Then Φ is $\mathcal{T}$-satisfiable.

Theorems 3, 4 and 5 are proved in the appendix.

5.3   Strengthening Propositional Rules

Clearly, DPLL is a subsystem of NODPLL, but its rules UnitPropag, Conflict and Explain are less permissive than the corresponding rules Infer$_{\mathbb{B}}$, Conflict$_{\mathbb{B}}$ and Explain$_{\mathbb{B}}$ of NODPLL. If we change these three rules of NODPLL with the equally named rules in Figure 7, then the correspondence would be exact. This change would not affect NODPLL in any significant way. In particular, the proof of correctness properties of NODPLL given in the appendix would apply verbatim to the modified system.

5.4   Why Are the Literals Labeled?

Every literal that gets added to any of the local stacks is a logical consequence of the decision literals and the local constraints Ψ_i. When a conflict is reached, we need to identify a subset of decision literals that is sufficient for the conflict. The "explanation" mechanism serves this purpose; starting with a conflicting set of literals, it picks a non-decision literal from the set, detects the inference step that created it, and replaces the literal with a subset of the local stack that was used by the inference step. The result is a new conflicting set of literals that is in a precise sense "older", so that repeating the literal explanation process will terminate (with a conflicting set of decision literals).

$$\textsf{Infer}_{\mathbb{B}} \quad \frac{l \in L_{\mathbb{B}} \qquad l, \bar{l} \notin M_{\mathbb{B}} \qquad l \vee l_1 \vee \cdots \vee l_k \in \Psi \qquad \bar{l}_1, \ldots, \bar{l}_k \in M_{\mathbb{B}}}{M_{\mathbb{B}} := M_{\mathbb{B}} + \langle l, \mathbb{B} \rangle}$$

$$\textsf{Conflict}_{\mathbb{B}} \quad \frac{C = \mathsf{no\_cflct} \qquad \langle l_1, i_1 \rangle, \ldots, \langle l_k, i_k \rangle \in M_{\mathbb{B}} \qquad \bar{l}_1 \vee \cdots \vee \bar{l}_k \in \Psi_{\mathbb{B}}}{C := \{\langle l_1, i_1 \rangle, \ldots, \langle l_k, i_k \rangle\}}$$

$$\textsf{Explain}_{\mathbb{B}} \quad \frac{\langle l, \mathbb{B} \rangle \in C \qquad \langle l_1, i_1 \rangle, \ldots, \langle l_k, i_k \rangle \prec_{M_{\mathbb{B}}} \langle l, \mathbb{B} \rangle \qquad l \vee \bar{l}_1 \vee \cdots \vee \bar{l}_k \in \Psi_{\mathbb{B}}}{C := C \cup \{\langle l_1, i_1 \rangle, \ldots, \langle l_k, i_k \rangle\} \smallsetminus \{\langle l, \mathbb{B} \rangle\}}$$

Fig. 7. Rules of DPLL within NODPLL

Detecting the inference step that created a particular literal is the main purpose of labels: the label in a labeled literal simply signifies the theory responsible for its derivation. Without labels, the explanation process would be too ambiguous and potentially circular—the phenomenon termed "too new explanations" in [16]. As an illustration, consider the five-step execution of NODPLL in Figure 8, where we indicate only the changes of local stacks $M_{\mathbb{B}}, M_1, M_2$, the other parts of the NODPLL state being unaffected. We assume that $\bar{l} \vee l' \in \Psi_{\mathbb{B}}$ and $\Psi_2, l' \models_2 l$—the facts responsible for the $\textsf{Infer}_{\mathbb{B}}$ and $\textsf{Infer}_2$ steps.

$$M_{\mathbb{B}} : [] \xrightarrow{(2)} [l] \xrightarrow{(3)} [l, l'] \qquad\qquad M_{\mathbb{B}} : [] \xrightarrow{(2)} [\langle l, 1 \rangle] \xrightarrow{(3)} [\langle l, 1 \rangle, \langle l', \mathbb{B} \rangle]$$

$$M_1 : [] \xrightarrow{(1)} [l] \qquad\qquad\qquad M_1 : [] \xrightarrow{(1)} [\langle l, 1 \rangle]$$

$$M_2 : [] \xrightarrow{(4)} [l'] \xrightarrow{(5)} [l', l] \qquad\qquad M_2 : [] \xrightarrow{(4)} [\langle l', \mathbb{B} \rangle] \xrightarrow{(5)} [\langle l', \mathbb{B} \rangle, \langle l, 2 \rangle]$$

Fig. 8. A five-step run: (1) $\textsf{Infer}_1$, (2) $\textsf{LitPropag}_1$, (3) $\textsf{Infer}_{\mathbb{B}}$, (4) $\textsf{LitDispatch}_2$, (5) $\textsf{Infer}_2$

Suppose that, as shown on the left in Figure 8, we use non-labeled literals in the local stacks. Assume that sometime in the future a conflict arises, with the conflict set that contains l but not l'. Say, $C = \{l\} \cup D$. Then $\textsf{Explain}_2$ applies and changes C to $\{l'\} \cup D$. But then $\textsf{Explain}_{\mathbb{B}}$ applies and changes C back to $\{l\} \cup D$. So the system can repeat explaining l and l' with each other forever.

The same situation, but with labeled literals, is shown on the right in Figure 8: The conflict set C is now $\{\langle l, 2 \rangle\} \cup D$. It becomes $\{\langle l', \mathbb{B} \rangle\} \cup D$ after $\textsf{Explain}_2$, and then becomes $\{\langle l, 1 \rangle\} \cup D$ after $\textsf{Explain}_{\mathbb{B}}$. At this point, we cannot explain $\langle l, 1 \rangle$ with $\langle l', \mathbb{B} \rangle$, and this prevents the circularity that was possible when labels were not used. Instead, rule $\textsf{Explain}_1$ will have to explain $\langle l, 1 \rangle$ with the (in this case, empty) set of literals that were used in the $\textsf{Infer}_1$ step.

5.5   Basic Extensions

The system NODPLL can be extended with new rules to capture secondary features, often without significantly complicating correctness proofs.

The rules Forget Restart, and ThLearn in Figure 6 are used in practice to improve the boolean search. Reasonably restricting their use to preserve termination, they can be safely added to the basic NODPLL. This has been addressed in [16].

Extending NODPLL with the rule ThLearn makes it possible to propagate disjunctions of shared equalities; one can prove, by an argument that goes back to [15], that with this rule the system becomes complete even for non-convex theories.

NODPLL keeps the variable and constraint sets V_i, Ψ_i constant, except for $\Psi_\mathbb{B}$, which grows with each Learn or ThLearn step and shrinks with Forget or Restart. However, it is useful to also have rules that modify V_i and/or Ψ_i. A simple rule that replaces Ψ_i with an equisatisfiable Ψ_i' that may even use fresh variables [7,16] would allow us to generate $(x \notin u \wedge x \in v) \vee (x \in u \wedge x \notin v)$ when $u \neq v$ (in set theory) and $u = 3x - 1 \wedge v = 2x + 1$ when $2u + 3y = 1$ (in integer arithmetic), where in both cases x is fresh. Adding new variables (proxies of theory facts) to $V_\mathbb{B}$ is the essence of "splitting on demand" [3]; together with the above Ψ_i-modifying rule and ThLearn, it models Extended T-Learn of [3]. Termination is an issue again, but manageable, as shown in [3].

5.6 Equality Proxying and Propagation

If in Example 2 we had a proxy for $y = u$, say $r \Leftrightarrow y = u$, with this definitional form put in both Ψ_{Int} and Ψ_{UF}, and with r in $V_\mathbb{B}$, then instead of propagating $y = u$ from M_{UF} to M_{Int} with EqPropag and EqDispatch in steps 12 and 13, we can equivalently propagate r with LitPropag and LitDispatch.

The DELAYED THEORY COMBINATION (DTC) approach of *MathSAT* [5] takes this idea to the extreme: at the initialization time, introduce a proxy boolean variable e_{xy} for every equality $x = y$ between shared variables and put the definitional form $e_{xy} \Leftrightarrow x = y$ in Ψ_i for all i such that $x, y \in V_i$. Then let NODPLL communicate equalities only through their boolean proxies e_{xy}. This way we can eliminate the rules EqPropag and EqDispatch altogether.

DTC guarantees completeness even if participating theories are not convex; see case (ii) of Theorem 5. It is also conceptually simple and so is used in the theoretical system $DPLL(T_1, \ldots T_n)$ [3]. The disadvantage is that it requires addition of a potentially large set of new variables. *Yices* [10] adopts DTC but goes a step further and curtails proliferation of proxies e_{xy} by introducing them only "on demand", thus ignoring provably useless ones. On the other hand, in *Simplify* [9] and in *CVC Lite* [2] propagation of equalities can occur directly, without creating propositional proxy variables.

Techniques for equality propagation clearly deserve further study and experimentation; NODPLL provides a flexible medium to express various approaches.

5.7 Participating Solvers

The requirements on the deductive strength of individual solvers can be read off from Figure 5 and are exactly as specified by the $DPLL(T)$ framework [16]. Infer needs deduction of new literals from those in the local stack and Explain needs a subset (preferably small) of the local stack that suffices for that deduction. Conflict requires detection of inconsistency and an inconsistent (small again) subset of the local stack. How complete a solver needs to be with respect to Infer and Conflict depends on the approach taken with equality proxying (and on the convexity if of the theory) and is discussed in [16].

There is also an explicit requirement to deal with cardinality constraints, which sometimes can be delegated to the equality module and the SAT solver by introducing clauses saying that every variable of a specific finite type is equal to one of (representatives of) elements of that type [10]. This issue has been only recently raised [12] and is awaiting proper treatment.

6   Conclusion

Gaps between published algorithms and their actual implementations are inevitable, but in the SMT area they are often too large. Clarification efforts are needed and recent work on the $DPPL(T)$ architecture [16] shows how such efforts pay off with superior implementations. Our involvement in the design of a comprehensive SMT solver prompted the question of what exactly is "$DPLL(T)$ with Nelson-Oppen", but the available answers were lacking in various ways. With the transition system NODPLL presented in this paper, we have identified an abstraction layer for describing SMT solvers that is fully tractable by formal analysis and comfortably close to implementation. It gives a precise setting in which one can see the features of existing systems, search for improvements, and recount them.

Acknowledgments. We thank Jim Grundy, Murali Talupur and Cesare Tinelli for their comments, and Leonardo de Moura for explaining some *Yices* details.

References

1. Baader, F., Nipkow, T.: Term Rewriting and All That. Cambridge University Press, Cambridge (1998)
2. Barrett, C.: Checking Validity of Quantifier-free Formulas in Combinations of First-Order Theories. PhD thesis, Stanford University (2002)
3. Barrett, C., Nieuwenhuis, R., Oliveras, A., Tinelli, C.: Splitting on demand in SAT Modulo Theories. In: Hermann, M., Voronkov, A. (eds.) LPAR 2006. LNCS (LNAI), vol. 4246, Springer, Heidelberg (2006)
4. Bonacina, M.P., Ghilardi, S., Nicolini, E., Ranise, S., Zucchelli, D.: Decidability and undecidability results for Nelson-Oppen and rewrite-based decision procedures. In: Furbach, U., Shankar, N. (eds.) IJCAR 2006. LNCS (LNAI), vol. 4130, Springer, Heidelberg (2006)
5. Bozzano, M., Bruttomesso, R., Cimatti, A., Junttila, T., van Rossum, P., Ranise, S., Sebastiani, R.: Efficient theory combination via boolean search. Information and Computation 204(10), 1493–1525

6. Bryant, R., Lahiri, S., Seshia, S.: Modeling and verifying systems using a logic of counter arithmetic with lambda expressions and uninterpreted functions. In: Brinksma, E., Larsen, K.G. (eds.) CAV 2002. LNCS, vol. 2404, Springer, Heidelberg (2002)
7. Conchon, S., Krstić, S.: Strategies for combining decision procedures. Theoretical Computer Science 354(2), 187–210 (2006)
8. Davis, M., Logemann, G., Loveland, D.: A machine program for theorem-proving. Commun. ACM 5(7), 394–397 (1962)
9. Detlefs, D., Nelson, G., Saxe, J.B.: Simplify: A theorem prover for program checking. Journal of the ACM 52(3), 365–473 (2005)
10. Dutertre, B., de Moura, L.: The Yices SMT solver. Technical report, SRI International (2006)
11. Eén, N., Sörensen, N.: An extensible SAT solver. In: Giunchiglia, E., Tacchella, A. (eds.) SAT 2003. LNCS, vol. 2919, Springer, Heidelberg (2004)
12. Krstić, S., Goel, A., Grundy, J., Tinelli, C.: Combined satisfiability modulo parametric theories. In: TSDM 2000. LNCS, vol. 4424, Springer, Heidelberg (2007) (extended version) available at ftp://ftp.cs.uiowa.edu/pub/tinelli/papers/KrsGGT-RR-06.pdf
13. Mitchell, J.C.: Foundations of Programming Languages. MIT Press, Cambridge (1996)
14. Moskewicz, M.W., Madigan, C.F., Zhao, Y., Zhang, L., Malik, S.: Chaff: engineering an efficient sat solver. In: Conference on Design Automation (DAC), ACM Press, New York (2001)
15. Nelson, G., Oppen, D.C.: Simplification by cooperating decision procedures. ACM Transactions on Programming Languages and Systems 1(2), 245–257 (1979)
16. Nieuwenhuis, R., Oliveras, A., Tinelli, C.: Solving SAT and SAT Modulo Theories: From an abstract Davis-Putnam-Logemann-Loveland procedure to DPLL(T). Journal of the ACM 53(6), 937–977 (2006)
17. Ranise, S., Ringeissen, C., Zarba, C.G.: Combining data structures with nonstably infinite theories using many-sorted logic. In: Gramlich, B. (ed.) Frontiers of Combining Systems. LNCS (LNAI), vol. 3717, Springer, Heidelberg (2005)
18. Reynolds, J.C.: Types, abstraction and parametric polymorphism. In: Mason, R.E.A., (ed.) Information Processing: 9th World Computer Congress, pp. 513–523. North-Holland (1983)
19. Tinelli, C., Harandi, M.: A new correctness proof of the Nelson-Oppen combination procedure. In: Frontiers of Combining Systems (FroCoS), vol. 3 of Applied Logic, pp. 103–120 (1996)
20. Tinelli, C., Zarba, C.: Combining nonstably infinite theories. Journal of Automated Reasoning 34(3), 209–238 (2005)

A   Appendix

Proof of Theorem 2

There is little here that is not contained in the proofs of Theorems 3, 4, 5. Yet, we give a full proof of Theorem 2 because it may be of independent interest and because it may serve as an introduction to the more involved proofs that follow.

Starting the proof of termination of DPLL, define the relation $M \preceq M'$ on checkpointed sequences to mean that either $M = M'$, or for some m, $M^{[m]}$ is a proper prefix of $M'^{[m]}$. It is easy to prove that $\preceq$ is a partial order.

Observe that with respect to the ordering $\preceq$, the rules Decide, UnitPropag and BackJump increase the M-component of the DPLL state, while the other three rules leave M unchanged. Observe also that the set of all possible values for M is finite, as a consequence of this easily checked invariant of DPLL:

$$\text{If } l \text{ occurs in } M, \text{ then it occurs only once and } \bar{l} \text{ does not occur at all.} \tag{3}$$

It follows now that in every run

$$s_{\text{init}} \rightarrow s_1 \rightarrow s_2 \rightarrow \ldots \tag{4}$$

of DPLL, only finitely many steps are based on Decide, UnitPropag and BackJump. Since there must be a BackJump between any two occurrences of Conflict (to restore $C = \text{no\_cflct}$), the number of occurrences of Conflict in (4) is also finite. The same is true about Learn because there are only finitely many clauses to add to Ψ. Thus, the only possibility for (4) to be infinite is that from some point on, all steps are based on the rule Explain. To see that every sequence of Explain-based steps must be finite, observe first an easy invariant of DPLL:

$$\text{Every literal in } C \text{ occurs in } M. \tag{5}$$

Notice then that, leaving M intact, Explain replaces a literal l of C with a set of literals that precede l in M. Thus, with each application of Explain, the set C gets smaller in the multised ordering that the ordering of M induces on subsets of M.[5]

For the rest of the proof, assume that $s_\diamond = \langle \Psi_\diamond, M_\diamond, C_\diamond \rangle$ is a final state obtained by running DPLL initialized with the set of clauses Ψ_{init}. It remains to prove

$$C_\diamond = \text{no\_cflct} \text{ or } C_\diamond = \varnothing; \tag{6}$$

$$\text{If } C_\diamond = \varnothing \text{ then } \Psi_{\text{init}} \text{ is unsatisfiable;} \tag{7}$$

$$\text{If } C_\diamond = \text{no\_cflct}, \text{ then } M_\diamond \text{ is a model for } \Psi_{\text{init}}. \tag{8}$$

Proof of (6). Assuming the contrary, suppose $C_\diamond$ is a non-empty set and let l be an arbitrary element of it. By (5), l occurs in $M_\diamond$. Considering a particular run $s_{\text{init}} \rightarrow s_1 \rightarrow s_2 \ldots \rightarrow s_\diamond$, let s_n be the last state in this run such that $s_n.M$ does not contain l. Note that the transition $s_n \rightarrow s_{n+1}$ must be based on Decide, UnitPropag, or BackJump, since the other three rules do not update M. Note that $s_{n+1}.M = s_n.M + l$ and also that

$$s_{n+1}.M \text{ is a prefix of } s_i.M \text{ for all } i > n. \tag{9}$$

Indeed, if (9) is not true, then in the execution $s_{n+1} \rightarrow \cdots \rightarrow s_\diamond$ there must be a BackJump to the level smaller than the level of l, and it must remove l from M, contradicting the assumption that l occurs in $s_i.M$ for all $i > n$.

---

[5] "$M \sqsupset_{\text{mul}} N$ holds iff you can get from M to N by carrying out the following procedure one or more times: remove an element x and add a finite number of elements, all of which are smaller than x." [1]

If the transition $s_n \rightarrow s_{n+1}$ is a UnitPropag or BackJump, then Explain is applicable to s_{n+1} and so by (9), Explain is applicable to $s_\diamond$ as well, contradicting the finality of $s_\diamond$. Thus, our transition must be based on the rule Decide, and so l is a *decision literal* (a literal immediately following an occurrence of $\Box$) in $s_\diamond.M$. Since l was by assumption an arbitrary element of $C_\diamond$, it follows that *all* elements of $C_\diamond$ are decision literals. As a consequence, the levels of literals in $C_\diamond$ are all distinct. Now, depending on whether the clause $\bigvee_{l \in C_\diamond} \bar{l}$ is in Ψ or not, either BackJump or Learn applies to $s_\diamond$. In both cases we run into contradiction with the finality of $s_\diamond$.

Proof of (7). We prove by simultaneous induction that the following two properties are invariants of DPLL. Note that (7) is a special case of (11) when $k = 0$.

$$\Psi \text{ is equivalent with } \Psi_{\text{init}} \tag{10}$$
$$\text{If } C = \{l_1, \ldots, l_k\}, \text{ then } \Psi_{\text{init}} \models \bar{l}_1 \vee \cdots \vee \bar{l}_k \tag{11}$$

Both properties are trivially true for initial states. Assuming $s \rightarrow s'$ is a transition based on a rule R of DPLL, and s satisfies (10) and (11), we proceed to prove that s' satisfies these conditions too.

If R is not Learn, then $s'.\Psi = s.\Psi$ and so s' satisfies (10) by induction hypothesis. If R is Learn, the proof that s' satisfies (10) is a simple application of the induction hypotheses (10) and (11). Thus, s' satisfies (10) in all cases.

Now we prove that s' satisfies (11). The only non-trivial cases are when R is Conflict$_i$ or Explain$_i$, since in all other cases we have $s'.C = s.C$. When R is Conflict$_i$, from the guard $\bar{l}_1 \vee \cdots \vee \bar{l}_k \in s.\Psi$ and (10), we obtain the desired relation $\Psi_{\text{init}} \models \bar{l}_1 \vee \cdots \vee \bar{l}_k$ immediately.

Suppose R is Explain$_i$ and let γ be the clause consisting of the inverses of literals of $s.C - \{l\}$. By induction hypothesis, we have $\Psi_{\text{init}} \models \gamma \vee \bar{l}$. Also, the guard of Explain and (10) imply $\Psi_{\text{init}} \models \bar{l}_1 \vee \cdots \vee \bar{l}_k \vee l$. The required relation $\Psi_{\text{init}} \models \gamma \vee \bar{l}_1 \vee \cdots \vee \bar{l}_k$ follows immediately.

Proof of (8). From (5) and non-applicability of Decide, it follows that $M_\diamond$ is an assignment: for every $l \in L$, it contains either l or $\bar{l}$. By (10), we only need to prove $M_\diamond \models \gamma$ for every clause $\gamma = l_1 \vee \cdots \vee l_k$ in $\Psi_\diamond$. But if this were not true, we would have $\bar{l}_i \in M_\diamond$ for $i = 1, \ldots, k$ and so Conflict would be applicable to the stat $s_\diamond$, contradicting its finality.

Proof of Theorems 3 and 4

Assuming that the input formula Φ is fixed, we will write s_{init} for s_{init}^Φ. For any state s, the union of local constraints $s.\Psi_\text{B}, s.\Psi_\text{E}, s.\Psi_1, \ldots, s.\Psi_n$ will be denoted $s.\Psi$.

Let us start with a set of invariants of NODPLL:

$$\text{All local stacks contain the same number of occurrences of } \Box; \tag{12}$$
$$\text{In any local stack, any literal can occur at most once;} \tag{13}$$
$$\text{If } l \text{ occurs in } M_\text{B}, \text{ then } \bar{l} \text{ does not occur in } M_\text{B}. \tag{14}$$

All these properties are obviously true in the initial state. Directly examining all rules, we can easily check that if $s \to s'$ and s satisfies the properties, then so does s'.

Consider an arbitrary execution sequence (finite or infinite)

$$\pi : \; s_{\text{init}} = s_0 \to s_1 \to s_2 \to \dots \qquad (15)$$

For each state s_k in π we will collect the local stacks $s_k.M_i$ ($i = \mathbb{B}, \mathbb{E}, 1, \dots, n$) into the GLOBAL STACK $s_k.O$ that interleaves them all. The elements of that stack will be triples $\langle l, j, i \rangle$, denoting the occurrence of $\langle l, j \rangle$ in M_i. The global stacks $s_k.O$ are defined inductively as follows. First, $s_{\text{init}}.O$ is the empty sequence. Then, if the transition $s_k \to s_{k+1}$ is based on the rule R, let $s_{k+1}.O = s_k.O$ if R is Learn, Conflict$_i$ or Explain$_i$; if R is BackJump, let $s_{k+1}.O = (s_k.O)^{[m]} + \langle \bar{l}, \mathbb{B}, \mathbb{B} \rangle$; finally, if R is one of the remaining six rules, let $s_{k+1}.O = s_k.O + U$, where U is given in the following table:

R :	Decide	Infer$_i$	LitDispatch$_i$	EqDispatch$_i$	LitPropag$_i$	EqPropag$_i$
U :	$\square + \langle p^\epsilon, \mathbb{B}, \mathbb{B} \rangle$	$\langle l, i, i \rangle$	$\langle p^\epsilon, j, i \rangle$	$\langle x = y, j, i \rangle$	$\langle p^\epsilon, i, \mathbb{B} \rangle$	$\langle x = y, i, \mathbb{E} \rangle$

It follows immediately from the definition that $\langle l, i, j \rangle$ occurs in $s.O$ if and only if $\langle l, i \rangle$ occurs in $s.M_j$. The ordering of occurrence triples in $s.O$ will be denoted $\sqsubseteq$.

Lemma 1. *The following properties hold for all states in* π.

(a) If $\langle l, j \rangle \prec_{M_i} \langle l', j' \rangle$ then $\langle l, j, i \rangle \sqsubseteq \langle l', j', i \rangle$.
(b) If $\langle l, i \rangle$ occurs in M_j, then it also occurs in M_i and we have $\langle l, i, i \rangle \sqsubseteq \langle l, i, j \rangle$.

Proof. Straightforward induction. $\qquad\qquad\qquad\qquad\qquad\qquad\qquad\qquad\qquad\square$

Corollary 1. *If the rule* LitDispatch$_i$ *or* EqDispatch$_i$ *applies to a reachable state, then $j \neq i$. (The number j here is from the rule as stated in Figure 5.)*

Proof. Let s be a state in which LitDispatch$_i$ applies. (We omit the discussion of the entirely analogous EqDispatch case.) Using an execution sequence π that contains s, we have $\langle p^\epsilon, j, i \rangle \in s.O$ and so, by part *(b)* of Lemma 1, $\langle p^\epsilon, j, j \rangle \in s.O$. In particular $p^\epsilon \in M_j$, which together with the guard $p^\epsilon \notin M_i$ implies $i \neq j$. $\square$

For each state s, define

$$s.C^* = \begin{cases} \text{no\_cflct} & \text{if } s.C = \text{no\_cflct} \\ \{\langle l, i, i \rangle \mid \langle l, i \rangle \in s.C\} & \text{otherwise} \end{cases}$$

Lemma 2. *(a) For every reachable state s with $s.C \neq$ no_cflct, all elements of $s.C^*$ occur in $s.O$.*
(b) If s is a reachable state and $s \to s'$ is a transition based on the rule Explain$_i$, *then $s'.C^* \sqsubset_{\text{mul}} s.C^*$, where $\sqsubseteq_{\text{mul}}$ is the multiset ordering[6] induced by the relation $\sqsubseteq$ on the set of triples occurring in $s'.O = s.O$.*

---

[6] The guard of Explain$_i$ implies that neither $s.C^*$ nor $s'.C^*$ can be no_cflct, so they can be compared by $\sqsubseteq_{\text{mul}}$.

Proof. First we prove *(a)* by induction. Let s, s' be two consecutive states in any execution sequence π and let the transition $s \rightarrow s'$ be based on a rule R. If R is any of the first six rules in Figure 5, or if R is Learn, then $s'.C^* = s.C^*$ and $s'.O$ contains $s.O$. If R is BackJump, then $s'.C \neq$ no_cflct. In all these cases, there is nothing to check. Finally, if R is either Conflict$_i$ or Explain$_i$, then $s'.O = s.O$, and $s'.C - s.C$ consists of pairs $\langle l_\nu, i_\nu \rangle$ that occur in $s.M_i$. Thus, $\langle l_\nu, i_\nu, i \rangle$ occurs in $s.O$, and by Lemma 1*(a)*, the new element $\langle l_\nu, i_\nu, i_\nu \rangle$ of $s.C^*$ occurs in $s.O$ too.

For part *(b)*, we have

$$s'.C = s.C - \{\langle l, i \rangle\} + \{\langle l_1, i_1 \rangle, \ldots, \langle l_k, i_k \rangle\},$$

where $\langle l_1, i_1 \rangle, \ldots, \langle l_k, i_k \rangle \prec_{s.M_i} \langle l, i \rangle$. Thus, by Lemma 1*(a,b)*,

$$\langle l_\nu, i_\nu, i_\nu \rangle \sqsubseteq \langle l_\nu, i_\nu, i \rangle \sqsubset \langle l, i, i \rangle$$

for $\nu = 1, \ldots, k$. $\qquad\square$

Proof of Theorem 3. Part 1: Termination. Immediately from the definition of the global stack, for every NODPLL transition $s \rightarrow s'$ we have $s.O = s'.O$ if the transition is based on Learn, Conflict, or Explain, and $s.O \prec s'.O$ if the transition is based on any other rule. The ordering $\prec$ here is that of checkpointed sequences, introduced in the proof of Theorem 2.

Assume now the theorem is not true and suppose the execution sequence π in (15) is infinite. From the previous paragraphs, we have

$$s_{\text{init}}.O \preceq s_1.O \preceq s_2.O \preceq \ldots \qquad (16)$$

The invariant (13) (unique occurrence of literals in local stacks) implies that the set of all possible tuples $s.O$ where s is a NODPLL state is finite. This immediately implies that only finitely many inequalities in (16) can be strict.

Since (16) is thus an eventually constant sequence, the first six rules of NODPLL and BackJump (which all necessarily change $s.O$) can occur only finitely many times in π. Since Conflict applies only when $C =$ no_cflct and replaces it with a set, and since only BackJump can make $C =$ no_cflct again, we derive that Conflict also can occur only finitely many times in π. Since there are only finitely many clauses that Learn might add to $\Psi_\mathbb{B}$, this rule also occurs finitely many times. Therefore, all but finitely many transitions in π are based on Explain.

Now, for some m, we have that all transitions in the subsequence $s_m \rightarrow s_{m+1} \rightarrow \ldots$ of π are based on Explain. By Lemma 2, this yields an infinite descending chain $s_m.C^* \sqsupseteq_{\text{mul}} s_{m+1}.C^* \sqsupseteq_{\text{mul}} \ldots$, contradicting well-foundedness of the multiset ordering. This finishes the proof that NODPLL is terminating. $\square$

Recall that a *decision literal* in a state s is any labeled literal $\langle l, \mathbb{B} \rangle$ that occurs immediately after $\square$ in $s.M_\mathbb{B}$. Let M_{dec} be the subsequence of $M_\mathbb{B}$ consisting of all decision literals and let $M_{\text{dec}}^{[n]}$ be the sequence of the first n decision literals. We will also need the notation for conflict clauses: if $s.C = \{l_1, \ldots, l_k\}$, define $s.C^{\text{cls}} = \bar{l}_1 \vee \cdots \vee \bar{l}_k$, and if $s.C =$ no_cflct, define $s.C^{\text{cls}} =$ true. Note that $s.C^{\text{cls}} =$ false if $s.C = \varnothing$.

Lemma 3. *The following are invariants of* NODPLL:

(a) $\Psi \models_\mathcal{T} \Psi_{\text{init}}$ *and* $\Psi_{\text{init}} \models_\mathcal{T} \Psi$;
(b) $\Psi_{\text{init}} \models_\mathcal{T} C^{\text{cls}}$;
(c) For every i, $\Psi_{\text{init}}, M_{\text{dec}} \models_\mathcal{T} M_i$.

Proof. The initial state obviously satisfies all three conditions.

We prove (a) and (b) by simultaneous induction. If $s \rightarrow s'$ is a transition based on a rule R of NODPLL, and s satisfies (a) and (b), we prove that s' satisfies these conditions too.

If R is not Learn, then $s'.\Psi = s.\Psi$ and so s' satisfies (a) by induction hypothesis. If R is Learn, then $s'.\Psi = s.\Psi \cup \{s.C^{\text{cls}}\}$, so the proof that s' satisfies (a) is a simple application of the induction hypotheses (a) and (b).

Now we prove that s' satisfies (b): $\Psi_{\text{init}} \models_\mathcal{T} s'.C^{\text{cls}}$. The only non-trivial cases are when R is Conflict$_i$ or Explain$_i$, since in all other cases we have either $s'.C = s.C$ or $s'.C = \text{true}$ (the latter happens if R is BackJump). When R is Conflict$_i$, the truth of the guard $s.\Psi_i, l_i, \ldots, l_k \models_i \text{false}$ directly implies $s.\Psi_i \models_i s'.C^{\text{cls}}$. By induction hypothesis (a) $\Psi_{\text{init}} \models_\mathcal{T} s.\Psi_i$. Combining the two facts proves our goal.

Suppose finally R is Explain$_i$. The clause $s'.C^{\text{cls}}$ is obtained from $s.C^{\text{cls}}$ by removing the literal $\bar{l}$ and adding literals $\bar{l}_1, \ldots, \bar{l}_k$. We have $s.\Psi_i, l_i, \ldots, l_k \models_i l$ from the guard of our rule. We also have $\Psi_{\text{init}} \models_\mathcal{T} s.C^{\text{cls}}$ and $\Psi_{\text{init}} \models_\mathcal{T} s.\Psi_i$ from the induction hypotheses (b) and (a) respectively. Combining these facts proves that s' satisfies (b) too.

Having proved that (a) and (b) hold for all reachable states, it only remains to prove (c). We will prove that the following generalization of (c) holds for all reachable states.

$$\text{For every } i \text{ and } n, \ \Psi_{\text{init}}, M_{\text{dec}}^{[n]} \models_\mathcal{T} M_i^{[n]}. \tag{17}$$

Again, we reason by induction. If R, the rule used in a transition $s \rightarrow s'$, is one of the first six (from Decide to EqPropag) in Figure 5, it is easy to see by direct examination that s' satisfies (17) if s satisfies it. For the next three rules we have $s'M_i = s.M_i$ (for all i), so there is nothing to prove. Thus, we may assume that the transition $s \rightarrow s'$ is based on BackJump. The only fact needed to prove that s' satisfies (17) that is not immediately implied by the induction hypothesis is $\Psi_{\text{init}}, M_{\text{dec}}^{[m]} \models_\mathcal{T} \bar{l}$, where m and l are as in the rule BackJump in Figure 5. This follows from two facts: (1) $\Psi_{\text{init}} \models_\mathcal{T} s.C^{\text{cls}}$, and (2) $\Psi_{\text{init}}, M_{\text{dec}}^{[m]} \models_\mathcal{T} l'$ for every $l' \in s.C - \{l\}$. Fact (1) is part (b) of our lemma, and fact (2) follows from our induction hypothesis, because the guard of BackJump implies that $l' \in s.M_{\mathbb{B}}^{[m]}$ for every $l' \in s.C - \{l\}$. $\square$

Proof of Theorem 3. Part 2: Final States. Suppose s is a final state with $s.C \neq$ no_cflct and let $s_{\text{init}} \rightarrow s_1 \rightarrow s_2 \rightarrow \ldots \rightarrow s$ be a run leading to s. Arguing by contradiction, assume $s.C \neq \varnothing$. Note that $\bigvee_{l \in C} \bar{l} \in \Psi_{\mathbb{B}}$, because otherwise Learn would apply to s. We claim that in this situation all elements of C are decision literals. Since no two decision literals can have the same level, this claim implies that BackJump applies to s, which is a contradiction.

It remains now to prove our claim: every element $\langle l, i \rangle$ of $s.C$ is a decision literal. By Lemma 2 (a), $\langle l, i \rangle$ occurs in $s.M_j$ for some j, and then by Lemma 1 (b), $\langle l, i \rangle \in s.M_i$. Let n be the largest integer such that $\langle l, i, i \rangle \notin s_n.O$. Let R be the rule used in the transition $s_n \rightarrow s_{n+1}$. By definition of the global stack, we have $s_{n+1}.O = s_n.O^{[m]} + \langle l, i, i \rangle$ (when R is BackJump), $s_{n+1}.O = s_n.O + \square + \langle l, i, i \rangle$ (when R is Decide), or $s_{n+1}.O = s_n.O + \langle l, i, i \rangle$, in the remaining cases. The "remaining cases" actually consist only of Infer_i; the propagation rules change the global stack by adding to it triples $\langle l', i', j' \rangle$ with $i' \neq j'$, and the same is true of the dispatch rules by Corollary 1. If R is Decide, we are done. Thus, it only remains to eliminate the possibilities when R is Infer_i or BackJump.

Note that in all cases $s_{n+1}.O$ must be a prefix of $s.O$, because otherwise there would have been a BackJump to a level smaller than the level of $\langle l, i, i \rangle$ in the execution $s_{n+1} \rightarrow \cdots \rightarrow s$, and it would have removed $\langle l, i, i \rangle$ from the global stack, contradicting the assumption that $\langle l, i, i \rangle$ occurs in $s_i.O$ for all $i \geq n+1$. Thus, $s_{n+1}.M_i$ is a prefix of $s.M_i$.

Suppose R is Infer_i. The guard of Infer_i implies $\Psi_i, l_1, \ldots, l_k \models_i l$ for some $l_1, \ldots, l_k \in s_n.M_i$. Since $s_n.M_i$ is a prefix of $s_{n+1}.M_i$, it is also a prefix of $s.M_i$. This implies that $\mathsf{Explain}_i$ is enabled at s—a contradiction because s is final.

Suppose now R is BackJump: $s_{n+1}.O = s_n.O^{[m]} + \langle l, i, i \rangle$. We have $i = \mathbb{B}$ and $\langle l, i \rangle = \langle \bar{l}_0, \mathbb{B} \rangle$, where $s_n.C = \{\langle l_0, i_0 \rangle, \langle l_1, i_1 \rangle, \ldots, \langle l_k, i_k \rangle\}$ and level $l_0 > k \geq$ level l_ν ($\nu = 1, \ldots k$). The levels here are computed with respect to s_n. Thus, $l_1, \ldots, l_k \in s_n.M_{\mathbb{B}}$. Moreover, since the backjumping level in the transition $s_n \rightarrow s_{n+1}$ is m, from the guard of BackJump we have that the literals $l_1, \ldots, l_k$ occur in $(s_n.M_{\mathbb{B}})^{[m]}$ (the level of each is at most m). Since $s_{n+1}.M_{\mathbb{B}} = s_n.M_{\mathbb{B}}^{[m]} + \langle \bar{l}_0, \mathbb{B}, \mathbb{B} \rangle$ and $s_{n+1}.M_{\mathbb{B}}$ is a prefix of $s.M_{\mathbb{B}}$, these literals occur in $s.M_{\mathbb{B}}$ as well, and their occurrences in $s.M_{\mathbb{B}}$ precede the occurrence of $\bar{l}_0$. The guard of BackJump implies also that the clause $\bar{l}_0 \vee \bar{l}_1 \vee \cdots \vee \bar{l}_k$ is in $s_n.\Psi_{\mathbb{B}}$, and so it must be in $s.\Psi_{\mathbb{B}}$ too (any transition that changes $\Psi_{\mathbb{B}}$ makes it larger). The facts just collected immediately imply that $\mathsf{Explain}_{\mathbb{B}}$ applies to s, which (again) is not possible because s is final. $\square$

Proof of Theorem 4. This is a special case of Lemma 3(b), since $C^{\mathsf{cls}} = \mathsf{false}$ when $C = \varnothing$. $\square$

Proof of Theorem 5

By Theorem 1, to prove that Φ is $\mathcal{T}$-satisfiable, it suffices to find an assignment M to variables occurring in $\Phi_{\mathbb{B}}$ and an arrangement Δ of other shared variables in Φ such that

$$M \models \Phi_{\mathbb{B}} \tag{18}$$

$$(\Phi_i \cup \Delta)^{\mathsf{pure}} \cup \Phi_i^{\mathsf{card}} \cup M \text{ is } \mathcal{T}_i\text{-satisfiable for every } i \in \{\mathbb{E}, 1, \ldots, n\} \tag{19}$$

Since $\Psi_i = \Phi_i^{\mathsf{pure}} \cup \Phi_i^{\mathsf{card}}$, the condition (19) can be restated as

$$\Psi_i \cup \Delta \cup M \text{ is } \mathcal{T}_i\text{-satisfiable for every } i \in \{\mathbb{E}, 1, \ldots, n\}. \tag{20}$$

Now, suppose we are in a final state s of NODPLL. We will first see how s determines M and Δ such that (18) holds. Then we will show that (20) holds if we assume either of the conditions $(i), (ii)$.

Define M to be $s.M_\mathbb{B}$. In s, as in any final state, $s.M_\mathbb{B}$ contains every variable in $V_\mathbb{B}$ or its negation—otherwise the rule Decide would apply. Thus, M can be seen as a full assignment to propositional variables in $V_\mathbb{B}$. Since all variables of $s.\Psi_\mathbb{B}$ are in $V_\mathbb{B}$, we must have either $M \models s.\Psi_\mathbb{B}$ or $M \models \neg(s.\Psi_\mathbb{B})$. In the latter case, M would have to falsify some clause of $s.\Psi_\mathbb{B}$, so the rule Conflict$_\mathbb{B}$ would apply, which is not true since we are in a final state. Thus, $M \models s.\Psi_\mathbb{B}$. Since $\Psi_\mathbb{B}$ is initially $\Phi_\mathbb{B}$ and can only grow with applications of NODPLL rules, the desired relation $M \models \Phi_\mathbb{B}$ holds.

For the rest of the proof, observe that rules of NODPLL do not modify local constraints other than $\Psi_\mathbb{B}$; thus, $s.\Psi_i = \Psi_i$ holds for every $i \neq \mathbb{B}$.

Recall that $\Phi_\mathbb{E}$ consists of formulas of the form $p \Leftrightarrow (x = y)$, where $p \in V_\mathbb{B}$ and x, y are shared variables. Since $M = s.M_\mathbb{B}$ is an assignment to $V_\mathbb{B}$, we have either $p \in M$, or $\bar{p} \in M$. In the first case, we must have $p \in s.M_\mathbb{E}$, and in the second case, we must have $\bar{p} \in s.M_\mathbb{E}$—otherwise, LitDispatch$_\mathbb{E}$ would apply to s. (Note that $p, \bar{p} \in L_\mathbb{E}$.) Since $\Psi_\mathbb{E} \cup s.M_\mathbb{E}$ is consistent (otherwise, Conflict$_\mathbb{E}$ would apply to s), it follows that the set $\Psi_\mathbb{E} \cup s.M_\mathbb{E} \cup M$ is consistent too. Consider an arbitrary model of this set and define Δ to be the arrangement of $V_\mathbb{E}$ determined by that model. Clearly, (20) holds for $i = \mathbb{E}$.

Arguing by contradiction, assume (20) is not true for some i. This implies that $\Psi_i \cup \Delta_i \cup M$ is not $\mathcal{T}_i$-satisfiable, where Δ_i is the subset of Δ containing the (dis)equalities between variables in V_i. Indeed, if one has a $\mathcal{T}_i$-model for $\Psi_i \cup \Delta_i \cup M$, then this model extends to a model of $\Psi_i \cup \Delta \cup M$ by interpreting the non-V_i variables of Δ as arbitrary elements constrained only by equalities and disequalities of $\Delta - \Delta_i$. (It is easy to argue that such extensions exist.)

Notice that for unsatisfiability of $\Psi_i \cup \Delta_i \cup M$, propositional literals that occur in M but not in Ψ_i are irrelevant. Thus, $\Psi_i \cup \Delta_i \cup M^i$ is $\mathcal{T}_i$-unsatisfiable, where M^i is the subsequence of M containing only variables in $V_\mathbb{B} \cap V_i$ and their negations. Now, every element of M^i must also be in M_i, because otherwise the rule LitDispatch would apply. As a consequence, $\Psi_i \cup \Delta_i \cup M_i$ is not $\mathcal{T}_i$-satisfiable.

At this point, we have to use our assumptions (i) or (ii).

Case 1: Assume (i) holds. Write $\Delta_i = \Delta^+ \cup \Delta^-$, where Δ^+ and Δ^- contain equalities and disequalities respectively. Then $\Psi_i, M_i, \Delta^+ \models_i \neg \Delta^-$. For each definitional form $p \Leftrightarrow \phi$ in Ψ_i, either p or $\bar{p}$ occurs in M_i (because $p \in V_\mathbb{B} \cap V_i$ and M is an assignment to all variables in $V_\mathbb{B}$). Obtain Ψ_i' from Ψ_i by replacing $p \Leftrightarrow \phi$ with ϕ or $\neg\phi$, depending on whether M_i contains p or $\neg p$. Clearly, $\Psi_i, M_i \models_i \Psi_i'$ and $\Psi_i', \Delta^+ \models_i \neg \Delta^-$. Now, $\Psi_i' \cup \Delta^+$ is a set of $\mathcal{T}_i$-literals (here we use the assumption that Ψ_i contains no cardinality constraints) and Δ^- is a disjunction of equalities. Since $\mathcal{T}_i$ is convex, we must have $\Psi_i' \cup \Delta^+ \models_i x = y$ for some $x, y \in V_i$ such that $(x \neq y) \in \Delta^-$. In other words, $\Psi_i, M_i \models_i x = y$ for some x, y such that $\langle x, y \rangle \notin \delta$. Since Infer$_i$ does not apply, we must have $(x = y) \in M_i$. Then, since EqPropag$_i$ does not apply, we must have $(x = y) \in s.M_\mathbb{E}$. This contradicts consistency of $s.M_\mathbb{E} \cup \Delta$ that has already been established, finishing the proof.

Case 2: Assume (ii) holds. Since $\Psi_i \cup \Delta_i \cup M_i$ is $\mathcal{T}_i$-unsatisfiable, we have $\Psi_i, M_i \models_i \neg\Delta_i$, and so $\Psi_i, M_i \models_i \neg\phi$ for some $\phi \in \Delta_i$. Now, ϕ is either $x = y$ or $x \neq y$, for some $x, y \in V_i$. By assumption (ii), there is a variable $p \in V_\mathbb{B} \cap V_i$ such that $p \Leftrightarrow (x = y)$ is in $\Psi_\mathbb{E}$. As we already argued, we have either $p \in M_i$ and $p \in s.M_\mathbb{E}$, or $\bar{p} \in M_i$ and $\bar{p} \in s.M_\mathbb{E}$. Assume first $p \in M_i$; then $(x = y) \in \Delta$ (by definition of Δ), so ϕ must be $(x = y)$, so $\Psi_i, M_i \models_i \neg p$, which implies $\Psi_i, M_i \models_i$ false and therefore applicability of Conflict$_i$ to our final state. This is a contradiction. In the same way the contradiction is obtained in the remaining case $\bar{p} \in M_i$. □

Note that in case (i), the proof relies on the full strength of rules Infer$_i$ for inferring equalities between variables. In case (ii), however, the proof relies only on the full strength of the rules Conflict$_i$ and it would go through even if the rules Infer$_i$ ($i = 1, \ldots, n$) were removed from the system.

Note also that completeness can be proved on the *per theory* basis, where different theories satisfy different sufficient conditions for completeness. For example, instead of requiring in Theorem 5 that one of the conditions (i), (ii) holds, it suffices to make these requirements per theory. Precisely, we can change the last assumption of Theorem 5 to read as follows: for every $i \in \{1, \ldots, n\}$, one of the following conditions holds:

(i') $\mathcal{T}_i$ is convex and $\Phi_i^{\mathrm{card}} = \varnothing$;
(ii') for every pair $x, y \in V_i$ of shared variables of the same type, $\Phi_\mathbb{E}$ contains a definitional form $p \Leftrightarrow (x = y)$.

The proof above would apply with minimal changes.

Finally, we give an example showing that in case (i) the completeness does not necessarily hold without the assumption $\Phi_i^{\mathrm{card}} = \varnothing$.

Example 3. Let x_1, x_2, x_3, x_4 be variables of type α, and let Φ be the $\mathcal{T}_\times$-query consisting of the cardinality constraint $\alpha \doteq 2$ and all constraints $\langle x_i, x_j \rangle \neq \langle x_k, x_l \rangle$, where (i, j, k, l) is a permutation of $(1, 2, 3, 4)$. It is easy to see that Φ is satisfiable and that in every model $\langle \iota, \rho \rangle$ of Φ, three of the variables x_1, x_2, x_3, x_4 are mapped by ρ to the same element of $\iota(\alpha)$, while the fourth is mapped to the other element of the two-element set $\iota(\alpha)$.

Now suppose we have five variables x_i of type α, five disjoint theories $\mathcal{T}_i$ and queries Φ_i such that the variables occurring in Φ_i are x_j, where $j \in \{1, \ldots, 5\} \setminus \{i\}$. Suppose also that each Φ_i contains the cardinality constraint $\alpha \doteq 2$ and that—as in the example of $\mathcal{T}_\times$ and Φ above—for every i, the query Φ_i is $\mathcal{T}_i$-satisfiable, but that every model requires the four variables in Φ_i to be mapped to the two elements of the domain set in a 3:1 fashion (three variables mapped to the same element, the fourth to a distinct element).

The union of the queries $\Phi_1, \ldots, \Phi_5$ is unsatisfiable: there is no partition of a set of five elements that when restricted to any four-element subset produces a 3:1 partition.

From KSAT to Delayed Theory Combination: Exploiting DPLL Outside the SAT Domain*

Roberto Sebastiani

DIT, Università di Trento, via Sommarive 14, I-38050 Povo, Trento, Italy
roberto.sebastiani@dit.unitn.it

Abstract. In the last two decades we have witnessed an impressive advance in the efficiency of propositional satisfiability techniques (SAT), which has brought large and previously-intractable problems at the reach of state-of-the-art SAT solvers. Most of this success is motivated by the impressive level of efficiency reached by current implementations of the DPLL procedure. Plain propositional logic, however, is not the only application domain for DPLL. In fact, DPLL has also been successfully used as a boolean-reasoning kernel for automated reasoning tools in much more expressive logics.

In this talk I overview a 12-year experience on integrating DPLL with logic-specific decision procedures in various domains. In particular, I present and discuss three main achievements which have been obtained in this context: the DPLL-based procedures for modal and description logics, the lazy approach to Satisfiability Modulo Theories, and Delayed Theory Combination.

1 Introduction

In the last two decades we have witnessed an impressive advance in the efficiency of propositional satisfiability techniques (SAT), which has brought large and previously-intractable problems at the reach of state-of-the-art SAT solvers. As a consequence, many hard real-world problems have been successfully solved by encoding into SAT. E.g., SAT solvers are now a fundamental tool in most formal verification design flows for hardware systems.

Most of the success of SAT technologies is motivated by the impressive level of efficiency reached by current implementations of the Davis-Putnam-Logemann-Loveland procedure (DPLL) [13,12], in its most-modern variants (see, e.g., [43]).

Plain propositional logic, however, is not the only application domain for DPLL. In fact, DPLL has also been successfully used as a boolean-reasoning kernel for automated reasoning tools in much more expressive logics, including modal and description logics, and decidable subclasses of first-order logic. In most cases, this has produced a boost in the overall performances, which rely

---

* This work has been partly supported by ORCHID, a project sponsored by Provincia Autonoma di Trento, by the EU project S3MS "Security of Software and Services for Mobile System" contract n. 27004, and by a grant from Intel Corporation.

B. Konev and F. Wolter (Eds.): FroCos 2007, LNAI 4720, pp. 28–46, 2007.

both on the improvements in DPLL technology and on clever integration between DPLL and the logic-specific decision procedures.

In this talk I overview a 12-year experience on integrating DPLL with logic-specific decision procedures in various domains. In particular, I present and discuss three main achievements which have been obtained in this context.

The first (§2) is the introduction of DPLL inside *satisfiability procedures for modal and description logics* [23,24,37,27,35,28,25,21,22,26], which caused a boost in performances wrt. previous state-of-the-art procedures, which used Smullyan's analytic tableaux [39] as propositional-reasoning engine.

The second (§3) is the *lazy approach to Satisfiability Modulo Theories* (lazy SMT) [1,41,15,3,4,18,19,6,16], in which DPLL is combined with satisfiability procedures for (sets of literals in) expressive decidable first-order theories. Current lazy SMT tools have reached a high degree of efficiency, so that they are increasingly used in formal verification.

The third (§4) is *Delayed Theory Combination (*DTC*)* [7,8,9,17,14], a general method for tackling the problem of theory combination within the context of lazy *SMT*. DTC exploits the power of DPLL also for assigning truth values for the interface equalities that the $\mathcal{T}$-*solver*'s are not capable of inferring. Thus, it does not rely on (possibly very expensive) deduction capabilities of the component procedures —although it can fully benefit from them— and nicely encompasses the case of non-convex theories.

2   DPLL for Modal Logics

We assume the reader is familiar with the basic notions on modal logics and of first-order logic. Some very-basic background on SAT (see, e.g., [43]) and on decision procedures and their combination (see, e.g., [31]) is also assumed.

We adopt the following terminology and notation. We call an *atom* any formula which cannot be decomposed propositionally (e.g., A_1, $\Box_r(A_1 \wedge \Box_r A_2)$), and a *literal* an atom or its negation. We call a *truth assignment* μ for a formula φ any set/conjunction of top-level literals in φ. Positive literals $\Box_r \alpha_i$, A_k [resp. negative literals $\neg\Box_r \beta_i$, $\neg A_k$] mean that the corresponding atom is assigned to true [resp. false]. We say that a truth assignment μ for φ *propositionally satisfies* φ, written $\mu \models_p \varphi$, iff it tautologically entails φ. E.g., $\{A_1, \neg\Box_r(A_2 \wedge \Box_r A_3)\} \models_p (A_1 \wedge (A_2 \vee \neg\Box_r(A_2 \wedge \Box_r A_3)))$.

2.1   From Tableau-Based to DPLL-Based Procedures

We call "tableau-based" a system that implements and extends to other logics the Smullyan's propositional tableau calculus [39]. E.g., a typical Tableau-based procedure for modal K_m consists on some control strategy applied to the following rules:

$$\frac{\Gamma, \varphi_1 \wedge \varphi_2}{\Gamma, \varphi_1, \varphi_2}\ (\wedge) \qquad \frac{\Gamma, \varphi_1 \vee \varphi_2}{\Gamma, \varphi_1 \quad \Gamma, \varphi_2}\ (\vee) \qquad \frac{\mu}{\alpha_1 \wedge \ldots \wedge \alpha_m \wedge \neg\beta_j}\ (\Box_r / \neg\Box_r) \quad (1)$$

for each box-index $r \in \{1, ..., m\}$. Γ is an arbitrary set of formulas, and μ is a set of literals which includes $\neg\Box_r\beta_j$ and whose only positive $\Box_r$-atoms are $\Box_r\alpha_1, ..., \Box_r\alpha_m$.

We call "DPLL-based" any system that implements and extends to other logics the Davis-Putnam-Longeman-Loveland procedure (DPLL) [13,12]. DPLL-based procedures basically consist on the combination of a DPLL procedure handling the purely-propositional component of reasoning, and some procedure handling the purely-modal component. Thus, for instance, in our terminology KSAT [23], FACT [27], DLP [35], RACER [26] are DPLL-based systems.[1] From a purely-logical viewpoint, it is possible to conceive a DPLL-based framework by substituting the propositional tableaux rules with some rules implementing the DPLL algorithms in a tableau-based framework [37]. A formal framework for representing DPLL and DPLL-based procedures has been proposed in [40,33].

2.2   Basic Modal DPLL for K_m

The first DPLL-based procedure for a modal logic, KSAT, was introduced in [23,25] (Figure 1). This schema evolved from that of the PTAUT procedure in [2], and is based on the "classic" DPLL procedure [13,12]. KSAT takes in input a modal formula φ and returns a truth value asserting whether φ is K_m-satisfiable or not. KSAT invokes K-DPLL passing as arguments φ and (by reference) an empty assignment $\top$. K-DPLL tries to build a K_m-satisfiable assignment μ propositionally satisfying φ. This is done recursively, according to the following steps:

- (base) If $\varphi = \top$, then μ propositionally satisfies φ. Thus, if μ is K_m-satisfiable, then φ is K_m-satisfiable. Therefore K-DPLL invokes K-SOLVER(μ), which returns a truth value asserting whether μ is K_m-satisfiable or not.
- (backtrack) If $\varphi = \bot$, then μ does not satisfy φ, so that K-DPLL returns *False*.
- (unit) If a literal l occurs in φ as a unit clause, then l must be assigned $\top$. To obtain this, K-DPLL is invoked recursively with arguments the formula returned by $assign(l, \varphi)$ and the assignment obtained by adding l to μ.
- (split) If none of the above situations occurs, then $choose\text{-}literal(\varphi)$ returns an unassigned literal l according to some heuristic criterion. Then K-DPLL is first invoked recursively with arguments $assign(l, \varphi)$ and $\mu \wedge l$. If the result is negative, then K-DPLL is invoked with $assign(\neg l, \varphi)$ and $\mu \wedge \neg l$.

K-DPLL is a variant of the "classic" DPLL algorithm [13,12]. The K-DPLL schema differs from that of classic DPLL by only two steps.

The first is the "base" case: when standard DPLL finds an assignment μ which propositionally satisfies the input formula, it simply returns "*True*". K-DPLL,

---

[1] Notice that there is not an universal agreement on the terminology "tableau-based" and "DPLL-based". E.g., tools like FACT, DLP, and RACER are often called "tableau-based", although they use a DPLL-like algorithm instead of propositional tableaux for handling the propositional component of reasoning [27,35,28,26].

function KSAT (φ)
    return K-DPLL $(\varphi, \top)$;

function K-DPLL (φ, μ)
    if $(\varphi == \top)$ /* base   */
        then return K-SOLVER (μ);
    if $(\varphi == \bot)$ /* backtrack */
        then return *False*;
    if $\{$a unit clause (l) occurs in $\varphi\}$ /* unit   */
        then return K-DPLL $(assign(l, \varphi), \mu \wedge l)$;
    $l := choose\text{-}literal(\varphi)$;   /* split   */
    return   K-DPLL $(assign(l, \varphi), \mu \wedge l)$ **or**
                K-DPLL $(assign(\neg l, \varphi), \mu \wedge \neg l)$;

/* μ is $\bigwedge_i \Box_1 \alpha_{1i} \wedge \bigwedge_j \neg\Box_1 \beta_{1j} \wedge \ldots \wedge \bigwedge_i \Box_m \alpha_{mi} \wedge \bigwedge_j \neg\Box_m \beta_{mj} \wedge \bigwedge_k A_k \wedge \bigwedge_h \neg A_h$ */
function K-SOLVER (μ)
    for each box index $r \in \{1...m\}$ **do**
        for each literal $\neg\Box_r \beta_{rj} \in \mu$ **do**
            if not $(\text{KSAT}(\bigwedge_i \alpha_{ri} \wedge \neg\beta_{rj}))$
                then return *False*;
    return *True*;

Fig. 1. The basic version of KSAT algorithm. $assign(l, \varphi)$ substitutes every occurrence of l in φ with $\top$ and evaluates the result.

instead, is also supposed to check the K_m-satisfiability of the corresponding set of literals, by invoking K-SOLVER on μ. If the latter returns *true*, then the whole formula is satisfiable and K-DPLL returns *True* as well; otherwise, K-DPLL backtracks and looks for the next assignment.

The second is in the fact that in K-DPLL the pure-literal step [12] is removed.[2] In fact the sets of assignments generated by DPLL with pure-literal might be incomplete and might cause incorrect results. This fact is shown by the following example.

Example 1. Let φ be the following formula:

$$(\Box_1 A_1 \vee A_1) \wedge (\Box_1(A_1 \to A_2) \vee A_2) \wedge (\neg\Box_1 A_2 \vee A_2) \wedge (\neg A_2 \vee A_3) \wedge (\neg A_2 \vee \neg A_3).$$

φ is K_m-satisfiable, because $\mu = \{A_1, \neg A_2, \Box_1(A_1 \to A_2), \neg\Box_1 A_2\}$ is a K_m-consistent assignment propositionally satisfying φ. It is easy to see that no satisfiable assignment propositionally satisfying φ assigns $\Box_1 A_1$ to true. As $\Box_1 A_1$ occurs only positively in φ, DPLL with the pure literal rule would assign $\Box_1 A_1$ to true as first step, which would lead the procedure to return *False*.

With these simple modifications, the embedded DPLL procedures works as an enumerator of a complete set of assignments, whose K_m-satisfiability is recursively

---

[2] Alternatively, the application of the pure-literal rule is restricted to atomic propositions only.

checked by K-SOLVER. K-SOLVER is a straightforward application of the $(\Box_r/\neg\Box_r)$-rule in (1).

The above schema has lately been extended to other modal and description logics [27,28,22]. Moreover, the schema has been lately adapted to work with modern DPLL procedures, and many optimizations have been conceived. Some of them will be described in §3.3 in the context of Satisfiability Modulo Theories.

2.3 DPLL-Based vs. Tableaux-Based Procedures

[23,24,25,20,21,28,29] presented extensive empirical comparisons, in which DPLL-based procedures outperformed tableau-based ones, with orders-of-magnitude performance gaps. (Similar performance gaps between tableau-based vs. DPLL-based procedures were obtained lately also in a completely-different context [1].) Remarkably, most such results were obtained with tools implementing variants of the "classic" DPLL procedure of §2.2, still very far from the efficiency of current DPLL implementations.

Both tableau-based and DPLL-based procedures for K_m-satisfiability work (i) by enumerating truth assignments which propositionally satisfy the input formula φ and (ii) by recursively checking the K_m-satisfiability of the assignments found. As both algorithms perform the latter step in the same way, the key difference relies in the way they handle propositional inference. In [24,25] we remarked that, regardless the quality of implementation and the optimizations performed, DPLL-based procedures do not suffer from two intrinsic weaknesses of tableau-based procedures which significantly affect their efficiency, and whose effects are amplified up to exponentially when using them in modal inference. We consider these weaknesses in turn.

Syntactic vs. semantic branching. In a propositional tableaux truth assignments are generated as branches induced by the application of the ∨-rule to disjunctive subformulas of the input formula φ. Thus, they perform *syntactic branching* [24], that is, the branching in the search tree is induced by the syntactic structure of φ. As discussed in [11], an application of the ∨-rule generates two subtrees which can be mutually consistent, i.e., which may share propositional models.[3] Therefore, the set of truth assignments enumerated by a propositional tableau grows exponentially with the number of disjunctions occurring positively in φ, regardless the fact that it may contain up to exponentially-many duplicated and/or subsumed assignments.

Things get even worse in the modal case. When testing K_m-satisfiability, unlike the propositional case where they look for *one* assignment satisfying the input formula, the propositional tableaux are used to enumerate up to *all* satisfying assignments, which must be recursively checked for K_m-consistency. This requires checking recursively possibly-many sub-formulas of the form $\bigwedge_i \alpha_{ri} \wedge \neg\beta_j$

---

[3] As pointed out in [11], propositional tableaux rules are unable to represent *bivalence*: "every proposition is either true or false, *tertium non datur*". This is a consequence of the elimination of the cut rule in cut-free sequent calculi, from which propositional tableaux are derived.

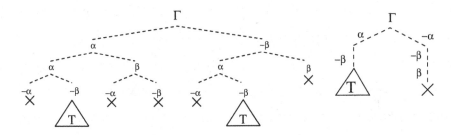

Fig. 2. Search trees for the formula $\Gamma = (\alpha \vee \neg\beta) \wedge (\alpha \vee \beta) \wedge (\neg\alpha \vee \neg\beta)$. Left: a tableau-based procedure. Right: a DPLL-based procedure.

of depth $d - 1$, for which a propositional tableau will enumerate all satisfying assignments, and so on. At every level of nesting, a redundant truth assignment introduces a redundant modal search tree. Thus, with modal formulas, the redundancy of the propositional case propagates up-to-exponentially with the modal depth.

DPLL instead, performs a search which is based on *semantic branching* [24], i.e., a branching on the *truth value* of sub-formulas ψ of φ (typically atoms): [4]

$$\frac{\varphi}{\varphi[\psi/\top] \qquad \varphi[\psi/\bot],}$$

where $\varphi[\psi/\top]$ is the result of substituting with $\top$ all occurrences of ψ in φ and then simplify the result. Thus, every branching step generates two *mutually-inconsistent* subtrees. Thus, DPLL always generates non-redundant sets of assignments. This avoids search duplications and, in the case of modal search, the recursive exponential propagation of redundancy.

Example 2. Consider the formula $\Gamma = (\alpha \vee \neg\beta) \wedge (\alpha \vee \beta) \wedge (\neg\alpha \vee \neg\beta)$, where α and β are modal atoms s.t. $\alpha \wedge \neg\beta$ is K_m-inconsistent, and let d be the depth of Γ. The only assignment propositionally satisfying Γ is $\mu = \alpha \wedge \neg\beta$. Consider Figure 2, left. Two distinct but identical open branches are generated, both representing the assignment μ. Then the tableau expands the two open branches in the same way, until it generates two identical (and possibly-big) closed modal sub-trees T of modal depth d, each proving the K_m-unsatisfiability of μ.

This phenomenon may repeat itself at the lower level in each sub-tree T, and so on. For instance, if $\alpha = \Box_1((\alpha' \vee \neg\beta') \wedge (\alpha' \vee \beta'))$ and $\beta = \Box_1(\alpha' \wedge \beta')$, then at the lower level we have a formula Γ' of depth $d - 1$ analogous to Γ. This propagates exponentially the redundancy with the depth d.

Finally, notice that if we considered the formula $\Gamma^K = \bigwedge_{i=1}^{K}(\alpha_i \vee \neg\beta_i) \wedge (\alpha_i \vee \beta_i) \wedge (\neg\alpha_i \vee \neg\beta_i)$, the tableau would generate 2^K identical truth assignments $\mu^K = \bigwedge_i \alpha_i \wedge \neg\beta_i$, and things would get exponentially worse.

---

[4] Notice that the notion of "semantic branching" introduced in [24] is stronger than that lately used in [27,28]; the former coarsely corresponds to the latter plus the usage of unit-propagation.

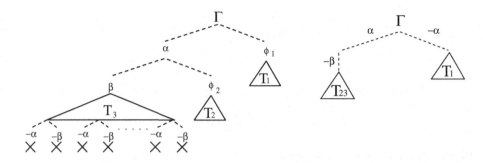

Fig. 3. Search trees for the formula $\Gamma = (\alpha \vee \phi_1) \wedge (\beta \vee \phi_2) \wedge \phi_3 \wedge (\neg\alpha \vee \neg\beta)$. Left: a tableau-based procedure. Right: a DPLL-based procedure.

Look at Figure 2, right. A DPLL-based procedure branches asserting $\alpha = \top$ or $\alpha = \bot$. The first branch generates $\alpha \wedge \neg\beta$, whilst the second gives $\neg\alpha \wedge \neg\beta \wedge \beta$, which immediately closes. Therefore, only one instance of $\mu = \alpha \wedge \neg\beta$ is generated. The same applies to μ^K.

Detecting constraint violations. A propositional formula φ can be seen as a set of constraints for the truth assignments which possibly satisfy it. For instance, a clause $A_1 \vee A_2$ constrains every assignment not to set both A_1 and A_2 to $\bot$. Unlike tableaux, DPLL prunes a branch as soon as it violates some constraint of the input formula. (For instance, in KSAT this is done by the function *assign*.)

Example 3. Consider the formula $\Gamma = (\alpha \vee \phi_1) \wedge (\beta \vee \phi_2) \wedge \phi_3 \wedge (\neg\alpha \vee \neg\beta)$, α and β being atoms, ϕ_1, ϕ_2 and ϕ_3 being sub-formulas, such that $\alpha \wedge \beta \wedge \phi_3$ is propositionally satisfiable and $\alpha \wedge \phi_2$ is K_m-unsatisfiable. Look at Figure 3, left. Again, assume that, in a tableau-based procedure, the $\vee$-rule is applied in order, left to right. After two steps, the branch α, β is generated, which violates the constraint imposed by the last clause $(\neg\alpha \vee \neg\beta)$. A tableau-based procedure is not able to detect such a violation until it explicitly branches on that clause, that is, only after having generated the whole sub-tableau T_3 for $\alpha \wedge \beta \wedge \phi_3$, which may be rather big. DPLL instead (Figure 3, right) avoids generating the violating assignment detects the violation and immediately prunes the branch.

3   Integrating DPLL and Theory Solvers: Lazy SMT

Satisfiability Modulo Theories is the problem of deciding the satisfiability of a first-order formula with respect to some decidable first-order theory $\mathcal{T}$ $(SMT(\mathcal{T}))$. Examples of theories of interest are, those of Equality and Uninterpreted Functions $(\mathcal{EUF})$, Linear Arithmetic $(\mathcal{LA})$, both over the reals $(\mathcal{LA}(\mathbb{Q}))$ and the integers $(\mathcal{LA}(\mathbb{Z}))$, its subclasses of Difference Logic $(\mathcal{DL})$ and Unit-Two-Variable-Per-Inequality $(\mathcal{UTVPI})$, the theories of bit-vectors $(\mathcal{BV})$, of arrays $(\mathcal{AR})$ and of lists $(\mathcal{LI})$.

Efficient *SMT* solvers have been developed in the last five years, called *lazy SMT solvers*, which combine DPLL with decision procedures (*T-solvers*) for many theories of interest (e.g., [1,41,15,3,4,18,19,6,16]).

3.1 Theory Solvers

In its simplest form, a *Theory Solver* for T (*T-solver*) is a procedure which takes as input a collection of T-literals μ and decides whether μ is T-satisfiable. In order to be effectively used within a lazy *SMT* solver, the following features of *T-solver* are often important or even essential.

Model generation: when *T-solver* is invoked on a T-consistent set μ, it is able to produce a T-model $\mathcal{I}$ witnessing the consistency of μ, i.e., $\mathcal{I} \models_T \mu$.

Conflict set generation: when *T-solver* is invoked on a T-inconsistent set μ, it is able to produce the (possibly minimal) subset η of μ which has caused its inconsistency. η is called a *theory conflict set* of μ.

Incrementality: *T-solver* "remembers" its computation status from one call to the other, so that, whenever it is given in input a set $\mu_1 \cup \mu_2$ such that μ_1 has just been proved T-satisfiable, it avoids restarting the computation from scratch.

Backtrackability: it is possible for the *T-solver* to undo steps and return to a previous status on the stack in an efficient manner.

Deduction of unassigned literals: when *T-solver* is invoked on a T-consistent set μ, it can also perform a set of deductions in the form $\eta \models_T l$, s.t. $\eta \subseteq \mu$ and l is a literal on a not-yet-assigned atom in φ.

Deduction of interface equalities: when returning Sat, *T-solver* can also perform a set of deductions in the form $\mu \models_T e$ (if T is convex) or $\mu \models_T \bigvee_j e_j$ (if T is not convex) s.t. $e, e_1, ..., e_n$ are equalities between variables or terms occurring in atoms in μ. We denote the equality $(v_i = v_j)$ by e_{ij}, and we call e_{ij}-*deduction* a deduction of (disjunctions of) e_{ij}'s. A *T-solver* is e_{ij}-*deduction-complete* if it always capable to inferring the (disjunctions of) e_{ij}'s which are entailed by the input set of literals. Notice that here the deduced equalities need not occur in the input formula φ.

3.2 Lazy Satisfiability Modulo Theories

We adopt the following terminology and notation. The bijective function $T2B$ ("theory-to-propositional"), called *boolean abstraction*, maps propositional variables into themselves, ground T-atoms into fresh propositional variables, and is homomorphic w.r.t. boolean operators and set inclusion. The function $B2T$ ("propositional-to-theory"), called *refinement*, is the inverse of $T2B$. The symbols φ, ψ denote T-formulas, and μ, η denote sets of T-literals; φ^p, ψ^p denote propositional formulas, μ^p, η^p denote sets of propositional literals (i.e., truth assignments) and we often use them as synonyms for the boolean abstraction of φ, ψ, μ, and η respectively, and vice versa (e.g., φ^p denotes $T2B(\varphi)$, μ denotes $B2T(\mu^p)$). If $T2B(\varphi) \models \bot$, then we say that φ is *propositionally unsatisfiable*, written $\varphi \models_p \bot$.

```
1.     SatValue T-DPLL (T-formula φ, T-assignment & μ) {
2.        if (T-preprocess(φ,μ) == Conflict);
3.           return Unsat;
4.        φᵖ = T2P(φ); μᵖ = T2P(μ);
5.        while (1) {
6.           T-decide_next_branch(φᵖ,μᵖ);
7.           while (1) {
8.              status = T-deduce(φᵖ,μᵖ);
9.              if (status == Sat) {
10.                 μ = P2T(μᵖ);
11.                 return Sat; }
12.              else if (status == Conflict) {
13.                 blevel = T-analyze_conflict(φᵖ,μᵖ);
14.                 if (blevel == 0)
15.                    return Unsat;
16.                 else T-backtrack(blevel,φᵖ,μᵖ);
17.              }
18.              else break;
19.  } } }
```

Fig. 4. Schema of T-DPLL based on modern DPLL

Figure 4 represent the schema of a T-DPLL procedure based on a modern DPLL engine. This schema evolved from that of the DPLL-based procedures for modal logics, see §2.2. The input φ and μ are a T-formula and a reference to an (initially empty) set of T-literals respectively. The DPLL solver embedded in T-DPLL reasons on and updates φ^p and μ^p, and T-DPLL maintains some data structure encoding the set $Lits(\varphi)$ and the bijective mapping $T2P/P2T$ on literals.

T-preprocess simplifies φ into a simpler formula, and updates μ if it is the case, so that to preserve the T-satisfiability of $\varphi \wedge \mu$. If this process produces some conflict, then T-DPLL returns Unsat. T-preprocess combines most or all the boolean preprocessing steps for DPLL with some theory-dependent rewriting steps on the T-literals of φ. (The latter are described in §3.3.)

T-decide_next_branch selects the next literal like in standard DPLL (but it may consider also the semantics in T of the literals to select).

T-deduce, in its simplest version, behaves similarly to standard BCP in DPLL: it iteratively deduces boolean literals l^p deriving propositionally from the current assignment (i.e., s.t. $\varphi^p \wedge \mu^p \models l^p$) and updates φ^p and μ^p accordingly, until one of the following facts happens:

(i) μ^p propositionally violates φ^p ($\mu^p \wedge \varphi^p \models \bot$). If so, T-deduce behaves like deduce in DPLL, returning Conflict.

(ii) μ^p propositionally satisfies φ^p ($\mu^p \models \varphi^p$). If so, T-deduce invokes T-solver on μ: if the latter returns Sat, then T-deduce returns Sat; otherwise, T-deduce returns Conflict.

(iii) no more literals can be deduced. If so, $\mathcal{T}$-deduce returns Unknown. A slightly more elaborated version of $\mathcal{T}$-deduce can invoke $\mathcal{T}$-solver on μ at this intermediate stage: if $\mathcal{T}$-solver returns Unsat, then $\mathcal{T}$-deduce returns Conflict. (This enhancement, called *early pruning*, is discussed in §3.3.)

A much more elaborated version of $\mathcal{T}$-deduce can be implemented if $\mathcal{T}$-solver is able to perform deductions of unassigned literals $\eta \models_{\mathcal{T}} l$ s.t. $\eta \subseteq \mu$, as in §3.1. If so, $\mathcal{T}$-deduce can iteratively deduce and propagate also the corresponding literal l^p. (This enhancement, called $\mathcal{T}$-*propagation*, is discussed in §3.3.)

$\mathcal{T}$-analyze_conflict is an extensions of analyze_conflict of DPLL [42,43]: if the conflict produced by $\mathcal{T}$-deduce is caused by a boolean failure (case (i) above), then $\mathcal{T}$-analyze_conflict produces a boolean conflict set η^p and the corresponding value of blevel; if the conflict is caused by a $\mathcal{T}$-inconsistency revealed by $\mathcal{T}$-solver (case (ii) or (iii) above), then $\mathcal{T}$-analyze_conflict produces the boolean abstraction η^p of the theory conflict set $\eta \subseteq \mu$ produced by $\mathcal{T}$-solver, or computes a mixed boolean+theory conflict set by a backward-traversal of the implication graph starting from the conflicting clause $\neg \eta^p$ (see §3.3). Once the conflict set η^p and blevel have been computed, $\mathcal{T}$-backtrack behaves analogously to backtrack in DPLL: it adds the clause $\neg \eta^p$ to φ^p, either temporarily or permanently, and backtracks up to blevel. (These features, called $\mathcal{T}$-*backjumping* and $\mathcal{T}$-*learning*, are discussed in §3.3.)

$\mathcal{T}$-DPLL differs from the standard DPLL [42,43] because it exploits:

- an extended notion of *deduction of literals*: not only *boolean deduction* ($\mu^p \wedge \varphi^p \models l^p$), but also *theory deduction* ($\mu \models_{\mathcal{T}} l$);
- an extended notion of *conflict*: not only *boolean conflict* ($\mu^p \wedge \varphi^p \models_p \bot$), but also *theory conflict* ($\mu \models_{\mathcal{T}} \bot$), or even *mixed boolean+theory conflict* ($(\mu \wedge \varphi) \models_{\mathcal{T}} \bot$).

Example 4. Consider the $\mathcal{LA}(\mathbb{Q})$-formulas φ and its boolean abstraction φ^p of Figure 5. Suppose $\mathcal{T}$-decide_next_branch selects, in order, $\mu^p := \{\neg B_5, B_8, B_6, \neg B_1\}$ (in c_4, c_7, c_6, and c_1). $\mathcal{T}$-deduce cannot unit-propagate any literal. By the enhanced version of step (iii), it invokes $\mathcal{T}$-solver on $\mu := \{\neg(3x_1 - x_3 \leq 6), (x_3 = 3x_5 + 4), (x_2 - x_4 \leq 6), \neg(2x_2 - x_3 > 2)\}$. The enhanced $\mathcal{T}$-solver not only returns Sat, but also it deduces $\neg(3x_1 - 2x_2 \leq 3)$ (c_3 and c_5) as a consequence of the first and last literals. The corresponding boolean literal $\neg B_3$, is added to μ^p and propagated ($\mathcal{T}$-propagation). Hence A_1, A_2 and B_2 are unit-propagated from c_5, c_3 and c_2.

Let μ'^p be the resulting assignment $\{\neg B_5, B_8, B_6, \neg B_1, \neg B_3, A_1, A_2, B_2\}$). By step (iii), $\mathcal{T}$-deduce invokes $\mathcal{T}$-solver on μ': $\{\neg(3x_1 - x_3 \leq 6), (x_3 = 3x_5 + 4), (x_2 - x_4 \leq 6), \neg(2x_2 - x_3 > 2), \neg(3x_1 - 2x_2 \leq 3), (x_1 - x_5 \leq 1)\}$ which is inconsistent because of the 1st, 2nd, and 6th literals, so that returns Unsat, and hence $\mathcal{T}$-deduce returns Conflict. Then $\mathcal{T}$-analyze_conflict and $\mathcal{T}$-backtrack learn the corresponding boolean conflict clause

$$c_8 =_{def} B_5 \vee \neg B_8 \vee \neg B_2$$

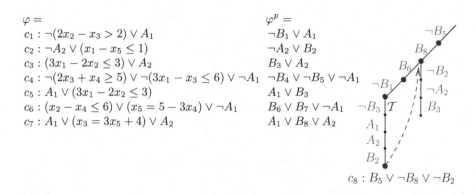

$\varphi =$

$c_1 : \neg(2x_2 - x_3 > 2) \lor A_1$

$c_2 : \neg A_2 \lor (x_1 - x_5 \leq 1)$

$c_3 : (3x_1 - 2x_2 \leq 3) \lor A_2$

$c_4 : \neg(2x_3 + x_4 \geq 5) \lor \neg(3x_1 - x_3 \leq 6) \lor \neg A_1$

$c_5 : A_1 \lor (3x_1 - 2x_2 \leq 3)$

$c_6 : (x_2 - x_4 \leq 6) \lor (x_5 = 5 - 3x_4) \lor \neg A_1$

$c_7 : A_1 \lor (x_3 = 3x_5 + 4) \lor A_2$

$\varphi^p =$

$\neg B_1 \lor A_1$

$\neg A_2 \lor B_2$

$B_3 \lor A_2$

$\neg B_4 \lor \neg B_5 \lor \neg A_1$

$A_1 \lor B_3$

$B_6 \lor B_7 \lor \neg A_1$

$A_1 \lor B_8 \lor A_2$

$c_8 : B_5 \lor \neg B_8 \lor \neg B_2$

Fig. 5. Boolean search (sub)tree in the scenario of Example 4. (A diagonal line, a vertical line and a vertical line tagged with "$\mathcal{T}$" denote literal selection, unit propagation and $\mathcal{T}$-propagation respectively; a bullet "•" denotes a call to $\mathcal{T}$-solver.)

and backtrack, popping from μ^p all literals up to $\{\neg B_5, B_8\}$, and then unit-propagate $\neg B_2$ on c_8 ($\mathcal{T}$-backjumping and $\mathcal{T}$-learning). Then, starting from $\{\neg B_5, B_8, \neg B_2\}$, also $\neg A_2$ and B_3 are unit-propagated on c_2 and c_3 respectively.

As in standard DPLL, an excessive number of $\mathcal{T}$-learned clauses may cause an explosion in size of φ. Thus, many lazy *SMT* tools introduce techniques for *discharging* $\mathcal{T}$-learned clauses when necessary. Moreover, like in standard DPLL, $\mathcal{T}$-DPLL can be *restarted* from scratch in order to avoid dead-end portions of the search space. The learned clauses prevent $\mathcal{T}$-DPLL to redo the same steps twice. Most lazy *SMT* tools implement restarting mechanisms as well.

3.3 Enhancements

In the schema of Figure 4, even assuming that the DPLL engine and the $\mathcal{T}$-*solver* are extremely efficient as a stand-alone procedures, their combination can be extremely inefficient. This is due to a couple of intrinsic problems.

– The DPLL engine assigns truth values to (the boolean abstraction of) $\mathcal{T}$-atoms in a blind way, receiving no information from $\mathcal{T}$-*solver* about their semantics. This may cause up to an huge amount of calls to $\mathcal{T}$-*solver* on assignments which are obviously $\mathcal{T}$-inconsistent, or whose $\mathcal{T}$-inconsistency could have been easily derived from that of previously-checked assignments.
– The $\mathcal{T}$-*solver* is used as a memory-less subroutine, in a master-slave fashion. Therefore $\mathcal{T}$-*solver* may be called on assignments that are subsets of, supersets of or similar to assignments it has already checked, with no chance of reusing previous computations.

Therefore, it is essential to improve the integration schema so that the DPLL solver is driven in its boolean search by $\mathcal{T}$-dependent information provided by

$\mathcal{T}$-*solver*, whilst the latter is able to take benefit from information provided by the former, and it is given a chance of reusing previous computation.

We describe some of the most effective techniques which have been proposed in order to optimize the interaction between DPLL and $\mathcal{T}$-*solver*. (We refer the reader to [36] for a much more extensive and detailed survey.) Some of them, like Normalizing $\mathcal{T}$-atoms, Early pruning, $\mathcal{T}$-backjumping and pure-literal filtering, derive from those developed in the context of DPLL-based procedures for modal logics.

Normalizing $\mathcal{T}$-atoms. In order to avoid the generation of many trivially-unsatisfiable assignments, it is wise to preprocess $\mathcal{T}$-atoms so that to map as many as possible $\mathcal{T}$-equivalent literals into syntactically-identical ones. This can be achieved by applying some rewriting rules, like, e.g.:

- *Drop dual operators*: $(x_1 < x_2)$, $(x_1 \geq x_2) \Rightarrow \neg(x_1 \geq x_2)$, $(x_1 \geq x_2)$.
- *Exploit associativity*: $(x_1 + (x_2 + x_3) = 1)$, $((x_1 + x_2) + x_3) = 1) \Rightarrow (x_1 + x_2 + x_3 = 1)$.
- *Sort*: $(x_1 + x_2 - x_3 \leq 1)$, $(x_2 + x_1 - 1 \leq x_3) \Rightarrow (x_1 + x_2 - x_3 \leq 1))$.
- *Exploit $\mathcal{T}$-specific properties*: $(x_1 \leq 3)$, $(x_1 < 4) \Rightarrow (x_1 \leq 3)$ if $x_1 \in \mathbb{Z}$.

The applicability and effectiveness of these mappings depends on the theory $\mathcal{T}$.

Static learning. On some specific kind of problems, it is possible to quickly detect a priori short and "obviously $\mathcal{T}$-inconsistent" assignments to $\mathcal{T}$-atoms in $Atoms(\varphi)$ (typically pairs or triplets). Some examples are:

- *incompatible values* (e.g., $\{x = 0, x = 1\}$),
- *congruence constraints* (e.g., $\{(x_1 = y_1), (x_2 = y_2), \neg(f(x_1, x_2) = f(y_1, y_2))\}$),
- *transitivity constraints* (e.g., $\{(x - y \leq 2), (y - z \leq 4), \neg(x - z \leq 7)\}$),
- *equivalence constraints* ($\{(x = y), (2x - 3z \leq 3), \neg(2y - 3z \leq 3)\}$).

If so, the clauses obtained by negating the assignments (e.g., $\neg(x = 0) \vee \neg(x = 1)$) can be added a priori to the formula before the search starts. Whenever all but one literals in the inconsistent assignment are assigned, the negation of the remaining literal is assigned deterministically by unit propagation, which prevents the solver generating any assignment which include the inconsistent one. This technique may significantly reduce the boolean search space, and hence the number of calls to $\mathcal{T}$-*solver*, producing very relevant speed-ups [1,6].

Intuitively, one can think to static learning as suggesting a priori some small and "obvious" $\mathcal{T}$-valid lemmas relating some $\mathcal{T}$-atoms of φ, which drive DPLL in its boolean search. Notice that the clauses added by static learning refer only to atoms which already occur in the original formula, so that the boolean search space is not enlarged.

Early pruning. Another optimization, here generically called *early pruning – EP*, is to introduce an intermediate call to $\mathcal{T}$-*solver* on intermediate assignment μ. (I.e., in the $\mathcal{T}$-DPLL schema of Figure 4, this is represented by the "slightly more elaborated" version of step (iii) of $\mathcal{T}$-**deduce**.) If $\mathcal{T}$-*solver*(μ) returns Unsat, then all possible extensions of μ are unsatisfiable, so that $\mathcal{T}$-DPLL returns Unsat and backtracks, avoiding a possibly big amount of useless search.

In general, EP may introduce a drastic reduction of the boolean search space, and hence of the number of calls to $\mathcal{T}$-*solvers*. Unfortunately, as EP may cause useless calls to $\mathcal{T}$-*solver*, the benefits of the pruning effect may be partly counter-balanced by the overhead introduced by the extra EP calls. To this extent, many different improvements to EP and strategies for interleaving calls to $\mathcal{T}$-*solvers* and boolean reasoning steps [41,19,3,6,10] have been proposed.

$\mathcal{T}$-propagation. As discussed in §3.1, for some theories it is possible to implement $\mathcal{T}$-*solver* so that a call to $\mathcal{T}$-*solver*(μ) returning Sat can also perform one or more deduction(s) in the form $\eta \models_{\mathcal{T}} l$, s.t. $\eta \subseteq \mu$ and l is a literal on an unassigned atom in φ. If this is the case, then $\mathcal{T}$-*solver* can return l to $\mathcal{T}$-DPLL, so that l^p is added to μ^p and unit-propagated [1,3,19]. This process, which is called $\mathcal{T}$-propagation, may induce a beneficial loop with unit-propagation. As with early-pruning, there are different strategies by which $\mathcal{T}$-propagation can be interleaved with unit-propagation [1,3,19,6,10,33].

Notice that $\mathcal{T}$-*solver* can return the deduction(s) performed $\eta \models_{\mathcal{T}} l$ to $\mathcal{T}$-DPLL, which can add the deduction clause $(\eta^p \rightarrow l^p)$ to φ^p, either temporarily and permanently. The deduction clause will be used for the future boolean search, with benefits analogous to those of $\mathcal{T}$-learning (see §3.3).

$\mathcal{T}$-backjumping and $\mathcal{T}$-learning. Modern implementations inherit the back-jumping mechanism of current DPLL tools: $\mathcal{T}$-DPLL learns the conflict clause $\neg\eta^p$ and backtracks to the highest point in the stack where one $l^p \in \eta^p$ is not assigned, and unit propagates $\neg l^p$ on $\neg\eta^p$. Intuitively, DPLL backtracks to the highest point where it would have done something different if it had known in advance the conflict clause $\neg\eta^p$ from the $\mathcal{T}$-*solver*.

As hinted in §3.2, it is possible to use either a theory conflict η (i.e., $\neg\eta$ is a $\mathcal{T}$-valid clause) or a *mixed boolean+theory conflicts sets* η', i.e., s.t. an inconsistency can be entailed from $\eta' \wedge \varphi$ by means of a combination of boolean and theory reasoning ($\eta' \wedge \varphi \models_{\mathcal{T}} \bot$). Such conflict sets/clauses can be obtained starting from the theory-conflicting clause $\neg\eta^p$ by applying the backward-traversal of the implication graph, until one of the standard conditions (e.g., 1UIP) is achieved. Notice that it is possible to learn *both* clauses $\neg\eta$ and $\neg\eta'$.

Example 5. The scenario depicted in Example 4 represents a form of $\mathcal{T}$-backjumping and $\mathcal{T}$-learning, in which the conflict clause c_8 used is a $\mathcal{LA}(\mathbb{Q})$-conflict clause (i.e., $\mathcal{P}2\mathcal{T}(c_8)$ is $\mathcal{LA}(\mathbb{Q})$-valid). However, $\mathcal{T}$-analyze_conflict could instead look for a mixed boolean+theory conflict clause by treating c_8 as a conflicting clause and backward-traversing the implication graph, that is, by resolving backward c_8 with c_2 and c_3, (i.e., with the antecedent clauses of B_2 and A_2) and with the deduction clause c_9 (which "caused" the propagation of $\neg B_3$):

$$\dfrac{\dfrac{\overbrace{B_5 \vee \neg B_8 \vee \neg B_2}^{c_8:\ theory\ conflicting\ clause}\qquad \overbrace{\neg A_2 \vee B_2}^{c_2}}{B_5 \vee \neg B_8 \vee \neg A_2}\ (B_2)\quad \overbrace{B_3 \vee A_2}^{c_3}}{\dfrac{B_5 \vee \neg B_8 \vee B_3}{\underbrace{B_5 \vee \neg B_8 \vee B_1}_{c_8':\ mixed\ boolean+theory\ conflict\ clause}}\ (\neg A_2)\quad \overbrace{B_5 \vee B_1 \vee \neg B_3}^{c_9}\ (B_3)}$$

finding the mixed boolean+theory conflict clause c_8' : $B_5 \vee \neg B_8 \vee B_1$. (Notice that, $\mathcal{P}2\mathcal{T}(c_8') = (3x_1 - x_3 \leq 6) \vee \neg(x_3 = 3x_5 + 4) \vee (2x_2 - x_3 > 2)$ is not $\mathcal{LA}(\mathbb{Q})$-valid.) If so then $\mathcal{T}$-backtrack pops from μ^p all literals up to $\{\neg B_5, B_8\}$, and then unit-propagates B_1 on c_8', and hence A_1 on c_1.

As with static learning, the clauses added by $\mathcal{T}$-learning refer only to atoms which already occur in the original formula, so that no new atom is added. [18] proposed an interesting generalization of $\mathcal{T}$-learning, in which learned clause may contain also new atoms. [7,8] used a similar idea to improve the efficiency of Delayed Theory Combination (see §4).

Pure-literal filtering. If we have non-boolean $\mathcal{T}$-atoms occurring only positively [resp. negatively] in the input formula, we can safely drop every negative [resp. positive] occurrence of them from the assignment to be checked by $\mathcal{T}$-solver [41,22,3,6,36].[5] We call this technique, *pure-literal filtering*.

There are two potential benefits for this behavior. Let μ' be the reduced version of μ. First, μ' might be $\mathcal{T}$-satisfiable despite μ is $\mathcal{T}$-unsatisfiable. If so, and if μ propositionally satisfies φ, then $\mathcal{T}$-DPLL can stop, potentially saving a lot of search. Second, if μ' (and hence μ) is $\mathcal{T}$-unsatisfiable, then checking the consistency of μ' rather than that of μ can be faster and cause smaller conflict sets, so that to improve the effectiveness of $\mathcal{T}$-backjumping and $\mathcal{T}$-learning.

Moreover, this technique is particularly useful in some situations. For instance, many $\mathcal{T}$-solvers for $\mathcal{DL}(\mathbb{Z})$ and $\mathcal{LA}(\mathbb{Z})$ cannot efficiently handle disequalities (e.g., $(x_1 - x_2 \neq 3)$), so that they are forced to split them into the disjunction of strict inequalities $(x_1 - x_2 > 3) \vee (x_1 - x_2 < 3)$. This causes an enlargement of the search, because the two disjuncts must be investigated separately. In many problems, however, it is very frequent that most equalities $(t_1 = t_2)$ occur with positive polarity only. If so, then pure-literal filtering avoids adding $(t_1 \neq t_2)$ to μ when $(t_1 = t_2)^p$ is assigned to false by $\mathcal{T}$-DPLL, so that no split is needed [3].

4   DPLL for Theory Combination: DTC

We consider the *SMT* problem in the case of combined theories, $SMT(\mathcal{T}_1 \cup \mathcal{T}_2)$. In the original Nelson-Oppen method [31] and its variant due to Shostak

---

[5] If both $\mathcal{T}$-propagation and pure-literal filtering are implemented, then the filtered literals must be dropped not only from the assignment, but also from the list of literals which can be $\mathcal{T}$-deduced, so that to avoid the $\mathcal{T}$-propagation of literals which have already been filtered away.

[38] (hereafter referred as *deterministic N.O.*[6]) the two $\mathcal{T}$-*solvers* cooperate by inferring and exchanging equalities between shared terms (interface equalities), until either one $\mathcal{T}$-*solver* detects unsatisfiability (Unsat case), or neither can perform any more entailment (Sat case). In case of a non-convex theory $\mathcal{T}_i$, the $\mathcal{T}_i$-*solver* may generate a disjunction of interface equalities; consequently, a $\mathcal{T}_i$-*solver* receiving a disjunction of equalities from the other one is forced to case-split on each disjunct. Deterministic N.O. requires that each $\mathcal{T}$-*solver* is always capable to inferring the (disjunctions of) equalities which are entailed by the input set of literals (see §3.1). Whilst for some theories this feature can be implemented very efficiently (e.g., $\mathcal{EUF}$ [32]), for some others it can be extremely expensive (e.g., $\mathcal{DL}(\mathbb{Z})$ [30]).

*Delayed Theory Combination (*DTC*)* is a general method for tackling the problem of theory combination within the context of lazy *SMT* [7,8]. As with N.O., we assume that $\mathcal{T}_1$, $\mathcal{T}_2$ are two signature-disjoint stably-infinite theories with their respective $\mathcal{T}_i$-*solvers*. Importantly, no assumption is made about the e_{ij}-deduction capabilities of the $\mathcal{T}_i$-*solvers* (§3.1): for each $\mathcal{T}_i$-*solver*, every intermediate situation from complete e_{ij}-deduction (like in deterministic N.O.) to no e_{ij}-deduction capabilities (like in non-deterministic N.O.) is admitted.

In a nutshell, in DTC the embedded DPLL engine not only enumerates truth assignments for the atoms of the input formula, but also assigns truth values for the interface equalities that the $\mathcal{T}$-*solver*'s are not capable of inferring, and handles the case-split induced by the entailment of disjunctions of interface equalities in non-convex theories. The rationale is to exploit the full power of a modern DPLL engine by delegating to it part of the heavy reasoning effort previously due to the $\mathcal{T}_i$-*solvers*.

An implementation of DTC [8,9] is based on the schema of Figure 4, exploiting early pruning, $\mathcal{T}$-propagation, $\mathcal{T}$-backjumping and $\mathcal{T}$-learning. Each of the two $\mathcal{T}_i$-*solvers* interacts only with the DPLL engine by exchanging literals via the truth assignment μ in a stack-based manner, so that there is no direct exchange of information between the $\mathcal{T}_i$-*solvers*. Let $\mathcal{T}$ be $\mathcal{T}_1 \cup \mathcal{T}_2$. The $\mathcal{T}$-DPLL algorithm is modified to the following extents [8,9]:[7]

- $\mathcal{T}$-DPLL must be instructed to assign truth values not only to the atoms in φ, but also to the interface equalities not occurring in φ. $\mathcal{P}2\mathcal{T}$ and $\mathcal{T}2\mathcal{P}$ are modified accordingly. In particular, $\mathcal{T}$-decide_next_branch is modified to select also new interface equalities not occurring in the original formula.
- μ^p is partitioned into three components $\mu^p_{\mathcal{T}_1}$, $\mu^p_{\mathcal{T}_2}$ and μ^p_e, s.t. $\mu_{\mathcal{T}_i}$ is the set of i-pure literals and μ_e is the set of interface (dis)equalities in μ.
- $\mathcal{T}$-deduce is modified to work as follows: for each $\mathcal{T}_i$, $\mu^p_{\mathcal{T}_i} \cup \mu^p_e$, is fed to the respective $\mathcal{T}_i$-*solver*. If both return Sat, then $\mathcal{T}$-deduce returns Sat, otherwise it returns Conflict.
- Early-pruning is performed; if some $\mathcal{T}_i$-*solver* can deduce atoms or single interface equalities, then $\mathcal{T}$-propagation is performed. If one $\mathcal{T}_i$-solver

---

[6] We also call *nondeterministic N.O.* the non-deterministic variant of N.O. method first presented in [34].

[7] For simplicity, we assume φ is pure, although this condition is not necessary.

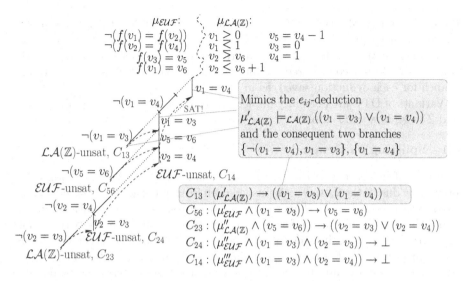

Fig. 6. The DTC search tree for Example 6 on $\mathcal{LA}(\mathbb{Z}) \cup \mathcal{EUF}$, with no e_{ij}-deduction. $v_1, \ldots, v_6$ are interface terms. μ'_{T_i}, μ''_{T_i}, μ'''_{T_i} denote generic subsets of μ_{T_i}, $T \in \{\mathcal{EUF}, \mathcal{LA}(\mathbb{Z})\}$.

performs the e_{ij}-deduction $\mu^* \models_{T_i} \bigvee_{j=1}^{k} e_j$, s.t. $\mu^* \subseteq \mu_{T_i} \cup \mu_e$, each e_j being an interface equality, then the deduction clause $T2\mathcal{B}(\mu^* \rightarrow \bigvee_{j=1}^{k} e_j)$ is learned.

- T-analyze_conflict and T-backtrack are modified so that to use the conflict set returned by one T_i-solver for T-backjumping and T-learning. Importantly, such conflict sets may contain interface equalities.

In order to achieve efficiency, other heuristics and strategies have been further suggested in [7,8,9], and more recently in [17,14].

Example 6. [9] Consider the set of $\mathcal{EUF} \cup \mathcal{LA}(\mathbb{Z})$-literals $\mu =_{def} \mu_{\mathcal{EUF}} \cup \mu_{\mathcal{LA}(\mathbb{Z})}$ of Figure 6. We assume that both the $\mathcal{EUF}$- and $\mathcal{LA}(\mathbb{Z})$-solvers have no e_{ij}-deduction capabilities (like with non-deterministic N.O.). For simplicity, we also assume that both T_i-solvers always return conflict sets which do not contain redundant interface disequalities $\neg e_{ij}$. (We adopt here a strategy for DTC which is described in detail in [9].) In short, T-DPLL performs a boolean search on the e_{ij}'s, backjumping on the T-conflicting clauses C_{13}, C_{56}, C_{23}, C_{24} and C_{14}, which in the end causes the unit-propagation of ($v_1 = v_4$). Then, T-DPLL selects a sequence of $\neg e_{ij}$'s without generating conflicts, and concludes that the formula is $T_1 \cup T_2$-satisfiable. Notice that the backjumping steps on the clauses C_{13}, C_{56}, and C_{25} mimic the effects of performing e_{ij}-deductions.

By adopting T-*solvers* with different e_{ij}-deduction power, one can trade part or all the e_{ij}-deduction effort for extra boolean search. [9] shows that, if the T-*solvers* have full e_{ij}-deduction capabilities, then no extra boolean search on the e_{ij}'s is required; otherwise, the boolean search is controlled by the quality of the conflict sets returned by the $\mathcal{T}$-*solvers*: the more redundant $\neg e_{ij}$'s are removed from the conflict sets, the more boolean branches are pruned. If the conflict sets do not contain redundant $\neg e_{ij}$'s, the extra effort is reduced to one branch for each deduction saved, as in Example 6.

Variants of DTC are currently implemented in the MATHSAT [8], YICES [17], and Z3 [14] lazy *SMT* tools.

4.1 Splitting on Demand

The idea of delegating to the DPLL engine part of the heavy reasoning effort previously due to the $\mathcal{T}_i$-*solvers* is pushed even further in the *Splitting on demand* technique proposed in [5]. This work is built on top of the observation that for many theories, in particular for non-convex ones, $\mathcal{T}$-*solvers* must perform lots of internal case-splits in order to decide the satisfiability of a set of literals. Unfortunately most $\mathcal{T}$-*solvers* cannot handle boolean search internally, so that they cannot do anything better then doing naive case-splitting on all possible combinations of the alternatives.

With splitting on demand, whenever the $\mathcal{T}$-*solver* encounters the need of a case-split, it gives back the control to the DPLL engine by returning (the boolean abstraction of) a clause encoding the alternatives, which is learned and split upon by the DPLL engine. (Notice that the atoms encoding the alternatives in the learned clause may not occur in the original formula.) This is repeated until the $\mathcal{T}$-*solver* can decide the $\mathcal{T}$-satisfiability of its input literals without case-splitting. Therefore the $\mathcal{T}$-*solver* delegates the boolean search induced by the case-splits to the DPLL solver, which presumably handles it in a much more efficient way.

References

1. Armando, A., Castellini, C., Giunchiglia, E.: SAT-based procedures for temporal reasoning. In: Jaffar, J. (ed.) Principles and Practice of Constraint Programming – CP'99. LNCS, vol. 1713, Springer, Heidelberg (1999)
2. Armando, A., Giunchiglia, E.: Embedding Complex Decision Procedures inside an Interactive Theorem Prover. Annals of Mathematics and Artificial Intelligence 8(3–4), 475–502 (1993)
3. Audemard, G., Bertoli, P., Cimatti, A., Korniłowicz, A., Sebastiani, R.: A SAT Based Approach for Solving Formulas over Boolean and Linear Mathematical Propositions. In: Voronkov, A. (ed.) Automated Deduction - CADE-18. LNCS (LNAI), vol. 2392, Springer, Heidelberg (2002)
4. Barrett, C., Dill, D., Stump, A.: Checking Satisfiability of First-Order Formulas by Incremental Translation to SAT. In: 14th International Conference on Computer-Aided Verification (2002)
5. Barrett, C., Nieuwenhuis, R., Oliveras, A., Tinelli, C.: Splitting on Demand in SAT Modulo Theories. In: Hermann, M., Voronkov, A. (eds.) LPAR 2006. LNCS (LNAI), vol. 4246, Springer, Heidelberg (2006)
6. Bozzano, M., Bruttomesso, R., Cimatti, A., Junttila, T., van Rossum, P., Schulz, S., Sebastiani, R.: MathSAT: A Tight Integration of SAT and Mathematical Decision Procedure. Journal of Automated Reasoning 35(1-3) (2005)

7. Bozzano, M., Bruttomesso, R., Cimatti, A., Junttila, T., van Rossum, P.: Efficient Satisfiability Modulo Theories via Delayed Theory Combination. In: Etessami, K., Rajamani, S.K. (eds.) CAV 2005. LNCS, vol. 3576, Springer, Heidelberg (2005)
8. Bozzano, M., Bruttomesso, R., Cimatti, A., Junttila, T., van Rossum, P., Ranise, S., Sebastiani, R.: Efficient Theory Combination via Boolean Search. Information and Computation 204(10) (2006)
9. Bruttomesso, R., Cimatti, A., Franzén, A., Griggio, A., Sebastiani, R.: Delayed Theory Combination vs. Nelson-Oppen for Satisfiability Modulo Theories: a Comparative Analysis. In: Hermann, M., Voronkov, A. (eds.) LPAR 2006. LNCS (LNAI), vol. 4246, Springer, Heidelberg (2006)
10. Cotton, S., Maler, O.: Fast and Flexible Difference Logic Propagation for DPLL(T). In: Biere, A., Gomes, C.P. (eds.) SAT 2006. LNCS, vol. 4121, Springer, Heidelberg (2006)
11. D'Agostino, M., Mondadori, M.: The Taming of the Cut. Journal of Logic and Computation 4(3), 285–319 (1994)
12. Davis, M., Longemann, G., Loveland, D.: A machine program for theorem proving. Journal of the ACM 5(7) (1962)
13. Davis, M., Putnam, H.: A computing procedure for quantification theory. Journal of the ACM 7, 201–215 (1960)
14. de Moura, L., Bjorner, N.: Model-based Theory Combination. In: Proc. 5th workshop on Satisfiability Modulo Theories, SMT'07 (2007) (to appear)
15. de Moura, L., Rueß, H., Sorea, M.: Lemmas on Demand for Satisfiability Solvers. In: Proc. SAT'02 (2002)
16. Dutertre, B., de Moura, L.: A Fast Linear-Arithmetic Solver for DPLL(T). In: Ball, T., Jones, R.B. (eds.) CAV 2006. LNCS, vol. 4144, Springer, Heidelberg (2006)
17. Dutertre, B., de Moura, L.: System Description: Yices 1.0. In: Proc. on 2nd SMT competition, SMT-COMP'06 (2006), Available at yices.csl.sri.com/yices-smtcomp06.pdf.
18. Flanagan, C., Joshi, R., Ou, X., Saxe, J.B.: Theorem Proving Using Lazy Proof Explication. In: Hunt Jr., W.A., Somenzi, F. (eds.) CAV 2003. LNCS, vol. 2725, Springer, Heidelberg (2003)
19. Ganzinger, H., Hagen, G., Nieuwenhuis, R., Oliveras, A., Tinelli, C.: DPLL(T): Fast Decision Procedures. In: Alur, R., Peled, D.A. (eds.) CAV 2004. LNCS, vol. 3114, Springer, Heidelberg (2004)
20. Giunchiglia, E., Giunchiglia, F., Sebastiani, R., Tacchella, A.: More evaluation of decision procedures for modal logics. In: Proc. KR'98, Trento, Italy (1998)
21. Giunchiglia, E., Giunchiglia, F., Sebastiani, R., Tacchella, A.: SAT vs. Translation based decision procedures for modal logics: a comparative evaluation. Journal of Applied Non-Classical Logics 10(2), 145–172 (2000)
22. Giunchiglia, E., Giunchiglia, F., Tacchella, A.: SAT Based Decision Procedures for Classical Modal Logics. Journal of Automated Reasoning. Special Issue: Satisfiability at the start of the year 2000 (2001)
23. Giunchiglia, F., Sebastiani, R.: Building decision procedures for modal logics from propositional decision procedures - the case study of modal K. In: CADE 1996. LNCS (LNAI), Springer, Heidelberg (1996)
24. Giunchiglia, F., Sebastiani, R.: A SAT-based decision procedure for ALC. In: Proc. KR'96, Cambridge, MA, USA (November 1996)
25. Giunchiglia, F., Sebastiani, R.: Building decision procedures for modal logics from propositional decision procedures - the case study of modal K(m). Information and Computation 162(1/2) (2000)

26. Haarslev, V., Moeller, R.: RACER System Description. In: Goré, R.P., Leitsch, A., Nipkow, T. (eds.) IJCAR 2001. LNCS (LNAI), vol. 2083, Springer, Heidelberg (2001)

27. Horrocks, I.: Using an expressive description logic: FaCT or fiction? In: 6th International Conference on Principles of Knowledge Representation and Reasoning (KR'98), pp. 636–647 (1998)

28. Horrocks, I., Patel-Schneider, P.F.: Optimizing Description Logic Subsumption. Journal of Logic and Computation 9(3), 267–293 (1999)

29. Horrocks, I., Patel-Schneider, P.F., Sebastiani, R.: An Analysis of Empirical Testing for Modal Decision Procedures. Logic Journal of the IGPL 8(3), 293–323 (2000)

30. Lahiri, S.K., Musuvathi, M.: An Efficient Decision Procedure for UTVPI Constraints. In: Gramlich, B. (ed.) FroCos 2005. LNCS (LNAI), vol. 3717, Springer, Heidelberg (2005)

31. Nelson, G., Oppen, D.C.: Simplification by Cooperating Decision Procedures. ACM Trans. on Programming Languages and Systems 1(2), 245–257 (1979)

32. Nieuwenhuis, R., Oliveras, A.: Proof-Producing Congruence Closure. In: Giesl, J. (ed.) RTA 2005. LNCS, vol. 3467, Springer, Heidelberg (2005)

33. Nieuwenhuis, R., Oliveras, A., Tinelli, C.: Solving SAT and SAT Modulo Theories: from an Abstract Davis-Putnam-Logemann-Loveland Procedure to DPLL(T). Journal of the ACM 53(6), 937–977 (2006)

34. Oppen, D.C.: Complexity, convexity and combinations of theories. Theoretical Computer Science 12, 291–302 (1980)

35. Patel-Schneider, P.F.: DLP System Description. In: Proc. Int. Workshop on Description Logics. In: DL'98 (1998)

36. Sebastiani, R.: Lazy Satisfiability Modulo Theories. Technical Report dtr-07-022, DIT, University of Trento, Italy (April 2007), Available at http://eprints.biblio.unitn.it/archive/00001196/01/dtr-07-022.pdf.

37. Sebastiani, R., Villafiorita, A.: SAT-based decision procedures for normal modal logics: a theoretical framework. In: Giunchiglia, F. (ed.) AIMSA 1998. LNCS (LNAI), vol. 1480, Springer, Heidelberg (1998)

38. Shostak, R.E.: Deciding Combinations of Theories. Journal of the ACM 31, 1–12 (1984)

39. Smullyan, R.M.: First-Order Logic. Springer, Heidelberg (1968)

40. Tinelli, C.: A DPLL-based Calculus for Ground Satisfiability Modulo Theories. In: Flesca, S., Greco, S., Leone, N., Ianni, G. (eds.) JELIA 2002. LNCS (LNAI), vol. 2424, pp. 308–319. Springer, Heidelberg (2002)

41. Wolfman, S., Weld, D.: The LPSAT Engine & its Application to Resource Planning. In: Proc. IJCAI (1999)

42. Zhang, L., Madigan, C.F., Moskewicz, M.W., Malik, S.: Efficient conflict driven learning in boolean satisfiability solver. In: ICCAD, pp. 279–285 (2001)

43. Zhang, L., Malik, S.: The quest for efficient boolean satisfiability solvers. In: Brinksma, E., Larsen, K.G. (eds.) CAV 2002. LNCS, vol. 2404, pp. 17–36. Springer, Heidelberg (2002)

Hierarchical and Modular Reasoning in Complex Theories: The Case of Local Theory Extensions

Viorica Sofronie-Stokkermans

Max-Planck-Institut für Informatik, Stuhlsatzenhausweg 85, Saarbrücken, Germany
sofronie@mpi-sb.mpg.de

Abstract. We present an overview of results on hierarchical and modular reasoning in complex theories. We show that for a special type of extensions of a base theory, which we call *local*, hierarchic reasoning is possible (i.e. proof tasks in the extension can be hierarchically reduced to proof tasks w.r.t. the base theory). Many theories important for computer science or mathematics fall into this class (typical examples are theories of data structures, theories of free or monotone functions, but also functions occurring in mathematical analysis). In fact, it is often necessary to consider complex extensions, in which various types of functions or data structures need to be taken into account at the same time. We show how such local theory extensions can be identified and under which conditions locality is preserved when combining theories, and we investigate possibilities of efficient modular reasoning in such theory combinations.

We present several examples of application domains where local theories and local theory extensions occur in a natural way. We show, in particular, that various phenomena analyzed in the verification literature can be explained in a unified way using the notion of locality.

1 Introduction

Many problems in mathematics and computer science can be reduced to proving the satisfiability of conjunctions of literals in a background theory (which can be the extension of a base theory with additional functions – e.g., free, monotone, or recursively defined – or a combination of theories). It is therefore very important to identify situations where reasoning in complex theories can be done efficiently and accurately. Efficiency can be achieved for instance by:

(1) reducing the search space (preferably without loosing completeness);
(2) modular reasoning, i.e., delegating some proof tasks which refer to a specific theory to provers specialized in handling formulae of that theory.

Identifying situations where the search space can be controlled without loss of completeness is of utmost importance, especially in applications where efficient algorithms (in space, but also in time) are essential. To address this problem, essentially very similar ideas occurred in various areas: proof theory and automated deduction, databases, algebra and verification.

B. Konev and F. Wolter (Eds.): FroCos 2007, LNAI 4720, pp. 47–71, 2007.
© Springer-Verlag Berlin Heidelberg 2007

Local inference systems. Possibilities of restricting the search space in inference systems without loss of completeness were studied by McAllester and Givan in [17,21,18]. They introduced so-called "local inference systems", which can be modeled by sets of rules (or sets of Horn clauses N) with the property that for any ground Horn clause G, it is guaranteed that if G can be proved using N then G can already be proved by using only those instances $N[G]$ of N containing only ground terms occurring in G or in N. For local inference systems, validity of ground Horn clauses can be checked in polynomial time. In [5,4], Ganzinger and Basin define a more general notion, *order locality*, and establish links between order-locality and saturation w.r.t. ordered resolution with a special notion of redundancy. These results were used for automated complexity analysis.

The work on local inference systems and local theories can be seen as an extension of ideas which occurred in the study of *deductive databases*. The inference rules of a deductive database are usually of a special form (known as datalog program): typically a set of universal Horn clauses which do not contain function symbols. Any datalog program defines an inference relation for which entailment of ground clauses is decidable in polynomial time [33,34].

Locality and algebra. Similar ideas also occurred in algebra. To prove that the uniform word problem for lattices is decidable in polynomial time, Skolem [26] used the following idea: replace the lattice operations $\vee$ and $\wedge$ by ternary relations $r_\vee$ and $r_\wedge$, required to be functional, but not necessarily total. The lattice axioms were translated to a relational form, by flattening them and then replacing every atom of the form $x \vee y \approx z$ with $r_\vee(x, y, z)$ (similarly for $\wedge$-terms). Additional axioms were added, stating that equality is an equivalence and that the relations are compatible with equality and functional. This new presentation, consisting only of Horn, function-free clauses, can be used for deciding in polynomial time the uniform word problem for lattices. The correctness and completeness of the method relies on the fact that every partially-ordered set (where $\vee$ and $\wedge$ are partially defined) embeds into a lattice. A similar idea was used by Evans in the study of classes of algebras with a PTIME decidable word problem [12]. The idea was extended by Burris [8] to quasi-varieties of algebras. He proved that if a quasi-variety axiomatized by a set $\mathcal{K}$ of Horn clauses has the property that *every finite partial algebra which is a partial model of the axioms in $\mathcal{K}$ can be extended to a total algebra model of $\mathcal{K}$* then the uniform word problem for $\mathcal{K}$ is decidable in polynomial time. In [13], Ganzinger established a link between the proof theoretic notion of locality and embeddability of partial into total algebras. In [14,27] the notion of locality for Horn clauses is extended to the notion of *local extension* of a base theory.

Locality and verification. Apparently independently, similar phenomena were studied in the verification literature, mainly motivated by the necessity of devising methods for efficient reasoning in theories of data structures. In [23], McPeak and Necula investigate local reasoning in pointer data structures, with the goal of efficiently proving invariants in programs dealing with pointers. They present a methodology of specifying shapes of data structures using a class of specifications which they call *local*. It is then shown that the class of local specifications has the property that in order to disprove a (ground) formula, only certain ground instances of the specification are needed, referring to a part of the data structure which is situated in the "neighborhood" of the counterexample. The essence of the method devised by McPeak and Necula is to perform case analysis based on memory writes, and generate facts that must be proved unsatisfiable by using a *finite number of instantiations* of the axioms defining the properties of the data structures. They show that for local specifications finite sets of instances can be found, without loss of completeness. Locality considerations also occur in the study of a theory of arrays by Bradley, Manna and Sipma [6]. They identified a fragment of the theory of arrays for which universal quantification over indices can be replaced by taking a (well-determined) set of ground instances for the index variables. We will show that all these phenomena are instances of a general concept, and present possibilities of recognizing various types of locality of theories and theory extensions.

It is equally important to be able to reason efficiently in complex theories.

Modular reasoning in combinations of theories. Modular methods for checking satisfiability of conjunctions of ground literals in combinations of theories which have *disjoint signatures*, or only share constants are well studied. The Nelson-Oppen combination procedure [24] for instance, can be applied for combining decision procedures of *stably infinite* theories over disjoint signatures. Resolution-based methods have also been used in this context [2,1]. Recently, attempts have been made to extend the Nelson-Oppen combination procedure to more general theories. Extensions have been achieved either by relaxing the requirement that the theories to be combined are stably-infinite [32][1]; or by relaxing the requirement that the theories to be combined have disjoint signatures [3,31,15]. Note that these extensions are still restrictive, as the conditions imposed on the base theory and on the component theories are very strong, and of a model theoretic nature. For instance, due to the limitations on the shared theory for decidability transfer in combinations of theories as studied in [15], only locally finite shared theories (hence no numerical domains) can be handled when applying these results to verification in [16]. In contrast, the notion of local extensions we studied [27] imposes no restrictions on using numerical domains as a base theory.

The notion of locality of a theory extension allows us to address at the same time the two aspects important for efficient reasoning mentioned above, namely restricting the search space and modular reasoning. Locality is used for restricting the search space, but as a side-effect it allows to reduce proof tasks in the extension, hierarchically, to proof tasks w.r.t. the base theory. We will present these results here. We will also present recent results on preservation of locality of theories (resp. theory extensions) under theory combination, and on possibilities of modular reasoning in such combinations. In particular, we are interested in characterizing the type of information which needs to be exchanged between

---

[1] It is interesting that, although the approach of [32] is orthogonal to the notion of locality of a theory extension [27], many of the examples considered there can also be explained using semantical characterizations of locality.

provers for the component theories in order to guarantee completeness of the procedure. This last problem is strongly related to the problem of studying the form of interpolants in theory combinations. This is why we will also mention some of our results on interpolation in local theory extensions.

Structure of the paper: The paper is structured as follows: Section 2 contains generalities on theories, local theories, partial algebras, weak validity and embeddability of partial algebras into total algebras. In Section 3 the notion of local theory extension is introduced, and a method for hierarchical reasoning in such extensions is presented. Section 4 presents two possibilities of identifying local theory extensions: one based on links between embeddability and locality (Section 4.1) and one which in addition allows to use resolution-based methods (Section 4.2). These methods are used in Section 5 to provide various examples of local theory extensions. We illustrate the method for hierarchical reasoning in Section 3.1 on several examples. In Section 6 we investigate conditions under which locality is preserved when combining theories, and in Section 7 we investigate possibilities of efficient modular reasoning in such theory combinations.

2   Preliminaries

Theories. Theories can be regarded as sets of formulae or as sets of models. Let T be a Π-theory and ϕ, ψ be Π-formulae. We say that $T \wedge \phi \models \psi$ (written also $\phi \models_T \psi$) if ψ is true in all models of T which satisfy ϕ.

In what follows we consider extensions of theories, in which the signature is extended by new *function symbols* (i.e. we assume that the set of predicate symbols remains unchanged in the extension). If a theory is regarded as a set of formulae, then its extension with a set of formulae is set union. If T is regarded as a collection of models then its extension with a set $\mathcal{K}$ of formulae consists of all structures (in the extended signature) which are models of $\mathcal{K}$ and whose reduct to the signature of T_0 is in T_0.

Let T_0 be an arbitrary theory with signature $\Pi_0 = (S_0, \Sigma_0, \mathsf{Pred})$, where S_0 is a set of sorts, Σ_0 a set of function symbols, and Pred a set of predicate symbols. We consider extensions T_1 of T_0 with signature $\Pi = (S, \Sigma, \mathsf{Pred})$, where the set of sorts is $S = S_0 \cup S_1$ and the set of function symbols is $\Sigma = \Sigma_0 \cup \Sigma_1$ (i.e. the signature is extended by new sorts and function symbols). We assume that T_1 is obtained from T_0 by adding a set $\mathcal{K}$ of (universally quantified) clauses in the signature Π. Thus, $\mathsf{Mod}(T_1)$ consists of all Π-structures which are models of $\mathcal{K}$ and whose reduct to Π_0 is a model of T_0.

Local theories. This notion was introduced by Givan and McAllester in [17,21]. A *local theory* is a set of Horn clauses $\mathcal{K}$ such that, for any ground Horn clause C, $\mathcal{K} \models C$ only if already $\mathcal{K}[C] \models C$ (where $\mathcal{K}[C]$ is the set of instances of $\mathcal{K}$ in which all terms are subterms of ground terms in either $\mathcal{K}$ or C).

The size of $\mathcal{K}[G]$ is polynomial in the size of G for a fixed $\mathcal{K}$. Since satisfiability of sets of ground Horn clauses can be checked in linear time [11], it follows that for local theories, validity of ground Horn clauses can be checked in polynomial time. Givan and McAllester proved that every problem which is decidable in PTIME can be encoded as an entailment problem of ground clauses w.r.t. a local theory [18]. An example of a local theory (cf. [18]) is the set of axioms of a monotone function w.r.t. a transitive relation $\leq$:

$$\mathcal{K} = \{x \leq y \wedge y \leq z \rightarrow x \leq z, \quad x \leq y \rightarrow f(x) \leq f(y)\}.$$

Another example provided in [18] is a local axiom set for reasoning about a lattice (similar to that proposed by Skolem in [26]). In [5,4], Ganzinger and Basin defined the more general notion of *order locality* and showed how to recognize (order-)local theories and how to use these results for automated complexity analysis. Given a term ordering $\succ$, we say that a set $\mathcal{K}$ of clauses entails a clause C bounded by $\succ$ (notation: $\mathcal{K} \models_{\preceq} C$), if and only if there is a proof of $\mathcal{K} \models C$ from those ground instances of clauses in $\mathcal{K}$ in which (under $\succeq$) each term is smaller than or equal to some term in C.

Definition 1 ([5,4]). *A set of clauses $\mathcal{K}$ is local with respect to $\succ$ if whenever $\mathcal{K} \models C$ for a ground clause C, then $\mathcal{K} \models_{\preceq} C$.*

Theorem 1 ([5,4]). *Let $\succ$ be a (possibly partial) term ordering and $\mathcal{K}$ be a set of clauses. Assume that $\mathcal{K}$ is saturated with respect to $\succ$-ordered resolution, and let C be a ground clause. Then $\mathcal{K} \models C$ for a ground clause C if and only if $\mathcal{K} \models_{\preceq} C$, i.e. $\mathcal{K}$ is local with respect to $\succ$.*

The converse of this theorem is not true in general. Ganzinger and Basin established conditions under which the converse holds – they use a hyperresolution calculus and identify conditions when for Horn clauses order locality is equivalent to so-called *peak saturation* (Theorems 4.4–4.7 in [4]). These results are obtained for first-order logic without equality. In [13], Ganzinger established a link between proof theoretic and semantic concepts for polynomial time decidability of uniform word problems which had already been studied in algebra [26,12,8]. He defined two notions of locality for equational Horn theories, and established relationships between these notions of locality and corresponding semantic conditions, referring to embeddability of partial algebras into total algebras. Theorem 1 also can be used for recognizing equational Horn theories:

Theorem 2 ([13]). *Let $\mathcal{K}$ be a set of Horn clauses. Then $\mathcal{K}$ is a local theory in logic with equality if and only if $\mathcal{K} \cup EQ$ is a local theory in logic without equality, where EQ denotes the set of equality axioms consisting of reflexivity, symmetry, transitivity, and of congruence axioms for each function symbol in the signature.*

Theorems 2 and 1 were used in [13] for proving the locality of the following presentation Int of the set of integers with successor and predecessor by saturation:

(1) $p(x) \approx y \rightarrow s(y) \approx x$ (3) $p(x) \approx p(y) \rightarrow y \approx x$
(2) $s(x) \approx y \rightarrow p(y) \approx x$ (4) $s(x) \approx s(y) \rightarrow y \approx x$

The presentation Int$'$ of integers with successor and predecessor consisting of the axioms (1) and (2) alone (without the injectivity conditions (3) and (4)) is not local but it is *stably local*: in order to disprove a ground set G of clauses only those ground instances $\mathsf{Int}'^{[G]}$ of Int' are needed where variables are mapped to subterms occurring in G. (Note that $\mathsf{Int}' \cup EQ$ is not saturated under ordered resolution; when saturating it the injectivity axioms are generated.)

In [14,27] the notion of locality for Horn clauses is extended to the notion of *local extension* of a base theory (cf. Section 3). In the study of local theory extensions we will refer to *total* models of a theory and to *partial models* of a theory. The necessary notions on partial structures are defined below.

Partial structures. Let $\Pi = (S, \Sigma, \mathsf{Pred})$ be a S-sorted signature where Σ is a set of function symbols and Pred a set of predicate symbols. A *partial Π-structure* is a structure $A = (\{A_s\}_{s \in S}, \{f_A\}_{f \in \Sigma}, \{P_A\}_{P \in \mathsf{Pred}})$, where for every $s \in S$, A_s is a non-empty set and for every $f \in \Sigma$ with arity $s_1 \ldots s_n \to s$, f_A is a partial function from $\prod_{i=1}^{n} A_{s_i}$ to A_s. A is called a *total structure* if all functions f_A are total. (In the one-sorted case we will denote both an algebra and its support with the same symbol.) Details on partial algebras can be found in [7]. The notion of evaluating a term t with variables $X = \{X_s \mid s \in S\}$ w.r.t. an assignment $\{\beta_s : X_s \to A_s \mid s \in S\}$ for its variables in a partial structure A is the same as for total many-sorted algebras, except that the evaluation is undefined if $t = f(t_1, \ldots, t_n)$ with $a(f) = (s_1 \ldots s_n \to s)$, and at least one of $\beta_{s_i}(t_i)$ is undefined, or else $(\beta_{s_1}(t_1), \ldots, \beta_{s_n}(t_n))$ is not in the domain of f_A.

A *weak Π-embedding* between the partial structures $A = (\{A_s\}_{s \in S}, \{f_A\}_{f \in \Sigma}, \{P_A\}_{P \in \mathsf{Pred}})$ and $B = (\{B_s\}_{s \in S}, \{f_B\}_{f \in \Sigma}, \{P_B\}_{P \in \mathsf{Pred}})$ is a (many-sorted) family $i = (i_s)_{s \in S}$ of total maps $i_s : A_s \to B_s$ such that

- if $f_A(a_1, \ldots, a_n)$ is defined then also $f_B(i_{s_1}(a_1), \ldots, i_{s_n}(a_n))$ is defined and $i_s(f_A(a_1, \ldots, a_n)) = f_B(i_{s_1}(a_1), \ldots, i_{s_n}(a_n))$, provided $a(f) = s_1 \ldots s_n \to s$;
- for each s, i_s is injective and an embedding w.r.t. Pred i.e. for every $P \in \mathsf{Pred}$ with arity $s_1 \ldots s_n$ and every $a_1, \ldots, a_n$ where $a_i \in A_{s_i}$, $P_A(a_1, \ldots, a_n)$ if and only if $P_B(i_{s_1}(a_1), \ldots, i_{s_n}(a_n))$.

In this case we say that A *weakly embeds* into B.

In what follows we will denote a many-sorted variable assignment $\{\beta_s : X_s \to A_s \mid s \in S\}$ as $\beta : X \to A$. For the sake of simplicity all definitions below are given for the one-sorted case. They extend in a natural way to many-sorted structures.

Definition 2 (Weak validity). *Let* $(A, \{f_A\}_{f \in \Sigma}, \{P_A\}_{P \in \mathsf{Pred}})$ *be a partial structure and* $\beta : X \to A$.

(1) $(A, \beta) \models_w t \approx s$ if and only if (a) $\beta(t)$ and $\beta(s)$ are both defined and equal; or (b) at least one of $\beta(s)$ and $\beta(t)$ is undefined.

(2) $(A, \beta) \models_w t \not\approx s$ if and only if (a) $\beta(t)$ and $\beta(s)$ are both defined and different; or (b) at least one of $\beta(s)$ and $\beta(t)$ is undefined.

(3) $(A, \beta) \models_w P(t_1, \ldots, t_n)$ if and only if (a) $\beta(t_1), \ldots, \beta(t_n)$ are all defined and $(\beta(t_1), \ldots, \beta(t_n)) \in P_A$; or (b) at least one of $\beta(t_1), \ldots, \beta(t_n)$ is undefined.

(4) $(A, \beta) \models_w \neg P(t_1, \ldots, t_n)$ if and only if (a) $\beta(t_1), \ldots, \beta(t_n)$ are all defined and $(\beta(t_1), \ldots, \beta(t_n)) \notin P_A$; or (b) at least one of $\beta(t_1), \ldots, \beta(t_n)$ is undefined.

(A, β) weakly satisfies a clause C (notation: $(A, \beta) \models_w C$) if $(A, \beta) \models_w L$ for at least one literal L in C. A weakly satisfies C (notation: $A \models_w C$) if $(A, \beta) \models_w C$ for all assignments β. A weakly satisfies a set of clauses $\mathcal{K}$ (notation: $A \models_w \mathcal{K}$) if $A \models_w C$ for all $C \in \mathcal{K}$.

Definition 3 (Evans validity). *Evans validity is defined similarly, with the difference that (1) is replaced with:*

*(1') $(A, \beta) \models t \approx s$ if and only if (a) $\beta(t)$ and $\beta(s)$ are both defined and equal; or
(b) $\beta(s)$ is defined, $t = f(t_1, \ldots, t_n)$ and $\beta(t_i)$ is undefined for at least one of the direct subterms of t; or (c) both $\beta(s)$ and $\beta(t)$ are undefined.*

Evans validity extends to (sets of) clauses in the usual way. We use the notation: $(A, \beta) \models L$ for a literal L; $(A, \beta) \models C$ and $A \models C$ for a clause C, etc.

Example 1. *Let A be a partial Σ-algebra, where $\Sigma = \{\mathsf{car}/1, \mathsf{nil}/0\}$. Assume that nil_A is defined and $\mathsf{car}_A(\mathsf{nil}_A)$ is not defined. Then:*

- $A \not\models \mathsf{car}(\mathsf{nil}) \approx \mathsf{nil}$ *(since $\mathsf{car}_A(\mathsf{nil})$ is undefined in A, but nil is defined in A);*
- $A \models \mathsf{car}(\mathsf{nil}) \not\approx \mathsf{nil}$;
- $A \models_w \mathsf{car}(\mathsf{nil}) \approx \mathsf{nil}$, $A \models_w \mathsf{car}(\mathsf{nil}) \not\approx \mathsf{nil}$ *(since $\mathsf{car}(\mathsf{nil})$ is not defined in A).*

Definition 4. *A partial Π-algebra A is a* weak partial model *(resp.* partial model*) of $\mathcal{T}_1$ with totally defined Σ_0-function symbols if (i) $A_{|\Pi_0}$ is a model of $\mathcal{T}_0$ and (ii) $A \models_w \mathcal{K}$ (resp. $A \models \mathcal{K}$).*

If the base theory $\mathcal{T}_0$ and its signature are clear from the context, we will refer to *(weak) partial models* of $\mathcal{T}_1$. We will use the following notation:

- $\mathsf{PMod}(\Sigma_1, \mathcal{T}_1)$ is the class of all partial models of $\mathcal{T}_1$ in which the functions in Σ_1 are partial, and all other function symbols are total;
- $\mathsf{PMod_w}(\Sigma_1, \mathcal{T}_1)$ is the class of all weak partial models of $\mathcal{T}_1$ in which the Σ_1-functions are partial and all the other function symbols are total;
- $\mathsf{Mod}(\mathcal{T}_1)$ denotes the class of all total models of $\mathcal{T}_1$.

We will also consider small variations of the notion of weak partial model:

- $\mathsf{PMod_w^f}(\Sigma_1, \mathcal{T}_1)$ is the class of all finite weak partial models of $\mathcal{T}_1$ in which the Σ_1-functions are partial and all the other function symbols are total;
- $\mathsf{PMod_w^{fd}}(\Sigma_1, \mathcal{T}_1)$ is the class of all weak partial models of $\mathcal{T}_1$ in which the Σ_1-functions are partial and their definition domain is a finite set, and all the other function symbols are total.

and similar variations $\mathsf{PMod^f}(\Sigma_1, \mathcal{T}_1)$, $\mathsf{PMod^{fd}}(\Sigma_1, \mathcal{T}_1)$ of the notion of partial model.

Embeddability. For theory extensions $\mathcal{T}_0 \subseteq \mathcal{T}_1 = \mathcal{T}_0 \cup \mathcal{K}$, where $\mathcal{K}$ is a set of clauses, we consider the following conditions:

(Emb) Every $A \in \mathsf{PMod}(\Sigma_1, \mathcal{T}_1)$ weakly embeds into a total model of $\mathcal{T}_1$.
(Emb$_w$) Every $A \in \mathsf{PMod_w}(\Sigma_1, \mathcal{T}_1)$ weakly embeds into a total model of $\mathcal{T}_1$.

We also define a stronger notion of embeddability, which we call *completability*:

(Comp$_w$)   Every $A \in \mathsf{PMod}_w(\Sigma_1, \mathcal{T}_1)$ weakly embeds into a total model B of $\mathcal{T}_1$ such that $A_{|\Pi_0}$ and $B_{|\Pi_0}$ are isomorphic.

(Comp) is defined analogously (w.r.t. $\mathsf{PMod}(\Sigma_1, \mathcal{T}_1)$).

Conditions which only refer to embeddability of *finite* partial models are denoted by (Emb$_w^f$), (Comp$_w^f$), resp. (Emb^f), (Comp^f). Conditions referring to embeddability of partial models in which the extension functions have a finite definition domain (i.e. in $\mathsf{PMod}_w^{fd}(\Sigma_1, \mathcal{T}_1)$) are denoted by (Emb$_w^{fd}$), resp. (Comp$_w^{fd}$).

3   Local Theory Extensions

The notion of local theories introduced and studied by Givan and McAllester [17,21,18] can be extended in a natural way to extensions of a base theory with a set of additional function symbols constrained by a set $\mathcal{K}$ if clauses.

Let $\mathcal{K}$ be a set of clauses in the signature $\Pi = (S, \Sigma, \mathsf{Pred})$, where $S = S_0 \cup S_1$ and $\Sigma = \Sigma_0 \cup \Sigma_1$. In what follows, when we refer to sets G of ground clauses we assume that they are in the signature $\Pi^c = (S, \Sigma \cup \Sigma_c, \mathsf{Pred})$, where Σ_c is a set of new constants. If Ψ is a set of ground $\Sigma_0 \cup \Sigma_1 \cup \Sigma_c$-terms, we denote by $\mathcal{K}_\Psi$ the set of all instances of $\mathcal{K}$ in which all terms starting with a Σ_1-function symbol are ground terms in the set Ψ. We denote by $\mathcal{K}^\Psi$ the set of all instances of $\mathcal{K}$ in which all variables occurring below a Σ_1-function symbol are instantiated with ground terms in the set $T_{\Sigma_0}(\Psi)$ of Σ_0-terms generated by Ψ.

If G is a set of ground clauses and $\Psi = \mathsf{st}(\mathcal{K}, G)$ is the set of ground subterms occurring in either $\mathcal{K}$ or G then we write $\mathcal{K}[G] := \mathcal{K}_\Psi$, and $\mathcal{K}^{[G]} := \mathcal{K}^\Psi$.

We will focus on the following type of locality of a theory extension $\mathcal{T}_0 \subseteq \mathcal{T}_1$, where $\mathcal{T}_1 = \mathcal{T}_0 \cup \mathcal{K}$ with $\mathcal{K}$ a set of (universally quantified) clauses:

(Loc)   For every set G of ground clauses $\mathcal{T}_1 \cup G \models \perp$ iff $\mathcal{T}_0 \cup \mathcal{K}[G] \cup G$ has no weak partial model in which all terms in $\mathsf{st}(\mathcal{K}, G)$ are defined.

(SLoc)   For every set G of ground clauses $\mathcal{T}_1 \cup G \models \perp$ iff $\mathcal{T}_0 \cup \mathcal{K}^{[G]} \cup G$ has no partial model in which all terms in $\mathsf{st}(\mathcal{K}, G)$ are defined.

Weaker notions (Loc^f), resp. (SLoc^f) can be defined if we require that the respective conditions only hold for *finite* sets G of ground clauses. An intermediate notion of locality (Loc^{fd}) can be defined if we require that the respective conditions only hold for sets G of ground clauses containing only a finite set of terms starting with a function symbol in Σ_1. A more general notion of locality (ELoc) is presented at the end of Section 4.1.

An extension $\mathcal{T}_0 \subseteq \mathcal{T}_1$ is *local* (*stably local*) if it satisfies condition (Loc^f) (resp. (SLoc^f)). A local (stably local) theory [13] is a local extension of the empty theory. In (stably) local theory extensions hierarchical reasoning is possible.

3.1   Hierarchical Reasoning in Local Theory Extensions

Consider a local theory extension $\mathcal{T}_0 \subseteq \mathcal{T}_0 \cup \mathcal{K}$. The locality conditions defined above require that, for every set G of ground clauses, $\mathcal{T}_1 \cup G$ is satisfiable if and only if $\mathcal{T}_0 \cup \mathcal{K}*[G] \cup G$ has a (Evans, weak, finite) partial model with additional properties, where, depending on the notion of locality, $\mathcal{K} * [G]$ is $\mathcal{K}[G]$ or $\mathcal{K}^{[G]}$. All clauses in $\mathcal{K} * [G] \cup G$ have the property that the function symbols in Σ_1 have as arguments only ground terms. Therefore, $\mathcal{K} * [G] \cup G$ can be flattened and purified (i.e. the function symbols in Σ_1 are separated from the other symbols) by introducing, in a bottom-up manner, new constants c_t for subterms $t = f(g_1, \ldots, g_n)$ with $f \in \Sigma_1$, g_i ground $\Sigma_0 \cup \Sigma_c$-terms (where Σ_c is a set of constants which contains the constants introduced by flattening, resp. purification), together with corresponding definitions $c_t \approx t$. The set of clauses thus obtained has the form $\mathcal{K}_0 \cup G_0 \cup D$, where D is a set of ground unit clauses of the form $f(g_1, \ldots, g_n) \approx c$, where $f \in \Sigma_1$, c is a constant, $g_1, \ldots, g_n$ are ground terms without function symbols in Σ_1, and $\mathcal{K}_0$ and G_0 are clauses without function symbols in Σ_1. Flattening and purification preserve both satisfiability and unsatisfiability with respect to total algebras, and also with respect to partial algebras in which all ground subterms which are flattened are defined [27].

For the sake of simplicity in what follows we will always flatten and then purify $\mathcal{K} * [G] \cup G$. Thus we ensure that D consists of ground unit clauses of the form $f(c_1, \ldots, c_n) \approx c$, where $f \in \Sigma_1$, and $c_1, \ldots, c_n, c$ are constants.

Lemma 3 ([27]). *Let $\mathcal{K}$ be a set of clauses and G a set of ground clauses, and let $\mathcal{K}_0 \cup G_0 \cup D$ be obtained from $\mathcal{K} * [G] \cup G$ by flattening and purification, as explained above. Assume that $\mathcal{T}_0 \subseteq \mathcal{T}_0 \cup \mathcal{K}$ is a local theory extension. Then the following are equivalent:*

(1) $\mathcal{T}_0 \cup \mathcal{K}*[G] \cup G$ has a partial model in which all terms in $\mathsf{st}(\mathcal{K}, G)$ are defined.
(2) $\mathcal{T}_0 \cup \mathcal{K}_0 \cup G_0 \cup D$ has a partial model with all terms in $\mathsf{st}(\mathcal{K}_0, G_0, D)$ defined.
(3) $\mathcal{T}_0 \cup \mathcal{K}_0 \cup G_0 \cup N_0$ has a (total) model, where

$$N_0 = \{ \bigwedge_{i=1}^n c_i \approx d_i \rightarrow c = d \mid f(c_1, \ldots, c_n) \approx c, f(d_1, \ldots, d_n) \approx d \in D \}.$$

Theorem 4 ([27]). *Assume that the theory extension $\mathcal{T}_0 \subseteq \mathcal{T}_1$ either (1) satisfies condition (Loc^f), or (2) satisfies condition (SLoc^f) and $\mathcal{T}_0$ is locally finite. Then:*

(a) If all variables in the clauses in $\mathcal{K}$ occur below some function symbol from Σ_1 and if the universal theory of $\mathcal{T}_0$ is decidable, then the universal theory of $\mathcal{T}_1$ is decidable.
(b) Assume some variables in $\mathcal{K}$ do not occur below any function symbol in Σ_1. If the $\forall \exists$ theory of $\mathcal{T}_0$ is decidable then the universal theory of $\mathcal{T}_1$ is decidable.

In case (a) above locality allows to reduce reasoning in $\mathcal{T}_1$ to reasoning in an extension of $\mathcal{T}_0$ with free function symbols (for this an SMT procedure can be used). In case (b) this is not possible, as $\mathcal{K} * [G]$ is not a set of ground clauses.

We will illustrate the applicability of Lemma 3 and Theorem 4 for specific examples of local theory extensions in Section 5.

4   Identifying Local Theory Extensions

We discuss two different ways of recognizing the locality of a theory extension. The first is semantical, based on possibilities of embedding partial models of a theory extension into total models. The second is proof theoretical, and at the moment part of work in progress: we present some results based on possibilities of saturating the extension axioms with respect to ordered resolution.

4.1   Locality and Embeddability

Links between *locality of a theory* and *embeddability* were established by Ganzinger in [13]. Similar results can also be obtained for *local theory extensions*.

In what follows we say that a non-ground clause is Σ_1-*flat* if function symbols (including constants) do not occur as arguments of function symbols in Σ_1. A Σ_1-flat non-ground clause is called Σ_1-*linear* if whenever a variable occurs in two terms in the clause which start with function symbols in Σ_1, the two terms are identical, and if no term which starts with a function symbol in Σ_1 contains two occurrences of the same variable.

For sets of Σ_1-flat clauses locality implies embeddability. This generalizes results presented in the case of local theories in [13].

Theorem 5. *Assume that $\mathcal{K}$ is a family of Σ_1-flat clauses in the signature Π.*

(1) If the extension $\mathcal{T}_0 \subseteq \mathcal{T}_1 := \mathcal{T}_0 \cup \mathcal{K}$ satisfies (Loc) then it satisfies (Emb$_w$).
(2) If the extension $\mathcal{T}_0 \subseteq \mathcal{T}_1 := \mathcal{T}_0 \cup \mathcal{K}$ satisfies (Loc^f) then it satisfies (Emb$_w^f$).
(3) If the extension $\mathcal{T}_0 \subseteq \mathcal{T}_1 := \mathcal{T}_0 \cup \mathcal{K}$ satisfies (Loc^{fd}) then it satisfies (Emb$_w^{fd}$).
(4) If $\mathcal{T}_0$ is compact and the extension $\mathcal{T}_0 \subseteq \mathcal{T}_1$ satisfies (Loc^f), then $\mathcal{T}_0 \subseteq \mathcal{T}_1$ satisfies (Emb$_w$).

Conversely, embeddability implies locality. The following results appear in [27], [30] and allow us to give several examples of local theory extensions (cf. Sect. 5).

Theorem 6 ([27,30]). *Let $\mathcal{K}$ be a set of Σ_1-flat and Σ_1-linear clauses.*

(1) If the extension $\mathcal{T}_0 \subseteq \mathcal{T}_1$ satisfies (Emb$_w$) then it satisfies (Loc).
(2) Assume that $\mathcal{T}_0$ is a locally finite universal theory, and that $\mathcal{K}$ contains only finitely many ground subterms. If the extension $\mathcal{T}_0 \subseteq \mathcal{T}_1$ satisfies (Emb$_w^f$), then $\mathcal{T}_0 \subseteq \mathcal{T}_1$ satisfies (Loc^f).
(3) $\mathcal{T}_0 \subseteq \mathcal{T}_1$ satisfies (Emb$_w^{fd}$). Then $\mathcal{T}_0 \subseteq \mathcal{T}_1$ satisfies (Loc^{fd}).

Theorem 7 ([27]). *Let $\mathcal{T}_0$ be a universal theory and $\mathcal{K}$ be a set of clauses. Then:*

(1) If the extension $\mathcal{T}_0 \subseteq \mathcal{T}_1$ satisfies (Emb) then it satisfies (SLoc).
(2) Assume that $\mathcal{T}_0$ is a locally finite universal theory, and that $\mathcal{K}$ contains only finitely many ground subterms. If the extension $\mathcal{T}_0 \subseteq \mathcal{T}_1$ satisfies (Emb^f), then $\mathcal{T}_0 \subseteq \mathcal{T}_1$ satisfies (SLoc^f).

Analyzing the proofs of Theorems 6 and 7 we notice that the embeddability conditions (Comp) and (Comp$_w$) imply, in fact, stronger locality conditions. Consider a theory extension $T_0 \subseteq T_0 \cup \mathcal{K}$ with a set $\mathcal{K}$ of formulae of the form $\forall x_1 \ldots x_n (\Phi(x_1, \ldots, x_n) \vee C(x_1, \ldots, x_n))$, where $\Phi(x_1, \ldots, x_n)$ is an *arbitrary first-order formula* in the base signature Π_0 with free variables $x_1, \ldots, x_n$, and $C(x_1, \ldots, x_n)$ is a *clause* in the signature Π.

We can extend the notion of locality of an extension accordingly:

(ELoc)   For every formula $\Gamma = \Gamma_0 \cup G$, where Γ_0 is a Π_0-sentence and G is a set of ground clauses, $T_1 \cup \Gamma \models \bot$ iff $T_0 \cup \mathcal{K}[\Gamma] \cup \Gamma$ has no weak partial model in which all terms in $\mathsf{st}(\mathcal{K}, G)$ are defined.

A stable locality condition (ESLoc) can be defined similarly. The proofs of Theorems 6 and 7 can be adapted with minimal changes to prove a stronger result:

Theorem 8 ([27]). *(1) Assume all terms of $\mathcal{K}$ starting with a Σ_1-function are flat and linear. If the extension $T_0 \subseteq T_1$ satisfies* (Comp$_w$) *then it satisfies* (ELoc).

(2) Assume that T_0 is a universal theory. If the extension $T_0 \subseteq T_1$ satisfies (Comp) *then it satisfies* (ESLoc).

4.2   Locality and Saturation

In Section 2, the results of Basin and Ganzinger [5,4] were mentioned, in which links between saturation w.r.t. ordered resolution of a set of clauses $\mathcal{K}$ and the (order)-locality of $\mathcal{K}$ were established. It is natural to ask if similar results can be obtained for local theory extensions. Local theory extensions are extensions T_1 of a base theory T_0 by means of a set of new sorts S_1 and a set of new function symbols Σ_1 constrained by a set of clauses $\mathcal{K}$. We investigate the link between the locality of the set $\mathcal{K}$ of clauses and the locality of the extension $T_0 \subseteq T_0 \cup \mathcal{K}$. This is work in progress, from which we present a first result:

Theorem 9. *Let T_0 be a first-order theory with signature $\Pi_0 = (S_0, \Sigma_0, \mathsf{Pred})$. Let $T_1 = T_0 \cup \mathcal{K}$ with signature $\Pi = (S_0 \cup S_1, \Sigma_0 \cup \Sigma_1, \mathsf{Pred})$. Assume that:*

- *all functions in Σ_1 occurring in $\mathcal{K}$ have their output sort in S_1;*
- *$\mathcal{K}$ is a set of clauses which only contain function symbols in Σ_1;*
- *the set $\mathcal{K}$ of clauses is local (resp. stably local).*

Then the extension $T_0 \subseteq T_0 \cup \mathcal{K}$ is also local (resp. stably local).

Proof: (Sketch) Let $P = (\{P_s\}_{s \in S_0 \cup S_1}, \{f_P\}_{f \in \Sigma_0 \cup \Sigma_1}, \{R_P\}_{R \in \mathsf{Pred}})$ be a weak partial model of $T_0 \cup \mathcal{K}$ in which all Σ_0-functions are totally defined. We will denote by $P_{|\Sigma_1}$ the partial structure obtained from P by forgetting all operation symbols in Σ_0. P (hence also $P_{|\Sigma_1}$) is a weak partial model of $\mathcal{K}$. By the locality of $\mathcal{K}$, $P_{|\Sigma_1} = (\{P_s\}_{s \in S_0 \cup S_1}, \{f_P\}_{f \in \Sigma_1}, \{R_A\}_{R \in \mathsf{Pred}})$ weakly embeds (via an embedding i) into a total model $A = (\{A_s\}_{s \in S_0 \cup S_1}, \{f_A\}_{f \in \Sigma_1}, \{R_A\}_{R \in \mathsf{Pred}})$ of $\mathcal{K}$. Let A^* be the substructure of A having the same supports as A for the sorts in S_1 and support $i_s(P_s)$ for each sort $s \in S_0$. (Since we assumed that all function symbols in Σ_1 have output sort in S_1, A^* is closed under all Σ_1-operations.)

Let $B = (\{B_s\}_{s \in S_0 \cup S_1}, \{f_B\}_{f \in \Sigma_0 \cup \Sigma_1}, \{R_B\}_{R \in \mathsf{Pred}})$, where for $s \in S_0$, $B_s = i_s(P_s)$, for $s \in S_1$, $B_s = A_s$, for $f \in \Sigma_0$, f_B coincides with f_P, for $f \in \Sigma_1$, f_B coincides with f_{A^*}, and all predicate symbols coincide with those in A^*. Then $B_{|\Pi_0}$ is isomorphic to $P_{|\Pi_0}$, hence is a model of $\mathcal{T}_0$ and $B_{|\Sigma_1} = A^*$, hence $B \models \mathcal{K}$. $\qquad\square$

The locality of $\mathcal{K}$ can be checked e.g. by testing whether $\mathcal{K} \cup EQ$ is saturated under ordered resolution (w.r.t. the (strict) subterm ordering) using Theorems 1 and 2 (cf. also [5,4,13]) but now extended to a many-sorted framework. The advantage is that even if $\mathcal{K}$ is not saturated, if $\mathcal{K}^*$ is a finite saturation of $\mathcal{K} \cup EQ$ under ordered resolution, then $\mathcal{T}_0 \cup \mathcal{K}^*$ can be used to extract a presentation which defines a (local) theory extension which has the same total models as $\mathcal{T}_0 \cup \mathcal{K}$.

Note: The idea in the proof of Theorem 9 can also be used to show that (under the assumptions in Theorem 9) if $\mathcal{K}$ satisfies Comp (resp. (Comp$_w$)) then the extension $\mathcal{T}_0 \subseteq \mathcal{T}_0 \cup \mathcal{K}$ also satisfies Comp (resp. (Comp$_w$)).

5   Examples of Local Theory Extensions

We present several examples of theory extensions for which embedding conditions among those mentioned above hold and are thus local, and illustrate the possibilities of local reasoning in such extensions.

5.1   Extensions with Free Functions

Any extension $\mathcal{T}_0 \cup \mathsf{Free}(\Sigma)$ of a theory $\mathcal{T}_0$ with a set Σ of free function symbols satisfies condition (Comp$_w$).

Example 2. Let $\mathcal{T}_0$ be the theory $\mathsf{LI}(\mathbb{Q})$ of linear rational arithmetic, and let $\mathcal{T}_1 = \mathsf{LI}(\mathbb{Q}) \cup \mathsf{Free}(\{f, g, h\})$ be the extension of $\mathcal{T}_0$ with the free functions f, g, h, and let $G = g(a) = c+5 \land f(g(a)) \geq c+1 \land h(b) = d+4 \land d = c+1 \land f(h(b)) < c+1$. We show that G is unsatisfiable in $\mathsf{LI}(\mathbb{Q}) \cup \mathsf{Free}(\{f, g, h\})$ as follows:

Step 1: Flattening; purification. G is purified and flattened by replacing the terms starting with f, g, h with new variables. We obtain the following purified form:

$$G_0: \quad a_1 = c+5 \;\land\; a_2 \geq c+1 \;\land\; b_1 = d+4 \;\land\; d = c+1 \;\land\; b_2 < c+1,$$
$$\mathsf{Def}: \quad a_1 = g(a) \;\land\; a_2 = f(a_1) \;\land\; b_1 = h(b) \;\land\; b_2 = f(b_1).$$

Step 2: Hierarchical reasoning. By Lemma 3, G is unsatisfiable in $\mathsf{LI}(\mathbb{Q}) \cup \mathsf{Free}(\{f, g, h\})$ iff $G_0 \land N_0$ is unsatisfiable in $\mathsf{LI}(\mathbb{Q})$, where N_0 corresponds to the consequences of the congruence axioms for those ground terms which occur in the definitions Def for the newly introduced variables.

Def	G_0	N_0
$a_1 = g(a) \land a_2 = f(a_1)$	$a_1 = c+5 \land a_2 \geq c+1$	$N_0: \; b_1 = a_1 \rightarrow b_2 = a_2$
$b_1 = h(b) \land b_2 = f(b_1)$	$b_1 = d+4 \land d = c+1 \land b_2 < c+1$	

To prove that $G_0 \land N_0$ is unsatisfiable in $\mathsf{LI}(\mathbb{Q})$, note that $G_0 \models_{\mathsf{LI}(\mathbb{Q})} a_1 = b_1$. Hence, $G_0 \land N_0$ entails $a_2 = b_2 \land a_2 \geq c+1 \land b_2 < c+1$, which is inconsistent.

5.2 Shallow Theory Extensions

We now consider the case of shallow extensions of a base theory T_0 first considered in [14]. Let Π be the signature of the theory extension. We assume that all extension functions have a codomain in the set S_0 of (base) sorts. A Π-clause is called *shallow* if extension function symbols in Σ_1 occur in C only positively and only at the root of terms. The theory extension $T_0 \subseteq T_0 \cup \mathcal{K}$ is *shallow* if $\mathcal{K}$ consists only of shallow clauses. Typical examples of shallow clauses are tail-recursive definitions of an extension function.

Theorem 10 ([14]). *Assume that $T_0 \subseteq T_0 \cup \mathcal{K}$ is a theory extension by a set $\mathcal{K}$ of shallow clauses w.r.t. the family of all extension functions with a codomain in S_0. Then the extension satisfies condition* Comp *and hence is stably local.*

5.3 Extensions with Monotone Functions

In [27] and [30] we analyzed extensions with monotonicity conditions for an n-ary function f w.r.t. a subset $I \subseteq \{1, \ldots, n\}$ of its arguments:

$$(\mathsf{Mon}_f^I) \qquad \bigwedge_{i \in I} x_i \leq_i y_i \wedge \bigwedge_{i \notin I} x_i = y_i \rightarrow f(x_1, .., x_n) \leq f(y_1, .., y_n).$$

If $I = \{1, \ldots, n\}$ we speak of monotonicity in all arguments; we denote $\mathsf{Mon}_f^{\{1, \ldots, n\}}$ by Mon_f. If $I = \emptyset$, $\mathsf{Mon}_f^\emptyset$ is equivalent to the congruence axiom for f. Monotonicity in some arguments and antitonicity in other arguments is modeled by considering functions $f : \prod_{i \in I} P_i^{\sigma_i} \times \prod_{j \notin I} P_j \rightarrow P$ with $\sigma_i \in \{-, +\}$, where $P_i^+ = P_i$ and $P_i^- = P_i^\partial$, the order dual of the poset P_i. The corresponding axioms are denoted by Mon_f^σ, where for $i \in I$, $\sigma(i) = \sigma_i \in \{-, +\}$, and for $i \notin I$, $\sigma(i) = 0$.

Theorem 11 ([27,30]). *The following hold:*

1. *Let T_0 be a class of (many-sorted) bounded semilattice-ordered Σ_0-structures. Let Σ_1 be disjoint from Σ_0 and $T_1 = T_0 \cup \{\mathsf{Mon}_f^\sigma | f \in \Sigma_1\}$. Then the extension $T_0 \subseteq T_1$ satisfies* (Comp_w^{fd}), *hence is local.*
2. *Any extension of the theory of posets with functions in a set Σ_1 satisfying $\{\mathsf{Mon}_f^\sigma \mid f \in \Sigma_1\}$ satisfies condition* (Emb_w), *hence is local.*

This provides us with a large number of concrete examples.

Corollary 12 ([27,30]). *The extensions with functions satisfying monotonicity axioms Mon_f^σ of the following classes of algebras are local:*

(1) *any class of algebras with a bounded (semi)lattice reduct, a bounded distributive lattice reduct, or a Boolean algebra reduct ((Comp_w^{fd}) holds);*
(2) *T, the class of totally-ordered sets; $\mathcal{DO}$, the theory of dense totally-ordered sets ((Comp_w^{fd}) holds);*
(3) *the class $\mathcal{P}$ of partially-ordered sets ((Emb_w) holds).*

Corollary 13 ([27,30]). *Any (possibly many-sorted) extension of a class of algebras with a semilattice reduct, a (distributive) lattice reduct, or a Boolean algebra reduct, as well as any extension of the theory of reals (integers) with functions satisfying* Mon_f^σ *into an infinite numeric domain is local ((*Comp$_w^{fd}$*) holds).*

Example 3. Let T_0 be a theory (with a binary predicate $\leq$), and T_1 a local extension of T_0 with two monotone functions f, g. Consider the following problem:

$$T_0 \cup \mathrm{Mon}_f \cup \mathrm{Mon}_g \models \forall x, y, z, u, v(x \leq y \wedge f(y \vee z) \leq g(u \wedge v) \rightarrow f(x) \leq g(v))$$

The problem reduces to the problem of checking whether $T_0 \cup \mathrm{Mon}_f \cup \mathrm{Mon}_g \cup G \models \bot$, where $G = c_0 \leq c_1 \wedge f(c_1 \vee c_2) \leq g(c_3 \wedge c_4) \wedge f(c_0) \not\leq g(c_4)$.

The locality of the extension $T_0 \subseteq T_1$ means that, in order to test if $T_0 \cup \mathrm{Mon}_f \cup \mathrm{Mon}_g \cup G \models \bot$, it is sufficient to test whether $T_0 \cup \mathrm{Mon}_f[G] \cup \mathrm{Mon}_g[G] \cup G \models_w \bot$, where $\mathrm{Mon}_f[G], \mathrm{Mon}_g[G]$ consist of those instances of the monotonicity axioms for f and g in which the terms starting with f and g already occur in G:

$$\mathrm{Mon}_f[G] = \begin{array}{l} c_0 \leq c_1 \vee c_2 \rightarrow f(c_0) \leq f(c_1 \vee c_2) \\ c_1 \vee c_2 \leq c_0 \rightarrow f(c_1 \vee c_2) \leq f(c_0) \end{array} \quad \mathrm{Mon}_g[G] = \begin{array}{l} c_4 \leq c_3 \wedge c_4 \rightarrow g(c_4) \leq g(c_3 \wedge c_4) \\ c_3 \wedge c_4 \leq c_4 \rightarrow g(c_3 \wedge c_4) \leq g(c_4) \end{array}$$

In order to check the satisfiability of the latter formula, we purify it, introducing definitions for the terms below the extension functions $d_1 = c_1 \vee c_2, d_2 = c_3 \wedge c_4$ as well as for the terms starting with the extension functions themselves: $f(d_1) = e_1, f(c_0) = e_3, g(c_4, e_4), g(d_2, e_2)$, and add the following (purified) instances of the congruence axioms: $d_1 = c_0 \rightarrow e_1 = e_3$ and $c_4 = d_2 \rightarrow e_4 = e_2$. We obtain the following set of clauses:

Def	G_0	N_0	K_0
$f(d_1) = e_1$	$c_0 \leq c_1$	$d_1 = c_0 \rightarrow e_1 = e_3$	$d_1 \leq c_0 \rightarrow e_1 \leq e_3$
$f(c_0) = e_3$	$d_1 = c_1 \vee c_2$	$d_2 = c_4 \rightarrow e_2 = e_4$	$c_0 \leq d1 \rightarrow e_3 \leq e_1$
$g(c_4) = e_4$	$d_2 = c_3 \wedge c_4$		$d_2 \leq c_4 \rightarrow e_2 \leq e_4$
$g(d_2) = e_2$	$e_1 \leq e_2 \ \wedge \ e_3 \not\leq e_4$		$d_4 \leq d_2 \rightarrow e_4 \leq e_2$

We illustrate the hierarchical reduction to testing satisfiability in the base theory for the following examples of local extensions:

(1) Let $T_0 = \mathcal{DL}$, the theory of distributive lattices or $T_0 = \mathcal{B}$, the theory of Boolean algebras. The universal clause theory of $\mathcal{DL}$ (resp. $\mathcal{B}$) is the theory of the two element lattice (resp. two element Boolean algebra), so testing Boolean satisfiability is sufficient (this is in NP); any SAT solver can be used for this.

(2) If $T_0 = \mathcal{L}$ we can reduce the problem above to the problem of checking the satisfiability of a set of ground Horn clauses. This can be checked in PTIME.

(3) If $T_0 = \mathbb{R}$ we first need to explain what $\vee$ and $\wedge$ are. For this, we replace $d_1 = c_1 \vee c_2$ with $(c_1 \leq c_2 \rightarrow d_1 = c_2) \wedge (c_2 < c_1 \rightarrow d_1 = c_2)$ and similarly for $d_2 = c_3 \wedge c_4$. We proved unsatisfiability using the REDLOG demo [10].

We can therefore conclude that in all cases above:
$$T_1 \models \forall x, y, z, u, v(x \leq y \wedge f(y \vee z) \leq g(u \wedge v) \rightarrow f(x) \leq g(v)). \qquad \square$$

Blockwise and piecewise monotonicity also define local theory extensions if the base theory (for indices) T_0 is a theory endowed with a total order relation $\leq$. The extensions below are similar to some examples considered in [6] but slightly more general since we do not restrict T_0 to be Presburger arithmetic.

Theorem 14. *Let T_0 be a theory endowed with a total order relation $\leq$.*

Piecewise monotonicity. *Assume that $l_1, \ldots, l_m, u_1, \ldots, u_m$ are constants such that $l_1 \leq u_1 < l_2 \leq u_2 < \cdots < l_m \leq u_m$. Let f be a unary function symbol. Any piecewise-monotone extension $T_0 \wedge (\mathsf{GMon}_f)$ of T_0 is local. Here $(\mathsf{GMon}_f) = (\mathsf{GMon}_f^{[l_1, u_1]}) \wedge \cdots \wedge (\mathsf{GMon}_f^{[l_m, u_m]})$, where:*

$$(\mathsf{GMon}_f^{[l_i, u_i]}) \qquad \forall x, y(l_i \leq x \leq y \leq u_i \;\rightarrow\; f(x) \leq f(y)).$$

Blockwise monotonicity. *Assume that $l_1, \ldots, l_m, u_1, \ldots, u_m$ are given constants such that $l_1 \leq u_1 < l_2 \leq u_2 < \cdots < l_m \leq u_m$. Let f be a unary function. Any blockwise-monotone extension $T_0 \wedge (\mathsf{BMon}_f)$ of T_0 is local. Here $(\mathsf{BMon}_f) = \bigwedge_{i=1}^{m-1}(\mathsf{BMon}_f^{[l_i, u_i], [l_{i+1}, u_{i+1}]})$, where:*

$$(\mathsf{BMon}_f^{[l_i, u_i], [l_{i+1}, u_{i+1}]}) \qquad \forall x, y(l_i \leq x \leq u_i < l_{i+1} \leq y \leq u_{i+1} \rightarrow f(x) \leq f(y)).$$

Similar conditions can be defined for n-ary functions and/or many-sorted functions bridging several theories endowed with total orders.

Strict monotonicity. Strict monotonicity can be handled too, under the assumption of density of the codomain of the functions [20].

5.4 Boundedness Conditions

Any extension of a theory for which $\leq$ is reflexive with functions satisfying (Mon_f^σ) and boundedness (Bound_f^t) conditions is local [28,30].

$$(\mathsf{Bound}_f^t) \qquad \forall x_1, \ldots, x_n(f(x_1, \ldots, x_n) \leq t(x_1, \ldots, x_n))$$

where $t(x_1, \ldots, x_n)$ is a term in the base signature Π_0 with variables among $x_1, \ldots, x_n$ (such that in any model the associated function has the same monotonicity as f). Similar results can be established for *guarded monotonicity conditions* with mutually disjoint guards [28].

Theorem 15. *Any extension of T_0 with a function $f \notin \Sigma_0$ satisfying boundedness (Bound_f^t) or guarded boundedness (GBound_f^t) conditions is local.*

$$(\mathsf{Bound}_f^t) \qquad \forall x_1, \ldots, x_n(f(x_1, \ldots, x_n) \leq t(x_1, \ldots, x_n))$$
$$(\mathsf{GBound}_f^t) \qquad \forall x_1, \ldots, x_n(\phi(x_1, \ldots, x_n) \rightarrow f(x_1, \ldots, x_n) \leq t(x_1, \ldots, x_n))$$

where $t(x_1, \ldots, x_n)$ is a term in the base signature Π_0 with variables among $x_1, \ldots, x_n$ and $\phi(x_1, \ldots, x_n)$ a conjunction of literals in signature Π_0 with variables among $x_1, \ldots, x_n$.

Theorem 16 (Piecewise boundedness for free functions). *Let* $m \in \mathbb{N}$. *For* $i \in \{1, \ldots, m\}$, *let* $t_i(x_1, \ldots, x_n)$ *and* $s_i(x_1, \ldots, x_n)$ *be terms in the signature* Π_0 *with variables among* $x_1, \ldots, x_n$, *and let* $\phi_i(x_1, \ldots, x_n)$, $i \in \{1, \ldots, m\}$ *be conjunctions of literals in the base signature* Π_0, *with variables among* $x_1, \ldots, x_n$, *i.e. such that for every* $i \neq j$, $\phi_i \wedge \phi_j \models_{\mathcal{T}_0} \perp$. *Any "piecewise-bounded" extension* $\mathcal{T}_0 \wedge (\mathsf{GBound}_f)$, *where* $f \notin \Sigma_0$, *is local. Here* $(\mathsf{GBound}_f) = \bigwedge_{i=1}^{m} (\mathsf{GBound}_f^{[s_i, t_i], \phi_i})$;

$(\mathsf{GBound}_f^{[s_i, t_i], \phi_i})$ $\quad \forall \overline{x}(\phi_i(\overline{x}) \rightarrow s_i(\overline{x}) \leq f(\overline{x}) \leq t_i(\overline{x}))$.

Combinations of (strict) monotonicity with (guarder) boundedness often occur in applications. We present a simple example in the verification of a train controller (for details and more realistic rules we refer to [20]).

Example 4 ([20]). We consider a controller which communicates with all the trains on a given linear track. Trains report their position in given time intervals (Δt) and the controller then communicates them how they can move. The trains adjust their speed accordingly (between given minimum and maximum speeds). These update rules can be described by the following set of clauses where the positions of trains are stored in arrays a (for the current moment of time) and a' for their positions at the next evaluation point (after Δt seconds).

(F1) $\forall i$ $(i = 0 \quad \rightarrow \quad a(i) + \Delta t * \min \leq_{\mathbb{R}} a'(i) \leq_{\mathbb{R}} a(i) + \Delta t * \max)$

(F2) $\forall i$ $(0 < i < n \quad \wedge \quad a(p(i)) >_{\mathbb{R}} 0 \quad \wedge \quad a(p(i)) - a(i) \geq_{\mathbb{R}} l_{\mathsf{alarm}}$
$\rightarrow a(i) + \Delta t * \min \leq_{\mathbb{R}} a'(i) \leq_{\mathbb{R}} a(i) + \Delta t * \max)$

(F3) $\forall i$ $(0 < i < n \quad \wedge \quad a(p(i)) >_{\mathbb{R}} 0 \quad \wedge \quad a(p(i)) - a(i) <_{\mathbb{R}} l_{\mathsf{alarm}}$
$\rightarrow a'(i) = a(i) + \Delta t * \min)$

(F4) $\forall i$ $(0 < i < n \quad \wedge \quad a(p(i)) \leq_{\mathbb{R}} 0 \quad \rightarrow \quad a'(i) = a(i))$.

The following constants are considered either given or parameters: $\Delta t > 0$ (time between evaluations of the system); minimum/maximum speed of trains $0 \leq \min \leq \max$; l_{alarm} (the distance between trains which is deemed secure); n (the number of trains). An example of an invariant to be checked is collision freeness. At a very abstract level, this can be expressed as a monotonicity axiom,

$$\mathsf{CF}(a) \quad \forall i, j \ (0 \leq i < j \leq n \rightarrow a(i) >_{\mathbb{R}} a(j)),$$

where $<$ is an ordering which expresses train precedence and $>_{\mathbb{R}}$ is the usual ordering on the real numbers (i.e. for all trains i, j on the track, if i precedes j then i should be positioned strictly ahead of j). For a more realistic encoding of collision freeness which takes into account the length of trains cf. [20]. To check that collision freeness is an invariant, we check that the initial state is collision free and that collision freeness is preserved by the updating rules $\mathcal{K} = \{\mathsf{F_1}, \ldots, \mathsf{F_4}\}$.

Let $\mathcal{T}_0$ be a many-sorted combination of real arithmetic – for reasoning about positions, sort num – with an index theory – for describing precedence between trains, sort i. Let $\mathcal{T}$ be the extension of $\mathcal{T}_0$ with the two functions a and a'. We need to check that $\mathcal{T} \models \mathcal{K} \wedge \mathsf{CF}(a) \rightarrow \mathsf{CF}(a')$, i.e.

$$\mathcal{T} \wedge \mathcal{K} \wedge \mathsf{CF}(a) \wedge \neg \mathsf{CF}(a') \models \perp.$$

For this, in [20] we considered two successive extensions of the base theory $\mathcal{T}_0$:

- the extension $\mathcal{T}_1$ of $\mathcal{T}_0$ with a strictly monotone function a, of sort i $\rightarrow$ num,
- the extension $\mathcal{T}_2$ of $\mathcal{T}_1$ with a function a' satisfying the update axioms $\mathcal{K}$.

By using the previous results we can prove that both these extensions are local. We can theorefore reduce successively, in a hierarchical way (using Lemma 3) the test of satisfiability of a set G of ground clauses w.r.t. T_2 first to a satisfiability test for a set G' of ground clauses w.r.t. T_1, and then to a satisfiability test for a set G'' of ground clauses w.r.t. T_0. This hierarchical approach can also be used for determining constraints between the parameters of the system $(\Delta t, \mathsf{min}, \mathsf{max}, n, l_{\mathsf{alarm}})$ which guarantee collision freeness.

5.5 Data Structures: Theories of Constructors/Selectors

Many data structures important in verification have local or stably local axiomatizations, or can be defined by using chains of local theory extensions. Some examples are given below.

Extensions with selector functions [27]. Let T_0 be a theory with signature $\Pi_0 = (\Sigma_0, \mathsf{Pred})$, let $c \in \Sigma_0$ with arity n, and let $\Sigma_1 = \{s_1, \dots, s_n\}$ consist of n unary function symbols. Let $T_1 = T_0 \cup \mathsf{Sel}_c$ (a theory with signature $\Pi = (\Sigma_0 \cup \Sigma_1, \mathsf{Pred})$) be the extension of T_0 with the set Sel_c of clauses below. Assume that T_0 satisfies the (universally quantified) formula Inj_c (i.e. c is injective in T_0) then the extension $T_0 \subseteq T_1$ satisfies condition $(\mathsf{Comp}_\mathsf{w})$ [27].

$$(\mathsf{Sel}_c) \qquad s_i(c(x_1, \dots, x_n)) \approx x_i \qquad i \in \{1, \dots, n\}$$
$$x \approx c(x_1, \dots, x_n) \to c(s_1(x), \dots, s_n(x)) \approx x$$

$$(\mathsf{Inj}_c) \qquad c(x_1, \dots, x_n) \approx c(y_1, \dots, y_n) \to (\bigwedge_{i=1}^{n} x_i \approx y_i)$$

A general study of the locality of various presentations of theories of constructors and selectors, as well as of theories of arrays is subject of ongoing work jointly with Swen Jacobs and Carsten Ihlemann [19]; it will not be mentioned here. Below, we present a simple example concerning an axiomatization of doubly-linked lists with additional information fields. Then we analyze a class of alternative axiomatizations of pointer structures (studied by Necula and McPeak [23]) and show that these also define stably local theory extensions.

Example 5. Let T_1 be the theory of doubly-linked lists with information on elements, with sorts cell (list cell) and s (scalar, referring to the information stored in the cells). The signature contains the functions s and p (arity cell $\to$ cell) and a family of functions $\{\mathsf{info}_i\}_{i \in I}$ (arity cell $\to$ s). We assume that s and p satisfy the axioms (1)–(4) in Section 2 (listed directly after Theorem 2 as an axiomatization for Int) and $\{\mathsf{info}_i \mid i \in I\}$ are not constrained by any other axioms. We can view the theory T_1 as the extension of the theory Int in Section 2 with an additional sort s and free function symbols $\{\mathsf{info}_i \mid i \in I\}$. Thus, satisfiability tests for ground clauses w.r.t. T_1 can be reduced in a hierarchical way, in one step to satisfiability tests for ground clauses w.r.t. Int (a local theory). A direct locality proof can also be given. By imposing additional axioms on the info_i functions we still define local extensions: this would for instance be the case if adding guarded boundedness constraints on some of the info_i's, or local sets of axioms $\mathcal{K}$ on $\{\mathsf{info}_i \mid i \in I\}$ subject to the conditions in Theorem 9.

5.6   Verification of Pointer Programs: Local Data Structures

In [23], McPeak and Necula investigate reasoning in pointer data structures. The language used has two sorts (a pointer sort p and a scalar sort s). Sets Σ_p and Σ_s of pointer resp. scalar fields are given. They can be modeled by functions of sort p $\to$ p and p $\to$ s, respectively. A constant null of sort p exists. The only predicate of sort p is equality between pointers; predicates of scalar sort can have any arity. In this language one can define pointer (dis)equalities and arbitrary scalar constraints. The local axioms considered in [23] are of the form

$$\forall p \quad \mathcal{E} \vee \mathcal{C} \tag{1}$$

where $\mathcal{E}$ contains disjunctions of pointer equalities and $\mathcal{C}$ contains scalar constraints (sets of both positive and negative literals). It is assumed that for all terms $f_1(f_2(\dots f_n(p)))$ occurring in the body of an axiom, the axiom also contains the disjunction $p = \text{null} \vee f_n(p) = \text{null} \vee \dots \vee f_2(\dots f_n(p))) = \text{null}$. This has the rôle of excluding null pointer errors. Examples of axioms (for doubly linked data structures with state and priorities) which are considered there are:

$$\forall p \quad p \neq \text{null} \wedge \text{next}(p) \neq \text{null} \qquad \to \text{prev}(\text{next}(p)) = p$$
$$\forall p \quad p \neq \text{null} \wedge \text{next}(p) \neq \text{null} \qquad \to \text{state}(p) = \text{state}(\text{next}(p))$$
$$\forall p \quad p \neq \text{null} \wedge \text{next}(p) \neq \text{null} \wedge \text{state}(p) = \text{RUN} \to \text{priority}(p) \geq \text{priority}(\text{next}(p))$$

(the first axiom states that prev is a left inverse for next, the second axiom tells how a state can be updated; the third axiom is a monotonicity condition on the function priority with values in a partially ordered domain).

For the sake of simplicity, in what follows we assume that in (1) the disjunctions contain also definedness guards on the scalar fields. The special form of the axioms ensures that all partial models can be embedded into total models.

Theorem 17. *Let T_1 be the two-sorted extension $T_0 \cup \mathcal{K}$ of a Π_0-theory T_0 (or sort s, the theory of scalars), with signature $\Pi = (S, \Sigma, \text{Pred})$, where $S = \{p, s\}$, $\Sigma = \Sigma_p \cup \Sigma_s \cup \Sigma_0$ axiomatized by a set $\mathcal{K}$ of axioms $\forall p(\mathcal{E} \vee \mathcal{C})$ of type (1). Then T is a stably local extension of T_0.*

Proof: Let $P = (P_p, P_s, \{f_P\}_{f \in \Sigma_p \cup \Sigma_s} \cup \{g_P\}_{g \in \Sigma_0}, \{R_P\}_{R \in \text{Pred}}) \in \text{PMod}(\Sigma_p \cup \Sigma_s, T_1)$. We construct a total model A starting from P as follows. The universes of A are the same as those of P. For every $f \in \Sigma_p$ and every $p \in P_p$, we define $f_A(p) := f_P(p)$ if $f_P(p)$ is defined, and $f_A(p) := \text{null}$ otherwise. For every $f \in \Sigma_s$ and every $q \in P_p$ we define $f_A(q) := f_P(q)$ if $f_P(q)$ is defined, and $f_A(p) := \text{null}_s$ otherwise. We show that B is a model of T_1: Clearly, $B_{|\Pi_0} = P_{|\Pi_0} = (P_s, \{g_P\}_{g \in \Sigma_0}, \{R_P\}_{R \in \text{Pred}})$ is a total model of T_0. We show that $B \models \mathcal{K}$. Let $C = \forall p(\mathcal{E} \vee \mathcal{C}) \in \mathcal{K}$ and let $\beta : X_p \to B_p$. If there exists any $t = \text{null}$ in $\mathcal{E}$ with any $\beta(t) = \text{null}$, $\beta \models C$. Assume now that $\beta(t) \neq \text{null}$ for all terms occurring below a function symbol in Σ_p or Σ_s in C. This means that $\beta(t)$ is defined also in P for all such terms. As $(P, \beta) \models C$, there exists a literal L in C such that $(P, \beta) \models L$. We distinguish the following cases: (a) $L = t \approx s$ and both $\beta(t), \beta(s)$ are defined in P. Then they are defined and equal also in B, so $(B, \beta) \models C$. (b)

$L = t \approx s$, $\beta(s)$ is defined, $t = f(t_1, \ldots, t_n)$, where $f \in \Sigma_p \cup \Sigma_s$, and $\beta(t_i)$ is undefined for at least one of $t_1, \ldots, t_n$. This case cannot occur since we assumed that $\beta(t_i) \neq$ null for all i; if they were undefined in P the value assigned to them in B would have been null. (c) $L = t \approx s$, $\beta(t)$ and $\beta(s)$ are both undefined. Then the value assigned to them in B is either null if they are of pointer sort, or null_s if they are of scalar sort. Therefore $(B, \beta) \models C$ also in this case. (d) $L = (\neg)R(t_1, \ldots, t_n)$, where $t_1, \ldots, t_n$ are terms of scalar sort. An argument similar to that used in (b) shows that (if clauses are guarded by definedness conditions for the scalar terms) $\beta(t_i)$ is defined in P for all i so $(P, \beta) \models L$, i.e. $(B, \beta) \models C$. Thus, $(B, \beta) \models C$ for all $\beta : X_p \to B_p$ and all $C \in \mathcal{K}$. This shows that $B \in \text{Mod}(\mathcal{T}_1)$.[2] $\square$

6 Combinations of Local Extensions

In this section we study the locality of combinations of local theory extensions. In the light of the results in Section 4.1 we concentrate on studying which embeddability properties are preserved under combinations of theories. For the sake of simplicity, in what follows we only consider conditions (Emb_w) and (Comp_w). Analogous results can be given for conditions (Emb_w^f), (Comp_w^f), resp. (Emb_w^{fd}), (Comp_w^{fd}) and combinations thereof. Full proofs are contained in [29].

We first consider the situation when both components satisfy the embeddability condition (Comp_w).

Theorem 18. *Let $\mathcal{T}_0$ be a first order theory with signature $\Pi_0 = (\Sigma_0, \text{Pred})$ and (for $i \in \{1,2\}$) $\mathcal{T}_i = \mathcal{T}_0 \cup \mathcal{K}_i$ be an extension of $\mathcal{T}_0$ with signature $\Pi_i = (\Sigma_0 \cup \Sigma_i, \text{Pred})$. Assume that both extensions $\mathcal{T}_0 \subseteq \mathcal{T}_1$ and $\mathcal{T}_0 \subseteq \mathcal{T}_2$ satisfy condition (Comp_w), and that $\Sigma_1 \cap \Sigma_2 = \emptyset$. Then the extension $\mathcal{T}_0 \subseteq \mathcal{T} = \mathcal{T}_0 \cup \mathcal{K}_1 \cup \mathcal{K}_2$ satisfies condition (Comp_w). If, additionally, in $\mathcal{K}_i$ all terms starting with a function symbol in Σ_i are flat and linear, for $i = 1, 2$, then the extension is local.*

Example 6. *The following combinations of theories (seen as extensions of a first-order theory $\mathcal{T}_0$) satisfy condition (Comp_w) (in case (4) condition (Comp_w^{fd})):*

(1) $\mathcal{T}_0 \cup \text{Free}(\Sigma_1)$ and $\mathcal{T}_0 \cup \text{Sel}_c$ if $\mathcal{T}_0$ is a theory and $c \in \Sigma_0$ is injective in $\mathcal{T}_0$.
(2) $\mathbb{R} \cup \text{Free}(\Sigma_1)$ and $\mathbb{R} \cup \text{Lip}_c^\lambda(f)$, where $f \notin \Sigma_1$. Here $\text{Lip}_c^\lambda(f)$ is the λ-Lipschitz condition[3] for f at point $c \in \mathbb{R}$ (for $\lambda > 0$):
$$(\text{Lip}_c^\lambda(f)) \qquad \forall x \; |f(x) - f(c)| \leq \lambda \cdot |x - c|.$$

(3) $\mathbb{R} \cup \text{Lip}_{c_1}^{\lambda_1}(f)$ and $\mathbb{R} \cup \text{Lip}_{c_2}^{\lambda_2}(g)$, where $f \neq g$.

---

[2] Analyzing the proof of Theorem 7 (embeddability implies stable locality), one can see that for any valuation β and set Ψ of ground terms of sort p closed under subterms the proof only uses embeddability into total models of a special type of partial models P, namely those for which for $f \in \Sigma_p \cup \Sigma_s$, $f_P(p_1, \ldots, p_n)$ is defined iff there exist terms $t_1, \ldots t_n$ in Ψ which evaluate to $p_1, \ldots, p_n$ w.r.t. β. With such restrictions the definedness guards on scalar terms are not necessary for proving stable locality.

[3] We proved in [27] that for every function f and constants c and λ with $\lambda > 0$ the extension $\mathbb{R} \subseteq \mathbb{R} \cup (\text{Lip}_c^\lambda(f))$ satisfies (Comp_w), hence it is local.

(4) $T_0 \cup \mathsf{Free}(\Sigma_1)$ and $T_0 \cup \mathsf{Mon}_f^\sigma$, where $f \notin \Sigma_1$ has arity n, $\sigma : \{1, \ldots, n\} \rightarrow \{-1, 1, 0\}$, if T_0 is, e.g., a theory of algebras with a bounded semilattice reduct.

This result can be extended to the more general situation in which one extension satisfies condition $(\mathsf{Emb_w})$ and the other satisfies $(\mathsf{Comp_w})$ or $(\mathsf{Emb_w})$.

Theorem 19. *Let T_0 be a first order theory with signature $\Pi_0 = (\Sigma_0, \mathsf{Pred})$, and let $T_1 = T_0 \cup \mathcal{K}_1$ and $T_2 = T_0 \cup \mathcal{K}_2$ be two extensions of T_0 with signatures $\Pi_1 = (\Sigma_0 \cup \Sigma_1, \mathsf{Pred})$ and $\Pi_2 = (\Sigma_0 \cup \Sigma_2, \mathsf{Pred})$, respectively. Assume that:*

(1) $T_0 \subseteq T_1$ satisfies condition $(\mathsf{Comp_w})$,
(2) $T_0 \subseteq T_2$ satisfies condition $(\mathsf{Emb_w})$,
(3) $\mathcal{K}_1$ is a set of Σ_1-flat clauses in which all variables occur below a Σ_1-function.

Then the extension $T_0 \subseteq T_0 \cup \mathcal{K}_1 \cup \mathcal{K}_2$ satisfies $(\mathsf{Emb_w})$. If in $\mathcal{K}_i$ all terms starting with a function symbol in Σ_i are flat and linear (for $i=1, 2$) the extension is local.

Theorem 20. *Let T_0 be an arbitrary theory in signature $\Pi_0 = (\Sigma_0, \mathsf{Pred})$. Let $\mathcal{K}_1$ and $\mathcal{K}_2$ be two sets of clauses over signatures $\Pi_i = (\Sigma_0 \cup \Sigma_i, \mathsf{Pred})$, where Σ_1 and Σ_2 are disjoint. We make the following assumptions:*

(A1) The class of models of T_0 is closed under direct limits of diagrams in which all maps are embeddings (or, equivalently, T_0 is a $\forall \exists$ theory).
(A2) $\mathcal{K}_i$ is Σ_i-flat and Σ_i-linear for $i = 1, 2$, and $T_0 \subseteq T_0 \cup \mathcal{K}_i$, $i = 1, 2$ are both local extensions of T_0.
(A3) For all clauses in $\mathcal{K}_1$ and $\mathcal{K}_2$, every variable occurs below some extension function.

Then $T_0 \cup \mathcal{K}_1 \cup \mathcal{K}_2$ is a local extension of T_0.

Example 7. *The following combinations of theories (seen as extensions of the theory T_0) satisfy condition $(\mathsf{Emb_w})$, hence are local:*

(1) $\mathcal{E}q \subseteq \mathsf{Free}(\Sigma_1) \cup \mathcal{L}$, where $\mathcal{E}q$ is the pure theory of equality, without function symbols, and $\mathcal{L}$ the theory of lattices.
(2) $T_0 \subseteq (T_0 \cup \mathsf{Free}(\Sigma_1)) \cup (T_0 \cup \mathsf{Mon}(\Sigma_2))$, where $\Sigma_1 \cap \Sigma_2 = \emptyset$, $\mathsf{Mon}(\Sigma_2) = \bigwedge_{f \in \Sigma_2} \mathsf{Mon}_f^{\sigma(f)}$ and T_0 is, e.g., the theory of posets.
(3) The combination of the theory of lattices and the theory of integers with injective successor and predecessor is local (local extension of the theory of pure equality).

7 Modular Reasoning

In what follows we discuss some issues related to modular reasoning in combinations of local theory extensions. We analyze, in particular, the form of information which needs to be exchanged between provers for the component theories when reasoning in combinations of local theory extensions.

7.1   Reasoning in Local Combinations of Theory Extensions

Let $T_1 = T_0 \cup K_1$ and $T_2 = T_0 \cup K_2$ be theories with signatures $\Pi_1 = (\Sigma_0 \cup \Sigma_1, \mathsf{Pred})$ and $\Pi_2 = (\Sigma_0 \cup \Sigma_2, \mathsf{Pred})$, and G a set of ground clauses in the joint signature with additional constants $\Pi^c = (\Sigma_0 \cup \Sigma_1 \cup \Sigma_2 \cup \Sigma_c, \mathsf{Pred})$. We want to decide whether $T_1 \cup T_2 \cup G \models \bot$.

The set G of ground clauses can be flattened and purified as explained above. For the sake of simplicity, everywhere in what follows we will assume w.l.o.g. that $G = G_1 \wedge G_2$, where G_1, G_2 are flat and linear sets of clauses in the signatures Π_1, Π_2 respectively, i.e. for $i = 1, 2$, $G_i = G_i^0 \wedge G_0 \wedge D_i$, where G_i^0 and G_0 are clauses in the base theory and D_i a conjunction of unit clauses of the form $f(c_1, \ldots, c_n) = c, f \in \Sigma_i$.

Corollary 21. *Assume that $T_1 = T_0 \cup K_1$ and $T_2 = T_0 \cup K_2$ are local extensions of a theory T_0 with signature $\Pi_0 = (\Sigma_0, \mathsf{Pred})$, and that the extension $T_0 \subseteq T_0 \cup K_1 \cup K_2$ is local. Let $G = G_1 \wedge G_2$ be a set of flat, linear are purified ground clauses, such that $G_i = G_i^0 \wedge G_0 \wedge D_i$ are as explained above. Then the following are equivalent:*

(1) $T_1 \cup T_2 \cup (G_1 \wedge G_2) \models \bot,$
(2) $T_0 \cup (K_1 \cup K_2)[G_1 \wedge G_2] \cup (G_1^0 \wedge G_0 \wedge D_1) \wedge (G_2^0 \wedge G_0 \wedge D_2) \models \bot,$
(3) $T_0 \cup K_1^0 \cup K_2^0 \cup (G_1^0 \cup G_0) \cup (G_2^0 \cup G_0) \cup N_1 \cup N_2 \models \bot,$ *where*

$$N_i = \{ \bigwedge_{i=1}^{n} c_i \approx d_i \rightarrow c = d \mid f(c_1, \ldots, c_n) \approx c, f(d_1, \ldots, d_n) \approx d \in D_i \}, i = 1, 2,$$

and K_i^0 is the formula obtained from $K_i[G_i]$ after purification and flattening, taking into account the definitions from D_i.

A more precise characterization of the formulae that need to be exchanged between provers for the components is provided by results on interpolation.

7.2   Interpolation in Local Theory Extensions

A theory T has *interpolation* if, for all formulae ϕ and ψ in the signature of T, if $\phi \models_T \psi$ then there exists a formula I containing only symbols which occur in both ϕ and ψ such that $\phi \models_T I$ and $I \models_T \psi$. First order logic has interpolation [9], but for an arbitrary first order theory T, the interpolants may contain (alternations of) quantifiers even for very simple formulae ϕ and ψ. It is important to identify situations in which ground clauses have ground interpolants.

A theory T has the *ground interpolation property* if for all ground clauses $A(\bar{c}, \bar{d})$ and $B(\bar{c}, \bar{e})$, if $A(\bar{c}, \bar{d}) \wedge B(\bar{c}, \bar{e}) \models_T \bot$ then there exists a ground formula $I(\bar{c})$, containing only the constants $\bar{c}$ occurring both in A and B, such that $A(\bar{c}, \bar{d}) \models_T I(\bar{c})$ and $B(\bar{c}, \bar{e}) \wedge I(\bar{c}) \models_T \bot$.

In [28] we identify a class of theory extensions $T_0 \subseteq T_1$ for which interpolants can be computed hierarchically using a procedure for generating interpolants in the base theory $\mathcal{T}_0$. This allows to exploit specific properties of $\mathcal{T}_0$ for obtaining simple interpolants in $\mathcal{T}_1$. We make the following assumptions[4] about $\mathcal{T}_0$ and $\mathcal{T}_1$:

Assumption 1: $\mathcal{T}_0$ is *convex* w.r.t. the set Pred of all predicates (including equality $\approx$), i.e., for all conjunctions Γ of ground atoms, relations $R_1, \ldots, R_m \in$ Pred and ground tuples of corresponding arity $\bar{t}_1, \ldots, \bar{t}_n$, if $\Gamma \models_{\mathcal{T}_0} \bigvee_{i=1}^{m} R_i(\bar{t}_i)$ then there exists a $j \in \{1, \ldots, m\}$ such that $\Gamma \models_{\mathcal{T}_0} R_j(\bar{t}_j)$.

Assumption 2: $\mathcal{T}_0$ is *P-interpolating*, i.e. for all conjunctions A and B of ground literals, all binary predicates $R \in P$ and all constants a and b such that a occurs in A and b occurs in B (or vice versa), if $A \wedge B \models_{\mathcal{T}_0} aRb$ then there exists a term t containing only constants common to A and B with $A \wedge B \models_{\mathcal{T}_0} aRt \wedge tRb$.

Assumption 3: $\mathcal{T}_0$ has ground interpolation.

Assumption 4: $\mathcal{T}_1 = \mathcal{T}_0 \cup \mathcal{K}$, where $\mathcal{K}$ consists of the combinations of clauses:

$$\begin{cases} x_1 R_1 s_1 \wedge \cdots \wedge x_n R_n s_n \rightarrow f(x_1, \ldots, x_n) R g(y_1, \ldots, y_n) \\ x_1 R_1 y_1 \wedge \cdots \wedge x_n R_n y_n \rightarrow f(x_1, \ldots, x_n) R f(y_1, \ldots, y_n) \end{cases} \tag{2}$$

where $n \geq 1$, $x_1, \ldots, x_n$ are variables, $R_1, \ldots, R_n, R$ are binary relations with $R_1, \ldots, R_n \in P$ and R transitive, and each s_i is either a variable among the arguments of g, or a term of the form $f_i(z_1, \ldots, z_k)$, where $f_i \in \Sigma_1$ and all the arguments of f_i are variables occurring among the arguments of g.

Theorem 22 ([28]). *If the theory extension $\mathcal{T}_0 \subseteq \mathcal{T}_1$ satisfies the assumptions above then ground interpolants for $\mathcal{T}_1$ exist and can be computed hierarchically.*

In [25] we adapt and apply the idea of Theorem 22 for efficiently computing interpolants with a simple form for extensions of linear arithmetic with free function symbols, as an alternative to the method proposed by McMillan [22].

As a consequence of the results in [28], the following theory extensions have ground interpolation, and interpolants can be computed hierarchically.

(a) Extensions with free function symbols of any of the base theories: $\mathcal{Eq}$ (pure equality), $\mathcal{P}$ (posets), $\mathsf{LI}(\mathbb{Q}), \mathsf{LI}(\mathbb{R})$ (linear rational, resp. real arithmetic), $\mathcal{S}$ (semilattices), $\mathcal{DL}$ (lattices), $\mathcal{B}$ Boolean algebras.

(b) Extensions with monotone functions of any of the base theories: $\mathcal{P}$ (posets), $\mathcal{S}$ (semilattices), $\mathcal{DL}$ (lattices), $\mathcal{B}$ Boolean algebras.

(c) Extensions of any of the base theories in (b) with $\mathsf{Leq}(f, g) \wedge \mathsf{Mon}_f$.

(d) Extensions of any of the base theories in (b) with $\mathsf{SGc}(f, g_1) \wedge \mathsf{Mon}(f, g_1)$.

(e) Extensions of any of the base theories in (a) with Bound_f^t or GBound_f^t (where t is a term and ϕ a set of literals in the base theory).

(f) Extensions of any base theory in (b) with $\mathsf{Mon}_f \wedge \mathsf{Bound}_f^t$, if t is monotone.

7.3   Application: Information Exchange in Combinations of Theories

The method for hierarchic reasoning described in Corollary 21 is modular, in the sense that once the information about $\Sigma_1 \cup \Sigma_2$-functions was separated into a

---

[4] Examples of theories which have these properties are provided in [28].

Σ_1-part and a Σ_2-part, it does not need to be recombined again. For reasoning in the combined theory one can proceed as follows:

- Purify (and flatten) the goal G, and thus transform it into an equisatisfiable conjunction $G_1 \wedge G_2$, where G_i consists of clauses in the signature Π_i, for $i = 1, 2$, and $G_i = G_i^0 \wedge G_0 \wedge D_i$, as in Corollary 21.
- The problem of testing the validity of the formulae containing extension functions in the signature Σ_i, $\mathcal{K}_i[G_i] \wedge G_i$ are reduced (using Lemma 3) to testing the validity of the formula $\mathcal{K}_i^0 \wedge G_i^0 \wedge G_0 \wedge N_i$ in the base theory.
- The conjunction of all the formulae obtained this way, for all component theories, is used as input for a decision procedure for the base theory.

We show that, in fact, only information exchange over the shared signature (i.e. shared functions and constants) is necessary.

Theorem 23 ([28]). *Let $\mathcal{T}_0 \subseteq \mathcal{T}_0 \cup \mathcal{K}_i$ be local extensions, $i = 1, 2$ where $\mathcal{K}_i$ are Σ_i-flat and Σ_i-linear and all variables in clauses in $\mathcal{K}_i$ occur below a Σ_i-symbol. Assume the extension $\mathcal{T}_0 \subseteq \mathcal{T}_0 \cup \mathcal{K}_1 \cup \mathcal{K}_2$ is local. Let $G = G_1 \wedge G_2$ be as constructed before with $\mathcal{T}_0 \cup (\mathcal{K}_1 \wedge G_1) \wedge (\mathcal{K}_2 \wedge G_2) \models \bot$. Then we can construct a ground formula I which contains only function symbols in $\Sigma_0 = \Sigma_1 \cap \Sigma_2$ and constants shared by G_1, G_2 such that $(\mathcal{T}_0 \cup \mathcal{K}_1) \wedge G_1 \models I$ and $(\mathcal{T}_0 \cup \mathcal{K}_2) \wedge G_2 \wedge I \models \bot$.*

8 Conclusions

We presented an overview of results on hierarchical and modular reasoning in complex theories. We show that for *local* and *stably local* theory extensions hierarchic reasoning is possible (i.e. proof tasks in the extension can be hierarchically reduced to proof tasks w.r.t. the base theory). We showed how local theory extensions can be identified and provided various examples from mathematics and verification. In particular, we identified phenomena analyzed in the verification literature which can be explained using the notion of locality.

We then presented criteria for recognizing situations in which combinations of theory extensions of a base theory are again local extensions of the base theory. These results allow to recognize even wider classes of local theory extensions, and open the way for studying possibilities of modular reasoning in such extensions. For this, it is interesting to analyze the exact amount of information which needs to be exchanged between provers for the component theories. We characterized the form of this information in the case of local combinations of local extensions. We plan to investigate whether there are any links between the results described in this paper and other methods for reasoning in combinations of theories over non-disjoint signatures e.g. by Ghilardi [15].

Acknowledgement. This work was partly supported by the German Research Council (DFG) as part of the Transregional Collaborative Research Center "Automatic Verification and Analysis of Complex Systems" (SFB/TR 14 AVACS). See www.avacs.org for more information.

References

1. Armando, A., Bonacina, M.P., Ranise, S.: On a rewriting approach to satisfiability procedures: extension, combination of theories and an experimental appraisal. In: Gramlich, B. (ed.) FroCos 2005. LNCS (LNAI), vol. 3717, pp. 65–80. Springer, Heidelberg (2005)
2. Armando, A., Ranise, S., Rusinowitch, M.: A rewriting approach to satisfiability procedures. Information and Computation 183(2), 140–164 (2003)
3. Baader, F., Tinelli, C.: Deciding the word problem in the union of equational theories sharing constructors. Information and Computation 178(2), 346–390 (2002)
4. Basin, D., Ganzinger, H.: Automated complexity analysis based on ordered resolution. Journal of the ACM 48(1), 70–109 (2001)
5. Basin, D.A., Ganzinger, H.: Complexity analysis based on ordered resolution. In: Proc. 11th IEEE Symposium on Logic in Computer Science (LICS'96), pp. 456–465. IEEE Computer Society Press, Los Alamitos (1996)
6. Bradley, A.R., Manna, Z., Sipma, H.B.: What's decidable about arrays? In: Emerson, E.A., Namjoshi, K.S. (eds.) VMCAI 2006. LNCS, vol. 3855, pp. 427–442. Springer, Heidelberg (2005)
7. Burmeister, P.: A Model Theoretic Oriented Approach to Partial Algebras: Introduction to Theory and Application of Partial Algebras, Part I. In: Mathematical Research, vol. 31, Akademie-Verlag, Berlin (1986)
8. Burris, S.: Polynomial time uniform word problems. Mathematical Logic Quarterly 41, 173–182 (1995)
9. Craig, W.: Linear reasoning. A new form of the Herbrand-Gentzen theorem. J. Symb. Log. 22(3), 250–268 (1957)
10. Dolzmann, A., Sturm, T.: Redlog: Computer algebra meets computer logic. ACM SIGSAM Bulletin 31(2), 2–9 (1997)
11. Dowling, W.F., Gallier, J.H.: Linear-time algorithms for testing the satisfiability of propositional Horn formulae. J. Logic Programming 1(3), 267–284 (1984)
12. Evans, T.: The word problem for abstract algebras. J. London Math. Soc., 26, 64–71 (1951)
13. Ganzinger, H.: Relating semantic and proof-theoretic concepts for polynomial time decidability of uniform word problems. In: Proc. 16th IEEE Symposium on Logic in Computer Science (LICS'01), pp. 81–92. IEEE Computer Society Press, Los Alamitos (2001)
14. Ganzinger, H., Sofronie-Stokkermans, V., Waldmann, U.: Modular proof systems for partial functions with Evans equality. Information and Computation 204(10), 1453–1492 (2006)
15. Ghilardi, S.: Model theoretic methods in combined constraint satisfiability. Journal of Automated Reasoning 33(3-4), 221–249 (2004)
16. Ghilardi, S., Nicolini, E., Ranise, S., Zucchelli, D.: Combination methods for satisfiability and model-checking of infinite-state systems. In: Pfenning, F. (ed.) CADE 2007, LNCS, vol. 4603, Springer, Heidelberg (2007)
17. Givan, R., McAllester, D.: New results on local inference relations. In: Principles of Knowledge Representation and reasoning. Proceedings of the Third International Conference (KR'92), pp. 403–412. Morgan Kaufmann Press, San Francisco (1992)
18. Givan, R., McAllester, D.A.: Polynomial-time computation via local inference relations. ACM Transactions on Computational Logic 3(4), 521–541 (2002)
19. Ihlemann, C., Jacobs, S., Sofronie-Stokkermans, V.: Locality and data structures. Work in progress (2007)

20. Jacobs, S., Sofronie-Stokkermans, V.: Applications of hierarchical reasoning in the verification of complex systems. Electronic Notes in Theoretical Computer Science 174(8), 39–54 (2007)
21. McAllester, D.: Automatic recognition of tractability in inference relations. Journal of the ACM 40(2), 284–303 (1993)
22. McMillan, K.L.: An interpolating theorem prover. Theoretical Computer Science 345(1), 101–121 (2005)
23. McPeak, S., Necula, G.C.: Data structure specifications via local equality axioms. In: Etessami, K., Rajamani, S.K. (eds.) CAV 2005. LNCS, vol. 3576, pp. 476–490. Springer, Heidelberg (2005)
24. Nelson, G., Oppen, D.C.: Simplification by cooperating decision procedures. ACM Transactions on Programming Languages and Systems (1979)
25. Rybalchenko, A., Sofronie-Stokkermans, V.: Constraint solving for interpolation. In: Cook, B., Podelski, A. (eds.) VMCAI 2007. LNCS, vol. 4349, Springer, Heidelberg (2007)
26. Skolem, T.: Logisch-kombinatorische Untersuchungen über die Erfüllbarkeit und Beweisbarkeit mathematischen Sätze nebst einem Theoreme über dichte Mengen. Skrifter utgit av Videnskabsselskapet i Kristiania, I. Matematisk-naturvidenskabelig klasse. vol. 4, pp. 1–36 (1920)
27. Sofronie-Stokkermans, V.: Hierarchic reasoning in local theory extensions. In: Nieuwenhuis, R. (ed.) Automated Deduction – CADE-20. LNCS (LNAI), vol. 3632, pp. 219–234. Springer, Heidelberg (2005)
28. Sofronie-Stokkermans, V.: Interpolation in local theory extensions. In: Furbach, U., Shankar, N. (eds.) IJCAR 2006. LNCS (LNAI), vol. 4130, pp. 235–250. Springer, Heidelberg (2006)
29. Sofronie-Stokkermans, V.: On combinations of local theory extensions (Submitted for publication) (2006)
30. Sofronie-Stokkermans, V., Ihlemann, C.: Automated reasoning in some local extensions of ordered structures. In: Proceedings of ISMVL-2007, IEEE Computer Society, Los Alamitos (2007), http://dx.doi.org/10.1109/ISMVL.2007.10
31. Tinelli, C., Ringeissen, C.: Unions of non-disjoint theories and combinations of satisfiability procedures. Theoretical Computer Science 290(1), 291–353 (2003)
32. Tinelli, C., Zarba, C.: Combining nonstably infinite theories. Journal of Automated Reasoning 34(3), 209–238 (2005)
33. Ullman, J.: Principles of Database and Knowledge-Base Systems. Computer Science Press (1988)
34. Ullman, J.: Bottom-up beats top-down for datalog. In: Proceedings of the 8th ACM SIGACT-SIGMOD-SIGART Symposium on the Principles of Database Systems, pp. 140–149 (1989)

Temporalising Logics: Fifteen Years After

Michael Zakharyaschev

School of Computer Science and Information Systems,
Birkbeck College, London, UK
michael@dcs.bbk.ac.uk

A straightforward way of adding a temporal dimension to a logical system is to combine it with a suitable temporal logic. Typical examples are first-order temporal logic [3], temporal description logics [1] or spatio-temporal logics [4]. In 1992, Finger and Gabbay [2] started an investigation of possible ways of temporalising abstract logical systems.

In this paper, I analyse the existing methodologies of temporalising logics and illustrate them by recent results on the computational properties and expressive power of temporal description, spatio-temporal and dynamic topological logics.

References

1. Artale, A., Franconi, E.: Temporal description logics. In: Fisher, M., Gabbay, D., Vila, L. (eds.) Handbook of Temporal Reasoning in Artificial Intelligence, pp. 375–388. Elsevier, Amsterdam (2005)
2. Finger, M., Gabbay, D.M.: Adding a temporal dimension to a logic system. Journal of Logic, Language, and Information 1(3), 203–233 (1992)
3. Gabbay, D., Hodkinson, I., Reynolds, M.: Temporal Logic: Mathematical Foundations and Computational Aspects, vol. 1. Oxford University Press, Oxford (1994)
4. Gabelaia, D., Kontchakov, R., Kurucz, A., Wolter, F., Zakharyaschev, M.: Combining spatial and temporal logics: expressiveness vs. complexity. Journal of Artificial Intelligence Research (JAIR) 23, 167–243 (2005)

B. Konev and F. Wolter (Eds.): FroCos 2007, LNAI 4720, p. 72, 2007.
© Springer-Verlag Berlin Heidelberg 2007

Termination of Innermost Context-Sensitive Rewriting Using Dependency Pairs*

Beatriz Alarcón and Salvador Lucas

DSIC, Universidad Politécnica de Valencia, Spain
{balarcon, slucas}@dsic.upv.es

Abstract. Innermost context-sensitive rewriting has been proved useful for modeling computations of programs of algebraic languages like Maude, OBJ, etc. Furthermore, innermost termination of rewriting is often easier to prove than termination. Thus, under appropriate conditions, a useful strategy for proving termination of rewriting is trying to prove termination of innermost rewriting. This phenomenon has also been investigated for context-sensitive rewriting (*CSR*). Up to now, only few transformations have been proposed and used to prove termination of innermost *CSR*. In this paper, we investigate direct methods for proving termination of innermost *CSR*. We adapt the recently introduced context-sensitive dependency pairs approach to innermost *CSR* and show that they can be advantageously used for proving termination of innermost *CSR*. We have implemented them as part of the termination tool MU-TERM.

1 Introduction

The *dependency pairs method* [3] is one of the most powerful techniques for proving termination of Term Rewriting Systems (TRSs [21,22]). Roughly speaking, given a TRS $\mathcal{R}$, the dependency pairs associated with $\mathcal{R}$ form a new TRS $\mathsf{DP}(\mathcal{R})$ which (together with $\mathcal{R}$) determines the so-called *dependency chains* which characterize termination of $\mathcal{R}$. The dependency pairs can be presented as a *dependency graph*, where the absence of infinite chains can be analyzed by considering the *cycles* in the graph. In [1], the dependency pairs method has been adapted for proving termination of *context-sensitive rewriting* (*CSR* [15,18]). With *CSR* we can *achieve* a terminating behavior for non-terminating TRSs by pruning (all) infinite rewrite sequences. In *CSR* we only rewrite μ-replacing subterms. Here, μ is a *replacement map*, i.e., a mapping $\mu : \mathcal{F} \to \mathcal{P}(\mathbb{N})$ satisfying $\mu(f) \subseteq \{1, \ldots, k\}$, for each k-ary symbol f of the signature $\mathcal{F}$ [15]. We use them to indicate the argument positions on which the rewriting steps are allowed. Then, t_i is a μ-replacing subterm of $f(t_1, \ldots, t_k)$ if $i \in \mu(f)$; every term t (as a whole) is μ-replacing by definition.

---

* This work has been partially supported by the EU (FEDER) and the Spanish MEC, under grants TIN 2004-7943-C04-02 and HA 2006-2007, and the Generalitat Valenciana under grant GV06/285. Beatriz Alarcón was partially supported by the Spanish MEC under FPU grant AP2005-3399.

B. Konev and F. Wolter (Eds.): FroCos 2007, LNAI 4720, pp. 73–87, 2007.

For other subterms we proceed inductively in this way. Then, for a given TRS $\mathcal{R}$ and a replacement map μ, we obtain a restriction of rewriting which we call *context-sensitive rewriting*. A pair $(\mathcal{R}, \mu)$ is often called a context-sensitive TRS (CS-TRS). Proving termination of *CSR* is an interesting problem with several applications in the fields of term rewriting and programming languages (see [20] for further motivation). Furthermore, termination of *innermost CSR* (i.e., the variant of *CSR* where only the deepest μ-replacing redexes are contracted) has proved useful for proving termination of programs in programming languages like Maude and OBJ* which permit to control the program execution by means of such context-sensitive annotations [16,17].

Proving innermost termination of rewriting is often easier than proving termination of rewriting [3] and, for some relevant classes of TRSs, innermost termination of rewriting is even equivalent to termination of rewriting [10,11]. In [7,12] it is proved that the equivalence between termination of innermost *CSR* and termination of *CSR* holds in some interesting cases (e.g., for *orthogonal* CS-TRSs).

Example 1. Consider the following orthogonal TRS $\mathcal{R}$ which is a variant of an example in [4]:

```
from(X) -> cons(X,from(s(X)))
sel(0,cons(X,XS)) -> X
sel(s(N),cons(X,XS)) -> sel(N,XS)
minus(X,0) -> X
minus(s(X),s(Y)) -> minus(X,Y)
quot(0,s(Y)) -> 0
quot(s(X),s(Y)) -> s(quot(minus(X,Y),s(Y)))
zWquot(nil,nil) -> nil
zWquot(cons(X,XS),nil) -> nil
zWquot(nil,cons(X:XS)) -> nil
zWquot(cons(X,XS),cons(Y,YS))->cons(quot(X,Y),zWquot(XS,YS))
```

together with $\mu(\texttt{cons}) = \{1\}$ and $\mu(f) = \{1, \dots, ar(f)\}$ for all other symbols f. According to [6], innermost μ-termination of $\mathcal{R}$ implies its μ-termination as well. We will show how $\mathcal{R}$ can easily be proved innermost μ-terminating (and hence μ-terminating) by using the results in this paper.

In this paper, we extend the context-sensitive dependency pairs approach in [1] for proving termination of innermost *CSR*. Actually, techniques for proving termination of innermost *CSR* have already been investigated [7,16]. However, these papers only consider *transformational* techniques, where the original CS-TRS $(\mathcal{R}, \mu)$ is transformed into a TRS $\mathcal{R}_\Theta^\mu$ (where Θ represents the transformation which has been used) whose *innermost* termination implies the innermost termination of *CSR* for $(\mathcal{R}, \mu)$. Up to now, no direct method has been proposed to prove termination of innermost *CSR*. As shown in [2], proofs of termination using context-sensitive dependency pairs (CSDPs) are much more powerful and faster than any other technique for proving termination of *CSR*. Dealing with innermost *CSR*, we have a similar situation.

Example 2. Consider the following TRS $\mathcal{R}$:

```
b -> c(b)
f(c(X),X) -> f(X,X)
```

together with $\mu(\mathtt{f}) = \{1, 2\}$ and $\mu(\mathtt{c}) = \varnothing$. This system is *not* μ-terminating:

$$\mathtt{f}(\underline{\mathtt{b}},\mathtt{b}) \hookrightarrow \underline{\mathtt{f}(\mathtt{c}(\mathtt{b}),\mathtt{b})} \hookrightarrow \mathtt{f}(\underline{\mathtt{b}},\mathtt{b}) \hookrightarrow \ldots$$

where $\hookrightarrow$ denotes a context-sensitive rewriting step. However $\mathcal{R}$ is innermost μ-terminating. We can give a very easy automatic proof of this fact because the *innermost* context-sensitive dependency graph has *no cycle*. In contrast, by using available transformations for proving innermost termination of *CSR* (see [8] for a survey), we could not obtain a proof by using tools (like AProVE or TTT) supporting innermost termination proofs (of rewriting).

In the dependency pairs approach, proofs of termination of innermost rewriting are easier than proofs of termination of rewriting because: (1) the estimated innermost dependency graph is more accurate, (2) it is possible to limit the attention on the so-called *usable* rules of the TRS (for a given cycle).

After some preliminaries in Section 2, in Section 3 we prove that termination of innermost *CSR* can be characterized by using an appropriate definition of chain of CSDPs. In Section 4 we show how to prove automatically innermost termination of *CSR* by using the *innermost context-sensitive dependency graph*. Section 5 adapts the notion of usable rules to deal with innermost *CSR*. Section 6 provides a first experimental evaluation of our techniques.

2 Preliminaries

Terms. Throughout the paper, $\mathcal{X}$ denotes a countable set of variables and $\mathcal{F}$ denotes a signature, i.e., a set of function symbols $\{\mathtt{f}, \mathtt{g}, \ldots\}$, each having a fixed arity given by a mapping $ar : \mathcal{F} \to \mathbb{N}$. The set of terms built from $\mathcal{F}$ and $\mathcal{X}$ is $\mathcal{T}(\mathcal{F}, \mathcal{X})$. Positions $p, q, \ldots$ are represented by chains of positive natural numbers used to address subterms of t. Given positions p, q, we denote their concatenation as $p.q$. Positions are ordered by the standard prefix ordering $\leq$. If p is a position, and Q is a set of positions, $p.Q = \{p.q \mid q \in Q\}$. We denote the topmost position by Λ. The set of positions of a term t is $\mathcal{P}os(t)$. Positions of non-variable symbols in t are denoted as $\mathcal{P}os_{\mathcal{F}}(t)$ while $\mathcal{P}os_{\mathcal{X}}(t)$ are the positions of variables. The subterm at position p of t is denoted as $t|_p$ and $t[s]_p$ is the term t with the subterm at position p replaced by s. We write $t \trianglerighteq s$ if $s = t|_p$ for some $p \in \mathcal{P}os(t)$ and $t \rhd s$ if $t \trianglerighteq s$ and $t \neq s$. The symbol labelling the root of t is denoted as $root(t)$. A *context* is a term $C \in \mathcal{T}(\mathcal{F} \cup \{\Box\}, \mathcal{X})$ with zero or more 'holes' $\Box$ (a fresh constant symbol).

Term rewriting. A rewrite rule is an ordered pair (l, r), written $l \to r$, with $l, r \in \mathcal{T}(\mathcal{F}, \mathcal{X})$, $l \notin \mathcal{X}$ and $\mathcal{V}ar(r) \subseteq \mathcal{V}ar(l)$. The left-hand side (*lhs*) of the rule is l and r is the right-hand side (*rhs*). A TRS is a pair $\mathcal{R} = (\mathcal{F}, R)$ where R is a set of rewrite rules. Given $\mathcal{R} = (\mathcal{F}, R)$, we consider $\mathcal{F}$ as the disjoint union $\mathcal{F} = \mathcal{C} \uplus \mathcal{D}$ of symbols $c \in \mathcal{C}$, called *constructors* and symbols $f \in \mathcal{D}$, called *defined functions*, where $\mathcal{D} = \{root(l) \mid l \to r \in R\}$ and $\mathcal{C} = \mathcal{F} - \mathcal{D}$.

Context-sensitive rewriting. A mapping $\mu : \mathcal{F} \to \mathcal{P}(\mathbb{N})$ is a *replacement map* (or $\mathcal{F}$-map) if $\forall f \in \mathcal{F}$, $\mu(f) \subseteq \{1, \ldots, ar(f)\}$ [15]. Let $M_{\mathcal{F}}$ be the set of all $\mathcal{F}$-maps (or $M_{\mathcal{R}}$ for the $\mathcal{F}$-maps of a TRS $(\mathcal{F}, R)$). A binary relation R on terms is μ-monotonic if $t \, R \, s$ implies $f(t_1, \ldots, t_{i-1}, t, \ldots, t_k) \, R \, f(t_1, \ldots, t_{i-1}, s, \ldots, t_k)$ for all $f \in \mathcal{F}$, $i \in \mu(f)$, and $t, s, t_1, \ldots, t_k \in \mathcal{T}(\mathcal{F}, \mathcal{X})$. The set of μ-*replacing positions* $\mathcal{P}os^{\mu}(t)$ of $t \in \mathcal{T}(\mathcal{F}, \mathcal{X})$ is: $\mathcal{P}os^{\mu}(t) = \{\Lambda\}$, if $t \in \mathcal{X}$ and $\mathcal{P}os^{\mu}(t) = \{\Lambda\} \cup \bigcup_{i \in \mu(root(t))} i.\mathcal{P}os^{\mu}(t|_i)$, if $t \notin \mathcal{X}$. The set of μ-*replacing* variables of t is $\mathcal{V}ar^{\mu}(t) = \{x \in \mathcal{V}ar(t) \mid \exists p \in \mathcal{P}os^{\mu}(t), t|_p = x\}$. The μ-replacing subterm relation $\unrhd_{\mu}$ is given by $t \unrhd_{\mu} s$ if there is $p \in \mathcal{P}os^{\mu}(t)$ such that $s = t|_p$. We write $t \rhd_{\mu} s$ if $t \unrhd_{\mu} s$ and $t \neq s$. In *context-sensitive rewriting* (*CSR* [15]), we (only) contract μ-*replacing* redexes: s μ-rewrites to t, written $s \hookrightarrow_{\mu} t$ (or $s \hookrightarrow_{\mathcal{R},\mu} t$ and even $s \hookrightarrow t$, if $\mathcal{R}$ and μ are clear from the context), if $s \xrightarrow{p}_{\mathcal{R}} t$ and $p \in \mathcal{P}os^{\mu}(s)$. A μ-normal form is a term which cannot be μ-rewritten. Let $\mathsf{NF}_{\mu}(\mathcal{R})$ (or just NF_{μ} if no confusion arises) be the set of μ-normal forms of a TRS $\mathcal{R}$. A μ-innermost redex is a redex t whose μ-replacing subterms are μ-normal forms: $t = \sigma(l)$ for some substitution σ and rule $l \to r \in \mathcal{R}$ and for all $p \in \mathcal{P}os^{\mu}(t)$, $t|_p \in \mathsf{NF}_{\mu}$. A term s innermost μ-rewrites to t, written $s \overset{i}{\hookrightarrow} t$, if $s \xrightarrow{p}_{\mathcal{R}} t$, $p \in \mathcal{P}os^{\mu}(s)$, and $s|_p$ is an μ-innermost redex. A TRS $\mathcal{R}$ is μ-terminating if $\hookrightarrow_{\mu}$ is terminating. A term t is μ-terminating if there is no infinite μ-rewrite sequence $t = t_1 \hookrightarrow_{\mu} t_2 \hookrightarrow_{\mu} \cdots \hookrightarrow_{\mu} t_n \hookrightarrow_{\mu} \cdots$ starting from t. A TRS $\mathcal{R}$ is innermost μ-terminating if $\overset{i}{\hookrightarrow}_{\mu}$ is terminating. We write $s \overset{i}{\hookrightarrow}^!_{\mathcal{R}} t$ if $s \overset{i}{\hookrightarrow}^*_{\mathcal{R}} t$ and $t \in \mathsf{NF}_{\mu}$.

A pair $(\mathcal{R}, \mu)$ where $\mathcal{R}$ is a TRS and $\mu \in M_{\mathcal{R}}$ is often called a CS-TRS.

Reduction pairs. A reduction pair $(\succeq, \sqsupset)$ consists of a stable and weakly monotonic quasi-ordering $\succeq$, and a stable and well-founded ordering $\sqsupset$ satisfying either $\succeq \circ \sqsupset \subseteq \sqsupset$ or $\sqsupset \circ \succeq \subseteq \sqsupset$. Note that *monotonicity is not required* for $\sqsupset$.

3   Termination of Innermost *CSR* with Dependency Pairs

In the following definition, given a term $t = f(t_1, \ldots, t_k) \in \mathcal{T}(\mathcal{F}, \mathcal{X})$, we write $t^{\sharp}$ to denote the *marked* term $f^{\sharp}(t_1, \ldots, t_k)$, where $f^{\sharp}$ is a new fresh symbol (called *tuple* symbol [3]). Given a signature $\mathcal{F}$, we let $\mathcal{F}^{\sharp}$ be the extension of $\mathcal{F}$ containing all tuple symbols for $\mathcal{F}$: $\mathcal{F}^{\sharp} = \mathcal{F} \cup \{f^{\sharp} \mid f \in \mathcal{F}\}$. Similarly, if $t = f^{\sharp}(t_1, \ldots, t_k)$ is a marked term, we write $t^{\natural}$ to denote the unmarked term $f(t_1, \ldots, t_k)$.

Definition 1 (CS-dependency pairs [1]). *Let* $\mathcal{R} = (\mathcal{F}, R) = (\mathcal{C} \uplus \mathcal{D}, R)$ *be a TRS and* $\mu \in M_{\mathcal{R}}$. *We define* $\mathsf{DP}(\mathcal{R}, \mu) = \mathsf{DP}_{\mathcal{F}}(\mathcal{R}, \mu) \cup \mathsf{DP}_{\mathcal{X}}(\mathcal{R}, \mu)$ *to be the set of* context-sensitive *dependency pairs* (*CS-DPs*) *where:*

$$\mathsf{DP}_{\mathcal{F}}(\mathcal{R}, \mu) = \{l^{\sharp} \to s^{\sharp} \mid l \to r \in R, r \unrhd_{\mu} s, root(s) \in \mathcal{D}, l \ntrianglerighteq_{\mu} s\}$$

and $\mathsf{DP}_{\mathcal{X}}(\mathcal{R}, \mu) = \{l^{\sharp} \to x \mid l \to r \in R, x \in \mathcal{V}ar^{\mu}(r) - \mathcal{V}ar^{\mu}(l)\}$. *We extend* $\mu \in M_{\mathcal{F}}$ *into* $\mu^{\sharp} \in M_{\mathcal{F}^{\sharp}}$ *by* $\mu^{\sharp}(f) = \mu(f)$ *if* $f \in \mathcal{F}$, *and* $\mu^{\sharp}(f^{\sharp}) = \mu(f)$ *if* $f \in \mathcal{D}$.

Example 3. Consider the CS-TRS $(\mathcal{R}, \mu)$ in Example 2. There is only one context-sensitive dependency pair:

```
F(c(X),X) -> F(X,X)
```

with $\mu^{\sharp}(\mathbf{F}) = \{1, 2\}$.

In the CS-DP approach, termination of *CSR* is characterized as the absence of infinite chains of CS-DPs [1, Definition 2]. In innermost *CSR*, we only perform reduction steps on *innermost replacing redexes*. Therefore, we have to restrict the definition of chains in order to obtain an appropriate notion corresponding to innermost *CSR*. Regarding innermost reductions, arguments of a redex should be in *normal form* before the redex is contracted and, regarding *CSR*, the redex to be contracted has to be in a *replacing* position.

Definition 2 (Innermost μ-chain). *Given a CS-TRS $(\mathcal{P}, \mu^{\sharp})$ of CS-DPs associated to a CS-TRS $(\mathcal{R}, \mu)$, an innermost $(\mathcal{R}, \mathcal{P}, \mu^{\sharp})$-chain is a sequence of pairs $u_j \to v_j \in \mathcal{P}$ such that there is a substitution σ such that $\sigma(u_j) \in \mathsf{NF}_\mu(\mathcal{R})$ and such that, for all $j \geq 1$,*

1. $\sigma(v_j) \overset{i}{\hookrightarrow}^{!}_{\mathcal{R},\mu^{\sharp}} \sigma(u_{j+1})$, if $u_j \to v_j \in \mathsf{DP}_{\mathcal{F}}(\mathcal{R}, \mu)$, and
2. if $u_j \to v_j = u_j \to x_j \in \mathsf{DP}_{\mathcal{X}}(\mathcal{R}, \mu)$, then there is some $s_j \in \mathcal{T}(\mathcal{F}, \mathcal{X})$ such that $\sigma(x_j) \unrhd_\mu s_j$ and $s_j^{\sharp} \overset{i}{\hookrightarrow}^{!}_{\mathcal{R},\mu^{\sharp}} \sigma(u_{j+1})$.

As usual we assume that different occurrences of dependency pairs do not share any variables (renamings are used if necessary). An innermost $(\mathcal{R}, \mathcal{P}, \mu^{\sharp})$-chain is minimal if for all $u_j \to v_j \in \mathcal{P}$ and $j \geq 1$, $\sigma(v_j)$ is innermost μ-terminating (whenever $u_j \to v_j \in \mathsf{DP}_{\mathcal{F}}(\mathcal{R}, \mu)$) and $s_j^{\sharp}$ is innermost μ-terminating (whenever $u_j \to v_j \in \mathsf{DP}_{\mathcal{X}}(\mathcal{R}, \mu)$).

Theorem 1. *A CS-TRS $(\mathcal{R}, \mu)$ is innermost μ-terminating if and only if no infinite minimal innermost μ-chain exists.*

Let $\mathcal{M}_{\infty,\mu}$ be a set of minimal non-μ-terminating terms in the following sense [1]: t belongs to $\mathcal{M}_{\infty,\mu}$ if t is non-μ-terminating and every strict μ-*replacing* subterm s of t (i.e., $t \rhd_\mu s$) is μ-terminating. The proof of this result uses the following result.

Proposition 1. *[1, Proposition 1] Let $\mathcal{R} = (\mathcal{C} \uplus \mathcal{D}, R)$ be a TRS and $\mu \in M_{\mathcal{R}}$. Then for all $t \in \mathcal{M}_{\infty,\mu}$, there exist $l \to r \in R$, a substitution σ and a term $u \in \mathcal{M}_{\infty,\mu}$ such that $t \overset{>\Lambda}{\hookrightarrow}^{*} \sigma(l) \overset{\Lambda}{\to} \sigma(r) \unrhd_\mu u$ and either (1) there is a μ-replacing subterm s of r such that $u = \sigma(s)$, or (2) there is $x \in \mathcal{V}ar^{\mu}(r) - \mathcal{V}ar^{\mu}(l)$ such that $\sigma(x) \unrhd_\mu u$.*

Proof. (of Theorem 1) We prove the *if* part by contradiction. We show that for any infinite innermost μ-rewriting sequence we can construct an infinite innermost $(\mathcal{R}, \mathsf{DP}(\mathcal{R}, \mu), \mu^{\sharp})$-chain. Let innermost μ-rewriting below the root be $\overset{\geq i}{\hookrightarrow} = (\overset{>\Lambda}{\hookrightarrow} \cap \overset{i}{\hookrightarrow})$. If $\mathcal{R}$ is not innermost μ-terminating, then, by Proposition 1, there is a term $t \in \mathcal{M}_{\infty,\mu}$, a rule $l \to r \in R$, a substitution σ, and a term $u \in \mathcal{M}_{\infty,\mu}$ such that $t \stackrel{\geq i}{\hookrightarrow} \sigma(l) \stackrel{\Lambda}{\to} \sigma(r) \trianglerighteq_\mu u$ (where every immediate replacing subterm of $\sigma(l)$ is a μ-normal form), u is not innermost μ-terminating and either

1. there is a μ-replacing subterm s of r such that $u = \sigma(s)$, or
2. there is $x \in Var^\mu(r) - Var^\mu(l)$ such that $\sigma(x) \trianglerighteq_\mu u$.

In the first case above, we have a dependency pair $l^\sharp \to s^\sharp \in \mathsf{DP}_\mathcal{F}(\mathcal{R},\mu)$ such that $u = \sigma(s) \in \mathcal{M}_{\infty,\mu}$, i.e., we can start an innermost $(\mathcal{R}, \mathsf{DP}(\mathcal{R},\mu), \mu^\sharp)$-chain beginning with $\sigma(l^\sharp) \hookrightarrow_{\mathsf{DP}(\mathcal{R},\mu),\mu^\sharp} \sigma(s^\sharp)$. Note that $\sigma(l^\sharp) \in \mathsf{NF}_\mu(\mathcal{R})$.

In the second case above, since $u \in \mathcal{M}_{\infty,\mu}$, there is a rule $\lambda \to \rho$ such that $u \stackrel{>i}{\hookrightarrow^!} \sigma(\lambda)$ (since we can assume that the variables in this rule do not occur in l, we can use the same –conveniently extended– substitution σ) and $\sigma(\rho)$ contains a subterm in $\mathcal{M}_{\infty,\mu}$. Hence, $u^\sharp \stackrel{i}{\hookrightarrow^!}_{\mathcal{R},\mu^\sharp} \sigma(\lambda^\sharp)$. Furthermore, there is a dependency pair $l^\sharp \to x \in \mathsf{DP}_\mathcal{X}(\mathcal{R},\mu)$ such that $\sigma(x) \trianglerighteq_\mu u$; thus, according to Definition 2 we can start an $(\mathcal{R}, \mathsf{DP}(\mathcal{R},\mu), \mu^\sharp)$-chain beginning with

$$\sigma(l^\sharp) \hookrightarrow_{\mathsf{DP}(\mathcal{R},\mu),\mu^\sharp} u^\sharp$$

and then continuing with a dependency pair $u' \to v'$ such that $u' = \lambda^\sharp$ and $u^\sharp \stackrel{i}{\hookrightarrow^!}_{\mathcal{R},\mu^\sharp} \sigma(u')$. Note that $\sigma(l^\sharp), \sigma(\lambda^\sharp) \in \mathsf{NF}_\mu(\mathcal{R})$.

Thus, in both cases we can start an innermost $(\mathcal{R}, \mathsf{DP}(\mathcal{R},\mu), \mu^\sharp)$-chain which could be infinitely extended in a similar way by starting from $u^\sharp$. This contradicts our initial assumption.

On the other hand, in order to show that the criterion is also *necessary* for innermost termination of context-sensitive rewriting we assume that there exists an infinite innermost μ-chain that implies the existence of an infinite innermost μ-rewrite sequence. If there is an infinite innermost $(\mathcal{R}, \mathsf{DP}(\mathcal{R},\mu), \mu^\sharp)$-chain, then there is a substitution σ and dependency pairs $u_i \to v_i \in \mathsf{DP}(\mathcal{R},\mu)$ such that considering the first dependency pair $u_1 \to v_1$ in the sequence:

1. If $u_1 \to v_1 \in \mathsf{DP}_\mathcal{F}(\mathcal{R},\mu)$, then $v_1^\sharp$ is a μ-replacing subterm of the right-hand-side r_1 of a rule $l_1 \to r_1$ in $\mathcal{R}$. Therefore, $r_1 = C_1[v_1^\sharp]_{p_1}$ for some $p_1 \in \mathcal{P}os^\mu(r_1)$ and, since $\sigma(u_1) \in \mathsf{NF}_\mu$, we can perform the innermost μ-rewriting step $t_1 = \sigma(u_1^\sharp) \stackrel{i}{\hookrightarrow}_{\mathcal{R},\mu} \sigma(r_1) = \sigma(C_1)[\sigma(v_1^\sharp)]_{p_1} = s_1$, where $\sigma(v_1^\sharp)^\sharp = \sigma(v_1) \stackrel{i}{\hookrightarrow^!}_{\mathcal{R},\mu^\sharp} \sigma(u_2)$ and $\sigma(u_2)$ also initiates an infinite innermost $(\mathcal{R}, \mathsf{DP}(\mathcal{R},\mu), \mu^\sharp)$-chain. Note that $p_1 \in \mathcal{P}os^\mu(s_1)$.
2. If $u_1 \to x \in \mathsf{DP}_\mathcal{X}(\mathcal{R},\mu)$, then there is a rule $l_1 \to r_1$ in $\mathcal{R}$ such that $u_1 = l_1^\sharp$, and $x \in Var^\mu(r_1) - Var^\mu(l_1)$, i.e., $r_1 = C_1[x]_{q_1}$ for some $q_1 \in \mathcal{P}os^\mu(r_1)$. Furthermore, since there is a subterm s such that $\sigma(x) \trianglerighteq_\mu s$ and $s^\sharp \stackrel{i}{\hookrightarrow^!}_{\mathcal{R},\mu^\sharp} \sigma(u_2)$, we can write $\sigma(x) = C_1'[s]_{p_1'}$ for some $p_1' \in \mathcal{P}os^\mu(\sigma(x))$. Therefore, since $\sigma(u_1) = \sigma(l_1)^\sharp \in \mathsf{NF}_\mu$, we can perform the innermost μ-rewriting step $t_1 = \sigma(l_1) \stackrel{i}{\hookrightarrow}_{\mathcal{R},\mu} \sigma(r_1) = \sigma(C_1)[C_1'[s]_{p_1'}]_{q_1} = s_1$ where $s^\sharp \stackrel{i}{\hookrightarrow^!}_{\mathcal{R},\mu^\sharp} \sigma(u_2)$ (hence

$s \stackrel{i}{\hookrightarrow}^! u_2^\natural)$ and $\sigma(u_2)$ initiates an infinite innermost $(\mathcal{R}, \mathsf{DP}(\mathcal{R}, \mu), \mu^\natural)$-chain. Note that $p_1 = q_1.p_1' \in \mathcal{P}os^\mu(s_1)$.

Since $\mu^\natural(f^\natural) = \mu(f)$, and $p_1 \in \mathcal{P}os^\mu(s_1)$, we have that $s_1 \stackrel{i}{\hookrightarrow}^!_{\mathcal{R},\mu} t_2[\sigma(u_2)]_{p_1} = t_2$ and $p_1 \in \mathcal{P}os^\mu(t_2)$. Therefore, we can build in that way an infinite μ-rewrite sequence

$$t_1 \stackrel{i}{\hookrightarrow}_{\mathcal{R},\mu} s_1 \stackrel{i}{\hookrightarrow}^!_{\mathcal{R},\mu} t_2 \stackrel{i}{\hookrightarrow}_{\mathcal{R},\mu} \cdots$$

which contradicts the innermost μ-termination of $\mathcal{R}$.

Example 4. Consider again the CS-TRS $\mathcal{R}$ in Example 2. As shown in Example 3, there is only one CS-DP:

    F(c(X),X) -> F(X,X)

Since $\mu^\natural(\mathsf{F}) = \{1, 2\}$, if a substitution σ satisfies $\sigma(\mathsf{F(c(X),X)}) \in \mathsf{NF}_\mu(\mathcal{R})$, then $\sigma(X) = s$ is in μ-normal form. Assume that the dependency pair is part of an innermost CS-DP-chain. Since there is no way to μ-rewrite $F(s, s)$, there must be $F(s, s) = F(c(t), t)$ for some term t, which means that $s = t$ and $c(t) = s$, i.e., $t = c(t)$ which is not possible. Thus, there is no infinite innermost chain of CS-DPs for $\mathcal{R}$, which is proved innermost terminating by Theorem 1.

Of course, ad-hoc reasonings like in Example 4 do not lead to automation. In the following section we discuss how to prove termination of innermost *CSR* by giving *constraints* on terms that can be solved by using standard methods.

4 Checking Innermost μ-Termination Automatically

The analysis of infinite sequences of dependency pairs can be handled by looking at (the cycles $\mathfrak{C}$ of) the dependency graph associated to the TRS $\mathcal{R}$ [3].

The Innermost Context-Sensitive dependency graph of a TRS $\mathcal{R}$ is the directed graph whose nodes are the CS-dependency pairs; there is an arc from $u \to v$ to $u' \to v'$ if $u \to v$, $u' \to v'$ is an innermost μ-chain.

In [2] we have investigated the structure of context-sensitive sequences in order to improve the CS-dependency graph. A μ-rewrite sequence can proceed in two ways: by means of *visible* parts of the rules that is, μ-replacing subterms in the right-hand sides which are rooted by a defined symbol, or showing up *hidden* non-μ-terminating subterms which are activated by *migrating* variables of a rule $l \to r$, i.e. those variables that are not μ-replacing in l and become μ-replacing in r.

Definition 3 (Hidden symbol [2]). *Let $\mathcal{R} = (\mathcal{F}, R)$ be a TRS and $\mu \in M_\mathcal{R}$. We say that $f \in \mathcal{F}$ is a* hidden symbol *if there is a rule $l \to r \in R$ where f occurs at a non-μ-replacing position. Let $\mathcal{H}(\mathcal{R}, \mu)$ (or just $\mathcal{H}$, if $\mathcal{R}$ and μ are clear from the context) be the set of all hidden symbols in $(\mathcal{R}, \mu)$.*

Obviously, as innermost μ-chains are restricted chains (also restricted μ-chains!), the Innermost Context-Sensitive dependency graph (in the following ICSDG or ICS-dependency graph for short) is a subgraph of the dependency graph.

Definition 4 (Innermost CSDG). *Let $\mathcal{R}$ be a TRS and $\mu \in M_{\mathcal{R}}$. The innermost context-sensitive dependency graph consists of the set $\mathsf{DP}(\mathcal{R}, \mu)$ of context-sensitive dependency pairs and arcs which connect them as follows:*

1. *There is an arc from a dependency pair $u \to v \in \mathsf{DP}_{\mathcal{F}}(\mathcal{R}, \mu)$ to a dependency pair $u' \to v' \in \mathsf{DP}(\mathcal{R}, \mu)$ if there are substitutions σ and θ such that $\sigma(v) \overset{i}{\hookrightarrow}^! \theta(u')$ and $\sigma(u)$ and $\theta(u') \in \mathsf{NF}_{\mu}(\mathcal{R})$.*
2. *There is an arc from a dependency pair $u \to v \in \mathsf{DP}_{\mathcal{X}}(\mathcal{R}, \mu)$ to a dependency pair $u' \to v' \in \mathsf{DP}(\mathcal{R}, \mu)$ if $root(u')^{\natural} \in \mathcal{H}(\mathcal{R}, \mu)$ and u and $u' \in \mathsf{NF}_{\mu}(\mathcal{R})$.*

Example 5. Consider the following CS-TRS $\mathcal{R}$ in [6]:

$$\texttt{f(g(b)) -> f(g(a))} \qquad \texttt{f(a) -> f(a)} \qquad \texttt{a -> b}$$

together with $\mu(\texttt{f}) = \{1\}$ and $\mu(\texttt{g}) = \varnothing$. Then $\mathsf{DP}(\mathcal{R}, \mu)$ is:

$$\texttt{F(g(b)) -> F(g(a))} \qquad \texttt{F(a) -> F(a)} \qquad \texttt{F(a) -> A}$$

and $\mu^{\natural}(\texttt{F}) = \{1\}$. The CSDG contains a single cycle $\{\texttt{F(a) -> F(a)}\}$. However, the ICSDG is empty.

4.1   Approximating the ICSDG

In order to automatically build the Innermost Context-Sensitive Dependency Graph it is necessary to approximate it since for two dependency pairs $u \to v$ and $u' \to v'$ it is undecidable to know if there exist two substitutions σ and θ such that $\sigma(v)$ μ-reduces innermost to $\theta(u')$ and $\sigma(u)$ and $\theta(u')$ are instantiated to μ-normal forms. For this reason, we have to approximate the graph by computing a supergraph containing it in the same way as previous approaches [3,1]. In the context-sensitive setting, we have adapted functions CAP and REN to be applied only on μ-*replacing* subterms [1]. On the other hand, in the innermost setting it is not necessary to use REN since all variables are always instantiated to normal forms and cannot be reduced and CAP(v) substitutes every subterm with a defined root symbol by fresh variables only if the term is not equal to subterms of u. To approximate the ICS-dependency graph, however, we have to combine both of them: we use $\mathrm{CAP}_u^{\mu}(v)$ to replace all μ-replacing subterm rooted with a defined symbol whenever the term was not equal to a μ-replacing subterm of the left-hand side of the dependency pair u. We use $\mathrm{REN}_u^{\mu}(v)$ to replace by fresh variables those ones that are replacing in v but not in u since they are not μ-normalized. Given a term u, we let CAP_u^{μ} be given as follows: let D be a set of defined symbols (in our context, $D = \mathcal{D} \cup \mathcal{D}^{\natural}$):

$$\mathrm{CAP}_u^{\mu}(x) = x \;\; \text{if } x \text{ is a variable}$$
$$\mathrm{CAP}_u^{\mu}(f(t_1, \dots, t_k)) = \begin{cases} y & \text{if } f \in D \\ f([t_1]_1^f, \dots, [t_k]_k^f) & \text{otherwise} \end{cases}$$

where y is a new, fresh variable which has not yet been used and given a term s, $[s]_i^f = \mathrm{CAP}_u^{\mu}(s)$ if $i \in \mu(f)$ and s is not equal to a μ-replacing subterm of u and $[s]_i^f = s$ otherwise. Given a term u, we let REN_u^{μ} be given by: $\mathrm{REN}_u^{\mu}(x) = y$ if x is a variable and $\mathrm{REN}_u^{\mu}(f(t_1, \dots, t_k)) = f([t_1]_1^f, \dots, [t_k]_k^f)$ for evey k-ary symbol

f, where given a term $s \in T^{\sharp}(\mathcal{F}, \mathcal{X})$, $[s]_i^f = \text{REN}_u^{\mu}(s)$ if $i \in \mu(f)$ and the variable is not μ-replacing in u and $[s]_i^f = s$ otherwise.

We have an arc from $u \rightarrow v$ to $u' \rightarrow v'$ in the ICS-dependency graph if $\text{REN}_u^{\mu}(\text{CAP}_u^{\mu}(v))$ and u' are unifiable by some mgu σ such that $\sigma(u), \sigma(u') \in \text{NF}_{\mu}(\mathcal{R})$; following [3], we say that v and u' are *innermost μ-connectable*. The following result whose proof is similar to that of [3, Theorem 39] formalizes the correctness of this approach (we only need to take into account the replacement restrictions indicated by the replacement map μ).

Proposition 2. *Let $(\mathcal{R}, \mu)$ be a CS-TRS. If there is an arc from $u \rightarrow v$ to $u' \rightarrow v'$ in the ICS-dependency graph, then v and u' are innermost μ-connectable.*

Example 6. (Continuing Example 2) Since $\text{REN}_u^{\mu^{\sharp}}(\text{CAP}_u^{\mu^{\sharp}}(\text{F(X,X)})) = \text{F(X,X)}$ and F(c(Y),Y) do not unify we conclude (and this can easily be implemented) that the ICS-dependency graph for the CS-TRS $(\mathcal{R}, \mu)$ in Example 2 contains no cycles.

We know how to approximate the ICS-dependency graph by means of the functions CAP_u^{μ} and REN_u^{μ}. The next step is checking the innermost μ-termination with the ICSDG automatically.

4.2 Proofs of Termination of Innermost *CSR* Using the ICSDG

The absence of infinite innermost $(\mathcal{R}, \text{DP}(\mathcal{R}, \mu), \mu^{\sharp})$-chains is checked in the ICSDG by finding (possibly different) μ-reduction pairs $(\gtrsim_{\mathfrak{C}}, \sqsupset_{\mathfrak{C}})$ for each cycle $\mathfrak{C}$. Here, a μ-reduction pair is a pair $(\gtrsim, \sqsupset)$ where $\gtrsim$ is a stable and μ-monotonic quasi-ordering which is compatible with the well-founded and stable ordering $\sqsupset$, i.e., satisfying either $\gtrsim \circ \sqsupset \subseteq \sqsupset$ or $\sqsupset \circ \gtrsim \subseteq \sqsupset$.

Theorem 2 (Use of the ICSDG). *Let $\mathcal{R}$ be a TRS and $\mu \in M_{\mathcal{R}}$. Then, $\mathcal{R}$ is innermost μ-terminating iff for each cycle $\mathfrak{C}$ in the innermost context-sensitive dependency graph there is a μ-reduction pair $(\gtrsim_{\mathfrak{C}}, \sqsupset_{\mathfrak{C}})$ such that $\mathcal{R} \subseteq \gtrsim_{\mathfrak{C}}$, $\mathfrak{C} \subseteq \gtrsim_{\mathfrak{C}} \cup \sqsupset_{\mathfrak{C}}$, and*

1. *If $\mathfrak{C} \cap \text{DP}_{\mathcal{X}}(\mathcal{R}, \mu) = \varnothing$, then $\mathfrak{C} \cap \sqsupset_{\mathfrak{C}} \neq \varnothing$*
2. *If $\mathfrak{C} \cap \text{DP}_{\mathcal{X}}(\mathcal{R}, \mu) \neq \varnothing$, then $\unrhd_{\mu} \subseteq \gtrsim_{\mathfrak{C}}$, and*
   (a) $\mathfrak{C} \cap \sqsupset_{\mathfrak{C}} \neq \varnothing$ and $f(x_1, \ldots, x_k) \gtrsim_{\mathfrak{C}} f^{\sharp}(x_1, \ldots, x_k)$ for all $f^{\sharp}$ in $\mathfrak{C}$, or
   (b) $f(x_1, \ldots, x_k) \sqsupset_{\mathfrak{C}} f^{\sharp}(x_1, \ldots, x_k)$ for all $f^{\sharp}$ in $\mathfrak{C}$.

The proof is similar to that of [1, Theorem 4]. The practical use of Theorem 2 concerns the so-called *strongly connected components* (SCCs) of the dependency graph, rather than the cycles themselves (which are exponentially many) [13,14].

Example 7. There are many examples that are easily solved when trying to build the ICS-dependency graph since they do not contain cycles. This is the case for Example 2 and Example 5.

The use of *argument filterings*, which is standard in the current formulations of the dependency pairs method, also adapts without changes to this setting.

Also the *subterm criterion* [13], can be used to ignore certain cycles of the dependency graph. In [1], we have adapted it to *CSR*.

5   Usable CS-Rules

An interesting feature in the treatment of innermost termination problems using the dependency pairs approach is that, since the variables in the right-hand side of the dependency pairs are in normal form, the rules which can be used to connect contiguous dependency pairs are usually a proper subset of the rules in the TRS. This leads to the notion of *usable rules* [3, Definition 32] which simplifies the proofs of innermost termination of rewriting. We adapt this notion to the context-sensitive setting.

Definition 5 (Basic usable CS-rules). *Let $\mathcal{R}$ be a TRS and $\mu \in M_{\mathcal{R}}$. For any symbol f let $Rules(\mathcal{R}, f)$ be the set of rules defining f and such that the left-hand side l has no redex as proper μ-replacing subterm. For any term t the set of basic usable rules $\mathbf{U}_0(\mathcal{R}, t)$ is as follows:*

$$\mathbf{U}_0(\mathcal{R}, x) = \varnothing$$
$$\mathbf{U}_0(\mathcal{R}, f(t_1, \ldots, t_n)) = Rules(\mathcal{R}, f) \cup \bigcup_{i \in \mu(f)} \mathbf{U}_0(\mathcal{R}', t_i) \cup \bigcup_{l \to r \in Rules(\mathcal{R}, f)} \mathbf{U}_0(\mathcal{R}', r)$$

where $\mathcal{R}' = \mathcal{R} - Rules(\mathcal{R}, f)$. If $\mathfrak{C} \subseteq \mathsf{DP}(\mathcal{R}, \mu)$, then $\mathbf{U}_0(\mathcal{R}, \mathfrak{C}) = \bigcup_{l \to r \in \mathfrak{C}} \mathbf{U}_0(\mathcal{R}, r)$.

Interestingly, although our definition is a straightforward extension of the classical one (which just takes into account that μ-rewritings are possible only on μ-replacing subterms), some subtleties arise due to the presence of *non-conservative* rules. Here, a rule $l \to r$ of a TRS $\mathcal{R}$ is μ-conservative if $Var^\mu(r) \subseteq Var^\mu(l)$, i.e., it does not contain migrating variables; $\mathcal{R}$ is μ-conservative if all its rules are (see [20]).

Definition 6 (Conservative CSDPs). *Let $\mathcal{R}$ be a TRS and $\mu \in M_{\mathcal{R}}$. The set of conservative CSDPs $\mathsf{DP}_{\mathsf{Co}}(\mathcal{R}, \mu)$ is $\mathsf{DP}_{\mathsf{Co}}(\mathcal{R}, \mu) = \{u \to v \in \mathsf{DP}(\mathcal{R}, \mu) \mid Var^{\mu^\sharp}(v) \subseteq Var^{\mu^\sharp}(u)\}$.*

Note that $\mathsf{DP}_{\mathsf{Co}}(\mathcal{R}, \mu) \subseteq \mathsf{DP}_{\mathcal{F}}(\mathcal{R}, \mu)$. Basic usable rules in Definition 5 can be applied to cycles $\mathfrak{C}$ consisting of *conservative* CS-dependency pairs provided that $\mathbf{U}_0(\mathcal{R}, \mathfrak{C})$ is also conservative. This is proved in Theorem 3 below. First, we need some auxiliary results.

Proposition 3. *Let $\mathcal{R}$ be a TRS and $\mu \in M_{\mathcal{R}}$. Let $t, s \in \mathcal{T}(\mathcal{F}, \mathcal{X})$ and σ be a substitution such that $s = \sigma(t)$ and $\forall x \in Var^\mu(t)$, $\sigma(x) \in \mathsf{NF}_\mu(\mathcal{R})$. If $s \overset{i}{\hookrightarrow} s'$ by applying a rule $l \to r \in \mathcal{R}$, then there is a substitution σ' such that $s' = \sigma'(t')$ for $t' = t[r]_p$ and $p \in \mathcal{P}os_{\mathcal{F}}^\mu(t)$.*

Proof. Let $p \in \mathcal{P}os^\mu(s)$ be the position of an innermost redex $s|_p = \theta(l)$ for some substitution θ. Since $s = \sigma(t)$ and for all replacing variables in t, we have $\sigma(x) \in \mathsf{NF}_\mu(\mathcal{R})$, it follows that p is a non-variable (replacing) position of t. Therefore, $p \in \mathcal{P}os_{\mathcal{F}}^\mu(t)$. Since $s = \sigma(t)$, we have that $s' = \sigma(t)[\theta(r)]_p$ and since $p \in \mathcal{P}os_{\mathcal{F}}^\mu(t)$, by defining $\sigma'(x) = \sigma(x)$ for all $x \in Var(t)$ and $\sigma(x) = \theta(x)$ for all $x \in Var(r)$ (as usual, we assume $Var(t) \cap Var(r) = \varnothing$), we have $s' = \sigma'(t[r]_p)$.

Proposition 4. *Let $\mathcal{R}$ be a TRS and $\mu \in M_{\mathcal{R}}$. Let $t, s \in \mathcal{T}(\mathcal{F}, \mathcal{X})$ and σ be a substitution such that $s = \sigma(t)$ and $\forall x \in Var^\mu(t)$, $\sigma(x) \in NF_\mu(\mathcal{R})$. If $s \overset{i}{\hookrightarrow} s'$ by applying a conservative rule $l \to r \in \mathcal{R}$, then there is a substitution σ' such that $s' = \sigma'(t')$ for $t' = t[r]_p$, $p \in \mathcal{P}os_{\mathcal{F}}^\mu(t)$ and $\forall x \in Var^\mu(t')$, $\sigma'(x) \in NF_\mu(\mathcal{R})$.*

Proof. By Proposition 3, we know that σ', as in Proposition 3, satisfies $s' = \sigma'(t')$ for θ as in Proposition 3 and some $p \in \mathcal{P}os_{\mathcal{F}}^\mu(t)$. Since $s|_p$ is an innermost μ-replacing redex, we have that $\forall y \in Var^\mu(l)$, $\theta(y) \in NF_\mu(\mathcal{R})$. Since the rule $l \to r$ is conservative, $Var^\mu(r) \subseteq Var^\mu(l)$, hence $\forall z \in Var^\mu(r)$, $\sigma'(z) \in NF_\mu(\mathcal{R})$. Since $Var^\mu(t[r]_p) \subseteq Var^\mu(t) \cup Var^\mu(r)$, we have that $\forall x \in Var^\mu(t')$, $\sigma'(x) \in NF_\mu(\mathcal{R})$.

Proposition 5. *Let $\mathcal{R}$ be a TRS and $\mu \in M_{\mathcal{R}}$. Let $t, s \in \mathcal{T}(\mathcal{F}, \mathcal{X})$ and σ be a substitution such that $s = \sigma(t)$ and $\forall x \in Var^\mu(t)$, $\sigma(x) \in NF_\mu(\mathcal{R})$. If $\mathbf{U}_0(\mathcal{R}, t)$ is conservative and $s \overset{i}{\hookrightarrow}_{\mathcal{R}}^* u$ then $s \overset{i}{\hookrightarrow}_{\mathbf{U}_0(\mathcal{R}, t)}^* u$.*

Proof. By induction on the length of the sequence $s \overset{i}{\hookrightarrow}_{\mathcal{R}}^* u$. If $s = \sigma(t) = u$, it is trivial. Otherwise, if $s \overset{i}{\hookrightarrow}_{\mathcal{R}} s' \overset{i}{\hookrightarrow}_{\mathcal{R}}^* u$, we first prove that the result also holds in $s \overset{i}{\hookrightarrow}_{\mathcal{R}} s'$. By Proposition 3, $s = \sigma(t)$, and $s' = \sigma'(t')$ for $t' = t[r]_p$ is such that $s|_p = \theta(l)$ and $s'|_p = \theta(r)$ for some $p \in \mathcal{P}os_{\mathcal{F}}^\mu(t)$. Thus, $root(l) = root(t|_p)$ and by Definition 5, we can conclude that $l \to r \in \mathbf{U}_0(\mathcal{R}, t)$. By hypothesis, $\mathbf{U}_0(\mathcal{R}, t)$ is conservative. Thus, $l \to r$ is conservative and by Proposition 4, $s' = \sigma'(t')$ and $\forall x \in Var^\mu(t')$, $\sigma'(x) \in NF_\mu(\mathcal{R})$. Since $t' = t[r]_p$ and $root(t|_p) = root(l)$, we have that $\mathbf{U}_0(\mathcal{R}, t') \subseteq \mathbf{U}_0(\mathcal{R}, t)$ and (since $\mathbf{U}_0(\mathcal{R}, t)$ is conservative) $\mathbf{U}_0(\mathcal{R}, t')$ is conservative as well. By the induction hypothesis we know that $s' \overset{i}{\hookrightarrow}_{\mathbf{U}_0(\mathcal{R}, t')}^* u$. Thus we have $s \overset{i}{\hookrightarrow}_{\mathbf{U}_0(\mathcal{R}, t)} s' \overset{i}{\hookrightarrow}_{\mathbf{U}_0(\mathcal{R}, t)}^* u$ as desired.

Theorem 3. *Let $\mathcal{R} = (\mathcal{F}, R)$ be a TRS, $\mu \in M_{\mathcal{F}}$, and $\mathfrak{C} \subseteq DP_{Co}(\mathcal{R}, \mu)$. If there is a $\mu^\sharp$-reduction pair $(\succsim, \sqsupset)$ such that, $\mathbf{U}_0(\mathcal{R}, \mathfrak{C})$ is conservative, $\mathbf{U}_0(\mathcal{R}, \mathfrak{C}) \subseteq \succsim$, $\mathfrak{C} \subseteq \succsim \cup \sqsupset$, and $\mathfrak{C} \cap \sqsupset \neq \varnothing$, then there is no minimal innermost $(\mathcal{R}, \mathfrak{C}, \mu^\sharp)$-chain.*

Proof. We proceed by contradiction. If $\mathcal{R}$ is not innermost μ-terminating, then by Theorem 1 there is an infinite innermost $(\mathcal{R}, DP(\mathcal{R}, \mu), \mu^\sharp)$-chain:

$$\sigma(u_1) \hookrightarrow_{DP(\mathfrak{C}, \mu), \mu^\sharp} \sigma(v_1) \overset{i\,!}{\hookrightarrow}_{\mathcal{R}} \sigma(u_2) \hookrightarrow_{DP(\mathfrak{C}, \mu), \mu^\sharp} \sigma(v_2) \overset{i\,!}{\hookrightarrow}_{\mathcal{R}} \sigma(u_3) \hookrightarrow_{DP(\mathfrak{C}, \mu), \mu^\sharp} \cdots$$

for a substitution σ and $u_i \to v_i \in DP_{\mathcal{F}}(\mathfrak{C}, \mu)$ for $i \geq 1$. Since $u_i \to v_i \in DP_{Co}(\mathcal{R}, \mu)$, and $\sigma(u_i) \in NF_\mu(\mathcal{R})$, this implies that $\forall x \in Var^\mu(v_i)$, $\sigma(x) \in NF_\mu(\mathcal{R})$ and by Proposition 5 the sequence can be seen as:

$$\sigma(u_1) \hookrightarrow_{DP(\mathfrak{C}, \mu), \mu^\sharp} \sigma(v_1) \overset{i\,!}{\hookrightarrow}_{(\mathbf{U}_0(\mathcal{R}, \mathfrak{C}), \mu^\sharp)} \sigma(u_2) \hookrightarrow_{DP(\mathfrak{C}, \mu), \mu^\sharp} \sigma(v_2) \overset{i\,!}{\hookrightarrow}_{(\mathbf{U}_0(\mathcal{R}, \mathfrak{C}), \mu^\sharp)} \sigma(u_3) \hookrightarrow \cdots$$

By stability of $\sqsupset$, we have $\sigma(u_i) \sqsupset \sigma(v_i)$ and by stability, μ-monotonicity and transitivity of $\succsim$ we have that $\sigma(v_i) \succsim \sigma(u_{i+1})$. By using the compatibility conditions of the μ-reduction pair, we obtain an infinite decreasing $\sqsupset$-sequence which contradicts well-foundedness of $\sqsupset$.

Unfortunately, dealing with non-conservative CSDPs, considering the basic usable CS-rules does *not* ensure a correct approach.

Example 8. Consider again the TRS $\mathcal{R}$:

```
b -> c(b)
f(c(X),X)-> f(X,X)
```

together with $\mu(\mathtt{f}) = \{1\}$ and $\mu(\mathtt{c}) = \varnothing$. There are *two* non-conservative CS-DPs (note that $\mu^{\sharp}(\mathtt{F}) = \mu(\mathtt{f}) = \{1\}$):

```
F(c(X),X) -> F(X,X)
F(c(X),X) -> X
```

and only one cycle in the ICSDG:

```
F(c(X),X) -> F(X,X)
```

Note that $\mathbf{U}_0(\mathcal{R}, \mathtt{F}(\mathtt{X},\mathtt{X})) = \varnothing$. Since this CS-DP is strictly compatible with, e.g., an LPO, we would conclude the innermost μ-termination of $\mathcal{R}$. However, this system is *not* innermost μ-terminating:

$$\mathtt{f}(\underline{\mathtt{b}},\mathtt{b}) \overset{i}{\hookrightarrow} \underline{\mathtt{f}(\mathtt{c}(\mathtt{b}),\mathtt{b})} \overset{i}{\hookrightarrow} \mathtt{f}(\underline{\mathtt{b}},\mathtt{b}) \overset{i}{\hookrightarrow} \cdots$$

The problem is that we have to take into account the special status of variables in the right-hand side of a non-conservative CS-DP. Instances of such variables are *not* guaranteed to be μ-normal forms. For this reason, when a cycle contains at least one non-conservative CS-DP, we have to consider the whole set of rules of the system.

Furthermore, conservativeness of $\mathbf{U}_0(\mathcal{R}, \mathfrak{C})$ cannot be dropped either since we could infer an incorrect result as shown by the following example.

Example 9. Consider the TRS $\mathcal{R}$:

```
b -> c(b)
f(c(X),X) -> f(g(X),X)
g(X) -> X
```

together with $\mu(\mathtt{f}) = \{1\}$ and $\mu(\mathtt{g}) = \mu(\mathtt{c}) = \varnothing$. There is only one conservative cycle: $\{\mathtt{F}(\mathtt{c}(\mathtt{X}),\mathtt{X}) \rightarrow \mathtt{F}(\mathtt{g}(\mathtt{X}),\mathtt{X})\}$ having only one usable (but non-conservative!) rule $\mathtt{g}(\mathtt{X}) \rightarrow \mathtt{X}$. This is compatible with the μ-reduction pair induced by the following polynomial interpretation:

$$[\mathtt{f}](x,y) = 0 \qquad [\mathtt{c}](x) = x+1 \qquad [\mathtt{g}](x) = x \qquad [\mathtt{F}](x,y) = x$$

However the system is not innermost μ-terminating:

$$\underline{\mathtt{f}(\mathtt{c}(\mathtt{b}),\mathtt{b})} \overset{i}{\hookrightarrow} \mathtt{f}(\underline{\mathtt{g}(\mathtt{b})},\mathtt{b}) \overset{i}{\hookrightarrow} \mathtt{f}(\underline{\mathtt{b}},\mathtt{b}) \overset{i}{\hookrightarrow} \underline{\mathtt{f}(\mathtt{c}(\mathtt{b}),\mathtt{b})} \overset{i}{\hookrightarrow} \cdots$$

Nevertheless, Theorem 3 is useful to improve the proofs of termination of innermost *CSR* as the following example shows.

Example 10. Consider again the TRS $\mathcal{R}$ in example 1. The system contains three cycles in the ICSDG:

```
{ SEL(s(N),cons(X,XS)) -> SEL(N,XS) }
{ MINUS(s(X),s(Y)) -> MINUS(X,Y) }
{ QUOT(s(X),s(Y)) -> QUOT(minus(X,Y),s(Y)) }
```

The first two cycles can be solved by using the subterm criterion. However, without the notion of usable rules, the last one is difficult to solve. The cycle is conservative and the obtained usable rules are also conservative: minus(X,0) -> X and minus(s(X),s(Y)) -> minus(X,Y). According to Theorem 3, the cycle can be easily solved by using a polynomial interpretation:

$$[\text{minus}](x, y) = x \qquad\qquad [0] = 0$$
$$[\text{s}](x) = x + 1 \qquad [\text{QUOT}](x, y) = x$$

6 Experiments

We have implemented the techniques described in the previous sections as part of the tool MU-TERM [19]. In order to evaluate the techniques which are reported in this paper we have made some benchmarks. We have considered the examples in the Termination Problem Data Base (TPDB, version 3.2) available through the URL:

http://www.lri.fr/~marche/tpdb/

Although there is no special TPDB category for innermost termination of *CSR* (yet) we have used the TRS/CSR directory in order to test our techniques for proving termination of innermost *CSR* (Theorems 2, 3). It contains 90 examples of CS-TRSs. We are able to give an automatic proof of innermost μ-termination for 62 examples. In order to evaluate our direct techniques in comparison with the transformational approach of [7,8,16], where termination of innermost *CSR* for a CS-TRS $(\mathcal{R}, \mu)$ is proved by proving innermost termination of a transformed TRS $\mathcal{R}_\Theta^\mu$, where Θ specifies a particular transformation (see [6,7] for a survey on this topic), we have transformed the set of examples by using the transformations that are correct for proving innermost termination of *CSR*: Giesl and Middeldorp's correct transformations for proving termination of innermost *CSR*, see [7], although we use the 'authors-based' notation introduced in [20]: GM and C for transformations 1 and 2 for proving termination of *CSR* introduced in [8], and iGM for the specific transformation for proving termination of innermost *CSR* introduced in [7]. Then we have proved innermost termination of the set of examples with AProVE [9], which is able to prove innermost termination of standard rewriting. In fact, AProVE is currently the most powerful tool for proving termination and innermost termination of TRSs but as we have said, MU-TERM is nowadays the only termination tool that proves innermost termination of *CSR*. The results are summarized in Table 1. Further details can be found here:

http://www.dsic.upv.es/~balarcon/FroCoS07/benchmarks

Indirectly, we have also made the first benchmarks to evaluate the existing correct transformations for proving innermost termination of *CSR* (see Table 1)

Table 1. Comparing techniques for proving termination of innermost *CSR*

	iCSDPs	Transformations
YES score	62	44
YES average time	0.13 sec.	5 sec.

	C	GM	iGM
YES score	24	41	30

showing that, quite surprisingly, the iGM transformation (which is in principle the more suitable one for proving innermost termination of *CSR*) obtains worse results than GM.

7   Conclusions and Future Work

In this paper, we have extended the context-sensitive dependency pairs approach in [1] for proving termination of innermost *CSR*. We have introduced the notion of an innermost μ-chain (Definition 2) and proved that it can be used to characterize innermost μ-termination (Theorem 1). We have also shown how to automatically prove innermost μ-termination by means of the ICS-dependency graph (Definition 4, Theorem 2). We have formulated the notion of basic usable rules showing how to use them in proofs of innermost termination of *CSR* (Definition 5, Theorem 3). We have implemented these techniques in MU-TERM and have made some benchmarks.

Up to now, no direct method has been proposed to prove termination of innermost *CSR*. So this is the first proposal of a direct method for proving termination of innermost *CSR*. We have extended Arts and Giesl's approach to prove innermost termination of TRSs to *CSR* (thus also extending [1,2]). The main issue which is left open is a general notion of *usable rules*, which can be used with non-conservative CSDPs. As in the standard case, this would probably help us to achieve better results. Even without them, though, our benchmarks show that the use of CSDPs dramatically improves the performance of existing (transformational) methods for proving termination of innermost *CSR*.

Acknoledgements. We thank the anonymous referees for many useful remarks.

References

1. Alarcón, B., Gutiérrez, R., Lucas, S.: Context-Sensitive Dependency Pairs. In: Arun-Kumar, S., Garg, N. (eds.) FSTTCS 2006. LNCS, vol. 4337, pp. 297–308. Springer, Heidelberg (2006)
2. Alarcón, B., Gutiérrez, R., Lucas, S.: Improving the context-sensitive dependency graph. Electronic Notes in Theoretical Computer Science (2007) (to appear)
3. Arts, T., Giesl, J.: Termination of Term Rewriting Using Dependency Pairs. Theoretical Computer Science 236, 133–178 (2000)
4. Borralleras, C.: Ordering-based methods for proving termination automatically. PhD Thesis, Departament de Llenguatges i Sistemes Informàtics, Universitat Politècnica de Catalunya (May 2003)

5. Giesl, J., Arts, T., Ohlebusch, E.: Modular Termination Proofs for Rewriting Using Dependency Pairs. Journal of Symbolic Computation 34(1), 21–58 (2002)
6. Giesl, J., Middeldorp, A.: Innermost termination of context-sensitive rewriting. Aachener Informatik-Berichte (AIBs) 2002-04, RWTH Aachen (2002)
7. Giesl, J., Middeldorp, A.: Innermost termination of context-sensitive rewriting. In: Ito, M., Toyama, M. (eds.) DLT 2002. LNCS, vol. 2450, pp. 231–244. Springer, Heidelberg (2003)
8. Giesl, J., Middeldorp, A.: Transformation techniques for context-sensitive rewrite systems. Journal of Functional Programming 14(4), 379–427 (2004)
9. Giesl, J., Schneider-Kamp, P., Thiemann, R.: AProVE 1.2: Automatic Termination Proofs in the Dependency Pair Framework. In: Furbach, U., Shankar, N. (eds.) IJCAR 2006. LNCS (LNAI), vol. 4130, pp. 281–286. Springer, Heidelberg (2006)
10. Gramlich, B.: Abstract Relations between Restricted Termination and Confluence Properties of Rewrite Systems. Fundamenta Informaticae 24, 3–23 (1995)
11. Gramlich, B.: On Proving Termination by Innermost Termination. In: Ganzinger, H. (ed.) RTA 1996. LNCS, vol. 1103, pp. 93–107. Springer, Heidelberg (1996)
12. Gramlich, B., Lucas, S.: Modular Termination of Context-Sensitive Rewriting. In: Proc. of PPDP'02, pp. 50–61. ACM Press, New York (2002)
13. Hirokawa, N., Middeldorp, A.: Dependency Pairs Revisited. In: van Oostrom, V. (ed.) RTA 2004. LNCS, vol. 3091, pp. 249–268. Springer, Heidelberg (2004)
14. Hirokawa, N., Middeldorp, A.: Automating the dependency pair method. Information and Computation 199, 172–199 (2005)
15. Lucas, S.: Context-sensitive computations in functional and functional logic programs. Journal of Functional and Logic Programming 1998(1), 1–61 (1998)
16. Lucas, S.: Termination of Rewriting With Strategy Annotations. In: Nieuwenhuis, R., Voronkov, A. (eds.) LPAR 2001. LNCS (LNAI), vol. 2250, pp. 669–684. Springer, Heidelberg (2001)
17. Lucas, S.: Termination of on-demand rewriting and termination of OBJ programs. In: Proc. of PPDP'01, pp. 82–93. ACM Press, New York (2001)
18. Lucas, S.: Context-sensitive rewriting strategies. Information and Computation 178(1), 293–343 (2002)
19. Lucas, S.: MU-TERM: A Tool for Proving Termination of Context-Sensitive Rewriting. In: van Oostrom, V. (ed.) RTA 2004. LNCS, vol. 3091, pp. 200–209. Springer, Heidelberg (2004)
20. Lucas, S.: Proving termination of context-sensitive rewriting by transformation. Information and Computation 204(12), 1782–1846 (2006)
21. Ohlebusch, E.: Advanced Topics in Term Rewriting. Springer, Heidelberg (2002)
22. TeReSe (ed.).: Term Rewriting Systems. Cambridge University Press, Cambridge (2003)

A Compressing Translation from Propositional Resolution to Natural Deduction

Hasan Amjad

University of Cambridge Computer Laboratory, William Gates Building,
15 JJ Thomson Avenue, Cambridge CB3 0FD, UK
Hasan.Amjad@cl.cam.ac.uk

Abstract. We describe a translation from SAT solver generated propositional resolution refutation proofs to classical natural deduction proofs. The resulting proof can usually be checked quicker than one that simply simulates the original resolution proof. We use this result in interactive theorem provers, to speed up reconstruction of SAT solver generated proofs. The translation is efficient, running in time linear in the length of the original proof, and effective, easily scaling up to large proofs with millions of inferences.

1 Introduction

Interactive theorem provers like PVS [11], HOL4 [3] or Isabelle [12] traditionally support rich specification logics. Automation for these logics is limited in theory and hard in practice, and proving a non-trivial theorem usually requires manual guidance by an expert user. Automatic proof procedures on the other hand, while designed for simpler logics, have become increasingly powerful over the past few years. By integrating automated procedures with interactive systems, we can preserve the richness of our specification logic and at the same time increase the degree of proof automation for useful fragments of that logic [13].

Formal verification is an important application area of interactive theorem proving. Problems in verification can often be reduced to Boolean satisfiability (SAT) and so the performance of an interactive prover on propositional problems may be of significant practical importance. SAT solvers [10] are powerful proof procedures for propositional logic and it is natural to wish to use them as proof engines for interactive provers.

There are many approaches to such an integration. The pragmatic approach is to trust the result of the SAT solver and assert it as a theorem in the prover. The danger is that of soundness bugs in the solver but more likely in the relatively untested interface code, which may involve complex translations to propositional logic. The safest approach would be execute the SAT solver algorithm within the prover, but we reject this on the grounds of efficiency. A good middle ground is to verify the SAT solver proof, and this is the approach we take. The extra assurance of soundness is particularly suited for those industrial applications where the focus is on certification rather than debugging.

B. Konev and F. Wolter (Eds.): FroCos 2007, LNAI 4720, pp. 88–102, 2007.
© Springer-Verlag Berlin Heidelberg 2007

Recent work [2,16] showed how interactive provers could use SAT solvers as non-trusted decision procedures for propositional logic, by simulating propositional resolution in their proof systems. We now show how to translate the resolution proof to a natural deduction proof that can be replayed faster than a natural deduction proof that directly simulates the resolution proof. The idea is to memoise parts of the proof by adapting standard data compression techniques. The treatment is tool independent, and assumes only that the interactive prover supports propositional logic and can simulate classical natural deduction.

The next section gives all the background required to keep the paper reasonably self-contained. In §3 and §4, we look at proof reconstruction and memoisation respectively. Finally, we give experimental results in §5.

2   Preliminaries

2.1   SAT Solver Proof Structure

We restrict ourselves to proofs produced by conflict driven clause learning SAT solvers based on the DPLL algorithm [8]. A SAT solver takes as input a term in conjunctive normal form (CNF), a conjunction of disjunctions of *literals*. A literal is a possibly negated atomic proposition. Each disjunct term of the conjunction is called a *clause*. Since both conjunction and disjunction are associative, commutative and idempotent, clauses can also be thought of as sets of literals, and the entire formula as a set of clauses.

The *propositional resolution* proof system is

$$\frac{C_0 \cup \{p\} \qquad C_1 \cup \{\bar{p}\}}{(C_0 - p) \cup (C_1 - \bar{p})} \bar{p}$$

where the literal $\bar{p}$ is the *pivot*. We set the convention that the pivot is given by its literal occurrence in the second input clause of the resolution. The first clause contains the negation of the pivot. The conclusion clause is the *resolvent*.

A SAT solver generated refutation proof consists of a list of *chains* of resolutions. The last chain in the list derives the empty clause ⊥. We abbreviate a chain c

$$\frac{C_2 \quad \dfrac{C_0 \quad C_1}{R_1} p_1}{R_2} p_2$$
$$\vdots$$
$$\frac{C_n \quad R_{n-1}}{R_n} p_n \qquad\qquad (1)$$

by using the linear form $c \equiv C_0(p_1)C_1(p_2)C_2 \ldots (p_n)C_n$ and order literals, so clauses are ordered sets. Each R_n is assigned a numeric ID that can be referenced by chains occuring later in the proof. The C_i are clause IDs (typically indexes into the clause database) and the pivots p_i are encoded as numbers.

Each chain corresponds to a conflict clause derivation during the SAT solver's execution. Since the solver uses backtracking search, many such derived clauses are never used in the final proof. The derivations that are relevant to the final proof can be easily and cheaply extracted from the SAT solver trace. Henceforth, whenever we refer to the SAT solver generated proof, we mean the smaller extracted version. It is beyond the scope of this work to discuss *why* SAT solver resolution proofs are restricted to this format [8].

2.2   Natural Deduction and Fully Expansive Proof

Classical natural deduction, call it **N**, is a well known inference system. Figure 1 gives a two-sided sequent style presentation of the rules, primitive and derived, that we shall use. **N** has rules for other connectives and for quantifiers, but we shall not be needing those.

$$\frac{}{\{A\} \vdash A}\text{ASSUME} \qquad \frac{\Gamma \vdash A \quad \Delta \vdash A \Rightarrow B}{\Gamma \cup \Delta \vdash B}\text{MP} \qquad \frac{\Gamma \vdash A \Rightarrow \bot}{\Gamma \vdash \neg A}\neg I$$

$$\frac{\Gamma \vdash A}{\Gamma - \{B\} \vdash B \Rightarrow A}\Rightarrow I \qquad \frac{\Gamma \vdash A \Rightarrow B}{\Gamma \cup \{A\} \vdash B}\Rightarrow E \qquad \frac{\Delta \vdash A \quad \Gamma \cup A \vdash B}{(\Gamma - A) \cup \Delta \vdash B}\text{CUT}$$

Fig. 1. Inference rules

Implementations of system **N** form the deductive engine for the theorem provers HOL4, Isabelle/HOL and HOL Light [5], and other well-known interactive provers such as Coq [7], MetaPRL and PVS can simulate system **N** easily. It thus forms a good starting point for our investigations.

A *fully expansive* or *LCF style* prover is one in which all proof must use a small *kernel* of simple inference rules. The small kernel is easy to get right, and all proof is then sound by construction. For this reason, all the provers mentioned above, except perhaps[1] PVS, are fully expansive.

The penalty for fully expansive proof is performance, because complex inferences must be implemented in terms of the existing kernel rather than in a more direct and efficient manner. It is therefore standard practice when implementing proof procedures for fully expansive provers to use an efficient external engine to find the proof, and then check the proof in-logic. One approach is to reflect a verified proof checker into efficient code [4]. Another is to replay the proof within the prover. We take the latter approach, since many interactive provers do not support reflection (except indirectly via unverified code generation).

We shall be using the HOL4 theorem prover as our initial test bed. The HOL4 kernel can efficiently simulate all the rules of Figure 1.

---

[1] The designation "fully expansive" is a philosophical one: implementations vary in both the size of the kernel and the complexity of the rules.

2.3 Generalised Suffix Trees

A generalised suffix tree (GST) is a data structure that supports efficient substring matching. Let A be an *alphabet*. An alphabet is a set of distinct atomic labels, called *characters*. Sequences of characters are called *strings*. The length $|s|$ of a string s is the number of characters in it. Strings are of finite length. A *substring* $s[i..j]$ is a contiguous subsequence of s, starting from the character of s at index i and going up to and including the character of s at index j.

Given a set of strings T over A and a string P, a GST for T can report all substrings of elements of T that are substrings of P, in time $O(|P|)$. The GST for T itself can be constructed in time $O(\Sigma_{s \in T}|s|)$ and takes up space $O(\Sigma_{s \in T}|s|)$, assuming A is fixed. If this is not the case, all complexity results acquire a factor of $\log_2 A$.

An online algorithm for GST construction is known, due to E. Ukkonen [15]. Ukkonen's algorithm is for constructing the suffix tree of one string, but can easily be extended to GSTs by adding a terminal character $ to the end of each string, where $ \notin A$.

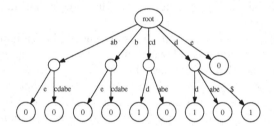

Fig. 2. Example GST for *abcdabe* and *cdd*

A GST stores all suffixes of each string in T, in a structure resembling a threaded Patricia trie [9]. As an example, Figure 2 gives the GST for the strings *abcdabe* and *cdd*, with pointers (or ID's) 0 and 1 respectively. The threads are not shown, and edges are labelled with substrings for readability.

Intuitively, a string is added by considering increasingly longer prefixes of it, and adding each suffix of that prefix to the tree. A final step adds on the $ character so that only the actual suffixes of s are represented. Suffixes are added by following from the root node the unique path corresponding to that suffix, and then creating new nodes (perhaps breaking an existing edge into two edges) and edges if some suffix of that suffix is not already present.

The concatenation of edge labels along the path from the root to a node is called the *path label* of the node. Note that a leaf node is labelled with the IDs of all strings that end at that node. Thus, the longest substring common to a set of strings is the deepest (w.r.t. the length of its path label) internal node such that all leaf nodes below it are labelled by IDs of only that set of strings. In the example, this would be *cd*.

3   Proof Reconstruction

To show that a propositional term t is a tautology, we convert $\bar{t}$ to CNF, and replay in the theorem prover the SAT solver generated proof of the unsatisfiability of $\bar{t}$, thus concluding $\vdash t$ (for details see [16]).

SAT solvers maintain a set of clauses, called the clause database (typically a dynamic array). Initially these are the problem clauses. The database is then extended by conflict clauses derived during the proof search. The proof search itself consists of trying out assignments of $\top$ or $\bot$ to the variables of the problem. A conflict (a clause in the database becoming false under the current assignment set) causes a backtrack where part or all of the current sequence of assignments may be undone. A conflict clause is then derived, encoding what the algorithm hopes are the critical assignments within the current assignment set that caused the conflict (for details see [8].

However, having conflict clauses does not mean that similar or identical subsequences of assignments can never occur in the future. Indeed, in problems with structure, such as most verification problems, there is some locality in the sense that given a certain assignment sequence, it is likely that the next variable to be assigned, and the value it is assigned, are the same as for an earlier identical assignment subsequence.

Since clause IDs are numbers and pivots are encoded as numbers, a chain can be seen as a string of numbers. Thus, locality in variable assignments translates into chains having identical substrings. During reconstruction of the proof within the interactive prover, such common substrings mean duplication of computational effort. We now show how such common substrings can be used to derive the same proof at lower cost. Section 4 will show how common substrings are actually found in the SAT solver proof and factored out. Chronologically, that happens first, but it is more instructive to first look at proof reconstruction.

To avoid clutter, we identify literals and clauses with their numeric IDs.

3.1   Simulating Resolution

The first step is see how propositional resolution can be efficiently simulated using the rules of Figure 1 [16]. A clause would normally be represented by a term $p_0 \vee \ldots \vee p_n$. However, performing resolution using this representation is inefficient because of tedious associative-commutative reasoning required to pick out the pivots. Instead, the clause is represented by the theorem $\{p_0 \vee \ldots \vee p_n, \bar{p}_0, \ldots, \bar{p}_n\} \vdash \bot$. This theorem form asserts exactly the clause concerned.

Now consider two clauses represented in theorem form. If the clauses are $s \equiv p_0 \vee \ldots \vee p_n \vee \bar{v}$ and $t \equiv q_0 \vee \ldots \vee q_m \vee v$, we may resolve them, with v as the pivot, as follows:

$$\cfrac{\cfrac{\cfrac{\{s, \bar{p}_0, \ldots, \bar{p}_n, v\} \vdash \bot}{\{s, \bar{p}_0, \ldots, \bar{p}_n\} \vdash v \Rightarrow \bot} \Rightarrow I}{\{s, \bar{p}_0, \ldots, \bar{p}_n\} \vdash \bar{v}} \neg I \qquad \{t, \bar{q}_0, \ldots, \bar{q}_m, \bar{v}\} \vdash \bot}{\{s, t, \bar{p}_0, \ldots, \bar{p}_n, \bar{q}_0, \ldots, \bar{q}_m\} \vdash \bot} \text{CUT}$$

We package this derivation into a single rule written as a function $\mathsf{RES}(s, t)$, where s and t are understood to be in theorem form, and the output is also a theorem. We assume only one variable occurs with opposite signs in the argument clauses, so there is no need to supply the pivot. This way, RES can be generalised to chains, i.e, $\mathsf{RES}(C_0, \ldots, C_n) = R_n$ for derivation 1 of §2.1, where the C_i are again understood to be theorems. The final resolvent theorem, and indeed any theorem intended to represent a clause, is called a *clause theorem*.

The clause theorem for the resolvent can be used as an input into another RES and the process continued until the hypotheses contain only terms corresponding to full clauses and no literals. At this point, we have derived the required refutation. To avoid clutter, we shall use the $\square$ symbol to represent all those hypotheses of a clause theorem that represent clauses. The choice of notation is deliberate, representing a "hole" rather than an identifier bound to specific terms. The hole collects all the initial clauses of the problem that participate in the refutation.

If hypotheses sets are implemented as such (e.g., they are implemented as red-black sets in HOL4), computing a single resolution inference requires two set deletions and one set union. In HOL4, hypothesis set deletions and insertions are logarithmic in the number of hypotheses, whereas unions are linearithmic[2].

3.2   Using Memoised Pieces of Chains

The memoisation algorithm (§4) generates a new, memoised proof from the SAT solver proof. It detects shared parts of the proof and writes them out before their first use, and later in the proof at the point of use inserts pointers to the shared part. We now show how this sharing is used in the theorem prover.

Let a *semi-chain* be a strictly alternating sequence of pivots and clauses, starting with a pivot and ending with a clause. Semi-chains are written using the same linear form as chains. The length or size of a semi-chain is the number of pivots in it. Given a chain $c \equiv C_0(p_1)C_1(p_2)C_2 \ldots (p_n)C_n$, a semi-chain $(p_i)C_i \ldots (p_j)C_j$ is denoted by $c[i..j]$ for $i > 0$, analogous to substring notation. We allow semi-chain notation in RES, i.e.,

$$\mathsf{RES}(C_0, C_1, C_2, \ldots, C_n)$$
$$=\mathsf{RES}(C_0, c[1..n])$$
$$=\mathsf{RES}(C_0, \ldots, C_{i-1}, c[i..j], C_{j+1}, \ldots, C_n)$$

Further, we use $\mathsf{RES}(c)$ for $\mathsf{RES}(C_0, c[1..n])$, and let c^i for $i > 0$ be the ith pivot in a (semi-)chain c.

We plan to use our memoisation algorithm (§4) to identify semi-chains common to more than one chain in the proof. Suppose the algorithm has found a semi-chain s with m pivots, such that $s = c_1[i..i + m]$ and $s = c_2[i'..i' + m]$ for chains c_1 and c_2, where c_1 is the same as the chain c in §2.1.

---

[2] $O(n\log(n))$

The aim is compute the resolutions in s only once. The immediate problem is that the semi-chain has no first clause with which to begin computing its resolutions. To get around this, we construct the first clause for s as follows:

$$\frac{\overline{\{s^1 \Rightarrow \ldots \Rightarrow s^m \Rightarrow \bot\} \vdash s^1 \Rightarrow \ldots \Rightarrow s^m \Rightarrow \bot}}{\{s^1 \Rightarrow \ldots \Rightarrow s^m \Rightarrow \bot, s^1, \ldots, s^m\} \vdash \bot} \text{ ASSUME} \atop \vdots \Rightarrow E \qquad (2)$$

We shall call such a clause the *starter clause* for a semi-chain, and denote it by $\hat{s}$. The reader can confirm that

$$\text{RES}(\hat{s}, s) = \{\Box, s^1 \Rightarrow \ldots \Rightarrow s^m \Rightarrow \bot, \bar{q}_0, \ldots, \bar{q}_k\} \vdash \bot$$

where the q_i are the non-pivot literals occuring in the clauses of s.

We can now see why semi-chains do not begin with a clause: if they did, the pivot to be removed from that clause would vary from one use of the semi-chain to another, making it impossible to cache $\text{RES}(\hat{s}, s)$.

Now, we wish to derive $\text{RES}(c_1)$ without computing $\text{RES}(C_{i-1}, c[i..i+n])$. The first step is

$$\frac{\begin{array}{c} \text{RES}(C_0, c_1[1..i-1]) \\ \vdots \Rightarrow I \\ \{\Box, \bar{q}_0, \ldots, \bar{q}_k\} \vdash s^1 \Rightarrow \ldots \Rightarrow s^m \Rightarrow \bot \quad \text{RES}(\hat{s}, s) \end{array}}{\{\Box, \bar{q}_0, \ldots, \bar{q}_{k'}\} \vdash \bot} \text{ CUT} \qquad (3)$$

where the q_i are again the non-pivot literals of the clauses of c_1, up to that point in the derivation. Then,

$$\text{RES}(c_1) = \text{RES}(\{\Box, \bar{q}_0, \ldots, \bar{q}_{k'}\} \vdash \bot, c_1[i+m+1..n])$$

This derivation works because $\Rightarrow I$ does not require that the antecedent being introduced should occur in the hypotheses of the theorem; if it does, it is deleted from the hypotheses as an additional step. This is easily generalised for multiple non-overlapping semi-chains in the same chain. Overlaps will be discussed in §3.3. $\text{RES}(c_2)$ is computed in a similar manner.

For every memoised semi-chain there is a one-time cost of the construction of the starter clause, which is m set insertions (one for each $\Rightarrow E$). For every use of a memoised semi-chain, we need one CUT and m number of $\Rightarrow I$, giving one set union and $m+1$ set deletions. However, since even a non-deductive use of the semi-chain would require one set union and one set deletion, our true net overhead is only m set deletions per use of a semi-chain. Even if only two chains share this semi-chain, we have still saved m set unions, and set union is a far more expensive operation than insertion or deletion.

3.3   Merging Overlapping Semi-chains

When a common semi-chain s is discovered, it is written out to the proof before the chains which will use it. The chains that use s have the s part of themselves replaced by a semi-chain of size one, consisting of the first pivot of s and a clause ID that points to $\mathsf{RES}(\hat{s}, s)$ in the clause database.

This can create unsoundness when semi-chains overlap, because pivots (that fall in the overlap of two semi-chains) that have been removed using one semi-chain are re-introduced using the next one, so that the clause theorem of the underlying chain changes from what the SAT solver intended. It is too limiting to forbid our semi-chain matching algorithm from detecting more than one match per chain. Instead, we can *merge* the clause theorems of overlapping semi-chains, to obtain a clause theorem that is usable without compromising soundness.

We show how to merge two overlapping semi-chains; it is easy to extend the method to more than two. We assume that the semi-chains do overlap and that neither is contained entirely within the other. The memoisation algorithm will guarantee this.

Suppose in a chain c we have we have two overlapping semi-chains $s_1 = c[i_1..j_1]$ and $s_2 = c[i_2..j_2]$, where $i_1 < i_2$. The merged semi-chain, s_3, is then $c[i_1..j_2]$. We first compute the list of pivots of s_3, $[c^{i_1}, \ldots, c^{j_2}]$. The next step is to construct the starter clause $\hat{s}_3$. This is done exactly as in derivation 2 of §3.2, except that we now use the list we just computed. Once that is done, we have,

$$
\begin{array}{c}
\hat{s}_3 \\
\vdots \;\Rightarrow I \\
\cfrac{\{\square, \bar{q}_0, \ldots, \bar{q}_k\} \vdash c^{i_1} \Rightarrow \ldots \Rightarrow c^{j_1} \Rightarrow \bot \quad \mathsf{RES}(\hat{s}_1, s_1)}{\{\square, \bar{q}_0, \ldots, \bar{q}_{k'}, c^{i_1} \Rightarrow \ldots \Rightarrow c^{j_2} \Rightarrow \bot\} \vdash \bot} \;\text{CUT} \\
\vdots \;\Rightarrow I \\
\cfrac{\{\square, \bar{q}_0, \ldots, \bar{q}_{k''}\} \vdash c^{i_2} \Rightarrow \ldots \Rightarrow c^{j_2} \Rightarrow \bot \qquad\qquad \mathsf{RES}(\hat{s}_2, s_2)}{\{\square, \bar{q}_0, \ldots, \bar{q}_{k'''}, c^{i_1} \Rightarrow \ldots \Rightarrow c^{j_2} \Rightarrow \bot\} \vdash \bot} \;\text{CUT}
\end{array}
$$

$$(4)$$

where the q_i play the same role as before, and $\mathsf{RES}(\hat{s}_1, s_1)$ and $\mathsf{RES}(\hat{s}_2, s_2)$ have already been computed using derivation 3 of §3.2. Then we can set

$$
\mathsf{RES}(\hat{s}_3, s_3) = \{\square, \bar{q}_0, \ldots, \bar{q}_{k'''}, c^{i_1} \Rightarrow \ldots \Rightarrow c^{j_2} \Rightarrow \bot\} \vdash \bot
$$

It is tedious but not hard to show that this clause theorem is precisely the clause theorem that would be generated from scratch (i.e., by performing all the resolutions) for the semi-chain s_3. $\mathsf{RES}(c)$ can now be computed as in derivation 3 of §3.2, using $\mathsf{RES}(\hat{s}_3, s_3)$.

However, a merge comes at a cost. There is the cost for $\hat{s}_3$, plus two CUT rules and $(j_1 - i_1) + (j_2 - i_2)$ applications of $\Rightarrow I$ (in the case of only two overlapping semi-chains). There is nothing against which to offset this cost, since merging does not save us anything: we are only doing it to preserve soundness. Worse, the computation of $\mathsf{RES}(\hat{s}_1, s_1)$ and $\mathsf{RES}(\hat{s}_2, s_2)$ computes the overlapping resolutions twice. However, we can add some tradeoff analysis to the memoisation algorithm to ensure we never lose time overall (see §4.1). We cannot, of course, discard s_1 and s_2 in favour of s_3, since they are separately used elsewhere.

4   Proof Memoisation

We now turn to the generation of the memoised proof itself. The input is the SAT solver generated proof (from which unused chains have already been filtered out). The output is a memoised proof that factors out shared semi-chains and additionally indicates when merging is required.

Since SAT solver proofs can have millions of inferences, we need an efficient way of detecting shared semi-chains. The algorithm proceeds in two stages. In the *read* stage, we make a pass though the proof, adding chains to a GST and collecting information about matches. In the *write* stage, we write out the memoised proof, ensuring that all semi-chains are written out before their point of first use.

4.1   Read Stage: Detecting Shared Semi-chains

Let V be the set of literals (hence potential pivots) and C be the set of clause IDs. Then our alphabet A is $V + C$, the $+$ here indicating disjoint union. Every semi-chain is a string, but not all strings are semi-chains. A *sub-semi-chain* of a semi-chain is any substring of the semi-chain that begins at an even numbered index (string indexes begin at zero) and is of even length.

In the read stage, our strategy will be to drop the first clause from each chain we encounter, and add the resulting semi-chain to our GST, as a string. Then, when reading in later chains, we shall match in the GST the longest sub-semi-chain(s) of the chain being read. Since not all strings (and hence not all substrings) are semi-chains, we will need to modify the GST matching algorithm to return only valid semi-chains. We could let (literal,clause ID) pairs be the alphabet, but then $A = V \times C$ and the constant factors in the complexity results would become very high.

The modification is easily done by filtering matching substrings. When the GST returns a match, it is possible to check in constant time that the starting index of the match is even numbered in both matching chains, and that the length of the match is even. If so, it is a valid semi-chain.

Detecting a match. In §2.3 we noted the longest common substring is the path label of the deepest node below which all leaves are marked only with the IDs of the strings we are interested in. This requires the use of sophisticated lowest common ancestor algorithms. Fortunately, we are interested in finding a match with any string, to only the string currently being added. So we can limit ourselves to leaves marked with the ID of the current string. But we can do better.

Once a variable has been assigned during a SAT solver's search, it is not assigned again unless there is a conflict and the variable becomes unassigned during backtracking. What this means for us is that a pivot never occurs twice in a (semi-)chain. This means that the GST algorithm, when adding the current string, will never revisit a node that was created earlier during the addition of the same string [15]. Nodes (or leaf edges from a node) are created whenever we are unable to find a way to extend a suffix of a prefix of the current string without explicitly adding the next character in that suffix to the current path in the tree that we have followed from the root node. This means that the suffix up to but not including the next character is a substring of an earlier chain, as well as a substring of the chain being added.

So, thanks to our knowledge of the structure of the strings, we can detect matches on the fly as we add the current string. The parent edge of any node just created was labelled with the ID of the string (or equivalently, the clause ID of the chain) during the addition of which that edge was created. This string/chain is called the *owner* of the match, and we are guaranteed not only that it contains the matched semi-chain, but also that it is the very first string that contains the matched semi-chain, since edges' string ID labels are assigned only when the edge is created.

Choosing the best match. Adding a string can return multiple overlapping matches. We have considered three different schemes for retaining these matches:

1. Retain only the longest size match.
2. Retain all matches.
3. Greedily retain maximal non-overlapping matches.

Since each retained match is converted into a memoised semi-chain in the output proof, the retention scheme affects how much merging will be required. Scheme 1 minimises merging (merging can still occur, in the owning chain), but may miss many opportunities for sharing work. Scheme 2 does not miss anything, but maximises merging. Scheme 3 attempts to find a middle of the road solution, and in experiments so far it appears to be superior.

It is too expensive to find the optimal maximal non-overlapping matches. Matches are always reported in increasing order of starting index (recall the GST algorithm considers prefixes of increasing size), so Scheme 3 adopts a greedy approach as follows, where set R is the set of reported matches that will be returned by the GST, and s is the string being added:

1. $R \leftarrow \emptyset, M \leftarrow \emptyset, max_j \leftarrow -1$
2. $s[i..j] \leftarrow next\_match$
3. **if** $i > max_j$ **then** $R \leftarrow R \cup \{\text{max\_substring}(M)\}, M \leftarrow \{s[i..j]\}$
   else $M \leftarrow M \cup \{s[i..j]\}, max_j \leftarrow \max(j, max_j)$
4. **if** $last\_match$ **then** $R \leftarrow R \cup \{\text{max\_substring}(M)\}$
   else goto 2

For each match that is reported, pointers to information about the match are recorded keyed on both the current and the owning string, for use during the write stage. These are literally pointers, so there is no wasted memory.

Tradeoff analysis. We do not report matches of length two, since these correspond to semi-chains of length one. In that case, the overhead for using the semi-chain outweighs the savings. The situation is slightly more complicated for semi-chains of length two. Here, if we have only a single match, we save two set unions and two set insertions, but use up two set unions and four set insertions and deletions in using the semi-chains, so again there is a net loss. However, if a semi-chain of length two matches in more than two chains, then we make a net profit in terms of set unions saved. For semi-chains of length three or more, we always profit (ignoring merges for the moment).

Therefore, for each semi-chain, we keep a count of how many times it has matched. This information is used in the write stage to decide which matches to retain, because by then we know how many times every semi-chain matched. The semi-chain match count information is recorded in a map whose key is a 64 bit unsigned integer constructed as follows:

1. The first 32 bits give the owner string's ID
2. The next 16 bits give the starting index in the owner
3. The next 16 bits give the ending index in the owner

This hash is perfect because a distinct matched semi-chain will always be owned by the string of the very first chain to contain that semi-chain. 32 bits for the clause ID is sufficient. 16 bits for the indices is not as safe, though we have yet to come across any proofs where a conflict clause derivation contained more than 2^{16} pivots. This may be because we have not attempted any large problems as yet.

4.2 Write Stage: Merging and Splitting

Once the read stage is over, we have for each chain information on all its matches, including those for which it is the owner. We now make another pass through the chains, writing out semi-chains s_i, merging information, and the chains themselves. For a chain c, we give a abstract view of the write stage (details follow):

foreach $s_i \in$ owned_by(c)

   record s_i

sort matched_in(c) **by** *starting_index*

foreach $S \subseteq$ matched_in(c)

   if overlap($s_i \in S$) **then** **record** merge(S)

record c

An example will make this more concrete.

Example. Suppose c matched semi-chains $s_1 \equiv c[i_1..j_1]$, $s_2 \equiv c[i_2..j_2]$ and $s_3 \equiv c[i_3..j_3]$, of which it owns all but s_1. Suppose further that s_1 and s_2 overlap in c. Then the proof output for c would be as follows (where we elide all clauses except the first clause C_0 of c and let c[i] $\equiv c^i$).

```
id2: S c[i_2] ... c[j_2]
id3: S c[i_3] ... c[j_3]
id4: M id1 c[i_1] c[j_1] id2 c[i_2] c[j_2]
id5: C C_0 c[1] ... c[i_1] id4 ... c[i_3] id3 ...
```

The idn denote clause IDs, which are added here for readability but are implicitly assigned by order of appearance in the actual proof. id1 is the ID of s_1, which was recorded earlier since c does not own it. An S indicates a semi-chain, recorded as a sequence of alternating pivot and clause IDs. An M indicates merging information, recorded as a list of (id,start index,end index) triples, in increasing order of start index, which is sufficient information for the methods of §3 to compute the required clause theorems. Finally, a C indicates the chain itself, with references to the clause IDs of semi-chains or merged semi-chains as required.   □

The only point of interest when writing semi-chains is that if a semi-chain is contained entirely within another (in which case c owns both), we write out both semi-chains separately since they may be required elsewhere, but ignore the contained semi-chain completely when writing out the C line.

Detecting merges. We need to check if semi-chains overlap each other, and in what order. There may be more than one M line if there was more than one disconnected set of overlapping semi-chains.

At this point it will be helpful to abstract the semi-chains $c[i..j]$ to closed intervals $[i, j]$ on the natural number line. The first step is to sort the intervals by start index. This can be done in any standard way. We use a heap H, the top most interval having the smallest start index.

The next step is to partition this interval set into *merge sets* such that an interval in one merge set overlaps with at most two intervals in the same set but has at least one pivot not overlapped by any interval, no interval is entirely contained in another, and no interval overlaps with an interval in another merge set. The intuition is that each merge set corresponds to a single M line. Merge sets keep their intervals sorted by start index. The merge sets are created as follows, where L is the final list of merge sets (@ is list append):

1. $L \leftarrow [\emptyset]$
2. **if** empty(H) **then** **return** L **else** $[i, j] \leftarrow$ pop(H)
3. **if** $j - i = 1 \wedge$ times_matched($c[i..j]$) $= 1$ **then** **goto** 2
4. $[i', j'] \leftarrow$ last(last(L))
5. **if** $j' \geq i$

   if $j \leq j' \vee i' \geq i$ **then** last(L) $\leftarrow$ last(L) $\cup \{[\min(i, i'), \max(j, j')]\}$

   else last(L) $\leftarrow$ last(L) $\cup \{[i, j]\}$

   else $L \leftarrow L@\{[i, j]\}$
6. **goto** 2

Note we take care to filter out intervals contained entirely within others. This procedure is linear in the number of intervals.

Splitting merged semi-chains. At this point we are ready to write out the merge information, each merge set in L contributing one M line. However, recall that we wish to avoid doing merges if possible, due to the overhead. Also, if two semi-chains overlap, then the resolutions in the overlapping part are computed twice, once for each semi-chain. We can sometimes avoid this situation by splitting two overlapping semi-chains into three semi-chains, corresponding to the non-overlapping part of the first semi-chain, the overlapping part, and the non-overlapping part of the second semi-chain. The three new semi-chains do not require merging, since they do not overlap, and the overlapped part is now computed only once.

Since semi-chains matched in c but not owned by c, have already been written out, a split can only happen if both the involved semi-chains are owned by c. We could get around this by making a third pass over the proof, which knows in advance what splits are required, but the gains from this are uncertain.

Even when we can split an overlap, it does not always pay to do so. The resulting semi-chains could be of length two, so that using them may result in a net increase in computational effort, as noted towards the end of §4.1. Further, if there is a choice between which overlap to split, we need to be careful since that split could affect whether or not we split any remaining overlaps.

Therefore, for each merge set, we sort overlaps by size, and begin by splitting the biggest one, for maximum savings. We avoid splitting overlaps where the resulting middle semi-chain would be of size two or less. The splitting information does not have to be recorded in the proof: all we get is a few more S lines and few less M lines. This optimisation made a marked difference in practice.

5   Experimental Results

Since the shortening of resolution proofs is believed to be an intractable problem [1], the algorithm is of heuristic value only, and requires benchmarking for performance evaluation. The memoisation algorithm itself is easily seen to be linear in the length of the proof: the read stage adds chains and detects matches in time linear in the length of the chain, and the write stage takes worst case linear time to analyse merging information (the sorting in §4.2 is an abstraction only, as the GST reports matched intervals ordered by starting index).

We tried out our algorithm on a few problems from the SATLIB benchmarks library for SAT solvers. We used the ZChaff SAT solver [10] to generate the proofs, which were then memoised using a C++ implementation, and then reconstructed in HOL4. The results are summarised in Table 1. The columns are, respectively: problem name, number of variables, number of clauses, SAT solver time, proof replay time, compression time, compressed proof replay time, number of resolutions, number of resolutions in compressed proof, net speed up. The benchmark machine was an Intel P4 3GHz CPU with 4GB of RAM.

The program crashed when reconstructing the memoised proof for ip50. The crash was not in our code but in the Moscow ML runtime engine on top of which HOL4 runs. We are investigating this.

As hoped, the proof replay times in the theorem prover do improve when using the memoising algorithm. The payoff column measures the reduction in

Table 1. Times in seconds. Resolutions in inference steps. Pay off in % time.

Problem	Vars	Clauses	ZChaff	HOL4	Memo	HOL4+M	Res	Res+M	Pay off
c7552.miter	11282	69529	78	104	3	76	242509	225439	24%
ip36	47273	153368	218	1706	22	1219	1141756	1022449	27%
ip38	49967	162142	237	1831	23	1222	1109932	996248	32%
ip50	66131	214786	1077	9034	118	-	3957973	3568362	-
6pipe	15800	394739	200	396	7	286	310813	267972	26%
6pipe.ooo	17064	545612	384	1093	15	735	782903	694019	31%
7pipe	23910	751118	584	1010	19	793	497019	437060	20%

total time and is always positive. We note here that directly verifying the proof in C++ is much faster. However, our aim here is not to debug SAT solvers, but to use them as untrusted oracles for fully expansive theorem provers.

As expected, the number of resolution steps is also lower in the memoised proof. This does not tell the full story since the memoised proof contains inferences other than RES inferences. Rather than counting all the different kinds of inferences, we normalised the computational cost in terms of set unions, deletions and insertions. The memoised proofs have more primitive inferences, but after factoring out the inferences due to simulating RES, we observed that the remaining inferences are mostly set deletions/insertions due to starter clause construction and merging. These operations are cheaper than set unions, so we conclude that the time savings come from the reduction in the number of costly set unions that occur in applications of the RES rule.

6   Conclusion

Other than the already cited work [2,16] we are not aware of any work on integration of DPLL based SAT solvers with interactive theorem provers. Harrison integrated a SAT solver based on Stålmarck's method into HOL90 [6], and the theorem provers PVS, Coq and HOL Light have been integrated with SMT solvers at various times. Certainly, we are not aware of any work on memoisation of SAT solver generated proofs. The closest work we could find is on merging chains using extended resolution, but both the method and the aim of that work are completely different from our own [14].

More interesting is to normalise chains by reordering the pivots, to increase the number of string matches. This will either require explicit knowledge of pivot occurrences in the chain clauses, or an implicit idea of which pivots' resolutions must precede the others. The former would require effectively doing all the resolutions, an expensive proposition. The latter would require analysing the implication graph of the SAT solver when a conflict occurs. Not only would this sacrifice tool independence, it would also be hard to do efficiently since we do not know a priori which conflicts are used in the final proof.

References

1. Alekhnovich, M., Razborov, A.A.: Resolution is not automatizable unless W[P] is tractable. In: FOCS, pp. 210–219. IEEE Computer Society Press, Los Alamitos (2001)
2. Fontaine, P., Marion, J.-Y., Merz, S., Nieto, L.P., Tiu, A.F.: Expressiveness + automation + soundness: Towards combining SMT solvers and interactive proof assistants. In: Hermanns, H., Palsberg, J. (eds.) TACAS 2006 and ETAPS 2006. LNCS, vol. 3920, pp. 167–181. Springer, Heidelberg (2006)
3. Gordon, M.J.C., Melham, T.F.: Introduction to HOL: A theorem-proving environment for higher order logic. Cambridge University Press, Cambridge (1993)
4. Harrison, J.: Metatheory and reflection in theorem proving: A survey and critique. Technical Report CRC-053, SRI International (1995)
5. Harrison, J.: HOL Light: A tutorial introduction. In: Srivas, M., Camilleri, A. (eds.) FMCAD 1996. LNCS, vol. 1166, pp. 265–269. Springer, Heidelberg (1996)
6. Harrison, J.: Stålmarck's algorithm as a HOL derived rule. In: von Wright, J., Grundy, J., Harrison, J. (eds.) TPHOLs 1996. LNCS, vol. 1125, pp. 221–234. Springer, Heidelberg (1996)
7. Huet, G., Kahn, G., Paulin-Mohring, C.: The Coq proof assistant: A tutorial: Version 7.2. Technical Report RT-0256, INRIA (February 2002)
8. Mitchell, D.G.: A SAT solver primer. In: EATCS Bulletin (The Logic in Computer Science Column), vol. 85, pp. 112–133 (February 2005)
9. Morrison, D.R.: PATRICIA-Practical Algorithm To Retrieve Information Code. In Alphanumeric. J. ACM 15(4), 514–534 (1968)
10. Moskewicz, M.W., Madigan, C.F., Zhao, Y., Zhang, L., Malik, S.: Chaff: Engineering an efficient SAT solver. In: Proceedings of the 38th Design Automation Conference, pp. 530–535. ACM Press, New York (2001)
11. Owre, S., Rushby, J.M., Shankar, N.: PVS: A prototype verification system. In: Kapur, D. (ed.) CADE 1992. LNCS, vol. 607, pp. 748–752. Springer, Heidelberg (1992)
12. Paulson, L.C.: A Generic Theorem Prover. In: Paulson, L.C. (ed.) Isabelle. LNCS, vol. 828, Springer, Heidelberg (1994)
13. Shankar, N.: Using decision procedures with a higher-order logic. In: Boulton, R.J., Jackson, P.B. (eds.) TPHOLs 2001. LNCS, vol. 2152, pp. 5–26. Springer, Heidelberg (2001)
14. Sinz, C.: Compressing propositional proofs by common subproof extraction. In: Pichler, F. (ed.) Euro Conference on Computer Aided Systems Theory (2007)
15. Ukkonen, E.: Online construction of suffix trees. Algorithmica 14(3), 249–260 (1995)
16. Weber, T., Amjad, H.: Efficiently checking propositional refutations in HOL theorem provers.JAL (special issue on Empirically Successful Computerized Reasoning) (to appear, 2007)

Combining Algorithms for Deciding Knowledge in Security Protocols[*]

Mathilde Arnaud[1], Véronique Cortier[2], and Stéphanie Delaune[2]

[1] École Normale Supérieure de Cachan, Computer Science department, France
[2] LORIA, CNRS & INRIA project Cassis, Nancy, France

Abstract. In formal approaches, messages sent over a network are usually modeled by terms together with an equational theory, axiomatizing the properties of the cryptographic functions (encryption, exclusive or, ...). The analysis of cryptographic protocols requires a precise understanding of the attacker knowledge. Two standard notions are usually considered: deducibility and indistinguishability. Those notions are well-studied and several decidability results already exist to deal with a variety of equational theories. However most of the results are dedicated to specific equational theories.

We show that decidability results can be easily combined for any disjoint equational theories: if the deducibility and indistinguishability relations are decidable for two disjoint theories, they are also decidable for their union. As an application, new decidability results can be obtained using this combination theorem.

1 Introduction

Security protocols are paramount in today's secure transactions through public channels. It is therefore essential to obtain as much confidence as possible in their correctness. Formal methods have proved their usefulness for precisely analyzing the security of protocols. Understanding security protocols often requires reasoning about knowledge of the attacker. In formal approaches, two main definitions have been proposed in the literature to express knowledge. They are known as message deducibility and indistinguishability relations.

Most often, the knowledge of the attacker is described in terms of message deducibility [17,19,18]. Given some set of messages ϕ representing the knowledge of the attacker and another message M, intuitively the secret, one can ask whether an attacker is able to compute M from ϕ. To obtain such a message he uses his deduction capabilities. For instance, he may encrypt and decrypt using keys that he knows.

This concept of deducibility does not always suffice for expressing the knowledge of an attacker. For example, if we consider a protocol that transmits an encrypted Boolean value (e.g. the value of a vote), we may ask whether an attacker can learn this value by eavesdropping on the protocol. Of course, it is

---

[*] This work has been partly supported by the RNTL project POSÉ and the ACI Jeunes Chercheurs JC9005.

B. Konev and F. Wolter (Eds.): FroCos 2007, LNAI 4720, pp. 103–117, 2007.
© Springer-Verlag Berlin Heidelberg 2007

completely unrealistic to require that the Boolean true and false are not deducible. We need to express the fact that the two transcripts of the protocol, one running with the Boolean value true and the other one with false are *indistinguishable*. Besides allowing more careful formalization of secrecy properties, indistinguishability can also be used for proving the more involved notion of cryptographic indistinguishability [6,1,16]: two sequences of messages are cryptographically indistinguishable if their distributions are indistinguishable to any attacker, that is to any probabilistic polynomial Turing machine.

In both cases, deduction and indistinguishability apply to observations on messages at a particular point in time. They do not take into account the dynamic behavior of the protocol. For this reason the indistinguishability relation is called *static equivalence*. Nevertheless those relations are quite useful to reason about the dynamic behavior of a protocol. For instance, the deducibility relation is often used as a subroutine of many decision procedures [20,7,11]. In the applied-pi calculus framework [3], it has been shown that observational equivalence (relation which takes into account the dynamic behavior) coincides with labeled bisimulation which corresponds to checking static equivalences and some standard bisimulation conditions.

Both of these relations rely on an underlying equational theory axiomatizing the properties of the cryptographic functions (encryption, exclusive or, ...). Many decision procedures have been provided to decide these relations under a variety of equational theories. For instance algorithms for deduction have been provided for exclusive or [11], homomorphic operators [13], Abelian groups with distributive encryption [15] and subterm theories [2]. These theories allow basic equations for functions such as encryption, decryption and digital signature. There are also some results on static equivalence. For instance, a general decidability result to handle the class of subterm convergent equational theories is given in [2]. Also in [2], some abstract conditions on the underlying equational theory are proposed to ensure decidability of deduction and static equivalence. Note that the use of this result requires checking some assumptions, which might be difficult to prove. This result has been applied to several interesting equational theories such as exclusive or, blind signature and other associative and commutative functions.

For all the previous results, decidability is provided for particular fixed theories or for particular classes of theories. In this paper, we provide a general combination result for both deduction and static equivalence: if the deducibility and indistinguishability relations are decidable for two disjoint theories E_1 and E_2 (that is, the equations of E_1 and E_2 do not share any symbol), they are also decidable for their union $E_1 \cup E_2$. Our algorithm for combining theories is polynomial (in the DAG-size of the inputs). It ensures in particular that if the deducibility and indistinguishability relations are decidable for two disjoint theories in polynomial time, they are decidable in polynomial time for their union.

The interest of our result is twofold: first, it allows us to obtain new decidability results from any combination of the existing ones: for example, we obtain that static equivalence is decidable for the theory of encryption combined with exclusive or (and also for example with blind signature), which was not known before. Second, our result allows a modular approach. Deciding interesting equational theories that could not be considered before can be done simply by reducing to the decision of simpler and independent theories.

Our combination result relies on combination algorithms for solving unification problem modulo an equational theory [21,5]. It follows the approach of Chevalier and Rusinowitch [8], who show how to combine decision algorithms for the deducibility problem in the presence of an active attacker. However, they do not consider static equivalence at all, which is needed to express larger classes of security properties. Moreover, even for deduction, they do not state any combination result in the passive case, though this result might be obtained by adapting their proof. Considering static equivalence notoriously involves more difficulties since static equivalence is defined through overall quantification. In particular, proving static equivalence requires a careful understanding of the (infinite) set of equalities satisfied by a sequence of terms.

Outline of the paper. In Section 2 we introduce notation and definitions as well as the two notions of knowledge. Section 3 provides some material for our combination algorithms. Then Sections 4 and 5 are devoted to the study of deduction and static equivalence respectively. In Section 6, we sum up our results and provide new results obtained as a consequence of our main theorems. Due to lack of space, some proofs are omitted. They can be found in [4].

2   Preliminaries

2.1   Basic Definitions

A *signature* Σ consists of a finite set of function symbols, such as enc and pair, each with an arity. A function symbol with arity 0 is a constant symbol. Given a signature Σ, an infinite set of names $\mathcal{N}$, and an infinite set of variables $\mathcal{X}$, we denote by $\mathcal{T}(\Sigma)$ (resp. $\mathcal{T}(\Sigma, \mathcal{X})$) the set of *terms* over $\Sigma \cup \mathcal{N}$ (resp. $\Sigma \cup \mathcal{N} \cup \mathcal{X}$). The former is called the set of ground terms over Σ, while the latter is simply called the set of terms over Σ. The concept of names is borrowed from the applied pi calculus [3] and corresponds to the notion of free constant used for instance in [8]. We write $fn(M)$ (resp. $fv(M)$) for the set of names (resp. variables) that occur in the term M. A context C is a term with holes, or (more formally) a linear term. When C is a context with n distinguished variables $x_1, \ldots, x_n$, we may write $C[x_1, \ldots, x_n]$ instead of C in order to show the variables, and when $T_1, \ldots, T_n$ are terms we may also write $C[T_1, \ldots, T_n]$ for the result of replacing each variable x_i with the corresponding term T_i. A *substitution* σ is a mapping from a finite subset of $\mathcal{X}$ called its domain and written $dom(\sigma)$ to $\mathcal{T}(\Sigma, \mathcal{X})$. Substitutions are extended to endomorphisms of $\mathcal{T}(\Sigma, \mathcal{X})$ as usual. We use a postfix notation for their application.

An *equational presentation* $\mathcal{H} = (\Sigma, \mathsf{E})$ is defined by a set E of equations $u = v$ with $u, v \in \mathcal{T}(\Sigma, \mathcal{X})$ and u, v without names. For any equational presentation $\mathcal{H}$, the relation $=_{\mathcal{H}}$ denotes the equational theory generated by (Σ, E) on $\mathcal{T}(\Sigma, \mathcal{X})$, that is the smallest congruence containing all instances of axioms of E. Abusively, we shall not distinghuish between an equational presentation $\mathcal{H}$ over a signature Σ and a set E of equations presenting it. Hence, we write $M =_E N$ instead of $M =_{\mathcal{H}} N$ when the signature is clear from the context. A theory E is *consistent* if there do not exist two distinct names n_1 and n_2 such that $n_1 =_E n_2$. Note that, in an inconsistent theory, the problem we are interested in, *i.e.* deduction (defined in Section 2.3) and static equivalence (defined in Section 2.4) are trivial.

Example 1. Let Σ_{xor} be the signature made up of the constant symbol 0 and the binary function $\oplus$ and E_{xor} be the following set of equations:

$$x \oplus (y \oplus z) = (x \oplus y) \oplus z \quad x \oplus 0 = x$$
$$x \oplus y = y \oplus x \quad x \oplus x = 0$$

We have that $n_1 \oplus (n_2 \oplus n_1) =_{E_{xor}} n_2$.

Definition 1 (syntactic subterm). *The set $St_s(M)$ of* syntactic subterms *of a term M is defined recursively as follows:*

$$St_s(M) = \begin{cases} \{M\} & \text{if } M \text{ is a variable, a name or a constant} \\ \{M\} \cup \bigcup_{i=1}^{\ell} St_s(M_i) & \text{if } M = f(M_1, \ldots, M_\ell) \end{cases}$$

The positions in a term M are defined recursively as usual (*i.e.* sequences of integers with ϵ being the empty sequence). We denote by $M|_p$ the syntactic subterm of M at position p. The term obtained by replacing $M|_p$ by N is denoted $M[N]_p$.

2.2   Assembling Terms into Frames

At a particular point in time, while engaging in one or more sessions of one or more protocols, an attacker may know a sequence of messages $M_1, \ldots, M_\ell$. This means that he knows each message but he also knows in which order he obtained the messages. So it is not enough for us to say that the attacker knows the set of terms $\{M_1, \ldots, M_\ell\}$. Furthermore, we should distinguish those names that the attacker knows from those that were freshly generated by others and which remain secret from the attacker; both kinds of names may appear in the terms.

In the applied pi calculus [3], such a sequence of messages is organized into a *frame* $\phi = \nu\tilde{n}.\sigma$, where $\tilde{n}$ is a finite set of *restricted* names (intuitively the fresh ones), and σ is a substitution of the form:

$$\{{}^{M_1}/_{x_1}, \ldots, {}^{M_\ell}/_{x_\ell}\} \quad \text{with} \quad dom(\sigma) = \{x_1, \ldots, x_\ell\}.$$

The variables enable us to refer to each M_i and we always assume that the terms M_i are ground. The names $\tilde{n}$ are bound and can be renamed. Moreover names that do not appear in ϕ can be added or removed from $\tilde{n}$. In particular, we can always assume that two frames share the same set of restricted names.

2.3   Deduction

Given a frame ϕ that represents the information available to an attacker, we may ask whether a given ground term M may be deduced from ϕ. Given an equational theory E on Σ, this relation is written $\phi \vdash_{\mathsf{E}} M$ and is axiomatized by the following rules:

$$\frac{}{\nu\tilde{n}.\sigma \vdash_{\mathsf{E}} M} \text{ if } \exists x \in dom(\sigma) \text{ s.t. } x\sigma = M \qquad \frac{}{\nu\tilde{n}.\sigma \vdash_{\mathsf{E}} s} \; s \in \mathcal{N} \smallsetminus \tilde{n}$$

$$\frac{\phi \vdash_{\mathsf{E}} M_1 \;\; \ldots \;\; \phi \vdash_{\mathsf{E}} M_\ell}{\phi \vdash_{\mathsf{E}} f(M_1,\ldots,M_\ell)} \; f \in \Sigma \qquad \frac{\phi \vdash_{\mathsf{E}} M}{\phi \vdash_{\mathsf{E}} M'} \; M =_{\mathsf{E}} M'$$

Intuitively, the deducible messages are the messages of ϕ and the names that are not protected in ϕ, closed by equality in E and closed by application of function symbols. Note that ϕ and M might be built on a signature Σ' that possibly contains some additional function symbol not in Σ. When $\nu\tilde{n}.\sigma \vdash_{\mathsf{E}} M$, any occurrence of names from $\tilde{n}$ in M is bound by $\nu\tilde{n}$. So $\nu\tilde{n}.\sigma \vdash_{\mathsf{E}} M$ could be formally written $\nu\tilde{n}.(\sigma \vdash_{\mathsf{E}} M)$. It is easy to prove by induction the following characterization of deduction.

Lemma 1 (characterization of deduction). *Let M be a ground term and $\nu\tilde{n}.\sigma$ be a frame built on Σ'. Then $\nu\tilde{n}.\sigma \vdash_{\mathsf{E}} M$ if and only if there exists a term $\zeta \in \mathcal{T}(\Sigma, \mathcal{X})$ such that $fn(\zeta) \cap \tilde{n} = \emptyset$ and $\zeta\sigma =_{\mathsf{E}} M$. Such a term ζ is a recipe of the term M.*

Example 2. Consider the signature $\Sigma_{enc} = \{\mathsf{dec}, \mathsf{enc}, \mathsf{pair}, \mathsf{proj}_1, \mathsf{proj}_2\}$. The symbols $\mathsf{dec}, \mathsf{enc}$ and pair are functional symbols of arity 2 that represent respectively the decryption, encryption and pairing functions whereas proj_1 and proj_2 are functional symbols of arity 1 that represent the projection function on respectively the first and the second component of a pair. As usual, we may write $\langle x, y \rangle$ instead of $\mathsf{pair}(x, y)$. The equational theory of pairing and symmetric encryption, denoted by E_{enc}, is defined by the following equations:

$$\mathsf{dec}(\mathsf{enc}(x, y), y) = x, \quad \mathsf{proj}_1(\langle x, y \rangle) = x \text{ and } \mathsf{proj}_2(\langle x, y \rangle) = y.$$

Let $\phi = \nu k, s_1.\{^{\mathsf{enc}(\langle s_1, s_2 \rangle, k)}/_{x_1}, ^{k}/_{x_2}\}$. We have that $\phi \vdash_{\mathsf{E}_{enc}} k$, $\phi \vdash_{\mathsf{E}_{enc}} s_1$ and also that $\phi \vdash_{\mathsf{E}_{enc}} s_2$. Indeed x_2, $\mathsf{proj}_1(\mathsf{dec}(x_1, x_2))$ and s_2 are recipes of the terms k, s_1 and s_2 respectively.

We say that deduction is decidable for the equational theory (Σ, E) if the following problem is decidable.

Entries A frame ϕ and a term M built on Σ
Question $\phi \vdash_{\mathsf{E}} M$?

2.4   Static Equivalence

Deduction does not always suffice for expressing the knowledge of an attacker, as discussed in the introduction. Sometimes, the attacker can deduce exactly the same set of terms from two different frames but he could still be able to tell the difference between these two frames.

Definition 2 (static equivalence). *Let ϕ be a frame built on Σ' and M and N be two terms. We say that M and N are equal in the frame ϕ under the theory E, and write $(M =_\mathsf{E} N)\phi$, if there exists $\tilde{n}$ such that $\phi = \nu\tilde{n}.\sigma$, $(fn(M) \cup fn(N)) \cap \tilde{n} = \emptyset$ and $M\sigma =_\mathsf{E} N\sigma$. We say that two frames $\phi = \nu\tilde{n}.\sigma$ and $\phi' = \nu\tilde{n}.\sigma'$ built on Σ' are statically equivalent w.r.t. (Σ, E), and write $\phi \approx_\mathsf{E} \phi'$ (or shortly $\phi \approx \phi'$) when*

– *$dom(\phi) = dom(\phi')$, and*
– *for all $M, N \in \mathcal{T}(\Sigma, \mathcal{X})$ we have that $(M =_\mathsf{E} N)\phi \Leftrightarrow (M =_\mathsf{E} N)\phi'$.*

Example 3. Consider the equational theory $(\Sigma_{\mathsf{enc}}, \mathsf{E}_{\mathsf{enc}})$ provided in Example 2. Let $\phi = \nu k.\sigma$, $\phi' = \nu k.\sigma'$ where $\sigma = \{^{\mathsf{enc}(s_0,k)}/_{x_1}, {}^k/_{x_2}\}$, $\sigma' = \{^{\mathsf{enc}(s_1,k)}/_{x_1}, {}^k/_{x_2}\}$. Intuitively, s_0 and s_1 could be the two possible (public) values of a vote. We have $\mathsf{dec}(x_1, x_2)\sigma =_{\mathsf{E}_{\mathsf{enc}}} s_0$ whereas $\mathsf{dec}(x_1, x_2)\sigma' \neq_{\mathsf{E}_{\mathsf{enc}}} s_0$. Therefore we have $\phi \not\approx \phi'$. However, note that $\nu k.\{^{\mathsf{enc}(s_0,k)}/_{x_1}\} \approx \nu k.\{^{\mathsf{enc}(s_1,k)}/_{x_1}\}$.

Let (Σ, E) be an equational theory. We define $\mathsf{Eq}_\mathsf{E}(\phi)$ to be the set of equations satisfied by the frame $\phi = \nu\tilde{n}.\sigma$ in the equational theory E:

$$\mathsf{Eq}_\mathsf{E}(\phi) = \{(M, N) \in \mathcal{T}(\Sigma, \mathcal{X}) \times \mathcal{T}(\Sigma, \mathcal{X}) \mid (M =_\mathsf{E} N)\phi\}.$$

We write $\psi \models \mathsf{Eq}_\mathsf{E}(\phi)$ if $(M =_\mathsf{E} N)\psi$ for any $(M, N) \in \mathsf{Eq}_\mathsf{E}(\phi)$.

Checking for static equivalence is clearly equivalent to checking whether the frames satisfy each other equalities.

Lemma 2 (characterization of static equivalence). *Let $\phi_1 = \nu\tilde{n}.\sigma_1$ and $\phi_2 = \nu\tilde{n}.\sigma_2$ be two frames. We have*

$$\phi_1 \approx_\mathsf{E} \phi_2 \quad \Leftrightarrow \quad \phi_2 \models \mathsf{Eq}_\mathsf{E}(\phi_1) \text{ and } \phi_1 \models \mathsf{Eq}_\mathsf{E}(\phi_2).$$

We say that static equivalence is decidable for the equational theory (Σ, E) if the following problem is decidable.

Entries Two frames ϕ_1 and ϕ_2 built on Σ
Question $\phi_1 \approx_\mathsf{E} \phi_2$?

3   Material for Combination Algorithms

We consider two equational theories $\mathcal{H}_1 = (\Sigma_1, \mathsf{E}_1)$ and $\mathcal{H}_2 = (\Sigma_2, \mathsf{E}_2)$ that are disjoint $(\Sigma_1 \cap \Sigma_2 = \emptyset)$ and consistent. We denote by Σ the union of the signatures Σ_1 and Σ_2 and by E the union of the equations E_1 and E_2. The *union* of the two equational theories is $\mathcal{H} = (\Sigma, \mathsf{E})$. Note that the equational theories $\mathcal{H}_1$ and $\mathcal{H}_2$ share symbols (namely names) that can be used to represent agent identities, keys or nonces. In other words, two ground terms t_1 and t_2 such that $t_1 \in \mathcal{T}(\Sigma_1)$ and $t_2 \in \mathcal{T}(\Sigma_2)$ may share some symbols. We simply require that $\Sigma_1 \cap \Sigma_2 = \emptyset$, that is intuitively, the two equational theories do not share cryptographic operators.

3.1 Factors, Subterms

We denote by $\mathsf{sign}(\cdot)$ the function that associates to each term M, the signature (Σ_1 or Σ_2) of the function symbol at position ϵ (root position) in M. For $M \in \mathcal{N} \cup \mathcal{X}$, we define $\mathsf{sign}(M) = \bot$, where $\bot$ is a new symbol. The term N is *alien* to M if $\mathsf{sign}(N) \neq \mathsf{sign}(M)$. We now introduce our notion of *subterms*. A similar notion is also used in [8].

Definition 3 (factors, subterms). *Let $M \in \mathcal{T}(\Sigma, \mathcal{X})$. The* factors *of M are the maximal syntactic subterms of M that are alien to M. This set is denoted $Fct(M)$. The set of its subterms, denoted $St(M)$, is defined recursively by*

$$St(M) = \{M\} \cup \bigcup_{N \in Fct(M)} St(N)$$

These notations are extended as expected to sets of terms and frames. Sometimes we will use $St(\phi, M)$ instead of $St(\phi) \cup St(M)$.

Let $M \in \mathcal{T}(\Sigma, \mathcal{X})$. The size $|M|$ of a term M is defined $|M| = 0$ if M is a name or a variable and by $1 + \sum_{i=1}^{n} |N_i|$ if $M = C[N_1, \ldots, N_n]$ where C is a context built on Σ_1 (or Σ_2) and $N_1, \ldots N_n$ are the factors of M.

Example 4. Consider the equational theories $\mathsf{E}_{\mathsf{enc}}$ and $\mathsf{E}_{\mathsf{xor}}$. Let M be the term $\mathsf{dec}(\langle n_1 \oplus \langle n_2, n_3 \rangle, \mathsf{proj}_1(n_1 \oplus n_2)\rangle, n_3)$. The term $n_1 \oplus \langle n_2, n_3 \rangle$ is a syntactic subterm of M alien to M since $\mathsf{sign}(n_1 \oplus \langle n_2, n_3 \rangle) = \Sigma_{\mathsf{xor}}$ and $\mathsf{sign}(M) = \Sigma_{\mathsf{enc}}$. We have that $Fct(M) = \{n_1 \oplus \langle n_2, n_3 \rangle,\ n_1 \oplus n_2,\ n_3\}$ and $St(M) = Fct(M) \cup \{M, n_1, n_2, \langle n_2, n_3 \rangle\}$. Moreover, we have that $|M| = 4$. Indeed, we have that

$$|M| = 1 + |n_1 \oplus \langle n_2, n_3 \rangle| + |n_1 \oplus n_2| + |n_3| = 1 + 2 + 1 + 0 = 4$$

This notion of size of terms is quite non-standard and does not correspond to the actual size of a term. It is only used for proving our lemmas by induction. Our complexity results stated later on in the paper relies on the more usual notion of DAG-size.

3.2 Ordered Rewriting

Most of the definitions and results in this subsection are borrowed from [9] since we use similar techniques. We consider the notion of *ordered rewriting* defined in [14], which is a useful tool that has been used (*e.g.* [5]) for proving correctness of combination of unification algorithms. Let $\prec$ be a simplification ordering[1] on ground terms assumed to be total and such that the minimum for $\prec$ is a name n_{min} and the constants in Σ are smaller than any non-constant ground term. We define Σ_0 to be the set of the constant symbols of Σ_1 and Σ_2 plus the name n_{min}.

Given a possibly infinite set of equations $\mathcal{O}$ we define the ordered rewriting relation $\to_{\mathcal{O}}$ by $M \to_{\mathcal{O}} M'$ if and only if there exists an equation $N_1 = N_2 \in \mathcal{O}$, a position p in M and a substitution τ such that:

---

[1] By definition $\prec$ satisfies that for all ground terms M, N_1, N_2, we have $N_1 \prec M[N_1]$ when M is not the empty context and $N_1 \prec N_2$ implies $M[N_1] \prec M[N_2]$.

$$M = M[N_1\tau]_p, \quad M' = M[N_2\tau]_p \text{ and } N_2\tau \prec N_1\tau.$$

It has been shown (see [14]) that by applying the *unfailing completion procedure* to a set of equations E we can derive a (possibly infinite) set of equations $\mathcal{O}$ such that on ground terms:

1. the relations $=_{\mathcal{O}}$ and $=_{\mathsf{E}}$ are equal on $\mathcal{T}(\Sigma)$,
2. the rewriting system $\rightarrow_{\mathcal{O}}$ is convergent on $\mathcal{T}(\Sigma)$.

Applying unfailing completion to $\mathsf{E} = \mathsf{E}_1 \cup \mathsf{E}_2$, it is easy to notice [5] that the set of generated equations $\mathcal{O}$ is the disjoint union of the two systems $\mathcal{O}_1$ and $\mathcal{O}_2$ obtained by applying unfailing completion procedures to E_1 and to E_2 respectively. The relation $\rightarrow_{\mathcal{O}}$ being convergent on ground terms we can define $M\downarrow_{\mathsf{E}}$ (or briefly $M\downarrow$) as the unique normal form of the ground term M for $\rightarrow_{\mathcal{O}}$. We denote by $M\downarrow_{\mathsf{E}_1}$ (resp. $M\downarrow_{\mathsf{E}_2}$) the unique normal form of the ground term M for $\rightarrow_{\mathcal{O}_1}$ (resp. $\rightarrow_{\mathcal{O}_2}$). We can easily prove the following lemmas.

Lemma 3. *Let M be a ground term such that all its factors are in normal form. Then*

- *either $M\downarrow \in Fct(M) \cup \{n_{min}\}$,*
- *or $\mathsf{sign}(M) = \mathsf{sign}(M\downarrow)$ and $Fct(M\downarrow) \subseteq Fct(M) \cup \{n_{min}\}$.*

Lemma 4. *Let M be a ground term such that $\mathsf{sign}(M) = \Sigma_i$ ($i = 1, 2$) and all its factors are in normal form. Then $M\downarrow = M\downarrow_{\mathsf{E}_i}$.*

3.3   Normalization and Replacements

If Π is a set of positions in a term M, we denote by $M[\Pi \leftarrow N]$ the term obtained by replacing all term at a position in Π by N. We denote by $\delta_{N,N'}$ the replacement of the occurrences of N which appears at a subterm position by N'. It is easy to establish the following lemma.

Lemma 5. *Let M be a ground term such that all its factors are in normal form. Let $N \in Fct(M)$ and N' be a term alien to M. We have that*

$$(M\delta_{N,N'})\downarrow = ((M\downarrow)\delta_{N,N'})\downarrow).$$

Example 5. Consider the equational theories E_{enc} and E_{xor}. Let $M = \mathsf{dec}(\mathsf{enc}(\langle n_1 \oplus n_2, n_1 \oplus n_2 \oplus n_3\rangle, n_1 \oplus n_2), n_1 \oplus n_2)$, $N = n_1 \oplus n_2$ and $N' = n$. We have that

- $M\delta_{N,N'} = \mathsf{dec}(\mathsf{enc}(\langle n, n_1 \oplus n_2 \oplus n_3\rangle, n), n)$,
- $M\downarrow\delta_{N,N'} = \langle n, n_1 \oplus n_2 \oplus n_3\rangle$.

Hence, we have that $M\delta_{N,N'}\downarrow = M\downarrow\delta_{N,N'}\downarrow = \langle n, n_1 \oplus n_2 \oplus n_3\rangle$.

Let $\rho : F \rightarrow \tilde{n}_F$ be a replacement (that is a function) from a finite set of terms F to names $\tilde{n}_F$. Let $F = \{t_1, \ldots, t_k\}$ be a set such that whenever t_i is a syntactic subterm of t_j then $i > j$. For any term M, we denote by M^ρ the term obtained by replacing in M (in an order that is consistent with the subterm relation) any subterm N that is equal modulo E to some $N' \in F$ by $\rho(N')$. Formally, $M^\rho = (M\delta_{t_1,\rho(t_1)}) \cdots \delta_{t_k,\rho(t_k)}$. This extends in a natural way to sets of terms, substitutions, frames ...

Example 6. Consider the equational theories E_{enc} and E_{xor} and the term $t = \mathsf{dec}(\langle n_1 \oplus \langle n_1 \oplus n_2, n_3 \rangle, \mathsf{proj}_1(n_1 \oplus n_2) \rangle, n_1 \oplus n_2)$. Let ρ_2 be the replacement $\{n_1 \oplus \langle n_1 \oplus n_2, n_3 \rangle \rightarrow k_1,\ n_1 \oplus n_2 \rightarrow k_2\}$. $t^{\rho_2} = \mathsf{dec}(\langle k_1, \mathsf{proj}_1(k_2) \rangle, k_2)$.

4   Combining Algorithms for Deduction

This section is devoted to the (sketch of) proof of the following theorem.

Theorem 1. *Let (Σ_1, E_1) and (Σ_2, E_2) be two consistent equational theories such that $\Sigma_1 \cap \Sigma_2 = \emptyset$. If deduction is decidable for (Σ_1, E_1) and (Σ_2, E_2) then deduction is decidable for $(\Sigma_1 \cup \Sigma_2, \mathsf{E}_1 \cup \mathsf{E}_2)$.*

Our algorithm consists in reducing the problem to decide whether $\phi \vdash_\mathsf{E} M$ ($\mathsf{E} = \mathsf{E}_1 \cup \mathsf{E}_2$) to several deduction problems. Each of them will be solved either in the equational theory E_1 or in the theory E_2. Our procedure first relies on the existence of a *local proof* of $\phi \vdash M$ which involves only terms in $St(\phi, M)$.

Lemma 6 (locality lemma). *Let $\phi = \nu\tilde{n}.\sigma$ be a frame and M be a ground term built on Σ such that terms in ϕ and M are in normal form. If $\phi \vdash_\mathsf{E} M$ then there exists a term ζ built on Σ such that $fn(\zeta) \cap \tilde{n} = \emptyset$ and $\zeta\sigma =_\mathsf{E} M$, and for all $\zeta' \in St(\zeta)$, we have that*

- *$\zeta'\sigma\downarrow \in St(\phi, \zeta\sigma\downarrow) \cup \{n_{min}\}$, and*
- *$\zeta'\sigma\downarrow \in St(\phi) \cup \{n_{min}\}$ when $\mathsf{sign}(\zeta') \neq \mathsf{sign}(\zeta'\sigma\downarrow)$.*

Example 7. Consider the theory $\mathsf{E} = \mathsf{E}_{enc} \cup \mathsf{E}_{xor}$, the term $M = n_2 \oplus n_3$ and the frame $\phi = \nu n_2, n_3.\{{}^{\mathsf{enc}(\langle n_1 \oplus n_2, n_3 \rangle, n_4)}/_{x_1}\}$. We have that $\phi \vdash_\mathsf{E} M$. The recipe $\zeta = \mathsf{proj}_1(\mathsf{dec}(x_1, n_4)) \oplus \mathsf{proj}_2(\mathsf{dec}(x_1, n_4)) \oplus n_1$ satisfies the conditions given in Lemma 6.

We also need to decide deducibility in the theory E_1 (resp. E_2) for terms built on $\Sigma_1 \cup \Sigma_2$. Therefore, we show that we can abstract the alien factors by new names.

Lemma 7. *Let ϕ be a frame and M be a ground term built on Σ such that terms in ϕ and M are in normal form. Let $F_2 = \{N \mid N \in St(\phi, M) \text{ and } \mathsf{sign}(N) = \Sigma_2\}$, $\tilde{n}_{F_2}$ be a set of names, distinct from the names occurring in ϕ and M, of the same cardinality as F_2 and $\rho_2 : F_2 \rightarrow \tilde{n}_{F_2}$ be a replacement. We have that*

$$\phi \vdash_{\mathsf{E}_1} M \text{ if and only if } \nu\tilde{n}_{F_2}.(\phi \vdash_{\mathsf{E}_1} M)^{\rho_2}.$$

A similar result holds by inverting the indices 1 and 2.

We show the lemmas above by using Lemmas 3, 4 and 5 stated in Section 3. Then, our algorithm proceeds by saturation of ϕ by the subterms in $St(\phi, M)$ which are deducible either in (Σ_1, E_1) or in (Σ_2, E_2).

Algorithm. Given a frame ϕ and a term M, we saturate ϕ as follows.

- We start with $\phi_0 = \phi \cup \{n_{min}\}$.
- For any term $T \in St(\phi, M)$, if $\nu\tilde{n}_{F_2}.(\phi_k \vdash_{\mathsf{E}_1} T)^{\rho_2}$ or $\nu\tilde{n}_{F_1}.(\phi_k \vdash_{\mathsf{E}_2} T)^{\rho_1}$ where F_1, F_2, ρ_1, ρ_2 are defined like in Lemma 7, we add T in the set of deducible subterms: $\phi_{k+1} = \phi_k \cup \{T\}$.

We start the procedure over until there are no more $T \in St(\phi, M)$ such that $\nu\tilde{n}_{F_2}.(\phi_k \vdash_{\mathsf{E}_1} M)^{\rho_2}$ or $\nu\tilde{n}_{F_1}.(\phi_k \vdash_{\mathsf{E}_1} M)^{\rho_1}$. Let ϕ^* be the saturated set. Using Lemma 6, we can show that ϕ^* contains exactly the set of all deducible subterms of $St(\phi, M)$. We deduce that $\phi \vdash_{\mathsf{E}_1 \cup \mathsf{E}_2} M$ if and only if $M \in \phi^*$.

Example 8. Consider again Example 7, we successively add in the frame the terms $n_1 \oplus n_2$, n_3 and $n_2 \oplus n_3$.

Complexity. Our reduction is polynomial. Our notion of size for terms was introduced for proving our lemmas by induction. It does not correspond to the actual size of a term since our notion of subterms does not take into account intermediate syntactic subterms. In addition, complexity results for deduction and static equivalence are usually given as functions of the DAG-size of the terms. Thus we express the complexity of our procedure as function of the DAG-size. The DAG-size of a term T, denoted $t_{\mathsf{dag}}(T)$, is the number of distinct syntactic subterms. We assume that $\phi \vdash_{\mathsf{E}_i} M$ can be decided in time $f_i(t_{\mathsf{dag}}(\phi) + t_{\mathsf{dag}}(M))$ where $f_i : \mathbb{N} \to \mathbb{R}$, $i \in \{1, 2\}$. Saturating ϕ requires at most $|St(\phi, M)| \leq t_{\mathsf{dag}}(\phi) + t_{\mathsf{dag}}(M)$ steps. At each step, we check whether $\nu\tilde{n}_{F_2}.(\phi_k \vdash_{\mathsf{E}_1} T)^{\rho_2}$ or $\nu\tilde{n}_{F_1}.(\phi_k \vdash_{\mathsf{E}_2} T)^{\rho_1}$ for each $T \in St(\phi, M)$. We deduce that ϕ^* can be computed in time $\mathcal{O}((t_{\mathsf{dag}}(\phi) + t_{\mathsf{dag}}(M))^2 [f_1(2(t_{\mathsf{dag}}(\phi) + t_{\mathsf{dag}}(M))) + f_2(2(t_{\mathsf{dag}}(\phi) + t_{\mathsf{dag}}(M)))])$. In particular, if deciding $\vdash_{\mathsf{E}_i}$ can be done in polynomial time for $i \in \{1, 2\}$ then deciding $\vdash_{\mathsf{E}_1 \cup \mathsf{E}_2}$ is also polynomial.

5   Combination Algorithm for Static Equivalence

This section is devoted to the (sketch of) proof of the following theorem.

Theorem 2. *Let (Σ_1, E_1) and (Σ_2, E_2) be two equational theories such that $\Sigma_1 \cap \Sigma_2 = \emptyset$. If deduction and static equivalence are decidable for (Σ_1, E_1) and (Σ_2, E_2) then static equivalence is decidable for $(\Sigma_1 \cup \Sigma_2, \mathsf{E}_1 \cup \mathsf{E}_2)$.*

We more precisely show that whenever static equivalence is decidable for (Σ_1, E_1) and (Σ_2, E_2) and deduction is decidable for (Σ, E), then static equivalence is decidable for (Σ, E) where $\Sigma = \Sigma_1 \cup \Sigma_2$ and $\mathsf{E} = \mathsf{E}_1 \cup \mathsf{E}_2$. Thanks to our combination result for deduction (Theorem 1), we know it is sufficient for deduction to be decidable for (Σ_1, E_1) and (Σ_2, E_2). Note that the decidability of $\vdash_{\mathsf{E}_i}$ is not necessarily a consequence of the decidability of $\approx_{\mathsf{E}_i}$. The encoding proposed in [2] works only when there exists a free function symbol in Σ_1.

Our decision procedure works as follows. We first add to the frames all their deducible subterms. This is the reason why we require the decidability of $\vdash_{\mathsf{E}}$. Then, we show that to decide whether $\phi_1 \models \mathsf{Eq}_{\mathsf{E}}(\phi_2)$, it is sufficient to check whether $\phi_1 \models \mathsf{Eq}_{\mathsf{E}_1}(\phi_2)$ and $\phi_1 \models \mathsf{Eq}_{\mathsf{E}_2}(\phi_2)$. Lastly, we abstract alien subterms by fresh names in order to reduce the signature.

5.1 Step 1: Adding Deducible Subterms to the Frames

Given $\phi_1 = \nu\tilde{n}.\sigma_1$ and $\phi_2 = \nu\tilde{n}.\sigma_2$ such that $dom(\phi_1) = dom(\phi_2)$, we define the frame $\overline{\phi_2}^{\phi_1}$ by extending ϕ_2 with some of its deducible terms: those for which there exists a recipe ζ such that $\zeta\sigma_1\!\downarrow$ is a subterm of ϕ_1.

$$\overline{\phi_2}^{\phi_1} \stackrel{\text{def}}{=} \phi_2 \cup \{{}^{\zeta_1\sigma_2\downarrow}/_{y_1}, \ldots, {}^{\zeta_n\sigma_2\downarrow}/_{y_n}\}.$$

where y_i is a fresh variable and ζ_i is a recipe of t_i in ϕ_1, i.e. $\zeta_i\sigma_1\!\downarrow = t_i$ and $fn(\zeta_i) \cap \tilde{n} = \emptyset$ such that:

- $t_i \in St(\phi_1) \cup \{n_{min}\}$, and
- t_i is not in the image of ϕ_1, that is $t_i \neq x\sigma$ for any $x \in dom(\phi_1)$.

Example 9. Let $\mathsf{E} = \mathsf{E}_{\mathsf{enc}}$ and consider the frames $\phi_2 = \nu n_1, n_2.\{{}^{\mathsf{enc}(n_1,n_2)}/_{x_1}\}$ and $\phi_1 = \nu n_1, n_2.\{{}^{\langle n_1, n_2\rangle}/_{x_1}\}$. We have that

$$\overline{\phi_2}^{\phi_1} = \nu n_1, n_2.\{{}^{\mathsf{enc}(n_1,n_2)}/_{x_1}, {}^{\mathsf{proj}_1(\mathsf{enc}(n_1,n_2))}/_{y_1}, {}^{\mathsf{proj}_2(\mathsf{enc}(n_1,n_2))}/_{y_2}, {}^{n_{min}}/_{y_3}\}$$

The three corresponding recipes are $\mathsf{proj}_1(x_1)$, $\mathsf{proj}_2(x_1)$ and n_{min}.

In particular, we have that $\overline{\phi}^{\phi} = \phi \cup \{{}^{t_1}/_{y_1}, \ldots, {}^{t_n}/_{y_n}\}$ where t_i are the deducible subterms of ϕ. When $\overline{\phi}^{\phi} = \phi$, we say that a frame ϕ contains all its deducible subterms.

Example 10. Consider the frame $\phi = \nu n_2, n_3.\{{}^{\mathsf{enc}(\langle n_1 \oplus n_2, n_3\rangle, n_4)}/_{x_1}\}$ given in Example 7 and let $\mathsf{E} = \mathsf{E}_{\mathsf{enc}} \cup \mathsf{E}_{\mathsf{xor}}$. We have that

$$\overline{\phi}^{\phi} = \nu n_2, n_3.\{{}^{\mathsf{enc}(\langle n_1 \oplus n_2, n_3\rangle, n_4)}/_{x_1}, {}^{n_1 \oplus n_2}/_{y_1}, {}^{n_2}/_{y_2}, {}^{n_3}/_{y_3}, {}^{n_1}/_{y_4}, {}^{n_4}/_{y_5}, {}^{n_{min}}/_{y_6}\}.$$

The following lemma ensures that extending frames preserves static equivalence.

Lemma 8. *Let ϕ_1 and ϕ_2 be two frames such that $dom(\phi_1) = dom(\phi_2)$. For any frame ψ such that $dom(\psi) = dom(\phi_1)$, we have that*

$$\overline{\phi_2}^{\psi} \models \mathsf{Eq}_{\mathsf{E}}(\overline{\phi_1}^{\psi}) \quad \text{if and only if} \quad \phi_2 \models \mathsf{Eq}_{\mathsf{E}}(\phi_1).$$

In particular, we deduce that $\phi_1 \approx_{\mathsf{E}} \phi_2$ if and only if $\overline{\phi_1}^{\phi_2} \approx_{\mathsf{E}} \overline{\phi_2}^{\phi_2}$. Since $\overline{\phi_1}^{\phi_2}$ may not contain all its deducible subterms, we need to extend again the frames with the deducible subterms of $\overline{\phi_1}^{\phi_2}$. However, $\overline{(\overline{\phi_2}^{\phi_2})}^{\overline{(\overline{\phi_1}^{\phi_2})}}$ might not contains its deducible subterms anymore. Lemma 9 states that actually, extending a frame preserves the property of containing all its deducible subterms. The proof of this lemma relies on the locality lemma (Lemma 6) stated in Section 4.

Lemma 9. *Let ϕ be a frame such that $\overline{\phi}^{\phi} = \phi$ and ψ be any frame such that $dom(\psi) = dom(\phi)$. Let $\phi' = \overline{\phi}^{\psi}$. We have that ϕ' contains all its deducible subterms, i.e. $\overline{\phi'}^{\phi'} = \phi'$.*

Thanks to Lemma 8, we deduce that deciding whether $\phi_1 \approx_E \phi_2$ is thus equivalent to deciding whether $\overline{(\overline{\phi_1}^{\phi_2})}^{\overline{(\overline{\phi_1}^{\phi_2})}} \approx_E \overline{(\overline{\phi_2}^{\phi_2})}^{\overline{(\overline{\phi_1}^{\phi_2})}}$ where $\overline{(\overline{\phi_1}^{\phi_2})}^{\overline{(\overline{\phi_1}^{\phi_2})}}$ and $\overline{(\overline{\phi_2}^{\phi_2})}^{\overline{(\overline{\phi_1}^{\phi_2})}}$ contain all their deducible subterms.

Computing $\overline{\phi}^{\psi}$. To compute $\overline{\phi}^{\psi}$, we need to compute the set of deducible subterms of ψ. Moreover, for each deducible subterm T of ψ, we also need to compute a recipe ζ_T such that $(\zeta_T =_E T)\psi$. Such a recipe can usually be deduced from the decision algorithm applied to $\psi \vdash_E T$ [2]. However, if it is not the case, once we know that $\psi \vdash_E T$ (using the decision algorithm), we can enumerate all the recipes until we find ζ such that $(\zeta_T =_E T)\psi$.

5.2 Step 2: Checking for Equalities in $\mathsf{Eq}_{\mathsf{E}_i}$

Checking for $\phi \approx_E \psi$ is equivalent to checking for $\phi \models \mathsf{Eq}_E(\psi)$ and $\psi \models \mathsf{Eq}_E(\phi)$. We show that checking for $\psi \models \mathsf{Eq}_E(\phi)$ can actually be done using only equalities in E_1 and E_2.

Proposition 1. *Let ϕ and ψ be two frames such that $\overline{\phi}^{\phi} = \phi$. We have that $\psi \models \mathsf{Eq}_E(\phi)$ if and only if $\psi \models \mathsf{Eq}_{\mathsf{E}_1}(\phi)$ and $\psi \models \mathsf{Eq}_{\mathsf{E}_2}(\phi)$.*

It is straightforward that $\psi \models \mathsf{Eq}_E(\phi)$ implies $\psi \models \mathsf{Eq}_{\mathsf{E}_1}(\phi)$ and $\psi \models \mathsf{Eq}_{\mathsf{E}_2}(\phi)$. The converse is more difficult. We first introduce some ordering on pairs of terms. We have $(M, N) < (M', N')$ if

$$(\max(|M|, |N|), |M| + |N|) <_{lex} (\max(|M'|, |N'|), |M'| + |N'|)$$

where $<_{lex}$ is the lexicographic order. Now, assuming that $\psi \models \mathsf{Eq}_{\mathsf{E}_1}(\phi)$ and $\psi \models \mathsf{Eq}_{\mathsf{E}_2}(\phi)$, we show by induction on the order on (M, N) that $(M, N) \in \mathsf{Eq}_E(\phi)$ implies $(M, N) \in \mathsf{Eq}_E(\psi)$. The key lemma for the induction step is as follows.

Lemma 10. *Let ϕ and ψ be two frames such that $\overline{\phi}^{\phi} = \phi$, $\psi \models \mathsf{Eq}_{\mathsf{E}_1}(\phi)$ and $\psi \models \mathsf{Eq}_{\mathsf{E}_2}(\phi)$. Let $(M, N) \in \mathsf{Eq}_E(\phi)$ and assume that for all terms M', N'*

$$(M', N') < (M, N) \quad implies \quad (M' =_E N')\phi \Rightarrow (M' =_E N')\psi.$$

Let $\phi = \nu\tilde{n}.\sigma$ such that $(fn(M) \cup fn(N)) \cap \tilde{n} = \emptyset$. If there exists $\zeta \in St(M)$ such that $\mathsf{sign}(\zeta\sigma) \neq \mathsf{sign}(\zeta\sigma\downarrow)$, then there exists M_1 such that $|M_1| < |M|$, $(M =_E M_1)\phi$ and $(M =_E M_1)\psi$.

5.3 Step 3: Abstraction of Alien Subterms

Since ψ and ϕ are built on Σ (and not on Σ_i), we cannot check whether $\psi \approx_{E_i} \phi$ using the decision algorithm for $\approx_{E_i}$. We show however that we can simply abstract the alien subterms by fresh names.

Lemma 11. *Let ϕ and ψ be two frames built on Σ and in normal form. Let $F_2 = \{N \in St(\phi \cup \psi) \mid \mathsf{sign}(N) = \Sigma_2\}$, $\tilde{n}_{F_2}$ be a set of names, distinct from the names occurring in ϕ and ψ, of same cardinality as F_2 and $\rho_2 : F_2 \to \tilde{n}_F$ a replacement. We have that*

$$\phi \models \mathsf{Eq}_{E_1}(\psi) \quad \text{if and only if} \quad \nu\tilde{n}_{F_2}.\phi^{\rho_2} \models \mathsf{Eq}_{E_1}(\nu\tilde{n}_{F_2}.\psi^{\rho_2})$$

A similar result holds when inverting the indices 1 and 2.

5.4 Combination Algorithm for Static Equivalence

To sum up, checking for $\phi_1 \approx_E \phi_2$ is performed in two steps:

1. Computing $\phi_1' = \overline{(\overline{\phi_1}^{\phi_2})}^{(\overline{\phi_1}^{\phi_2})}$ and $\phi_2' = \overline{(\overline{\phi_2}^{\phi_2})}^{(\overline{\phi_1}^{\phi_2})}$.
2. checking for $\nu\tilde{n}_{F_2}.(\phi_1')^{\rho_2} \approx_{E_1} \nu\tilde{n}_{F_2}.(\phi_2')^{\rho_2}$ and $\nu\tilde{n}_{F_1}.(\phi_1')^{\rho_1} \approx_{E_2} \nu\tilde{n}_{F_1}.(\phi_2')^{\rho_1}$.

Complexity. The complexity of the procedure mostly depends on the complexity of computing ϕ_1' and ϕ_2' and on their size. In particular, it depends on the time for computing recipes and on their size. Assume that

- $\phi \vdash_E M$ can be decided in $f_3(t_{\mathsf{dag}}(\phi) + t_{\mathsf{dag}}(M))$,
- a recipe ζ such that $(\zeta =_E M)\phi$ can be computed in $f_4(t_{\mathsf{dag}}(\phi) + t_{\mathsf{dag}}(M))$ and that we control the size of the recipe $t_{\mathsf{dag}}(\zeta) \leq f_5(t_{\mathsf{dag}}(\phi) + t_{\mathsf{dag}}(M))$
- $\phi \approx_{E_i} \psi$ can be decided in $f_i(t_{\mathsf{dag}}(\phi) + t_{\mathsf{dag}}(M))$ for $i \in \{1, 2\}$.

Then it is easy to check that $\phi \approx_E \psi$ can be decided in time polynomial in the $f_i(t_{\mathsf{dag}}(\phi) + t_{\mathsf{dag}}(M))$ with $i \in \{1, \ldots, 5\}$. In particular, if the f_i are polynomial, $\approx_E$ is decidable in polynomial time.

6 Application to New Decidability Results

Deduction and static equivalence are decidable in polynomial time (in the DAG-size of the inputs) for any convergent subterm theory [2]. A convergent subterm theory is an equational theory induced by a finite set of equations of the form $u = v$ where v is a subterm of u or v is a constant and such that the associate rewriting system is convergent. For example, E_{enc} is a convergent subterm theory. From [12], we also know that deduction and static equivalence are decidable in polynomial time for the equational theory E_{xor} of the exclusive or and also for the theory E_{AG} of Abelian group. Applying Theorems 1 and 2, we get the following new decidability result.

Proposition 2. *Let* E *be a convergent subterm theory. Deduction and static equivalence are decidable in polynomial time for* $E \cup E_{xor}$ *and* $E \cup E_{AG}$.

Since deduction and static equivalence are also decidable for the theories of blind signature, homomorphic encryption, exclusive or, and other associative-commutative functions [2], we get that deduction and static equivalence are decidable for any combination of these theories.

As further work, we consider extending our combination result for non disjoint theories. This would allow us to consider some fragments of the modular exponentiation theory such as the Diffie-Hellman one, *i.e.* the axioms $\exp(x, 1) = x$ and $\exp(\exp(x, y), z) = \exp(x, y \times z)$ where $\times$ is an Abelian group operator; or to take into account the equation $\exp(x, y) \cdot \exp(x, z) = \exp(x, y + z)$. We might use for example a notion of hierarchy between theories like in [10].

References

1. Abadi, M., Baudet, M., Warinschi, B.: Guessing attacks and the computational soundness of static equivalence. In: Aceto, L., Ingólfsdóttir, A. (eds.) FOSSACS 2006 and ETAPS 2006. LNCS, vol. 3921, pp. 398–412. Springer, Heidelberg (2006)
2. Abadi, M., Cortier, V.: Deciding knowledge in security protocols under equational theories. Theoretical Computer Science 387(1-2), 2–32 (2006)
3. Abadi, M., Fournet, C.: Mobile values, new names, and secure communication. In: Proceedings of the 28th ACM Symposium on Principles of Programming Languages (POPL'01), pp. 104–115. ACM Press, New York (2001)
4. Arnaud, M., Cortier, V., Delaune, S.: Combining algorithms for deciding knowledge in security protocols. Research Report 6118, INRIA, p. 28 (February 2007)
5. Baader, F., Schulz, K.U.: Unification in the union of disjoint equational theories: Combining decision procedures. Journal of Symbolic Computation 21(2), 211–243 (1996)
6. Baudet, M., Cortier, V., Kremer, S.: Computationally sound implementations of equational theories against passive adversaries. In: Caires, L., Italiano, G.F., Monteiro, L., Palamidessi, C., Yung, M. (eds.) ICALP 2005. LNCS, vol. 3580, pp. 652–663. Springer, Heidelberg (2005)
7. Chevalier, Y., Küsters, R., Rusinowitch, M., Turuani, M.: An NP decision procedure for protocol insecurity with XOR. In: Proceedings of 18th Annual IEEE Symposium on Logic in Computer Science (LICS'03), Ottawa (Canada), IEEE Computer Society Press, Los Alamitos (2003)
8. Chevalier, Y., Rusinowitch, M.: Combining intruder theories. In: Caires, L., Italiano, G.F., Monteiro, L., Palamidessi, C., Yung, M. (eds.) ICALP 2005. LNCS, vol. 3580, pp. 639–651. Springer, Heidelberg (2005)
9. Chevalier, Y., Rusinowitch, M.: Combining intruder theories. Technical Report 5495, INRIA (2005), http://www.inria.fr/rrrt/rr-5495.html
10. Chevalier, Y., Rusinowitch, M.: Hierarchical combination of intruder theories. In: Pfenning, F. (ed.) RTA 2006. LNCS, vol. 4098, pp. 108–122. Springer, Heidelberg (2006)

11. Comon-Lundh, H., Shmatikov, V.: Intruder deductions, constraint solving and insecurity decision in presence of exclusive or. In: Proceedings of 18th Annual IEEE Symposium on Logic in Computer Science (LICS'03), Ottawa (Canada), IEEE Computer Society Press, Los Alamitos (2003)
12. Cortier, V., Delaune, S.: Deciding knowledge in security protocols for monoidal equational theories. In: Proc. of the Joint Workshop on Foundations of Computer Security and Automated Reasoning for Security Protocol Analysis (FCS-ARSPA'07), Wrocław, Poland (to appear, 2007)
13. Delaune, S.: Easy intruder deduction problems with homomorphisms. Information Processing Letters 97(6), 213–218 (2006)
14. Dershowitz, N., Jouannaud, J.-P.: Rewrite systems. In: Handbook of Theoretical Computer Science, vol. B, ch. 6, Elsevier, Amsterdam (1990)
15. Lafourcade, P., Lugiez, D., Treinen, R.: Intruder deduction for the equational theory of Abelian groups with distributive encryption. Information and Computation (to appear, 2007)
16. Lakhnech, Y., Mazaré, L., Warinschi, B.: Soundness of symbolic equivalence for modular exponentiation. In: Proceedings of the Second Workshop on Formal and Computational Cryptography (FCC'06), pp. 19–23, Venice, Italy (July 2006)
17. Lowe, G.: Breaking and fixing the Needham-Schroeder public-key protocol using FDR. In: Margaria, T., Steffen, B. (eds.) TACAS 1996. LNCS, vol. 1055, pp. 147–166. Springer, Heidelberg (1996)
18. Millen, J., Shmatikov, V.: Constraint solving for bounded-process cryptographic protocol analysis. In: Proceedings of the 8th ACM Conference on Computer and Communications Security (CCS'01), ACM Press, New York (2001)
19. Paulson, L.C.: The inductive approach to verifying cryptographic protocols. Journal of Computer Security 6(1-2), 85–128 (1998)
20. Rusinowitch, M., Turuani, M.: Protocol insecurity with a finite number of sessions, composed keys is NP-complete. Theoretical Computer Science 1-3(299), 451–475 (2003)
21. Schmidt-Schauß, M.: Unification in a combination of arbitrary disjoint equational theories. Journal of Symbolic Computation 8(1/2), 51–99 (1989)

Combining Classical and Intuitionistic Implications[*]

Carlos Caleiro and Jaime Ramos

SQIG-IT and CLC, Department of Mathematics, IST, TU Lisbon, Portugal

Abstract. We present a simple logic that combines, in a conservative way, the implicative fragments of both classical and intuitionistic logics, thus settling a problem posed by Dov Gabbay in [5]. We also show that the logic can be given a nice complete axiomatization by adding four simple mixed axioms to the usual axiomatizations of classical and intuitionistic implications.

1 Introduction

In [5], Dov Gabbay pointed out a difficulty with the fibring methodology for combining logics [6,1] that became known as *the collapsing problem*. The argument given there suggested that there would be no way of combining classical and intuitionistic propositional logics, *CPL* and *IPL* respectively, in a way that would not collapse the intuitionistic connectives into classical ones. Following this spirit, Andreas Herzig and Luis Fariñas del Cerro have proposed in [4] a combined logic $C + J$ that starts from the expected combined semantic setting, that could be axiomatized, not by adding the axiomatizations of *CPL* and *IPL* together with some interaction rules, but rather by modifying these axioms along with their scope of applicability.

Actually, Gabbay's argument, which depends only on the implicative fragments of the logics, holds in fact for any logic combining classical and intuitionistic reasoning in a way that preserves the *deduction theorem* for both implications. However, a simple combination of the usual axiomatizations of classical and intuitionistic implications yields a system where none of the deduction theorems seems to hold. The question is how to prove this. A semantic argument would need to consider suitable, non-trivial, combined models. The natural place to look for such combined models would be to consider a *fibred semantics*. Still, a fibred model cannot do the job, because fibring classical and intuitionistic models together will only result in models where the intuitionistic implication becomes classical. Indeed, the semantic fibring of two logics does not always result in a conservative extension of the logics being combined. Looking for a way around this problem, we have proposed in [2,3] an extension of the fibring

---

[*] This work was partially supported by FCT and EU FEDER, namely via the recently approved KLog project PTDC/MAT/68723/2006 of SQIG-IT, and also the QuantLog project POCI/MAT/55796/2004 of CLC.

B. Konev and F. Wolter (Eds.): FroCos 2007, LNAI 4720, pp. 118–132, 2007.

methodology, called *cryptofibring*. In the new setting, we have obtained a more general notion of combined model and have managed to identify situations as the above mentioned collapsing problem as particular cases of non-conservative combinations. As a by-product, we have shown that a conservative extension of *CPL* and *IPL* is possible, and suggested a simple way to construct combined non-trivial models. A characterization of this (large) class of models, as well as a number of general results about cryptofibring, can be found in [2,3].

In this paper we study in detail the implicative fragment of the combined logic characterized by a subclass of these models. We prove that the resulting logic, *CIPL*, which features both a classical and an intuitionistic implication, is a conservative extension of the implicative fragments of both classical and intuitionistic logics. We also show that *CIPL* can be given a nice complete axiomatization by adding four simple mixed axioms to the usual axiomatizations of classical and intuitionistic implications. These mixed axioms will guarantee, in particular, that the classical implication be strictly stronger than the intuitionistic one. We assume nothing but acquaintance with textbook logic. A useful source on intuitionistic logic is [12].

In Section 2, we review Gabbay's argument for the collapse when combining classical and intuitionistic logics, namely at the light of the logic $C + J$ of Herzig and del Cerro, and show how to overcome these difficulties by introducing the class of models for the combined logic *CIPL*. Then, in Section 3, we study a number of interesting properties of these models, that will eventually lead us to showing that *CIPL* is indeed a conservative extension of the implicative fragments of both *CPL* and *IPL*. Particular emphasis will be put on studying the interactions between classical and intuitionistic implications. Section 4 is devoted to proposing an axiomatization of *CIPL*, and to proving, using standard techniques, its soundness and completeness with respect to the semantics. We conclude, in Section 5, with a discussion of related and future work.

2 Combining Models

Let us consider a set P of classical propositional symbols, and let us use $\Rightarrow$ to denote classical implication. It is well known that the implicative fragment of *CPL*, corresponding to the language defined by the grammar $\mathcal{L}_c ::= P \mid (\mathcal{L}_c \Rightarrow \mathcal{L}_c)$, can be characterized deductively by the axioms

> **(C1)** $A \Rightarrow (B \Rightarrow A)$
> **(C2)** $(A \Rightarrow (B \Rightarrow C)) \Rightarrow ((A \Rightarrow B) \Rightarrow (A \Rightarrow C))$
> **(C3)** $((A \Rightarrow B) \Rightarrow A) \Rightarrow A$

and the inference rule

$$\frac{A \quad (A \Rightarrow B)}{B} \quad \textbf{(CMP)}.$$

Note that **C3** is *Peirce's law* and **CMP** the rule of *Modus Ponens*. We use $\vdash_c$ to denote the resulting deductive consequence relation, that is, we write $\Gamma \vdash_c A$

to denote the fact that there exists a derivation of A from the set of hypotheses Γ using **C1-C3** and **CMP**.

Analogously, let us consider a set Q of intuitionistic propositional symbols, and let us use $\to$ to denote classical implication. The implicative fragment of *IPL*, corresponding to the language defined by $\mathcal{L}_i ::= Q \mid (\mathcal{L}_i \to \mathcal{L}_i)$, is also well known to be characterized deductively by the axioms

$$\textbf{(I1)} \quad A \to (B \to A)$$
$$\textbf{(I2)} \quad (A \to (B \to C)) \to ((A \to B) \to (A \to C))$$

and the inference rule

$$\frac{A \quad (A \to B)}{B} \quad \textbf{(IMP)}.$$

Comparing with the classical case, we have just excluded Peirce's law and rephrased the first two axioms and Modus Ponens using the intuitionistic arrow. We use now $\vdash_i$ to denote the resulting deductive consequence relation. Obviously, classical implication is stronger than intuitionistic implication. In particular, we have $\vdash_c ((A \Rightarrow B) \Rightarrow A) \Rightarrow A$ but $\nvdash_i ((A \to B) \to A) \to A$. Recall also that both implications enjoy the *deduction theorem*, that is

- $\Gamma, A \vdash_c B$ iff $\Gamma \vdash_c A \Rightarrow B$, where $\Gamma \cup \{A, B\} \subseteq \mathcal{L}_c$, and
- $\Gamma, A \vdash_i B$ iff $\Gamma \vdash_i A \to B$, where $\Gamma \cup \{A, B\} \subseteq \mathcal{L}_i$.

In order to combine the two fragments of *CPL* and *IPL*, let us consider adding together the axioms **C1-C3**, **I1-I2**, and the rules **CMP**, **IMP**, now over the combined language given by $\mathcal{L} ::= P \mid Q \mid (\mathcal{L} \Rightarrow \mathcal{L}) \mid (\mathcal{L} \to \mathcal{L})$. Henceforth, we will assume that the sets of classical and intuitionistic propositional symbols are disjoint, that is, $P \cap Q = \emptyset$. Denoting by $\vdash$ the resulting consequence relation, it will be reasonable to expect that $A \to B \vdash A \Rightarrow B$. However, the converse would be highly undesirable, not only because classical implication should be strictly stronger than intuitionistic implication, but also because the two would collapse. Gabbay's argument for the collapse of $\to$ into $\Rightarrow$ after the combination [5] was based on the assumption that the deduction theorem of each of the two implications in isolation would be transported to their combination. If that was the case, since we have $A \Rightarrow B, A \vdash B$ simply by using **CMP**, we could use the deduction theorem for $\to$ and immediately obtain $A \Rightarrow B \vdash A \to B$. Still, in this setting, it is not at all obvious that we can still use the deduction theorem over the combined language. Actually, although $\vdash A \to B$ implies $\vdash A \Rightarrow B$, it is even unclear how to obtain $A \to B \vdash A \Rightarrow B$ in the first place. If we take a little time trying to prove any meaningful interaction between $\to$ and $\Rightarrow$ using $\vdash$ we will soon be convinced that most probably the two implications do not collapse. Clearly, it would suffice to prove that $\nvdash ((A \to B) \to A) \to A$. Of course, we might try to prove this using some sort of combinatory argument over the possible deductions. But it will be much more enlightening to try and use a semantic argument, that is, to look for some sort of combined model m that falsifies $((A \to B) \to A) \to A$.

Let $\mathcal{M}_c$ stand for the class of all classical two-valued models. That is, a model in $\mathcal{M}_c$ is simply a function $v : P \to \{\bot, \top\}$ where, as usual, we define satisfaction of classical formulas inductively by:

- $v \Vdash_c p$ iff $v(p) = \top$;
- $v \Vdash_c A \Rightarrow B$ iff $v \nVdash_c A$ or $v \Vdash_c B$.

We will use $\vDash_c$ to denote the induced *entailment relation*, that is, given $\Gamma \cup \{A\} \subseteq \mathcal{L}_c$, we have $\Gamma \vDash_c A$ provided that $v \Vdash \Gamma$ implies $v \Vdash A$ for every $v \in \mathcal{M}_c$. It will be helpful to view classical models as *logical matrices* [13]. Given $v \in \mathcal{M}_c$, its associated matrix is $M(v) = \langle \{\bot, \top\}, \top, \cdot_v \rangle$, where $\{\bot, \top\}$ is the set of possible *truth-values*; $\top$ is the *designated* value; $p_v = v(p)$; and $\Rightarrow_v$ is given by the usual truth table, shown below.

$\Rightarrow_v$	$\bot$	$\top$
$\bot$	$\top$	$\top$
$\top$	$\bot$	$\top$

Clearly, v satisfies the formula A if and only $A_v = \top$, the designated truth-value.

For intuitionistic logic, we shall consider $\mathcal{M}_i$ to be the usual class of *rooted Kripke models*. That is, a model $k \in \mathcal{M}_i$ is a tuple $k = \langle W, \leq, V \rangle$ where W is a nonempty set partially ordered by $\leq$ and with a least element, that we will denote by w_0, and $V : Q \to \mathcal{U}_\leq$ is a function, where $\mathcal{U}_\leq$ is the set of all *uppersets* of $\langle W, \leq \rangle$, that is, all sets $U \subseteq W$ such that if $w \in U$ and $w \leq w'$ then also $w' \in U$. Recall that $k \Vdash_i A$ iff $(k, w) \Vdash_i A$ for every $w \in W$, where the local satisfaction relation at a fixed world w is defined inductively by

- $(k, w) \Vdash_i q$ iff $w \in V(q)$;
- $(k, w) \Vdash_i A \to B$ iff for every $w' \geq w$, $(k, w') \nVdash_i A$ or $(k, w') \Vdash_i B$.

As above, we will use $\vDash_i$ to denote the induced *entailment relation*. Given $\Gamma \cup \{A\} \subseteq \mathcal{L}_i$, we have $\Gamma \vDash_i A$ provided that $k \Vdash \Gamma$ implies $k \Vdash A$ for every $k \in \mathcal{M}_i$. The logical matrix corresponding to an intuitionistic model $k = \langle W, \leq, V \rangle \in \mathcal{M}_i$, is $M(k) = \langle \mathcal{U}_\leq, W, \cdot_k \rangle$, where the truth-values are the uppersets; the designated upperset is W; $q_k = V(q)$; and $U_1 \to_k U_2 = \{w \in W : \text{ if } w \leq w' \text{ and } w' \in U_1 \text{ then } w' \in U_2\}$. It is clear that k satisfies the formula A if and only $A_k = W$.

It is obvious that the sort of combined models for $C + J$ considered by Herzig and del Cerro in [4] does not fit our purposes, since their target was rather to stick with the obvious way of extending the intuitionistic models with an interpretation for classical implication, as is done in the usual Kripke structures for modal logic, and to axiomatize these models using adapted versions of the original axioms. Concretely, they considered an extended satisfaction relation $\Vdash$ over an intuitionistic model k such that

- $(k, w) \Vdash A \Rightarrow B$ iff $(k, w) \nVdash A$ or $(k, w) \Vdash B$.

However, as they show, these models will turn the axiomatization of intuitionistic implication unsound.

A second alternative would be to look for a convenient combined model obtained by *fibring* [6,1] a classical and an intuitionistic model. However, this is well-known to fail too because every fibred model will collapse the two implications. In order to understand why this happens, it suffices to note that fibring $v \in \mathcal{M}_c$ and $k \in \mathcal{M}_i$ requires that both models, seen as logical matrices, share the same set of truth-values and the same designated value (modulo possible renaming). Since every possible v yields exactly two truth-values, we get stuck with intuitionistic models $k = \langle W, \leq, V \rangle$ such that $\mathcal{U}_\leq$ has exactly two elements: $\emptyset$ and W. This means that there is only one world, i.e., $W = \{w_0\}$. By letting $\bot = \emptyset$ and $\top = W$ we can then get a fibred model, but one where intuitionistic implication is interpreted as $\rightarrow_k$, whose classical truth-table is shown below.

$\rightarrow_k$	$\emptyset$	W
$\emptyset$	W	W
W	$\emptyset$	W

However, as explained in [3], cryptofibring offers another option. We need a combined model m that behaves like v and k on the classical and intuitionistic fragments, respectively, but which is as free as possible on combined formulas, that is, a model m that extends k with an interpretation for $\Rightarrow$ that behaves as v on $\bot = \emptyset$ and $\top = W$. The model should also guarantee the persistence requirement that is essential for the soundness of the intuitionistic axioms. Clearly, $\rightarrow_k$ as defined above always yields an upperset. It is easy to see that $U_1 \rightarrow_k U_2$ is precisely the largest upperset contained in $X = (W \setminus U_1) \cup U_2$, like the *interior* operation in a topological space. We just compute X and get rid of the worlds $w \in X$ for which there exists w' such that $w \leq w'$ but $w' \notin X$. Still, there are other ways of achieving this. Our proposal is to interpret classical implication in such a way that $U_1 \Rightarrow_m U_2$ is the least upperset containing X, mimicking now the *closure* operation in a topological space. That is, we just compute X and add w' provided that there exists $w \in X$ such that $w \leq w'$ and $w' \notin X$. To interpret the classical propositional symbols we must add a copy of the classical valuation v to each world of k. The interpretation of classical symbols will be persistent in a very strong way: either p holds at all worlds, or at none.

Definition 1 (Combined models)

A *combined model* for the language $\mathcal{L}$ is a tuple $m = \langle W, \leq, \overline{V} \rangle$ where $\langle W, \leq \rangle$ is a partial order with a least element and $\overline{V} : P \cup Q \rightarrow \wp(W)$ is such that

- $\overline{V}(p) \in \{\emptyset, W\}$ for every $p \in P$;
- $\overline{V}(q) \in \mathcal{U}_\leq$ for every $q \in Q$.

The satisfaction of a formula $A \in \mathcal{L}$ is defined by $m \Vdash A$ if and only if $(m, w) \Vdash A$ for every $w \in W$, where the satisfaction at a world is defined inductively by

- $(m, w) \Vdash p$ iff $w \in \overline{V}(p)$;
- $(m, w) \Vdash q$ iff $w \in \overline{V}(q)$;
- $(m, w) \Vdash A \Rightarrow B$ iff there exists $w' \leq w$ such that $(m, w') \nVdash A$ or $m, w' \Vdash B$;
- $(m, w) \Vdash A \rightarrow B$ iff for every $w' \geq w$, $(m, w') \nVdash A$ or $(m, w') \Vdash B$.

We denote by $\mathcal{M}$ the class of all combined models.

We now define the semantics of our combined logic *CIPL*. Let $\Gamma \cup \{A\} \subseteq \mathcal{L}$.

Definition 2 (*CIPL*)
The *entailment relation* $\vDash$ of *CIPL* over the language $\mathcal{L}$ is defined, as usual, from satisfaction: $\Gamma \vDash A$ if $m \Vdash \Gamma$ implies $m \Vdash A$ for every $m \in \mathcal{M}$.

Our work, in the next sections, will be to study *CIPL* in detail.

3   Interacting Implications

To start our study of *CIPL*, via a semantic analysis of the class of models $\mathcal{M}$, we first note that there is a direct correspondence between combined models and pairs of classical and intuitionistic models. Given a combined model $m = \langle W, \leq, \overline{V} \rangle$, we can define classical and intuitionistic models

- $m|_c : P \to \{\bot, \top\}$ with $m|_c(p) = \begin{cases} \top \text{ if } \overline{V}(p) = W \\ \bot \text{ if } \overline{V}(p) = \emptyset \end{cases}$; and
- $m|_i = \langle W, \leq, \overline{V}|_Q \rangle$.

Conversely, given $v \in \mathcal{M}_c$ and $k = \langle W, \leq, V \rangle$ we can define a combined model

- $v \oplus k = \langle W, \leq, \overline{V} \rangle$ with $\overline{V}(p) = \begin{cases} W \text{ if } v(p) = \top \\ \emptyset \text{ if } v(p) = \bot \end{cases}$ and $\overline{V}(q) = V(q)$.

Proposition 1. *Let $m \in \mathcal{M}$, $v \in \mathcal{M}_c$ and $k \in \mathcal{M}_i$. We have:*

1. $m|_c \in \mathcal{M}_c$ and $m|_i \in \mathcal{M}_i$;
2. $v \oplus k \in \mathcal{M}$;
3. $m|_c \oplus m|_i = m$;
4. $(v \oplus k)|_c = v$ and $(v \oplus k)|_i = k$.

As a consequence, $\mathcal{M} = \{v \oplus k : v \in \mathcal{M}_c, k \in \mathcal{M}_i\}$.

Proof. The properties 1–4 are all straightforward from the definitions. The fact $\mathcal{M} = \{v \oplus k : v \in \mathcal{M}_c, k \in \mathcal{M}_i\}$ is a simple consequence of these properties. $\square$

A simple observation is that a combined model $v \oplus k$ indeed extends v and k, in the respective fragments.

Proposition 2. *Let $m \in \mathcal{M}$, $x \in \{c, i\}$ and $A \in \mathcal{L}_x$. We have $m \Vdash A$ if and only if $m|_x \Vdash_x A$.*

Proof. We first prove the result for $x = c$. Given any $w \in W$, it suffices to show that $(m, w) \Vdash A$ if and only if $m|_c \Vdash_c A$. The proof follows by induction on $A \in \mathcal{L}_c$. For a classical propositional symbol p, we have $(m, w) \Vdash p$ iff $w \in \overline{V}(p)$ iff $\overline{V}(p) \neq \emptyset$ iff $\overline{V}(p) = W$ iff $m|_c(p) = \top$ iff $m|_c \Vdash_c p$. Consider now the case $A \Rightarrow B \in \mathcal{L}_c$. Then, $(m, w) \Vdash A \Rightarrow B$ iff there exists $w' \leq w$ such that $(m, w') \not\Vdash A$ or $(m, w') \Vdash B$ iff, by induction hypothesis, $m|_c \not\Vdash_c A$ or $m|_c \Vdash_c B$ iff $m|_c \Vdash_c A \Rightarrow B$.

The proof for $x = i$ and $A \in \mathcal{L}_i$ is similar. Given any $w \in W$, it suffices to show that $(m, w) \Vdash A$ if and only if $(m|_i, w) \Vdash_i A$. The proof follows by induction on A. Consider first the case of an intuitionistic propositional symbol q. Then, $(m, w) \Vdash q$ iff $w \in \overline{V}(q)$ iff $w \in \overline{V}|_Q(q)$ iff $(m|_i, w) \Vdash_i q$. Consider now the case $A \to B \in \mathcal{L}_i$. Then, $(m, w) \Vdash A \to B$ iff $(m, w') \not\Vdash A$ or $(m, w') \Vdash B$, for every $w' \geq w$, iff, by induction hypothesis, $(m|_i, w') \not\Vdash_i A$ or $(m|_i, w') \Vdash_i B$, for every $w' \geq w$, iff $(m|_i, w) \Vdash_i A \to B$. $\qquad\square$

What we already know is enough to prove that *CIPL* is indeed a conservative extension of both the implicative fragments of *CPL* and *IPL*.

Theorem 1 (Conservativeness). *Let $x \in \{c, i\}$ and $\Gamma \cup \{A\} \subseteq \mathcal{L}_x$. We have $\Gamma \vDash A$ if and only if $\Gamma \vDash_x A$.*

Proof. The proof of the left-to-right implication is a direct application of Propositions 1–2, using the fact that both $\mathcal{M}_c \neq \emptyset$ and $\mathcal{M}_i \neq \emptyset$. Namely, for $x = c$, assume that $\Gamma \cup \{A\} \subseteq \mathcal{L}_c$ and $\Gamma \vDash A$. Let $v \in \mathcal{M}_c$ be such that $v \Vdash_c \Gamma$. Since $\mathcal{M}_i \neq \emptyset$ we can pick any intuitionistic model $k \in \mathcal{M}_i$ and build $v \oplus k \in \mathcal{M}$, according to Proposition 1. Hence, by using Proposition 2, we also know that $v \oplus k \Vdash \Gamma$ and by definition of entailment it follows that $v \oplus k \Vdash A$. Again using Proposition 2 we can conclude that $v \Vdash_c A$ and thus $\Gamma \vDash_c A$. The proof for $x = i$ is analogous.

The right-to-left implication is just a consequence of Proposition 2. $\qquad\square$

Let us now investigate, in detail, the properties of our combined models. Recall that we claimed, as a justification for their definition, that even the interpretation of classical formulas would be persistent.

Theorem 2 (Persistence)
Let $m = \langle W, \leq, \overline{V} \rangle \in \mathcal{M}$, $w \in W$ and $A \in \mathcal{L}$. If $(m, w) \Vdash A$ and $w \leq w'$ then $(m, w') \Vdash A$.

Proof. The proof follows by case analysis on the structure of formulas. The cases of atomic formulas, both classical and intuitionistic, follow straightforwardly from the definition of $\overline{V}$.

If $(m, w) \Vdash A \Rightarrow B$ then there exists $w'' \leq w$ such that $(m, w'') \not\Vdash A$ or $(m, w'') \Vdash B$. But, $w'' \leq w'$ and so $(m, w') \Vdash A \Rightarrow B$.

If $(m, w) \Vdash A \to B$ then either $(m, w'') \not\Vdash A$ or $(m, w'') \Vdash B$, for all $w'' \geq w$. It is straightforward to see that for any $w' \geq w$, $(m, w') \Vdash A \to B$. $\qquad\square$

Note that, as a corollary of persistence, the satisfaction of any formula $A \in \mathcal{L}$ by a model m can be simply checked at the root world w_0.

Corollary 1 (Satisfaction at the root)
Let $m \in \mathcal{M}$ and $A \in \mathcal{L}$. We have $m \Vdash A$ if and only if $(m, w_0) \Vdash A$.

Another direct consequence of Theorem 2 is that the satisfaction of formulas involving classical implication can be simplified.

Corollary 2 (Satisfaction of classical implication)
Let $A, B \in \mathcal{L}$, $m \in \mathcal{M}$ and $w \in W$. We have $(m, w) \Vdash A \Rightarrow B$ if and only if $(m, w_0) \not\Vdash A$ or $(m, w) \Vdash B$.

As should be expected, formulas in the classical fragment are even more than persistent, they are constant.

Proposition 3. *Let $m = \langle W, \leq, \overline{V} \rangle \in \mathcal{M}$, $w, w' \in W$ and $A \in \mathcal{L}_c$. We have $(m, w) \Vdash A$ if and only if $(m, w') \Vdash A$.*

Proof. The proof follows by induction on the structure of A. The case of atomic formulas is straightforward from the definition of $\overline{V}$. Consider $A \Rightarrow B \in \mathcal{L}_c$. Then, $(m, w) \Vdash A \Rightarrow B$ iff $(m, w_0) \not\Vdash A$ or $(m, w) \Vdash B$ iff, by induction hypothesis, $(m, w_0) \not\Vdash A$ or $(m, w') \Vdash B$ iff $(m, w') \Vdash A \Rightarrow B$. $\qquad\square$

We can now start to inspect closely the relationship between the two implications. As desired, we will show that classical implication is strictly stronger than intuitionistic implication.

Proposition 4. *Let $A, B \in \mathcal{L}$, $m = \langle W, \leq, \overline{V} \rangle \in \mathcal{M}$ and $w \in W$. If $(m, w) \Vdash A \to B$ then $(m, w) \Vdash A \Rightarrow B$. As a consequence, we have $A \to B \vDash A \Rightarrow B$.*

Proof. Assume that $(m, w) \Vdash A \to B$. Then, for every $w' \geq w$, either $(m, w') \not\Vdash A$ or $(m, w') \Vdash B$. Assume now, by absurd, that $(m, w) \not\Vdash A \Rightarrow B$. Then, $(m, w_0) \Vdash A$ and $(m, w) \not\Vdash B$. Since $(m, w_0) \Vdash A$ and $w_0 \leq w$, by persistence, we must also have $(m, w') \Vdash A$. Therefore, it must be the case that $(m, w') \Vdash B$ for every $w' \geq w$. But then, if we let $w' = w$ we obtain $(m, w) \Vdash B$, a contradiction. $\qquad\square$

The converse of the previous result does not hold, in general. Consider two intuitionistic propositional symbols q_1 and q_2, and take the model $m = \langle \{w_0, w_1\}, \leq, \overline{V} \rangle$ such that $w_0 \leq w_1$, $\overline{V}(q_1) = \{w_1\}$ and $\overline{V}(q_2) = \emptyset$. It is straightforward to see that $m \Vdash q_1 \Rightarrow q_2$ but $m \not\Vdash q_1 \to q_2$. Consequently, he have that $q_1 \Rightarrow q_2 \not\vDash q_1 \to q_2$. Still, there are certain particular situations in which the two implications coincide. A simple sufficient condition is that A be a classical formula.

Proposition 5. *Let $A \in \mathcal{L}_c$, $B \in \mathcal{L}$, $m = \langle W, \leq, \overline{V} \rangle \in \mathcal{M}$ and $w \in W$. Then, $(m, w) \Vdash (A \Rightarrow B) \to (A \to B)$. As a consequence, we have $\vDash (A \Rightarrow B) \to (A \to B)$.*

Proof. Suppose, by absurd, that $(m, w) \not\Vdash (A \Rightarrow B) \to (A \to B)$, for A classic. Then, there exists $w' \geq w$ such that $(m, w') \Vdash A \Rightarrow B$ and $(m, w') \not\Vdash A \to B$. On one hand, there exists $w'' \geq w'$ such that $(m, w'') \Vdash A$ and $(m, w'') \not\Vdash B$. On the other hand, either $(m, w_0) \not\Vdash A$ or $(m, w') \Vdash B$. As A is classic, by Proposition 3, the first condition is not possible. By Theorem 2, the second condition is also impossible. Hence, we have a contradiction. $\qquad\square$

Note that, as a consequence of the previous result, if A is classical then $A \Rightarrow B \models A \to B$. The essential ingredient of the proof is that the value of classical formulas does not change as one goes up the order on worlds. Actually, even if A is not classical, a similar situation arises as long as the value of A can be guaranteed not to change, that is, if A holds.

Proposition 6. *Let* $A, B \in \mathcal{L}$, $m = \langle W, \leq, \overline{V} \rangle \in \mathcal{M}$ *and* $w \in W$. *Then,* $(m, w) \Vdash A \Rightarrow ((A \Rightarrow B) \to (A \to B))$. *As a consequence,* $\models A \Rightarrow ((A \Rightarrow B) \to (A \to B))$.

Proof. Suppose, by absurd, that $(m, w) \not\Vdash A \Rightarrow ((A \Rightarrow B) \to (A \to B))$. Then, $(m, w_0) \Vdash A$ and $(m, w) \not\Vdash (A \Rightarrow B) \to (A \to B)$. Hence, there exists $w' \geq w$ such that $(m, w') \Vdash A \Rightarrow B$ and $(m, w') \not\Vdash A \to B$. On one hand, there exists $w'' \geq w'$ such that $(m, w'') \Vdash A$ and $(m, w'') \not\Vdash B$. On the other hand, either $(m, w_0) \not\Vdash A$ or $(m, w') \Vdash B$. The first condition is clearly impossible. The second condition is also impossible, by Theorem 2, since $w \leq w' \leq w''$.   □

The two implication connectives further interact in a number of interesting ways. Namely, note that if A holds in a world then also does $B \Rightarrow A$.

Proposition 7. *Let* $A, B \in \mathcal{L}$, $m = \langle W, \leq, \overline{V} \rangle \in \mathcal{M}$ *and* $w \in W$. *Then,* $(m, w) \Vdash A \to (B \Rightarrow A)$. *As a consequence we have* $\models A \to (B \Rightarrow A)$.

Proof. Assume, by absurd, that $(m, w) \not\Vdash A \to (B \Rightarrow A)$. Then, there exists $w' \geq w$ such that $(m, w') \Vdash A$ and $(m, w') \not\Vdash B \Rightarrow A$. Hence, $(m, w_0) \Vdash B$ and, more importantly, $(m, w') \not\Vdash A$ which is a contradiction.   □

Another interesting fact is that classical implication distributes over intuitionistic implication.

Proposition 8. *Given* $A, B \in \mathcal{L}$ *and* $m \in \mathcal{M}$, *then* $(m, w) \Vdash (X \Rightarrow (A \to B)) \to ((X \Rightarrow A) \to (X \Rightarrow B))$. *Consequently* $\models (X \Rightarrow (A \to B)) \to ((X \Rightarrow A) \to (X \Rightarrow B))$.

Proof. Assume, by absurd, that $(m, w) \not\Vdash (X \Rightarrow (A \to B)) \to ((X \Rightarrow A) \to (X \Rightarrow B))$. Then, there exists $w' \geq w$ such that $(m, w') \Vdash X \Rightarrow (A \to B)$ and $(m, w') \not\Vdash (X \Rightarrow A) \to (X \Rightarrow B)$. Hence, there is $w'' \geq w'$ such that $(m, w'') \Vdash X \Rightarrow A$ and $(m, w'') \not\Vdash X \Rightarrow B$. So, $(m, w_0) \Vdash X$ and $(m, w'') \not\Vdash B$. This implies that $(m, w'') \Vdash A$ and $(m, w') \Vdash A \to B$, which is impossible because $w' \leq w''$, $(m, w'') \Vdash A$ and $(m, w'') \not\Vdash B$.   □

Finally, we should note that a semantic form of the deduction theorem for classical implication holds.

Proposition 9. *Let* $\Gamma \cup \{A, B\} \subseteq \mathcal{L}$. *We have* $\Gamma, A \models B$ *if and only if* $\Gamma \models A \Rightarrow B$.

Proof. Assume that $\Gamma, A \models B$ and let $m \in \mathcal{M}$ be such that $m \Vdash \Gamma$. We need to prove that $(m, w_0) \Vdash A \Rightarrow B$. If $(m, w_0) \not\Vdash A$ we are done. Let us suppose, otherwise, that $(m, w_0) \Vdash A$. Then, we know that $m \Vdash A$ as well and by definition of entailment it follows that $m \Vdash B$ and, in particular, that $(m, w_0) \Vdash A \Rightarrow B$. Hence, we have $\Gamma \vDash A \Rightarrow B$.

Conversely, assume that $\Gamma \vDash A \Rightarrow B$ and let $m \in \mathcal{M}$ be such that $m \Vdash \Gamma$ and $m \Vdash A$. By entailment, we also known that $m \Vdash A \Rightarrow B$. Therefore, we have $(m, w_0) \Vdash A \Rightarrow B$ and $(m, w_0) \Vdash A$, and it follows immediately that $(m, w_0) \Vdash B$, that is, $m \Vdash B$. Thus, we get $\Gamma, A \vDash B$. □

For intuitionistic implication, however, the deduction theorem does not hold in general. Given the previous result, this is not unexpected since we already know that the two implications, in general, do not coincide. Note, in particular, that $A \Rightarrow B, A \vDash B$ but $A \Rightarrow B \nvDash A \rightarrow B$.

4   Axiomatization and Completeness

At this point, we are ready to propose an axiomatization for the combined logic *CIPL*.

Definition 3. The axiomatization of *CIPL* consists of the axioms

(C1)	$A \Rightarrow (B \Rightarrow A)$
(C2)	$(A \Rightarrow (B \Rightarrow C)) \Rightarrow ((A \Rightarrow B) \Rightarrow (A \Rightarrow C))$
(C3)	$((A \Rightarrow B) \Rightarrow A) \Rightarrow A$
(I1)	$A \rightarrow (B \rightarrow A)$
(I2)	$(A \rightarrow (B \rightarrow C)) \rightarrow ((A \rightarrow B) \rightarrow (A \rightarrow C))$
(X1)	$A \rightarrow (B \Rightarrow A)$
(X2)	$(A \Rightarrow B) \rightarrow (A \rightarrow B)$, for A classical
(X3)	$A \rightarrow ((A \Rightarrow B) \rightarrow (A \rightarrow B))$
(X4)	$(X \Rightarrow (A \rightarrow B)) \rightarrow ((X \Rightarrow A) \rightarrow (X \Rightarrow B))$

and the inferences rules

$$\frac{A \quad (A \Rightarrow B)}{B} \quad \textbf{(CMP)}$$

$$\frac{A \quad (A \rightarrow B)}{B} \quad \textbf{(IMP)}.$$

We denote by $\vdash$ the corresponding deductive consequence relation.

As we had promised, the axiomatization was obtained by adding together the axiomatizations of classical implication, **C1-C3** and **CMP**, and intuitionistic implication, **I1-I2** and **IMP**, with four interaction axioms **X1-X4**. Note that each of these interaction axioms has already been discussed in the preceding section, namely at Propositions 7, 5, 6 and 8, respectively. The soundness of these axioms and rules can be easily obtained.

Theorem 3 (Soundness)
Let $\Gamma \cup \{A\} \subseteq \mathcal{L}$. If $\Gamma \vdash A$ then $\Gamma \vDash A$.

Proof. It suffices to show that each of the axioms and rules are sound. Let m be a model.

Let us take **C1**. Assume that $m \not\Vdash A \Rightarrow (B \Rightarrow A)$, i.e. $(m, w) \not\Vdash A \Rightarrow (B \Rightarrow A)$, for some $w \in W$. Then, $(m, w_0) \Vdash A$ and $(m, w) \not\Vdash B \Rightarrow A$, i.e. $(m, w_0) \Vdash B$ and $(m, w) \not\Vdash A$. By Proposition 2, $(m, w_0) \Vdash A$ and $(m, w) \not\Vdash A$ constitute a contradiction. Hence, $m \Vdash A \Rightarrow (B \Rightarrow A)$.

The proofs for **C2** and **C3** are similar. Let us now consider the rule **CMP**. Assume that $m \Vdash A$ and $m \Vdash A \Rightarrow B$. Furthermore, assume by absurd that $m \not\Vdash B$. Then, there is w such that $(m, w) \not\Vdash B$ and by Proposition 2, $(m, w_0) \not\Vdash B$. On the other hand, $(m, w_0) \Vdash A$ and $(m, w_0) \Vdash A \Rightarrow B$ which implies that $(m, w_0) \Vdash B$, contradicting our assumption.

Take now **I1** and assume that $m \not\Vdash A \rightarrow (B \rightarrow A)$, i.e. $(m, w) \not\Vdash A \rightarrow (B \rightarrow A)$, for some $w \in W$. Then, there is $w' \geq w$ such that $(m, w') \Vdash A$ and $(m, w') \not\Vdash B \rightarrow A$. This implies that there is $w'' \geq w'$ such that $(m, w'') \Vdash B$ and $(m, w'') \not\Vdash A$. By Proposition 2, as $w'' \geq w'$, we have a contradiction.

The proof for **I2** is similar. Let us now consider the rule **IMP**. Assume that $m \Vdash A$ and $m \Vdash A \rightarrow B$. Furthermore, assume, by absurd, that $m \not\Vdash B$. Then, there exists $w \in W$ such that $(m, w) \not\Vdash B$. On the other hand, $(m, w) \Vdash A$ and $(m, w) \Vdash A \rightarrow B$ which imply that $(m, w) \Vdash B$, which, again, is a contradiction.

Finally, the soundness for the interaction axioms **X1-X4** was already established in Propositions 5-8. $\qquad \square$

We now proceed to establishing the completeness of the proposed axiomatization. As a preliminary step, we begin by obtaining the deduction theorem for classical implication.

Theorem 4 (Classical deduction theorem (CDED))
Let $\Gamma \cup \{A, B\} \subseteq \mathcal{L}$. We have $\Gamma, A \vdash B$ if and only if $\Gamma \vdash A \Rightarrow B$.

Proof. Assume that $\Gamma, A \vdash B$. We prove that $\Gamma \vdash A \Rightarrow B$ by induction on the length of the derivation of $\Gamma, A \vdash B$. If B is an axiom then:

$$\begin{array}{lll}
1.\ B & & \mathbf{Ax} \\
2.\ B \Rightarrow (A \Rightarrow B) & & \mathbf{C1} \\
3.\ A \Rightarrow B & & \mathbf{CMP} : 1, 2
\end{array}$$

Hence, $\Gamma \vdash A \Rightarrow B$. If $B \in \Gamma$ then the proof is similar. If B is A then $\Gamma \vdash A \Rightarrow A$, which can be derived as usual in classical logic.

If B resulted from $C \Rightarrow B$ and C using **CMP** then, by induction hypothesis, there are derivations for $\Gamma \vdash A \Rightarrow (C \Rightarrow B)$ and $\Gamma \vdash A \Rightarrow C$. Then:

$$\begin{array}{lll}
\quad \vdots & & \\
n.\ A \Rightarrow (C \Rightarrow B) & & \text{Hyp.} \\
\quad \vdots & & \\
n'.\ A \Rightarrow C & & \text{Hyp.} \\
n'+1.\ A \Rightarrow (C \Rightarrow B) \Rightarrow ((A \Rightarrow C) \Rightarrow (A \Rightarrow B)) & & \mathbf{C3} \\
n'+2.\ (A \Rightarrow C) \Rightarrow (A \Rightarrow B) & & \mathbf{CMP} : n, n'+1 \\
n'+3.\ A \Rightarrow B & & \mathbf{CMP} : n', n'+2
\end{array}$$

Note that this derivation depends only on Γ, thus $\Gamma \vdash A \Rightarrow B$.

Assume now that B resulted from $C \to B$ and C using **IMP**. Then, by induction hypothesis, there are derivations for $\Gamma \vdash A \Rightarrow C$ and $\Gamma \vdash A \Rightarrow (C \to B)$. Hence:

$$\vdots$$
$$n.\ A \Rightarrow (C \to B) \qquad\qquad\qquad\qquad \text{Hyp.}$$
$$\vdots$$
$$n'.\ A \Rightarrow C \qquad\qquad\qquad\qquad\qquad \text{Hyp.}$$
$$n'+1.\ (A \Rightarrow (C \to B)) \to ((A \Rightarrow C) \to (A \Rightarrow B)) \quad \textbf{X4}$$
$$n'+2.\ (A \Rightarrow C) \to (A \Rightarrow B) \qquad\qquad\ \ \textbf{IMP} : n, n'+1$$
$$n'+3.\ A \Rightarrow B \qquad\qquad\qquad\qquad\qquad\ \ \textbf{IMP} : n', n'+2$$

Once again, this derivation depends only on Γ, thus $\Gamma \vdash A \Rightarrow B$.

The converse is straightforward, using **CMP**. $\qquad\qquad\qquad\qquad\qquad$ $\square$

Although it fails in general, it is possible to formulate and prove a form of deduction theorem for the intuitionistic implication. For the purpose, we just need to consider derivations obtained without using the rule of classical *Modus Ponens*. Henceforth, we write $\Gamma \vdash_\to A$ to denote the fact that there is a derivation of A from Γ using only the axioms and the rule **IMP**. Obviously, if $\Gamma \vdash_\to A$ then $\Gamma \vdash A$.

Theorem 5 (Intuitionistic deduction theorem (IDED))
Let $\Gamma \cup \{A, B\} \subseteq \mathcal{L}$. We have $\Gamma, A \vdash_\to B$ if and only if $\Gamma \vdash_\to A \to B$.

Proof. Straightforward. $\qquad\qquad\qquad\qquad\qquad\qquad\qquad\qquad\qquad\qquad$ $\square$

Another useful result is that, as a consequence of the corresponding deduction theorems, each of the implications enjoys a form of *hypothetical syllogism*.

Corollary 3 (Hypothetical syllogism)
The following deductions hold for every $A, B, C \in \mathcal{L}$.

$$\textbf{(CHS)} \qquad A \Rightarrow B, B \Rightarrow C \vdash A \Rightarrow C$$
$$\textbf{(IHS)} \qquad A \to B, B \to C \vdash_\to A \to C$$

Going now towards the completeness proof, let us use $\Gamma^\vdash$ to denote the *theory* $\{A \in \mathcal{L} : \Gamma \vdash A\}$. We will also use $\Gamma^{\vdash_\to}$ to denote the set $\{A \in \mathcal{L} : \Gamma \vdash_\to A\}$. As usual, given a formula A, we will say that a theory Γ is *maximal relatively to A* if $\Gamma \not\vdash A$ but $\Gamma, B \vdash A$ for every $B \notin \Gamma$.

Theorem 6 (Completeness)
Let $\Gamma \cup \{A\} \subseteq \mathcal{L}$. If $\Gamma \models A$ then $\Gamma \vdash A$.

Proof. Assume that $\Gamma \not\vdash A$. We will show how to build a model m of Γ that does not satisfy A. Let Δ_0 be a theory extending Γ, such that Δ_0 is maximal relatively to A. Note that the existence of such a Δ_0 is guaranteed by the general form of Lindenbaum's lemma [13]. Consider now the sets $\Delta_s \subseteq \mathcal{L}$ satisfying the following conditions:

- $\Delta_0 \subseteq \Delta_s$;
- $\Delta_s \cap P = \Delta_0 \cap P$;
- $\Delta_s = \Delta_s^{\vdash\to}$.

Consider the tuple $m = \langle W, \subseteq, \overline{V} \rangle$ where W is the set of all Δ_s sets, and $\overline{V}$ is such that $\overline{V}(q) = \{\Delta_s : q \in \Delta_s\}$. We first observe that Δ_0 fulfills the above conditions on the sets Δ_s and, consequently, $\Delta_0 \in W$. Then, we also observe that $\langle W, \subseteq \rangle$ is a partial order with a least element which, by construction, is Δ_0. Furthermore, we also have that if $p \in P$ then either $p \in \Delta_0$ and $\overline{V}(p) = W$ or $p \notin \Delta_0$ and $V(p) = \emptyset$. Finally, if $q \in Q$, $\Delta_s \in \overline{V}(q)$ and $\Delta_s \subseteq \Delta_{s'}$ then $q \in \Delta_{s'}$ and so $\Delta_{s'} \in \overline{V}(q)$, i.e. q is persistent. All these conditions imply that $m \in \mathcal{M}$. We prove some auxiliary results about m.

Lemma 1. $B \in \Delta_0$ if and only if $B \Rightarrow A \notin \Delta_0$.

Proof. Assume that $B \in \Delta_0$. If $B \Rightarrow A \in \Delta_0$ then $A \in \Delta_0$, by **CMP**, which is a contradiction. Assume now that $B \notin \Delta_0$. As Δ_0 is maximal relatively to A, then $\Delta_0, B \vdash A$ and by **CDED** we have $B \Rightarrow A \in \Delta_0$.   □

Lemma 2. $B \Rightarrow C \in \Delta_0$ if and only if $B \notin \Delta_0$ or $C \in \Delta_0$.

Proof. If $B \Rightarrow C \in \Delta_0$ and $B \in \Delta_0$ then by **CMP** $C \in \Delta_0$. Assume now that $C \in \Delta_0$. Then, by **C1** and **CMP**, we have $B \Rightarrow C \in \Delta_0$. If $B \notin \Delta_0$ then, by Lemma 1, $B \Rightarrow A \in \Delta_0$. On the other hand, using **C3**, $((A \Rightarrow C) \Rightarrow A) \Rightarrow A \in \Delta_0$. Hence, by Lemma 1, $(A \Rightarrow C) \Rightarrow A \notin \Delta_0$. Again by Lemma 1, $A \Rightarrow C \in \Delta_0$. If $B \Rightarrow A \in \Delta_0$ and $A \Rightarrow C \in \Delta_0$ then, by **CHS**, $B \Rightarrow C \in \Delta_0$.   □

Lemma 3. For every $\Delta_s \in W$, $A \Rightarrow B \in \Delta_s$ if and only if $A \notin \Delta_0$ or $B \in \Delta_s$.

Proof. Assume that $A \Rightarrow B \in \Delta_s$ and that $A \in \Delta_0 \subseteq \Delta_s$. By **X3**, $A \Rightarrow ((A \Rightarrow B) \to (A \to B)) \in \Delta_0$ and using **CMP**, $(A \Rightarrow B) \to (A \to B) \in \Delta_0 \subseteq \Delta_s$. As Δ_s is closed for **IMP** it follows that $A \to B \in \Delta_s$. Again by **IMP** we have $B \in \Delta_s$.

If $A \notin \Delta_0$ then, by Lemma 2, $A \Rightarrow B \in \Delta_0 \subseteq \Delta_s$. If $B \in \Delta_s$ then, using **X1** and the fact that Δ_s is closed for **IMP**, it follows that $A \Rightarrow B \in \Delta_s$.   □

Lemma 4. For every $\Delta_s \in W$, $B \to C \in \Delta_s$ if and only if for every Δ_s' such that $\Delta_s \subseteq \Delta_s'$, if $B \in \Delta_s'$ then $C \in \Delta_s'$.

Proof. The left-to-right implication is straightforward by **IMP**. For the converse, consider the set $\Delta_s' = (\Delta_s \cup \{B\})^{\vdash\to}$ and assume that $C \in \Delta_s'$. Then, either Δ_s' has the same classical propositional symbols as Δ_0 or not. Let us assume first that Δ_s' has the same classical propositional symbols as Δ_0. Then $\Delta_s, B \vdash_\to C$ and by **IDED**, it follows that $B \to C \in \Delta_s$. Assume now that Δ_s' does not have the same classical propositional symbols as Δ_0. Then, $\Delta_s, B \vdash_\to p$, for some $p \in P$ such that $p \notin \Delta_0$. By **IDED**, $\Delta_s \vdash B \to p$. On the other hand, by Lemma 1, $p \Rightarrow A \in \Delta_0$, and by Lemma 2, $A \Rightarrow C \in \Delta_0$. So, by **CHS**, $p \Rightarrow C \in \Delta_0 \subseteq \Delta_s$. As p is classic, by **X2**, $(p \Rightarrow C) \to (p \to C) \in \Delta_s$ and by **IMP** it follows that $p \to C \in \Delta_s$. So, by **IHS**, we can conclude that $B \to C \in \Delta_s$.   □

Finally, we prove that, for $\Delta_s \in W$, $(m, \Delta_s) \Vdash B$ if and only if $B \in \Delta_s$. We proceed by induction on B. If B is a propositional symbol the result follows from the construction of $\overline{V}$. Consider now the case $B \Rightarrow C$. Then $(m, \Delta_s) \Vdash B \Rightarrow C$ iff either $(m, \Delta_0) \nVdash B$ or $(m, \Delta_s) \Vdash C$ iff, by induction hypothesis, either $B \notin \Delta_0$ or $C \in \Delta_s$ iff, by Lemma 3, $B \Rightarrow C \in \Delta_s$. Finally, consider the case $B \rightarrow C$. In this case, $(m, \Delta_s) \Vdash B \rightarrow C$ iff for every $\Delta'_s \supseteq \Delta_s$, either $(m, \Delta'_s) \nVdash B$ or $(m, \Delta'_s) \Vdash C$ iff for every $\Delta'_s \supseteq \Delta_s$, either $B \notin \Delta'_s$ or $C \in \Delta'_s$, by induction hypothesis, iff $B \rightarrow C \in \Delta_s$, by Lemma 4.

Hence, we conclude that $m \Vdash \Gamma$ and $(m, \Delta_0) \nVdash A$, and so $\Gamma \nVdash A$.

5 Concluding Remarks

In this paper we have introduced an extended Kripke semantics for both *CPL* and *IPL*, where classical and intuitionistic implications are shown not to coincide. We have also shown that the implicative fragment of the resulting combined logic *CIPL* is a conservative extension of the implicative fragments of both *CPL* and *IPL*, thus settling a problem raised by Dov Gabbay in [5]. In addition, we have provided a simple complete axiomatization for the combined logic, which adds four simple interaction axioms to the usual axiomatizations of classical and intuitionistic implications.

The logic *CIPL* is, to the best of our knowledge, the first logic that extends classical and intuitionistic logics in a conservative way. Note that the completeness theorem was obtained using fairly classical tools. It is interesting to note that our axiomatization works only for rooted models. Actually, if we consider arbitrary Kripke models we will get a logic that is similar in most respects to the one obtained here, with the exception of axiom **X3**. However, we were unable to find a property that would replace the role played by **X3** in the completeness proof. This is an open question for future research. Other topics for further investigation concern studying the combination of the full languages of *CPL* and *IPL*, as well as the decidability and algebraizability of the logics obtained. Note, however, that the *amalgamation*-like flavour of our class of models as expressed by Proposition 1 will still guarantee conservativeness, as well as a few other interesting independence properties, in a way similar to *Robinson's consistency theorem* for first-order theories. It is also worth mentioning that the assumption that $P \cap Q = \emptyset$ plays an important role here: the combined logic will only be a conservative extension of the classical and intuitionistic logics built over non-shared symbols.

It is interesting to note that our extended Kripke semantics, namely where classical implication is concerned, is very closely related to other extensions of intuitionistic Kripke semantics that can be found in the literature. Most notably, we should mention the *coimplication* of [11,14], but also Humberstone's *anticipation* operator [9], or the logic of *bunched implications* of [10]. A thorougher comparison with our *CIPL*, namely with respect to their topological semantic aspects is certainly needed. Of course, from the point of view of Grzegorczyk's logic of scientific reasoning [8], there is a simple meaning for our interpretation of classical implication. However, it is hard to say whether there is any connection to constructive proofs. In any case, developments in type theories have found that classical implication plays an essential role in typing certain control structures occurring in functional programs [7]. This is a line of research that is certainly worth exploring.

References

1. Caleiro, C., Carnielli, W.A., Rasga, J., Sernadas, C.: Fibring of logics as a universal construction. In: Gabbay, D., Guenthner, F. (eds.) Handbook of Philosophical Logic, 2nd edn., vol. 13, pp. 123–187. Springer, Heidelberg (2005)
2. Caleiro, C., Ramos, J.: Cryptomorphisms at work. In: Fiadeiro, J.L., Mosses, P.D., Orejas, F. (eds.) WADT 2004. LNCS, vol. 3423, pp. 45–60. Springer, Heidelberg (2005)
3. Caleiro, C., Ramos, J.: From fibring to cryptofibring: a solution to the collapsing problem. Logica Universalis 1(1), 71–92 (2007)
4. Cerro, L.F.d., Herzig, A.: Combining classical and intuitionistic logic. In: Baader, Schulz (eds.) Frontiers of combining systems, vol. 3, pp. 93–102. Kluwer Academic Publishers, Dordrecht (1996)
5. Gabbay, D.: An overview of fibred semantics and the combination of logics. In: Baader, F., Schulz, K.U. (eds.) Frontiers of Combining Systems, vol. 3, pp. 1–56. Kluwer Academic Publishers, Dordrecht (1996)
6. Gabbay, D.: Fibring Logics. Oxford University Press, Oxford (1999)
7. Griffin, T.: A formulae-as-type notion of control. In: POPL '90. Proc. 17th ACM Symp. Principles of Programming Languages, pp. 47–58. ACM Press, New York (1990)
8. Grzegorczyk, A.: A philosophically plausible formal interpretation of intuitionistic logic. Indagationes Mathematicae 26, 596–601 (1964)
9. Humberstone, L.: The pleasures of anticipation: enriching intuitionistic logic. Journal of Philosophical Logic 30, 395–438 (2001)
10. Pym, D.: The Semantics and Proof Theory of the Logic of Bunched Implications. Kluwer Academic Publishers, Dordrecht (2002)
11. Rauszer, C.: Semi-Boolean algebras and their applications to intuitionistic logic with dual operators. Fudamenta Mathematicae 83, 219–249 (1974)
12. Van Dalen, D.: Intuitionistic logic. In: Gabbay, D., Guenthner, F. (eds.) Handbook of Philosophical Logic, vol. 3, pp. 225–340. Reidel
13. Wójcicki, R.: Theory of Logical Calculi. Kluwer Academic Publishers, Dordrecht (1988)
14. Wolter, F.: On logics with coimplication. Journal of Philosophical Logic 27, 353–387 (1998)

Towards an Automatic Analysis of Web Service Security

Yannick Chevalier[1], Denis Lugiez[2], and Michaël Rusinowitch[3,*]

[1] IRIT, Team LiLac, Université de Toulouse, France
ychevali@irit.fr
[2] LIF, CNRS, Aix-Marseille Université, France
lugiez@lif.univ-mrs.fr
[3] LORIA-INRIA-Lorraine, France
rusi@loria.fr

Abstract. Web services send and receive messages in XML syntax with some parts hashed, encrypted or signed, according to the WS-Security standard. In this paper we introduce a model to formally describe the protocols that underly these services, their security properties and the rewriting attacks they might be subject to. Unlike other protocol models (in symbolic analysis) ours can handle non-deterministic receive/send actions and unordered sequence of XML nodes. Then to detect the attacks we have to consider the services as combining multiset operators and cryptographic ones and we have to solve specific satisfiability problems in the combined theory. By non-trivial extension of the combination techniques of [3] we obtain a decision procedure for insecurity of Web services with messages built using encryption, signature, and other cryptographic primitives. This combination technique allows one to decide insecurity in a modular way by reducing the associated constraint solving problems to problems in simpler theories.

Keyword: Security, Web services, verification, cryptographic protocols, combination of decision procedures, equational theories, rewriting.

1 Introduction

Web services promise to be a standard technology for Internet and enterprise networks. They require the ability to transmit securely messages in XML syntax using the SOAP protocol. Messages that travel over the networks can be observed and modified by intruders. Hence the protocol was extended by W3C for allowing one to sign and encrypt some parts of the contents. Nevertheless, as for classical protocols, cryptographic mechanisms are not sufficient for securing Web services. They can be subject to the same attacks (e.g. man-in-the middle) as classical cryptographic protocols, but the XML syntax and the specific way messages are

---

* This work has been supported by ACI-Jeunes Chercheurs Crypto, ACI-SI SATIN and ARA SSIA Cops.

B. Konev and F. Wolter (Eds.): FroCos 2007, LNAI 4720, pp. 133–147, 2007.

processed (e.g. not examining the full content) gives the opportunity to mount a new class of attacks, such as XML rewriting attacks, as shown in [1].

Recently many decision procedures have been proposed for analysing cryptographic protocols. These procedures rely on automated deduction and constraint solving procedures extending semantic unification. Our objective in this work is to investigate whether these results can be lifted to Web services. First it appears immediately that the flexible XML format requires one to consider message contents as sets of terms rather than terms: this introduces a first difficulty since no security decidability results exist yet for protocols using such a data structure. Second, since messages are only partially parsed by SOAP, the answer to a request might depend on the implementation: in other words we have to model a non-deterministic behaviour of the Web service protocols.

A role-based protocol model has been proposed in previous works [2]. This model admits two versions. In the first one, the *equational model*, operations (including decryption) are explicit and the basic operations are deterministic. We believe that this constraint is inherent to the model, as non-determinism in equational theories leads to inconsistency. The second model, the *pattern-matching model*, relies on patterns to filter incoming messages. It has been widely studied but proofs in this model are often complex and obscure, and there is no general combination result that would permit one to extend existing decision procedures to a new operation (the multiset operator, in our case).

Motivated by these facts, and also for the sake of deriving a uniform framework, we propose a protocol model that is more general than the two commonly used ones. It represents XML messages as multisets of terms and simulates nondeterministic behaviours. Moreover decidability and combination results (previous known only for the equational model [3]) have been lifted to this model. The proofs are involved and cannot be obtained from the ones in simpler models.

Related work. The Samoa Project project [1] offers a language to express SOAP-based security protocols which is compiled into the applied π calculus on which the resolution based system ProVerif is run to verify secrecy and authentication properties. Our approach is a complementary one since it provides decision procedures that are complete for finitely many sessions, even with an associative-commutative XML message constructor and other operators such as Dolev Yao encryption/decryption. A lot of work has been dedicated to security analysis of protocols modulo algebraic properties (see e.g. [4,5,6]). However no decidability results have been reported for associative or associative-commutative operators, supporting the combination with useful cryptographic primitives (such as XOR). To our knowledge, the ones we report here are the first of this kind, and we show how they apply to deciding security properties of XML services. Our results rely on extensive use of term rewriting and unification techniques [7].

Paper organization. First, we describe an example of XML-rewriting attacks in Sec. 2, then we recall the notions of term rewriting we use on our model in Sec. 3. Sec. 4 formally models service executions by the deductions that can be performed by intruders and honest agents. In particular we introduce *symbolic derivations* as parameterized deductions. They can be viewed as a variant of *strand spaces*, a fundamental concept in protocol analysis [8]. Security in this model reduces to a constraint satisfiability problem. We give an algorithm for solving it for the case of plain Web services in Sec. 5. Sec. 6 presents a combination scheme that applies to multiset and cryptographic operators: it provides us with a decidable analysis of XML protocols.

The long version [9] of this paper contains all missing lemmas and proofs.

2   An Example of Web Service and XML Rewriting Attack

Web services can be described as a set of receive/send action between clients and the provider, where the messages are XML terms following the SOAP format. Messages are constructed and parsed according to the security policy of the service which usually requires that some parts of the message are encrypted, signed using known algorithms like sha1, rsa,..., may contain timestamps, make reference to trusted third parties,.... A SOAP message is an envelope consisting of a mandatory body and of an optional header. The header contains the useful information about the message and usually has a security part that follows the WS-security specification defined by the OASIS organization. For instance, Alice may order a ticket for Bremen for herself to be charged to her account by sending send the following message to Bob, her correspondent in the travel agency:

```
<Envelope>
  <Header>
    <To> http://www.travel-for-free.com/~bob </>
    <Security>
      <timestamp>2007-04-16T09:56:43Z</>
      <signature>
        <signedInfo>
          <reference URI=#1>a string</>
          <signatureValue>another string </>
      </></></></>
    <Body>
      <Order id=1>
        <beneficiary>Alice</>
        <account>Alice</>
        <trip>Bremen</>
    </></></>
```

In the header, the first string is a digest of the body, and the other string is the encryption of this digest using the private key of Alice. For efficiency purposes, only parts of the messages are encrypted or signed. Since a node labelled by a tag 'a' may have an arbitrary number of elements, we introduce a unary symbol $a(\_)$ for each tag 'a' and an associative-commutative multiset constructor. For instance, the body of the above message corresponds to the term $Body(Order(beneficiary(Alice) \cdot account(Alice) \cdot trip(Bremen)))$ where $e_1 \cdot \ldots \cdot e_n$ denotes the multiset $\{e_1, \ldots, e_n\}$. Another possibility is to replace the multiset operator by an associative operator for sequences. In Web services, components of messages are selected by their tag and security policies usually refer to this name and don't consider the possibility of multiple occurrences of the same tag.

In our example, the recipient Bob performs several security checks, including the verification of the signature, then looks for a part of the *Body* labelled *Order*, orders a ticket for the requested trip and charges Alice's account. Then, he sends to Alice a SOAP message with a security header containing the digest of the original message and a body containing an accesscode for the trip encoded by the public key of the beneficiary (that Alice will transfer to the beneficiary). Like in the study of cryptographic protocols, we assume that cryptography is perfect, but we don't make any particular hypothesis on the implementation of parsing XML trees. An attacker Charlie may intercept the message and forge a new one that inserts a new *Order* item to the *Body*:

```
<Order id=2>
  <beneficiary>Charlie </>
  <account>Alice</>
  <trip> Hawaii</>
</>
```

before the previous *Order*. An implementation of the service may lead to a successful verification of the signature and to sending the accesscode to Charlie depending on how the XML term is parsed. If the first match of *Order* is chosen, then Charlie gets the accesscode, since the signature is correct because the reference to the initial *Order* is still used. Another implementation could parse the children of a node from right to left and select the correct *Order* subterm. Therefore the behavior of the protocol is non-deterministic which we model by rules that select a element *Order(_)* in a multiset. We shall model the service by deduction rules and equations that model all the operations that the participants can do and all algebraic relations that may hold between the operators A possible abstraction of the security protocol $\mathcal{P}$ that supports the service is:

$$A \rightarrow B : se(h(order(x,y,z)), SK_A) \cdot order(x,y,z)$$
$$B \rightarrow A : se(h(order(x,y,z)), PK_A) \cdot se(accesscode(z), PK_x)$$

where h denotes a hashing function, $order(x,y,z)$ denotes the request for trip z for beneficiary x, with y the account to charge, h is a hash function, *accesscode(z)* is the code requested to get the ticket from automata, $se(x,y)$ denotes the encryption of x using key y, PK_x is the public key of x, SK_x is the private key of x. The intruder deductive power is given by the classical Dolev-Yao rules (see [10,11]) extended by a rule that allows us to select any element in a multiset. Some realistic implementations of the service (like the one in Section 4) are subject to the following attack (assuming that $C = I$ or C is compromised):

$$A \rightarrow I_B : se(h(order(A, A, Bremen)), SK_A) \cdot order(A, A, Bremen)$$
$$I_A \rightarrow B : se(h(order(A, A, Bremen)), SK_A) \cdot order(C, A, Hawaii) \cdot order(A, A, Bremen)$$
$$B \rightarrow I_A : se(h(order(A, A, Bremen)), PK_A) \cdot se(accesscode(Hawaii), PK_C)$$

where I_A (resp. I_B) denotes a malicious agent I masquerading the honest participant A (resp. B), and the secret key SK_C is known by I.

3   Terms, Subterms and Ordered Rewriting

Basic notions. We consider an infinite set of free constants C and an infinite set of variables X. For all signatures $\mathcal{F}$ (*i.e.* a set of function symbols with arities), we denote by $T(\mathcal{F})$ (resp. $T(\mathcal{F}, X)$) the set of terms over $\mathcal{F} \cup C$ (resp. $\mathcal{F} \cup C \cup X$). The former is called the set of ground terms over $\mathcal{F}$, while the later is simply called the set of terms over $\mathcal{F}$. Variables are denoted by x, y, terms are denoted by s, t, u, v, and finite sets of terms are written $E, F, ...$, and decorations thereof, respectively. For finite sets of terms, we abbreviate $E \cup F$ by E, F and the union $E \cup \{t\}$ by E, t.

Given a signature $\mathcal{F}$ a *constant* is either a free constant or a function symbol of arity 0 in $\mathcal{F}$. For a term t, $\mathrm{Var}(t)$ is the set of variables occurring in t and by $\mathrm{Cons}(t)$ is the set of constants occurring in t. An *atom* is either a variable or a constant and we denote by $\mathrm{Atoms}(t)$ the set $\mathrm{Var}(t) \cup \mathrm{Cons}(t)$. The application of a substitution σ to a term t (resp. a set of terms E) is denoted $t\sigma$ (resp. $E\sigma$). An *equational presentation* $\mathcal{H} = (\mathcal{F}, A)$ is defined by a set A of equations $r = t$ with $r, t \in T(\mathcal{F}, X)$. For any equational presentation $\mathcal{H}$ the relation $=_{\mathcal{H}}$ denotes the equational theory generated by $(\mathcal{F}, A)$ on $T(\mathcal{F}, X)$. An $\mathcal{H}$-*Unification system* S is a finite set of pairs of terms in $T(\mathcal{F}, X)$ denoted by $(u_i \overset{?}{=} v_i)_{i \in \{1,...,n\}}$. The ground substitution σ satisfies S, denoted by $\sigma \models S$, iff for all $i \in \{1, \ldots, n\}$ $u_i\sigma =_{\mathcal{H}} v_i\sigma$. Syntactic subterms and positions are defined as usual (see [12,13]), and the replacement of the subterm of t by s at position p is denoted by $t[p \leftarrow s]$, for a set of positions Π, $t[\Pi \leftarrow s]$ denotes the replacement of all subterms at position $p \in \Pi$ by s.

Congruences and ordered rewriting. Let $<$ be a simplification ordering on $T(\mathcal{F})^1$, total on $T(\mathcal{F})$, such that (i) the minimal element for $<$ is a constant $c_{\min} \in C$; (ii) each non-free constant is smaller than any non-constant ground term. C_{spe} denotes the set containing the constants in $\mathcal{F}$ and $c_{\min}$. Given a possibly infinite set of equations O on the signature $T(\mathcal{F})$ the ordered rewriting relation $\rightarrow_O$ is defined by $t \rightarrow_O t'$ iff there exists a position p in t, an equation $l = r$ in O, a substitution τ such that $t = t[p \leftarrow l\tau]$, $t' = t[p \leftarrow r\tau]$, and $l\tau > r\tau$.

It has been shown that by applying the *unfailing completion procedure* to a set of equations $\mathcal{H}$ yields a (possibly infinite) set of equations O such that: (i) the congruence relations $=_O$ and $=_{\mathcal{H}}$ are equal on $T(\mathcal{F})$, (ii) the ordered rewrite relation $\rightarrow_O$ is convergent (*i.e.* terminating and confluent) on $T(\mathcal{F})$. We say that O is an *o-completion* of $\mathcal{H}$. Since the rewrite system $\rightarrow_O$ is convergent on ground terms, we can define $(t)\!\downarrow_O$ as the unique normal form of the ground term t for $\rightarrow_O$. A ground term t is in *normal form*, or *normalised*, if $t = (t)\!\downarrow_O$. Given a ground substitution σ we denote by $(\sigma)\!\downarrow_O$ the substitution with the same support such that $x(\sigma)\!\downarrow_O = (x\sigma)\!\downarrow_O$ for all variables x in the support of σ. A substitution σ is *normal* if $\sigma = (\sigma)\!\downarrow_O$.

---

[1] By definition $<$ satisfies for all $s, t, u \in T(\mathcal{F})$ $s < t[s]$ and $s < u$ implies $t[s] < t[u]$.

4   Modelling Service Execution

4.1   A Model for Secure Web Services

Let us first briefly review the situation we want to model. Some simple Web services are akin to functions in a library. Their execution is triggered by the reception of a request from a client, to which they immediately respond. These services are advertised by a WSDL specification that defines among other things the contents of the input and output messages. It is also possible to specify some cryptographic protection for integrity, confidentiality and authenticity of a request by means of a published security policy. This policy will constrain acceptable requests by mandating that some parts have to be signed, encrypted or integrity protected. These parts are expressed either by identifiers or by XPath expressions, and we say that these services are *protected*. Finally, some WS standards, *e.g.* BPEL, WS-SecureConversation, and others, permit to express sequences of simple service invocations, which we call *workflows*. We call totally ordered sequences *workflow executions*, as they also correspond to traces of service workflows.

The analysis of Web services is thus very similar to the one of cryptographic protocols. A protected service workflow is a composition of *roles* (client, service,...), and a workflow execution is akin to a protocol execution. *Agents* impersonate the roles in a workflow execution.

This similarity shall not, however, hide the differences at the level of messages. In the case of cryptographic protocols, the patterns of admissible messages are fixed, and known by the intruder, whereas security policies just express constraints on the presence of some particular subterms at some position in a message. Moreover, and since services are in most cases automatically generated, the verification of a message is likely to be independent of the construction of a response. Finally, some implementations may return only one node in a hedge when several ones correspond to an XPath expression, thereby allowing for XML injection attacks. The work described in this paper focuses on security policies expressing paths of subterms from the root (envelope) of the message, leaving general XPath constraints to future work.

Example 1. A client A invokes a service B by sending $se(h(order(x, y, z)), SK_A) \cdot order(x, y, z)$, where x, y and z are instantiated parameters of the client. Then it receives a response r which is parsed to check that it contains the nodes $se(z, PK_A)$ and $se(u, v)$ at its root, with $v = PK_x$ and $z = h(order(x, y, z))$.

The intruder and the insecurity problem. In the Dolev-Yao model [10], attacks on protocols are modelled by the addition of a malicious participant, called the intruder, that controls the network. It can intercept, block and/or redirect all messages sent by honest agents. It can also masquerade its identity and take part in the protocol under the identity of an honest participant. Its control of the communication network is modelled by assuming that all messages sent by honest agents are sent directly to the intruder and that all messages received by the honest agents are always sent by the intruder. Besides the control on the net, the intruder has specific rules to deduce new values and compute messages.

From the intruder's point of view a finite execution of a protocol is therefore the interleaving of a finite sequence of messages it has to send and a finite sequence of messages it receives (and add to its knowledge). Therefore the intruder is simply an additional role that runs concurrently with the honest participants.

The protocol is insecure if some secret knowledge is revealed during the execution of the protocol, which is modelled by adding a last step that reveals the secret. The insecurity problem amounts to finding a sequence of actions of the intruder such that its composition with the extended protocol is executable.

4.2   Deduction Systems

We give a formal model for roles and the execution of roles (including the intruder). Messages are ground terms and deduction rules are rewrite rules on sets of messages representing the knowledge of an agent. Each role derives new messages from a given (finite) set of messages by using deduction rules. Furthermore, these derivations are considered *modulo* the equational congruence $=_{\mathcal{H}}$ generated by the equational axioms satisfied by the function symbols of the signature $\mathcal{F}$. Let O be an o-completion of $\mathcal{H}$. We write $(t)\!\downarrow$ as a short-hand for $(t)\!\downarrow_O$.

Definition 1. *A* deduction rule *is a rule* $d : t_1, \ldots, t_n \to t$ *with* $t_1, \ldots, t_n, t$ *terms s.t.* $\mathrm{Const}((t\sigma)\!\downarrow) \subseteq \cup_{i=1}^n \mathrm{Const}((t_i\sigma)\!\downarrow) \cup \mathrm{C}_{\mathrm{spe}}$ *for any ground substitution* σ.

This condition is very similar to the *origination* condition for well-definedness in [14]. When the equational theory is regular (i.e. the same variables occur on each side of axioms) then this condition holds iff $\mathrm{Var}(t) \subseteq \mathrm{Var}(t_1, \ldots, t_n)$.

Example 2. $x, y \to \langle x, y \rangle$ is a deduction rule when assuming that the set of equational axioms is empty. This rules allows an agent (who can be the intruder) to construct a new pair from two values already known.

Deduction rules are the basic ingredients for deduction systems.

Definition 2. *A* deduction system $\mathcal{D}$ *is a triple* $\langle \mathcal{F}, \mathcal{R}, \mathcal{H} \rangle$ *where* $\mathcal{F}$ *is a signature,* $\mathcal{R}$ *is a set of deduction rules and* $\mathcal{H}$ *is a set of equations between terms in* $\mathrm{T}(\mathcal{F}, \mathcal{X})$. *For each deduction rule* $d : t_1, \ldots, t_n \to t \in \mathcal{R}$, *the set* $\mathrm{GI}(d)$ *denotes the set of ground instances of the rule* d *modulo* $\mathcal{H}$:

$$\mathrm{GI}(d) = \{l \to r \,|\, \exists \sigma, \text{ ground substitution on } \mathcal{F}, \ l =_{\mathcal{H}} t_1\sigma, \ldots, t_n\sigma \text{ and } r =_{\mathcal{H}} t\sigma\}$$

where $=_{\mathcal{H}}$ *is extended to sets of terms in the natural way. The set of rules* $\mathrm{GI}_{\mathcal{D}}$ *is defined as the union of the sets* $\mathrm{GI}(d)$ *for all* $d \in \mathcal{R}$.

Example 3. Let $\mathcal{F} = \{\langle \_, \_ \rangle, \mathrm{se}(\_, \_), \cdot, a(\_)\}$, $\mathcal{R}_{\mathcal{D}} = \{x, y \to \langle x, y \rangle \,; x, y \to \mathrm{se}(x, y);$ $\mathrm{se}(x, y), y \to x; \langle x_1, x_2 \rangle \to x_i; x, y \to x \cdot y; x \cdot y \to x; a(x) \to x; x \to a(x)\}$, $\mathcal{H} = \{x \cdot y = y \cdot x, x \cdot (y \cdot z) = (x \cdot y) \cdot z\}$. The rules associated with a are extended to any n-ary operator added to the signature representing an XML node. Then the deduction system $\mathcal{D} = \langle \mathcal{F}, \mathcal{R}_{\mathcal{D}}, \mathcal{H} \rangle$ describes the classical Dolev-Yao model with the addition of an associative-commutative operation $\cdot$ and of the rules that allow us to build multisets with $\cdot$ or to extract parts of a multiset.

Each deduction rule $l \rightarrow r$ in $\mathrm{GI}_{\mathcal{D}}$ defines an deduction relation $\rightarrow_{l \rightarrow r}$ between finite sets of terms: given two finite sets of terms E and F we define $E \rightarrow_{l \rightarrow r} F$ if and only if $l \subseteq E$ and $F = E, r$. We denote $\rightarrow_{\mathcal{D}}$ the union of the relations $\rightarrow_{l \rightarrow r}$ for all $l \rightarrow r$ such that $l \rightarrow r \in \mathrm{GI}(d)$ for some $d \in \mathcal{R}$, and by $\rightarrow_{\mathcal{D}}^{*}$ the transitive closure of $\rightarrow_{\mathcal{D}}$. We simply denote by $\rightarrow$ the relation $\rightarrow_{\mathcal{D}}$ when there is no ambiguity about the deduction system $\mathcal{D}$.

Definition 3. *A derivation D of length $n \geq 0$, is a sequence $E_0 \rightarrow_{\mathcal{D}} E_1 \rightarrow_{\mathcal{D}} \cdots \rightarrow_{\mathcal{D}} E_n$ where $E_0, \ldots E_n$ are finite set of ground terms such that $E_i = E_{i-1}, t_i$ for every $i \in \{1, \ldots, n\}$. The term t_n is called the goal of the derivation.*

Example 4. The previous deduction system has a derivation:

$$\{K_a, \langle \mathrm{se}(s, K_a), a \rangle, a, b\} \rightarrow_{\mathcal{D}} \{K_a, \langle \mathrm{se}(s, K_a), a \rangle, \mathrm{se}(s, K_a), a, b\}$$
$$\rightarrow_{\mathcal{D}} \{K_a, \langle \mathrm{se}(s, K_a), a \rangle, \mathrm{se}(s, K_a), s, a, b\}$$

that shows the discovering of a secret s by an intruder that knows the encryption key K_a, identity of agents and intercepts a message $\langle \mathrm{se}(s, K_a), a \rangle$. The ground deduction rules employed are $\langle \mathrm{se}(s, K_a), a \rangle \rightarrow \mathrm{se}(s, K_a)$ and $\mathrm{se}(s, K_a), K_a \rightarrow s$

$\mathrm{Der}_{\mathcal{D}}(E) = \{t \mid \exists F \text{ s.t. } E \rightarrow_{\mathcal{D}}^{*} F \text{ and } t \in F\}$ is the set of terms derivable from E is. We write $\mathrm{Der}(E)$ instead of $\mathrm{Der}_{\mathcal{D}}(E)$ when there is no ambiguity on $\mathcal{D}$.

4.3 Symbolic Derivation

Given a deduction system $\langle \mathcal{F}, \mathcal{R}, \mathcal{E} \rangle$, a role applies rules in $\mathcal{R}$ to construct the response of step i and tests equalities to check the well-formedness of a message. Hence the activity of a role can be expressed by a fixed symbolic derivation:

Definition 4. *(Symbolic Derivation) A symbolic derivation for deduction system $\langle \mathcal{F}, \mathcal{R}, \mathcal{E} \rangle$ is a tuple $(\mathcal{V}, \mathcal{S}, \mathcal{K}, \mathrm{IN}, \mathrm{OUT})$ where $\mathcal{V}$ is a finite sequence of variables, $(x_i)_{i \in Ind}$, indexed by a linearly ordered set $(Ind, <)$, $\mathcal{K}$ is a set of ground terms (the initial knowledge) $\mathrm{IN}, \mathrm{OUT}$ are disjoint subsets of Ind and $\mathcal{S}$ is a set of equations such that for all $x_i \in \mathcal{V}$ one of the following holds:*

- *$i \in \mathrm{IN}$*
- *There exists a ground term $t \in \mathcal{K}$ and an equation $x_i \overset{?}{=} t$ in $\mathcal{S}$;*
- *There exists a rule $l_1, \ldots, l_m \rightarrow r \in \mathcal{R}$ such that $\mathcal{S}$ contains the equations $x_i \overset{?}{=} r$ and $x_{\alpha_j} \overset{?}{=} l_j$ for $j \in \{1, \ldots, m\}$ with $\alpha_j < i$.*

A symbolic derivation is closed if $\mathrm{IN} = \mathrm{OUT} = \emptyset$, in which case it may be simply denoted by $(\mathcal{V}, \mathcal{S}, \mathcal{K})$. A substitution σ satisfies a closed symbolic derivation if $\sigma \models_{\mathcal{E}} \mathcal{S}$.

To improve readability of the examples, we replace every index i in a set of indices I by the variable x_i associated to this index, and we do not model the equations $x_i \overset{?}{=} t$ for $t \in \mathcal{K}$, writing t directly when x_i is needed, nonetheless keeping track of these variables in a set $\mathcal{V}_{\mathcal{K}}$. We will also employ _ to denote a variable appearing only once.

Example 5. The client A of $\mathcal{P}$ can be described by the deduction system $\mathcal{D}$ of Ex. 3. Starting from the initial knowledge $\mathcal{K}_A = \{a, b, Bremen, SK_a, PK_a\}$, the client applies the following ground instances of deduction rules. First it builds $x_1^A = order(a, a, Bremen)$ from $a, Bremen \in \mathcal{K}_A$ (ground instance of the rule $x, y, z \to order(x, y, z)$), then builds $x_2^A = h(x_1^A)$ from x_1^A and $x_3^A = se(x_2^A, SK_a)$. Finally it computes and sends $x_4^A = x_3^A \cdot x_1^A$, and waits for the response x_5^A. From x_5^A it extracts two components x_6^A and x_7^A, decrypts x_6^A with SK_a and checks that the result is equal to x_2^A and finally decrypts x_7^A to obtain the accesscode. A symbolic derivation for this role is $(\mathcal{V}_{\mathcal{K}_A} \cup (x_i^A)_{1 \leq i \leq 9}, S, \mathcal{K}_A, \{x_5^A\}, \{x_4^A\})$ with:

$$S = \begin{cases} x_1^A \overset{?}{=} order(a, a, Bremen) & x_2^A \overset{?}{=} h(x_1^A) & x_3^A \overset{?}{=} se(x_2^A, SK_a) \\ x_4^A \overset{?}{=} x_3^A \cdot x_1^A & x_5^A \overset{?}{=} x_6^A \cdot \_ & x_5^A \overset{?}{=} x_7^A \cdot \_ \\ x_6^A \overset{?}{=} se(x_8^A, PK_a) & x_7^A \overset{?}{=} se(x_9^A, PK_a) & x_8^A \overset{?}{=} x_2^A \end{cases}$$

To compose two symbolic derivations we identify some input variables of one derivation with some output variables of the other and vice-versa. This connection should be compatible with the variable orderings inherited from each component, as detailed in the following definition:

Definition 5. *Let* $C_1 = (\mathcal{V}_1, S_1, \mathcal{K}_1, \text{IN}_1, \text{OUT}_1)$, $C_2 = (\mathcal{V}_2, S_2, \mathcal{K}_2, \text{IN}_2, \text{OUT}_2)$ *be two symbolic derivations, with disjoint sets of variables and index sets* $(Ind_1, <_1)$ *and* $(Ind_2, <_2)$ *respectively. Let* I_1, I_2, O_1, O_2 *be subsets of* $\text{IN}_1, \text{IN}_2, \text{OUT}_1, \text{OUT}_2$ *respectively. and assume that there is an order-preserving bijection* ϕ *from* $I_1 \cup I_2$ *to* $O_1 \cup O_2$ *such that* $\phi(I_1) = O_2$ *and* $\phi(I_2) = O_1$. *A composition of two symbolic derivations along the sets* I_1, O_1, I_2, O_2 *is a symbolic derivation*

$$C = (\mathcal{V}, \phi(S_1 \cup S_2), \mathcal{K}_1 \cup \mathcal{K}_2, (\text{IN}_1 \cup \text{IN}_2) \setminus (I_1 \cup I_2), (\text{OUT}_1 \cup \text{OUT}_2) \setminus (O_1 \cup O_2))$$

where ϕ *is extended to a substitution on terms by setting* $\phi(x_i) = x_j$ *if* $\phi(i) = j$, $\mathcal{V}$ *is a sequence of variables indexed by* $Ind = (Ind_1 \setminus I_1) \cup (Ind_2 \setminus I_2)$, *ordered by a linear extension of the transitive closure of the relation:*

$$<_1 \cup <_2 \cup \{(u, v) \mid v = \phi(w) \text{ and } u <_1 w \text{ or } u <_2 w\}$$

and such that the variable of index i *in* $\mathcal{V}$ *is equal to the variable of index* i *in* $\mathcal{V}_1$ *if* $i \in Ind_1$, *and to the variable of index* i *in* $\mathcal{V}_2$ *if* $i \in Ind_2$.

A composition of two symbolic derivations is also a symbolic derivation and we can compose an arbitrary number of symbolic derivations in the same way.

Example 6. Let us consider the symbolic derivation of the previous example, and let us assume that the variables are ordered as $y_1^A, x_1^A, y_1^B, y_2^B, x_2^A, y_2^A$. The normal execution of the protocol $\mathcal{P}$ corresponds to a composition of the two symbolic derivations of the previous example along $I_1 = \{x_2^A\}, O_1 = \{y_1^A\}, I_2 = \{x_1^B\}, O_2 = \{y_1^B\}$, *i.e.* where x_2^A (resp. x_1^B) is replaced by y_1^B (resp. y_1^A).

4.4   The Formal Statement of Protocol Insecurity

As mentioned in Section 4.1, protocol insecurity can be reduced to the executability of the protocol extended by a step revealing a secret. Since we are interested to decide insecurity for combined deduction systems we will define a slightly more general problem that is also more modular:

Ordered Satisfiability

Input: a symbolic derivation C_h for $\langle \mathcal{F}, \mathcal{R}, \mathcal{E} \rangle$ (protocol), a set of terms $\mathcal{K}_i$ (intruder knowledge), X the set of all variables, C the set of free constants occurring in C_h and a linear ordering $\prec$ on $X \cup C$.

Output: SAT iff there exists a symbolic derivation $C_i = (\mathcal{V}_i, S_i, \mathcal{K}_i, \mathrm{IN}_i, \mathrm{OUT}_i)$ for $\langle \mathcal{F}, \mathcal{R}, \mathcal{E} \rangle$, a closed composition C_a of C_i and C_h, and a substitution σ such that σ satisfies C_a and: $\forall c \in C, x \prec c$ implies $c \notin \mathrm{Const}(x\sigma)$

4.5   Comparison with Pattern-Matching and Equational Models

The pattern-matching model. In this model pattern-matching is used to extract the components of incoming messages, independently of the feasibility of the operation by the agent. For instance, if a role A must execute the receive/send sequence $se(x, y) \rightarrow se(x, K)$ and if the actual message is $se(N_B, K)$, then pattern-matching yields the relation $x = N_b$. This allows us to get rid of the algebraic properties of explicit destructors (like decryption or projection) and provides the *syntactic Dolev-Yao model*. But when the algebraic properties of other operations like the exclusive or $\oplus$ are added to the model, this may lead to meaningless protocols (e.g. not *well-defined*): a step $x \oplus y \rightarrow x$ is unrealistic, but pattern matching succeeds. In our setting symbolic derivations are well-defined and can be translated into a well-defined protocol. Therefore decidability results on well-defined protocols for some signature transfer immediately to symbolic derivations on the same signature.

The equational model. The original Dolev-Yao model [10] used explicit constructors (*e.g.* for encryption) and destructors (*e.g.* for decryption) and the corresponding equational theory. To retrieve components of a message, pattern-matching is replaced by an explicit computation using destructors. For instance, to retrieve x in $m = se(x, K)$ yields the equation $x = sd(m, K)$. The executability of the protocol is guaranteed by the satisfiability of the system of equations modulo the equational theory enriched by axioms stating that a destructor is the inverse of a constructor. This approach is sound for classical cryptographic protocols but this no longer the case for non-deterministic security protocols arising in Web services. If f_a extracts the component $a(\_)$ in a multiset m, we get that $f_a(m) = a(x_1)$ and $f_a(m) = a(x_2)$ for $m = a(x_1) \cdot a(x_2)$, hence we get $a(x_1) = a(x_2)$ which leads to some inconsistencies (all terms headed by a are equal modulo the equational theory.)

5   Plain Web Services

In a first abstraction, Web services are protocols that exchange multisets of nodes. Hence we will consider first a signature that is reduced to a multiset operator, a constant (the empty multiset) and unary operators. We call *Plain Web services* protocols defined on this signature. We shall present now a procedure to decide ordered satisfiability for plain Web services. We note first that the ordered satisfiability for a deduction system in which one can enclose data in a node a (rule $x \rightarrow a(x)$) or expose the data contained in the node a (rule $a(x) \rightarrow x$) is easily decidable (by [15] and the fact that the deduction system is local and the equational theory is empty). Then for applying the combination result of next section, it remains to decide ordered satisfiability problems for the deduction system associated to the multiset operator that is employed in the construction and analysis of XML messages. We believe that the proof can be adapted for sets (with union and subset extraction). A related result for words (*i.e.* when the ordering of nodes matters) can be found in [16].

We consider the signature $\mathcal{F} = \{\cdot, 1\}$ with the following equational theory:

$$\mathcal{E} = \{x \cdot (y \cdot z) = (x \cdot y) \cdot z \ (A), x \cdot y = y \cdot x \ (C), x \cdot 1 = x \ (U)\}$$

(usually denoted ACU). Our decidability result is independent of the presence or absence of the (U) axiom. The deduction rules are:

$$\mathcal{R} = \{x \cdot y \rightarrow x, \quad x, y \rightarrow x \cdot y, \quad \rightarrow 1\}$$

This theory is regular and the set of variables of the right-hand side is included in the set of variables of the left-hand side for each rule, hence the rules are indeed deduction rules. We state now some some basic facts on $\mathcal{M} = \langle \mathcal{F}, \mathcal{R}, \mathcal{E} \rangle$.

Proposition 1. *Let E and t be respectively a set of terms and a term in normal form modulo $\mathcal{E}$. We have: (i)* $\mathrm{Const}(E) \subseteq \mathrm{Der}_{\mathcal{D}}(E)$, *(ii)* $E \subseteq \mathrm{Der}_{\mathcal{D}}(\mathrm{Const}(E))$; *(iii)* $\mathrm{Der}_{\mathcal{D}}(E) = \mathrm{Der}_{\mathcal{D}}(\mathrm{Const}(E))$; *(iv)* $t \in \mathrm{Der}_{\mathcal{D}}(E)$ *iff* $\mathrm{Const}(t) \subseteq \mathrm{Const}(E)$.
PROOF. Let $c \in \mathrm{Const}(E)$ be a constant, and $e \in E$ be a term such that $c \in \mathrm{Const}(e)$. We have therefore $e = e' \cdot c$. Thus in one step we have $E \rightarrow E, c$. Since c is arbitrary, we have $\mathrm{Const}(E) \subseteq \mathrm{Der}_{\mathcal{D}}(E)$. We easily see that we also have $E \subseteq \mathrm{Der}_{\mathcal{D}}(\mathrm{Const}(E))$ and (i) follows. From this, (ii) follows by double inclusion. For (iii) we have $t \in \mathrm{Der}_{\mathcal{D}}(E)$ is equivalent to $\mathrm{Der}_{\mathcal{D}}(E) = \mathrm{Der}_{\mathcal{D}}(E, t)$, and thus by (ii) it is equivalent to $\mathrm{Der}_{\mathcal{D}}(\mathrm{Const}(E)) = \mathrm{Der}_{\mathcal{D}}(\mathrm{Const}(E, t))$. By contradiction assume there exists $c \in \mathrm{Const}(t) \setminus \mathrm{Const}(E)$. Given the constraint on constants in deduction rules we have $c \notin \mathrm{Der}_{\mathcal{D}}(\mathrm{Const}(E))$ whereas c trivially is in $\mathrm{Der}_{\mathcal{D}}(\mathrm{Const}(E, t))$, which contradicts the equality, and thus $t \in \mathrm{Der}_{\mathcal{D}}(E)$ □

The decision procedure is given by Algorithm 1. The completeness of this algorithm is easy and the correctness derives from Proposition 1.
Complexity. Step one and checking satisfiability of linear equation systems over positive integers are in NP. Step three can be performed in PTIME.

Theorem 1. *Ordered satisfiability of multiset deduction systems is in NP.*

Similar results have been obtained for pure AC-symbols under some restrictions in [17] but they do not cover our case.

Algorithm 1. Ordered satisfiability for multiset deduction systems

---

Input: - $C = (\mathcal{V}, \mathcal{S}, \mathcal{K}, \text{IN}, \text{OUT})$;
   - A finite set of ground terms $K_{\mathcal{D}}$;
   - An ordering $\prec$ on $\text{Var}(C) \cup \text{Const}(C)$.

1: For each variable x in $\mathcal{V}$ guess the set of constants $P_x = \{a_1, \ldots, a_k\}$ that may occur in the solution, where $a_i \prec x$ for $i = 1, \ldots, k$.
2: Check the satisfiability of $\mathcal{S}$ by reduction to satisfiability of a set of linear equations over $\mathbb{N}$ by setting $x = \Sigma_{c \in P_x}(\lambda_{x,c} + 1)c$ for each variable $x \in \mathcal{V}$.
3: Check for each variable $x \in \text{IN}$ that $P_x \subseteq \text{Const}(\mathcal{K}_{\mathcal{D}}) \cup \bigcup_{\substack{x' \in \text{OUT} \\ x' <_\psi x}} P_{x'}$
4: If both checks are successful return SAT else FAIL

---

6   Protected Web Services

Protected Web services are Web services that contain cryptographic operators. Many results have been obtained for proving security of cryptographic protocols with various equational theories (xor, . . .), and we want to be able to use these results in our framework. [2]. In this last section we present a combination algorithm that allows us to reuse previous results, *either from the equational model or the pattern-matching model.* In particular it provides the first modularity result covering the pattern-matching model for cryptographic protocols.

From now on, we shall assume that $\mathcal{F}$ is the disjoint union of two signatures $\mathcal{F}_1$ and $\mathcal{F}_2$, and we assume that $\mathcal{E}_1$ (resp. $\mathcal{E}_2$) is a consistent equational theory on $\mathcal{F}_1$ (resp. $\mathcal{F}_2$). We recall that C is an infinite set of free constants, that $\mathcal{X}$ is an infinite set of variables and that $\text{T}(\mathcal{F}_1, \mathcal{X})$ (resp. $\text{T}(\mathcal{F}_2, \mathcal{X})$) denotes the set of terms on $\mathcal{F}_1 \cup \text{C}$ (resp. $\mathcal{F}_2 \cup \text{C}$). The ordering $<$ is a simplification ordering on $\text{T}(\mathcal{F}, \mathcal{X})$ total on $\text{T}(\mathcal{F})$ and the constant $c_{\min}$ is the minimal element for $<$.

A term t in $\text{T}(\mathcal{F}_1, \mathcal{X})$ (resp. in $\text{T}(\mathcal{F}_2, \mathcal{X})$) is called a *pure 1-term* (resp. a *pure 2-term*). The term s is *alien* to the term u if the top operators of s and u are not both in $\mathcal{F}_1$ or both in $\mathcal{F}_2$.

Definition 6. *Let t be a term in $\text{T}(\mathcal{F}_1 \cup \mathcal{F}_2, \mathcal{X})$. The set of its* factors *is denoted* $\text{Factors}(t)$ *and is the set of maximal syntactic strict subterms of t that are either alien to t or atoms. The set of its* subterm values *is denoted by $\text{Sub}(t)$ and is defined recursively by $\text{Sub}(t) = \{t\} \cup \bigcup_{u \in \text{Factors}(t)} \text{Sub}(u)$.*

For a set of terms E, the set $\text{Sub}(E)$ is the union of the subterm values of the elements of E. A set of equations $\mathcal{S}$ is called *homogeneous* iff it contains only pure equations. We denote by $t\delta_s$ the term obtained by replacing all *subterm* occurrences of s in t by $c_{\min}$.

Lemma 1. *Let $l \to r$ be a rule in $\text{GI}(d)$ with $d : t_1, \ldots, t_n \to t$ and $s \notin \text{C}_{\text{spe}}$ alien to some t_i or t. Then $(l\delta_s)\!\downarrow \to (r\delta_s)\!\downarrow$ is also a rule in $\text{GI}(d)$.*

---

[2] The freshness of nonces will be handled as for protocols and not discussed here.

PROOF. Let σ be a ground normal substitution such that $(t_1\sigma, \ldots, t_n\sigma)\!\downarrow = l$ and $(t\sigma)\!\downarrow = r$. Let us prove that for $u \in \{t_1, \ldots, t_n, t\}$ one has $((u\sigma)\!\downarrow\delta_s)\!\downarrow = (u(\sigma\delta_s))\!\downarrow$. This suffices to find a ground instance $(l\delta_s)\!\downarrow \rightarrow (r\delta_s)\!\downarrow$ in GI(d). If u is a variable then σ in normal form implies $(u\sigma)\!\downarrow = u\sigma$ and thus $((u\sigma)\delta_s)\!\downarrow = ((u\sigma)\!\downarrow\delta_s)\!\downarrow$. Otherwise, and since the rule is pure, the assumption implies that s is alien to u. Since σ is a normal substitution, and since for $u \in \{t_1, \ldots, t_n, t\}$ the term u is pure, the factors of $u\sigma$ are in normal form.

These facts and Lemma 10 from [9] imply that for all $u \in \{t_1, \ldots, t_n, t\}$ one has $((u\sigma)\!\downarrow\delta_s)\!\downarrow = ((u\sigma)\delta_s)\!\downarrow$. Since s is alien to the term u we also have $(u\sigma)\delta_s = u(\sigma\delta_s)$. By applying a bottom-up normalisation we have $u(\sigma\delta_s) =_{\mathcal{E}} u(\sigma\delta_s)\!\downarrow$. Putting together these equalities we obtain a substitution $\sigma' = (\sigma\delta_s)\!\downarrow$ such that the rule d instantiated by σ' is $(l\delta_s)\!\downarrow \rightarrow (r\delta_s)\!\downarrow$. $\square$

Let $\langle \mathcal{F}_1, S_1, \mathcal{E}_1 \rangle$ and $\langle \mathcal{F}_2, S_2, \mathcal{E}_2 \rangle$ be two deduction systems on disjoint signatures. Our combination algorithm relies on the following lemma stating that a satisfiable closed symbolic derivation for the union of $\langle \mathcal{F}_1, S_1, \mathcal{E}_1 \rangle$ and $\langle \mathcal{F}_2, S_2, \mathcal{E}_2 \rangle$ can be split into satisfiable symbolic derivations on $\mathcal{F}_1$ and $\mathcal{F}_2$ respectively. The abstraction of a term t in a signature $\mathcal{F}_i$, denoted $\text{Abs}_i(t)$, consists in replacing the maximal subterms of t with root in $\mathcal{F}_j, j \neq i$ by new constants.

The abstraction $\text{Abs}_i(\sigma)$ of a substitution σ in $\mathcal{F}_i$ is the substitution such that for all x in the support of σ, $x\text{Abs}_i(\sigma)$ is the abstraction of $x\sigma$ in $\mathcal{F}_i$. In the statement of next lemma, $\text{Sig}(t)$ designates the signature to which the top symbol of the term t belongs. From a system of equations S, one notes that one can derive, by introducing new variables, an equisatisfiable homogeneous set of equations $S_1 \cup S_2$ such that terms in S_i are pure $\mathcal{F}_i$-terms for $i = 1, 2$.

The proof idea is to "abstract" a solution σ for a symbolic derivation $\mathcal{C}$ in deduction system $\langle \mathcal{F}_1 \cup \mathcal{F}_2, S_1 \cup S_2, \mathcal{E}_1 \cup \mathcal{E}_2 \rangle$ and to apply iteratively Lemma 1 in order to show for $i = 1, 2$ that $\text{Abs}_i(\sigma)$ is a solution of the symbolic derivation in the deduction system $\langle \mathcal{F}_i, S_i, \mathcal{E}_i \rangle$.

Lemma 2. *Let $\mathcal{C} = (\mathcal{V}, S, \mathcal{K})$ be a closed derivation satisfied by a normal substitution σ for the deduction system $\langle \mathcal{F}_1 \cup \mathcal{F}_2, S_1 \cup S_2, \mathcal{E}_1 \cup \mathcal{E}_2 \rangle$. For $i = 1, 2$ let S_i denote the purification of S [3] and:*

$$\mathcal{K}_i = \{\text{Abs}_i(t) \in \text{Sub}(\mathcal{K}) \mid \text{Sig}(t) = i \text{ and } \exists x \in \mathcal{V}, \ x\sigma = t\} \cup \{x \in \mathcal{V} \mid \text{Sig}(x\sigma) \neq i\}$$

Then two closed symbolic derivations $\mathcal{C}_i = (\mathcal{V}, S_i, \mathcal{K}_i)$ (for $i = 1, 2$) can be computed such that they are satisfied by $\text{Abs}_i(\sigma)$ for intruder $\langle \mathcal{F}_i, S_i, \mathcal{E}_i \rangle$ respectively.

Algorithm 2 reduces satisfiability of a $\mathcal{D}$-symbolic derivation $\mathcal{C}$ to satisfiability of $\mathcal{D}_1$ and $\mathcal{D}_2$, symbolic derivations augmented with ordering constraints on the variables of $\mathcal{C}$ and the ordering constraints between variables and constants of $\mathcal{C}$. A *partial* symbolic derivation denotes a symbolic derivation for which variables in $\mathcal{V}$ whose index is not in IN may have no associated equation in S. This leads to the following theorem:

---

[3] As in unification.

Theorem 2. *If the ordered satisfiability problem for closed symbolic derivation is decidable for two deduction systems $\langle \mathcal{F}_1, S_1, \mathcal{E}_1 \rangle$ and $\langle \mathcal{F}_2, S_2, \mathcal{E}_2 \rangle$ with disjoint signatures $\mathcal{F}_1$ and $\mathcal{F}_2$ then the ordered satisfiability problem for closed symbolic derivation is decidable for the deduction system $\langle \mathcal{F}_1 \cup \mathcal{F}_2, S_1 \cup S_2, \mathcal{E}_1 \cup \mathcal{E}_2 \rangle$.*

Algorithm 2. Combination Algorithm $\mathbf{Solve}_{\mathcal{D}}(\mathcal{C}, \prec)$

Input: $\mathcal{C} = (\mathcal{V}, \mathcal{S}, \mathcal{K}, \text{IN}, \text{OUT})$ where $\mathcal{S}$ homogeneous;
    A finite set of ground terms $K_{\mathcal{D}}$;
    A linear ordering $\prec$ on $\text{Var}(\mathcal{C}) \cup \text{Const}(\mathcal{C})$.

1: Choose a partial symbolic derivation $\mathcal{C}_{\mathcal{D}} = (\mathcal{V}_{\mathcal{D}}, \mathcal{S}_{\mathcal{D}}, \mathcal{K}_{\mathcal{D}}, \text{IN}_{\mathcal{D}}, \text{OUT}_{\mathcal{D}})$ such that:

  – $|\mathcal{V}_{\mathcal{D}}| \leq |\text{Sub}(\mathcal{C})| + |\text{IN}| + |\text{OUT}| + |\mathcal{K}_{\mathcal{D}}|$
  – $|\text{IN}_{\mathcal{D}}| = |\text{OUT}|$ and $|\text{OUT}_{\mathcal{D}}| = |\text{IN}|$
  – A composition $\mathcal{C} \circ \mathcal{C}_{\mathcal{D}}(\mathcal{K}_{\mathcal{D}})$ is defined
  – $\mathcal{S}_{\mathcal{D}}$ is homogeneous, contains equations $x \overset{?}{=} t$ with $t \in \text{Sub}(\mathcal{C}) \cup \mathcal{V}_{\mathcal{D}}$ and $x \in X$, a set of new variables with $|X| \leq |\text{Sub}(\mathcal{C}) \cup \mathcal{V}_{\mathcal{D}}|$, and defines an equivalence relation on $\text{Sub}(\mathcal{C}) \cup \mathcal{V}_{\mathcal{D}}$

2: Choose a linear ordering $\prec_X$ on variables in $X \cup \text{Const}(\mathcal{C}) \cup \text{Var}(\mathcal{C})$ extending $\prec$. Let X_1 and X_2 be two disjoint subsets of X
3: Form the closed partial symbolic derivation $\mathcal{C}' = \mathcal{C} \circ \mathcal{C}_{\mathcal{D}}$, and purify it into two pure symbolic derivations $\mathcal{C}_1$ and $\mathcal{C}_2$, where variables of X_1 (resp. X_2) are considered as constants in $\mathcal{C}_2$ (resp. $\mathcal{C}_1$).
4: If $\mathbf{Solve}_{\mathcal{D}_1}(\mathcal{C}_1, \prec_X)$ and $\mathbf{Solve}_{\mathcal{D}_2}(\mathcal{C}_2, \prec_X)$ return SAT else FAIL

The proof of completeness of Alg. 2 is intricate, and relies on a locality result for deductions and on a pumping lemma for solutions. Its correctness relies on the ordering $\prec_X$ to construct a solution σ from two partial solutions σ_1 and σ_2.

7 Conclusion

Web service XML messages are often vulnerable to rewriting attacks since the associated message format and processing model are quite tolerant to inclusion of new elements. We have developed a verification procedure that accounts for this and moreover can be extended with most existing protocol analysis procedures for algebraic operators. The combination algorithm applies in particular to encryption/decryption operators [18], list with associative concatenation [16], XOR [15], abelian groups [14]. Our framework allows us to describe specific implementation of XML/XPath library and we aim at extending this work to take the various security standards for Web services into account. We also plan to implement it in the AVISPA platform [19].

References

1. Bhargavan, K., Fournet, C., Gordon, A.D., Pucella, R.: Tulafale: A security tool for web services. In: de Boer, F.S., Bonsangue, M.M., Graf, S., de Roever, W.-P. (eds.) FMCO 2003. LNCS, vol. 3188, pp. 197–222. Springer, Heidelberg (2004)

2. Cervesato, I., Durgin, N.A., Lincoln, P., Mitchell, J.C., Scedrov, A.: A meta-notation for protocol analysis. In: CSFW, pp. 55–69 (1999)
3. Chevalier, Y., Rusinowitch, M.: Combining intruder theories. In: Caires, L., Italiano, G.F., Monteiro, L., Palamidessi, C., Yung, M. (eds.) ICALP 2005. LNCS, vol. 3580, pp. 639–651. Springer, Heidelberg (2005)
4. Basin, D.A., Mödersheim, S., Viganò, L.: Algebraic intruder deductions. In: Sutcliffe, G., Voronkov, A. (eds.) LPAR 2005. LNCS (LNAI), vol. 3835, pp. 549–564. Springer, Heidelberg (2005)
5. Comon-Lundh, H., Delaune, S.: The finite variant property: How to get rid of some algebraic properties. In: Giesl, J. (ed.) RTA 2005. LNCS, vol. 3467, Springer, Heidelberg (2005)
6. Goubault-Larrecq, J., Roger, M., Verma, K.N.: Abstraction and resolution modulo ac: How to verify diffie-hellman-like protocols automatically. J. Log. Algebr. Program. 64(2), 219–251 (2005)
7. Baader, F., Schulz, K.U.: Unification in the union of disjoint equational theories. J. Symb. Comput. 21(2), 211–243 (1996)
8. Thayer, F.J., Herzog, J.C., Guttman, J.D.: Strand spaces: Proving security protocols correct. Journal of Computer Security 7(1) (1999)
9. Chevalier, Y., Lugiez, D., Rusinowitch, M.: Towards an Automatic Analysis of Web Service Security. Technical report, INRIA (2007), http://www.inria.fr/rrrt/liste-2007.html
10. Dolev, D., Yao, A.: On the Security of Public-Key Protocols. IEEE Transactions on Information Theory 2(29) (1983)
11. Weidenbach, C.: Towards an automatic analysis of security protocols in first-order logic. In: Ganzinger, H. (ed.) CADE 1999. LNCS (LNAI), vol. 1632, pp. 314–328. Springer, Heidelberg (1999)
12. Dershowitz, N., Jouannaud, J.P.: Rewrite systems. In: Handbook of Theoretical Computer Science, vol. B, pp. 243–320. Elsevier, Amsterdam (1990)
13. Baader, F., Nipkow, T.: Term Rewriting and All That. Cambridge University Press, Cambridge (1998)
14. Millen, J., Shmatikov, V.: Symbolic protocol analysis with an abelian group operator or Diffie-Hellman exponentiation. Journal of Computer Security (2005)
15. Chevalier, Y., Kuesters, R., Rusinowitch, M., Turuani, M.:An NP Decision Procedure for Protocol Insecurity with XOR. In: Proceedings of the Logic In Computer Science Conference, LICS'03 (2003)
16. Chevalier, Y., Kourjieh, M.: A symbolic intruder model for hash-collision attacks. In: 11th Annual Asian Computing Science Conference. LNCS, Springer, Heidelberg (2006) ftp://ftp.irit.fr/IRIT/LILAC/main.pdf
17. Bursuc, S., Comon-Lundh, H., Delaune, S.: Associative-commutative deducibility constraints. In: Thomas, W., Weil, P. (eds.) STACS 2007. LNCS, vol. 4393, pp. 634–645. Springer, Heidelberg (2007)
18. Rusinowitch, M., Turuani, M.: Protocol insecurity with finite number of sessions is NP-complete. In: Proc.14th IEEE Computer Security Foundations Workshop, Cape Breton, Nova Scotia (2001)
19. Armando, A., et al.: The AVISPA tool for the automated validation of internet security protocols and applications. In: Etessami, K., Rajamani, S.K. (eds.) CAV 2005. LNCS, vol. 3576, pp. 281–285. Springer, Heidelberg (2005)

Certification of Automated Termination Proofs*

Evelyne Contejean[1], Pierre Courtieu[2], Julien Forest[2], Olivier Pons[2],
and Xavier Urbain[2]

[1] LRI, Université Paris-Sud, CNRS, INRIA Futurs, Orsay F-91405
[2] CÉDRIC – Conservatoire national des arts et métiers

Abstract. Nowadays, formal methods rely on tools of different kinds: proof assistants with which the user interacts to discover a proof step by step; and fully automated tools which make use of (intricate) decision procedures. But while some proof assistants can *check* the soundness of a proof, they lack automation. Regarding automated tools, one still has to be satisfied with their answers Yes/No/Do not know, the validity of which can be subject to question, in particular because of the increasing size and complexity of these tools.

In the context of rewriting techniques, we aim at bridging the gap between proof assistants that yield formal guarantees of reliability and highly automated tools one has to trust. We present an approach making use of both shallow and deep embeddings. We illustrate this approach with a prototype based on the C*i*ME rewriting toolbox, which can discover involved termination proofs that can be certified by the COQ proof assistant, using the COCCINELLE library for rewriting.

1 Introduction

Formal methods play an increasingly important role when it comes to guaranteeing good properties for complex, sensitive or critical systems. In the context of proving, they rely on tools of different kinds: proof assistants with which the user interacts step by step, and fully automated tools which make use of (intricate) decision procedures.

Reducing the cost of formal proofs amounts to using more and more automation. However, while some proof assistants can *check* the soundness of a proof, one still has to be satisfied with the answer of automated tools. Yet, since application fields include possibly critical sectors as security, code verification, cryptographic protocols, etc., *reliance on verification tools is crucial*.

Some proof assistants, like COQ [28], need to check mechanically the proof of each notion used. Among the strengths of these assistants are firstly a powerful specification language that can express both logical assertions and programs, hence properties of programs, and secondly a *highly reliable* procedure that checks the soundness of proofs.

For instance, COQ or ISABELLE/HOL [26] have a small and highly reliable *kernel*. In COQ, the kernel type-checks a *proof term* to ensure the soundness of a proof. Certified-programming environments based on these proof assistants find here an additional guarantee. Yet, among the weaknesses of these assistants, one may regret the lack of automation in the proof discovery process. Automation is indeed difficult to obtain in this framework: the proof assistant has to check a property proven by an external

---

* Work partially supported by A3PAT project of the French ANR (ANR-05-BLAN-0146-01).

B. Konev and F. Wolter (Eds.): FroCos 2007, LNAI 4720, pp. 148–162, 2007.

procedure before accepting it. Therefore, such a procedure has to return a *proof trace* checkable by the assistant.

We want to meet the important need of *proofs delegation* for some properties in the framework of rewriting techniques. We will focus on generic ways to provide reasonably-sized proof traces for complex properties, for instance *termination*.

Termination is the property of a program any execution of which always yields a result. Fundamental when recursion and induction are involved, it is an unavoidable preliminary for proving many various properties of a program. Confluence of a rewriting system, for instance, becomes decidable when the system terminates. More generally, proving termination is a boundary between *total* and *partial* correctness of programs. Hence, automating termination is of great interest for provers like CoQ, in which functions can be defined only if they are proven to be terminating.

The last decade has been very fertile w.r.t. automation of termination proofs, and yielded many efficient tools (APROVE [17], C*i*ME [8], JAMBOX [15], TPA [22], TTT [20] and others) referenced on the website of the Termination Competition [24]. Some of them display nice output for *human* reading. However, there is still a clear gap between proof assistants that provide *formal* guarantees of reliability and highly automated tools that do not. In the sequel, we aim at bridging this gap.

We present here a methodology for the particularly important challenge of automatically generating proof traces in the domain of *first order term rewrite systems* and in particular for termination proofs of such systems. We do not restrict to classical approaches of all-shallow embedding or, like Color [4], of all-deep embedding to model properties or techniques. Instead we use a mixed approach so as to get the best of both worlds. We implemented our principles and methodology within the rewrite tool box C*i*ME 2.99. This version uses parts of the termination engine of C*i*ME2.04; with our mixed approach it can certify (with CoQ) termination proofs of more than 370 problems (i.e. approximately 34.5% of the TPDB 3.2 directory TRS excluding termination modulo equational theories), and using involved criteria. This is made possible thanks to a CoQ library for rewriting (COCCINELLE) developed by E. Contejean in our project.

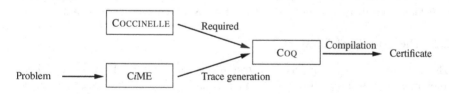

We make our notations precise and give some prerequisites about first order term rewriting and about the CoQ proof assistant in Section 2. Then, in Section 3, we present our modelling of termination of rewriting in CoQ, which mixes deep and shallow embeddings in order to take benefits of both. We briefly present the CoQ library COCCINELLE developed in the project to that purpose. In section 4 we present the certification of proofs using involved criteria such as Dependency Pairs [1] with graphs refinement, mixing orderings based on polynomial interpretations [23] or RPO [10] with AFS [1]. We shall adopt the end-user point of view and provide some experimental results of C*i*ME 2.99 in Section 5. Eventually we briefly compare with related works and conclude in Section 6.

2   Preliminaries

2.1   Rewriting

We assume the reader familiar with basic concepts of term rewriting [13, 2] and termination, in particular with the Dependency Pairs (DP) approach [1]. We recall usual notions, and give notations. A *signature* $\mathcal{F}$ is a finite set of *symbols* with arities. Let X be a countable set of *variables*; $T(\mathcal{F}, X)$ denotes the set of finite *terms* on $\mathcal{F}$ and X. $\Lambda(t)$ is the symbol at root position in term t. We write $t|_p$ for subterm of t at position p and $t[u]_p$ for term t where $t|_p$ has been replaced by u. *Substitutions* are mappings from variables to terms and $t\sigma$ denotes the application of a substitution σ to a term t.

A *term rewriting system* (TRS for short) over a signature $\mathcal{F}$ is a set R of *rewrite rules* $l \to r$ with $l, r \in T(\mathcal{F}, X)$. A TRS R defines a monotonic relation $\to_R$ closed under substitution (aka a *rewrite relation*) in the following way: $s \to_R t$ (*s reduces to t*) if there is a position p such that $s|_p = l\sigma$ and $t = s[r\sigma]_p$ for a rule $l \to r \in R$ and a substitution σ. In the following, we shall omit systems and positions that are clear from the context. We denote the reflexive-transitive closure of a relation $\to$ by $\to^*$. Symbols occurring at root position in the left-hand sides of rules in R are said to be *defined*, the others are said to be *constructors*.

A term is *R-strongly normalizing* (*R*-SN) if it cannot reduce infinitely many times for the relation defined by System R^1. A rewrite relation *terminates* if any term is SN. Termination is usually proven with the help of *reduction orderings* [11] or *ordering pairs* with *dependency pairs*. The set of *unmarked* dependency pairs[2] of a TRS R, denoted $DP(R)$ is defined as $\{\langle u, v\rangle$ such that $u \to t \in R$ and $t|_p = v$ and $\Lambda(v)$ is defined$\}$. An *ordering pair* is a pair $(\succeq, >)$ of relations over $T(\mathcal{F}, X)$ such that: 1) $\succeq$ is a stable and monotonic quasi-ordering, i.e. reflexive and transitive, 2) $>$ is a stable strict ordering, i.e. irreflexive and transitive, and 3) $> \cdot \succeq\, =\, >$ or $\succeq \cdot > \,=\, >$. An ordering pair is *well-founded* if there is no infinite strictly decreasing sequence $t_1 > t_2 > \ldots$

2.2   The COQ Proof Assistant

The COQ proof assistant is based on *type theory* and features: 1) A *formal language* to express objects, properties and proofs in a unified way; all these are represented as terms of an expressive λ-calculus: the *Calculus of Inductive Constructions* (CIC) [9]. λ-abstraction is denoted **fun** x:T => t, and application is denoted t u. 2) A *proof checker* which checks the validity of proofs written as CIC-terms. Indeed, in this framework, a term is a *proof* of its type, and checking a proof consists in typing a term. The tool's correctness relies on this type checker, which is a small kernel of 5 000 lines of OBJECTIVE CAML code.

For example the following simple terms are proofs of the following (tautological) types (remember that implication arrow $\to$ is right associative): the identity function

---

[1] When R is clear from the context, we shall write SN.

[2] For readability's sake we detail only unmarked DP, see Sec. 4.4 for how we deal with marks.

fun `x:A` => `x` is a proof of A $\rightarrow$ A, and **fun** `(x:A)` `(f:A`$\rightarrow$ B`)` => f `x` is a proof of A $\rightarrow$ (A $\rightarrow$ B) $\rightarrow$ B.

A very powerful feature of COQ is the ability to define *inductive types* to express inductive data types and inductive properties. For example the following inductive types define the data type `nat` of natural numbers, `O` and `S` (successor) being the two constructors[3], and the property `even` of being an even natural number.

```
Inductive nat : Set := | O : nat | S : nat → nat.
Inductive even : nat → Prop := | even_O : even O
  | even_S : ∀n : nat, even n → even (S (S n)).
```

Hence the term `even_S (S (S O)) (even_S O (even_O))` is of type `even (S (S (S (S O))))` so it is a proof that 4 is even.

2.3 Termination in COQ

We focus in this paper on termination. This property is defined in COQ standard library as the well-foundedness of an *ordering*. Hence we model TRS as *orderings* in the following. This notion is defined using the *accessibility* predicate. A term $t : A$ is accessible for an ordering $<$ if all its predecessors are, and $<$ is well-founded if all terms of type A are accessible (R y x stands for $y < x$):

```
Inductive Acc (A : Type) (R : A → A → Prop) (x : A) : Prop :=
  | Acc_intro : (∀ y : A, R y x → Acc R y) → Acc R x
Definition well_founded (A : Type) (R : A → A → Prop) :=
  ∀ a : A, Acc R a.
```

This inductive definition contains both the basis case (that is when an element has no predecessor w.r.t. the relation R) and the general inductive case. For example, in a relation R on `bool` defined by R `true false`, `true` is accessible because it has no predecessor, and so is `false` because its only predecessor is `true`. Hence `Acc R true` and `Acc R false` are provable, hence `well-founded R` is provable.

The usual ordering $<$ is not well-founded over the integers, there are infinite descending chains as for example $\ldots - (n+1) < -n < -(n-1) < \ldots < -1 < 0$. However, it is possible to reason by well-founded induction over the integer using a well-founded relation $<_{wf}$ defined by $x <_{wf} y$ if $|x| < |y|$ or ($|x| = |y|$ and $x > 0 > y$). The relation is of the form: $0 <_{wf} 1 <_{wf} -1 <_{wf} 2 <_{wf} -2 <_{wf} \ldots$

3 Modelling Termination of Rewriting in COQ

If R is the relation modelling a TRS $\mathcal{R}$, we should write R u t (which means $u < t$) when a term t rewrites to a term u. For the sake of readability we will use as much as possible the COQ notation: t -[R]> u (and t -[R]*> u for $t \rightarrow^* u$) instead.

The wanted final theorem stating that $\mathcal{R}$ is terminating has the following form:

Theorem `well_founded_R: well_founded R.`

---

[3] Note that this notion of constructors is different from the one in Section 2.1.

Since we want certified automated proofs, the definition of R and the proof of this theorem are discovered and generated in COQ syntax *with full automation* by our prototype. In order to ensure that the original rewriting system $\mathcal{R}$ terminates, the only things the user has to check is firstly that the generated relation R corresponds to $\mathcal{R}$ (which is easy as we shall see in Section 3.2), and secondly that the generated COQ files do compile.

3.1 Shallow vs Deep Embedding

In order to prove properties on our objects (terms, rewriting systems, polynomial interpretations...), we have to model these objects in the proof assistant by defining a theory of rewriting. There are classically two opposite ways of doing this: *shallow embedding* and *deep embedding*. When using shallow embedding, one defines *ad hoc translations* for the different notions, and proves criteria on the translation of each considered system. For instance TRSs will be inductive definitions with one constructor per rule.

When using deep embedding, one defines *generic* notions for rewriting and proves generic criteria on them, and then instantiates notions and criteria on the considered system. Both shallow and deep embedding have advantages and drawbacks. On the plus side of shallow embedding are: an easy implementation of rewriting notions, and the absence of need of meta notions (as substitutions or term well-formedness w.r.t. a signature). On the minus side, one cannot certify a criterion but only its *instantiation* on a particular problem, which often leads to large scripts and proof terms. Regarding deep embedding, it usually leads (not always as we explain below) to simpler scripts and proof terms since one can reuse generic lemmas but at the cost of a rather technical first step consisting in defining the generic notions and proving generic lemmas.

We present here an hybrid approach where some notions are deep (Σ-algebra, RPO) and others are shallow (rewriting system, dependency graphs, polynomial interpretations). The reason for this is mainly due to our *proof* concern which makes sometimes deep embedding not worth the efforts it requires: some premises of generic lemmas, which have to be proven on each considered problem, are as hard (if not harder) to prove than the shallow lemmas themselves. We will show that using both embeddings in a single proof is not a problem, and moreover that we can take full benefit of both.

3.2 The COCCINELLE Library

The deep part of the modelling is formalised in a public COQ library called COCCINELLE [6]. To start with, it contains a modelling of the mathematical notions needed for rewriting, such as term algebras, generic rewriting, generic and AC equational theories and RPO with status. It contains also proofs of properties of these notions, for example that RPO is well-founded whenever the underlying precedence is.

Moreover COCCINELLE is intended to be a mirror of the C*i*ME tool in COQ; this means that some of the types of COCCINELLE (terms, etc.) are translated from C*i*ME (in OBJECTIVE CAML) to COQ, as well as some functions (AC matching)[4].

---

[4] It should be noticed that COCCINELLE is not a *full* mirror of C*i*ME: some parts of C*i*ME are actually search algorithms for proving for instance equality of terms modulo a theory or termination of TRSs. These search algorithms are much more efficient when written in OBJECTIVE CAML than in COQ, they just need to provide a *trace* for COCCINELLE.

Translating functions and proving their full correctness obviously provide a certification of the underlying algorithm. Note that some proofs may require that *all* objects satisfying a certain property have been built: for instance in order to prove local confluence of a TRS, one need to get all critical pairs, hence a unification algorithm which is complete[5].

Since module systems in OBJECTIVE CAML and COQ are similar, both C*i*ME and COCCINELLE have the same structure, except that C*i*ME contains only types and functions whereas COCCINELLE also contains properties over these types and functions.

Terms. A signature is defined by a set of symbols with decidable equality, and a function `arity` mapping each symbol to its arity.

The arity is not simply an integer, it mentions also whether a symbol is free of arity n, AC or C (of implicit arity 2) since there is a special treatment in the AC/C case.

```
Inductive arity_type : Set :=
 | Free : nat → arity_type | AC : arity_type | C : arity_type.
```

```
Module Type Signature.
  Declare Module Export Symb : decidable_set.S.
  Parameter arity : Symb.A → arity_type.
End Signature.
```

Up to now, our automatic proof generator does not deal with AC nor C symbols, hence in this work all symbols have an arity `Free n`. However, AC/C symbols are used in other parts of COCCINELLE, in particular the formalisation of *AC matching* [5].

A term algebra is a module defined from its signature F and the set of variables X.

```
Module Type Term.
  Declare Module Import F : Signature.
  Declare Module Import X : decidable_set.S.
```

Terms are defined as variables or symbols applied to lists of terms. Lists are built from two constructors `nil` and `::`, and enjoy the usual `[ x ; y; ...]` notation.

```
Inductive term : Set :=
 | Var : variable → term | Term : symbol → list term → term.
```

This type allows to share terms in a standard representation as well as in a canonical form; but this also implies that terms may be ill-formed w.r.t. the signature. The module contains decidable definitions of well-formedness. However, the rewriting systems we consider do not apply on ill-formed terms, so we will not have to worry about it to prove termination.

The term module type contains other useful definitions and properties that we omit here for the sake of clarity. The COCCINELLE library contains also a *functor* `term.Make` which, given a signature and a set of variables, returns a module of type Term. We will not show its definition here.

```
Module Make (F1 : Signature) (X1 : decidable_set.S) : Term.
```

---

[5] Local confluence is not part of COCCINELLE yet.

Rewriting systems. TRSs provided as sets of rewrite rules are not modelled directly in
COCCINELLE. Instead, as explained in the introduction of this section, we use orderings
built from any arbitrary relation R : relation term (by definition relation A is
A → A → Prop). The usual definition can be retrieved obviously from a list of
rewrite rules (i.e. pairs of terms) $\mathcal{R}$ by defining R as:

$$\forall s, t \in T(\mathcal{F}, X), s \ -[\text{R}]> t \Longleftrightarrow (s \to t) \in \mathcal{R}$$

The COCCINELLE library provides a module type RWR which defines a reduction
relation (w.r.t. the "rules" R) and its properties.

Module Type RWR.
  Declare Module Import T : Term.

The first step toward definition of the rewrite relation is the closure by instantiation:

```
Inductive rwr_at_top (R : relation term) : relation term :=
| instance : ∀t1 t2 sigma, t1 -[R]> t2
  → (apply_subst sigma t1) -[rwr_at_top R]> (apply_subst sigma t2).
```

Then we define a rewrite step as the closure by context of the previous closure. Notice
the use of mutual inductive relations to deal with lists of terms.

```
(** One step at any position. *)
Inductive one_step (R : relation term) : relation term :=
| at_top : ∀t1 t2, t1 -[rwr_at_top R]> t2 → t1 -[one_step R]> t2
| in_context : ∀f l1 l2, l1 -[one_step_list R]> l2
                  → (Term f l1 -[one_step R]> Term f l2)
with one_step_list (R : relation term): relation (list term) :=
| head_step : ∀t1 t2 l, t1 -[one_step R]> t2
                  → (t1 :: l -[one_step_list R]> t2 :: l)
| tail_step : ∀t l1 l2, l1 -[one_step_list R]> l2
                  → (t :: l1) -[one_step_list R]> (t :: l2).
```

This module type contains properties declared using the keyword Parameter. This
means that to build a module of this type, one must prove these properties. For instance
it contains the following property stating that if $t_1 \to^+ t_2$ then $t_1\sigma \to^+ t_2\sigma$[6] for any
substitution σ.

```
  Parameter rwr_apply_subst :
  ∀ R t1 t2 sigma, t1 -[rwr R]> t2 →
    (apply_subst sigma t1 -[rwr R]> apply_subst sigma t2).
```

The library contains a functor rewriting.Make building a module of type RWR
from a module T of type Term. This functor *builds* in particular *the proof of all properties* required by RWR. For an R representing the rules of the TRS under consideration,
the final theorem we want to generate is:

Theorem well_founded_R: well_founded (one_step R).

To ensure that one_step R corresponds to the original TRS $\mathcal{R}$, it *suffices for the
user* to perform the easy check that R corresponds to the set of rules defining $\mathcal{R}$.

---

[6] The transitive closure of one_step is defined as rwr in COCCINELLE.

Note that since the datatype `term` represents any Σ-algebra (via application of the functor `Make`), we can say that terms are represented in a deep embedding. However, to simplify proofs, we avoid using substitutions by quantifying on subterms as much as possible. That makes our use of the type `term` slightly more shallow on this point.

4   Generation of Proof Traces

We will illustrate our approach by presenting proof generation techniques at work on a small example in our prototype, namely C*i*ME 2.99. While being based on the C*i*ME2 tool box, this prototype does not certify all its predecessor's termination power. For instance, modular criteria [29] and termination modulo equational theories are not supported yet. In the following, we restrict to (marked/unmarked) Dependency Pairs [1] with/without graphs refinements. The orderings we deal with include strictly the orderings that C*i*ME generates: (non-linear) polynomial interpretations (section 4.6) and RPO with status[7] (section 4.7).

4.1   Global Structure of a Generated Proof

A close look at different termination tools reveals a common underlying methodology which we use as the skeleton of our generated proofs. It consists in deriving recursively from a relation R a set of other relations R_i such that if all R_is are terminating, then so is R. For instance, this structure appears explicitly with the *processors* [18] of APROVE.

This recursive decomposition is done using *termination criteria* like DP criteria, (complex) graph criteria, modular criteria, etc. Some tools may use some backtracking but if the procedure succeeds, it means that an implicit tree was built:

$$
< \frac{
  < \frac{<_1 \text{ (poly. interp.)}}{\{\ldots \langle t_{1,i}, u_{1,i}\rangle \ldots\}}\quad
  \frac{\dfrac{<_2 \text{ (RPO)}}{\{\ldots \langle t_{2,1,i}, u_{2,1,i}\rangle \ldots\}}\quad \dfrac{<_3 \text{ (poly. interp.)}}{\{\ldots \langle t_{2,2,i}, u_{2,2,i}\rangle \ldots\}}}{\{\ldots \langle t_{2,i}, u_{2,i}\rangle \ldots\}}\ <\ \text{Sub-Graph}
}{
  R_{dp} = \{\ldots \langle t_i, u_i\rangle \ldots\}
} \ \ \begin{matrix}\text{Graph}\\\text{DP}\end{matrix}
$$
$$
R_{init} = \{\ldots l_i \to r_i \ldots\}
$$

This tree is rooted by the initial problem, namely the initial rewriting system and the first termination criterion used. Each intermediate node is also labelled by a relation and the termination criterion used to decompose the node into its children. Finally each leaf must be labelled by a relation R_i and a well-founded ordering which includes it.

The tree structure is reflected in the generated file. Indeed, for each criterion step (R replaced by sufficient conditions $\{R_i\}$), we will generate a lemma of the form:

```
Lemma wf_R_if_wf_Ri : well_founded R1 → well_founded R2 ...
  → well_founded R.
```

The proof of this lemma depends on the termination criterion used (Sec. 4.4 and 4.5).

Each time a leaf is proven using an ordering, we generate a lemma of the form:

```
Lemma wf_Ri : well_founded Ri.
```

---

[7] To date, C*i*ME can discover polynomials and LPO with AFS.

The proof is made by induction on the ordering built by the automated tool. Once all leaves have been proven this way, one can easily build the proof of the initial termination property by applying lemmas from leaves to the root:

```
Lemma final: well_founded R.
Proof. apply (wf_R_if_wf_Ri wf_R1 wf_R2 ...). Qed.
```

4.2 The Running Example

We illustrate our method with a very simple TRS $R = R_{ack} \cup R_{add}$ (over a signature $\mathcal{F}$) where R_{ack} computes the Ackerman function on Peano integers, and R_{add} computes addition on binary integers. *Digits* are denoted as postfix operators (_)0 and (_)1, whereas # is the constant 0 seen as a *number*, shared between binary and Peano integers.

$$
R \begin{cases}
R_{ack} \begin{cases}
ack(\#, y) \to s(y) & ack(s(x), \#) \to ack(x, s(\#)) \\
ack(s(x), s(y)) \to ack(x, ack(s(x), y))
\end{cases} \\
R_{add} \begin{cases}
(\#)0 \to \# & \# + x \to x & x + \# \to x \\
(x)0 + (y)0 \to (x + y)0 & (x)1 + (y)0 \to (x + y)1 \\
(x)0 + (y)1 \to (x + y)1 & (x)1 + (y)1 \to ((x + y) + (\#)1)0
\end{cases}
\end{cases}
$$

4.3 Generation of the TRS Definition

For sake of clarity we will use COQ notations that are different than in previous sections: Term X (Y::Z::...::nil) will now be denoted by X(Y,Z...).

The generation of the Σ-algebra corresponding to a signature in the automated tool is straightforward. We show here the signature corresponding to the Σ-algebra of $\mathcal{F}$. Notice the module type constraint <: Signature making COQ check that definitions and properties of SIGMA_F comply with Signature as defined in Section 3.2.

```
Module SIGMA_F <: Signature.
  Inductive symb : Set := | # : symb | s : symb ...
  Module Export Symb.
    Definition A := symb.
    Lemma eq_dec : ∀f1 f2 : symb, {f1 = f2} + {f1 <> f2}...
  End Symb.
  Definition arity (f:symb) : arity_type :=
    match f with | # => Free 0 | s => Free 1... end.
End SIGMA_F.
```

We define a module VARS for variables, apply functors building the term algebra and rewrite system on it, and then the rewriting system corresponding to R:

```
Module Import TERMS := term.Make(SIGMA)(VARS).
Module Import Rwr := rewriting.Make(TERMS).
Inductive R_rules : term → term → Prop :=
| R0 : ∀V1 : term, ack(#,V1) -[R_rules]> s(V1)...
Definition R := Rwr.one_step R_rules.
```

Notice that from now on notation T -[R]> U denotes that T rewrites to U in the sense of Section 2.1, i.e. there exists two subterms t and u at the same position in respectively T and U, such that R u t (see the definition of one_step in section 3.2).

4.4 Criterion: Dependency Pairs

The (unmarked) dependency pairs of R generated by *CiME* are the following:

$\langle \text{ack}(s(x), \#), \text{ack}(x, s(\#)) \rangle$
$\langle \text{ack}(s(x), s(y)), \text{ack}(x, \text{ack}(s(x), y)) \rangle$ $\langle \text{ack}(s(x), s(y)), \text{ack}(s(x), y)) \rangle$
$\langle (x)1 + (y)0, x + y \rangle$ $\langle (x)0 + (y)1, x + y \rangle$ $\langle (x)0 + (y)0, x + y \rangle$ $\langle (x)0 + (y)0, (x + y)0 \rangle$
$\langle (x)1 + (y)1, x + y \rangle$ $\langle (x)1 + (y)1, (x + y) + (\#)1 \rangle$ $\langle (x)1 + (y)1, ((x + y) + (\#)1)0 \rangle$

An inductive relation representing the *dependency chains* [1] is built automatically. A step of this relation models the (finite) reductions by R in the strict subterms of DP instances (e.g. $x_0 \rightarrow^\star s(V_0), \ldots$) *and* one step of the relevant dependency pair. We illustrate this on $\langle \text{ack}(s(x), \#), \text{ack}(x, s(\#)) \rangle$ with $\sigma = \{x \mapsto V_0\}$:

```
Inductive DPR : term → term → Prop :=
| DPR₀: ∀x₀ x₁ V₀, x₀ -[R]*> s(V₀) → x₁ -[R]*> #
          → ack(x₀,x₁) -[DPR]> ack(V₀,s(#))
```

The main lemma on DPs fits in the general structure we explained on Section 4.1:

Lemma wfR_if_wfDPR: well_founded DPR → well_founded R.

The proof follows a general scheme due to Hubert [21]. It involves several nested inductions instantiating the proof of the criterion in the particular setting of DPR and R.

Note that we can also prove this lemma in the case of an enhancement of DPs by Dershowitz [12] consisting in discarding DPs whose rhs is a subterm of the lhs[8].

Marked symbols. A refinement of the DP criterion consists in marking head symbols in lhs and rhs of dependency pairs in order to relax ordering constraints. We simply generate the symbol type with two versions of each symbol and adapt the definition of orderings. The proof strategy needs no change.

4.5 Criterion: Dependency Pairs with Graph

Not all DPs can follow one another in a dependency chain: one may consider the graph of possible sequences of DPs (*dependency graph*). This graph is not computable, so one uses graphs containing it. We consider here Arts & Giesl's simple approximation [1].

The graph criterion [1] takes benefit from working on the (approximated) graph. In its weak version, it consists in providing *for each strongly connected component* (SCC) an ordering pair that decreases strictly for all its nodes, and weakly for all rules. In its strong version, it considers *cycles*:

Theorem 1 (Arts and Giesl [1]). *A TRS R is terminating iff for each cycle P in its dependency graph there is a reduction pair $(\succeq_P, \succ_P)$ such that: (1) $l \succeq_P r$ for any $l \rightarrow r \in R$, (2) $s \succeq_P t$ for any $\langle s, t \rangle \in P$, and (3) $s \succ_P t$ for at least one pair in P.*

In practice, our tool uses a procedure due to Middledorp and Hirokawa [19] which splits recursively the graph into sub-components using different orders. The proof uses shallow embedding. One reason for this choice is that a generic theorem for a complex

---

[8] Such DPs cannot occur in minimal chains. Thus they can be discarded.

graph criterion is not easy to prove since it involves a substantial part of graph theory (e.g. the notion of cycle). Moreover, verifying the premises of such a theorem amounts to checking that all SCCs found by the prover are really SCCs and that they are terminating, but also to *proving* that it found *all* SCCs of the graph. That is tedious. On the contrary, using shallow embedding we use these facts *implicitly* by focusing on the termination proof of each component.

Weak version. The first thing we generate is the definition of each component as computed by CiME. To illustrate the graph criterion on our example we may take the whole system R. CiME detects two components (sub$_0$ with some DPs of R_{add}, sub$_1$ with some DPs of R_{ack}): we generate the two corresponding sub-relations of DPR.

```
Inductive DPR_sub₀ : term → term → Prop :=
| DPR_sub₀₀: ∀x₀ x₁ V₀, x₀ -[R]*> s(V₀) → x₁ -[R]*> #
→ ack(x₀,x₁)-[DPR_sub₀]> ack(V₀,s(#)) (*<ack(s(V₀),#), ack(V₀,s(#))>*)...
Inductive DPR_sub₁ : term → term → Prop := ...
```

The following lemma states the criterion and fits the general structure in Section 4.1.

```
Lemma wf_DPR_if_wf_sub₀_sub₁ : well_founded DPR_sub₀ →
well_founded DPR_sub₁ → well_founded DPR.
```

The proof of these lemmas uses the idea that if we collapse each SCC into one node, they form a DAG on which we can reason by cases on the edges in a depth-first fashion.

Strong version. In addition, when the strong version of the criterion is used, the termination of each sub-component may itself be proven from the termination of smaller components, each one with a different ordering. Due to lack of space, we will not go into the details of this methodology.

It remains to conclude by providing well-suited ordering pairs.

4.6 Orderings: Polynomial Interpretations

In our framework a polynomial interpretation is defined as a recursive function on terms. CiME outputs an interpretation for the SCC sub$_0$ (other symbols are mapped to 0):

```
[#]= 0; [0](X0)= X0 + 1; [1](X0)= X0 + 1; [+](X0,X1)= X1 + X0;
```

From this interpretation we produce a measure: term → Z:

```
Fixpoint measure_DPR_sub₀ (t:term) {struct t} : Z :=
match t with
| Var _ => 0 | # => 0
| 0(x₀) => measure_DPR x₀ + 1 | 1(x₀) => measure_DPR x₀ + 1
| plus (x₀, x₁) => measure_DPR x₁ + measure_DPR x₀ | _ => 0
end.
```

Notice that although our term definition is a deep embedding, the measure is defined as if we were in a shallow embedding[9]. Indeed it is defined by a direct recursive function on terms and does not refer to polynomials, substitutions or variables (x_0 above

---

[9] In particular it is completely handled by the trace generation part of CiME since our library COCCINELLE focuses on deep embedding.

is a COQ variable, it is not a rewriting variable which would be of the form $\mathtt{Var\ n}$). This choice makes, once again, our proofs simpler to generate. In a deep embedding we would need a theory for polynomials, and a generic theorem stating that a polynomial on positive integers with positive factors is monotonic. But actually this property instantiated on $\mathtt{measure\_DPR\_sub_0}$ above can be proven by a trivial induction on $\mathtt{t}$. So again the effort of a deep embedding is not worth this effort. The following lemma proves the well-foundedness of $\mathtt{measure\_DPR\_sub_0}$:

Lemma $\mathtt{Well\_founded\_DPR\_sub_0}$: $\mathtt{well\_founded\ DPR\_sub_0}$.

which is equivalent to $\forall\,\mathtt{x},\ \mathtt{Acc\ DPR\ x}$. This is proven firstly by induction on the value of $(\mathtt{measure\_DPR\_sub_0\ x})$, then by cases on each DP of $\mathtt{DPR\_sub_0}$, finally by applying the induction hypothesis using the fact that each pair is decreases w.r.t. $\mathtt{measure\_DPR\_sub_0}$. One concludes by polynomial comparison. It is well known that the comparison of non-linear polynomials on $\mathbb{N}$ is not decidable in general. We have a decision procedure for the particular kind of non linear polynomials CiME produces.

4.7   Orderings: RPO

The COCCINELLE library formalises RPO in a generic way, and proves it to be well-suited for ordering pairs. RPO is defined using a precedence (a decidable strict ordering $\mathtt{prec}$ over symbols) and a *status* (multiset/lexicographic) for each symbol.

```
Inductive status_type: Set := Lex:status_type | Mul:status_type.
Module Type Precedence.
  Parameter (A: Set)(prec: relation A)(status: A → status_type).
  Parameter prec_dec : ∀a1 a2 : A, {prec a1 a2} + {~prec a1 a2}.
  Parameter prec_antisym : ∀s, prec s s → False.
  Parameter prec_transitive : transitive A prec.
End Precedence.
```

A module type for an RPO should be built from a term algebra and a precedence:

```
Module Type RPO.
  Declare Module Import T : term.Term.
  Declare Module Import P : Precedence with Definition A:= T.symbol.
```

The library contains a functor $\mathtt{rpo.Make}$ building an RPO from two modules of type $\mathtt{Term}$ and $\mathtt{Precedence}$. It also builds among other usual properties of RPO, the proof that if the precedence is well-founded, then so is the RPO. This part of the library is in a deep embedding style. Proofs of termination using RPOs are very easy to generate as it is sufficient to generate the precedence, the proof that it is well-founded and to apply the functor $\mathtt{rpo.Make}$. It should be noticed that the fact that the generic RPO uses a strict precedence and a comparison from left to right in the lexicographic case is not a restriction in practice: a simple translation from terms to terms mapping equivalent symbols onto the same symbol, and performing the wanted permutation over the subterms under a given lexicographic symbol is both monotonic and stable. Hence the relation defined by comparing the translations of terms by the generic RPO still has the desired properties.

The generated definition of the RPO used for proving well-foundedness of sub$_1$ is:

```
Module precedence <: Precedence.
  Definition A : Set := symb.
  Definition prec (a b:symb) : Prop :=
    match a,b with | s,ack => True | _,_ => False end.
  Definition status: symb → status_type:= fun x => Lex.
  Lemma prec_dec: ∀a1 a2: symb, {prec a1 a2}+{~ prec a1 a2}. ...
  Lemma prec_antisym: ∀s, prec s s → False. ...
  Lemma prec_transitive: transitive symb prec. ...
End precedence.
```

And as previously: **Lemma** Well_founded_DPR_sub$_1$: well_founded DPR_sub$_1$.

Argument filtering systems The use of Dependency Pairs allows a wide choice of orderings by dropping the condition of strict monotonicity. Regarding path orderings, this can be achieved using argument filtering systems (AFS) [1]. We define AFSs as fixpoints and apply them at comparison time. This does not affect the (COQ) proof scheme.

5   Results and Benchmarks

CiME 2.99 can be downloaded and tested from the A3PAT website[10]. Once the system is defined, we have to choose the termination criterion and the orderings. For instance, we may select DP with graphs refinement and both linear polynomials (bound 2) and RPO with AFSs, then ask CiME to check termination and generate the proof trace:

```
CiME> termcrit "dp"; termcrit "nomarks"; termcrit "graph";
CiME> polyinterpkind {("linear",2);("rpo",1)}; termination R;
CiME> coq_certify_proof "example.v" R;
```

We used the *Termination Problems Data Base*[11] v3.2 as challenge. Until now we have produced a COQ certificate for 374 TRS that CiME proves terminating without using modular technique or AC termination[12]; this number rises over 545 on TPDB v4.0. We will now give some details on our experiments. We give below, depending on the use of graphs, the average and max. sizes of compiled COQ proofs, as well as the *average* compilation time (together with the number of problem solved) using marks on a 2GHz, 1GB machine, running Linux. RPO + Pol. means that selected orderings for proof search are RPOs and polynomials.

	with graph				without graph			
	s. av.	s. max	t. av	(nb)	s. av.	s. max	t. av	(nb)
RPO	3.6MB	9.09MB	9.9s	(228)	3.64MB	5.31MB	7.8s	(196)
Linear Pol.	0.72MB	12.27MB	7.8s	(295)	0.42MB	4.89MB	2.5s	(225)
Simple Pol.	0.84MB	12.40MB	10.1s	(314)	0.45MB	1.26MB	6.3s	(264)
RPO + Pol.	1.20MB	12.30MB	10.6s	(374)	0.69MB	4.91MB	8.7s	(300)

---

[10] http://www3.ensiie.fr/~urbain/a3pat/pub/index.en.html

[11] http://www.lri.fr/~marche/tpdb

[12] Not all the systems of the TPDB are terminating. Some are proven by the *full* termination engine of CiME 2.04 using techniques for which CiME 2.99 does not produce a certificate yet.

6   Related Works and Conclusion

There are several works to be mentioned w.r.t. the communication between automated provers and COQ. Amongst them, the theorem-prover ZÉNON [14], based on tableaux, produces COQ proof terms as certificates. ELAN enjoys techniques to produce COQ certificates for rewriting [25]. Bezem describes an approach regarding resolution [3]. However, these systems do not tackle the problem of termination proofs.

To our knowledge the only other approach to generate termination certificates for rewriting systems relies on the CoLoR/Rainbow libraries [4]. In this approach, term algebras and TRSs are handled via an embedding even deeper than in COCCINELLE, since a TRS is given by a set of pairs of terms. Rainbow is a relatively efficient tool thanks to orderings built with *matrix interpretations* (which we don't handle yet). But it does not handle the following techniques: *enhanced* or *marked* dependency pairs, *complex graphs*, RPO with AFS. We think that adding these techniques to CoLoR/Rainbow will be hard, due to the pure deep embedding approach. There are currently 167 out of 864 termination problems in TPDB (v3.2) proven by TPA [22] and certified by CoLoR/Rainbow using polynomial interpretations and the webpage mentions 237 problems certified using matrix interpretations.

We presented a methodology to make automated termination tools generate *traces* in a proof assistant format. The approach is validated by a prototype generating COQ traces. The performances of the prototype on the examples of the TPDB database are promising. Our approach is easy to extend, in particular because extensions may be done in deep or shallow embedding.

To apply this methodology on different tools and targeted proof assistants, one needs a *termination trace language*. An ongoing work in the A3PAT group is to define a more general language that can even tackle proofs of various rewriting properties such as termination, confluence (which needs termination), equational proofs [7], etc. We think that a good candidate could be based on the tree structure we explained on Section 4.1.

One particularly interesting follow-up of this work is the possibility to plug automated termination tools *as external termination tactics* for proof assistants. Indeed termination is a key property of many algorithms to be proven in proof assistants. Moreover, in type theory based proof assistants like COQ, one cannot define a function without simultaneously proving its termination. This would allow to define functions whose termination is not obvious without the great proof effort it currently needs.

References

1. Arts, T., Giesl, J.: Termination of term rewriting using dependency pairs. Theoretical Computer Science 236, 133–178 (2000)
2. Baader, F., Nipkow, T.: Term Rewriting and All That. Cambridge University Press, Cambridge (1998)
3. Bezem, M., Hendriks, D., de Nivelle, H.: Automated proof construction in type theory using resolution. J. Autom. Reasoning 29(3-4), 253–275 (2002)
4. Blanqui, F., Coupet-Grimal, S., Delobel, W., Hinderer, S., Koprowski, A.: Color, a coq library on rewriting and termination. In: Geser and Sondergaard [16]
5. Contejean, E.: A certified AC matching algorithm. In: van Oostrom, V. (ed.) RTA 2004. LNCS, vol. 3091, pp. 70–84. Springer, Heidelberg (2004)

6. Contejean, E.: Coccinelle (2005), http://www.lri.fr/~contejea/Coccinelle/coccinelle.html
7. Contejean, E., Corbineau, P.: Reflecting proofs in first-order logic with equality. In: Nieuwenhuis, R. (ed.) CADE 2005. LNCS (LNAI), vol. 3632, pp. 7–22. Springer, Heidelberg (2005)
8. Contejean, E., Marché, C., Monate, B., Urbain, X.: Proving termination of rewriting with cime. In: Rubio [27], pp. 71–73, http://cime.lri.fr
9. Coquand, T., Paulin-Mohring, C.: Inductively defined types. In: Martin-Löf, P., Mints, G. (eds.) COLOG-88. LNCS, vol. 417, Springer, Heidelberg (1990)
10. Dershowitz, N.: Orderings for term rewriting systems. Theoretical Computer Science 17(3), 279–301 (1982)
11. Dershowitz, N.: Termination of rewriting. Journal of Symbolic Computation 3(1), 69–115 (1987)
12. Dershowitz, N.: Termination Dependencies. In: Rubio [27] Technical Report DSIC II/15/03, Univ. Politécnica de Valencia, Spain
13. Dershowitz, N., Jouannaud, J.-P.: Rewrite systems. In: van Leeuwen, J. (ed.) Handbook of Theoretical Computer Science, vol. B, pp. 243–320. North-Holland, Amsterdam (1990)
14. Doligez, D.: Zenon. http://focal.inria.fr/zenon/
15. Endrullis, J.: Jambox, http://joerg.endrullis.de/index.html.
16. Geser, A., Sondergaard, H. (eds.).: Extended Abstracts of the 8th International Workshop on Termination, WST'06 (August 2006)
17. Giesl, J., Schneider-Kamp, P., Thiemann, R.: Aprove 1.2: Automatic termination proofs in the dependency pair framework. In: Furbach, U., Shankar, N. (eds.) IJCAR 2006. LNCS (LNAI), vol. 4130, Springer, Heidelberg (2006)
18. Giesl, J., Thiemann, R., Schneider-Kamp, P., Falke, S.: Mechanizing and Improving Dependency Pairs. Journal of Automated Reasoning 37(3), 155–203 (2006)
19. Hirokawa, N., Middeldorp, A.: Automating the dependency pair method. In: Baader, F. (ed.) CADE 2003. LNCS (LNAI), vol. 2741, pp. 32–46. Springer, Heidelberg (2003)
20. Hirokawa, N., Middeldorp, A.: Tyrolean termination tool. In: Giesl, J. (ed.) RTA 2005. LNCS, vol. 3467, pp. 175–184. Springer, Heidelberg (2005)
21. Hubert, T.: Certification des preuves de terminaison en Coq. Rapport de DEA, Université Paris 7, In French (September 2004)
22. Koprowski, A.: TPA, http://www.win.tue.nl/tpa
23. Lankford, D.S.: On proving term rewriting systems are Noetherian.Technical Report MTP-3, Mathematics Department, Louisiana Tech. Univ., (1979) Available at http://perso.ens-lyon.fr/pierre.lescanne/not_accessible.html
24. Marché, C., Zantema, H.: The termination competition 2006. In Geser and Sondergaard [16], http://www.lri.fr/~marche/termination-competition/
25. Nguyen, Q.H., Kirchner, C., Kirchner, H.: External rewriting for skeptical proof assistants. J. Autom. Reasoning 29(3-4), 309–336 (2002)
26. Nipkow, T., Paulson, L.C., Wenzel, M.: Isabelle/HOL — A Proof Assistant for Higher-Order Logic. In: Nipkow, T., Paulson, L.C., Wenzel, M. (eds.) Isabelle/HOL. LNCS, vol. 2283, Springer, Heidelberg (2002)
27. Rubio, A., (ed.).: Extended Abstracts of the 6th International Workshop on Termination, WST'03, Technical Report DSIC II/15/03, Univ. Politécnica de Valencia, Spain (June 2003)
28. The Coq Development Team. The Coq Proof Assistant Documentation – Version V8.1, (February 2007), http://coq.inria.fr.
29. Urbain, X.: Modular and incremental automated termination proofs. Journal of Automated Reasoning 32, 315–355 (2004)

Temporal Logic with Capacity Constraints

Clare Dixon, Michael Fisher, and Boris Konev

Department of Computer Science, University of Liverpool, Liverpool, U.K.
{C.Dixon, M.Fisher, B.Konev}@csc.liv.ac.uk

Abstract. Often when modelling systems, physical constraints on the resources available are needed. For example, we might say that at most N processes can access a particular resource at any moment or exactly M participants are needed for an agreement. Such situations are concisely modelled where propositions are constrained such that at most N, or exactly M, can hold at any moment in time. This paper describes both the logical basis and a verification method for propositional linear time temporal logics which allow such constraints as input. The method incorporates ideas developed earlier for a resolution method for the temporal logic TLX and a tableaux-like procedure for PTL. The complexity of this procedure is discussed and case studies are examined. The logic itself represents a combination of standard temporal logic with classical constraints restricting the numbers of propositions that can be satisfied at any moment in time.

1 Introduction

Although temporal logic is widely used in the specification and verification of concurrent and reactive systems [21,20] , there are cases where *full* temporal logic is *too* expressive. In particular, if we wish to describe the temporal properties of a restricted number of components, not all of which can occur at every moment in time, then the full temporal language forces us to describe the behaviour of all these components explicitly. In [8], it was shown that, simply by incorporating *"exactly one" constraints* into a propositional temporal logic, much better computational complexity could be achieved. Essentially, the basic set of propositions within the temporal logic was partitioned into *"exactly one" sets*. So

$$\mathsf{Props} \ = \ \mathsf{X}_1 \cup \mathsf{X}_2 \cup \ldots \cup \mathsf{X}_n$$

where each X_i is disjoint. Then the propositions within each "exactly one" set, for example

$$\mathsf{X}_1 \ = \ \{p_1, p_2, p_3, p_4\}$$

were implicitly constrained so that, at any moment in time, exactly one of p_1, p_2, p_3, or p_4 is satisfied. Not only did this allow the concise specification of examples such as the representation of automata, planning problems, and agent negotiation protocols, but also greatly reduced the complexity of the associated decision procedure [7,8]. Essentially, this is because (as the name suggests) *exactly* one element of each "exactly one" set must be satisfied at every temporal state. So, in the above example, we can only have exactly one of p_1, p_2, p_3, or p_4 in any state; we can never have combinations of these propositions holding at the same moment or none of them holding.

B. Konev and F. Wolter (Eds.): FroCos 2007, LNAI 4720, pp. 163–177, 2007.

Although being able to constrain the logic so that exactly *one* of a particular set of propositions is satisfied is useful, especially for representing finite automata, we have found this to be quite restrictive at times. So, in this paper, we will generalise the approach from [8] beyond simply "exactly one" sets. We will allow the specifier to constrain the logic so that *up to* k propositions, or *exactly* k propositions from some subset of propositions, are true at any moment in time. Thus, in this paper, rather than working with a temporal logic extended with "exactly one" sets, we instead use more flexible *constrained* sets, which provide more sophisticated restrictions on the capacity within the logic. Note that this approach involves reasoning *in the presence* of constraints rather than reasoning *about* them. That is, the resulting logic represents a combination of standard temporal logic with (fixed) constraints that restrict the numbers of propositions that can be satisfied at any moment in time.

This new approach is particularly useful for:

– ensuring that a fixed bound is kept on the number of propositions satisfied at any moment to prevent overload;
– in finite collections of communicating automata, ensuring that no more than k automata are in a particular state;
– modelling restrictions on resources, for example at most k vehicles are available or there are at most k seats available;
– modelling the necessity to elect exactly k from n participants.

Motivating Example. Consider a fixed number, n, of robots that can each $work$, $rest$ or $recharge$. We assume that that there are only $k < n$ recharging points and only $j < n$ workstations. Let:

– $work_i$ represent the fact that robot i is working;
– $rest_i$ represent the fact that robot i is resting; and
– $recharge_i$ represent the fact that robot i is recharging.

Now, we typically want to specify that exactly j of the n robots are working at any one time. In the syntax given later, such a logic might be defined as TLC($\mathcal{W}^{=j}, \mathcal{R}^{<k+1}$), where

$$\mathcal{W}^{=j} = \{work_1, \ldots, work_n\}$$
$$\mathcal{R}^{<k+1} = \{recharge_1, \ldots, recharge_n\}$$

This represents the logic with the constraints that exactly j robots must work at any moment and at most k can recharge at any moment.

The above represents exactly the kind of logical base and case studies we consider in this paper.

The paper is organised as follows. Section 2 gives the syntax and semantics of the constrained temporal logic, together with a normal form for this logic. Section 3 addresses its complexity. In Section 4 we show how to construct a structure representing the underlying models of formulae and relate satisfiability of the formula with a property of the structure. In Section 5 we provide examples and, in Section 6 we provide concluding remarks, incorporating both related and future work.

2   A Constrained Temporal Logic

The logic we consider is called "TLC", and its syntax and semantics essentially follow that of PTL [12], with models being isomorphic to the Natural Numbers, $\mathbb{N}$. The main novelty in TLC is that it is parameterised by (not necessarily disjoint) sets $\mathcal{P}_1^{r_1,d_1}$, $\mathcal{P}_2^{r_2,d_2}$,..., where $r_i \in \{=,<\}$ and $d_i \in \mathbb{N}$ and the formulae of TLC($\mathcal{P}_1^{r_1,d_1}$, $\mathcal{P}_2^{r_2,d_2}$, ...) are constructed under the restriction that, dependent on r_i *exactly* or *less than* d_i propositions from every set $\mathcal{P}_i^{r_i,d_i}$ are true in every state.

For example, consider TLC($\mathcal{P}^{<4}$, $\mathcal{Q}^{=2}$), where $\mathcal{P}^{<4} = \{a,b,c,d,e,f\}$, and $\mathcal{Q}^{=2} = \{x,y,z\}$. Then, at any moment in time, less than four of a, b, c, d, e, or f are true, and exactly two of x, y, or z are true.

Furthermore, we assume that there exists a set of propositions, $\mathcal{A}$, in addition to those defined by the parameters, and that these propositions are unconstrained as normal in PTL. The set $\mathcal{A}$ is disjoint with

$$\bigcup_i \mathcal{P}_i^{r_i,d_i}.$$

Thus, TLC with no parameters, i.e. TLC( ) is essentially a standard propositional, linear temporal logic, while TLC($\mathcal{P}^{=1},\mathcal{Q}^{=1},\mathcal{R}^{=1}$) is a temporal logic containing the sets of propositions $\mathcal{P}$, $\mathcal{Q}$, and $\mathcal{R}$, where these sets are constrained by a standard "exactly one" operator as in [7].

2.1   TLC Syntax

The future-time temporal connectives that we use include $\Diamond$ (*sometime in the future*), $\square$ (*always in the future*), $\bigcirc$ (*in the next moment in time*), $\mathcal{U}$ (*until*), and $\mathcal{W}$ (*unless, or weak until*). Formally, TLC($\mathcal{P}_1^{r_1,d_1}, \ldots \mathcal{P}_n^{r_n,d_n}$) formulae are constructed from the following elements:

- a set, Props $= \mathcal{P}_1^{r_1,d_1} \cup \ldots \mathcal{P}_n^{r_n,d_n} \cup \mathcal{A}$ of propositional symbols;
- propositional connectives, **true**, **false**, $\neg$, $\vee$, $\wedge$, and $\Rightarrow$; and
- temporal connectives, $\bigcirc$, $\Diamond$, $\square$, $\mathcal{U}$, and $\mathcal{W}$.

The set of well-formed formulae of TLC, denoted by WFF, is inductively defined as the smallest set satisfying the following.

- Any element of Props and **true** and **false** are in WFF.
- If A and B are in WFF then so are

$$\neg A \quad A \vee B \quad A \wedge B \quad A \Rightarrow B \quad \Diamond A \quad \square A \quad A\mathcal{U}B \quad A\mathcal{W}B \quad \bigcirc A.$$

A *literal* is defined as either a proposition symbol or the negation of a proposition symbol.

2.2 TLC Semantics

A model for TLC formulae can be characterised as a sequence of *states* of the form:

$$\sigma = t_0, t_1, t_2, t_3, \ldots$$

where each state, t_i, is a set of proposition symbols, representing those propositions which are satisfied in the ith moment in time. Note that every t_i should satisfy the constraints on propositions. For example, for TLC($\mathcal{Q}^{=2}$), every state t_i must contain exactly two propositions from the constraint set $\mathcal{Q}^{=2}$.

The notation $(\sigma, i) \models A$ denotes the truth of formula A in the model σ at state index $i \in \mathbb{N}$ defined as follows.

$$
\begin{array}{ll}
(\sigma, i) \models \mathbf{true} & \\
(\sigma, i) \not\models \mathbf{false} & \\
(\sigma, i) \models p & \text{iff } p \in t_i \text{ where } p \in \mathsf{Props} \\
(\sigma, i) \models A \wedge B & \text{iff } (\sigma, i) \models A \text{ and } (\sigma, i) \models B \\
(\sigma, i) \models A \vee B & \text{iff } (\sigma, i) \models A \text{ or } (\sigma, i) \models B \\
(\sigma, i) \models A \Rightarrow B & \text{iff } (\sigma, i) \models \neg A \text{ or } (\sigma, i) \models B \\
(\sigma, i) \models \neg A & \text{iff } (\sigma, i) \not\models A \\
(\sigma, i) \models \bigcirc A & \text{iff } (\sigma, i + 1) \models A \\
(\sigma, i) \models \Diamond A & \text{iff } \exists k \in \mathbb{N}. \ (k \geqslant i) \text{ and } (\sigma, k) \models A \\
(\sigma, i) \models \Box A & \text{iff } \forall j \in \mathbb{N}. \ \text{if } (j \geqslant i) \text{ then } (\sigma, j) \models A \\
(\sigma, i) \models A \mathcal{U} B & \text{iff } \exists k \in \mathbb{N}. \ k \geqslant i \text{ and } (\sigma, k) \models B \\
& \quad\quad \text{and } \forall j \in \mathbb{N}, \text{ if } i \leqslant j < k \text{ then } (\sigma, j) \models A \\
(\sigma, i) \models A \mathcal{W} B & \text{iff } (\sigma, i) \models A \mathcal{U} B \text{ or } (\sigma, i) \models \Box A
\end{array}
$$

For any formula A, model σ, and state index $i \in \mathbb{N}$, then either $(\sigma, i) \models A$ holds or $(\sigma, i) \models A$ does not hold, denoted by $(\sigma, i) \not\models A$. If there is some σ such that $(\sigma, 0) \models A$, then A is said to be *satisfiable*. If $(\sigma, 0) \models A$ for all models, σ, then A is said to be *valid* and is written $\models A$. Note that formulae here are interpreted at t_0; this is an *anchored* definition of satisfiability and validity [9].

2.3 Normal Form

To assist in the definition of the normal form we introduce a further (nullary) connective 'start' that holds only at the beginning of time, i.e.,

$$(\sigma, i) \models \mathbf{start} \quad \text{iff} \quad i = 0.$$

This allows the general form of the (clauses of the) normal form to be implications.

Assume we have n sets of constrained propositions $\mathcal{P}_1^{r_1, d_1} = \{p_{11}, \ldots p_{1N_1}\}, \ldots, \mathcal{P}_n^{r_n, d_n} = \{p_{n1}, \ldots p_{nN_n}\}$ and a set of additional propositions $\mathcal{A} = \{a_1, \ldots a_{N_a}\}$. In the following, small Latin letters, k_i, l_j, m represent literals in the language Props. A normal form for TLC is of the form $\Box \bigwedge_i C_i$ where each C_i is an *initial*, *step*, or *sometime* clause (respectively) as

$$\textbf{start} \Rightarrow \bigvee_i l_i \qquad \textit{(initial)}$$

$$\bigwedge_i k \Rightarrow \bigcirc \bigvee_j l_j \qquad \textit{(step)}$$

$$\textbf{true} \Rightarrow \Diamond m \qquad \textit{(sometime)}$$

Theorem 1. *[11] Any TLC formula can be transformed into an equi-satisfiable TLC formula in the normal form with at most a linear increase in the size of the problem.*

Transformation into the normal form may introduce new (unconstrained) propositions; note, however, that many temporal formulae stemming from realistic specifications are already in the normal form, or very close to the normal form and require few extra variables for the translation [13].

3 Complexity of TLC

We now prove the upper complexity bound on satisfiability of TLC by an explicit construction of a directed graph known as a *behaviour graph*. The notion of a behaviour graph for a set of clauses was introduced in [11]. It is a directed graph for a set of temporal clauses such that (after reductions) any infinite path through the graph is a model for the set of clauses. Satisfiability of TLC formulae is equivalent to a property of the graph; in what follows, we estimate the size of the graph and time needed both for its construction and for checking the property.

Given a formula φ in the normal form over a set of (both constrained and unconstrained) propositional symbols Props, we construct a finite directed graph G as follows. The nodes of G are interpretations of Props, satisfying the required constraints.

For each node, I, we construct an edge in G to a node I' if, and only if, the following condition is satisfied:

- For every step rule , $\bigwedge_i k \Rightarrow \bigcirc \bigvee_j l_j$, if $I \models \bigwedge_i k$ then $I' \models \bigvee_j l_j$.

A node, I, is designated an initial node of G if $I \models \bigvee_i l_i$ for every initial clause $\textbf{start} \Rightarrow \bigvee_i l_i$ of the given temporal formula.

The *behaviour graph*, H, of φ is the maximal subgraph of G given by the set of all nodes reachable from initial nodes. The *reduced behaviour graph*, H_R, of φ is a graph obtained from the behaviour graph of φ by repeated deletion of nodes I such that

a) I does not have a successor; or
b) for some eventuality clause $\textbf{true} \Rightarrow \Diamond m$ within φ, there is no path from I to a node J where m is true, that is, $J \models m$.

The following theorem can be obtained by an adaptation of results in [11,5] to the terminology of this paper.

Theorem 2. *[11,5] A TLC formula in the normal form φ is satisfied if, and only if, its reduced behaviour graph is non-empty.*

The link between the satisfiability of TLC formulae and properties of the behaviour graph allows us to prove the complexity bound for our logic.

Theorem 3. *Satisfiability of a $TLC(\mathcal{P}_1^{r_1,d_1}, \ldots \mathcal{P}_n^{r_n,d_n})$ formula φ can be decided in time*

$$O\left(|\varphi| \times \left(|\mathcal{P}_1^{r_1,d_1}|^{d_1} \times \ldots \times |\mathcal{P}_n^{r_n,d_n}|^{d_n} \times 2^{|A|}\right)^2\right)$$

where $|\varphi|$ is the length of φ, $|\mathcal{P}_i^{r_i,d_i}|$ is the size of the set $\mathcal{P}_i^{r_i,d_i}$ of constrained propositions, and $|A|$ is the size of the set A of non-constrained propositions.

Proof. There exist $O(|\mathcal{P}^{r_1,d_1}|^{d_1} \times \ldots \times |\mathcal{P}_n^{r_n,d_n}|^{d_n} \times 2^{|A|})$ different interpretations of propositions from Props; moreover, they can all be enumerated in time $O(|\mathcal{P}^{r_1,d_1}|^{d_1} \times \ldots \times |\mathcal{P}_n^{r_n,d_n}|^{d_n} \times 2^{|A|})$. Therefore, one can explicitly build the reduced behaviour graph H_R in time $O(|\varphi| \times (|\mathcal{P}^{r_1,d_1}|^{d_1} \times \ldots \times |\mathcal{P}_n^{r_n,d_n}|^{d_n} \times 2^{|A|})^2)$.

Corollary 1. *If the number n of sets of constrained propositions, the number d_i of propositions from the set $\mathcal{P}^{r_i,d_i}$ that can be true at any time, and the size $|A|$ of the set of non-constrained propositions is fixed, satisfiability of $TLC(\mathcal{P}_1^{r_1,d_1}, \ldots \mathcal{P}_n^{r_n,d_n})$ formulae can be decided in polynomial time.*

4   Checking Satisfiability

Based on the proof of complexity of TLC given in Section 3, one can provide an algorithm checking the satisfiability of TLC formulae as follows.

4.1   Incremental Algorithm

A straightforward approach is to construct the graph G representing all possible interpretations of Props, and then 'carve' the behaviour graph H from G. However, such a procedure might consider some nodes that are actually unreachable from the initial nodes and, thus, do excess work. In this section we present an incremental, tableaux-like algorithm, which avoids building these unnecessary nodes.

Let Assignments(φ, cons) be a procedure, which, when given a formula, φ, and a set of constraints on variables, cons, returns the set of *all* interpretations within the language Props that both satisfy the conditions cons and make φ true. Clearly, Assignments($\varphi, \{\mathcal{P}_1^{r_1,d_1}, \ldots, \mathcal{P}_n^{r_n,d_n}\}$) can be computed deterministically in time $O(int)$ where $int = (|\mathcal{P}^{r_1,d_1}|^{d_1} \times \ldots \times |\mathcal{P}_n^{r_n,d_n}|^{d_n} \times 2^{|A|})$ returning at most $O(int)$ interpretations for any φ.

Example. If Props $= \{p, q, r, s\}$ then Assignments($p \vee q, \{\{p,q,r,s\}^{=1}\}$) will return two interpretations: $\{p, \neg q, \neg r, \neg s\}$ and $\{\neg p, q, \neg r, \neg s\}$; whereas Assignments($p \vee q, \{\{p,q\}^{=1}, \{q,r,s\}^{=2}\}$) will return three: $\{p, \neg q, r, s\}$, $\{\neg p, q, r, \neg s\}$, and $\{\neg p, q, \neg r, s\}$.

Now, we use Assignments(φ, cons) to construct nodes of the behaviour graph H for a formula φ incrementally. Nodes of H can be *marked* or *unmarked*. A node is marked if all its successors are already represented in H, otherwise, it is unmarked. The incremental algorithm is given in detail in Fig. 1. Note that if the set of clauses contains no initial clauses, then the formula ψ in line 1 of the algorithm is **true**, and if the conjunction in line 7 is empty then χ is **true**. After the behaviour graph is constructed, we compute the reduced behaviour graph in time quadratic in the size of the behaviour graph.

1: Let $\psi = \bigwedge\{C_j \mid \textbf{start} \Rightarrow C_j \text{ is an initial clause}\}$
2: **for all** I in Assignments(ψ, cons) **do**
3:      Add an unmarked node I to H
4: **end for**
5: **while** Not all nodes in H are marked **do**
6:      Pick an unmarked node I and mark I
7:      Let $\chi = \bigwedge\{D_k \mid C_k \Rightarrow \bigcirc D_k \text{ is a step clause}, I \models C_k\}$
8:      **for all** J in Assignments(χ, cons) **do**
9:          **if** J is not already in H **then**
10:             Add an unmarked node J to H
11:         **end if**
12:         Add an edge (I, J) to H
13:     **end for**
14: **end while**

Fig. 1. Incremental behaviour graph construction algorithm

The following theorem follows from the Incremental Algorithm given in Figure 1.

Theorem 4. *Given a TLC formula ϕ, the incremental procedure terminates and builds the behaviour graph H of ϕ.*

5   Case Studies

In this section we will consider case studies and show how they can be specified and verified in TLC.

5.1   Multiprocessor Job-Shop Scheduling

The first problem we consider is a generalisation of the classic job-shop scheduling problem, called the *Multiprocessor Job-shop Scheduling* (MJS) problem [4,2]. Here, a set of jobs $(j_1, j_2, \ldots, j_n)$ have to be processed on a set of machines running in parallel. In general, each job might require several processor steps to complete but, to begin with we will assume each job is completed after only one step; see Fig. 2. While in these settings deciding if a schedule exists at all is comparatively easy, once we add constraints such that one job *must* be run before another, deciding the existence of a schedule becomes exponentially hard [2].

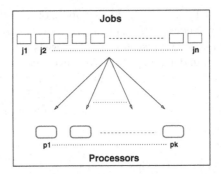

Fig. 2. Basic Multiprocessor Job Scheduling.

In what follows, we will begin with a basic specification (in TLC) corresponding to the easy form of the problem, but will then add formulae constraining particular jobs, thus giving a harder form of problem.

Basic Specification. We will now model this in TLC. Assume that we have just one constrained set

$$\{run_1, run_2, \ldots, run_n\}^{=k} .$$

Since this constrained set is of dimensionality k, then we know that at any moment in time, exactly k propositions from $run_1, run_2, \ldots, run_n$ are satisfied. (N.B., later we will relax this constraint and allow $< (k + 1)$ propositions to be satisfied at any moment.)

Now, we define other propositions using the following clauses in the normal form (for every $1 \leq i \leq n$):

$$\textbf{start} \Rightarrow \neg hasrun_i$$
$$(\neg hasrun_i \wedge \neg run_i) \Rightarrow \bigcirc \neg hasrun_i$$
$$run_i \Rightarrow \bigcirc hasrun_i$$
$$hasrun_i \Rightarrow \bigcirc hasrun_i$$

N.B., the last two clauses effectively define $run_i \Rightarrow \bigcirc \square hasrun_i$.

So, we have defined $hasrun_i$ to be true if j_i has been run in the past.

Now, to allow us to establish some simple properties, we will also constrain each job to only run once. So, we add (though we must translate to the normal form), for each $1 \leq i \leq n$

$$run_i \Rightarrow \bigcirc \square \neg run_i .$$

Synthesising a Schedule. Let us term the basic system, comprising the above clauses, as 'φ'. Now, we can simply ask whether

$$\textbf{start} \Rightarrow (\varphi \Rightarrow \Diamond \bigwedge_{i=1}^{n} hasrun_i)$$

is satisfiable or not. In other words, is there a point in the future by which time all jobs $j_1, \ldots, j_n$ have run?

If this is satisfiable, then there *is* a way to run the jobs such that exactly k run at every moment in time. If the above is not satisfiable, then it is not possible to find such a moment.

However, the strict k bound on the constrained set is a little restrictive, especially when n is *not* a multiple of k. So, we can reformulate the problem with a constrained set $\{run_1, run_2, \ldots, run_n\}^{<(k+1)}$, allowing *at most* k jobs to be run at any moment in time. Thus, checking that

$$\text{start} \ \Rightarrow (\varphi \Rightarrow \Diamond \bigwedge_{i=1}^{n} hasrun_i)$$

is satisfiable tells us whether there is a way to schedule the jobs successfully on k processors. Note that, since we build a behaviour graph for this, then if the above is satisfiable we can extract a satisfying linear path from the graph. This path corresponds to the schedule for achieving the required job runs.

Now, once we know that $\Diamond \bigwedge_{i=1}^{n} hasrun_i$ is satisfied, we can go further. We can check

$$\text{start} \ \Rightarrow (\varphi \Rightarrow \bigcirc^m \bigwedge_{i=1}^{n} hasrun_i) \, .$$

If this is satisfiable, then decrease m and try again; if it is unsatisfiable, increase m and try again. In this way, we find the minimum value of m such that

$$\bigcirc^m \bigwedge_{i=1}^{n} hasrun_i$$

is satisfied. Thus, there is no way to schedule the jobs any faster than in m steps — in this sense, we generate an *optimal* schedule through carrying out such satisfiability checks. Note that finding an optimal schedule for the MJS problem is typically an NP-hard problem [4].

Refined Specification. Now let us constrain this scenario still further. It is only to be expected that there will be dependencies between some of the jobs. We can also specify these simply in TLC. In order to show this, below are some examples.

- *job y must run immediately after job x:* $run_x \Rightarrow \bigcirc run_y$
- *job b must not run before job a has run:* $run_a \Rightarrow \bigcirc \Diamond run_b$
- *jobs p and q must only run at exactly the same time:* $\Box(run_p \Leftrightarrow run_q)$
- *jobs f and g must never run simultaneously* $\Box(\neg run_f \vee \neg run_g)$
- *and so on ...*

In this way we can specify job interdependencies and, via satisfiability checking, can extract the (optimal) schedule (if there is one)[1].

---

[1] We could also have specified jobs of varying durations (rather than just one step) in TLC. However, this would have taken more space than was available.

Note. It is obviously possible to generate a set of job interdependencies such that the specification is unsatisfiable, for example

$$\Box(run_1 \Leftrightarrow run_2) \wedge \Box(run_2 \Leftrightarrow run_3) \wedge \ldots \wedge \Box(run_{h-1} \Leftrightarrow run_h)$$

where $h > k$. Thus, it is natural to check satisfiability of the basic specification, φ, before checking $\Diamond \bigwedge\limits_{i=1}^{n} \Box \neg run_i$, etc.

5.2   Robots

Consider the robots example outlined earlier. Let us assume there are 5 robots and at any moment 3 must work and up to 2 may recharge. Further, each robot must do exactly one of *work*, *rest* or *recharge* at any moment. In the terminology we have provided, the problem is defined as $\text{TLC}(\mathcal{W}^{=3}, \mathcal{R}^{<3}, \mathcal{S}_1^{=1}, \mathcal{S}_2^{=1}, \mathcal{S}_3^{=1}, \mathcal{S}_4^{=1}, \mathcal{S}_5^{=1})$, where

$$\mathcal{W}^{=j} = \{work_1, \ldots, work_5\}$$
$$\mathcal{R}^{<3} = \{recharge_1, \ldots, recharge_5\}$$
$$\mathcal{S}_i^{=1} = \{work_i, rest_i, recharge_i\}$$

We assume that each robot has a specification relating to when it works, rests and recharges. For example, we could assume that each robot has the same specification and that after working for one time unit it must recharge for one time unit.

$$\Box(work_i \Rightarrow \bigcirc recharge_i)$$

We assume initially that robots 1,2 and 3 are working, i.e.

$$\textbf{start} \Rightarrow work_1$$
$$\textbf{start} \Rightarrow work_2$$
$$\textbf{start} \Rightarrow work_3$$

Informally we can see that this specification plus the constraints are unsatisfiable. This is because at any moment there must be exactly three robots working. The specification will then require that at the following moment all the three robots that were working in the previous moment are now recharging which will contradict the constraint relating to recharging.

Applying the Incremental Algorithm where $\psi = work_1 \wedge work_2 \wedge work_3$ and

$$\text{Assignments}(\psi, \text{cons}) = \left\{ \begin{array}{l} \{work_1, work_2, work_3, recharge_4, recharge_5\}, \\ \{work_1, work_2, work_3, rest_4, rest_5\}, \\ \{work_1, work_2, work_3, recharge_4, rest_5\}, \\ \{work_1, work_2, work_3, rest_4, recharge_5\} \end{array} \right\}$$

we add an unmarked node for each assignment to the behaviour graph. Consider the first of these assignments and call its related node I. Extending the structure we construct χ from the robot specification. Here $\chi = recharge_1 \wedge recharge_2 \wedge recharge_3$. Now when we try construct $\text{Assignments}(\chi, \text{cons})$ we obtain an empty set as χ and the constraints cannot be satisfied together. Reasoning is similar from the other unmarked nodes, hence the reduced behaviour graph is empty and the specification plus constraints must be unsatisfiable.

Next we loosen the robot specifications to say that if a robot has worked for two moments in time it must recharge in the next moment. To specify this we need an additional proposition for each robot, x_i which holds at the moment after $work_i$ holds. Informally, if x_i is true then either we are at the start of time, or the i-th robot has worked in the previous moment.

$$\Box(work_i \Rightarrow \bigcirc x_i)$$
$$\Box(work_i \wedge x_i \Rightarrow \bigcirc recharge_i)$$

Again we assume that robots 1, 2 and 3 must work initially. Now our behaviour graph construction has an extra five propositions. The specification is now satisfiable, a sample model being the following.

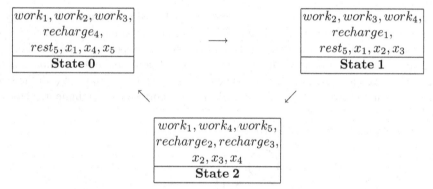

Further, we may want to strengthen the specification to ensure that each robot gets a chance to work infinitely often.

$$\mathbf{true} \Rightarrow \Diamond work_i$$

We can observe that this is satisfied in the above model.

Finally observing the model suggested above we can see that robot 5 never recharges as it just works intermittently. To avoid such a situation we may want to specify that the robot needs to recharge after working for two moments in time since last recharging even if these moments are not immediately one after the other. Again informally, if y_i is true then either we are at start of time or the i-th robot has worked one time unit since the last recharge.

$$\Box(work_i \Rightarrow \bigcirc y_i)$$
$$\Box(work_i \wedge y_i \Rightarrow \bigcirc recharge_i)$$
$$\Box(rest_i \wedge y_i \Rightarrow \bigcirc y_i)$$
$$\Box(recharge_i \Rightarrow \bigcirc \neg y_i)$$

Now extending the above model with suitable y_i propositions and removing the x_i propositions won't satisfy the new specification and constraints as robot 5 works infinitely often but never gets to recharge. However we can easily specify a model which does satisfy the new specification and constraints.

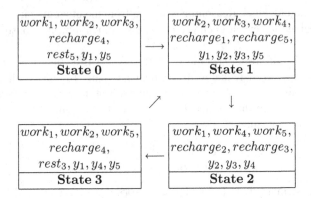

$work_1, work_2, work_3,$ $recharge_4,$ $rest_5, y_1, y_5$	$work_2, work_3, work_4,$ $recharge_1, recharge_5,$ y_1, y_2, y_3, y_5
State 0	**State 1**

$work_1, work_2, work_5,$ $recharge_4,$ $rest_3, y_1, y_4, y_5$	$work_1, work_4, work_5,$ $recharge_2, recharge_3,$ y_2, y_3, y_4
State 3	**State 2**

5.3 Petri Nets

Consider now 1-safe Petri nets (see for example [10]), which are used to model systems with limited resources. In 1-safe nets, every place may contain at most one token. This restriction allows us to represent 1-safe Petri nets in propositional temporal logic. Encoding places with propositions (proposition p_i is true if, and only if, a token is at place P_i), given a 1-safe Petri net $\mathcal{N}$, one can construct a PTL formula $\phi_{\mathcal{N}}$ of the size polynomial in the size of $\mathcal{N}$, such that models of $\phi_{\mathcal{N}}$ correspond to infinite trajectories of $\mathcal{N}$.

For example, the following transition

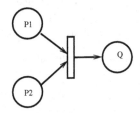

can be represented as

$$\Box(p_1 \wedge p_2 \Rightarrow \bigcirc(q \wedge \neg p1 \wedge \neg p2))$$

i.e. the transition fires if both P_1 and P_2 contain a token, plus suitable frame axioms to prevent tokens from arbitrarily appearing or disappearing. Similarly, reachability in these nets, for example the reachability of the state P_F corresponds to the satisfiability of $\Diamond p_F$ from an initial state. Since the reachability problem (as well as many other interesting problems) for 1-safe nets is PSPACE-complete [10], such translation is optimal.

We can then use capacity constraints to impose *place invariants*: for a subset of places in a Petri net, the total number of tokens in places from this subset remains constant. Such invariants are used, for example, in the verification of distributed protocols with Petri nets [18,19]. Note that imposing such extra restrictions actually makes the complexity of reasoning lower.

6   Concluding Remarks

In this paper we have introduced TLC, a propositional temporal logic that allows the specifier to put powerful additional constraints on how many propositions can be satisfied at any one time. This logic represents a combination of standard propositional linear-time temporal logic with constraints relating to restrictions on the number of propositions, for particular subsets of propositions, at each moment in time. This is not only an interesting extension of PTL, but can potentially be decided in polynomial, rather than exponential time. This improved complexity makes TLC a strong candidate for practical verification based upon temporal satisfiability.

We provide a graph construction algorithm to check satisfiability by enumerating only the reachable nodes that satisfy the required constraints. The definition of resolution rules incorporating these constraints appear complex and non-trivial. Similarly, the adaption of tableau algorithms for PTL [24] to this constrained situation lead, in some cases, to the generation of exponentially many successors to nodes in the tableau.

There is little related work in this area. Refinements of PTL have been considered, particularly in relation to model checking, by Demri and Schnoebelen [6]. Mutually exclusive conditions (stemming e.g. from automata representation) and numbers from a fixed range can often be handled through efficient *translation* — consider, for example, logarithmic encoding or property-driven partitioning used in model checking [23] and SAT [1] — however, we are not aware of others who have explicitly studied constraints directly *in the logic itself*, such as those described in this paper, apart from ourselves in earlier work just on XOR extensions of PTL [7,8].

Our explicit graph construction has a similar flavour to that of tableau algorithms developed for PTL [24,15] which attempt to explicitly construct a model for formulae. Here the expansion rules focus on formulae in the normal form rather than any well-formed formula. Implementations of the tableau procedures [22,17] are available within the logics workbench [16], and powerful tools for constructing automata from PTL formulae now exist [3,14].

Future Work. Work on TLC has uncovered a new, and potentially very sophisticated, approach to temporal specification. Rather than concentrating solely on the behaviour of components, the use of TLC encourages specifiers to partition the propositions, and also to consider what constraints need to be put upon these partitioned sets. Thus, this leads us towards the approach of *engineering* the sets and constraints first, *before* even addressing the temporal specification of the component behaviours.

Furthermore, the incremental algorithm in Fig. 1 can potentially be modified to allow for *dynamic* changes of the set of constraints. This allows us to accommodate constraints *into* the language as a logical connective. Let $\oplus^{=s}$ denote a logical operator of flexible arity, which states that exactly s of its arguments is true, while $\oplus^{<d}$ states that fewer than d of its arguments can be true. Expressions of the form

$$\bigwedge_i k \Rightarrow \bigcirc \oplus_j^{=d} l_j$$

are called $\oplus^{=d}$-*step clauses* ($\oplus^{<d}$-step clauses are defined similarly). If in the algorithm in Fig. 1, lines 6–12, $I \models \bigwedge_i k$, we look for interpretations, which make χ true and

satisfy *both* constraints, cons, and the right-hand side of the of $\oplus^{=d}$ step clause. A more elaborate language even allows us to dynamically *disallow* existing constraints as well as introduce new ones.

The development of an implementation of the algorithms discussed in this paper together with practical verification case studies, form the basis for our future work. Further, the extension to dynamic constraints and a deeper comparison to related methods are future work.

Acknowledgements. The authors were partially supported by EPSRC grants GR/S63182 (Dixon, Konev) and EP/D052548 (Fisher), and would also like to thank both Bo Chen and Leslie Goldberg for their input on complexity issues.

References

1. Bordeaux, L., Hamadi, Y., Zhang, L.: Propositional Satisfiability and Constraint Programming: A Comparative Survey. ACM Computing Surveys 38(4) (2006)
2. Chen, B.: Parallel Scheduling for Early Completion. In: Leung, J.Y.-T. (ed.) Handbook of Scheduling: Algorithms, Models, and Performance Analysis, ch. 9, Chapman & Hall/CRC Press (2004)
3. Daniele, M., Giunchiglia, F., Vardi, M.Y.: Improved Automata Generation for Linear Temporal Logic. In: Halbwachs, N., Peled, D.A. (eds.) CAV 1999. LNCS, vol. 1633, pp. 249–260. Springer, Heidelberg (1999)
4. Dauzére-Pérès, S., Paulli, J.: An Integrated Approach for Modeling and Solving the General Multiprocessor Job-shop Scheduling Problem using Tabu Search. Annals of Operations Research 70, 281–306 (1997)
5. Degtyarev, A., Fisher, M., Konev, B.: A Simplified Clausal Resolution Procedure for Propositional Linear-Time Temporal Logic. In: Egly, U., Fermüller, C. (eds.) TABLEAUX 2002. LNCS (LNAI), vol. 2381, pp. 85–99. Springer, Heidelberg (2002)
6. Demri, S., Schnoebelen, P.: The Complexity of Propositional Linear Temporal Logic in Simple Cases. Information and Computation 174(1), 84–103 (2002)
7. Dixon, C., Fisher, M., Konev, B.: Is There a Future for Deductive Temporal Verification? In: Proc. Thirteenth International Symposium on Temporal Representation and Reasoning (TIME), IEEE Computer Society Press, Los Alamitos (June 2006)
8. Dixon, C., Fisher, M., Konev, B.: Tractable Temporal Reasoning. In: Proc. International Joint Conference on Artificial Intelligence (IJCAI), AAAI Press, Stanford, California (2007)
9. Emerson, E.A.: Temporal and Modal Logic. In: van Leeuwen, J. (ed.) Handbook of Theoretical Computer Science, pp. 996–1072. Elsevier, Amsterdam (1990)
10. Esparza, J.: Decidability and Complexity of Petri Net Problems - An Introduction. In: Reisig, W., Rozenberg, G. (eds.) Lectures on Petri Nets I: Basic Models. LNCS, vol. 1491, pp. 374–428. Springer, Heidelberg (1998)
11. Fisher, M., Dixon, C., Peim, M.: Clausal Temporal Resolution. ACM Transactions on Computational Logic 2(1), 12–56 (2001)
12. Gabbay, D., Pnueli, A., Shelah, S., Stavi, J.: The Temporal Analysis of Fairness. In: Proc. Seventh ACM Symposium on the Principles of Programming Languages (POPL), pp. 163–173 (January 1980)
13. Gago, M.-C.F., Hustadt, U., Dixon, C., Fisher, M., Konev, B.: First-Order Temporal Verification in Practice. Journal of Automated Reasoning 34(3), 295–321 (2005)

14. Giannakopoulou, D., Lerda, F.: From States to Transitions: Improving Translation of LTL Formulae to Büchi Automata. In: Peled, D.A., Vardi, M.Y. (eds.) FORTE 2002. LNCS, vol. 2529, pp. 308–326. Springer, Heidelberg (2002)
15. Gough, G.D.: Decision Procedures for Temporal Logic. Master's thesis, Department of Computer Science, University of Manchester, October, Also University of Manchester, Department of Computer Science, Technical Report UMCS-89-10-1 (1984)
16. Jaeger, G., Balsiger, P., Heuerding, A., Schwendimann, S., Bianchi, M., Guggisberg, K., Janssen, G., Heinle, W., Achermann, F., Boroumand, A.D., Brambilla, P., Bucher, I., Zimmermann, H.: LWB–The Logics Workbench 1.1. University of Berne, Switzerland (2002), http://www.lwb.unibe.ch
17. Janssen, G.: Logics for Digital Circuit Verification: Theory, Algorithms, and Applications. PhD thesis, Eindhoven University of Technology, Eindhoven, The Netherlands (1999)
18. Kindler, E.: Petri Nets, Situations, and Automata. In: Esparza, J., Lakos, C.A. (eds.) ICATPN 2002. LNCS, vol. 2360, pp. 217–236. Springer, Heidelberg (2002)
19. Kindler, E., Reisig, W., Völzer, H., Walter, R.: Petri Net Based Verification of Distributed Algorithms: An Example. Formal Aspects of Computing 9(4), 409–424 (1997)
20. Lamport, L.: Specifying Systems: The TLA+ Language and Tools for Hardware and Software Engineers. Addison Wesley Professional, Reading (2003)
21. Manna, Z., Pnueli, A.: The Temporal Logic of Reactive and Concurrent Systems: Specification. Springer, Heidelberg (1992)
22. Schwendimann, S.: Aspects of Computational Logic. PhD thesis, University of Bern, Switzerland (1998)
23. Sebastiani, R., Tonetta, S., Vardi, M.Y.: Symbolic Systems, Explicit Properties: On Hybrid Approaches for LTL Symbolic Model Checking. In: Etessami, K., Rajamani, S.K. (eds.) CAV 2005. LNCS, vol. 3576, pp. 350–363. Springer, Heidelberg (2005)
24. Wolper, P.: The Tableau Method for Temporal Logic: An Overview. Logique et Analyse, 110–111,119–136, (June-September 1985)

Idempotent Transductions for Modal Logics

Tim French

School of Computer Science & Software Engineering
The University of Western Australia
tim@csse.uwa.edu.au

Abstract. We investigate the extension of modal logics by bisimulation quantifiers and present a class of modal logics which is decidable when augmented with bisimulation quantifiers. These logics are refered to as the idempotent transduction logics and are defined using the programs of propositional dynamic logic including converse and tests. This is a nontrivial extension of the decidability of the positive idempotent transduction logics which do not use converse operators in the programs (French, 2006). This extension allows us to apply bisimulation quantifiers to, for example, logics of knowledge, logics of belief and tense logics. We show the idempotent transduction logics preserve the axioms of propositional quantification and are decidable. The definition of idempotent transduction logics allows us to apply these results to a number of combined modal logics with a variety of interactions between modalities.

1 Introduction

Bisimulation quantifiers were introduced by Visser [1] and Ghilardi [2] as a semantic characterization of uniform interpolants in modal logics such as **K**, **Grz** and **GL**. More recently, bisimulation quantifiers have been investigated as an expressive extension of many modal logics such as **PDL** [3], and **S4** [4].

Syntactically, bisimulation quantifiers are the same as propositional quantifiers. Semantically, they quantify over all interpretations of the specified propositional atom *in all bisimilar models*. Thus bisimulation quantified modal logics are typically less expressive than standard propositional quantified modal logics (which are generally undecidable [5]).

The motivation for considering bisimulation quantifiers is to extend modal logics with the ability to reason about *hypothetical assignments of atoms*. That is we may express the property, "there could be an interpretation of atoms that agrees with the present interpretation on all atoms except x, that makes α true." To evaluate this statement we must decide what it means for two interpretations to *agree*. In our case we suppose two interpretations agree if they are structures that are bisimilar up to the proposition x. This is a very natural standard to apply. Bisimulations were defined by Milner [6], Park [7] and (as p-relations) van Benthem [8]. Stirling [9] surveys the relationships between bisimulations and modal logic. In [8] it is shown that properties definable in modal logic are exactly the first-order properties that are bisimulation invariant. Therefore modal formulas are unable to distinguish between bisimilar structures, and this degree of abstraction has allowed modal logics to be easily applied in a range of contexts (such as reasoning about time [10] or knowledge [11]). We consider quantification

B. Konev and F. Wolter (Eds.): FroCos 2007, LNAI 4720, pp. 178–192, 2007.
© Springer-Verlag Berlin Heidelberg 2007

modulo bisimulation because we would like to preserve this degree of abstraction whilst considering hypothetical assignments of atoms.

Bisimulation quantifiers were originally investigated in [1] and [2] as abbreviations for uniform interpolants in some modal logics. In [3] this characterization was extended to abbreviations for uniform interpolants in the modal μ-calculus. More recently, bisimulation quantifiers have been investigated independently of uniform interpolants. We briefly survey some of these results here: In [4] axiomatizations are given for the bisimulation quantified extension of **K** and the bisimulation quantified extension of **PDL**. In [12] bisimulation quantifiers are considered in the context of arbitrary modal logics. It is shown that there are cases where extension by bisimulation quantifiers does not preserve decidability, or the axioms for propositional quantification. The paper [13] explores the relationship between fixed-point operators and bisimulation quantifiers, and it is shown that there are cases where bisimulation quantified logics are more expressive than the corresponding fixed-point logic. The paper [14] introduces the *positive idempotent transduction logics*. This is a decidable class of bisimulation quantified logics which includes many of the well-known and applied modal logics (such as **K4**, **GL** and a fragment of **CTL**).

In this paper we enhance the results of [14]. We extend the definition of idempotent transduction logics in such a way as to capture the logics **S5**, **KD45** and many more besides[1]. The logic **S5** is applied for reasoning about knowledge and security [11] and **KD45** is used for reasoning about belief in agent systems, so there are practical reasons to extend the class of idempotent transduction logics to include such logics as these. We show that the idempotent transduction logics are decidable, and preserve the axioms of propositional quantification. This work is a non-trivial extension of the results of [14], which presented the class of positive idempotent transduction logics. Positive idempotent transductions specified modalities as μ-programs without converse, whereas idempotent transduction specify modalities as μ-programs with converse. While this significantly complicates the proofs, it allows us to extend our generalized results to combinations of logics including knowledge and belief.

These results have been presented in [15], although the proofs are improved here.

2 Preliminaries

In this section we give the basic notation, definitions and lemmas required throughout this paper.

2.1 Modal Logic

Definition 1. *Let Λ be a non-empty set. A Λ-frame is a tuple (S, R) where S is some set and $R : \Lambda \longrightarrow \wp(S \times S)$.*

The set S corresponds to the set of possible worlds, and for each $a \in \Lambda$, $R(a)$ refers to some relation between the possible worlds. A model adds a valuation to a Λ-frame

---

[1] Using the language of [15] we will refer to the idempotent transduction logics of [14] as *positive idempotent transduction logics*.

which defines which atomic propositions are true at each element of S, and identifies the *current world*.

Definition 2. *A Λ-$\mathcal{V}$-model is a tuple (S, R, ρ, s) where (S, R) is a Λ-frame, $\rho : S \longrightarrow \wp(\mathcal{V})$, and $s \in S$.*

Here $\mathcal{V}$ is a countable set of atomic propositions, ρ assigns those propositions to states (so that $x \in \rho(t)$ if and only if x is true at t), and s is the *current state of the model*. We will refer to Λ-$\mathcal{V}$-models as Λ-models when there is no ambiguity about $\mathcal{V}$. The use of the term *model* rather than *structure* or *system* is quite deliberate. A structure implies some concrete entity, whereas we consider the models to be abstractions of some real-world entity (but importantly, an abstraction that is equally as good as any other bisimilar model).

The syntax of the modal logic (L_Λ) is given with respect to the sets Λ (the set of modalities) and $\mathcal{V}$ (the set of atomic propositions).

$$\alpha ::= x \mid \neg\alpha \mid \alpha_1 \vee \alpha_2 \mid \Diamond_a\alpha \tag{1}$$

where $x \in \mathcal{V}$ and $a \in \Lambda$. Correspondingly, we will refer to Λ-$\mathcal{V}$-models as Λ-models when there is no ambiguity about $\mathcal{V}$. We let the abbreviations $\wedge$, $\rightarrow$, $\leftrightarrow$, $\top$ and $\bot$ be defined as usual and let $\Box_a\alpha$ abbreviate $\neg\Diamond_a\neg\alpha$. We let $var(\alpha)$ be the set of propositional atoms appearing in α.

The modal logic L_Λ has the following semantics. Given some Λ-model $M = (S, R, \rho, s)$ for each $t \in S$ let $M_t = (S, R, \rho, t)$. We then define:

$$M \models x \iff x \in \rho(s)$$
$$M \models \Diamond_a\alpha \iff \text{for some } (s, t) \in R(a),\ M_t \models \alpha$$

where $\neg$ and $\vee$ have their usual interpretation.

From a purely semantic view of logic, we can define a variety of modal logics by restricting the class of models over which formulas are evaluated.

Definition 3. *Given some set Λ, a Λ-class $\mathcal{C}$ is a class of Λ-frames. The logic $L_\mathcal{C}$ is the set of all L_Λ formulas which are true on all Λ-$\mathcal{V}$-models, (S, R, ρ, s), where $(S, R) \in \mathcal{C}$.*

In an abuse of notation we may refer to $M \in \mathcal{C}$, where $M = (S, R, \rho, s)$ and $(S, R) \in \mathcal{C}$.

2.2 Bisimulation Quantifiers

The *bisimulation quantified logic of $\mathcal{C}$* ($BQL_\mathcal{C}$) is the extension of $L_\mathcal{C}$ by bisimulation quantifiers. The syntax is given by:

$$\alpha ::= x \mid \neg\alpha \mid \alpha_1 \vee \alpha_2 \mid \Diamond_a\alpha \mid \exists x\alpha \tag{2}$$

where $x \in \mathcal{V}$ and $a \in \Lambda$. To give the formal semantics we require bisimulations. These are well-known and we extend this definition to Θ-bisimulations.

Definition 4. *Let $M = (S, R, \rho, s_0)$ and $N = (T, P, \lambda, t_0)$ be Λ-$\mathcal{V}$-models and suppose $\Theta \subseteq \mathcal{V}$. We say the models M and N are Θ-bisimilar (written $M \cong_\Theta N$) if there is some relation $B \subseteq S \times T$ such that:*

1. $(s_0, t_0) \in B$;
2. for all $(s,t) \in B$, $\rho(s)\backslash\Theta = \lambda(t)\backslash\Theta$;[2]
3. for all $(s,t) \in B$, for all $a \in \Lambda$, for all $u \in S$ such that $(s, u) \in R(a)$ there is some $v \in T$ such that $(u, v) \in B$ and $(t, v) \in P(a)$;
4. for all $(s,t) \in B$, for all $a \in \Lambda$, for all $v \in T$ such that $(t, v) \in P(a)$ there is some $u \in S$ such that $(u, v) \in B$ and $(s, u) \in R(a)$.

We call such a relation B a Θ-bisimulation from M to N and if $M \cong_{\{x\}} N$ we say M and N are x-bisimilar (written $M \cong_x N$).

Given $M = (S, R, \rho, s)$ is a $\mathcal{C}$-model the interpretation of $\exists x \alpha$ in $\text{BQL}_\mathcal{C}$ is $M \models_\mathcal{C} \exists x \alpha$ if and only if there is some $\mathcal{C}$-model N where $N \cong_x M$ and $N \models_\mathcal{C} \alpha$.

We note that the class $\mathcal{C}$ appears explicitly in the semantics, and thus has a direct effect on the meaning of formulas. For example, we might have some Λ-model M and some formula α such that for two classes, $\mathcal{C}$ and $\mathcal{D}$ $M \models_\mathcal{C} \alpha$ and $M \models_\mathcal{D} \neg\alpha$. Consider, for example, the formula $\alpha = \forall x(x \rightarrow \Diamond_a x)$, and suppose M is a $\{a\}$-model consisting of a single world related to itself by $R(a)$.

- In the class $\mathcal{C}$ of all reflexive $\{a\}$-frames we would have $M \models_\mathcal{C} \alpha$.
- However, in the class of all $\{a\}$-frames, $\mathcal{D}$, we have $M \models_\mathcal{D} \neg\alpha$, since M is $\{x\}$-bisimilar to some model (T, P, τ, t) where $x \in \tau(t)$ and $(t, t) \notin P(a)$.

This is in contrast to the case of pure modal logic, where there is one semantics for all logics, so that $L_\mathcal{C}$ and $L_\mathcal{D}$ will always agree on the meaning of a formula (i.e. whether a given formula is satisfied by a given model), but they may differ on whether a formula is valid.

In the remainder of this paper we will let BQL_Λ refer to the logic $\text{BQL}_\mathcal{C}$ where C is the class of all Λ-frames, and write $M \models_\Lambda \alpha$ to denote satisfaction in this class.

2.3 Amalgamation

It was shown in [12] that bisimulation quantifiers are not well behaved for all classes of frames. Particularly we can define a class of frames $\mathcal{C}$ such that $\text{BQL}_\mathcal{C}$ does not validate the standard rules of propositional quantification:

1. *Existential elimination*: If $\phi \rightarrow \psi$ is a validity and ψ does not contain free occurrences of the variable x, then $\exists x \phi \rightarrow \psi$ should also be a validity.
2. *Existential introduction*: Suppose α is a formula such that β is free for x in α. Then $\alpha[x\backslash\beta] \rightarrow \exists x\alpha$ is a validity.

Here $\alpha[x\backslash\beta]$ is the formula α with every free occurrence of the variable x replaced by the formula β, and β is *free for x in α* if and only if for every free variable, y, of β the variable x is not in the scope of a quantifier, $\exists y$, in α. In [15], it is shown that these laws, along with the tautologies of propositional logic, are sufficient to give a sound and complete axiomatization of the extension of propositional logic by propositional quantification.

Several classes of frames that do not validate these rules are presented in [12]. These rules are sound for all logics, $\text{BQL}_\mathcal{C}$, where $\mathcal{C}$ has the *amalgamation property*.

---

[2] Here, $\backslash$ is used to indicate set subtraction.

Definition 5. *We say the class of frames* C *has the* amalgamation property *(or* C *is amalgamative) if and only if for any* $\Theta_1, \Theta_2 \subset V$, *for any* C-*models* M *and* N *such that* $M \cong_{\Theta_1 \cup \Theta_2} N$, *there is some* C-*model,* K *such that* $M \cong_{\Theta_1} K$ *and* $N \cong_{\Theta_2} K$.

The following was shown in [12] (where amalgamation was refered to as safety).

Lemma 1. *If* C *enjoys amalgamation, then the rules* existential elimination *and* existential introduction *are sound for* BQL_C.

Note that the soundness of existential elimination rule implies bisimulation invariance, so as a corollary we have, if C is amalgamative, then BQL_C is bisimulation invariant.

3   Motivation and Examples

We will present some examples of bisimulation quantified modal logics, and then consider some of the applications for bisimulation quantifiers. The first two examples demonstrate the use of bisimulation quantifiers in the context of knowledge and belief. As the modalities of knowledge and belief are, respectively, symmetric and Euclidean [16], their interpretation relies on the converse relations. As such they cannot be presented using the positive idempotent transductions of [14].

3.1   Knowledge

We consider a very simple example in the context of epistemic logic. Suppose that $\Lambda = \{a, b\}$ (for *Alice* and *Bob*). We let C be the Λ-class of frames (S, R) where both $R(a)$ and $R(b)$ are equivalence relations. This corresponds to a very simple logic of knowledge where two worlds u and v are related by $R(a)$ if and only if Alice cannot distinguish between those two worlds, and thus $\Box_a \alpha$ is true at the current world if and only if α is true at every world that Alice cannot distinguish from the current world (i.e. Alice knows α). See [11] for a good introduction to epistemic logics.

Consider a simple model which consists of only two worlds, *locked* and *unlocked*, that Alice can distinguish, but which Bob cannot. That is, in all worlds the formula *locked* $\leftrightarrow \Box_a locked$ is true. Even though Bob does not know whether the door is locked or not, he does know that Alice knows. Now suppose that (hypothetically) Bob announces he is going to flip a coin and keep the result secret. We can consider the hypothetical proposition *heads*, where $\Box_b heads \wedge \neg \Box_a heads$ is true. As a bisimulation quantified formula this is expressed as $\exists heads(\Box_b heads \wedge \neg \Box_a heads)$ and its semantic interpretation is illustrated in Figure 1. The model on the right is $\{heads\}$-bisimilar to the one on the left, and satisfies $\Box_b heads \wedge \neg \Box_a heads$ at its bottom left world.

This is a very simple example, but we can see how bisimulation quantifiers can be applied in different contexts. In this example we supposed it was possible for Bob to be able to flip a coin and keep the result secret from Alice. However, if we restricted the class C so that the equivalence classes of $R(a)$ were always subsets of equivalence classes that belong to $R(b)$ we would have a semantic where Alice *always* knows more than Bob (for example Alice might be a super-user who has access to all of Bob's files). In this case $\exists heads(\Box_b heads \wedge \neg \Box_a heads)$ would not be satisfied. Such hierarchical logics of knowledge (without bisimulation quantifiers) are considered in [17]. In [18] a

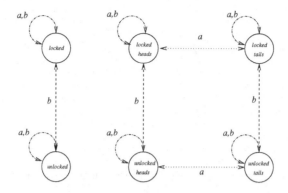

Fig. 1. Two models demonstrating the interpretation of the formula $\exists heads(\Box_b heads \wedge \neg\Box_a heads)$ in bisimulation quantified epistemic logic

bisimulation quantified logic of knowledge is presented, although several of the proofs are flawed. The results of this paper redress some of those errors.

3.2 Belief

Another interesting example of the application of bisimulation quantifiers is in the logic **KD45**, which is Kripke complete for the class of serial, transitive, Euclidean frames (a frame is Euclidean if any two successors of a world are related to each other). In $BQL_{\mathbf{KD45}}$,

$$\Diamond(\exists x(x \wedge \Box\neg x)) \tag{3}$$

is a validity, but $\exists x\Diamond(x \wedge \Box\neg x)$ is a contradiction. The unsatisfiability of the second follows from the fact that $\Box(x \rightarrow \Diamond x)$ is a validity of **KD45**. Figure 2 demonstrates how formula (3) is satisfied. Here, M is a **KD45** model, and $M_t \cong_x N_{t'}$, but there is no **KD45**-model $K = (U, Q, \gamma, u)$ where $K \cong_x M$ and $K_v \cong N_{t'}$ for some v where $(u, v) \in Q$. That is, the bisimulation quantifier does not necessarily commute with modalities, so bisimulation quantified **KD45** does not satisfy the Barcan formula, $\forall x\Box\alpha \rightarrow \Box\forall x\alpha$. This may appear to be a flaw in the interpretation of bisimulation quantifiers. However, **KD45** is the logic of belief and in this context it makes sense. An agent *believes* that some set of worlds are possible, and refuses to believe any other world is possible. Suppose that we are dealing with an informed agent that knows the difference between belief and knowledge. The agent would *believe* that in principle it is *possible* that he believes some (hypothetical) property to be true, even though that property is not satisfied at the current world. That is, $\Diamond\exists x(\neg x \wedge \Box x)$ is valid. However the agent would still not concede that any of the real, non-hypothetical properties (i.e. unquantified propositions) that he believes are false.

3.3 Expressing Refinement

We consider the applications of modal logic to the verification and modeling of computational systems. Such systems can be specified at many levels of abstraction, ranging

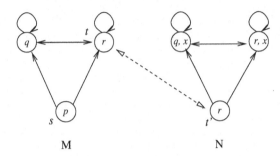

Fig. 2. A depiction of the validity (3) with respect to the class of **KD45** frames

from the individual transistors that make up a circuit, to objects of high level programming languages.

Abadi and Lamport [19] examine the problem of specifying and reasoning about systems at multiple levels of abstraction. They divide the properties at any level of abstraction into external properties and internal properties, where the external properties describe the visible behavior of a system. At a higher level of abstraction less properties are externally visible. Abadi and Lamport use finite state machines to represent the behavior of systems, and apply the notion of a *refinement mapping* [20] to verify if one specification implements another specification (or agrees with the external properties of that specification).

In the context of general modal logics, such refinements can be modeled by bisimulation quantifiers. For example two security protocols could be specified by the formulas of epistemic logic, $S_1(\overline{x}, \overline{y})$ and $S_2(\overline{x}, \overline{z})$, respectively. We are able to express that the specification S_1 always agrees with the specification S_2 with respect to the propositional atoms (or properties), $\overline{x}$ using the bisimulation quantified epistemic formula

$$\forall \overline{x} \forall \overline{y}(S_1(\overline{x}, \overline{y}) \rightarrow \exists \overline{z} S_2(\overline{x}, \overline{z})). \tag{4}$$

We note that the use of bisimulation quantifiers rather than naive propositional quantifiers is significant here. For example, it is possible that the specification $S_1(\overline{x}, \overline{y})$ is satisfiable in a model containing only three worlds, whilst $S_2(\overline{x}, \overline{z})$, can only be satisfied by models with more than three worlds. In such a case the formula (4) would not be valid.

We do not consider any particular specifications, or any specification languages here. Rather we simply note that bisimulation quantifiers seem to naturally capture the intuitive meaning of one specification *implementing another*. A general aim of this paper and other works [14,15,13] is to develop a formal framework for the iterative refinement of specifications in different ontologies.

4   The Modal μ-Calculus with Converse

In this section we examine the *modal μ-calculus with converse*[21]. The converse operators inverts the modal accessibility relation allowing us to "see" backwards along a relation. Including converse programs is important to allow us to capture the symmetric nature of the modal relations in **S5** and other similar logics. However, the converse operators also significantly increase the complexity of the decidability proof.

4.1 Syntax and Semantics

The *full μ-calculus*, μL_Λ is an extension of modal logic that includes the *least fixed point operator* μ, and converse modalities:

$$\alpha ::= x \mid \neg\alpha \mid \alpha \vee \alpha \mid \langle a \rangle \alpha \mid \langle a^- \rangle \alpha \mid \mu x \alpha \tag{5}$$

where $x \in \mathcal{V}$, $a \in \Lambda$ and in the recursion for $\mu x \alpha$ we require that x only occurs in the scope of an even number of negations in α. We let $\nu x \alpha$ be an abbreviation for $\neg\mu x \neg\alpha[x\backslash\neg x]$, (where $\alpha[x\backslash\neg x]$ is α with every free occurrence of x replaced by $\neg x$).

The interpretation of $\langle a \rangle \alpha$ is the same as the interpretation of $\Diamond_a \alpha$ and the interpretation of $\langle a^- \rangle \alpha$ is given as:

$$M_t \models \langle a^- \rangle \alpha \iff \text{for some } (s,t) \in R(a), \ M_s \models \alpha.$$

The interpretation of $\mu x \alpha$ is the least of all assignments of x such that x is true exactly where α is true, and the operator ν refers to the greatest such assignment[22].

4.2 Results for the Modal μ-Calculus with Converse

The modal μ-calculus without converse was introduced by Kozen in [22]. In [23] it was shown that μL_Λ corresponds to the bisimulation invariant fragment of monadic second-order logic. Emerson and Jutla presented an exponential time decision procedure for the modal μ-calculus in [24]. In [3] it was shown that the μ-calculus was closed under bisimulation quantifiers. That is, for all formulas of the μ-calculus α, for all atomic propositions x, there is some formula of the μ-calculus, $\tilde{\exists}x\alpha$, such that for all models, $M, M \models \tilde{\exists}x\alpha$ if and only if there is some model $N \cong_x M$ such that $N \models \alpha$.

The μ-calculus with converse (or the *full μ-calculus*) was shown to be decidable in [21]. The proof of decidability defined *two-way alternating automata* to accept models of full μ-calculus formulas, and then reduced the two-way alternating automata to (one-way) non-deterministic automata.

It is well-known that the μ-calculus can express *dynamic modalities* (or *programs*).

Definition 6. *Let Λ be a set of atomic programs. The μ-programs π over Λ (Prog$_\Lambda$) are:*

$$\pi := a \mid \pi; \pi \mid \pi \cup \pi \mid \pi^* \mid \pi^- \mid \alpha?;$$

where $a \in \Lambda$ and

$$\alpha := P \mid \neg\phi \mid \alpha \vee \alpha \mid \langle \pi \rangle \phi \mid \mu P \alpha,$$

provided P is under an even number of negations in α.

The modalities, $\langle \pi \rangle$, corresponding to programs, π are defined as usual by extending the function R to map all programs, π, to a binary relation over S, $R(\pi)$. This is done inductively where: the base case is given by $R(a)$ for $a \in \Lambda$; $R(\pi_1; \pi_2)$ is the composition of the relations $R(\pi_1)$ and $R(\pi_2)$; $R(\pi_1 \cup \pi_2)$ is the union of $R(\pi_1)$ and $R(\pi_2)$; $R(\pi^*)$ is the reflexive transitive closure of $R(\pi)$; $R(\pi^-)$ is the converse of the relation $R(\pi)$ (so that $(u, v) \in R(\pi^-)$ if and only if $(v, u) \in R(\pi)$); and α? is a *test* program defined by $R(\alpha?) = \{(u, u) \mid M_u \models_c \alpha\}$.

We use the μ-programs defined here to describe a large class of bisimulation quantified modal logics. Whilst these classes of logics may be defined using converse programs, the logics themselves only use forward modalities. To address this asymmetry we give the following definitions.

We first focus on translating the class of $\mathcal{C}_\Lambda$-models to a class of models where the converse of each atomic modality is explicitly represented by another atomic modality.

Definition 7. *1. Given the set $\Lambda = \{a_1, a_2, \ldots\}$, let Λ' be a set $\{b_1, b_2, \ldots\}$ such that $\Lambda \cap \Lambda' = \emptyset$. The converse closure of Λ, with respect to Λ', is the set $\overline{\Lambda} = \{a_1, b_1, a_2, b_2, \ldots\}$, and for all i, we let $\overline{a_i} = b_i$ and $\overline{b_i} = a_i$.*
2. *Given the Λ-class of frames $\mathcal{C}$, let the converse extension of $\mathcal{C}$ be the $\overline{\Lambda}$-class $\overline{\mathcal{C}} = \{(S, \overline{R}) \mid (S, R) \in \mathcal{C}\}$ where $\overline{R} : \overline{\Lambda} \longrightarrow S \times S$ is defined such that for all $a \in \Lambda$, $\overline{R}(a) = R(a)$ and $(u, v) \in \overline{R}(\overline{a})$ if and only if $(v, u) \in R(a)$.*
3. *Given the $\mathcal{C}$-model $M = (S, R, \rho, s)$ let the converse extension of M be the $\overline{\mathcal{C}}$-model $\overline{M} = (S, \overline{R}, \rho, s)$.*
4. *Given any $\mathcal{C}_{\overline{\Lambda}}$-model $M = (S, R, \rho, s)$ we define the converse closure of M to be the $\overline{\mathcal{C}_\Lambda}$-model $M^+ = (S, R^+, \rho, s)$ where for $o \in \overline{\Lambda}$, $R^+(o) = R(o) \cup \{(u, v) \mid (v, u) \in R(\overline{o})\}$.*

The following definition introduces *tree-like* models. Tree-like models are useful since they require that every world in the model is reachable from the current world. This allows us to interpret converse modalities in terms of atomic modalities.

Definition 8. *For any Λ, we say a Λ-model $M = (S, R, \rho, s)$ is tree-like if*

1. *for all $u \in S \setminus \{s\}$, there is exactly one pair $(o, v) \in \Lambda \times S$ such that $(v, u) \in R(o)$; and*
2. *for all $u \in S$, for all $o \in \Lambda$, $(u, s) \notin R(o)$*
3. *for all $u \in S \setminus \{s\}$, there is some finite sequence $u_0, u_1, \ldots, u_n$ such that $u_0 = s$, $u_n = u$ and for all $i < n$, there is some $o \in \Lambda$ such that $(u_i, u_{i+1}) \in R(o)$.*

Lemma 2. *For every $\mathcal{C}_\Lambda$-model M, there is some tree-like $\mathcal{C}_\Lambda$-model N such that $M \cong N$.*

The proof is given in [15] (Lemma 5.89).

Lemma 3. *For every $\overline{\mathcal{C}_\Lambda}$ model, M, for every tree-like $\mathcal{C}_{\overline{\Lambda}}$ model N where $N \cong_x M$, we have $N^+ \cong_x M$.*

The proof is given in [15] (Lemma 5.93).

Using these definitions, we can describe a translation from the modal μ-calculus with converse, to the modal μ-calculus without converse.

Theorem 1. *There exists a translation $(\cdot)'$ from μL_Λ with converse to $\mu L_{\overline{\Lambda}}$ without converse, such that for all tree-like $\overline{\Lambda}$-models M, for all μL_Λ formulas α, $M^+ \models \alpha$ if and only if $M \models \alpha'$.*

We sketch the proof of this theorem via alternating automata and μ-automata here (see [25] for an overview of these formalisms). As the language of alternating automata is equivalent to the modal μ-calculus we can define an alternating automaton, A (over the set of programs $\{a, a^- \mid a \in \Lambda\}$) such that A accepts M^+ if and only if $M^+ \models \alpha$.

From A, we can define a μ-automaton A^2, such that A^2 accepts tree-like $\overline{\Lambda}$-model M if and only if A accepts M^+. This is based on Vardi's construction [21] and a complete description is given in [15], Appendix C.

Finally, as there is an effective translation from μ-automata to the μ-calculus [23], we can convert A^2 to the $\mu L_{\overline{\Lambda}}$ formula α', so that $M^+ \models \alpha$ if and only if $M \models \alpha'$.

5 Idempotent Transductions

Here we consider a class of decidable bisimulation quantified modal logics which includes the bisimulation quantified extensions of **S4, GL, S5** and **KD45**. We refer to this class of logics as the *idempotent transduction logics*. Aside from the well-known logics above there are many other idempotent transduction logics. These logics are defined by encoding modalities as μ-programs, so potentially we can rapidly provide expressive and decidable logics for different ontologies "on the fly".

Recall the definition of $Prog_\Lambda$ (Definition 6).

Definition 9. *Given a finite set of modalities Λ, a Λ-transduction is a function Π : $\Lambda \longrightarrow Prog_\Lambda$.*

We can apply Λ-transductions to frames as described in the following definition:

Definition 10. *Given a Λ-transduction, Π, and a Λ-frame $F = (S, R)$ we define $F^\Pi = (S, R^\pi)$ where for all $u, v \in S$, $(u, v) \in R^\Pi(a)$ if and only if for all models $M = (S, R, \rho, s)$, $(u, v) \in R(\Pi(a))$. We define the transduction class of Π (written C_Π) to be the class of Λ-frames F^Π where F is any Λ-frame.*

Definition 11. *A Λ-transduction Π is an* idempotent transduction *if for all $a \in \Lambda$, $\Pi(a)$ contains no free atomic propositions and for all Λ-models M, for all tree-like Λ-models N such that $N \cong M^\Pi$ we have $M^\Pi \cong N^\Pi$. If Π is a idempotent transduction, then C_Π is an* idempotent transduction class *of frames and the logic* BQL_{C_Π} *is an idempotent transduction logic.*

Positive Idempotent transductions were identified for transductions that did not use the converse operator [14]. Positive idempotent transductions are truly idempotent (where idempotent means $M^\Pi = (M^\Pi)^\Pi$). To accommodate converse operators in the transductions the definition has been generalized.

5.1 Amalgamation for Idempotent Transduction Logics

Amalgamation is an important property as it allows us to use the tautologies of propositional quantification in a logic. We can show that all idempotent transduction logics enjoy amalgamation.

Lemma 4. *Given any two tree-like Λ-models M and N, and some Λ-transduction Π such that for all $a \in \Lambda$, $\Pi(a)$ contains no free atomic propositions from Θ, if $M \cong_\Theta N$ then $M^\Pi \cong_\Theta N^\Pi$*

The proof is given in [15] (Lemma 6.133).

Given any idempotent transduction, Π, we can show that $\mathcal{C}_\Pi$ enjoys the amalgamation property (Definition 5).

Lemma 5. *Every idempotent transduction class is amalgamative.*

Proof. Suppose that Π is an idempotent Λ-transduction, $M = (S, R, \rho, s)$ and $N = (T, P, \tau, t)$ are $\mathcal{C}_\Pi$-models and $M \cong_{\Theta \cup \Gamma} N$. By Lemma 2 there is some tree-like Λ-model $M' = (S', R', \rho', s')$ and some tree like Λ-model $N' = (T', P', \tau', t')$ such that $M' \cong M$ and $N' \cong N$. Therefore $M' \cong_{\Theta \cup \Gamma} N'$ via some bisimulation $B \subseteq S' \times T'$. Let $L = (B, Q, \eta, (s', t'))$ be a Λ-model where

1. for all $a \in \Lambda$, $((u, v), (w, z)) \in Q(a)$ if and only if $(u, w) \in R(a)$ and $(v, z) \in P(a)$, and
2. $\eta(u, v) = (\rho'(u) \backslash \Theta) \cup (\tau'(v) \backslash \Gamma)$.

Clearly, $L \cong_\Theta M'$ and $L \cong_\Gamma N'$. Again by Lemma 2 there is some tree-like Λ-model K such that $K \cong L$ and thus $K \cong_\Theta M'$ and $K \cong_\Gamma N'$. By Lemma 4 and the fact that Π is idempotent,

$$M \cong (M')^\Pi \cong_\Theta K^\Pi \cong_\Gamma (N')^\Pi \cong N,$$

so $\mathcal{C}_\Pi$ is amalgamative.

The following lemma can be shown by a simple induction over the complexity of programs.

Lemma 6. *Given any Λ-models, M and N such that $M \cong_\Theta^2 N$, and a Λ-transduction Π such that for all $a \in \Theta$, $\Pi(a)$ does not contain any free propositional atoms from Θ, we have $M^\Pi \cong_\Theta^2 N^\Pi$.*

5.2 Examples

Before we proceed with the proof of decidability, let us consider some examples. The logic **S4** has been shown to be equivalent to the pure modal logic of all reflexive, transitive frames. The class of all reflexive transitive $\{a\}$-frames (where a is some arbitrary label on a modality) is equivalent to the class $\mathcal{C}_\Pi$ where Π is the $\{a\}$-transduction defined by $\Pi(a) = a^*$. Therefore the bisimulation quantified extension of **S4** is an idempotent transduction logic. Similarly:

1. **S5** is the pure modal logic of all reflexive, symmetric and transitive frames. It is defined by the transduction $\Pi(a) = (a \cup a^-)^*$.
2. **GL** is the pure modal logic of all transitive, well-founded frames. It is defined by the transduction

$$\Pi(a) = (\mu x[a]x)?; a; a^*.$$

The test ensures the for all $(u, v) \in \Pi(a)$, every a-path starting at u is finite. The correctness of this transduction (using a different notation) is presented in [15], Lemma 6.139.

3. **KD45** is the pure modal logic of all serial, transitive, Euclidean frames (where a frame is Euclidean if every successor of any given world is related to one another, see Figure 2). It is defined by the transduction $\Pi(a) = ((a \cup a^-)^*; a) \cup ([a]\perp)?$.

Idempotent transductions also allow us to define the interactions between different modalities. Consider the following logic of hierarchical knowledge. Let $\mathbf{S5}_{\subseteq \mathbf{n}}$ be the class of Λ-frames, (S, R) where

- $\Lambda = \{1, 2, \ldots, n\}$,
- for all $i \in \Lambda$, $R(i)$ is reflexive, transitive and symmetric, and
- for all $i \in \Lambda$, for all $j < i$, $R(j) \subseteq R(i)$.

This describes a system of hierarchical knowledge so that $\square_i$ is a knowledge operator for agent i, and if $j < i$, agent j knows at least as much as agent i. See [17] for a discussion of logics of hierarchical knowledge. For each i in Λ we define $\Pi(i) = (1 \cup 1^- \cup \ldots \cup i \cup i^-)^*$.

An advantage of idempotent transduction logics is that they allow us to easily define powerful combinations of logics. For example, to reason about a system of belief and knowledge, we may suppose the standard interpretations for belief and knowledge hold, and also that knowledge implies belief, but not necessarily vice-versa. This situation can be described using the idempotent transduction, Π:

$$\Pi(k) = (k \cup k^- \cup b \cup b^-)^*$$
$$\Pi(b) = ((b \cup b^-)^*; b) \cup ([b]\perp)?$$

where $[k]\phi$ means the agent knows ϕ, and $[b]\phi$ means the agent believes ϕ.

5.3   The Decidability of Idempotent Transduction Logics

We can now show that all idempotent transduction logics are decidable by reducing their satisfiability problem to the satisfiability problem for the full μ-calculus.

Theorem 2. *For every idempotent Λ-transduction, Π, there is a translation $(\cdot)^\Pi$ from* $\mathrm{BQL}_{\mathcal{C}_\Pi}$ *to μL_Λ such that for all Λ-models, M*

$$M \models_{\mathcal{C}_\Pi} \alpha \iff M \models \alpha^\Pi. \tag{6}$$

Proof. The proof follows from the inductive construction of α^Π which we describe here. As the base of this induction we may suppose that α contains no bisimulation quantifiers at all. In this case we let $\alpha^\Pi = \alpha[a \backslash \Pi(a)]_{a \in \Lambda}$, where $\alpha[a \backslash \Pi(a)]_{a \in \Lambda}$ is the formula α with every modality, $\Diamond_a$, replaced by $\langle \Pi(a) \rangle$. By comparing the definition of M^Π with the semantics for μL_Λ extended with dynamic modalities (Definition 6), we can see

$$M^\Pi \models_{\mathcal{C}_\Pi} \alpha \iff M \models \alpha[a \backslash \Pi(a)]_{a \in \Lambda}. \tag{7}$$

Now we proceed by induction. For all operators except the bisimulation quantifier the constructions are trivial: $(\alpha_1 \vee \alpha_2)^\Pi = \alpha_1^\Pi \vee \alpha_2^\Pi$; $(\neg \alpha)^\Pi = \neg \alpha^\Pi$; and $\Diamond_a \alpha = \langle \Pi(a) \rangle \alpha$. The proofs follow directly from the semantic definitions of the operators.

We are left to define the translation for the bisimulation quantifier. Suppose that for all Λ-models N, $N^{\Pi} \models_{\mathcal{C}_{\Pi}} \alpha$ if and only if $N \models \alpha^{\Pi}$, and suppose that $M^{\Pi} \models_{\mathcal{C}_{\Pi}} \exists x \alpha$. By the definition,

$$M^{\Pi} \models_{\mathcal{C}_{\Pi}} \exists x \alpha \Longleftrightarrow \exists N^{\Pi} \in \mathcal{C}_{\Pi},\ N^{\Pi} \cong_{x} M^{\Pi},\ \text{and } N^{\Pi} \models_{\mathcal{C}_{\Pi}} \alpha. \tag{8}$$

Since Π is an idempotent transduction, if T is a tree-like Λ-model such that $T \cong N^{\Pi}$, then $T^{\Pi} \cong N^{\Pi}$. Let $\mathcal{T}_{\Lambda}$ the the set of tree-like Λ-models. By Lemma 2, the transitivity of bisimulation and Lemma 1

$$M^{\Pi} \models_{\mathcal{C}_{\Pi}} \exists x \alpha \Longleftrightarrow \exists T \in \mathcal{T}_{\Lambda},\ T \cong_{x} M^{\Pi},\ \text{and } T^{\Pi} \models_{\mathcal{C}_{\Pi}} \alpha. \tag{9}$$

Now, by applying the induction hypothesis it follows:

$$M^{\Pi} \models_{\mathcal{C}_{\Pi}} \exists x \alpha \Longleftrightarrow \exists T \in \mathcal{T}_{\Lambda},\ T \cong_{x} M^{\Pi},\ \text{and } T \models \alpha^{\Pi}. \tag{10}$$

The full μ-calculus is not closed under bisimulation quantifiers (since bisimulations only respect forward modalities). As α^{Π} is a formula of the full μ-calculus, by Theorem 1 there is a $\mu L_{\overline{\Lambda}}$ formula without converse, $(\alpha^{\Pi})'$, such that $T \models (\alpha^{\Pi})'$ if and only if $T^{+} \models \alpha^{\Pi}$. As T is a Λ-model (and thus a $\overline{\Lambda}$-model), we have $T \models \alpha^{\Pi}$ if and only if $T^{+} \models \alpha^{\Pi}$. Furthermore, we may suppose that $(\alpha^{\Pi})'$ does not contain converse modalities $\overline{a}$, (since $\langle \overline{a} \rangle \phi$ will always be false). Therefore $(\alpha^{\Pi})'$ is a formula of μL_{Λ} without converse, which is closed under bisimulation quantifiers [3]. That is, there is a computable μL_{Λ} formula, $\tilde{\exists}x(\alpha^{\Pi})'$ such that for all Λ-models N, $N \models \tilde{\exists}x(\alpha^{\Pi})'$ if and only if, for some model $K \cong_{x} N$, $K \models (\alpha^{\Pi})'$. Therefore

$$M^{\Pi} \models_{\mathcal{C}_{\Pi}} \exists x \alpha \Longleftrightarrow M^{\Pi} \models \tilde{\exists}x(\alpha^{\Pi})'. \tag{11}$$

Finally, from the semantic interpretation of the full modal μ-calculus we can see

$$M^{\Pi} \models_{\mathcal{C}_{\Pi}} \exists x \alpha \Longleftrightarrow M \models (\tilde{\exists}x(\alpha^{\Pi})')[a \backslash \Pi(a)]_{a \in \Lambda}, \tag{12}$$

where where $\alpha[a \backslash \Pi(a)]_{a \in \Lambda}$ is the formula α with every atomic program, a, replaced by $\Pi(a)$. To complete the proof we let $(\exists x \alpha)^{\Pi} = (\tilde{\exists}x(\alpha^{\Pi})')[a \backslash \Pi(a)]_{a \in \Lambda}$.

In [14] a more simple reduction that did not consider converse modalities was used to prove decidability for positive idempotent transduction logics. A more complex decidability proof for idempotent transduction logics is given in [15] (Theorem 6.136).

We proof in [15] relied on the following theorem for BQDL_{Λ}, (which is *propositional dynamic logic with converse programs* extended by bisimulation quantifiers).

Theorem 3. *Given any Λ, for all formulas α of BQDL_{Λ} there is some computable BQDL_{Λ} formula α^{*} such that for any Λ-class $\mathcal{C}$, for any $\mathcal{C}$-model M, $M \models_{\mathcal{C}} \alpha^{*}$ if and only if $M \models_{\Lambda} \alpha$.*

The proof is given in [15] (Theorem 5.108) and follows the same strategy as the proof of Theorem 2, where α^{*} is inductively defined to be μ-calculus formula equivalent to α. As the interpretation of the μ-calculus is independent of the class of frames, the Theorem follows.

6 Conclusion

This paper presents a general class of bisimulation quantified modal logics, the *idempotent transduction logics*, that are amalgamative and decidable. This class is defined by taking the fixed points (modulo bisimulation) of transductions defined by programs of propositional dynamic logic with converse.

The benefits of this approach are as follows:

1. This definition provides a powerful methodology for extending and combining bisimulation quantified modal logics. A number of logics can be combined, where the modalities interaction can be expressed using programs of propositional dynamic logic.
2. Including bisimulation quantifiers in a logic can greatly increase the expressivity of the logic, allowing us to represent operators such as the *until* operator of temporal logic or fixed point operators. Furthermore in [15] it is shown that $BQDL_\Lambda$ is non-elementarily more succinct than the modal μ-calculus.
3. Bisimulation quantifiers have a natural interpretation as a *hypothetical assignment of atoms*. This allows them to be applied directly to refinement and simulation problems in a variety of ontologies.

Future work will examine further generalizations of the class of idempotent transduction logics. However, we note that this great generality comes at the cost of complexity. Therefore, we will also consider sub-classes of the idempotent transduction logics and look for efficient model-checking procedures, decision procedures, and axiomatizations.

Acknowledgements. The author would like to thank the anonymous reviewers for their helpful suggestions and comments.

References

1. Visser, A.: Uniform interpolation and layered bisimulation. In: Godel '96. Lecture Notes Logic. vol. 6, pp. 139–164 (1996)
2. Ghilardi, S., Zawadowski, M.: Undefinability of propositional quantifiers in the modal system S4. Studia Logica 55, 259–271 (1995)
3. D'Agostino, G., Hollenberg, M.: Logical questions concerning the μ-calculus: interpolation, Lyndon and Los-Tarski. J. Symb. Log. 65(1), 310–332 (2000)
4. D'Agostino, G., Lenzi, G.: An axiomatization of bisimulation quantifiers via the μ-calculus. Theor. Comput. Sci. 338, 64–95 (2005)
5. Fine, K.: Propositional quantifiers in modal logic. Theoria 36, 336–346 (1970)
6. Milner, R.: A Calculus of Communication Systems. LNCS, vol. 92. Springer, Heidelberg (1980)
7. Park, D.: Concurrency and automata on infinite sequences. In: Deussen, P. (ed.) Theoretical Computer Science. LNCS, vol. 104, pp. 167–183. Springer, Heidelberg (1981)
8. van Benthem, J.: Correspondence theory. Handbook of Philosophical Logic 2, 167–247 (1984)
9. Stirling, C.: The joys of bisimulation. In: Brim, L., Gruska, J., Zlatuška, J. (eds.) MFCS 1998. LNCS, vol. 1450, pp. 142–151. Springer, Heidelberg (1998)

10. Pnueli, A.: The temporal logic of programs. In: Proceedings of the Eighteenth Symposium on Foundations of Computer Science, pp. 46–57 (1977)
11. Fagin, R., Halpern, J., Moses, Y., Vardi, M.: Reasoning about knowledge. MIT Press, Cambridge (1995)
12. French, T.: Bisimulation quantified logics: undecidability. In: Ramanujam, R., Sen, S. (eds.) FSTTCS 2005. LNCS, vol. 3821, pp. 396–407. Springer, Heidelberg (2005)
13. D'Agostino, G., Lenzi, G., French, T.: mu-programs, unifrom interpolation and bisimulation quantifiers. Journal of Applied Non-classical Logics 16, 297–310 (2006)
14. French, T.: Bisimulation quantified modal logics: decidability. Advances in Modal Logic 6, 147–166 (2006)
15. French, T.: Bisimulation quantifiers for modal logic. PhD thesis, The University of Western Australia (2006) Available from http://people.csse.uwa.edu.au/tim/
16. Gabbay, D., Kurucz, A., Wolter, F., Zakharayashev, M.: Many Dimensional Modal Logics: Theory and Applications. Elsevier, Amsterdam (2003)
17. Engelhardt, K., van der Meyden, R., Su, K.: Modal logics with a linear hierarchy of local propositional quantifiers. Advances in Modal Logic 4, 9–30 (2003)
18. French, T.: Decidability of propositionally quantified logics of knowledge. In: Australian Conference on Artificial Intelligence, pp. 352–363 (2003)
19. Abadi, M., Lamport, L.: The existence of refinement mappings. Theoretical Computer Science 82(2), 253–284 (1991)
20. Lamport, L.: Specifying concurrent program modules. ACM Trans. Program. Lang. Syst. 5(2), 190–222 (1983)
21. Vardi, M.: Reasoning about the past with two-way automata. In: Larsen, K.G., Skyum, S., Winskel, G. (eds.) ICALP 1998. LNCS, vol. 1443, pp. 628–641. Springer, Heidelberg (1998)
22. Kozen, D.: Results on the propositional mu-calculus. Theor. Comp. Sci. 27 (1983)
23. Janin, D., Walukiewicz, I.: Automata for the modal μ-calculus and related results. In: Hájek, P., Wiedermann, J. (eds.) MFCS 1995. LNCS, vol. 969, pp. 552–562. Springer, Heidelberg (1995)
24. Emerson, E.A., Jutla, C.S.: Tree automata, μ-calculus and determinacy. In: Proceedings of the 32nd annual symposium on Foundations of computer science, pp. 368–377. IEEE Computer Society Press, Los Alamitos (1991)
25. Gradel, E., Thomas, W., Wilke, T. (eds.): Automata, Logics, and Infinite Games. Springer, Heidelberg (2002)

A Temporal Logic of Robustness

Tim French, John C. McCabe-Dansted, and Mark Reynolds

University of Western Australia, Department of Computer Science and Software
Engineering
{tim,john,mark}@csse.uwa.edu.au

Abstract. It can be desirable to specify polices that require a system
to achieve some outcome even if a certain number of failures occur. This
paper proposes a logic, RoCTL*, which extends CTL* with operators
from Deontic logic, and a novel operator referred to as "Robustly". This
novel operator acts as variety of path quantifier allowing us to consider
paths which deviate from the desired behaviour of the system. Unlike
most path quantifiers, the Robustly operator must be evaluated over
a path rather than just a state; the Robustly operator quantifies over
paths produced from the current path by altering a single step. The
Robustly operator roughly represents the phrase "even if an additional
failure occurs now or in the future". This paper examines the expressivity
of this new logic, motivates its use and shows that it is decidable.

Keywords: RoCTL*, Decidability, Modal Logic, Robustness, Branching
Time Logic, QCTL*.

1 Introduction

Temporal logic has been particularly useful in reasoning about properties of
systems. In particular, the branching temporal logics CTL* [1] and CTL [2] have
been used to verify the properties of non-deterministic and concurrent programs.

The logic RoCTL* divides the set of all futures/histories of the CTL* model
into successful paths and faulty paths. There is a temporal aspect to faults, so
that after the final fault, the path is successful. That is, a path with a finite
number of failures has a successful suffix. We augment the operators of CTL*
with a Deontic operator, which quantifies over all successful paths, and a novel
operator "Robustly" which quantifies over paths which deviate from the current
path. Thus there are three path quantifiers in RoCTL*. These quantifiers will
be discussed below.

The CTL* "All paths" operator describes hard constraints on the behavior
of the system, statements which must be true regardless of how many failures
occur. A hard constraint may result from some law of physics, or it may represent
something that the system can always be expected to achieve. For example, a
real time system may be known to miss some deadlines, but never return an
incorrect result. RoCTL* is a conservative extension of LTL and CTL* [3].

To allow us to reason about the consequences of failures, we add an operator
"Robustly" (▲) that allows us to quantify over "deviations" from the current

B. Konev and F. Wolter (Eds.): FroCos 2007, LNAI 4720, pp. 193–205, 2007.

path. For a statement to be robustly true, it must be true on the current path and any path produced by altering a single step. We can represent the statement "if up to n additional failures occur" by chaining n instances of the Robustly operator. To strengthen the meaning of the Robustly operator, we allow the deviating event to be a success as well as a failure. The future after the deviating event may bear no resemblance to the current path. However, to preserve the intuition of the Robustly operator as introducing no more than a single additional failure, no failures occur after the deviating event.

The "Obligatory" operator from Standard Deontic Logic (SDL) is embedded in RoCTL*. This operator is used to describe what the future must be like if no further failures occur. All of the validities of O from SDL hold in RoCTL*. Additionally, as O is used as a path quantifier, all true state formulæ are obligatory in RoCTL*.

The addition of the Robustly operator and temporal operators to Deontic logic allows RoCTL* to deal with Contrary-to-Duty obligations. SDL is able to distinguish what ought to be true from what is true, but is unable to specify obligations that come into force only when we behave incorrectly. For example, SDL is inadequate to represent the obligation "if you murder, you must murder gently" [4]. Addition of temporal operators to Deontic logic allows us to specify correct responses to failures that have occurred in the past [5]. However, this approach alone is not sufficient [5] to represent obligations such as "You must assist your neighbour, and you must warn them iff you will not assist them". In RoCTL* these obligations can be represented if the obligation to warn your neighbour is robust but the obligation to assist them is not.

Other approaches to dealing with Contrary-to-Duty obligations exist. Defeasible logic is often used [6], and logics of agency, such as STIT [7], can be useful as they can allow obligations to be conditional on the agent's ability to carry out the obligation.

This paper provides some examples of robust systems that can be effectively represented in RoCTL*. It is easy to solve the coordinated attack problem if our protocol is allowed to assume that only n messages will be lost. The logic may also be useful to represent the resilience of some economy to temporary failures to acquire or send some resource. For example, a remote mining colony may have interacting requirements for communications, food, electricity and fuel. RoCTL* may be more suitable than Resource Logics (see e.g. [8]) for representing systems where a failure may cause a resource to become temporarily unavailable. This paper presents a simple example where the only requirement is to provide a cat with food when it is hungry.

A number of other extensions of temporal logics have been proposed to deal with Deontic or Robustness issues [9,10,11,12,13]. Each of these logics are substantially different from RoCTL*. Some of these logics are designed specifically to deal with deadlines [9,11]. An Agent Communication Language was formed by adding Deontic and other modal operators to CTL [13]; this language does not explicitly deal with robustness or failures. Hansson and Johnsson [11] proposed an extension of CTL to deal with reliability. However their logic reasons about reliability using probabilities rather than numbers of failures, and their paper does not contain any discussion of the relationship of their logic to Deontic logics. Like our embedding into QCTL*, Aldewereld et al. [12] uses a Viol atom to represent failure. However, their logic also uses probability instead of failure counts and is thus suited to a different class of problems than RoCTL*. Additionally, adding the Viol atom has different expressivity properties to the Robustly operator. CTL* with a special "Viol" atom can express statements such as "If at least one failure occurs" which cannot be expressed in RoCTL*, and it is not known whether all statements that can be expressed in RoCTL* can be trivially translated into CTL*. In particular, it is not known how to translate the phrase "even if a deviation from the current path occurs" into CTL*. None of these logics appear to have an operator that is substantially similar to the Robustly operator of RoCTL*.

Diagnosis problems in control theory [14,15] also deals with failures of systems. Diagnosis is in some sense the dual of the purpose of the RoCTL* logic, as diagnosis requires that failure cause something (detection of the failure) whereas robustness involves showing that failure will *not* cause something.

This paper shows that all RoCTL* statements can be expressed in QCTL*. Furthermore, it is easy to represent statements like "even if n failures occur" in CTL*. However, this paper will show how the RoCTL* logic can represent and make explicit different interactions between the time that failures occur and the time or duration of the effect. There is no known trivial embedding into CTL* that preserves these properties.

2   RoCTL* Logic

2.1   RoCTL* Syntax

RoCTL* extends CTL*, which uses the path operators from LTL:

Next $N\phi$ indicates that ϕ is true at the next step.
Globally $G\phi$ indicates that ϕ is true and will always be true.
Finally $F\phi$ indicates that ϕ will be true at some point in the future.
Until $\phi U\psi$ indicates that ϕ will be true until ψ is true
Weak until $\phi W\psi$ indicates that either $\phi U\psi$ or $G\phi$ is true.

CTL* includes two path-quantifiers:

Always $A\phi$ indicates that ϕ is true in all possible futures.
Exists $E\phi$ indicates that there is a future in which ϕ is true.

RoCTL* Includes the Deontic operators O and P as path-quantifiers.

Obligatory $O\phi$ indicates that in every failure-free future ϕ holds
Permissible $P\phi$ indicates that there is a failure-free future where ϕ holds

RoCTL* has a new pair of path-quantifiers to deal with failures. Unlike A and E which are S5 operators, $\blacktriangle$ is a T operator.

Robustly ▲ϕ indicates that ϕ is true on this path and any path that differs from this path by a single deviating event.

Prone to $\Delta\phi$ indicates that ϕ is true, either on this path or a path differing by a single deviating event, and is the dual of ▲.

The RoCTL* Logic has a set $\mathcal{V}$ of atomic propositions that we call <u>variables</u>. Where p varies over $\mathcal{V}$, the formulæ of RoCTL* are defined by the abstract syntax $\phi := \top \mid p \mid \neg\phi \mid (\phi \wedge \phi) \mid (\phi U \phi) \mid N\phi \mid A\phi \mid O\phi \mid ▲\phi$.

The $\top$, $\neg$, $\wedge$, N, U and A are the familiar "true", "not", "and", "next", "until" and "all paths" operators from CTL. The abbreviations $\bot$, $\vee$, F, G, W, E $\rightarrow$ and $\leftrightarrow$ are defined as in CTL* logic. As with SDL logic, we define $P \equiv \neg O\neg$. Finally, we define the abbreviation $\Delta \equiv \neg▲\neg$. We say that ϕ is a state formula iff ϕ is equivalent to $A\phi$.

2.2 RoCTL-Structures

Definition 1. *A <u>valuation</u> α is a map from a set of states A to the power set of the variables; we represent the statement "the variable p is true at state w" with $p \in \alpha(w)$.*

Definition 2. *A CTL-structure $M^* = (A^*, \rightarrow^*, \alpha^*)$ is a 3-tuple containing a set of states A^*, a serial (total) binary relation $\rightarrow^*$ and a valuation α^* on the set of states A^*. We define $\mathbb{C}$ as the class of such structures and $\mathbb{C}_t$ as the class of such structures where $\rightarrow^*$ forms a tree.*

Definition 3. *A RoCTL-structure M is a 4-tuple $(A, \overset{s}{\rightarrow}, \overset{f}{\rightarrow}, \alpha)$, consisting of a set of states A, a serial (total) binary "success" relation $\overset{s}{\rightarrow}$, a binary "failure" relation $\overset{f}{\rightarrow}$ and a valuation α on the set of states A. We define $\mathbb{M}$ as the class of such RoCTL-structures.*

Definition 4. *We use $\overset{sf}{\rightarrow}$ as an abbreviation for $\left(\overset{s}{\rightarrow} \cup \overset{f}{\rightarrow}\right)$. For all $n \in \mathbb{N}$ we call an ω-sequence $\sigma = \langle w_0, w_1, \ldots \rangle$ of states a <u>fullpath</u> iff for all non-negative integers i we have $w_i \overset{sf}{\rightarrow} w_{i+1}$. For all i in $\mathbb{N}$ we define $\sigma_{\geq i}$ to be the fullpath $\langle w_i, w_{i+1}, \ldots \rangle$, we define σ_i to be w_i and we define $\sigma_{\leq i}$ to be the sequence $\langle w_0, w_1, \ldots, w_i \rangle$.*

Definition 5. *We say that a fullpath σ is <u>failure-free</u> iff for all $i \in \mathbb{N}$ we have $\sigma_i \overset{s}{\rightarrow} \sigma_{i+1}$. We define $\mathcal{SF}(w)$ to be the set of all fullpaths in M starting with w and $S(w)$ to be the set of all failure-free fullpaths in M starting with w.*

Definition 6. *For two fullpaths σ and π we say that π is an <u>i-deviation</u> from σ iff $\sigma_{\leq i} = \pi_{\leq i}$ and $\pi_{\geq i+1} \in S(\pi_{i+1})$. We say that π is a <u>deviation</u> from σ if there exists a non-negative integer i such that π is an i-deviation from σ. We define a function δ from a fullpath to a set of fullpaths such that where σ and π are fullpaths, π is a member of $\delta(\sigma)$ iff π is a deviation from σ.*

Below is an example of an i-deviation π from a fullpath σ. The arrows not labeled with s can be either $\overset{s}{\rightarrow}$ or $\overset{f}{\rightarrow}$. After π diverges from σ, it avoids any failures that may have been on $\sigma_{>i}$. We require that a deviation not introduce any failures except for the deviating event itself, hence $\pi_{\geq i+1}$ is failure-free.

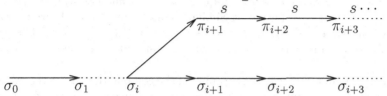

Note that after the deviation, all transitions must be success transitions while steps before the deviation may be either success or failure transitions. This follows from the intuition of Robustly representing "even if an additional failure occurs", as the failures that are prior to the deviation are already on the existing path. Additionally, allowing failures to occur before the deviation also allows n Robustly operators to be nested to represent the statement "even if n additional failures occur".

2.3 RoCTL* Semantics

We define truth of a RoCTL* formula ϕ on a fullpath $\sigma = \langle w_0, w_1, \ldots \rangle$ in RoCTL-structure M recursively as follows:

$$M, \sigma \vDash N\phi \text{ iff } M, \sigma_{\geq 1} \vDash \phi$$

$$M, \sigma \vDash \phi U\psi \text{ iff } \exists_{i \in \mathbb{N}} \text{ s.t. } M, \sigma_{\geq i} \vDash \psi \text{ and } \forall_{j \in \mathbb{N}} j < i \implies M, \sigma_{\geq j} \vDash \psi$$

$$M, \sigma \vDash A\phi \text{ iff } \forall_{\pi \in \mathscr{F}(\sigma_0)} M, \pi \vDash \phi$$

$$M, \sigma \vDash O\phi \text{ iff } \forall_{\pi \in S(\sigma_0)} M, \pi \vDash \phi$$

$$M, \sigma \vDash \blacktriangle\phi \text{ iff } \forall_{\pi \in \delta(\sigma)} M, \pi \vDash \phi \text{ and } M, \sigma \vDash \phi.$$

The definitions for $\top$, p, $\neg$ and $\wedge$ are as we would expect from classical logic. We say that a formula ϕ is valid in RoCTL* iff for all structures M in $\mathbb{M}$, for all fullpaths σ in M we have $M, \sigma \vDash \phi$.

The operator O is similar to A. If ψ is a CTL* formula and ψ' is ψ with all instances of A replaced with O, then $O\psi'$ is a validity of RoCTL* iff ψ is a validity [3]. It is also easy to show that if $\xrightarrow{f}$ is empty, the O and $\blacktriangle$ operators are equivalent to the A operator. Restricting the class of structures such that $\xrightarrow{s} \cap \xrightarrow{f} = \emptyset$ and/or such that $\xrightarrow{f}$ is serial does not affect the validities of the logic.

3 Properties of RoCTL*

The behaviour of the A operator is the same as in CTL*, and the behaviour of the O operator is similar to that of the O operator in SDL. It is easy to show [3] that the axiom class $O\phi \rightarrow P\phi$ is valid in RoCTL* (and SDL); neither the axiom class $\phi \rightarrow P\phi$, nor the axiom class $O\phi \rightarrow \phi$, is valid in RoCTL* (or SDL). However, unlike SDL, the axiom class $p \rightarrow Op$ is valid in RoCTL* [3]. This is due to O being a path quantifier in RoCTL*. In this section, combinations of operators and differences between the operators will be discussed.

3.1   Interpretations of Combinations of Operators

As both A and O are traditional path-quantifiers, AO and OA are of little use and reduce to O and A respectively. Similarly, $\blacktriangle O$ reduces to O. However, $O\blacktriangle$ does not reduce to $\blacktriangle$. Indeed, $\blacktriangle\phi$ is not a state formula, while $O\blacktriangle\phi$ is. The pair $O\blacktriangle$ quantifies over any path starting at the present state that has at most one failure.

The order of $\blacktriangle$ and N affects the meaning of the combination, $\blacktriangle N\phi$ represents the statement "Even if one or fewer deviations occur now or in the future, ϕ will be true at the next step". The formula $N\blacktriangle\phi$ is similar, but only requires ϕ to be true if the deviation occurs after the next step. As with the A path-quantifier from CTL*, $\blacktriangle N\phi \rightarrow N\blacktriangle\phi$ and $\blacktriangle G\phi \rightarrow G\blacktriangle\phi$ are valid in RoCTL* but $\blacktriangle N\phi \leftarrow N\blacktriangle\phi$ and $G\blacktriangle\phi \rightarrow \blacktriangle G\phi$ are not [3]. The statement $G\blacktriangle\phi$ indicates that for every state along the present path, ϕ holds at the beginning of all deviations; the statement $\blacktriangle G\phi$ indicates that ϕ will be true not only at the beginning of the deviation, but along the deviation as well.

The order of the N and O operators is important, even more so than of N and A. As with $NA\phi \rightarrow AN\phi$, the formula form $NO\phi \rightarrow ON\phi$ is not valid. However, unlike $AN\phi \rightarrow NA\phi$, the form $ON\phi \rightarrow NO\phi$ is not valid. The combination NO represents what will obligatory after the next transition, which might be a failure transition. The ON combination instead discusses what should be true at the next step. For further discussion of this combination, see Example 1.

It is easy to show that the following formulæ forms are valid in RoCTL*: $A\phi \rightarrow O\phi$, $AO\phi \leftrightarrow O\phi$, $OA\phi \leftrightarrow A\phi$, $A\phi \rightarrow \blacktriangle\phi$, $\blacktriangle\phi \rightarrow O\phi$, $A\blacktriangle\phi \leftrightarrow A\phi$, $\blacktriangle A\phi \leftrightarrow A\phi$ and $\blacktriangle O\phi \leftrightarrow O\phi$.

3.2   Differences Between A, $\blacktriangle$ and O

The A, $\blacktriangle$ and O operators have similar properties since they quantify over paths. The $\blacktriangle$ operator is an unusual path quantifier as $\blacktriangle\phi$ is not a state formula. This paper will not present a full axiomatization of RoCTL*. However, it will examine which axioms of A are also valid for $\blacktriangle$ and O . The axioms [16] that reference the A operator are:

C9	$A(\phi \rightarrow \psi) \rightarrow (A\phi \rightarrow A\psi)$	C13	$A\neg\phi \leftrightarrow \neg E\phi$
C10	$A\phi \rightarrow AA\phi$	C14	$p \rightarrow Ap$
C11	$A\phi \rightarrow \phi$	C15	$AN\phi \rightarrow NA\phi$
C12	$\phi \rightarrow AE\phi$		
LC	$AG(A\phi \rightarrow EN(A\psi U A\phi)) \rightarrow (A\phi \rightarrow EG(A\psi U A\phi))$.		

As the real world may not be in a desirable state, neither $O\phi \rightarrow \phi$ nor $\phi \rightarrow OP\phi$ are valid. As mentioned previously $ON\phi \rightarrow NO\phi$ is not valid in RoCTL*. It is easy to show that the C9, C10, C13, C14 and LC axioms are still valid if A is replaced with O.

The formula $\phi \rightarrow \blacktriangle\triangle\phi$ is not valid in RoCTL*. The reason for this is that a deviation can prevent any number of failures occurring in the future, but the second deviation can cause only a single new failure. The $\blacktriangle$ operator is not transitive, so $\blacktriangle\phi \rightarrow \blacktriangle\blacktriangle\phi$ is not valid in RoCTL*. The axiom forms C9,

C13, C14, C15 are still valid in RoCTL* if A is replaced with $\blacktriangle$. The formula $\blacktriangle G\,(A\phi \to PN\,(A\psi U A\phi)) \to (A\phi \to \Delta G\,(A\psi U A\phi))$ is also valid in RoCTL*.

4 Examples

In this section a number of examples are presented. The first example examines the difference between the formula $NO\phi$ and the formula $ON\phi$. The second example shows how RoCTL* may be used to specify a robust network protocol. Then an example of feeding a cat will be introduced to explain how we may reason about consequences of polices. These examples will frequently use the $\blacktriangle/\Delta$ operator to form the pair $O\blacktriangle$. In the final example we use the simple formula $O(\Delta Fe \to Fw)$ which nests $\blacktriangle/\Delta$ in a less trivial way.

Example 1. Here is an example of a simple Contrary-to-Duty obligation. This provides a counter example to both $ON\phi \to NO\phi$ and $NO\phi \to ON\phi$.

$ON(Gp)$: You should commit to the proper decision.
$NO\,(G\neg p \vee Gp)$: Once you have made your decision, you must stick with it.

It is consistent with the above that we do not make the proper decision ($N\neg p$). Once we have made the wrong decision we cannot satisfy Gp, so we must stick with the wrong decision $G\neg p$. Hence, in this case, both $ON(Gp)$ and $NO(G\neg p)$ are true. Likewise $ON(G\neg p)$ and $NO(Gp)$ are false. This demonstrates how obligations can change with time in RoCTL*. We will now give an example of a structure $M = (A, \overset{s}{\to}, \overset{f}{\to}, \alpha)$ that satisfies these formulae:

$$A = \{u, v, w\},$$
$$\overset{s}{\to} = \{(u,v),(v,v),(w,w)\},$$
$$\overset{f}{\to} = \{(u,w)\},$$
$$\alpha(v) = \{p\}, \quad \alpha(w) = \emptyset.$$

Let σ be the fullpath $\langle u, w, w, \ldots \rangle$ corresponding to making the wrong decision. We see that $M, \sigma_{\geq 1} \vDash \neg p$, so $M, \sigma_{\geq 1} \vDash O\neg p$ and $M, \sigma_{\geq 1} \vDash \neg Op$. Thus $M, \sigma \vDash NO\neg p$ and $M, \sigma \vDash N\neg Op$. It follows that $M, \sigma \vDash \neg NOp$.

Let $\pi = \langle v, v, \ldots \rangle$. We see that $M, \pi \vDash p$. We see that $S(u) = \{\langle u, v, v, \ldots \rangle\}$. Hence $M, \sigma \vDash ONp$ and it follows that $M, \sigma \vDash \neg O\neg Np$ and so $M, \sigma \vDash \neg ON\neg p$.

Hence $M, \sigma \vDash (ONp \wedge \neg NOp)$ and so $M, \sigma \nvDash (ON\phi \to NO\phi)$ where $\phi = p$. Likewise $M, \sigma \vDash (NO\neg p \wedge \neg ON\neg p)$, so $M, \sigma \nvDash (NO\phi \to ON\phi)$ where $\phi = \neg p$.

Example 2. In the coordinated attack problem we have two generals A and B. General A wants to organise an attack with B. A communication protocol will be presented such that a coordinated attack will occur if no more than one message is lost.

$AG\,(s_A \to ONr_B)$: If A sends a message, B should receive it at the next step.
$AG\,(\neg s_A \to \neg Nr_B)$: If A does not send a message now, B will not receive a message at the next step.

$AG(f_A \rightarrow AGf_A)$: If A commits to an attack, A cannot withdraw.
$AG(f_A \rightarrow \neg s_A)$: If A has committed to an attack, it is too late to send messages.
$A(\neg f_A W r_A)$: A cannot commit to an attack until A has received plans from B

Similar constraints to the above also apply to B. Below we add a constraints requiring A to be the general planning the attack

$A(\neg s_B W r_B)$: General B will not send a message until B has received a message.

No protocol exists to satisfy the original coordination problem, since an unbounded number of messages can be lost. Here we only attempt to ensure correct behaviour if one or fewer messages are lost.

$A(s_A U r_A)$: General A will send plans until a response is received.
$AG(r_A \rightarrow f_A)$: Once general A receives a response, A will commit to an attack.
$A(\neg r_B W(r_B \wedge (s_B \wedge Ns_B \wedge NNf_B)))$: Once general B receives plans, B will
    send two messages to A and then commit to an attack.

Having the formal statement of the policy above and the semantics of RoCTL* we may prove that the policy $\hat{\phi}$ is consistent and that it implies correct behaviour even if a single failure occurs:

$$\hat{\phi} \rightarrow O\blacktriangle F(f_A \wedge f_B) \, .$$

Indeed, we will show in Section 5 that such issues can be decided in finite time.

Example 3. We have a cat that does not eat the hour after it has eaten. If the cat bowl is empty we might forget to fill it. We must ensure that the cat never goes hungry, even if we forget to fill the cat bowl one hour. At the beginning of the first hour, the cat bowl is full. We have the following variables:

b "The cat bowl is full at the beginning of this hour"
d "This hour is feeding time"

We can translate the statements above into RoCTL* statements:

1. $AG(d \rightarrow \neg Nd)$: If this hour is feeding time, the next is not.
2. $AG((d \vee \neg b) \rightarrow \Delta N \neg b)$: If it is feeding time or the cat bowl was empty, a single failure may result in an empty bowl at the next step
3. $AG((\neg d \wedge b) \rightarrow Nb)$: If the bowl is full and it is not feeding time, the bowl will be full at the beginning of the next hour.
4. $O\blacktriangle G(d \rightarrow b)$: It is obligatory that, even if a single failure occurs, it is always the case that the bowl must be full at feeding time.
5. b: The cat bowl starts full.

Having the formalised the policy it can be proven that the policy is consistent and that the policy implies $O\blacktriangle GONb$, indicating that the bowl must be filled at every step (in case we forget at the next step), unless we have already failed twice. The formula $AGONb \rightarrow O\blacktriangle G(d \rightarrow b)$ can also be derived, indicating that following a policy requiring us to always attempt to fill the cat bowl ensures that we will not starve the cat even if we make a single mistake. Thus following this simpler policy is sufficient to discharge our original obligation.

Example 4. We define a system that will warn the user if the system enters an unsafe state:

1. $AGONs$: The system should always ensure that the system reaches a safe state by the next step.
2. $AG(s \to N\neg e)$: If the system is in a safe state an error e will not occur at the next step.
3. $s \wedge \neg e$: The system starts in a safe state with no error.
4. $AG(\neg s \to Nw)$: If the system is in an unsafe state, the system will warn the user at the next step.

We may prove that if an error e almost occurs, the system will finally warn the user, i.e. $O(\Delta Fe \to Fw)$.

See [3] for more examples, such as nesting Δ within $\blacktriangle$ to discuss liveness of failure detection.

5 Embeddings

In this section it will be shown that RoCTL* can be embedded in QCTL*, and hence is decidable.

5.1 Converting a RoCTL-Structure M to a CTL-Structure M^*

For a RoCTL-structure M we construct a CTL tree structure M^* as follows. We define an interim CTL-structure M^{sf}. The atoms of M^{sf} are the atoms of M plus an additional atom "Viol" representing the statement "The last transition was a failing (f) transition" and an additional set Y of anonymous atoms. For each state w of M we have two states w^s and w^f in M^{sf}, with Viol being true at w^f but not w^s. For each pair of states w_i and w_j in M, we have

$$w_i^s \to w_j^s \iff w_i \xrightarrow{s} w_j \qquad w_i^s \to w_j^f \iff w_i \xrightarrow{f} w_j$$
$$w_i^f \to w_j^s \iff w_i \xrightarrow{s} w_j \qquad w_i^f \to w_j^f \iff w_i \xrightarrow{f} w_j .$$

It is easy to rewrite a RoCTL* formula to use the Δ operator instead of $\blacktriangle$. To ease the embedding of the Δ operator we will add a countable set Y of atoms to M^{sf} and unwind it into a tree to form the tree structure M^*.

Translating a CTL tree structure $M^* = (A^*, \to^*, \alpha^*)$ with a Viol atom into a RoCTL-structure $M = (A, \xrightarrow{s}, \xrightarrow{f}, \alpha)$ is trivial. We set $A = A^*$ and let $\alpha^* = \alpha$. We set $\xrightarrow{s}$ and $\xrightarrow{f}$ such that for each pair of states w_i and w_j we have:

$$w_i \xrightarrow{s} w_j \iff (w_i \to^* w_j) \wedge (\text{Viol} \notin \alpha(w_j))$$
$$w_i \xrightarrow{f} w_j \iff (w_i \to^* w_j) \wedge (\text{Viol} \in \alpha(w_j)) .$$

5.2   Translating a RoCTL* Formula into a QCTL* Formula

Definition 7. *Given some CTL structure $M = (A, \rightarrow, \alpha)$ and some $x \in A$, an x-variant of M is some structure $M = (A, \rightarrow, \alpha')$ where $\alpha'(w)\backslash\{x\} = \alpha(w)\backslash\{x\}$ for all $w \in A$.*

QCTL* has the syntax $\phi := \top \,|\, p \,|\, \neg\phi \,|\, (\phi \wedge \phi) \,|\, (\phi U \phi) \,|\, N\phi \,|\, A\phi \,|\, \exists_p \phi$. The semantics of $\top$, p, $\neg$, $\wedge$, U, N, and A are the same as in CTL* and RoCTL*. Under the Kripke semantics for QCTL*, $\exists_p \phi$ is defined as

$$M, b \vDash \exists_p \alpha \iff \text{There is some } p\text{-variant } M' \text{ of } M \text{ such that } M', b \vDash \alpha.$$

This paper uses the tree semantics for QCTL*. These semantics are the same as the Kripke semantics except that, whereas the Kripke semantics evaluates validity over the class $\mathbb{C}$ of CTL-structures, the tree semantics evaluate validity over the class $\mathbb{C}_t$ of tree CTL-structures. This changes the validities of the logic as, unlike CTL* [17], QCTL* is sensitive to unwinding into a tree structure [18].

We let γ be the (Q)CTL* formula $NNG\neg$Viol. The γ formula is used to represent the requirement that all transitions after a deviation must be successes.

We define a translation function t^Δ such that for any formula ϕ^* and for some atom y not in ϕ^*:

$$t^\Delta(\phi^*) = \forall_y \left[Gy \rightarrow E\left[(Gy \vee F(y \wedge \gamma)) \wedge \phi^* \right] \right].$$

Note that for $t^\Delta(\phi^*)$ to hold, $E\left[(Gy \vee F(y \wedge \gamma)) \wedge \phi^* \right]$ must hold for all possible values of y that satisfy Gy, including the case where y is true only along the current fullpath σ^*. The diagram below shows a fullpath π^* that satisfies $F(y \wedge \gamma)$ for all such y.

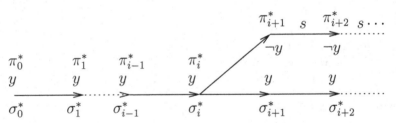

Lemma 1. *Say that ϕ is a RoCTL* formula and ϕ^* is a QCTL* formula such that for all M and σ it is the case that $M, \sigma \vDash \phi$ iff $M^*, \sigma^* \vDash \phi^*$. Then, for all M and σ it is the case that $M, \sigma \vDash \Delta\phi$ iff $M^*, \sigma^* \vDash t^\Delta(\phi^*)$.*

Proof. ($\Longrightarrow$) Say that $M, \sigma \vDash \Delta\phi$. Then $M, \sigma \vDash \phi$ or there exists a deviation π from σ such that $M, \pi \vDash \phi$. If $M, \sigma \vDash \phi$ then $M^*, \sigma^* \vDash \phi^*$ from which it follows that $M^*, \sigma^* \vDash \forall_y [Gy \rightarrow E[Gy \wedge \phi^*]]$, and so $M^*, \sigma^* \vDash t^\Delta(\phi^*)$.

If $M, \sigma \nvDash \phi$ then, for some i, there exists an i-deviation π from σ such that $M, \pi \vDash \phi$. If Gy holds along σ^* then y holds at $\pi_i^* = \sigma_i^*$. As π is an i-deviation, all transitions following π_{i+1} are success transitions, so $M^*, \pi_{\geq i}^* \vDash \gamma$ and $M^*, \pi^* \vDash F(y \wedge \gamma) \wedge \phi^*$ from which it follows that $M^*, \sigma^* \vDash t^\Delta(\phi^*)$.

($\Longleftarrow$) Say that $M^*, \sigma^* \vDash t^{\Delta}(\phi^*)$. Then

$$M^y, \sigma^* \vDash [Gy \rightarrow E\,[(Gy \vee F\,(y \wedge \gamma)) \wedge \phi^*]]\;,$$

where M^y is any tree structure that is y-bisimilar to M^*. Consider an M^y for which y is true at a state w iff $w \in \sigma^*$. Then $M^y, \sigma^* \vDash E\,[(Gy \vee F\,(y \wedge \gamma)) \wedge \phi^*]$. Thus there exists some fullpath σ^y such that $\sigma_0^y = \sigma_0^*$ and $M^y, \sigma^y \vDash F\,(y \wedge \gamma) \wedge \phi^*$ or $M^y, \sigma^y \vDash Gy \wedge \phi^*$.

If $M^y, \sigma^y \vDash Gy \wedge \phi^*$ then $\sigma^y = \sigma^*$, so $M^*, \sigma^* \vDash \phi^*$ and $M, \sigma \vDash \phi$. If $M^y, \sigma^y \vDash F\,(y \wedge \gamma) \wedge \phi^*$ then there exists an integer i such that $M^y, \sigma_{\geq i}^y \vDash y \wedge \gamma$. Let σ and π be translations of σ^* and σ^y respectively into fullpaths through the original structure M. As M^y is a tree structure and y is only true along σ^*, it follows that $\sigma_{\leq i}^y = \sigma_{\leq i}^*$ and $\pi_{\leq i} = \sigma_{\leq i}$. This, together with the fact that $M^y, \sigma_{\geq i}^y \vDash \gamma$, means that π is an i-deviation from σ. As $M^y, \sigma^y \vDash \phi^*$ it follows that $M, \pi \vDash \phi$, and so $M, \sigma \vDash \Delta\phi$.

Theorem 1. *We may express any RoCTL* formula ϕ of length n as a QCTL* formula ϕ^* of length $\mathcal{O}(n)$ that is equivalent to ϕ when ϕ^* is interpreted according to the tree semantics for QCTL*.*

Proof. Using $t^{\Delta}(\phi^*)$ defined above, $t^O(\phi^*) \equiv A\,(NG\neg\text{Viol} \rightarrow \phi^*)$, $t^{\neg}(\phi^*) \equiv \neg\phi^*$, $t^N(\phi^*) \equiv N\phi^*$, $t^A(\phi^*) \equiv A\phi^*$, $t^{\wedge}(\phi_1^*, \phi_2^*) \equiv \phi_1^* \wedge \phi_2^*$, $t^U(\phi_1^*, \phi_2^*) \equiv \phi_1^* U \phi_2^*$, $t^{\top} = \top$ and $t^p(p) \equiv p$, we may recursively translate any RoCTL* formula ϕ into a QCTL* formula ϕ^* such that $M, \sigma \vDash \phi$ iff $M^*, \sigma^* \vDash \phi^*$ where M^*, σ^* are the transformations of M, σ described above.

Corollary 1. *RoCTL* is decidable.*

Proof. In Section 5.1 we have shown that for every RoCTL-structure M there is a corresponding CTL tree structure M^* and visa versa. As the tree semantics for QCTL* are decidable [19,20], it is obvious from Theorem 1 that RoCTL* is decidable.

6   Conclusion

We have proposed a logic RoCTL* for reasoning about robust systems. This logic introduced a Robustly operator that provides a bridge between what should happen and what actually does. We have given examples of simple robust systems that can be represented in RoCTL*. We have proven that RoCTL* has a linear embedding into QCTL*, and hence is decidable. Never-the-less there is much more to be understood about this logic.

Although we can decide RoCTL* via QCTL*, it is important to find a more efficient decision procedure as QCTL* is not elementary [21,22]. Determining whether a particular model satisfies a RoCTL* policy is also useful. It is easy to show that the model checking problem is decidable via reduction to QCTL* and μ-calculus. However, a more efficient decision procedure is needed.

Restricting the expressivity of RoCTL* may lead to better complexity results. It may be productive to look for a restriction of RoCTL* that more closely resembles CTL or LTL than CTL*. However, as the Robustly operator is a path-quantifier that is not a state formulae, it is quite different from the operators found in CTL and LTL. For this reason, finding a restriction that preserves the usefulness and uniqueness of the Robustly operator while gaining some of the simplicity of CTL or LTL will be non-trivial.

Finding an axiomatization for RoCTL* may be a challenging task. Although this paper has compared the validities of the ▲ and O operators to the axioms for the A operator, we are far from finding a sound axiomatization of RoCTL*, and have not examined how to prove that such an axiomatization is complete.

More work needs to be done in applying RoCTL* to practical problems. This paper has presented some trivial examples where RoCTL* succinctly represents robustness properties of simple systems. To test the expressivity of RoCTL* and find real world applications, much larger and more complex examples need to be formalised and examined. For some uses, RoCTL* may need to be extended. RoCTL* can use the prone operator to discuss whether it is possible for a failure to be detected at a particular step. Diagnosis problems require that failures *will* be detected. For these purposes, an "If *at least* one additional failure occurs" operator and a knowledge operator are desirable. It would be useful to find an extension that satisfies these requirements while preserving decidability.

References

1. Emerson, E.A., Sistla, A.P.: Deciding full branching time logic. Technical report, University of Texas at Austin, Austin, TX, USA (1985)
2. Clarke, E., Emerson, E.: Synthesis of synchronization skeletons for branching time temporal logic. In: Proc. IBM Workshop on Log. of Progr., Yorktown Heights, pp. 52–71. Springer, Heidelberg (1981)
3. French, T., McCabe-Dansted, J.C., Reynolds, M.: A temporal logic of robustness, RoCTL*. Technical report, UWA (2007) http://dansted.org/RoCTL07.pdf
4. Forrester, J.W.: Gentle murder, or the adverbial samaritan. J. Philos. 81(4), 193–197 (1984)
5. van der Torre, L.W.N., Tan, Y.: The temporal analysis of Chisholm's paradox. In: Senator, T., Buchanan, B. (eds.) Proc. 14th Nation. Conf. on AI and 9th Innov. Applic. of AI Conf., Menlo Park, California, pp. 650–655. AAAI Press, Stanford, California (1998)
6. McCarty, L.T.: Defeasible deontic reasoning. Fundam. Inform. 21(1/2), 125–148 (1994)
7. Belnap, N.: Backwards and forwards in the modal logic of agency. Philos. Phenomen. Res. 51(4), 777–807 (1991)
8. de Weerdt, M., Bos, A., Tonino, H., Witteveen, C.: A resource logic for multi-agent plan merging. Annals of Math. and AI 37(1-2), 93–130 (2003)
9. Broersen, J., Dignum, F., Dignum, V., Meyer, J.J.C.: In: Designing a Deontic Logic of Deadlines. In: Lomuscio, A.R., Nute, D. (eds.) DEON 2004. LNCS (LNAI), vol. 3065, pp. 43–56. Springer, Heidelberg (2004)
10. Long, W., Sato, Y., Horigome, M.: Quantification of sequential failure logic for fault tree analysis. Reliab. Eng. Syst. Safe. 67, 269–274 (2000)

11. Hansson, H., Jonsson, B.: A logic for reasoning about time and reliability. Form. Asp. Comput. 6(5), 512–535 (1994)
12. Aldewereld, H., Grossi, D., Vazquez-Salceda, J., Dignum, F.: Designing normative behaviour by the use of landmarks. In: Agents, Norms and Institutions for Regulated Multiag. Syst., Utrecht, The Netherlands (2005)
13. Rodrigo, A., Eduardo, A.: Normative pragmatics for agent communication languages. In: Akoka, J., Liddle, S.W., Song, I.-Y., Bertolotto, M., Comyn-Wattiau, I., van den Heuvel, W.-J., Kolp, M., Trujillo, J., Kop, C., Mayr, H.C. (eds.) Perspectives in Conceptual Modeling. LNCS, vol. 3770, pp. 172–181. Springer, Heidelberg (2005)
14. Jéron, T., Marchand, H., Pinchinat, S., Cordier, M.O.: Supervision patterns in discrete event systems diagnosis. In: 8th Internat. Workshop on Discrete Event Syst., pp. 262–268 (2006)
15. Arnold, A., Vincent, A., Walukiewicz, I.: Games for synthesis of controllers with partial observation. TCS 303(1), 7–34 (2003)
16. Reynolds, M.: An axiomatization of full computation tree logic. J. Symb. Log. 66(3), 1011–1057 (2001)
17. Emerson, E.A.: Alternative semantics for temporal logics. TCS 26, 121–130 (1983)
18. Kupferman, O.: Augmenting branching temporal logics with existential quantification over atomic propositions. In: Comput. Aid. Verfic., Proc. 7th Int. Conf., Liege, pp. 325–338. Springer, Heidelberg (1995)
19. Emerson, E.A., Sistla, A.P.: Deciding branching time logic. In: STOC '84: Proc. 16th annual ACM sympos. on Theory of computing, New York, NY, USA, pp. 14–24. ACM Press, New York (1984)
20. French, T.: Decidability of quantifed propositional branching time logics. In: AI '01. Proc. 14th Austral. Joint Conf. on AI, London, UK, pp. 165–176. Springer, Heidelberg (2001)
21. Sistla, A.P., Vardi, M.Y., Wolper, P.: The complementation problem for buchi automata with applications to temporal logic. TCS 49(2-3), 217–237 (1987)
22. French, T.: Bisimulation Quantifiers for Modal Logics. PhD thesis, UWA (2006)

Noetherianity and Combination Problems

Silvio Ghilardi[1], Enrica Nicolini[2], Silvio Ranise[2], and Daniele Zucchelli[1,2]

[1] Dipartimento di Informatica, Università degli Studi di Milano, Italia
[2] LORIA & INRIA-Lorraine, Nancy, France

Abstract. In abstract algebra, a structure is said to be Noetherian if it does not admit infinite strictly ascending chains of congruences. In this paper, we adapt this notion to first-order logic by defining the class of Noetherian theories. Examples of theories in this class are Linear Arithmetics without ordering and the empty theory containing only a unary function symbol. Interestingly, it is possible to design a non-disjoint combination method for extensions of Noetherian theories. We investigate sufficient conditions for adding a temporal dimension to such theories in such a way that the decidability of the satisfiability problem for the quantifier-free fragment of the resulting temporal logic is guaranteed. This problem is firstly investigated for the case of Linear time Temporal Logic and then generalized to arbitrary modal/temporal logics whose propositional relativized satisfiability problem is decidable.

1 Introduction

Since full first-order temporal logics are known to be highly undecidable, researchers concentrated on finding fragments having good computational properties, such as the decidable monodic fragments investigated in, e.g., [17,9,12]. Although such fragments may also be used in verification, widely adopted formalisms for the specification of reactive or distributed systems (e.g., the one proposed by Manna and Pnueli [23] or the Temporal Logic of Actions by Lamport [19]) are such that the temporal part, used to describe the dynamic behavior of the systems, is parametric with respect to the underlying language of first-order logic, used to formalize the data structures manipulated by the systems. While the expressiveness of these formalisms helps in writing concise and abstract specifications, it is not clear how these can be amenable to automated analysis. The work presented in this paper contributes towards the solution of this problem, by analyzing what happens when we "add a temporal dimension" (in a sense similar to that investigated in [11]) to a decidable fragment of a *first-order theory* T with identity. By doing this, the hope is to transfer the decidability of the theory T to its "temporalized" version. This point of view has been pioneered by Plaisted in [29], where he further refined the semantics of the "temporalized T" by partitioning the symbols of the signature of T in *rigid* (whose interpretation is time-independent) and *flexible* (whose interpretation is time-dependent). This facilitates the expression of properties of both open and closed systems (see, e.g., [11] for more on this issue).

B. Konev and F. Wolter (Eds.): FroCos 2007, LNAI 4720, pp. 206–220, 2007.

In [14], we have presented a uniform framework where the approach in [29] has been clarified and extended. In particular, we have obtained undecidability and decidability results for quantifier-free satisfiability and model-checking problems in a temporal logic obtained by extending a decidable theory T with the operators of Linear time Temporal Logic (LTL). The key to obtain the results in [14] is a reduction of satisfiability and model-checking to the combination of (infinitely many) *partially renamed copies* of T (the symbols that are not renamed are those belonging to the rigid sub-signature Σ_r). The viewpoint of combination helps clarifying both decidability and undecidability issues. In fact, it is not always possible to transfer the decidability of the quantifier-free fragment of T to its "temporalized" version as shown by a simple reduction to known undecidable combination problems [5], even when the rigid subsignature Σ_r is empty. Fortunately, it is possible to use combination methods for non-disjoint theories in first-order logic [13] and find suitable requirements on the theory T to derive the decidability of both the satisfiability and the model-checking problem for the quantifier-free formulae of the "temporalized" version of T. The key ingredients are two. First (for correctness), it is assumed that T has a decidable universal fragment and is T_r-compatible [13], where T_r is the Σ_r-reduct of the universal fragment of T. Second (for termination), T_r is assumed to be locally finite [13]. Under these hypotheses, a (non-deterministic) combination schema can be obtained by using guessings over the finitely many (because of local finiteness) literals in the shared theory. This also simplifies the proof of correctness.

In this paper, we weaken the requirement of local finiteness to that of Noetherianity (cf. Section 3), and we focus our attention to the satisfiability problem, since model-checking is easily shown to be undecidable when considering Noetherian theories [15]. The *first contribution* of this paper is to show that our combinability requirements related to Noetherianity are met by any extension with a free unary function symbol of a stably infinite theory (cf. Section 3.2). The *second contribution* is to derive an amalgamation lemma (cf. Lemma 3.7) for combinations of (infinitely many) theories sharing a Noetherian theory (cf. Section 3.1). The combination procedure is more complex than in the locally finite case, since the exhaustive enumeration of guessings can no more be used to abstract away the exchange of now (possibly) infinitely many literals between the component theories and the combination results in [13,14] do not apply. The exchange mechanism is formalized by *residue enumerators*, i.e. computable functions returning entailed positive clauses in the shared theory. The *third contribution* of the paper is the application of the amalgamation lemma to show the decidability of the satisfiability problem for quantifier-free LTL formulae modulo a first order theory T, when T is an effectively Noetherian and T_r-compatible extension of T_r (cf. Section 4). Finally, the decidability result is extended to any modal/temporal logic whose propositional relativized satisfiability problem is decidable (cf. Section 5). Full proofs and all the technical details can be found in the extended version of this paper available online at the address http://homes.dsi.unimi.it/~zucchell

2   Formal Preliminaries

We adopt the usual first-order syntactic notions of signature, term, position, atom, (ground) formula, sentence, and so on. Let Σ be a first-order signature; we assume the binary equality predicate symbol '=' to be in any signature (so, if $\Sigma = \emptyset$, then Σ does not contain other symbols than equality). The signature obtained from Σ by adding it a set $\underline{a}$ of new constants (i.e., 0-ary function symbols) is denoted by $\Sigma^{\underline{a}}$. A *positive clause* is a disjunction of atoms. A *constraint* is a conjunctions of literals. A Σ-*theory* T is a set of sentences (called the axioms of T) in the signature Σ and it is *universal* iff it has universal closures of open formulae as axioms.

We also assume the usual first-order notion of interpretation and truth of a formula, with the proviso that the equality predicate $=$ is always interpreted as the identity relation. We let $\bot$ denote an arbitrary formula which is true in no structure. A formula φ is *satisfiable* in $\mathcal{M}$ iff its *existential* closure is true in $\mathcal{M}$. A Σ-structure $\mathcal{M}$ is a *model* of a Σ-theory T (in symbols $\mathcal{M} \models T$) iff all the sentences of T are true in $\mathcal{M}$. If φ is a formula, $T \models \varphi$ ('φ *is a logical consequence of* T') means that the universal closure of φ is true in all the models of T. A Σ-theory T is *complete* iff for every Σ-sentence φ, either φ or $\neg\varphi$ is a logical consequence of T. T admits *quantifier elimination* iff for every formula $\varphi(\underline{x})$ there is a quantifier-free formula $\varphi'(\underline{x})$ such that $T \models \varphi(\underline{x}) \leftrightarrow \varphi'(\underline{x})$ (notations like $\varphi(\underline{x})$ mean that φ contains free variables only among the tuple $\underline{x}$). T is *consistent* iff it has a model, i.e., if $T \not\models \bot$. A sentence φ is T-consistent iff $T \cup \{\varphi\}$ is consistent.

The *constraint satisfiability problem* for the constraint theory T is the problem of deciding whether a Σ-constraint is satisfiable in a model of T (or, equivalently, T-satisfiable). In the following, we use free constants instead of variables in constraint satisfiability problems, so that we (equivalently) redefine a constraint satisfiability problem for the theory T as the problem of *establishing the consistency of* $T \cup \Gamma$ *for a finite set* Γ *of ground* $\Sigma^{\underline{a}}$-*literals* (where $\underline{a}$ is a finite set of new constants). For the same reason, we abbreviate 'ground $\Sigma^{\underline{a}}$-constraint' with 'Σ-constraint,' when $\underline{a}$ is clear from the context.

If $\Sigma_0 \subseteq \Sigma$ is a subsignature of Σ and if $\mathcal{M}$ is a Σ-structure, the Σ_0-*reduct* of $\mathcal{M}$ is the Σ_0-structure $\mathcal{M}_{|\Sigma_0}$ obtained from $\mathcal{M}$ by forgetting the interpretation of function and predicate symbols from $\Sigma \setminus \Sigma_0$. A Σ-*embedding* (or, simply, an embedding) between two Σ-structures $\mathcal{M} = (M, \mathcal{I})$ and $\mathcal{N} = (N, \mathcal{J})$ is any mapping $\mu : M \longrightarrow N$ among the corresponding support sets satisfying the condition

$$\mathcal{M} \models \varphi \quad \text{iff} \quad \mathcal{N} \models \varphi \tag{1}$$

for all Σ^M-atoms φ (here $\mathcal{M}$ is regarded as a Σ^M-structure, by interpreting each additional constant $a \in M$ into itself and $\mathcal{N}$ is regarded as a Σ^M-structure by interpreting each additional constant $a \in M$ into $\mu(a)$). If $M \subseteq N$ and if the embedding $\mu : \mathcal{M} \longrightarrow \mathcal{N}$ is just the identity inclusion $M \subseteq N$, we say that $\mathcal{M}$ is a *substructure* of $\mathcal{N}$ or that $\mathcal{N}$ is an *extension* of $\mathcal{M}$. In case condition (1) holds for all first order formulae, the embedding μ is said to be *elementary*.

3   Noetherian Theories

In abstract algebra, the adjective Noetherian is used to describe structures that satisfy an ascending chain condition on congruences (see, e.g., [22]): since congruences can have special representations, Noetherianity concerns, e.g., chains of ideals in the case of rings and chains of submodules in the case of modules. Although this is somewhat non-standard, we may take a more abstract view and say that a *variety* (i.e. an equational class of structures) is Noetherian iff finitely generated free algebras satisfy the ascending chain condition for congruences or, equivalently, iff finitely generated algebras are finitely presented. Now, congruences over finitely generated free algebras may be represented as sets of equations among terms. This allows us to equivalently re-state the Noetherianity of varieties as "there are no infinite ascending chains of sets of equations modulo logical consequence". This observation was the basis for the abstract notion of Noetherian Fragment introduced in [16], here adapted for an arbitrary first-order theory.

Definition 3.1 (Noetherian Theory). *A Σ_0-theory T_0 is Noetherian if and only if for every* finite *set of free constants $\underline{a}$, every infinite ascending chain*

$$\Theta_1 \subseteq \Theta_2 \subseteq \cdots \subseteq \Theta_n \subseteq \cdots$$

of sets of ground $\Sigma_0^{\underline{a}}$-atoms is eventually constant modulo T_0, i.e. there is an n such that $T_0 \cup \Theta_n \models A$, for every natural number m and atom $A \in \Theta_m$.

Natural examples of Noetherian theories are the first-order axiomatization (in equational logic) of varieties like K-algebras, K-vector spaces, and R-modules, where K is a field and R is a Noetherian ring (see [22] for further details). *Abelian semigroups* are also Noetherian (cf. Theorem 3.11 in [8]). Notice that, since any extension (in the same signature) of a Noetherian theory is also Noetherian, any theory extending the theory of a single Associative-Commutative symbol is Noetherian. This shows that the family of Noetherian theories is important for verification because theories axiomatizing *integer addition* or *multiset union* formalize crucial aspects of a system to be verified (e.g., multisets may be used to check that the result of some operations like sorting on a collection of objects yields a permutation of the initial collection). More examples will be considered below.

   Before being able to describe our new combination method, we need to introduce some preliminary notions. In the remaining of this section, *we fix two theories $T_0 \subseteq T$ in their respective signatures $\Sigma_0 \subseteq \Sigma$.*

Definition 3.2 (T_0-basis). *Given a finite set Θ of ground clauses (built out of symbols from Σ and possibly further free constants) and a finite set of free constants $\underline{a}$, a T_0-basis for Θ w.r.t. $\underline{a}$ is a set Δ of positive ground $\Sigma_0^{\underline{a}}$-clauses such that*

(i) *$T \cup \Theta \models C$, for all $C \in \Delta$ and*
(ii) *if $T \cup \Theta \models C$ then $T_0 \cup \Delta \models C$, for every positive ground $\Sigma_0^{\underline{a}}$-clause C.*

Notice that only constants in $\underline{a}$ may occur in a T_0-basis for Θ w.r.t. $\underline{a}$, although Θ may contain constants not in $\underline{a}$.

Definition 3.3 (Residue Enumerator). *Given a finite set $\underline{a}$ of free constants, a T-residue enumerator for T_0 w.r.t. $\underline{a}$ is a computable function $Res_T^{\underline{a}}(\Gamma)$ mapping a Σ-constraint Γ to a finite T_0-basis of Γ w.r.t. $\underline{a}$.*

If Γ is T-unsatisfiable, then a residue enumerator can always return the singleton set containing the empty clause. The concept of (Noetherian) residue enumerator is inspired by the work on partial theory reasoning (see, e.g., [3]) and generalizes the notion of deduction complete procedure of [18]. Given a residue enumerator for constraints (cf. Definition 3.3), it is always possible to build one for clauses (this will be useful for the combination method, see below).

Lemma 3.4. *Given a finite set $\underline{a}$ of free constants and a T-residue enumerator for T_0 w.r.t. $\underline{a}$, there exists a computable function $Res_T^{\underline{a}}(\Theta)$ mapping a finite set of ground clauses Θ to a finite T_0-basis of Θ w.r.t. $\underline{a}$.*

If T_0 is Noetherian, then it is possible to show that a finite T_0-basis for Γ w.r.t. $\underline{a}$ always exists, for every Σ-constraint Γ and for every set $\underline{a}$ of constants, by using König lemma. Unfortunately, such a basis is not always computable; this motivates the following notion.

Definition 3.5. *The theory T is an effectively Noetherian extension of T_0 if and only if T_0 is Noetherian and there exists a T-residue enumerator for T_0 w.r.t. every finite set $\underline{a}$ of free constants.*

For example, the theory of commutative K-algebras is an effectively Noetherian extension of the theory of K-vector spaces, where K is a field (see [16,28] for details). Locally finite theories and Linear Real Arithmetic are further examples taken from the literature about automated theorem proving.

A Σ_0-theory T_0 is *locally finite* iff Σ_0 is finite and, for every finite set of free constants $\underline{a}$, there are finitely many ground $\Sigma_0^{\underline{a}}$-terms $t_1, \ldots, t_{k_{\underline{a}}}$ such that for every ground $\Sigma_0^{\underline{a}}$-term u, $T_0 \models u = t_i$ (for some $i \in \{1, \ldots, k_{\underline{a}}\}$). If such $t_1, \ldots, t_{k_{\underline{a}}}$ are effectively computable from $\underline{a}$, then T_0 is *effectively locally finite* and there are finitely many (*representative*) $\Sigma_0^{\underline{a}}$-atoms $\psi_1(\underline{a}), \ldots, \psi_m(\underline{a})$ such that for any $\Sigma_0^{\underline{a}}$-atom $\psi(\underline{a})$, there is some i such that $T_0 \models \psi_i(\underline{a}) \leftrightarrow \psi(\underline{a})$. Examples of effectively locally finite theories are Boolean algebras, Linear Integer Arithmetic modulo a given integer, and any theory over a finite purely relational signature. Also, theories consisting of sentences which are true in a fixed finite Σ_0-structure $\mathcal{M} = (M, \mathcal{I})$ are locally finite. Enumerated datatypes can be formalized by theories in this class. The class of locally finite theories is (strictly) contained in that of Noetherian theories: to see this, it is sufficient to notice that, once fixed a finite set of free constants $\underline{a}$, there are only finitely many $\Sigma_0^{\underline{a}}$-atoms which are not equivalent to each other modulo the locally finite theory. From this, it is obvious that any infinite ascending chain of sets of such atoms must be eventually constant. Under the hypotheses that T_0 is effectively locally finite and its extension T has decidable constraint satisfiability problem, it is straightforward to build a T-residue enumerator for T_0.

Example. Let us consider the signature $\Sigma = \{0, +, -, \{f_r\}_{r \in \mathbb{R}}, \leq\}$ where 0 is a constant, $-$ and f_r are unary function symbols, $+$ is a binary function symbol, $\leq$ is a binary predicate symbol, and $\Sigma_0 = \Sigma \setminus \{\leq\}$. We consider the theory $T_{\mathbb{R}}^{\leq} = Th_{\Sigma}(\mathbb{R})$, i.e. the set of all Σ-sentences true in $\mathbb{R}$, which is seen as an $\mathbb{R}$-vector space equipped with a linear ordering, where the f_r's represent the external product so that terms are all equivalent to homogeneous linear polynomials. Finally, let $T_{\mathbb{R}}$ be $Th_{\Sigma_0}(\mathbb{R})$, i.e. the set of all Σ_0-sentences true in $\mathbb{R}$, which is seen as an $\mathbb{R}$-vector space without the ordering (so $T_{\mathbb{R}}$ is the theory of the $\mathbb{R}$-vector spaces, not reduced to $\{0\}$). The Noetherianity of $T_{\mathbb{R}}$ follows from general algebraic properties (see, e.g., [22]). A $T_{\mathbb{R}}^{\leq}$-residue enumerator for $T_{\mathbb{R}}$ can be obtained as follows. Let $\Gamma = \{C_1, \ldots, C_m\}$ be a set of inequalities, i.e. Σ-atoms whose main predicate symbol is $\leq$. By Definition 3.2, a Σ_0-basis for Γ is the set of all the disjunctions of equalities implied by Γ. Actually, to compute a basis, it is sufficient to identify the set of *implicit* equalities in Γ, i.e. the equalities $C_i^=$ such that $T_{\mathbb{R}}^{\leq} \models \Gamma \to C_i^=$ (here $C_i^=$ is obtained from C_i by substituting $\leq$ with $=$). This is so because (i) $T_{\mathbb{R}}^{\leq}$ is Σ_0-*convex* (i.e. if $T_{\mathbb{R}}^{\leq} \models \Gamma \to (e_1 \vee \cdots \vee e_n)$, then there exists $i \in \{1, \ldots, n\}$ such that $T_{\mathbb{R}}^{\leq} \models \Gamma \to e_i$, for $n \geq 1$ and equalities $e_1, \ldots, e_n$) and (ii) given a system of inequalities Γ, if Δ is the collection of all the implicit equalities of Γ and e is an equality such that $T_{\mathbb{R}}^{\leq} \models \Gamma \to e$, then $T_{\mathbb{R}} \models \Delta \to e$ (see [21] for full details, [28] for the adaptation to our context). The interest of implicit equalities is that they can be easily identified by using the Fourier-Motzkin variable elimination method (see [20] for details on how to do this).

3.1   Combination over Noetherian Theories

Preliminarily, we recall the notion of T_0-compatibility [13] which is crucial for the completeness of our combination technique.

Definition 3.6 (T_0-compatibility [13]). *Let T be a theory in the signature Σ and let T_0 be a universal theory in a subsignature $\Sigma_0 \subseteq \Sigma$. We say that T is T_0-compatible iff $T_0 \subseteq T$ and there is a Σ_0-theory $T_0^\star$ such that (i) $T_0 \subseteq T_0^\star$; (ii) $T_0^\star$ has quantifier elimination; (iii) every model of T_0 can be embedded into a model of $T_0^\star$; and (iv) every model of T can be embedded into a model of $T \cup T_0^\star$.*

The requirements (i)-(iii) guarantee the uniqueness of the theory $T_0^\star$, provided it exists ($T_0^\star$ is the *model completion* of T_0, see e.g. [7]). Notice that if T_0 is the empty theory over the empty signature, then $T_0^\star$ is the theory axiomatizing an infinite domain, (i)-(iii) hold trivially, and (iv) can be shown equivalent to the stably infinite requirement of the Nelson-Oppen schema [27,31]. Examples of theories satisfying the compatibility condition are the following: (a) the theory of K-algebras is compatible with the theory of K-vector spaces, where K is a field (see [16,28]), (b) $T_{\mathbb{R}}^{\leq}$ is compatible with the universal fragment of $T_{\mathbb{R}}$ (this is so for $T_{\mathbb{R}}^{\leq} \supseteq T_{\mathbb{R}}$ and $T_{\mathbb{R}}$ eliminates quantifiers), (c) any equational extension over a larger signature of the theory BA of Boolean algebras is BA-compatible [13], and (d) any extension of T_0 whatsoever is T_0-compatible whenever T_0 eliminates quantifiers.

The following lemma is *our main technical tool* allowing us to reduce satisfiability in a "temporalized" extension of a (Noetherian) theory to satisfiability in first-order logic.

Lemma 3.7 (Amalgamation). *Let I be a (possibly infinite) set of indexes; $\Sigma_i^{\underline{c},\underline{a}_i}$ (for $i \in I$) be signatures (expanded with free constants $\underline{c}, \underline{a}_i$), whose pairwise intersections are all equal to a certain signature $\Sigma_r^{\underline{c}}$ (i.e. $\Sigma_i^{\underline{c},\underline{a}_i} \cap \Sigma_j^{\underline{c},\underline{a}_j} = \Sigma_r^{\underline{c}}$, for all distinct $i, j \in I$); T_i be Σ_i-theories (for $i \in I$) which are all T_r-compatible, where $T_r \subseteq \bigcap_i T_i$ is a universal Σ_r-theory; $\{\Gamma_i\}_{i \in I}$ be sets of ground $\Sigma_i^{\underline{c},\underline{a}_i}$-clauses; and $\mathcal{B}^\star$ be a set of positive ground $\Sigma_r^{\underline{c}}$-clauses not containing the empty clause and satisfying the following condition:*

$$\text{if } T_i \cup \Gamma_i \cup \mathcal{B}^\star \models C, \text{ then } C \in \mathcal{B}^\star,$$

for $i \in I$ and every positive ground $\Sigma_r^{\underline{c}}$-clause C. Then, there exists a $\bigcup_i (\Sigma_i^{\underline{c},\underline{a}_i})$-structure $\mathcal{M}$ such that $\mathcal{M} \models \bigcup_i (T_i \cup \Gamma_i)$ or, equivalently, there exist $\Sigma_i^{\underline{c},\underline{a}_i}$-structures $\mathcal{M}_i$ ($i \in I$) satisfying $T_i \cup \Gamma_i$, whose $\Sigma_r^{\underline{c}}$-reducts coincide.

This lemma can also be used to prove the "first-order version" of the combination result in [16], where residue enumerators permit the exchange of positive clauses between theories.

3.2   The Theory of a Free Unary Function Symbol

By collecting the observations above, it is easy to identify pairs of theories (T, T_0) such that T satisfies our relevant requirements to be 'combined over T_0' (i.e. T is such that $T_0 \subseteq T$ and T is a T_0-compatible effectively Noetherian extension of T_0). Here, we consider an entirely new (and somewhat remarkable) class of examples of such pairs (T, T_0) of theories.

Let f be a unary function symbol. If T is a theory, then T_f is the theory obtained from T by adding f to its signature (as a new free function symbol). So, e.g., if E the empty theory over the empty signature, E_f denotes the empty theory over the signature $\{f\}$.

Proposition 3.8. E_f *is Noetherian.*

A theory T is stably infinite (see, e.g., [27,31]) iff it is E-compatible, or, equivalently, iff any T-satisfiable constraint is satisfiable in a model of T whose domain is infinite.

Proposition 3.9. *If T is stably infinite and has decidable constraint satisfiability problem, then T_f is an effectively Noetherian extension of E_f.*

Proposition 3.10. *If T is stably infinite, then T_f is E_f-compatible.*

We are now ready to characterize our new class of theories.

Theorem 3.11. *Let T be a theory with decidable constraint satisfiability problem. If T is stably infinite, then T_f is an effectively Noetherian extension of E_f, which is also E_f-compatible.*

This result is a first step towards the integration in our framework of some theories that are useful for verification. For example, the theory of integer offsets can be seen as an extension of the theory of a loop-free unary function symbol (see, e.g., [1]). Properties of hardware systems can be expressed in a mixture of temporal logic – e.g., LTL or Computation Tree Logic (CTL) – and the theory of integer offsets [6]. Our decidability results on "temporalized" first-order theories below (see Theorems 4.11 and 5.4) can then be used to augment the degree of automation of tools attempting to solve this kind of verification problems.

4   Temporalizing a First-Order Theory

We introduce "temporalized" first-order theories, by using LTL to describe the temporal dimension. We use the formal framework introduced in [14] where formulae are obtained by applying temporal and Boolean operators (but no quantifiers) to first-order formulae over a given signature.

Definition 4.1 (LTL($\Sigma^{\underline{a}}$)-Sentences [14]). *Given a signature Σ and a (finite or infinite) set of free constants $\underline{a}$, the set of LTL($\Sigma^{\underline{a}}$)-sentences is inductively defined as follows: (a) if φ is a first-order $\Sigma^{\underline{a}}$-sentence, then φ is an LTL($\Sigma^{\underline{a}}$)-sentence and (b) if ψ_1, ψ_2 are LTL($\Sigma^{\underline{a}}$)-sentence, so are $\psi_1 \wedge \psi_2$, $\psi_1 \vee \psi_2$, $\neg\psi_1$, $X\psi_1$, $\square\psi_1$, $\Diamond\psi_1$, $\psi_1 U \psi_2$.*

The free constants $\underline{a}$ allowed in LTL($\Sigma^{\underline{a}}$)-sentences will be used to model the variables and the parameters of (reactive) systems.

Definition 4.2 ([14]). *Given a signature Σ and a set $\underline{a}$ of free constants, an LTL($\Sigma^{\underline{a}}$)-structure (or simply a structure) is a sequence $\mathcal{M} = \{\mathcal{M}_n = (M, \mathcal{I}_n)\}_{n \in \mathbb{N}}$ of $\Sigma^{\underline{a}}$-structures. The set M is called the domain (or the universe) and $\mathcal{I}_n$ is called the n-th level interpretation function of the LTL($\Sigma^{\underline{a}}$)-structure.*[1]

When considering a background Σ-theory T, the structures $\mathcal{M}_n = (M_n, \mathcal{I}_n)$ will be taken to be models of T (further requirements will be analyzed later on).

Definition 4.3 ([14]). *Given an LTL($\Sigma^{\underline{a}}$)-sentence φ and $t \in \mathbb{N}$, the notion of "φ being true in the LTL($\Sigma^{\underline{a}}$)-structure $\mathcal{M} = \{\mathcal{M}_n = (M, \mathcal{I}_n)\}_{n \in \mathbb{N}}$ at the instant t" (in symbols $\mathcal{M} \models_t \varphi$) is inductively defined as follows:*

- *if φ is an first-order sentence, $\mathcal{M} \models_t \varphi$ iff $\mathcal{M}_t \models \varphi$;*
- *$\mathcal{M} \models_t \neg\varphi$ iff $\mathcal{M} \not\models_t \varphi$;*
- *$\mathcal{M} \models_t \varphi \wedge \psi$ iff $\mathcal{M} \models_t \varphi$ and $\mathcal{M} \models_t \psi$;*
- *$\mathcal{M} \models_t \varphi \vee \psi$ iff $\mathcal{M} \models_t \varphi$ or $\mathcal{M} \models_t \psi$;*
- *$\mathcal{M} \models_t X\varphi$ iff $\mathcal{M} \models_{t+1} \varphi$;*
- *$\mathcal{M} \models_t \square\varphi$ iff for each $t' \geq t$, $\mathcal{M} \models_{t'} \varphi$;*
- *$\mathcal{M} \models_t \Diamond\varphi$ iff for some $t' \geq t$, $\mathcal{M} \models_{t'} \varphi$;*
- *$\mathcal{M} \models_t \varphi U \psi$ iff there exists $t' \geq t$ such that $\mathcal{M} \models_{t'} \psi$ and for each t'', $t \leq t'' < t' \Rightarrow \mathcal{M} \models_{t''} \varphi$.*

---

[1] In more detail, $\mathcal{I}_n$ is such that $\mathcal{I}_n(P) \subseteq M^k$ for every predicate symbols $P \in \Sigma$ of arity k, and $\mathcal{I}_n(f) : M^k \longrightarrow M$ for each function symbol $f \in \Sigma$ of arity k.

Let φ be an LTL($\Sigma^{\underline{a}}$)-sentence; we say that φ *is true in* $\mathcal{M}$ or, equivalently, that $\mathcal{M}$ *satisfies* φ (in symbols $\mathcal{M} \models \varphi$) iff $\mathcal{M} \models_0 \varphi$.

Since we distinguish between rigid (i.e. time-independent) and flexible (i.e. time-dependent) symbols of the signature, we need to introduce a notion of first-order theory that fixes a sub-signature and distinguish between two kinds of free constants.

Definition 4.4. *A* data-flow theory *is a 5-tuple* $\mathcal{T} = \langle \Sigma, T, \Sigma_r, \underline{a}, \underline{c} \rangle$ *where* Σ *is a signature,* T *is a* Σ-theory *(called the underlying theory of* $\mathcal{T}$*),* Σ_r *is the rigid subsignature of* Σ, $\underline{a}$ *is a set of free constants (called* system variables*), and* $\underline{c}$ *is a set of free constants (called* system parameters*).*

A data-flow theory $\mathcal{T} = \langle \Sigma, T, \Sigma_r, \underline{a}, \underline{c} \rangle$ is *totally flexible* iff Σ_r is empty and is *totally rigid* iff $\Sigma_r = \Sigma$. In [14], data-flow theories are called LTL-theories. Here, we prefer to use the more abstract term of data-flow theory in order to prepare for the generalization of the decidability result in the next section.

Definition 4.5 ([14]). *An* LTL($\Sigma^{\underline{a},\underline{c}}$)-*structure* $\mathcal{M} = \{\mathcal{M}_n = (M, \mathcal{I}_n)\}_{n \in \mathbb{N}}$ *is* appropriate *for a data-flow theory* $\mathcal{T} = \langle \Sigma, T, \Sigma_r, \underline{a}, \underline{c} \rangle$ *iff for all* $m, n \in \mathbb{N}$*, for all function symbol* $f \in \Sigma_r$*, for all relational symbol* $P \in \Sigma_r$*, and for all constant* $c \in \underline{c}$*, we have*

$$\mathcal{M}_n \models T, \quad \mathcal{I}_n(f) = \mathcal{I}_m(f), \quad \mathcal{I}_n(P) = \mathcal{I}_m(P), \quad \mathcal{I}_n(c) = \mathcal{I}_m(c).$$

The satisfiability problem *for* $\mathcal{T}$ *is the following: given an* LTL($\Sigma^{\underline{a},\underline{c}}$)*-sentence* φ*, decide whether there is an* LTL($\Sigma^{\underline{a},\underline{c}}$)*-structure* $\mathcal{M}$ *appropriate for* $\mathcal{T}$ *such that* $\mathcal{M} \models \varphi$*. The* ground satisfiability problem *for* $\mathcal{T}$ *is similarly introduced, but* φ *is assumed to be ground.*

Notice that appropriate structures are such that the equality symbol is always interpreted as the identity relation, since the equality is included in every signature (hence also in the rigid signature Σ_r).

In the sequel, we shall concentrate on the ground satisfiability problem for data-flow theories; for this reason, we shall assume from now on that **the underlying theory** T **of any data-flow theory** $\mathcal{T} = \langle \Sigma, T, \Sigma_r, \underline{a}, \underline{c} \rangle$ **has decidable constraint satisfiability problem.** Unfortunately, this assumption is insufficient to guarantee decidability.

Theorem 4.6 ([14]). *There exists a totally flexible data-flow theory* $\mathcal{T}$ *whose ground satisfiability problem is undecidable.*

Notwithstanding the undecidability of the ground satisfiability problem, the following compatibility requirement can be used to re-gain decidability.

Definition 4.7. *A data-flow theory* $\mathcal{T} = \langle \Sigma, T, \Sigma_r, \underline{a}, \underline{c} \rangle$ *is said to be* Noetherian compatible *iff there is a* Σ_r-universal theory T_r *such that* T *is an effectively Noetherian and* T_r-compatible *extension of* T_r*.*

The definition above refers to a Σ_r-theory T_r such that T is T_r-compatible. Although not relevant for the results in this paper, we notice that if such a theory T_r exists, then one can always take T_r to be the theory axiomatized by the universal Σ_r-sentences which are logical consequences of T.

4.1   A Decision Procedure for the Noetherian Compatible Case

Preliminarily, we recall that it is possible to define the notion of ground model-checking problem in our framework [14] and to show its undecidability when the underlying theory is Noetherian. The argument of the proof is a simple reduction to the (undecidable) reachability problem of Minsky machines [26,10] by using the reduct of Presburger Arithmetic obtained by forgetting addition and ordering, which is capable of encoding counters (see [15] for details). This is why here we focus on the ground satisfiability problem in the Noetherian compatible case.

Before developing our decision procedure, some preliminary notions are required.

Definition 4.8 (PLTL-Abstraction [14]). *Given a signature $\Sigma^{\underline{a}}$ and a set of propositional letters $\mathcal{L}$ of the appropriate cardinality, let $[\![\cdot]\!]$ be a bijection from the set of ground $\Sigma^{\underline{a}}$-atoms into $\mathcal{L}$. By translating identically Boolean and temporal connectives, the map is inductively extended to a bijective map (also called $[\![\cdot]\!]$) from the set of LTL($\Sigma^{\underline{a}}$)-sentences onto the set of propositional $\mathcal{L}$-formulae.*

Given a ground LTL($\Sigma^{\underline{a}}$)-sentence φ, we call $[\![\varphi]\!]$ the *PLTL-abstraction* of φ; moreover, if Θ is a set of ground LTL($\Sigma^{\underline{a}}$)-sentences, the PLTL-abstraction $[\![\Theta]\!]$ of Θ denotes the set $\{ [\![\varphi]\!] \mid \varphi \in \Theta \}$.

Definition 4.9 (φ-Guessing). *Let φ be a ground LTL($\Sigma^{\underline{a},\underline{c}}$)-sentence. A φ-guessing is a Boolean assignment to literals of φ (we view a guessing as the set $\{ \ell \mid \ell$ is an atom occurring in φ and ℓ is assigned to true$\} \cup \{ \neg \ell \mid \ell$ is an atom occurring in φ and ℓ is assigned to false$\}$).*

We say that a (non-empty) set of φ-guessings $\mathcal{G}_{(\varphi)} := \{ G_1, \ldots, G_k \}$ is φ-compatible if and only if $[\![\varphi \wedge \square \bigvee_{i=1}^{k} G_i]\!]$ is PLTL-satisfiable.

Let $\mathcal{T} = \langle \Sigma, T, \Sigma_r, \underline{a}, \underline{c} \rangle$ be a Noetherian compatible data-flow theory. The procedure NSAT (see Algorithm 1) takes a ground LTL($\Sigma^{\underline{a},\underline{c}}$)-sentence φ as input and returns *"satisfiable"* if there is an appropriate LTL($\Sigma^{\underline{a},\underline{c}}$)-structure $\mathcal{M}$ for $\mathcal{T}$ such that $\mathcal{M} \models \varphi$; otherwise, it returns *"unsatisfiable"*. The procedure relies on a decision procedure for the PLTL-satisfiability problem in order to recognize the φ-compatible sets of φ-guessings (cf. the outer loop of NSAT). Moreover, DP-T is a decision procedure for the satisfiability problem of arbitrary Boolean combinations of atoms of the theory T (i.e., it is capable of checking the T-satisfiability of sets of ground $\Sigma^{\underline{a},\underline{c}}$-clauses and not only of ground $\Sigma^{\underline{a},\underline{c}}$-literals). Notice that DP-T can be implemented by Satisfiability Modulo Theories solvers (see, e.g., [30]). Finally, $Res_T^{\underline{c}}$ is the T-residue enumerator for T_r w.r.t. $\underline{c}$.

In the outer loop of NSAT, all possible φ-compatible sets of φ-guessings are enumerated. Let $\mathcal{G}_{(\varphi)} := \{ G_1, \ldots, G_n \}$ be the current φ-guessing. The local variable $\mathcal{B}$ is initialized to the empty set (line 3) and then updated in the inner loop (lines 4-10) as follows: the T_r-bases $\mathcal{B}_i$ for $G_i \cup \mathcal{B}$ w.r.t. $\underline{c}$ are computed (for $i = 1, \ldots, n$), and the new value of $\mathcal{B}$ is set to $\bigcup_i \mathcal{B}_i$ (line 5 saves in $\mathcal{B}'$ the old value of $\mathcal{B}$). The inner loop is iterated until $\mathcal{B}$ is logically equivalent to $\mathcal{B}'$

Algorithm 1. The satisfiability procedure for the Noetherian compatible case

---

Require: φ ground LTL($\Sigma^{\underline{a},\underline{c}}$)-sentence
 1: **procedure** NSAT(φ)
 2:     **for all** φ-compatible set of φ-guessing $\mathcal{G}_{(\varphi)}$ **do**
 3:         $\mathcal{B} \leftarrow \emptyset$
 4:         **repeat**
 5:             $\mathcal{B}' \leftarrow \mathcal{B}$
 6:             **for all** $G_i \in \mathcal{G}_{(\varphi)}$ **do**
 7:                 $\mathcal{B}_i \leftarrow Res_T^{\underline{c}}(G_i \cup \mathcal{B})$
 8:             **end for**
 9:             $\mathcal{B} \leftarrow \bigcup_i \mathcal{B}_i$
10:         **until** DP-T($\mathcal{B}' \wedge \neg\mathcal{B}$) = *"unsatisfiable"*
11:         **if** DP-T($\mathcal{B}$) = *"satisfiable"* **then**
12:             **return** *"satisfiable"*
13:         **end if**
14:     **end for**
15:     **return** *"unsatisfiable"*
16: **end procedure**

---

modulo T. At this point, if $\mathcal{B}$ is T-consistent, the procedure stops and returns *"satisfiable"*; otherwise it tries another φ-compatible set of φ-guessings. If for all φ-compatible sets of φ-guessings the $\mathcal{B}$'s returned after the execution of the inner loop are T-inconsistent, the procedure returns *"unsatisfiable"*.

Proposition 4.10 (Correctness of NSat). *Let* $\mathcal{T} = \langle \Sigma, T, \Sigma_r, \underline{a}, \underline{c} \rangle$ *be a Noetherian compatible data-flow theory and* φ *be a ground LTL($\Sigma^{\underline{a},\underline{c}}$)-sentence. Then, NSAT($\varphi$) returns "satisfiable" iff there exists an LTL($\Sigma^{\underline{a},\underline{c}}$)-structure* $\mathcal{M}$ *appropriate for* $\mathcal{T}$ *such that* $\mathcal{M} \models \varphi$.

Indeed, the termination of NSAT is a consequence of the Noetherianity of the underlying theory of $\mathcal{T}$ by using the fact that every infinite ascending chain of sets of positive ground $\Sigma_r^{\underline{c}}$-clauses is eventually constant for logical consequence. The correctness and termination of NSAT yield our main decidability result.

Theorem 4.11. *The ground satisfiability problem for Noetherian compatible data-flow theories is decidable.*

The theories considered in the previous section (especially, those in Section 3.2) satisfy the hypothesis of the theorem above.

5   Extensions to Abstract Temporal Logics

By considering the proof of the correctness of NSAT, it becomes evident that only very few of the characteristic properties of LTL are used. It turns out that a simple generalization of NSAT can be used to decide satisfiability problems of "temporalized" extensions of Noetherian theories whose flow of time is not linear, e.g., branching as in CTL.

In order to formalize the observation above, we regard modal/temporal operators as functions operating on powerset Boolean algebras. In this way, logics for various flows of time, as well as CTL, Propositional Dynamic Logic (PDL), and the μ-calculus fall within the scope of our result (see [2] for a similar approach).

Definition 5.1. *An* abstract temporal signature[2] *I is a purely functional signature extending the signature BA of Boolean algebras.[3] An abstract temporal logic L is a class of I-structures, whose Boolean reducts are powerset Boolean algebras. Given an I-term t, deciding whether $t \neq 0$ is satisfied in some member of L is the* satisfiability *problem for L. Given I-terms t, u, deciding whether $u = 1 \,\&\, t \neq 0$ is satisfied in some member of L is the* relativized satisfiability *problem for L.*

In many cases (e.g., LTL, CTL, PDL, and the μ-calculus), it is possible to reduce the relativized satisfiability problem to that of satisfiability (by using the so-called "master modality"); however, there are logics for which the latter is decidable whereas the former is undecidable (see [12]).

Definition 5.2 ($I(\Sigma^{\underline{a}})$-sentence). *Given a signature Σ, a (finite or infinite) set of free constants $\underline{a}$, and an abstract temporal signature I, the set of $I(\Sigma^{\underline{a}})$-sentences is inductively defined as follows: (a) if φ is a first-order $\Sigma^{\underline{a}}$-sentence, then φ is an $I(\Sigma^{\underline{a}})$-sentence, (b) if φ_1, φ_2 are $I(\Sigma^{\underline{a}})$-sentences, so are $\varphi_1 \wedge \varphi_2, \varphi_1 \vee \varphi_2, \neg\varphi_1$, and (c) if $\psi_1, \ldots, \psi_n$ are $I(\Sigma^{\underline{a}})$-sentences and $O \in I \setminus BA$ has arity n, then $O(\psi_1, \ldots, \psi_n)$ is a $I(\Sigma^{\underline{a}})$-sentence.*

When I is LTL, $I(\Sigma^{\underline{a},\underline{c}})$-sentences coincide with LTL($\Sigma^{\underline{a},\underline{c}}$)-sentences (cf. Definition 4.1). We defined an abstract temporal logic L (based on I) as a class of I-structures based on powerset Boolean algebras: such structures (also called I-frames) will be denoted with $\mathcal{F} = (\wp(F), \{O^{\mathcal{F}}\}_{O \in I \setminus BA})$.

Definition 5.3. *Let a signature Σ, a set $\underline{a}$ of free constants, and an abstract temporal signature I be given; an $I(\Sigma^{\underline{a}})$-structure (or simply a structure) is a pair formed by an I-frame $\mathcal{F} = (\wp(F), \{O^{\mathcal{F}}\}_{O \in I \setminus BA})$ and a collection $\mathcal{M} = \{\mathcal{M}_n = (M, \mathcal{I}_n)\}_{n \in F}$ of $\Sigma^{\underline{a}}$-structures (all based on the same domain).*

An $I(\Sigma^{\underline{a}})$-sentence φ is true in the $I(\Sigma^{\underline{a}})$-structure $(\mathcal{F}, \mathcal{M})$ at $t \in F$ (noted $\mathcal{F}, \mathcal{M} \models_t \varphi$) iff the following holds: (a) if φ is a first-order sentence, then $\mathcal{F}, \mathcal{M} \models_t \varphi$ holds iff $\mathcal{M}_t \models \varphi$ and (b) if the main operator of φ is a Boolean connective, truth of φ is defined in a truth-table manner; (c) if φ is of the kind $O(\psi_1, \ldots, \psi_n)$, then $\mathcal{F}, \mathcal{M} \models_t \varphi$ holds iff $t \in O^{\mathcal{F}}(\{u \mid \mathcal{F}, \mathcal{M} \models_u \psi_1\}, \ldots, \{u \mid \mathcal{F}, \mathcal{M} \models_u \psi_n\})$.

---

[2] From the modal/temporal literature viewpoint, the adjective "intensional" might be preferable to "abstract temporal". We have chosen the latter, in order to emphasize that our results are deemed as significant for a class of logics whose modalities concern flows of time.

[3] This signature contains two binary function symbols for meet and join, a unary function symbol for complement, and two constants for zero and one (the latter are denoted with 0 and 1, respectively).

If a data-flow theory T is given, we say that an $I(\Sigma^{\underline{a}})$-structure is appropriate for T iff it satisfies the requirements of Definition 4.5. The (ground) satisfiability problem for an abstract temporal logic L (based on I) and for a data-flow theory T is now the following: given a (ground) $I(\Sigma^{\underline{a}})$-sentence φ, decide whether there is a $I(\Sigma^{\underline{a}})$-structure $(\mathcal{F}, \mathcal{M})$ appropriate for T, such that $\mathcal{F} \in L$ and such that $\mathcal{F}, \mathcal{M} \models_t \varphi$ holds for some t.

Theorem 5.4. *The ground satisfiability problem for T and L is decidable if (i) T is Noetherian compatible and (ii) the relativized satisfiability problem for L is decidable.*

When I is LTL, this result simplifies to Theorem 4.11. To prove Theorem 5.4, it is possible to re-use NSAT (cf. Algorithm 1) almost 'off-the-shelf', by preliminarily adapting the definition of PLTL-abstraction function $[\![\cdot]\!]$ (cf. Definition 4.8) to L in the obvious way. It turns out that only the compatibility of guessings should be changed: a finite set of φ-guessings $\mathcal{G}_{(\varphi)} := \{G_1, \ldots, G_k\}$ is φ-compatible if and only if the relativized satisfiability problem

$$[\![\varphi]\!] \neq 0 \quad \& \quad [\![\bigvee_{i=1}^{k} G_i]\!] = 1$$

is satisfiable in L (this is the only modification required to the definitions and proofs from Section 4.1).

While Theorem 4.11 is relevant to augment the degree of mechanization of deductive approaches for the verification of reactive systems based on LTL (e.g., the one put-forward by Manna and Pnueli [23]), one may wonder about the relevance of its generalization, i.e. Theorem 5.4. To see its usefulness, consider TLA [19]. For such a specification formalism, it is difficult to reuse techniques and tools for (classic) temporal/modal logic since TLA features some non-standard characteristics which are quite useful for practitioners (see [25] for an extensive discussion on this and related issues). On the other hand, deductive verification of TLA specifications can be supported by proof assistants (e.g., [24]). While applying the inference rules of TLA [19], it has been observed [25] that some of the resulting sub-goals may belong to a fragment of TLA which is equivalent to the modal logic S4.2 [4]. Now, the relativized satisfiability problem for this logic is decidable (see again [4]) so that NSAT can be used to automatically discharge some of the sub-goals, whenever the data-flow theory formalizing the data structure manipulated by the system modelled in TLA is Noetherian compatible.

6   Conclusions

We have investigated the role of Noetherianity for the decidability of the satisfiability problem for "temporalized" first-order theories (cf. Sections 4 and 5). The key technical contribution is Lemma 3.7, which allows us to obtain amalgamations of (possibly infinite) sequences of first-order structures corresponding to temporal structures. This lemma is the basis of a method for combinations of first-order theories over Noetherian theories. An important class of stably infinite theories extending the empty theory over a single unary function symbol has been shown to satisfy the hypotheses for the decidability of both the combination schema and the satisfiability of "temporalized" first-order theories (cf. Section 3.2).

The results in this paper extends those of [14] in two ways. First, the requirement of local finiteness of the (rigid) sub-theory is weakened to that of Noetherianity. Second, decidability is parametric w.r.t. a modal/temporal logic, provided that relativized satisfiability problem is decidable in the latter.

References

1. Armando, A., Bonacina, M.P., Ranise, S., Schulz, S.: On a rewriting approach to satisfiability procedures: extension, combination of theories and an experimental appraisal. In: Gramlich, B. (ed.) FroCoS 2005. LNCS (LNAI), vol. 3717, pp. 65–80. Springer, Heidelberg (2005)
2. Baader, F., Lutz, C., Sturm, H., Wolter, F.: Fusions of description logics and abstract description systems. Journal of A.I. Research 16, 1–58 (2002)
3. Baumgartner, P., Furbach, U., Petermann, U.: A unified approach to theory reasoning. Research Report 15–92, Universität Koblenz-Landau (1992)
4. Blackburn, P., de Rijke, M., Venema, Y.: Modal Logic. Cambridge University Press, Cambridge (2002)
5. Bonacina, M.P., Ghilardi, S., Nicolini, E., Ranise, S., Zucchelli, D.: Decidability and undecidability results for Nelson-Oppen and rewrite-based decision procedures. In: Furbach, U., Shankar, N. (eds.) IJCAR 2006. LNCS (LNAI), vol. 4130, pp. 513–527. Springer, Heidelberg (2006)
6. Bryant, R.E., Lahiri, S.K., Seshia, S.A.: Modeling and verifying systems using a logic of counter arithmetic with lambda expressions and uninterpreted functions. In: Brinksma, E., Larsen, K.G. (eds.) CAV 2002. LNCS, vol. 2404, pp. 78–92. Springer, Heidelberg (2002)
7. Chang, C.-C., Keisler, J.H.: Model Theory, 3rd edn. North-Holland, Amsterdam-London (1990)
8. Le Chenadec, P.: Canonical Forms in Finitely Presented Algebras. Research Notes in Theoretical Computer Science. Pitman-Wiley (1986)
9. Degtyarev, A., Fisher, M., Konev, B.: Monodic temporal resolution. ACM Transaction on Computational Logic 7(1), 108–150 (2006)
10. Ebbinghaus, H.-D., Flum, J., Thomas, W.: Mathematical logic. In: Undergraduate Texts in Mathematics, 2nd edn., Springer, Heidelberg (1994)
11. Finger, M., Gabbay, D.M.: Adding a temporal dimension to a logic system. Journal of Logic, Language, and Information 1(3), 203–233 (1992)
12. Gabbay, D.M., Kurucz, A., Wolter, F., Zakharyaschev, M.: Many-Dimensional Modal Logics: Theory and Applications. Studies in Logic and the Foundations of Mathematics, vol. 148, North-Holland, Amsterdam (2003)
13. Ghilardi, S.: Model theoretic methods in combined constraint satisfiability. Journal of Automated Reasoning 33(3-4), 221–249 (2004)
14. Ghilardi, S., Nicolini, E., Ranise, S., Zucchelli, D.: Combination methods for satisfiability and model-checking of infinite-state systems. In: Pfenning, F. (ed.) CADE 2007. LNCS, vol. 4603, pp. 362–378. Springer, Heidelberg (2007)

15. Ghilardi, S., Nicolini, E., Ranise, S., Zucchelli, D.: Combination methods for satisfiability and model-checking of infinite-state systems. Technical Report RI313-07, Università degli Studi di Milano (2007) Available at http://homes. dsi.unimi.it/ zucchell/publications/techreport/GhiNiRaZu-RI313-07.pdf

16. Ghilardi, S., Nicolini, E., Zucchelli, D.: A comprehensive framework for combined decision procedures. ACM Transactions on Computational Logic (to appear)

17. Hodkinson, I.M., Wolter, F., Zakharyaschev, M.: Decidable fragment of first-order temporal logics. Annals of Pure and Applied Logic 106(1–3), 85–134 (2000)

18. Kirchner, H., Ranise, S., Ringeissen, C., Tran, D.-K.: On superposition-based satisfiability procedures and their combination. In: Van Hung, D., Wirsing, M. (eds.) ICTAC 2005. LNCS, vol. 3722, pp. 594–608. Springer, Heidelberg (2005)

19. Lamport, L.: The temporal logic of actions. ACM Transactions on Programming Languages and Systems 16(3), 872–923 (1994)

20. Lassez, J.-L., Maher, M.J.: On Fourier's algorithm for linear arithmetic constraints. Journal of Automated Reasoning 9(3), 373–379 (1992)

21. Lassez, J.-L., McAloon, K.: A canonical form for generalized linear constraints. Journal of Symbolic Computation 13(1), 1–24 (1992)

22. MacLane, S., Birkhoff, G.: Algebra, 3rd edn. Chelsea Publishing, New York (USA) (1988)

23. Manna, Z., Pnueli, A.: Temporal Verification of Reactive Systems: Safety. Springer, Heidelberg (1995)

24. Merz, S.: Isabelle/TLA (1999), Available at http://isabelle.in.tum.de/ library/HOL/TLA.

25. Merz, S.: On the logic of TLA. Computing and Informatics 22, 351–379 (2003)

26. Minsky, M.L.: Recursive unsolvability of Post's problem of "tag" and other topics in the theory of Turing machines. Annals of Mathematics 74(3), 437–455 (1961)

27. Nelson, G., Oppen, D.C.: Simplification by cooperating decision procedures. ACM Transaction on Programming Languages and Systems 1(2), 245–257 (1979)

28. Nicolini, E.: Combined decision procedures for constraint satisfiability. PhD thesis, Dipartimento di Matematica, Università degli Studi di Milano (2007)

29. Plaisted, D.A.: A decision procedure for combination of propositional temporal logic and other specialized theories. Journal of Automated Reasoning 2(2), 171–190 (1986)

30. Ranise, S., Tinelli, C.: Satisfiability modulo theories. IEEE Magazine on Intelligent Systems 21(6), 71–81 (2006)

31. Tinelli, C., Harandi, M.T.: A new correctness proof of the Nelson-Oppen combination procedure. In: Proc. of FroCoS 1996, Applied Logic, pp. 103–120. Kluwer Academic Publishers, Dordrecht (1996)

Languages Modulo Normalization

Hitoshi Ohsaki[1] and Hiroyuki Seki[2]

[1] National Institute of Advanced Industrial Science and Technology
ohsaki@ni.aist.go.jp
[2] Nara Institute of Science and Technology
seki@is.naist.jp

Abstract. We propose a new class of tree automata, called *tree automata with normalization* (TAN). This framework is obtained by extending equational tree automata, and improves the results of the previous work, such as: recognized tree languages modulo the *idempotency* $f(x,x) = x$ are closed under complement, which are *not* closed in equational tree automata, besides we do not lose important decidability. In the paper, first we investigate the closure properties of this class for Boolean operations and the decidability relative to the equational tree automata. Next we consider the relationship to other automata frameworks, in particular, *hedge automata*, which is a class of unranked tree automata. Hedge automata have been recognized in the XML database community as a theoretical basis for modeling the manipulation of semi-structured data. Through the observation about transformations from hedge automata to tree automata, we discuss advantages in the expressiveness and complexity of TAN. As an application of our framework, we show an example that XML schema with constraints that can not be dealt with by other tree automata frameworks is manipulated by TAN.

Keywords: tree automata modulo axioms, equational rewriting, Boolean closedness, decidability, regularity, hedge automata and XML schema.

1 Introduction

Tree automata accept trees as word automata accept words. It is often considered that the class of tree automata inherits *by definition* the benefit from word automata that guarantees important bases for automated reasoning, including closure properties for Boolean operations and the positive decidability results. Propertywise there is no doubt in *regular* tree automata being a generalization of *regular* word automata, and in fact, several verification tools are designed based on useful properties of tree automata [9,11,12].

However, tree automata accept *irregular* words. That means, for instance, the set of trees $t_{i+1} = f(a, f(t_i, b))$ and $t_1 = f(a, b)$ is regular in the sense of tree automata, while $a^i b^i$, which are the leaves of t_i, are no longer regular in words. This is a natural consequence from the fact that trees accepted by regular tree automata are the derivation trees of context-free grammar, and thus, PUMPING LEMMA for regular tree automata, e.g. [3], can be seen as a variant of *uvwxy*-lemma for context-free grammar, where for every context-free grammar $\mathcal{G}$, there

B. Konev and F. Wolter (Eds.): FroCos 2007, LNAI 4720, pp. 221–236, 2007.

exists a natural number k such that, whenever a word z whose length $|z|$ is greater than k is generated by $\mathcal{G}$, z can be decomposed to be $uvwxy$ containing non-empty words v, x and for every $n \geqslant 0$, $uv^n wx^n y$ is generated by $\mathcal{G}$.

In the setting of equational tree automata, this becomes much more clear. We showed in [22] that the class of regular tree automata modulo associativity axioms is closely related to the class of context-free grammar. Moreover, *monotone* tree automata modulo associativity which are the super-class of regular tree automata modulo associativity are related to context-sensitive. These observations are obtained from the property that regular tree automata modulo associativity (for short, regular A-TA) are *not* closed under intersection or complement, and also from that the class of monotone tree automata modulo associativity (monotone A-TA) is *not* decidable in the emptiness, universality and inclusion problems. Furthermore, looking at the transition rules, regular rules $f(\alpha_1(x_1), \ldots, \alpha_n(x_n)) \rightarrow \beta(f(x_1, \ldots, x_n))$ in tree automata are the production rules $\beta \rightarrow \alpha_1 \cdots \alpha_n$ of context-free grammar, and monotone rules $f(\alpha_1(x_1), \ldots, \alpha_n(x_n)) \rightarrow f(\beta_1(x_1), \ldots, \beta_n(x_n))$ in tree automata are the rules $\beta_1 \cdots \beta_n \rightarrow \alpha_1 \cdots \alpha_n$ of context-sensitive grammar.

What should be then the counterpart of regular word languages in tree languages? In the paper, we introduce a new tree automata framework, called *tree automata with normalization*, that extends equational tree automata and generalizes the results of them. This class of tree automata includes regular tree automata with associativity normalization (regular TA + $\mathcal{R}_A$) that accept a candidate of the counterpart of regular word languages.

In equational tree automata, depending on the equational theory, we may lose the Boolean closedness or an important decidability result. In addition to the above-mentioned problems, it is known that regular tree automata modulo ACI theory (*associativity, commutativity and idempotency*) are not closed under complement. There is the same problem in the classes of tree automata modulo *exclusive-or* and *Abelian group* theories [29]. In the table below, we summarize the closure properties and decidability results. The class of languages accepted by *regular tree automata with associativity normalization* is closed under associativity ($=_A$), union ($\cup$), intersection ($\cap$) and complement (( )^C). The membership ($\in$?), emptiness ($=\varnothing$?), universality ($=T$?) and inclusion ($\subseteq$?) problems are decidable. In the table, the positive results are indicated by $\checkmark$, and the negative results are $-$. These results for regular TA + $\mathcal{R}_A$ and for other useful classes are the consequence of Theorems 1–5 in the following Sections 3 and 4.

		$=_A$	$\cup$	$\cap$	( )^C	$\in$?	$=\varnothing$?	$=T$?	$\subseteq$?
monotone A-TA	(CSG)	$\checkmark$	$\checkmark$	$\checkmark$	$\checkmark$	$\checkmark$	$-$	$-$	$-$
regular A-TA	(CFG)	$\checkmark$	$\checkmark$	$-$	$-$	$\checkmark$	$\checkmark$	$-$	$-$
regular TA + $\mathcal{R}_A$	(RG)	$\checkmark$	$\checkmark$	$\checkmark$	$\checkmark$	$\checkmark$	$\checkmark$	$\checkmark$	$\checkmark$

The class of the above regular TA + $\mathcal{R}_A$ is closely related to *hedge automata*. Hedge automata, originated from [27], are the automata which accepts *unranked* trees, whose transition rules have special patterns which matches regular sequence of state symbols as the arity of each function symbol is flexible. Every hedge automaton can be minimized, determinized and completely defined. Moreover, though the instances of transition rules are essentially not finite, most of the decidability questions are solvable. In Section 5, we investigate the relationship between the ranked and unranked tree automata frameworks.

As an early work of bi-directional translation between ranked and unranked tree languages, we should address the work of Carme, Niehren and Tommasi [2]. They showed that the hedges over the alphabet Σ are manipulated by a special class of regular tree automata, called *stepwise tree automata*, whose signature is constants from Σ and the binary symbol @. In our tree automata framework, their interpretation of hedges and the recognition in stepwise automata are performed by normalization and transition. We discuss the related work in Section 6, and then conclude this paper in Section 7.

2 Preliminaries

We assume the reader is familiar with term rewriting [1] and tree automata [3]. An *equational theory* is a pair $\mathcal{E} = (F, E)$ in which F is a finite set of function symbols, each with an associated *arity*, and E is a finite set of (orientation sensitive) axioms over the function symbols in F with possibly some variables from V. The binary relation $\rightarrow_{\mathcal{E}}$ induced by $\mathcal{E}$ is the rewrite relation, i.e. $s \rightarrow_{\mathcal{E}} t$ if there is an axiom $l = r$ in E, a context C and a substitution σ such that $s = C[l\sigma]$ and $t = C[r\sigma]$. The equivalence closure of $\rightarrow_{\mathcal{E}}$ is denoted by $=_{\mathcal{E}}$. Associative and commutative theory is an equational theory whose axioms are the associativity and commutativity for some of the binary function symbols. Given a binary function symbol $f \in F$, $f(f(x, y), z) = f(x, f(y, z))$ is an associativity (A) axiom, and $f(x, y) = f(y, x)$ is a commutativity (C) axiom.

An *equational rewriting system* is a pair $\mathcal{R} = (\mathcal{E}, R)$ in which R is a finite set of rewrite rules over F with V and $\mathcal{E}$ is an equational theory over the same signature F. The binary relation $\rightarrow_{\mathcal{R}}$ is a rewrite relation modulo axioms, i.e. $s \rightarrow_{\mathcal{R}} t$ if there is a rewrite rule $l \rightarrow r$ in R, a context C and a substitution σ such that $s =_{\mathcal{E}} C[l\sigma]$ and $t =_{\mathcal{E}} C[r\sigma]$. The reflexive transitive closure and the transitive closure of $\rightarrow_{\mathcal{R}}$ are denoted by $\rightarrow_{\mathcal{R}}^{*}$ and $\rightarrow_{\mathcal{R}}^{+}$, respectively. Given a term s, $s \rightarrow_{\mathcal{R}}^{!} t$ if $s \rightarrow_{\mathcal{R}}^{*} t$ and t is *some* normal form. We write $(s)\downarrow_{\mathcal{R}}^{!}$ to denote such t. For the set $\mathcal{T}(F)$ of ground terms over the signature F, $\mathrm{NF}_F(\mathcal{R})$ represents the set of normal forms of $\mathcal{R}$. An equational rewrite system $\mathcal{R}$ is weakly normalizing if for every term t, there exists some $(t)\downarrow_{\mathcal{R}}^{!}$. We say $\mathcal{R}$ (i.e. R modulo $\mathcal{E}$) is confluent / strongly normalizing if $\rightarrow_{\mathcal{R}}$ is confluent / strongly normalizing.

Given an equational theory $\mathcal{E} = (F, E)$ and an equational rewriting system $\mathcal{R} = (\mathcal{E}, R)$, the $\mathcal{E}$-*closure* of a subset L of terms, denoted by $\mathcal{E}(L)$, is the smallest set containing L closed under $=_{\mathcal{E}}$, i.e. if $s =_{\mathcal{E}} t$ and $s \in \mathcal{E}(L)$ then $t \in \mathcal{E}(L)$. The $\mathcal{R}$-*descendant closure* of L, $\mathcal{R}^{*}(L)$, is the smallest set containing L closed under $\rightarrow_{\mathcal{R}}^{*}$. Similarly, the $\mathcal{R}$-*ascendant closure* $(\mathcal{R}^{-1})^{*}(L)$ is the smallest set containing L closed under $\rightarrow^*_{\mathcal{R}^{-1}}$ and the $\mathcal{R}$-equivalence closure $(\mathcal{R} \cup \mathcal{R}^{-1})^*(L)$ is the smallest set containing L closed under $=_{\mathcal{R}}$.

A *tree automaton with normalization* (TAN) is a tuple $\mathcal{A} = (\mathcal{R}, Q, Q_{\text{fin}}, \Delta)$, consisting of the equational rewrite system $\mathcal{R} = (\mathcal{E}, R)$ with $\mathcal{E} = (F, E)$, a finite set Q of states disjoint from the symbols in F, a subset Q_{fin} of Q, and a finite set Δ of transition rules whose shapes are in the following forms:

(REGULAR)   (EPSILON)

$$f(\alpha_1(x_1), \ldots, \alpha_n(x_n)) \rightarrow \beta(f(x_1, \ldots, x_n)) \qquad \alpha(x_1) \rightarrow \beta(x_1)$$

for some $f \in F$ with $\mathsf{arity}(f) = n$ and $\alpha_1, \ldots, \alpha_n, \alpha, \beta \in Q$. Every state is a unary symbol, and variables x_i, x_j in the transition rule are different if $i \neq j$.

A *move relation* of $\mathcal{A}$ is concatenation of the two kinds of relations over $\mathcal{T}(F \cup Q)$, the normalization $\rightarrow^!_{\mathcal{R}}$ and the transition $\rightarrow_{\Delta}$ modulo $\mathcal{E}$, that means: $s \rightarrow_{\mathcal{A}} t$ if (1) there is a normal form u of s with respect to $\rightarrow_{\mathcal{R}}$ and (2) there is a transition rule $l \rightarrow r$ in Δ, a context C and a substitution σ such that $u =_{\mathcal{E}} C[l\sigma]$ and $t =_{\mathcal{E}} C[r\sigma]$. If there is no normal form $(s){\downarrow}^!_{\mathcal{R}}$, the transition fails.

A tree t is *accepted* by $\mathcal{A}$ if $t \in \mathcal{T}(F)$ and $t \rightarrow^*_{\mathcal{A}} \alpha(t')$ for some $\alpha \in Q_{\text{fin}}$ and $t' \in \mathcal{T}(F)$. The set of trees accepted by $\mathcal{A}$ is denoted by $\mathcal{L}(\mathcal{A})$. We say a TAN $\mathcal{A} = (\mathcal{R}, Q, Q_{\text{fin}}\Delta)$ with $\mathcal{R} = (F, E, R)$ is *regular* if transition rules in Δ are all in the REGULAR form. In case of $R = \varnothing$ and $E = \varnothing$, regular TAN are called regular tree automata. A tree language accepted by a regular tree automaton is called *regular*. These notions of regularity coincide with, if $R = \varnothing$ and $E = \varnothing$, the standard definition, e.g. [3]. *Leaves* of a tree t are the sequence in the left-to-right order of constants occurring in t. We denote leaf for the mapping $\mathsf{leaf}(f(t_1, \ldots, t_n)) = \mathsf{leaf}(t_1) \cdots \mathsf{leaf}(t_n)$ if $n \geqslant 1$; $\mathsf{leaf}(a) = a$, otherwise. The leaf language associated to a tree language L is the set of leaves obtained from L.

As an example, we consider the TAN $\mathcal{A}_1$ with

$R_1 \colon\ \mathsf{f}(\mathsf{h}(x), \mathsf{h}(x)) \rightarrow \mathsf{h}(x)$

$E_1 \colon\ \mathsf{f}(\mathsf{f}(x, y), z) = \mathsf{f}(x, \mathsf{f}(y, z)) \quad \mathsf{f}(x, y) = \mathsf{f}(y, x)$

$\Delta_1 \colon\ \mathsf{a} \rightarrow \alpha(\mathsf{a}) \quad \mathsf{g}(\alpha(x)) \rightarrow \alpha(\mathsf{g}(x)) \quad \mathsf{h}(\alpha(x)) \rightarrow \beta(\mathsf{h}(x))$

Let β be the final state, then $\mathsf{h}(\mathsf{g}(\mathsf{a}))$ is accepted by $\mathcal{A}_1$, since $\mathsf{h}(\mathsf{g}(\mathsf{a})) \rightarrow^!_{R_1} \mathsf{h}(\mathsf{g}(\mathsf{a}))$ and $\mathsf{h}(\mathsf{g}(\mathsf{a})) \rightarrow_{\Delta_1} \mathsf{h}(\mathsf{g}(\alpha(\mathsf{a})))$, and it turns out that $\mathsf{h}(\mathsf{g}(\mathsf{a})) \rightarrow^*_{\mathcal{A}_1} \beta(\mathsf{h}(\mathsf{g}(\mathsf{a})))$.

Regarding the language accepted by this example, we observe that

> if a tree t consists of nodes f with the same tree $\mathsf{h}(\mathsf{g}^i(\mathsf{a}))$ at each leaf position ($i \geqslant 0$), t is accepted by $\mathcal{A}_1$,

because for every such tree t, $t \rightarrow^!_{R_1} \mathsf{h}(\mathsf{g}^i(\mathsf{a}))$, and then $\mathsf{h}(\mathsf{g}^i(\mathsf{a})) \rightarrow^*_{\mathcal{A}_1} \beta(\mathsf{h}(\mathsf{g}^i(\mathsf{a})))$. For instance, $\mathsf{f}(\mathsf{h}(\mathsf{g}(\mathsf{a})), \mathsf{h}(\mathsf{g}(\mathsf{a}))) \rightarrow^!_{\mathcal{R}_1} \mathsf{h}(\mathsf{g}(\mathsf{a}))$, and thus $\mathsf{h}(\mathsf{g}(\mathsf{a})) \rightarrow^*_{\mathcal{A}_1} \beta(\mathsf{h}(\mathsf{g}(\mathsf{a})))$ from the above example.

In the next example, we compare the expressiveness between TAN and ETA. ETA (equational tree automata [23]) are the special class of TAN whose set R of rewrite rules is empty. We take the TAN $\mathcal{A}_2$ with the following components:

R_2: $f(h(x), h(x)) \to h(x)$

E_2: $f(f(x, y), z) = f(x, f(y, z))$ $f(x, y) = f(y, x)$

Δ_2: $a \to \alpha(a)$ $g(\alpha(x)) \to \alpha(g(x))$ $h(\alpha(x)) \to \beta(h(x))$

$\quad f(\beta(x), \beta(y)) \to \gamma(f(x, y))$

In this example, $\mathcal{A}_2$ has the the additional transition rule $f(\beta(x), \beta(y)) \to \gamma(f(x, y))$ with the final state γ. Similar to the previous example, we observe that

---

> if a tree t consists of nodes f with two different kinds of trees $h(g^i(a))$ and $h(g^j(a))$ at its leaf position $(i \neq j)$, t is accepted by $\mathcal{A}_2$.

For instance, $f(h(a), f(h(g(a)), h(a)))$ is accepted: $f(h(a), f(h(g(a)), h(a))) \to^!_{R_2} f(h(a), h(g(a)))$, and therefore $f(h(a), f(h(g(a)), h(a))) \to^*_{\mathcal{A}_2} \gamma(f(h(a), h(g(a))))$. However, $f(h(a), h(a))$ is not accepted by $\mathcal{A}_2$, because $f(h(a), h(a)) \to^!_{R_2} h(a)$ and $h(a) \to^*_{\mathcal{A}_2} \beta(h(a))$. In fact, $f(h(a), h(a)) \to^*_{\mathcal{A}_2} \beta(h(a))$.

Remark 1. The previous language $\mathcal{L}(\mathcal{A}_2)$ can not be represented by ETA if $E = \{ f(h(x), h(x)) = h(x),\ f(f(x, y), z) = f(x, f(y, z)),\ f(x, y) = f(y, x) \}$.

Furthermore, the language $\mathcal{L}(\mathcal{A}_2)$ is not accepted by multitree automata [14] or two-way equational tree automata [28] either.

3 Relative Decidability

We begin with the membership problem for the class of TAN. Hereafter in the following two sections, we suppose $\mathcal{E} = (F, E)$ and $\mathcal{R} = (\mathcal{E}, R)$.

Theorem 1. *The membership question for a TAN $\mathcal{A}$ is solvable if $\mathcal{R}$ is strongly normalizing over $T(F)$ and the membership question for an equational tree automaton $\mathcal{A}'$ is solvable, where $\mathcal{A}'$ is defined by replacing R in $\mathcal{A}$ with $\varnothing$.*   □

In the framework of TAN, the decidability result depends upon that of the corresponding equational tree automata, because $(\to^!_{\mathcal{R}} \cdot \to_{\mathcal{A}'})^+ \subseteq \to^!_{\mathcal{R}} \cdot \to^+_{\mathcal{A}'}$. To be precise, we state the following lemma.

Lemma 1. *Given $\mathcal{A} = (\mathcal{R}, Q, Q_{\text{fin}}, \Delta)$, let $\mathcal{A}' = (\mathcal{R}', Q, Q_{\text{fin}}, \Delta)$ and $\mathcal{R}' = (\mathcal{E}, \varnothing)$. Then for every $t \in T(F)$, if $t \to^+_{\mathcal{A}} t'$, there exists a normal form $(t){\downarrow}^!_{\mathcal{R}}$ such that $(t){\downarrow}^!_{\mathcal{R}} \to^*_{\mathcal{A}'} t'$.*   □

Accordingly, the question if $t \in \mathcal{L}(\mathcal{A})$ is determined by testing $(t){\downarrow}^!_{\mathcal{R}} \in \mathcal{L}(\mathcal{A}')$ for all $(t){\downarrow}^!_{\mathcal{R}}$. From König's Lemma, when $\mathcal{R}$ is strongly normalizing, there are only finitely many candidates for $(t){\downarrow}^!_{\mathcal{R}}$. In fact, in Theorem 1, strong normalization can not be weakened to weak normalization (Appendix A.2 [20]).

Every language accepted by a TAN $\mathcal{A} = (\mathcal{R}, Q, Q_{\text{fin}}, \Delta)$ is the $\mathcal{R}$-ascendant closure of some subset of normal forms: Let $\mathcal{A}' = ((\mathcal{E}, \varnothing), Q, Q_{\text{fin}}, \Delta)$,

(i) $\mathcal{L}(\mathcal{A}) = (\mathcal{R}^{-1})^*(\text{NF}_F(\mathcal{R}) \cap \mathcal{L}(\mathcal{A}'))$.

Moreover,

(ii) $\mathcal{E}(\mathcal{L}(\mathcal{A})) = \mathcal{L}(\mathcal{A})$,

(iii) $(\mathcal{R} \cup \mathcal{R}^{-1})^*(\mathcal{L}(\mathcal{A})) = \mathcal{R}^*(\mathcal{L}(\mathcal{A})) = \mathcal{L}(\mathcal{A})$ if $\mathcal{R}$ is confluent.

For instance, we consider the TAN $\mathcal{A}_1$ with

R: $\mathsf{f}(\mathsf{h}(x), \mathsf{h}(x)) \to \mathsf{h}(x)$

E: $\mathsf{f}(\mathsf{f}(x, y), z) = \mathsf{f}(x, \mathsf{f}(y, z))$ $\mathsf{f}(x, y) = \mathsf{f}(y, x)$

Δ: $\mathsf{a} \to \alpha(\mathsf{a})$ $\mathsf{g}(\alpha(x)) \to \alpha(\mathsf{g}(x))$ $\mathsf{h}(\alpha(x)) \to \beta(\mathsf{h}(x))$

We have $\mathcal{L}(\mathcal{A}_1) = (\mathcal{R}^{-1})^*(\mathcal{L}(\mathcal{A}_1'))$. This follows from Property (i) and $\text{NF}_F(\mathcal{R}) \cap \mathcal{L}(\mathcal{A}_1') = \mathcal{L}(\mathcal{A}_1')$. Furthermore, $(\mathcal{R} \cup \mathcal{R}^{-1})^*(\mathcal{L}(\mathcal{A}_1')) = \mathcal{L}(\mathcal{A}_1)$, because $\mathcal{L}(\mathcal{A}_1') \subseteq \mathcal{L}(\mathcal{A}_1)$ from $\mathcal{L}(\mathcal{A}_1) = (\mathcal{R}^{-1})^*(\mathcal{L}(\mathcal{A}_1'))$. Since $\mathcal{R}$ is confluent, $(\mathcal{R} \cup \mathcal{R}^{-1})^*(\mathcal{L}(\mathcal{A}_1)) = \mathcal{L}(\mathcal{A}_1)$ from Property (iii). Therefore, $(\mathcal{R}^{-1})^*(\mathcal{L}(\mathcal{A}_1')) \subseteq (\mathcal{R} \cup \mathcal{R}^{-1})^*(\mathcal{L}(\mathcal{A}_1')) \subseteq (\mathcal{R} \cup \mathcal{R}^{-1})^*(\mathcal{L}(\mathcal{A}_1))$.

Theorem 2. *The emptiness problem is decidable for tree automata with normalization if*

(1) there effectively exists an equational tree automaton (with the same equational theory) which accepts the set of normal forms of $\mathcal{R}$,

(2) this class of equational tree automata is closed under the intersection.

Proof. Let $\mathcal{A}_R = ((\mathcal{E}, R), P, P_{\text{fin}}, \Delta)$ and $\mathcal{A}_\varnothing = ((\mathcal{E}, \varnothing), P, P_{\text{fin}}, \Delta)$. The ETA $\mathcal{A}_\varnothing$ is obtained from the TAN $\mathcal{A}_R$ by replacing R with $\varnothing$. From the assumption (1), we obtain an ETA $\mathcal{B}$, equipped with the same theory $\mathcal{E} = (F, E)$, that accepts $\text{NF}_F(\mathcal{R})$. This implies from Property (i) that

$$\mathcal{L}(\mathcal{A}_R) = \varnothing \;\Leftrightarrow\; \mathcal{L}(\mathcal{A}_\varnothing) \cap \mathcal{L}(\mathcal{B}) = \varnothing.$$

From the assumption (2), we have an ETA $\mathcal{C} = ((F, E, \varnothing), Q, Q_{\text{fin}}, \Lambda)$ that accepts $\mathcal{L}(\mathcal{A}_\varnothing) \cap \mathcal{L}(\mathcal{B})$. Let $\mathcal{C}' = ((F, \varnothing, \varnothing), Q, Q_{\text{fin}}, \Lambda)$. Thanks to Lemma 1 [28], $\mathcal{L}(\mathcal{C})$ is the $\mathcal{E}$-closure of $\mathcal{L}(\mathcal{C}')$ regardless of E. (Cf. Lemma 2 [23].) This implies that $\mathcal{L}(\mathcal{A}_R) = \varnothing \;\Leftrightarrow\; \mathcal{L}(\mathcal{C}') = \varnothing$. By assumption, since $\mathcal{C}'$ is a regular tree automaton, the question if $\mathcal{L}(\mathcal{C}') = \varnothing$ can be solved.   □

The first equivalence in the above proof is rephrased as follows: $\mathcal{L}(\mathcal{A}_R) \neq \varnothing$ if and only if $\mathcal{L}(\mathcal{A}_\varnothing) \cap \text{NF}_F(\mathcal{R}) \neq \varnothing$. If $E = \varnothing$, checking $\mathcal{L}(\mathcal{A}_\varnothing) \cap \text{NF}_F(\mathcal{R}) \neq \varnothing$ is known to be an EXPTIME-complete problem, regardless of R [4].

Corollary 1. *If $E = \varnothing$, the conditions (1) and (2) can be omitted.*   □

Theorem 3. *The inclusion problem is decidable for tree automata with normalization if the conditions (1),(2) hold and the inclusion problem is decidable for this class of equational tree automata.* □

It is known that, if $\mathcal{E}$ is AC theory for a binary symbol f, the inclusion problem for ETA is decidable. Even if $\mathcal{E}$ also contains the axioms of $f(x,0) = x$ and/or $g(f(x,y)) = f(g(x),g(y))$, the inclusion problem is decidable.

Let $\mathcal{B}$ and $\mathcal{D}$ be ETA equipped with the equational theory $\mathcal{E}$, such that $\mathcal{B}$ accepts $\mathrm{NF}_F(\mathcal{R})$ and $\mathcal{D}$ accepts trees which are not normalizable. The universality question if $\mathcal{L}(\mathcal{A}_R) = \mathcal{T}(F)$ is equivalent to ask if $\mathcal{L}(\mathcal{B}) \subseteq \mathcal{L}(\mathcal{A}_\varnothing)$ and $\mathcal{L}(\mathcal{D}) = \varnothing$:

Theorem 4. *The universality is decidable for tree automata with normalization if the conditions (1),(3) hold and the inclusion problem is decidable for this class of equational tree automata:*

(3) there effectively exists an equational tree automaton (with the same equational theory) which accepts the set of non-normalizable trees. □

Corollary 2. *If $\mathcal{R}$ is weakly normalizing, the condition (3) can be omitted.* □

4   Closedness Under Boolean Operations

Theorem 5. *For every equational rewrite system $\mathcal{R} = (\mathcal{E}, R)$, the class of tree automata with $\mathcal{R}$-normalization is closed under Boolean operations if $\mathcal{R}$ is weakly normalizing and confluent over $\mathcal{T}(F)$ and the class of equational tree automata equipped with $\mathcal{E}$ is closed under Boolean operations.* □

In the above theorem, weak normalization is essential for closure under complement. Let us consider the rewrite system $\mathcal{R}_1 = ((\{\,a,\,b\,\}, \varnothing), \{\,a \to a\,\})$. Because a is not normalized, by definition, a is not accepted by any TAN with $\mathcal{R}_1$. The language accepted by $\mathcal{A}_1 = (\mathcal{R}_1, \{\,\alpha\,\}, \{\,\alpha\,\}, \{\,b \to \alpha(b)\,\})$ is $\{\,b\,\}$, but then the complement of $\mathcal{L}(\mathcal{A}_1)$ is not accepted by any TAN with $\mathcal{R}_1$.

Also, confluence is essential for closure under complement and intersection. We consider the TAN $\mathcal{A}_2 = (\mathcal{R}_2, \{\,\alpha\,\}, \{\,\alpha\,\}, \{\,b \to \alpha(b)\,\})$ with the rewrite system $\mathcal{R}_2 = ((\{\,a,\,b,\,c\,\}, \varnothing), \{\,a \to b,\,a \to c\,\})$. Because a is normalized to b, a is accepted by $\mathcal{A}_2$ as b is accepted. Every TAN with $\mathcal{R}_2$ accepting c accepts a, because $a \to^!_{\mathcal{R}_2} c$. This implies that the complement of $\mathcal{L}(\mathcal{A}_2)$ is not accepted by any TAN with $\mathcal{R}_2$. For confluence, we take $\mathcal{A}_3 = (\mathcal{R}_2, \{\,\alpha\,\}, \{\,\alpha\,\}, \{\,c \to \alpha(c)\,\})$. The intersection of the two languages $\mathcal{L}(\mathcal{A}_2)$ and $\mathcal{L}(\mathcal{A}_3)$, which is $\{\,a,\,b\,\} \cap \{\,a,\,c\,\}$, is not accepted by any TAN with $\mathcal{R}_2$, because every TAN with $\mathcal{R}_2$ accepting a accepts b or c.

However, weak normalization is not needed for closure under intersection. Moreover, weak normalization and confluence are not required for the union.

Example 1. Let $\mathcal{E}_{\mathsf{AC}} = (F, E_{\mathsf{AC}})$ whose second component E_{AC} is the set of AC axioms for f. For each $R \in \{\,R_\mathsf{U},\,R_\mathsf{I},\,R_\mathsf{N},\,R_\mathsf{D},\,R_\mathsf{UI},\,R_\mathsf{UN},\,R_\mathsf{UD},\,R_\mathsf{G}\,\}$ defined below, $(\mathcal{E}, R)$ is strongly normalizing and confluent over $\mathcal{T}(F)$:

R_U: $f(x,0) \rightarrow x$ R_{UI}: $R_U \cup R_I$ R_{UN}: $R_U \cup R_N$ R_{UD}: $R_U \cup R_D$

R_I: $f(x,x) \rightarrow x$

R_N: $f(x,x) \rightarrow 0$

R_D: $g(f(x,y)) \rightarrow f(g(x),g(y))$ $g(0) \rightarrow 0$ $g(g(x)) \rightarrow x$

R_G: $R_{UD} \cup \{\, f(x,g(x)) \rightarrow 0 \,\}$ (ABELIAN GROUP)

The above claim can be easily justified. Tool support, e.g. that of C*i*ME [5], is helpful in proving strongly normalization and checking all AC critical pairs to be joinable. Thus, from Theorem 5, the above observation yields that: for every $R \in \{\, R_U, R_I, R_N, R_D, R_{UI}, R_{UN}, R_{UD}, R_G \,\}$, the class of TAN with $(\mathcal{E}_{AC}, R)$ is closed under Boolean operations. Moreover, from Theorem 1, the membership problem is decidable for this class of TAN.

Remark 2. ETA with ACUI (resp. ACUN) axioms are *not* closed under complement. This is the same reason why two-way equational automata with ACUI (resp. ACUN) are *not* closed under complement [29]. Moreover, we can show that ETA with ACI (resp. ACN) axioms are also *not* closed under complement. In contrast, there is no such problem in TAN if we take R_I and R_N for I and N.

It is not obvious for ETA how we can deal with Boolean operations in the ACD or ACUD case. Though it is shown in [29] that the class of tree languages modulo ACUD is closed under Boolean operations, the computation algorithm is quite involved. In case of TAN, Boolean computation for TAN with $(\mathcal{E}_{AC}, R_{UD})$ can be manipulated by using the operations for AC tree automata. Furthermore,

Corollary 3. *The emptiness, universality and inclusion problems are decidable for TAN with R_U, R_D or R_{UD} modulo $\mathcal{E}_{AC}$.* $\square$

Because these problems are decidable for the class of AC tree automata, the above corollary follows from the fact that we can define AC tree automata, each of which accepts normal forms of R_U, R_D, R_{UD} modulo $\mathcal{E}_{AC}$. For instance, we consider $(\mathcal{E}_{AC}, R_U)$. Since R_U is left-linear, we have the tree automaton $\mathcal{A}_U = ((F, \varnothing, \varnothing), Q, Q_{fin}, \Delta_U)$ that accepts $\mathrm{NF}_F((F, \varnothing, R_U))$. Normal forms of $(\mathcal{E}_{AC}, R_U)$ are the $\mathcal{E}_{AC}$-closure of $\mathcal{L}(\mathcal{A}_U)$, which is accepted by $((F, \mathcal{E}_{AC}, \varnothing), Q, Q_{fin}, \Delta_U)$. Similarly, AC tree automata for $(\mathcal{E}_{AC}, R_D)$ and $(\mathcal{E}_{AC}, R_{UD})$ can be obtained.

However, it is unclear whether the emptiness problem is decidable for TAN with $(\mathcal{E}_{AC}, R)$ if R is R_I, R_N, R_{UI}, R_{UN} or R_G, because it is not known that the question if, given an AC tree automaton $\mathcal{A}$ and an AC rewrite system $\mathcal{R}$, $\mathcal{L}(\mathcal{A}) \cap \mathrm{NF}_F(\mathcal{R}) = \varnothing$ can be solved. According to the proof of Theorem 2, the decidability of the emptiness problem in the above cases is rephrased as follows.

Corollary 4. *The emptiness problem is decidable for TAN with R_I (resp. R_N) modulo $\mathcal{E}_{AC}$ if and only if the following question is decidable: given a tree automaton, does its language contain an instance of $f(x, x)$ modulo $\mathcal{E}_{AC}$?* $\square$

5   Regular Leaf Languages and Hedge Automata

When discussing the expressiveness of tree languages, we often take the images of them into word languages. Given a signature F, the mapping from trees to right-associative trees but whose leaves can be preserved is the rewrite system $\mathcal{R}_{\text{reg}}$ that consists of the rewrite rules, for arbitrary function symbols f, g in F,

$$f(x_1, \ldots, g(y_1, y_2, \ldots, y_k), x_i, \ldots, x_n) \to f(x_1, \ldots, y_1, g(y_2, \ldots, y_k, x_i), \ldots, x_n)$$

such that $\text{arity}(f) \geqslant 2$ and $\text{arity}(g) \geqslant 1$. Here f and g are possibly the same. Obviously, $\mathcal{R}_{\text{reg}}$ is strongly normalizing if $E = \varnothing$, but $\mathcal{R}_{\text{reg}}$ is *not* confluent, because $f(g(h(a, b), c), d) \to^!_{\mathcal{R}_{\text{reg}}} f(a, h(b, g(c, d)))$ and $f(g(h(a, b), c), d) \to^!_{\mathcal{R}_{\text{reg}}} f(a, g(b, h(c, d)))$.

The above rewrite system preserves the leaves when $E = \varnothing$:

Lemma 2. *For every s, t in $\mathcal{T}(F)$, $s =_{\mathcal{R}_{\text{reg}}} t$ if and only if* $\text{leaf}(s) = \text{leaf}(t)$. □

Trees in $\mathcal{R}_{\text{reg}}$-normal form, if $E = \varnothing$, are *right*-associative as derivation trees of regular word grammar are right-associative. For instance, when the grammar has the production rules $\alpha \to a\beta$, $\beta \to b\gamma$, $\gamma \to c$, we have $\alpha(a \circ \beta(b \circ \gamma(c)))$ for the derivation starting from α. The word abc is the leaves of this derivation tree. Meanwhile, in tree automata setting, the word abc can be represented to be $a \cdot (b \cdot c)$. Tree automaton accepting $a \cdot (b \cdot c)$ is equipped with the transition rules $a \to p_a(a)$, $p_a(x) \cdot \beta(y) \to \alpha(x \cdot y)$, $b \to p_b(b)$, $p_b(x) \cdot \gamma(y) \to \beta(x \cdot y)$, $c \to \gamma(c)$. Here we use the infix operators $\circ$ and $\cdot$ for denoting the branching node of derivations and the concatenation of alphabet.

Accordingly, trees which have such *regular* leaves should contain constants that appear on the left in a tree whenever non-constant trees appear at the same level in the tree. If $\mathcal{A}$ is a tree automaton, the leaf language $\{\, \text{leaf}(t) \mid (t)\downarrow^!_{\mathcal{R}_{\text{reg}}}$ accepted by $\mathcal{A}\,\}$ is regular, while $\{\, \text{leaf}(t) \mid t$ accepted by $\mathcal{A}\,\}$ is context-free. Since trees accepted by tree automata are derivation trees generated by context-free grammar, this observation can be easily obtained. But what about a tree automaton accepting $\{\, t \mid \text{leaf}(t)$ generated by $\mathcal{G}\,\}$?

Lemma 3. *Given a regular grammar $\mathcal{G} = (\Sigma, \mathcal{S}, s_0, \Lambda)$, we can construct a regular tree automaton $\mathcal{A}$ which accepts all trees whose leaves are generated by $\mathcal{G}$.* □

Corollary 5. *The above lemma can be extended to the case of an arbitrary signature F if F contains constants from Σ and a binary function symbol.* □

Of particular interest about Lemma 3 is that this property does not hold for context-free grammar. The proof of this observation is found in [20].

Lemma 4. *For every regular tree automaton $\mathcal{A}$, $\{\, t \mid (t)\downarrow^!_{\mathcal{R}_{\text{reg}}}$ accepted by $\mathcal{A}\,\}$ is a regular tree language.* □

Hence, the class of tree automata, each of which accepts all trees whose leaves is generated by a regular grammar, is a proper sub-class of regular tree automata. In the framework of TAN, this statement can be represented as follows.

Theorem 6. *The class of TAN with $\mathcal{R}_{\mathrm{reg}}$ is a sub-class of regular tree automata. Moreover, for every confluent sub-system $\mathcal{R}$ of $\mathcal{R}_{\mathrm{reg}}$, the class of TAN with $\mathcal{R}$ is also a sub-class of regular tree automata, and is*
  – *decidable in the membership, emptiness, universality and inclusion problems,*
  – *closed under $=_{\mathcal{R}}$,*
  – *closed under Boolean operations.*   □

An associativity rewrite system $\mathcal{R}_{\mathrm{A}}$, whose rewrite rules are $f(f(x,y),z) \to f(x, f(y,z))$ for some of the binary function symbols, is such an example of confluent sub-systems. Note that $\mathcal{R}_{\mathrm{A}}$ is a special case of $\mathcal{R}_{\mathrm{reg}}$. This class of rewrite systems is often used for modeling *unranked* tree automata by ranked signature.

In case of *unranked* signature, trees with regular leaves are manipulated by *hedge automata*. The hedge automata theory has been accepted in XML community [19], in which XML documents are considered as tree-structured objects, called *hedges*. Hence, as if an XML schema matches documents, a hedge automaton accepts the set of hedges. Hedges in $\mathrm{HDG}(\Sigma, C)$ over a finite set Σ of *label* symbols and a finite set C of *constants* are recursively defined as follows:

$$t \in \mathrm{HDG}(\Sigma, C) \quad \text{if } t = c \qquad \text{for some } c \in C$$
$$\text{if } t = a\langle w \rangle \quad \text{for some } a \in \Sigma,\ w \in \mathrm{HDGS}(\Sigma, C)$$

$$w \in \mathrm{HDGS}(\Sigma, C) \quad \text{if } w = \epsilon \qquad \text{(null hedge)}$$
$$\text{if } w = t \qquad \text{for some } t \in \mathrm{HDG}(\Sigma, C)$$
$$\text{if } w = u \circ v \quad \text{for some } u, v \in \mathrm{HDGS}(\Sigma, C)$$

The infix operator $\circ$ over hedges is associative over hedges with the identity axiom for ϵ. In the unranked setting, $t_1 \circ \cdots \circ t_n$ can be denoted as $\circ(t_1, \ldots, t_n)$, and it satisfies that $\circ(t_1, \ldots, t_i, \epsilon, t_{i+1}, \ldots, t_n) = \circ(t_1, \ldots, t_i, t_{i+1}, \ldots, t_n)$.

One should remark on hedges defined above. In the literature, e.g. [18] the null hedge ϵ and the sequence of hedges are defined as well-formed hedges. However, this leads us to confusion in distinguishing *elements* from *contents* in the context of XML. According to XML schema recommended by W3C [30], an *empty-element tag*, that corresponds to some c in C, is an element but is not the empty sequence of elements. On the other hand, an element (tagged a) with no content means the element having the empty sequence in between *start-tag* and *end-tag*, that corresponds $a\langle\ \rangle$.

A hedge automaton is a tuple $\mathcal{H} = (\Sigma, C, N, N_{\mathrm{fin}}, \Delta)$, in which N is a finite set of unary state symbols disjoint from Σ and C, N_{fin} is a set of final states with $N_{\mathrm{fin}} \subseteq N$, and Δ is a set of transition rules for Σ and C. Transition rules in Δ are in the two shapes of

$$c \to \beta(c)$$
$$a\langle \alpha_1(x_1) \circ \cdots \circ \alpha_n(x_n) \rangle \to \beta(a\langle x_1 \circ \cdots \circ x_n \rangle) \Leftarrow \alpha_1 \cdots \alpha_n \in \mathcal{L}(\mathcal{G})$$

with $a \in \Sigma$, $x_1, \ldots, x_n \in V$ and $\alpha_1, \ldots, \alpha_n, \beta \in N$.

The grammar $\mathcal{G}$ over N, that appears in the second type of rules, must be regular, but that can be different for each transition rule. The left-arrow ($\Leftarrow$)

together with the membership condition represents the guard, meaning that, if the sequence $\alpha_1 \cdots \alpha_n$ of states is generated by $\mathcal{G}$, the transition fires. Variables $x_1, \ldots, x_n$ in a rule are instantiated to certain hedges when the rule is applied. Formally, we should introduce *sequence variables* ([13]) for the second type of rules, so the left-hand side can match an arbitrary sequence $\alpha_1(x_1) \circ \cdots \circ \alpha_n(x_n)$. This implies in the sense of tree automata, that we allow hedge automata to contain in Δ infinite number of regular transition rules in special shapes.

In tree automata framework, hedges can be modeled over the signature

$$F_{\Sigma,C}: \{a \mid a \in \Sigma\} \quad \text{arity}(a) = 1 \text{ for each } a, \quad \{\circ\} \quad \text{arity}(\circ) = 2,$$
$$\{c \mid c \in C\} \quad \text{arity}(c) = 0 \text{ for each } c, \quad \{\epsilon\} \quad \text{arity}(\epsilon) = 0.$$

Hereafter, to discuss the translation from unranked to ranked signatures, we define the *unflattening* operation:

$$\text{unflat}(t) = \begin{cases} a(\text{unflat}(t_1) \circ \cdots (\text{unflat}(t_n) \circ \text{unflat}(t_{n+1})) \cdots) \\ \qquad \text{if } t = a\langle t_1 \cdots t_n\, t_{n+1}\rangle \text{ with } n \geqslant 0, \\ a(\epsilon) \qquad \text{if } t = a\langle\,\rangle, \\ t \qquad\quad \text{if } t \in C. \end{cases}$$

Moreover, we use flat for the reverse translation, e.g. $\text{flat}(f((a \circ b) \circ g(c))) = f\langle a \circ b \circ g\langle c\rangle\rangle$.

Proposition 1. *For every hedge automaton $\mathcal{H}$ over Σ and C, we can construct a tree automaton $\mathcal{A}_\mathcal{H}$ over the previous $F_{\Sigma,C}$ such that for every $t \in \text{HDG}(\Sigma, C)$, t is accepted by $\mathcal{H}$ if and only if $\text{unflat}(t)$ is accepted by $\mathcal{A}_\mathcal{H}$.* □

In the above setting, $f(a \circ (b \circ c))$ and $f((a \circ b) \circ c)$ are distinguished, because we *do not* assume that $(x \circ y) \circ z = x \circ (y \circ z)$ is given. However, due to Lemma 4, we can generalize Proposition 1 as follows.

Corollary 6. *For every hedge automaton $\mathcal{H}$ over Σ and C, we can construct a tree automaton $\mathcal{B}_\mathcal{H}$ over the previous $F_{\Sigma,C}$ such that for every $t \in T(F_{\Sigma,C})$, $\text{flat}(t)$ is accepted by $\mathcal{H}$ if and only if t is accepted by $\mathcal{B}_\mathcal{H}$.* □

One should notice that $\mathcal{L}(\mathcal{A}_\mathcal{H}) \subseteq \mathcal{L}(\mathcal{B}_\mathcal{H})$. The sizes $|\mathcal{A}_\mathcal{H}|$ and $|\mathcal{B}_\mathcal{H}|$ are $O(|\mathcal{H}|)$ and $O(|\mathcal{H}|^3)$, respectively. The time complexities are linear for the construction of $\mathcal{A}_\mathcal{H}$, and cubic for $\mathcal{B}_\mathcal{H}$ to the size of $\mathcal{H}$. In Corollary 6, we can take the TAN $\mathcal{A}_\mathcal{H}$ with $\mathcal{R}_A$, instead of $\mathcal{B}_\mathcal{H}$. In this case, Proposition 1 is generalized without losing the advantages of the size and time complexities. Detailed complexity analysis is found in [20].

As an application for XML manipulation, we consider the simple example (Fig. 1) that contains the hedge automaton $\mathcal{H}_{\text{in}}$, whose final state is γ. The language accepted by $\mathcal{H}_{\text{in}}$ consists of the hedges $f\langle g\langle a^*\rangle g\langle b^*\rangle\rangle$. Here $\circ$ is omitted, and a^* (b^*) denotes an arbitrary sequence of a (resp. b). In the example, we suppose that a and b are the elements with different types, and f and g are the tags, such that g contains a or b only. According to Lemma 4, we can construct tree automata $\mathcal{A}_{\mathcal{H}_{\text{in}}}$ over $F_{\Sigma,C}$, which corresponds to $\mathcal{H}_{\text{in}}$.

$$\mathcal{H}_{in}: \qquad f\langle \gamma(x) \circ \delta(y) \rangle \;\rightarrow\; \theta(f\langle x \circ y \rangle)$$

$$g\langle \alpha(z_1) \circ \cdots \circ \alpha(z_m) \rangle \;\rightarrow\; \gamma(g\langle z_1 \circ \cdots \circ z_m \rangle)$$

$$g\langle \beta(w_1) \circ \cdots \circ \beta(w_n) \rangle \;\rightarrow\; \delta(g\langle w_1 \circ \cdots \circ w_n \rangle)$$

$$a \;\rightarrow\; \alpha(a)$$

$$b \;\rightarrow\; \beta(b)$$

Fig. 1. Example of hedge automaton

Now we consider the constraint $\Psi_\leqslant$ for hedges, such that $\Psi_\leqslant(t)$ holds if $t = f\langle g\langle a^* \rangle g\langle b^* \rangle \rangle$ and the number of occurrences of a is less than or equals to the number of b. For instance, $\Psi_\leqslant(f\langle g\langle aa \rangle g\langle bbb \rangle \rangle)$ is true.

In tree automata framework, the above predicate $\Psi_\leqslant$ can be translated to the TAN $\mathcal{A}_\leqslant = (\mathcal{R}, Q, Q_{fin}, \Delta_\leqslant)$ with $\mathcal{R}_\leqslant = (F_{\Sigma,C}, \varnothing, R_\leqslant)$ as follows.

$\Delta_\leqslant:$ $f(\eta(x)) \rightarrow \theta(f(x))$ $\gamma(x) \circ \delta(y) \rightarrow \eta(x \circ y)$

$\qquad g(\alpha(x)) \rightarrow \gamma(g(x))$ $\epsilon \rightarrow \alpha(\epsilon)$

$\qquad g(\beta(x)) \rightarrow \delta(g(x))$ $\epsilon \rightarrow \beta(\epsilon)$ $b \rightarrow \beta(b)$ $\beta(x) \circ \beta(y) \rightarrow \beta(x \circ y)$

$Q:$ $\alpha \quad \beta \quad \gamma \quad \delta \quad \eta \quad \theta$

$Q_{fin}:$ θ

$R_\leqslant:$ $f(g(a \circ x) \circ g(b \circ y)) \rightarrow f(g(x) \circ g(y))$ $f(g(a) \circ g(b)) \rightarrow f(g(\epsilon) \circ g(\epsilon))$

$\qquad f(g(a \circ x) \circ g(b)) \rightarrow f(g(x) \circ g(\epsilon))$ $f(g(a) \circ g(b \circ y)) \rightarrow f(g(\epsilon) \circ g(y))$

$\qquad (x \circ y) \circ z \rightarrow x \circ (y \circ z)$ $\epsilon \circ x \rightarrow x$ $x \circ \epsilon \rightarrow x$

Lemma 5. $\mathcal{A}_\leqslant$ *with* $\mathcal{R}_\leqslant$ *accepts* t *if and only if* $\mathsf{flat}(t)$ *satisfies* $\Psi_\leqslant$. $\qquad\qquad \square$

Using a similar construction, we can define the TAN $\mathcal{A}_<$, $\mathcal{A}_\geqslant$, $\mathcal{A}_>$ for the constraints $\Psi_<$ (less than), $\Psi_\geqslant$ (greater than or equals to) and $\Psi_>$ (greater than).

Remark 3. The languages $\mathcal{L}(\mathcal{A}_\leqslant)$, $\mathcal{L}(\mathcal{A}_<)$, $\mathcal{L}(\mathcal{A}_\geqslant)$, $\mathcal{L}(\mathcal{A}_>)$ are not regular.

Furthermore, the class of TAN with the above $\mathcal{R}_\leqslant$ is closed under Boolean operations and the membership problem is decidable, because $\mathcal{R}_\leqslant$ is strongly normalizing and confluent as there are 9 critical pairs and they are all joinable. Besides, the emptiness, universality and inclusion problems are decidable, since $R_\leqslant$ is left-linear and $E = \varnothing$. Similar properties hold also for $\mathcal{R}_<$, $\mathcal{R}_\geqslant$ and $\mathcal{R}_>$.

6   Related Work

Recently, Dal Zilio and Lugiez [6] and Seidl *et al.* [25] proposed the extension of hedge automata in which a commutative infix operator over hedges is allowed.

We denote below this operator by $\otimes$. The concatenation of hedges by $\otimes$ is represented as $t_1 \otimes \cdots \otimes t_n$ in [6], and as the multiset $\{t_1, \ldots, t_n\}$ in [25]. Due to this extension, their frameworks require the additional sort of transition rules

$$a\langle \alpha_1(x_1) \otimes \cdots \otimes \alpha_n(x_n) \rangle \rightarrow \beta(a\langle x_1 \otimes \cdots \otimes x_n \rangle) \Leftarrow \alpha_1 \cdots \alpha_n \in \mathcal{L}(\mathcal{G}/\mathsf{C})$$

A *commutative regular grammar* $\mathcal{G}/\mathsf{C}$, which appear in the guard, is a regular grammar modulo the commutativity. The language generated by $\mathcal{G}/\mathsf{C}$ coincides with the commutative closure of $\mathcal{L}(\mathcal{G})$, meaning that: $u \in \mathcal{L}(\mathcal{G}/\mathsf{C})$ if and only if $u =_\mathsf{C} v$ and $v \in \mathcal{L}(\mathcal{G})$. Moreover, the Parikh image [24] of regular languages is characterized by Presburger arithmetic. Using this fact, Dal Zilio and Lugiez defined a query language for XML, called *sheaves logic*, in which the formulas may contain Presburger constraints over the number of occurrences of contents in XML documents.

In case of ranked signature, this extension to hedge automata can be simulated by assuming the associativity $(x \otimes y) \otimes z = x \otimes (y \otimes z)$ and commutativity $x \otimes y = y \otimes x$ axioms, and therefore, hedge automata equipped with this $\otimes$ are modeled by AC tree automata. For example, if we allow $\otimes$ in the schema $\mathcal{H}_{\mathrm{in}}$ in Section 5, it can be translated to an AC tree automaton. One should notice that the predicates $\Psi_\leqslant, \Psi_<, \Psi_\geqslant, \Psi_>$ are beyond this class of ETA, and moreover,

Remark 4. $\Psi_\leqslant, \Psi_<, \Psi_\geqslant, \Psi_>$ can not be expressed by sheaves logic.

Regarding the translation of hedge automata, the special class of tree automata, called *stepwise tree automata*, is studied [2]. The signature of this class consists of constant symbols from Σ and the binary symbol @. Their transition rules are in the two forms:

$$a \rightarrow \alpha(a) \qquad \alpha(x) @ \beta(y) \rightarrow \gamma(x @ y)$$

for some $a \in \Sigma$ and α, β, γ are state symbols. Epsilon transition rules $\alpha(x) \rightarrow \beta(x)$ can be permitted though they do not appear formally in the original definition. This class of tree automata has the bi-directional correspondence to hedge automata in terms of Proposition 1. We can simulate their *curried binary encoding* translation by TAN with the associativity rule $x @ (y @ z) \rightarrow (x @ y) @ z$ and the left- and right-identity for ϵ.

In the research of XML document processing, one of the prominent topics is the *type checking problem*. This question asks us if, for XML document types τ_{in} and τ_{out} and an XML transformer Φ, every document transformed by Φ from of type τ_{in} is of type τ_{out}. In practice, these document types τ_{in} and τ_{out} are described in an XML schema language, and this problem is represented as the inclusion problem $\{ t \mid \exists s \in \mathcal{L}(\tau_{\mathrm{in}}) : t = \Phi(s) \} \subseteq \mathcal{L}(\tau_{\mathrm{out}})$. For reasoning about this problem, Milo et al. [17] studied a special class of transformer on ranked trees, called k-*pebble tree transducer* (k-PTT), and they showed that the complexity of the type checking problem for k-PTT is k-tower of exponential. Engelfriet et al. showed in [7] that k-PTT is simulated by $(k + 1)$-fold compositions of another kind of transformer, called *stay macro tree transducers* (SMTT). Recently, Maneth et al. showed in [15] that the type checking can be solved in polynomial time if SMTT is *n-bounded copying*, that is, if nodes in an input tree are copied by transformer at most n-times in the output tree.

In rewriting, the type checking problem can be reformulated as the problem $\{ t \mid \exists s \in \mathcal{L}(\tau_{\text{in}}) : s \rightarrow^!_{\mathcal{R}_\Phi} t \} \subseteq \mathcal{L}(\tau_{\text{out}})$. In [26], Takai *et al.* proposed a class of rewrite systems that effectively preserves the regularity. This result enables us to handle the type checking problem whenever $\mathcal{R}_\Phi$ is in this class. For automated reasoning, Ohsaki and Takai have developed the verification tool *ACTAS* [21], and Genet *et al.* independently developed another tool *Timbuk* [8], that computes the exact and under-approximated $\mathcal{R}$-descendant closure of regular tree languages.

7   Conclusions

In rewriting community, equational rewriting has been studied over the years. This theory underlies several practical challenges, and in fact, there are many equational rewriting based software available for public, including executable specification languages, verification tools, and program optimization tools. Among elaborated studies on equational rewriting, tree automata with normalization (TAN) may have the roots in *normalized rewriting* [16]. The theory of normalized rewriting brought the idea in dealing with completion modulo axioms, and in practice that developed the software C*i*ME [5].

In the paper, we showed the decidability (Theorems 1–4 and Corollaries 1–3) and the closure properties (Theorem 5) of our tree automata framework. Corollary 4 can be improved if the intersection-emptiness of AC regular language and $R_!$-normal forms is a decidable question. In Section 5 we discussed advantages of TAN through the observation about the translation from unranked tree automata to ranked tree automata. In the example of XML manipulation, we demonstrated that the XML schema $\mathcal{H}_{\text{in}}$ (hedge automaton) and predicates $\Psi_\leqslant, \Psi_<, \Psi_\geqslant, \Psi_>$ can be translated to TAN, and showed that the recognized languages are effectively closed under Boolean operations and the decidability questions can be solved.

For further exploration, we have an interest in the extension of TAN, in the direction of PTA [10] and of monotone ETA [23]. The tool development based on our framework is useful in practice. Thanks to Lemma 1 and Properties (i)–(iii), a tool that supports AC tree automata computation (e.g. [21]) can easily manipulate TAN if the tool is equipped with plug-in functions for exporting data to and importing the result from rewriting engines.

Acknowledgments. The authors thank Ralf Treinen and Florent Jacquemard for their comments on the early draft, since we have done most of the preliminary work while Ohsaki visited in ENS de Cachan in 2006. Comments from four anonymous reviewers helped us for improving overall the paper. We also thank Stéphanie Delaune for her suggestion that improves Example 1.

References

1. Baader, F., Nipkow, T.: Term Rewriting and All That. Cambridge University Press, Cambridge (1998)
2. Carme, J., Niehren, J., Tommasi, M.: Querying Unranked Trees with Stepwise Tree Automata. In: van Oostrom, V. (ed.) RTA 2004. LNCS, vol. 3091, pp. 235–236. Springer, Heidelberg (2004)
3. Comon, H., Dauchet, M., Gilleron, R., Jacquemard, F., Lugiez, D., Tison, S., Tommasi, M.: Tree Automata Techniques and Applications, draft (2005), available at http://www.grappa.univ-lille3.fr/tata
4. Comon, H., Jacquemard, F.: Ground Reducibility is EXPTIME-Complete, Information and Computation, vol. 187(1), pp. 123–153. Elsevier, Amsterdam (2003)
5. Contejean, E., Marché, C., Monate, B., Urbain, X.: The CiME System: Version 2.02, Software and the document (2004), available at http://cime.lri.fr/
6. Dal Zilio, S., Lugiez, D.: XML Schema, Tree Logic and Sheaves Automata. In: Applicable Algebra in Engineering, Communication and Computing, vol. 17(5), pp. 337–377. Springer, Heidelberg (2006)
7. Engelfriet, J., Maneth, S.: A Comparison of Pebble Tree Transducers with Macro Tree Transducers. In: Acta Informatica, vol. 39, pp. 613–698. Springer, Heidelberg (2003)
8. Feuillade, G., Genet, T., Viet Triem Tong, V.: Reachability Analysis over Term Rewriting Systems. Journal of Automated Reasoning 33, 341–383 (2004)
9. Hendrix, J., Meseguer, J., Ohsaki, H.: A Sufficient Completeness Checker for Linear Order-Sorted Specifications Modulo Axioms. In: Furbach, U., Shankar, N. (eds.) IJCAR 2006. LNCS (LNAI), vol. 4130, pp. 151–155. Springer, Heidelberg (2006)
10. Hendrix, J., Ohsaki, H., Viswanathan, M.: Propositional Tree Automata. In: Pfenning, F. (ed.) RTA 2006. LNCS, vol. 4098, pp. 50–65. Springer, Heidelberg (2006)
11. Hosoya, H., Vouillon, J., Pierce, B.C.: Regular Expression Types for XML. In: Proc. of 5th ICFP, Montreal (Canada), SIGPLAN Notices. vol. 35(9), pp. 11–22. ACM, New York (2000)
12. Klarlund, N., Møller, A.: MONA Version 1.4 User Manual, BRICS Notes Series NS-01-1, Department of Computer Science, University of Aarhus (2001)
13. Kutsia, T.: Solving Equations Involving Sequence Variables and Sequence Functions. In: Buchberger, B., Campbell, J.A. (eds.) AISC 2004. LNCS (LNAI), vol. 3249, pp. 157–170. Springer, Heidelberg (2004)
14. Lugiez, D.: Multitree Automata That Count. In: Theoretical Computer Science, vol. 333(1–2), pp. 225–263. Elsevier, Amsterdam (2005)
15. Maneth, S., Perst, T., Seidl, H.: XML Type Checking in Polynomial Time. In: Schwentick, T., Suciu, D. (eds.) ICDT 2007. LNCS, vol. 4353, pp. 254–268. Springer, Heidelberg (2007)
16. Marché, C.: Normalized Rewriting: An Alternative to Rewriting Modulo a Set of Equations. Journal of Symbolic Computation 21(3), 253–288 (1996)
17. Milo, T., Suciu, D., Vianu, V.: Typechecking for XML Transformers. In: Proc. of 19th PODS, Dallas (Texas), pp. 11–22. ACM, New York (2000)
18. Murata, M.: Hedge Automata: A Formal Model for XML Schemata, draft (2000), available at http://citeseer.ist.psu.edu/murata99hedge.html
19. Murata, M., Prescod, P.: SGML/XML and Forest/Hedge Automata Theory, Online Resource for Markup Language Technologies, Cover Pages, OASIS (May 2001), Online document available at http://xml.coverpages.org/hedgeAutomata.html

20. Ohsaki, H., Seki, H.: Languages Modulo Normalization, draft (2007) Available at `http://staff.aist.go.jp/hitoshi.ohsaki/`
21. Ohsaki, H., Takai, T.: ACTAS: A System Design for Associative and Commutative Tree Automata Theory. In: Proc. of 5th RULE, Aachen (Germany), ENTCS. vol. 124, pp. 97–111. Elsevier, Amsterdam (2005)
22. Ohsaki, H., Takai, T.: Decidability and Closure Properties of Equational Tree Languages. In: Tison, S. (ed.) RTA 2002. LNCS, vol. 2378, pp. 114–128. Springer, Heidelberg (2002)
23. Ohsaki, H.: Beyond Regularity: Equational Tree Automata for Associative and Commutative Theories. In: Fribourg, L. (ed.) CSL 2001 and EACSL 2001. LNCS, vol. 2142, pp. 539–553. Springer, Heidelberg (2001)
24. Parikh, R.: On Context-Free Languages. In: JACM, vol. 13(4), pp. 570–581. ACM, New York (1966)
25. Seidl, H., Schwentick, T., Muscholl, A.: Numerical Document Queries. In: Proc. of 22nd PODS, San Diego (California), pp. 155–166. ACM Press, New York (2003)
26. Takai, T., Kaji, Y., Seki, H.: Right-Linear Finite Path Overlapping Term Rewriting Systems Effectively Preserve Recognizability. In: Bachmair, L. (ed.) RTA 2000. LNCS, vol. 1833, pp. 246–260. Springer, Heidelberg (2000)
27. Thatcher, J.W.: Characterizing Derivation Trees of Context-Free Grammars Through a Generalization of Automata Theory. Journal of Computer and System Sciences 1(4), 317–322 (1967)
28. Verma, K.N.: Two-Way Equational Tree Automata for AC-Like Theories: Decidability and Closure Properties. In: Nieuwenhuis, R. (ed.) RTA 2003. LNCS, vol. 2706, pp. 180–197. Springer, Heidelberg (2003)
29. Verma, K.N.: On Closure under Complementation of Equational Tree Automata for Theories Extending AC. In: Vardi, M.Y., Voronkov, A. (eds.) LPAR 2003. LNCS, vol. 2850, pp. 183–197. Springer, Heidelberg (2003)
30. Extensible Markup Language (XML) Schema 1.0, 3rd edn., W3C (2004) Document available at `http://www.w3.org/TR/2004/REC-xml-20040204/`

Combining Proof-Producing Decision Procedures

Silvio Ranise, Christophe Ringeissen, and Duc-Khanh Tran

LORIA & INRIA-Lorraine

Abstract. Constraint solvers are key modules in many systems with reasoning capabilities (e.g., automated theorem provers). To incorporate constraint solvers in such systems, the capability of producing conflict sets or explanations of their results is crucial. For expressiveness, constraints are usually built out in unions of theories and constraint solvers in such unions are obtained by modularly combining solvers for the component theories. In this paper, we consider the problem of modularly constructing conflict sets for a combined theory by re-using available proof-producing procedures for the component theories. The key idea of our solution to this problem is the concept of explanation graph, which is a labelled, acyclic and undirected graph capable of recording the entailment of some equalities. Explanation graphs allow us to record explanations computed by a proof-producing procedure and to refine the Nelson-Oppen combination method to modularly build conflict sets for disjoint unions of theories. We also study how the computed conflict sets relate to an appropriate notion of minimality.

1 Introduction

Constraint solvers are key modules in many systems, such as automated theorem provers, expert systems, and constraint logic programming (CLP) environments. To efficiently or correctly incorporate constraint solvers in such systems, the capability of producing conflict sets or explanations of the results of the solvers is crucial. For example, conflict sets are useful to prune the search space of Satisfiability Modulo Theories (SMT) solvers (see, e.g., [14]) or to direct backtracking in CLP systems [3] whereas explanations can be used to safely import the results of external reasoning modules (e.g., decision procedures for selected theories or unification algorithms) in skeptical proof assistants (see, e.g., [8]).

For expressiveness, constraints are usually built out in unions of theories and constraint solvers in such unions are obtained by modularly combining solvers for the component theories. So, it is desirable to build conflict sets or explanations in unions of theories by modularly combining the conflict sets computed by the available solvers for the component theories. In this paper, we consider the problem of modularly combining conflict sets or explanations produced by decision procedures for the satisfiability problem of conjunctions of quantifier-free literals in a first-order theory T. The hope is to reuse the work on extending

B. Konev and F. Wolter (Eds.): FroCos 2007, LNAI 4720, pp. 237–251, 2007.

satisfiability with proof-producing capabilities available in the literature (see, e.g., [7,4,11,17]).

The *main contribution* of this paper is an abstract account of how to extend the well-known and widely used Nelson-Oppen combination method [10,13] to build a satisfiability procedure capable of producing conflict sets in the union of theories T_1 and T_2, whenever the satisfiability procedures for T_1 and T_2 provide certain interface capabilities. To this end, we first introduce the concept of *explanation graph* (Section 3), a data structure which compactly encodes the fact that a certain equality between variables (called elementary equality) is a logical consequence of a set of elementary equalities. Explanation graphs can be easily implemented by using efficient algorithms based on the Union-Find data structure [18,5]. Then (Section 4), we show how to combine satisfiability procedures, called *explanation engines*, capable of building explanation graphs so as to obtain a satisfiability procedure with the capability of producing conflict sets in the union of the component theories. Then (Section 5), we introduce the concept of *quasi-conflict set*, which allows us to precisely characterize a (weak) form of minimality satisfied by the explanations computed by our combination method. Finally (Section 6), we show how to build explanation engines by adding explanation capabilities to a procedure for the theory of uninterpreted functions (Section 6.1) and one for an important fragment of Linear Arithmetic (Section 6.2, proofs can be found in [19] for lack of space).

2   Background

First-Order Logic. We assume the usual syntactic and semantic notions of term, formula, interpretation, satisfiability, etc. for first-order logic as given, e.g., in [6]. A *first-order theory* is a set of first-order sentences. A Σ-*theory* is a theory all of whose sentences have signature Σ. Since we are concerned with satisfiability, we may consider all symbols with arity 0 as constants since a formula is equisatisfiable to its existential closure and existentially quantified variables can be replaced by Skolem constants. This explains why we may talk about constants instead of variables depending on the context. A theory is *consistent* if it admits a model and *trivial* if the cardinality of each of its models is one. In this paper, we restrict ourselves to non-trivial and consistent theories. We will be concerned with the following theories. The theory of equality $\mathcal{E}$ whose signature contains a finite set of function and constant symbols, and such that the equality symbol $=$ is interpreted as the identity relation. The theory $\mathcal{E}^c$ consisting only of equalities or disequalities between constants. We will also refer to the literals of $\mathcal{E}^c$ as *elementary* equalities or disequalities and to $\mathcal{E}^c$ as the *theory of pure equality*. The quantifier-free fragment of Linear Rational Arithmetic is denoted with $\mathcal{LA}^{\leq}$ and its restriction to equalities or disequalities only is denoted with $\mathcal{LA}$. A term is *flat* if it is a variable or a term of the form $f(c_1, ..., c_n)$ where f is an n-ary function symbol and the c_i's are variables. A literal is *flat* if it has one of the following forms: $c_1 = c_2$, $\neg(c_1 = c_2)$ (also abbreviated with $c_1 \neq c_2$), $f(c_1, ..., c_n) = c_{n+1}$, $p(c_1, ..., c_n)$, or $\neg p(c_1, ..., c_n)$, where f (p) is an n-ary function (predicate, resp.) symbol and the c_i's are variables. A literal which is neither an elementary equality nor an elementary disequality is called *non-elementary*. In the following, φ denotes an arbitrary set of literals, Ω denotes a set of non-elementary flat literals, E denotes a set of elementary equalities, and Δ denotes a set of elementary disequalities. The set of variables occurring in φ is denoted by $Var(\varphi)$. The reflexive, symmetric and transitive closure of E is denoted by E^*. The set E of elementary equalities is *minimal* iff $E'^* \subset E^*$, for any $E' \subset E$.

A Σ-structure $\mathcal{M}$ is a model of a Σ-theory T if $\mathcal{M}$ satisfies every sentence in T. A Σ-formula is *satisfiable in T* (or T-satisfiable) if it is satisfiable in a model of T. Two Σ-formulas φ and ψ are *equisatisfiable in T* if for every model $\mathcal{M}$ of T, φ is satisfiable in $\mathcal{M}$ iff ψ is satisfiable in $\mathcal{M}$. We will omit the "Σ-" of Σ-theory, Σ-structure , ..., when it is clear from the context.

Satisfiability procedures and conflict sets. The *satisfiability problem* for a theory T amounts to establishing whether any (finite) quantifier-free conjunction of literals is T-satisfiable or not. We can use (free) constants instead of variables in a satisfiability problem, so that we can redefine it as the problem of establishing the satisfiability of $T \cup \Gamma$, for any (finite) set of ground literals. Below, we will indifferently use constants or variables when discussing notions related to satisfiability problems. A *satisfiability procedure* for T is any algorithm that solves the satisfiability problem for T. A *T-conflict set* is a T-unsatisfiable set of literals. A T-conflict set CS of literals is *minimal* if there is no $CS' \subset CS$ such that CS' is a T-conflict set. A *T-explanation* of an equality e is a T-satisfiable set φ of literals such that $T \models \varphi \Rightarrow e$. A T-explanation of e is *minimal* if there is no $\varphi' \subset \varphi$ such that $T \models \varphi' \Rightarrow e$. We will omit the theory T when it is clear from the context.

Proposition 1. *A T-satisfiable set of literals φ is a minimal T-explanation for an equality e iff $\varphi \cup \{\neg e\}$ is a minimal T-conflict set.*

Classes of theories and conflict sets. For simplicity, we will only consider convex and stably infinite theories in this paper. A set φ of T-literals is *convex* iff for any disjunction $x_1 = y_1 \vee \cdots \vee x_n = y_n$ for $n > 1$, where x_i, y_i are constants $(i = 1, ..., n)$ we have that $T \cup \varphi \models x_1 = y_1 \vee \cdots \vee x_n = y_n$ iff $T \cup \varphi \models x_i = y_i$ for some $i \in \{1, ..., n\}$. A theory T is *convex* iff all sets of T-literals are convex. We say that T is *stably infinite* if for every T-satisfiable set of literals φ there exists a model of T satisfying φ such that its interpretation domain is infinite. For example, $\mathcal{E}^c$, $\mathcal{E}$ and $\mathcal{LA}^\le$ (and its "reduct" $\mathcal{LA}$) are convex and stably infinite theories.

Proposition 2. *If T is a convex theory, then any minimal conflict set contains at most one disequality. If T is a convex theory axiomatized by a set of equalities, then any minimal conflict set contains exactly one disequality.*

For example, $\mathcal{E}^c$ and $\mathcal{E}$ are convex theories such that any minimal conflict set contains exactly one disequality. Notice that $\mathcal{LA}$, and hence also $\mathcal{LA}^\le$, does not satisfy this property (e.g., $\{x - y = 3, x - y = 2\}$ is a minimal $\mathcal{LA}$-conflict set).

Graphs. We use some standard notions as undirected graph, acyclic graph, sub-graph, connected graph, path, simple path, elementary path, and connected components. In the rest of the paper, we only consider acyclic undirected graphs, which will be often called graphs for the sake of simplicity. An undirected graph G is a pair (V, E) where V (also written as $Vertex(G)$) is a finite set and E (also written as $Edge(G)$) is a set of unordered pairs written as (v, w) for v, w in V. $G_{\emptyset}^V$ denotes the graph whose vertices are in the set V which are connected by no edges, i.e. $G_{\emptyset}^V = (V, \emptyset)$. The "is a sub-graph of" relation is denoted by $\subseteq$. Let $G = (V, E)$ be an acyclic undirected graph. The set $ElemPath(G, x, y)$ denotes the set of edges in an elementary path between x and y in G, i.e. if $v_0, ..., v_n$ is an elementary path where v_0 is x and v_n is y, then $ElemPath(G, x, y)$ is the set of edges $(v_{i-1}, v_i) \in Edge(G)$, for $i = 1, ..., n$. Given two distinct vertices x and y, $ElemPath(G, x, y)$ is empty iff x and y are not in the same connected component of G. The set of *pairs of connected vertices in G* is $CP(G) = \{(x, y) \mid x, y \in V \text{ and } ElemPath(G, x, y) \neq \emptyset\}$. Notice that the reflexive, symmetric, and transitive closure of E is equal to $CP(G) \cup \{(x, x) \mid x \in V\}$.

3   Explanation Graphs

Two preliminary remarks about the relationship between an acyclic undirected graph $G = (V, E)$ and a set of elementary equalities are useful. First, observe that an elementary equality can be regarded as an unordered pair and edges of G are unordered pairs. So, we will write $(x, y) \in E$ as $x = y$ and define the *set of elementary equalities of the graph G* as $Eq(G) = \bigcup_{x=y \in E}\{x = y\}$. Second, it is easy to see that a set of elementary equalities Γ is minimal iff there exists an acyclic undirected graph G such that $Eq(G) = \Gamma$; furthermore, Γ^* is equal to the reflexive, symmetric, and transitive closure of $Edge(G)^*$ or, equivalently, to $CP(G) \cup \{x = x \mid x \in Vertex(G)\}$. In other words, G avoids redundancy.

Roughly, an explanation graph for a set φ of literals and a theory T is an acyclic undirected graph $G = (V, E)$ such that $Eq(G)^*$ is equal to the sub-set of elementary equalities in φ and each edge $x = y \in Edge(G)$ is labelled by a satisfiable sub-set of φ implying $x = y$ in T. In a label, we may find literals occurring in φ as well as auxiliary elementary equalities which are entailed by other equalities in the graph.

Definition 1. *Let T be a theory, φ be a set of T-literals, and $G = (V, E)$ be an acyclic undirected graph such that E is a set totally ordered by some ordering $<_E$. G is an* explanation graph *of φ if (i) V is the set of constants occurring in φ, (ii) there exists a labelling function $\mathcal{L}_G$ with domain E and co-domain $2^{\varphi \cup CP(G)}$,[1] (iii) the following properties are satisfied for any $v_1 = v_2 \in E$:*

(iii.a) $\mathcal{L}_G(v_1 = v_2)$ is T-satisfiable and $T \models \mathcal{L}_G(v_1 = v_2) \Rightarrow v_1 = v_2$,
(iii.b) for each $v_1' = v_2'$ in $\mathcal{L}_G(v_1 = v_2) \backslash \varphi$ we have that $e <_E (v_1 = v_2)$, for any e in $ElemPath(G, v_1', v_2')$.

---

[1] Let X be a set, 2^X denotes the power-set of X.

The set of literals of φ in G *is* $Lit(G) = \varphi \cap (\bigcup_{e \in E} \mathcal{L}_G(e))$. *An edge* $v_1 = v_2 \in E$ *is* minimally explained *if* $\mathcal{L}_G(v_1 = v_2)$ *is a minimal* T-explanation for $v_1 = v_2$. *An* explanation graph is said edge-minimal *if all its edges are minimally explained.*

In the definition above, edges are ordered to express the fact that explanation graphs are built dynamically and this determines how explanations and conflict sets are computed. The ordering $<_E$ on edges corresponds to the order of insertion of edges in the graph. Adding an edge $x = y$ to the explanation graph $G = (V, E)$ of the set φ of literals is defined as follows: if x and y are two distinct vertices in V such that $x = y \notin CP(G)$, and L is a set of T-literals in $\varphi \cup CP(G)$ such that L is T-satisfiable and $T \models L \Rightarrow x = y$, then

$$Insert(G, x = y, L)$$

denotes the explanation graph $G' = (V, E')$, where $E' = E \cup \{x = y\}$, $\mathcal{L}_{G'}$ is such that $\mathcal{L}_{G'}(x = y) = L$, $\forall e \in E, \mathcal{L}_{G'}(e) = \mathcal{L}_G(e)$, and $<_{E'}$ is the smallest ordering containing $<_E$ such that $\forall e \in E, e <_{E'} x = y$. From now on, we assume that $<_{E'}$ and $<_E$ coincide on elements of E whenever $G = (V, E)$ and $G' = (V', E')$ are two explanation graphs such that $E \subseteq E'$.

We now consider the case of an explanation graph G obtained by adding a set of elementary equalities in a given order. (This will be important for our combination schema; see Section 4.1 below.) More precisely, G is obtained by adding one after the other each elementary equality in $E := \{e_1, ..., e_n\}$, according to an ordering $<_E$ (such that, wlog, $e_i <_E e_{i+1}$ for $i = 1, ..., n$) to $G_0 := G_\emptyset^{Var(\varphi)}$ (equipped with an empty labelling $\mathcal{L}_{G_0}$), i.e. $G := G_n$ where $G_{j+1} := Insert(G_j, e_j, \{e_j\})$ for $j = 0, ..., n - 1$. For the sake of conciseness, we will write $UF(E)$ to abbreviate the graph obtained by the sequence of insertions above.[2] If V is a set of variables, $UF^V(E)$ is the explanation graph obtained by adding V to the set of vertices of $UF(E)$. It is not difficult to see that for any set E of elementary equalities, $UF(E)$ is an edge-minimal explanation graph of E such that $Eq(UF(E))$ is a minimal set of elementary equalities (included in E).

For efficiency, it is important to consider explanation graphs from which all possible entailed elementary equalities can be extracted.

Definition 2. *Let* T *be a theory and let* φ *be a* T-satisfiable set of literals. A set of elementary equalities E is deduction complete *for* φ *(modulo* T*) if*

$$\forall x, y \in Var(\varphi), \; T \models \varphi \Rightarrow x = y \text{ iff } (x, y) \in E^*.$$

An explanation graph G *of a* T-satisfiable set φ *of literals is* deduction complete *(modulo* T*) if* $Eq(G)$ *is deduction complete for* φ *(modulo* T*).*

For example, $UF(E)$ is a deduction complete explanation graph of E (modulo $\mathcal{E}^c$). For convex theories, deduction complete explanation graphs allow us to handle elementary disequalities one by one.

---

[2] UF abbreviates Union-Find since the sequence of insertions is typically implemented using this data structure (see [7,4,11]).

Proposition 3. *Let T be a convex theory. Given a deduction complete explanation graph G of a T-satisfiable set of literals φ, and a set of elementary disequalities Δ, we have that $\varphi \cup \Delta$ is unsatisfiable if and only there exists $x \neq y \in \Delta$ such that $x = y \in CP(G)$.*

A naïve brute-force method to build explanation graphs consists in considering one by one each possible elementary equality made of disconnected vertices of the graph and check if it is implied by the input set of literals. Fortunately, there are satisfiability procedures with the capability of generating deduction complete and edge-minimal explanation graphs without resorting to such a brute-force method and are thus more efficient (see Section 6 for more on this issue).

4   Conflict Sets for Combination of Theories

We adapt the deterministic Nelson-Oppen combination method [10] to compute $T_1 \cup T_2$-conflict sets. This combination method allows us to build a satisfiability procedure for $T_1 \cup T_2$ by using satisfiability procedures known for T_1 and T_2, provided that T_1 and T_2 are signature-disjoint, convex, and stably-infinite. Informally, this combination method works as follows: entailed elementary equalities are exchanged between the two procedures until either unsatisfiability is derived by one of the two, or no more elementary equalities can be exchanged. In the first case, we derive the unsatisfiability of the input formula; in the second case, we derive its satisfiability. Thus, the unsatisfiability in $T_1 \cup T_2$ can be explained according to two kinds of explanations: (i) the explanation of entailed elementary equalities and (ii) the explanation of the unsatisfiability in a component theory. To develop our main combination result (cf. Section 4.1), we introduce the notion of *explanation engine*: a module capable of computing (i) and (ii) which may be obtained by re-using available proof-producing procedures (see Section 6).

Definition 3 (Explanation engine). *Let T be a theory, Ω be a set of non-elementary flat T-literals, and E be a minimal set of elementary equalities. A T-explanation engine is a T-satisfiability procedure, denoted by μEX_T, which computes an **edge-minimal** explanation graph G of $\Omega \cup E$ such that $E \subseteq Eq(G)$ and*

1. *if $\Omega \cup E$ is T-unsatisfiable, then μEX_T returns $false\{(\Omega', E', G)\}$ where $\Omega' \subseteq \Omega$, E' is a set of elementary equalities such that $\Omega' \cup E'$ is a **minimal** T-conflict set and $E' \subseteq CP(G)$.*
2. *if $\Omega \cup E$ is T-satisfiable, then μEX_T returns $true\{G\}$ where G is deduction complete for $\Omega \cup E$ modulo T.*

Given a T-satisfiability procedure equipped with the capabilities of computing minimal conflict sets (CS_T) and minimal explanations for entailed elementary equalities $(EX_T^{x=y})$, Figure 1 shows how to construct a T-explanation engine.

Function $\mu EX_T(\Omega, E)$
  $G := (Var(\Omega \cup E), E)$
  If $\Omega \cup E$ is T-unsatisfiable **Then**
    $\Omega' := CS_T(\Omega \cup E) \cap \Omega$
    $E' := CS_T(\Omega \cup E) \backslash \Omega$
    Return $false\{(\Omega', E', G)\}$
  Else
    Foreach $x = y$ such that $(x, y) \notin CP(G)$ and $T \models \Omega \cup E \Rightarrow x = y$
      $G := Insert(G, x = y, EX_T^{x=y}(\Omega \cup E))$
    EndForeach
    Return $true\{G\}$

Fig. 1. Construction of an explanation engine

4.1 Combination Algorithm

Figure 2 presents a variant of the Nelson-Oppen combination method for the union of two arbitrary signature-disjoint, stably infinite, and convex theories where explanation engines are used in place of satisfiability procedures. For example, it applies to $\mathcal{E} \cup \mathcal{LA}$ since $\mathcal{E}$ and $\mathcal{LA}$ are known to be stably infinite and convex, and it is possible to build explanation engines for both $\mathcal{E}$ and $\mathcal{LA}$ as shown in Section 6. The rules of Figure 2 (derived from [13]) aim at providing a $T_1 \cup T_2$-satisfiability procedure for sets of literals of the form $\varphi = \Omega_1 \cup \Omega_2 \cup E \cup \Delta$, where Ω_i is a set of non-elementary T_i-literals (for $i = 1, 2$), E is a set of elementary equalities and Δ is a set of elementary disequalities. Configurations manipulated by the rules consist of $\Omega_1, \Omega_2, \Delta$ together with an explanation graph G of φ. Initially, G is $UF^{Var(\varphi)}(E)$. The combination algorithm works as follows. Each explanation engine computes new entailed equalities stored (with their explanations) in a (local) explanation graph. Then, these are used to update the (global) explanation graph G for the union of the theories. This updating (formalized by the *Merge* in Figure 2) consists in adding some new edges to G. Unsatisfiability is detected either by an explanation engine (rule $\texttt{Unsat}_{=i}$, for $i = 1, 2$) or by a contradiction between the entailed elementary equalities stored in G and the elementary disequalities in Δ (rule $\texttt{Unsat}_{\neq}$). By the results in [13], one can easily show that the repeated application of rules in Figure 2 terminates with $false\{\cdots\}$ if and only if the initial configuration is unsatisfiable.

Theorem 1. *Let T_1 and T_2 be two signature-disjoint convex and stably infinite theories such that for each $i = 1, 2$, a T_i-explanation engine is available. Let Ω_i be a set of non-elementary T_i-literals for $i = 1, 2$, let E be a set of elementary equalities and let Δ be a set of elementary disequalities. Consider $\varphi = (\Omega_1 \cup \Omega_2 \cup \Delta \cup E)$ and fc be a final configuration obtained by the repeated application of the rules of Figure 2 on the initial configuration $\Omega_1; \Delta; UF^{Var(\varphi)}(E); \Omega_2$.*

  – If fc is of the form $false\{(\Omega', E', G)\}$, then φ is $T_1 \cup T_2$-unsatisfiable. Furthermore, $\Omega' \cup E'$ is a minimal conflict set such that $E' \subseteq CP(G)$.

$\text{Unsat}_{=1}$ $\quad \Omega_1; \Delta; G; \Omega_2$
$\qquad \vdash$
$\qquad false\{(\Omega_1', E_1', G')\}$
$\qquad \text{if} \begin{cases} \mu EX_1(\Omega_1, Eq(G)) = false\{(\Omega_1', E_1', G_1)\} \\ G' = Merge(G, G_1) \end{cases}$

$\text{Unsat}_{\neq}$ $\quad \Omega_1; \Delta; G; \Omega_2$
$\qquad \vdash$
$\qquad false\{(\{x \neq y\}, \{x = y\}, G)\}$
$\qquad \text{if } (x, y) \in CP(G) \text{ and } x \neq y \in \Delta$

Deduction_1 $\quad \Omega_1; \Delta; G; \Omega_2$
$\qquad \vdash$
$\qquad \Omega_1; \Delta; G'; \Omega_2$
$\qquad \text{if} \begin{cases} \mu EX_1(\Omega_1, Eq(G)) = true\{G_1\} \\ G' = Merge(G, G_1) \\ G' \neq G \end{cases}$

Legenda: Ω_i is a set of non-elementary T_i-literals, for $i = 1, 2$. Δ is a set of elementary disequalities. Symmetric rules are not depicted here for the sake of conciseness and they can be obtained by changing the subscript 1 into 2 in the rules above. The function $Merge$ is defined as follows:

Function $Merge(G, G')$
$\quad G'' := G$
$\quad$ **Foreach** $(x, y) \in Edge(G') \backslash Edge(G)$
$\qquad G'' := Insert(G'', x = y, \mathcal{L}_{G'}(x = y))$
$\quad$ **EndForeach**
$\quad$ **Return** G''

Fig. 2. Combination of explanation engines

- *Otherwise, fc is of the form $\Omega_1; \Delta; G; \Omega_2$ and φ is $T_1 \cup T_2$-satisfiable. Furthermore, G is deduction complete for φ modulo $T_1 \cup T_2$.*

Moreover, G is an **edge-minimal** *explanation graph of φ.*

Theorem 1 has an interesting consequence. The combination algorithm can be applied to a set of flat $T_1 \cup T_2$-literals without any disequalities, and in that case it provides a $T_1 \cup T_2$-explanation engine. Thus, we have a modular construction of explanation engines since $T_1 \cup T_2$ is convex and stably infinite when T_1 and T_2 are signature-disjoint, convex, and stably infinite theories.

Corollary 1 (Modular construction of explanation engines). *Let T_1 and T_2 be two signature-disjoint, convex, and stably infinite theories such that for each $i = 1, 2$, a T_i-explanation engine is known. Then, the combination rules depicted in Figure 2 provide a $T_1 \cup T_2$-explanation engine.*

This refinement of the Nelson and Oppen method allows us to obtain a truly modular combination method to build conflict sets in unions of n theories (with

$n \geq 2$) by combining explanation engines via the repeated application of the Corollary above.

Remark. It is not difficult to adapt the above method to combine the interface functionalities for computing conflict sets (CS_{T_i}) and explanations $(EX_{T_i}^{x=y})$ of the component theories. In this scenario, a single explanation graph is needed which is updated by CS_{T_i} and $EX_{T_i}^{x=y}$, for $i = 1, 2$; thereby avoiding the need of the *Merge* operation. We have not taken this option here, since it would have made more complex our study of the minimality of the conflict sets, as it will be apparent in the next Section where the output of explanation engines plays a key role.

5   Quasi-conflict Sets

In the previous combination algorithm, one can observe that some additional information, encoded as a triplet (ψ, E, G), is returned whenever an unsatisfiable set φ of literals is considered. This triplet contains two sets of literals ψ, E, and an explanation graph G such that $\psi \cup E$ is unsatisfiable, ψ is a satisfiable subset of φ, and E is a set of (entailed) elementary equalities explained in G. Strictly speaking, $\psi \cup E$ is not a conflict set of φ since it may contain literals which are not in φ. However, it is easy to extract a "real" conflict set from $\psi \cup E$ since E is entailed by φ and the related explanations are encoded in the associated explanation graph G. In the following, we investigate how to formalize this observation by defining the concept of *quasi-conflict set* as a triplet (ψ, E, G). The interest of this notion is that it is possible to define an ordering on such triplets and that the quasi-conflict sets computed by the combination algorithm in the previous Section are minimal according to this ordering.

Before being able to define the ordering on quasi-conflict sets, we need to introduce a suitable order on explanation graphs.

Definition 4. *Given two explanation graphs G and G' of φ, we define the relation $\sqsubseteq$ as follows:*

$$G' \sqsubseteq G \text{ if } Edge(G') \subseteq Edge(G) \text{ and } \forall e \in Edge(G'), \ \mathcal{L}_{G'}(e) \subseteq \mathcal{L}_G(e).$$

Given two explanation graphs G and G' of φ and four sets of literals ψ, E, ψ', E', we define the relation $\preceq$ as follows:

$$(\psi', E', G') \preceq (\psi, E, G) \text{ if } \psi' \subseteq \psi, \ E' \subseteq E \text{ and } G' \sqsubseteq G$$

It is not difficult to see that $\preceq$ is a quasi-ordering. The strict ordering $\prec$ induced by $\preceq$ will be used to define the notion of minimality.

Definition 5 (Quasi-conflict sets). *Let φ be an unsatisfiable set of literals, ψ be a subset of φ, G be an explanation graph of φ, and E be a set of equalities. The triplet (ψ, E, G) is a quasi-conflict set of φ if $E \subseteq CP(G)$, $\psi \cup E$ is unsatisfiable, and $E \neq \emptyset$ implies that ψ is satisfiable. The triplet (ψ, E, G) is a minimal quasi-conflict set if there is no $(\psi', E', G') \prec (\psi, E, G)$ such that (ψ', E', G') is a quasi-conflict set of φ.*

Notice that if (ψ, E, G) is a quasi-conflict set, then $E \neq \emptyset$ iff ψ is satisfiable. Also, if φ is a conflict set, then $(\varphi, \emptyset, G_\emptyset^{Var(\varphi)})$ is a quasi-conflict set.

Proposition 4. *If (ψ, E, G) is a quasi-conflict set of φ, then $\psi \cup Lit(G)$ is a conflict set of φ.*

Given a quasi-conflict set (ψ, E, G) of φ, $\psi \cup Lit(G)$ is the *conflict set associated to* (ψ, E, G). The set $Lit(G)$ provides an explanation of equalities in E, but it is a super-set of what we need: it is sufficient to consider the sub-graph of G obtained by focusing only on the paths in G "connecting" the equalities in E.

Definition 6. *Let G be an explanation graph of φ, $x = y \in CP(G)$ and $E \subseteq CP(G)$. The set of* explanation edges of $x = y$ in G *is the subset of $Edge(G)$ defined as follows:*

$$Exe(G, x = y) = ElemPath(G, x, y) \cup \left(\bigcup_{e \in ElemPath(G,x,y)} \bigcup_{e' \in \mathcal{L}_G(e) \setminus \varphi} Exe(G, e') \right).$$

The set of explanation edges of E in G *is $ExE(G, E) = \bigcup_{e \in E} Exe(G, e)$.*

The restriction of G to E is the sub-graph $G_{|E}$ of G such that $Edge(G_{|E}) = ExE(G, E)$ and $\forall e \in Edge(G_{|E})$, $\mathcal{L}_{G_{|E}}(e) = \mathcal{L}_G(e)$.

We are now ready to show how to compute minimal quasi-conflict sets.

Theorem 2. *Let (ψ, E, G) be a quasi-conflict set of φ such that $\psi \cup E$ is a minimal conflict set. If all edges of $G_{|E}$ are minimally explained then $(\psi, E, G_{|E})$ is a minimal quasi-conflict set of φ.*

Proof. $(\psi, E, G_{|E})$ is a quasi-conflict set since $E \subseteq CP(G_{|E})$ and $\psi \cup E$ is unsatisfiable.

Assume there exists a quasi-conflict set (ψ', E', G') of φ such that $(\psi', E', G') \prec (\psi, E, G_{|E})$. Since edges of $G_{|E}$ are minimally explained, we have necessarily $\forall e \in Edge(G')$, $\mathcal{L}_{G'}(e) = \mathcal{L}_{G_{|E}}(e)$, and the following cases:

1. $\psi' \subset \psi$, $E' \subseteq E$, $G' \subseteq G_{|E}$,
2. or $\psi' \subseteq \psi$, $E' \subset E$, $G' \subseteq G_{|E}$,
3. or $\psi' \subseteq \psi$, $E' \subseteq E$, $G' \subset G_{|E}$. In that case, suppose $E' = E$. Then, we have $E \subseteq CP(G')$. But this contradicts the fact that $G' \subset G_{|E}$. Consequently, $E' \subset E$.

In all cases, we get the strict inclusion $\psi' \cup E' \subset \psi \cup E$. Since $\psi \cup E$ is a minimal conflict set, $\psi' \cup E'$ is satisfiable. This contradicts the assumption. □

Theorem 2 is the key to study the minimality of the our proof-producing procedures.

Corollary 2. *Consider a T-explanation engine μEX.*
If $\mu EX(\Omega, E) = false\{(\Omega', E', G)\}$, then $\Omega' \cup E'$ is a minimal conflict set and $(\Omega', E', G_{|E'})$ is a **minimal quasi-conflict set**.

Cong $\Omega; G$
$\vdash$
$\quad \Omega; Insert(G, z = z', \{z = f(y_1, \ldots, y_n), z' = f(y'_1, \ldots, y'_n)\} \cup \bigcup_{j \in J}\{y_j = y'_j\})$

if $\begin{cases} z = f(y_1, \ldots, y_n), z' = f(y'_1, \ldots, y'_n) \in \Omega \\ z \neq z', (z, z') \notin CP(G) \\ I, J \text{ is a partition of } \{1, \ldots, n\} \text{ such that} \\ (\forall i \in I : y_i = y'_i), (\forall j \in J : (y_j, y'_j) \in CP(G)) \end{cases}$

Fig. 3. Congruence Closure with Explanation

Theorem 2 has also an interesting consequence when considering procedures for convex theories (cf. Proposition 3).

Corollary 3. *Let T be a convex (and non-trivial) theory. Given a deduction complete and **edge-minimal** explanation graph G of a T-satisfiable set of literals φ, and a set of elementary disequalities Δ, for any $x \neq y \in \Delta$ such that $(x, y) \in CP(G)$, $(\{x \neq y\}, \{x = y\}, G_{|\{x=y\}})$ is a **minimal quasi-conflict set** of $\varphi \cup \Delta$.*

6   Explaining Satisfiability Procedures

We briefly discuss the problem of constructing deduction complete and edge-minimal explanation graphs for $\mathcal{E}$ and $\mathcal{LA}$ and some of their extensions (e.g., the theory of lists or $\mathcal{LA}^{\leq}$). The purpose of this Section is to illustrate how readily available proof-producing procedures can be used in our framework, not to provide new insights into the problem of building proof-producing procedures for selected theories.

6.1   An $\mathcal{E}$-Explanation Engine

Preliminarily, recall that given a set E of elementary equalities, $UF(E)$ is a deduction complete and edge-minimal explanation graph for $\mathcal{E}^c$ (see Section 3). It is possible to build a congruence closure-like algorithm by using the rule Cong in Figure 3. In fact, it is sufficient to exhaustively apply the rule Cong with $(\Omega; UF^{Var(\Omega)}(E))$ as the initial configuration, where Ω is a set of non-elementary flat literals and E is a set of elementary equalities. It is easy to see that this process always terminates and the last component of a final configuration is a deduction complete and edge-minimal explanation graph. We observe that this abstract process can be efficiently implemented by using the algorithm in [11], where entailment of equalities is encoded by a proof forest. Such a notion is quite similar to that of explanation graph; the only difference being in the labelling of edges: in a proof forest, when an edge (x, y) is labelled by $\{x = f(x_1), y = f(y_1)\}$, the equality $x_1 = y_1$ is left implicit, whereas in an explanation graph, the label would be $\{x = f(x_1), y = f(y_1), x_1 = y_1\}$.

Unfortunately, the general method of Figure 1 to build explanations engines cannot be applied here since the congruence closure algorithm above allows us to

Function $\mu EX_{\mathcal{E}}(\Omega, E)$
$\quad G := UF^{Var(\Omega)}(E)$
$\quad$ **If** $(\exists G' : (\Omega; G) \vdash_{\text{Cong}} (\Omega; G'))$ **Then Return** $true\{G'\}$
$\quad$ **Else Return** $true\{G\}$

Fig. 4. An $\mathcal{E}$-explanation engine

compute neither minimal conflict sets nor minimal explanations.[3] Fortunately, it is not difficult to obtain an $\mathcal{E}$-explanation engine by using the rule Cong of Figure 3 as depicted in Figure 4, where $\vdash_{\text{Cong}}$ denotes the exhaustive application of Cong.

Remark. In [9], we have shown that rewriting-based satisfiability procedures are deduction complete for equational and Horn theories (e.g., the theory of lists) in the sense that deduction complete sets of elementary equalities (cf. Definition 2) can be extracted from saturated (w.r.t. a completion-like procedure) sets of clauses. It is not difficult to obtain explanation engines from such rewriting-based procedures by using the derived elementary equalities to build an explanation graph. The following observations suggest how. First, recall that any sets of equalities is satisfiable in equational and Horn theories. Second, the redundancy criteria of the completion process subsumes the redundancy notion of the explanation graph (cf. Section 3). Third, for every elementary equality e entailed by a satisfiable set φ of literals, the set E of elementary equalities returned by the procedure is such that $E \models e$ iff $e \in E^*$. Finally, the labels of the graph can easily be obtained by using the proof producing capabilities of many completion-based provers (such as the E-prover [16]). So, the idea is simply to add an edge to the explanation graph and label it with the set of literals used by the prover to derive it.

6.2   An $\mathcal{LA}$-Explanation Engine

We show how a variant of the Gauss elimination algorithm (see, e.g., [15]) can be used to build minimal conflict sets and explanations of elementary equalities. In this way, the method in Figure 1 can be used to obtain an $\mathcal{LA}$-explanation engine.

Below, GA denotes our variant of Gauss elimination. The input to GA is of the form $\Gamma|\Delta$, where Γ is a set of linear equalities and Δ is a set of disequalities. Observe that $l \neq r$ is equisatisfiable to $l - r = s \wedge s \neq 0$ where s is a fresh variable, also called *slack variable*. The first step of GA consists in replacing each disequality $l \neq r$ in Δ with the equality $l - r = s$, where s is a slack variable. From $\Gamma|\Delta$, we obtain a system $\Gamma|\Gamma'$ of equalities. The second step of GA is to perform Gauss elimination on $\Gamma|\Gamma'$ with the proviso that two equalities in Γ' should never be linearly combined[4] (in other words, only combinations of two

---

[3] To the best of our knowledge, this is a feature which is common to many proof-producing procedures for equality [7,4,11].

[4] We say that $e + k * e'$ (for some number $k \neq 0$) is a linear combination of the equality e of the form $a_1 * x_1 + \cdots + a_n * x_n = b$ and the equality e' of the form $a'_1 * x_1 + \cdots + a'_n * x_n = b'$ if it is the result of simplifying the equality $a_1 * x_1 + \cdots + a_n * x_n + k * (a'_1 * x_1 + \cdots + a'_n * x_n) = b + k * b'$.

equalities in Γ or an equality in Γ and one in Γ' are allowed). If we obtain an equality of the form $0 = c$ (where c is a non zero constant) from Γ, then GA returns the $\mathcal{LA}$-unsatisfiability of $\Gamma \cup \Delta$. Also, if we obtain an equality of the form $s = 0$ from Γ' where s is a slack variable, then GA returns the $\mathcal{LA}$-unsatisfiability of $\Gamma \cup \Delta$. Otherwise, GA returns the $\mathcal{LA}$-satisfiability of $\Gamma \cup \Delta$.

Generating minimal conflict sets. When considering a new equality e, GA labels it with a unique identifier ℓ producing $\ell : e$. If $\ell_1 : t_1 = 0$ and $\ell_2 : t_2 = 0$ are linearly combined so to obtain $t_1 + c * t_2 = 0$, then its label will be the expression $\ell_1 + c * \ell_2$. We also assume that expressions for labels are simplified according to the usual arithmetic rules. In this way, when an unsatisfiable equality $\ell : 0 = c$ (with $c \neq 0$) or $\ell : s = 0$ (with s a slack variable) is detected by GA, the identifiers occurring in the expression ℓ will yield a minimal conflict set. To illustrate the idea, consider the following example.

Example 1. Consider the input set Γ_I to GA, and the related output:

$$\Gamma_I := \begin{cases} \ell_1 : x_4 = x_1 \\ \ell_2 : x_5 = x_2 \\ \ell_3 : x_6 = x_3 \\ \ell_4 : x_5 + x_4 = 4 \\ \ell_5 : x_7 = x_4 \\ \ell_6 : x_7 = x_5 \\ \ell_7 : x_6 = 2 \\ \ell_8 : x_1 \neq x_2 \end{cases} \longrightarrow_{\mathsf{GA}} \begin{cases} \ell_1 : x_4 = x_1 \\ \ell_2 : x_5 = x_2 \\ \ell_3 : x_6 = x_3 \\ \ell_1 + \ell_2 - \ell_4 : x_1 + x_2 = 4 \\ \ell_5 - \ell_1 : x_7 = x_1 \\ 0.5\ell_6 - 0.5\ell_5 + 0.5\ell_4 - \ell_1 : x_1 = 2 \\ \ell_7 : x_6 = 2 \\ \ell_8 + \ell_6 + \ell_2 - \ell_5 - \ell_1 : s = 0 \end{cases}$$

Notice that the disequality $\ell_8 : x_1 \neq x_2$ in Γ_I has been translated to $\ell_8 : x_1 - x_2 = s$, where s is a slack variable. The unsatisfiable equation $s = 0$ (since s is a slack variable) in the output set is labelled by the expression $\ell_8 + \ell_6 + \ell_2 - \ell_5 - \ell_1$ and so the minimal conflict is $\{\ell_1, \ell_2, \ell_5, \ell_6, \ell_8\}$.

Explaining elementary equalities. Observe that if an equality $x = y$ is entailed by a system of linear equalities $t_i = 0$ for $i = 1, \ldots, n$, then $x - y$ must be a linear combination of t_i, $i \in \{1, \ldots, n\}$, i.e. $x - y = \sum_{i \in \{1, \ldots, n\}} \lambda_i * t_i$ such that $\lambda_k \neq 0$ for (at least one) k in $\{1, \ldots, n\}$. When GA cannot perform linear combinations any more, it back-substitutes variables in order to compute the most general solution of the system. As a consequence, equalities of the form $\ell'_i : x_i = t_i$ for $i = 1, \ldots n$ are obtained where x_i does not occur in t_i. Then, GA performs a guessing step, i.e. it picks two equalities $\ell'_i : x_i = t_i$ and $\ell'_j : x_j = t_j$ ($i \neq j$) and checks the syntactical identity of t_i and t_j. If this is the case, then $x_i - x_j = 0$ is entailed by the set of literals and its label is $\ell'_i - \ell'_j$.

Example 2. Consider the input set $\Gamma_I \setminus \{x_1 \neq x_2\}$ to GA, where Γ_I is the same of Example 1. It is easy to see that $\ell_6 - \ell_5 - \ell_1 - \ell_2 : x_1 - x_2 = 0$ is entailed by $\ell_1, \ldots, \ell_7$ since the right hand sides of the labelled equalities, namely $0.5\ell_6 - 0.5\ell_5 + 0.5\ell_4 - \ell_1 : x_1 = 2$ and $0.5\ell_5 + 0.5\ell_4 - \ell_2 - 0.5\ell_6 : x_2 = 2$ are identical. So, the minimal explanation of $x_1 = x_2$ is $\{\ell_1, \ell_2, \ell_5, \ell_6\}$.

GA can be efficiently implemented as explained in [3]. However, notice that GA has the additional capability to compute minimal explanations of elementary equalities, which is crucial to enable the application of the method in Figure 1.

Remark. The technique underlying GA can be extended to produce minimal conflict sets and explanations in $\mathcal{LA}^{\leq}$. The key idea is to couple GA with a variant of the Simplex algorithm (see, e.g., [15]) which keeps track of the constraints used during its pivoting phase in a way similar to the one described above for GA.

7   Discussion

In this paper, we have proposed a method to modularly build conflict sets in unions of theories by refining the Nelson-Oppen combination schema. The key concept is that of explanation graph, which allows us to encode the fact that a certain elementary equality is a logical consequence of a set of elementary equalities. Explanation engines formalize proof-producing procedures capable of computing explanation graphs. We have shown how to re-use (efficient) proof-producing procedures available in the literature to build explanation engines. Furthermore, explanation engines for unions of several theories can be obtained as a by-product of our combination method. A suitable notion of minimality (related to quasi-conflict sets) in unions of theories is also investigated.

In a slightly different context, our techniques could also be used to build "equational reasoners" having the capability of computing a (small) witness of unsatisfiability for equational problems such as unification, matching, and word problems. For equational theories, there are satisfiability procedures with the property of deriving elementary equalities (like unification or matching algorithms) and deductive combination methods based on the propagation of elementary equalities [1,12]. Applying the techniques developed here to more general equational reasoners appears to be a promising line of research.

Regarding the integration of constraint solvers in generic reasoning systems, (e.g., SMT solvers), an alternative approach to producing conflict sets in combinations of theories have been proposed [2], which does not require the (direct) combination of the solvers for the component theories. While the technique of [2] may yield better performances for SMT problems, we believe our combination method could become a key ingredient in the certification of the results produced by solvers to be integrated in skeptical proof assistants (see, e.g., [8]).

References

1. Boudet, A.: Combining unification algorithms. Journal of Symbolic Computation 16(6), 597–626 (1993)
2. Bozzano, M., Bruttomesso, R., Cimatti, A., Junttila, T., van Rossum, P., Ranise, S., Sebastiani, R.: Efficient Theory Combination via Boolean Search. J. of Information and Computation 10(204), 1411–1596 (2006)
3. Burg, J., Lang, S.-D., Hughes, C.E.: Intelligent Backtracking in CLP(R). Ann. Math. Artif. Intell. 17(3-4), 189–211 (1996)

4. de Moura, L., Rueß, H., Shankar, N.: Justifying Equality. In: Proc. of the Workshop on Pragmatics of Decision Procedures for Automated Reasoning (PDPAR'04), Also in ENTCS, vol. 125(3) (2004)
5. Downey, P.J., Sethi, R., Tarjan, R.E.: Variations on the common subexpression problem. J. ACM 27(4), 758–771 (1980)
6. Enderton, H.B.: A Mathematical Introduction to Logic. Academic Press, San Diego (1972)
7. Fontaine, P.: Techniques for Verification of Concurrent Systems with Invariants. PhD thesis, Université de Liège (2004)
8. Fontaine, P., Marion, J.-Y., Merz, S., Prensa Nieto, L., Tiu, A.F.: Expressiveness + Automation + Soundness: Towards Combining SMT Solvers and Interactive Proof Assistants. In: Hermanns, H., Palsberg, J. (eds.) TACAS 2006 and ETAPS 2006. LNCS, vol. 3920, pp. 167–181. Springer, Heidelberg (2006)
9. Kirchner, H., Ranise, S., Ringeissen, C., Tran, D.-K.: Automatic Combinability of Rewriting-Based Satisfiability Procedures. In: Hermann, M., Voronkov, A. (eds.) LPAR 2006. LNCS (LNAI), vol. 4246, pp. 542–556. Springer, Heidelberg (2006)
10. Nelson, G., Oppen, D.C.: Simplification by cooperating decision procedures. ACM Trans. on Programming Languages and Systems 1(2), 245–257 (1979)
11. Nieuwenhuis, R., Oliveras, A.: Proof-Producing Congruence Closure. In: Giesl, J. (ed.) RTA 2005. LNCS, vol. 3467, pp. 453–468. Springer, Heidelberg (2005)
12. Nipkow, T.: Combining matching algorithms: The regular case. Journal of Symbolic Computation 12, 633–653 (1991)
13. Ranise, S., Ringeissen, C., Tran, D.-K.: Nelson-Oppen, Shostak and the Extended Canonizer: A Family Picture with a Newborn. In: Liu, Z., Araki, K. (eds.) ICTAC 2004. LNCS, vol. 3407, Springer, Heidelberg (2005)
14. Ranise, S., Tinelli, C.: Satisfiability Modulo Theories. IEEE Magazine on Intelligent Systems 21(6), 71–81 (2006)
15. Schrijver, A.: Theory of linear and integer programming. John Wiley & Sons, Chichester (1986)
16. Schulz, S.: E – a brainiac theorem prover. AI Communications (2002)
17. Stump, A., Tang, L.-Y.: The Algebra of Equality Proofs. In: Giesl, J. (ed.) RTA 2005. LNCS, vol. 3467, pp. 469–483. Springer, Heidelberg (2005)
18. Tarjan, R.E.: Efficiency of a good but not linear set union algorithm. J. of the ACM 22(2), 215–225 (1975)
19. Tran, D.-K.: Conception de Procédures de Décision par Combinaison et Saturation. PhD thesis, Université Henri Poincaré, Nancy, France, Ch. 8 (in english) (2007)

Visibly Pushdown Languages and Term Rewriting

Jacques Chabin and Pierre Réty

LIFO - Université d'Orléans, B.P. 6759, 45067 Orléans cedex 2, France
{Jacques.Chabin, Pierre.Rety}@univ-orleans.fr
http://www.univ-orleans.fr/lifo/Members/rety

Abstract. To combine tree languages with term rewriting, we introduce a new class of tree languages, that both extends regular languages and restricts context-free languages, and that is closed under intersection (unlike context-free languages). To do it, we combine the concept of visibly pushdown language, with top-down pushdown tree automata, and we get the visibly pushdown tree automata. Then, we use them to express the sets of descendants for a sub-class of growing term rewrite systems, and thanks to closure under intersection, we get that joinability and (restricted) unifiability are decidable.

Keywords: tree languages, term rewriting.

1 Introduction

Tree languages allow to express, manipulate, and decide properties over infinite sets of first-order terms. This is why tree languages have been combined with several other domains, like term rewriting [3,9], logic programming [10], concurrency [12,5] (process algebra), protocol verification [4],...

We want to combine tree languages with term rewriting. However, to get something interesting, it is desirable that the considered tree languages have both a big expressivity and good properties. Since these two requirements are contradictory, one will look for a middle-way in between. Regular tree languages have good properties, but have a poor expressivity. Context-free tree languages are much more expressive, but have fewer good properties, in particular they are not closed under intersection. Some other expressive tree languages have the same disadvantages [14,5,11], or do not extend regular languages [7].

In this paper, we introduce a new class of tree languages, that both extends regular languages and restricts context-free languages, and that is closed under intersection. To do it, we combine the concept of visibly pushdown language, already used for string languages [2], with the top-down pushdown tree automata of I. Guessarian [6]. We call these new languages *Visibly Pushdown Tree Languages (VPTL)*, and show that they are closed under union and intersection. As a sub-class of context-free languages, membership and emptiness are decidable. This work is presented in Section 2.

B. Konev and F. Wolter (Eds.): FroCos 2007, LNAI 4720, pp. 252–266, 2007.

Next, we define the *Visibly Context-free Term Rewrite Systems (VCF-TRS)* as a sub-class of growing term rewrite systems. In [8] it is proved that the set of predecessors of a given regular tree language by a linear (weakened to left-linear in [13]) growing rewrite system, is also regular. Consequently reachability is decidable. However, nothing has been proved about descendants (successors). In this paper, we prove that the descendants of a given VPTL (which may be regular) by a linear VCF-TRS, is also a VPTL. Since VPTL's are closed under intersection, joinability is decidable in linear VCF-TRS's, whereas it is undecidable in growing rewrite systems. As a consequence, it is decidable whether two linear terms with disjoint variables are unifiable modulo a confluent linear VCF-TRS. Thanks to expressivity and closure under intersection, other applications of VPTL's should arise. This work is presented in Section 3.

2 Visibly Pushdown Tree Languages

A *pushdown alphabet* is a finite set $\Sigma = \Sigma_c \cup \Sigma_r \cup \Sigma_l$ where $\Sigma_c, \Sigma_r, \Sigma_l$ are disjoint. Σ_c is the set of *call symbols*, Σ_r is the set of *return symbols*, Σ_l is the set of *local symbols*. Intuitively, the automaton pushes onto the stack when it reads a call symbol, it pops the stack when it reads a return symbol, and it leaves the stack unchanged when it reads a local symbol.

Each symbol $f \in \Sigma$ has a unique arity, denoted by $ar(f)$. We consider a set of variables Var. The notions of first-order term, position, substitution, term rewriting, are defined as usual. Let us just precise some notations. T_Σ denotes the set of ground terms over Σ. For a term t, $Var(t)$ is the set of variables of t, $Pos(t)$ is the set of positions of t. For $p \in Pos(t)$, $t(p)$ is the symbol of $\Sigma \cup Var$ occurring at position p in t, and $t|_p$ is the subterm of t at position p. $PosVar(t) = \{p \in Pos(t) \mid t(p) \in Var\}$, $PosNonVar(t) = \{p \in Pos(t) \mid t(p) \notin Var\}$. Note that if $p \in PosNonVar(t)$, $t|_p = f(t_1, \ldots, t_n)$, and $i \in \{1, \ldots, n\}$, then $p.i$ is the position of t_i in t. For $p, p' \in Pos(t)$, $p < p'$ means that p occurs in t strictly above p'.

The automata defined below work top-down. States are binary symbols, whose first argument is a term in $T_{\Sigma \cup Var}$ and the second argument is a stack. Stacks are terms over the signature Π, which contains only unary symbols and one constant.

Definition 1. *A* Visibly Pushdown Tree Automaton (VPTA) *is a tuple* $A = (\Sigma, Q, q_0, \Pi, z_0, \Delta)$ *where* Σ *is a pushdown alphabet,* Q *is a finite set of states of arity 2,* $q_0 \in Q$ *is the initial state,* Π *is a finite set of stack symbols of arities in* $\{0, 1\}$ *which contains only one constant* z_0 *(z_0 is the empty stack),* Δ *is a set of rewrite rules, called* transitions, *of the form* $(q, q_1, \ldots, q_n \in Q, f \in \Sigma, e, e_1, \ldots, e_n \in \Pi, x_1, \ldots, x_n$ *and* z *are variables):*

- $q(f(x_1, \ldots, x_n), z) \rightarrow f(q_1(x_1, e_1(z)), \ldots, q_n(x_n, e_n(z)))$ *if* $f \in \Sigma_c$
- $q(f(x_1, \ldots, x_n), e(z)) \rightarrow f(q_1(x_1, z), \ldots, q_n(x_n, z))$ *if* $f \in \Sigma_r$
- $q(f(x_1, \ldots, x_n), z_0) \rightarrow f(q_1(x_1, z_0), \ldots, q_n(x_n, z_0))$ *if* $f \in \Sigma_r$

- $q(f(x_1, \ldots, x_n), z) \rightarrow f(q_1(x_1, z), \ldots, q_n(x_n, z))$ *if* $f \in \Sigma_l$
- $q(x, z) \rightarrow q_1(x, z)$ *(empty transition)*

f may be a constant, whereas $e, e_1, \ldots, e_n$ *are always unary.*

The language $L(A)$ *recognized by* A *is* $L(A) = \{t \in T_\Sigma \mid q_0(t, z_0) \rightarrow^*_\Delta t\}$. *A set of terms that can be recognized be a VPTA is called* Visibly Pushdown Tree Language (VPTL).

Note that the automaton can check the stack top only if it reads a return symbol.

Example 1. Let

$$E = \{ \quad c^n \quad \mid n \in \mathbb{N}\}$$

$$\begin{array}{c} c^n \\ | \\ f \\ / \ \backslash \\ g^n \quad s \\ | \quad | \\ a \quad h^n \\ | \\ a \end{array}$$

where $c^n = c(c(\cdots c(\ldots)))$ in which c occurs n times. E is a VPTL recognized by the automaton $A = (\Sigma, Q, q_0, \Pi, z_0, \Delta)$ where $\Sigma_c = \{c\}$, $\Sigma_r = \{g, h, a\}$, $\Sigma_l = \{f, s\}$, $Q = \{q_0, q_1, q_2, q_3\}$, $\Pi = \{e\}$, and $\Delta = \{$

$$q_0(c(x), z) \rightarrow c(q_0(x, e(z)))$$
$$q_0(f(x, y), z) \rightarrow f(q_1(x, z), q_2(y, z))$$
$$q_1(g(x), e(z)) \rightarrow g(q_1(x), z)$$
$$q_1(a, z_0) \rightarrow a$$
$$q_2(s(x), z) \rightarrow s(q_3(x, z))$$
$$q_3(h(x), e(z)) \rightarrow h(q_3(x), z)$$
$$q_3(a, z_0) \rightarrow a \}$$

Note that a checks that the current stack is the empty stack z_0, which ensures that there are exactly n occurrences of g and n occurrences of h.

Example 2. Let

$$E' = \{ \quad c^n \quad \mid n, i, j \in \mathbb{N} \wedge i + j = n\} \quad \text{and} \quad E'' = \{ \quad c^n \quad \mid n \in \mathbb{N}\}$$

$$\begin{array}{c} c^n \\ | \\ f \\ / \ \backslash \\ g^n \quad s^i \\ | \quad | \\ a \quad h^j \\ | \\ a \end{array} \qquad\qquad \begin{array}{c} c^n \\ | \\ f \\ / \ \backslash \\ g^n \quad s^n \\ | \quad | \\ a \quad h^n \\ | \\ a \end{array}$$

E' is a VPTL if s is a return symbol. E'' is not a VPTL : c should be call and s, h should be return to be able to count n, but reading one c necessarily pushes exactly one symbol onto the stack, and reading one s or one h pops exactly one symbol from the stack.

On the other hand, a language like $\{f(g^n(a), h^n(a)) \mid n \in \mathbb{N}\}$ is not a VPTL, since to check that the number of g and h are the same, we need to pop a stack of height n in both branches, and no symbol (it was c in Languages E and E') enables to build such a stack.

Theorem 2

- If L is a regular tree language over Σ, then L is also a visibly pushdown tree language over any partition $\Sigma_c \cup \Sigma_r \cup \Sigma_l$ of Σ.
- Every visibly pushdown tree language is a context-free language.

Proof 1) Since L is regular, it can be recognized by a top-down automaton without a stack $A = (\Sigma, Q, q_0, \Delta)$. Let $\Pi = \{e, z_0\}$, and Q' be the set composed of the states of Q considered as symbols of arity 2. Let Δ' be the set of transitions built as follows : for each non-empty transition $q(f(x_1, \ldots, x_n)) \to f(q_1(x_1), \ldots, q_n(x_n))$ of Δ, we add into Δ' :

- $q(f(x_1, \ldots, x_n), z) \to f(q_1(x_1, e(z)), \ldots, q_n(x_n, e(z)))$ if $f \in \Sigma_c$
- $q(f(x_1, \ldots, x_n), e(z)) \to f(q_1(x_1, z), \ldots, q_n(x_n, z))$ if $f \in \Sigma_r$
- $q(f(x_1, \ldots, x_n), z_0) \to f(q_1(x_1, z_0), \ldots, q_n(x_n, z_0))$ if $f \in \Sigma_r$
- $q(f(x_1, \ldots, x_n), z) \to f(q_1(x_1, z), \ldots, q_n(x_n, z))$ if $f \in \Sigma_l$

and for each empty transition $q(x) \to q_1(x)$ of Δ, we add into Δ' :

- $q(x, z) \to q_1(x, z)$

The automaton $A' = (\Sigma, Q', q_0, \Pi, z_0, \Delta')$ is a VPTA which also recognizes L.

2) VPTA's are particular cases of the top-down pushdown automata of [6], which recognize exactly context-free tree languages.

Although VPTL's are more expressive than regular tree languages, they still have good properties.

Theorem 3. *Visibly Pushdown Tree Languages are closed under union and intersection. Emptiness and membership are decidable.*

Unsurprisingly, the number of states (resp. transitions) of the union automaton is in the order of the sum of the number of states (resp. transitions) of the initial automata. The number of states (resp. transitions) of the intersection automaton is in the order of the product of the number of states (resp. transitions) of the initial automata if they have no empty transitions.

Proof. Let L_1 and L_2 be VPTL's over the same pushdown alphabet Σ. Let $A_1 = (\Sigma, Q_1, q_0^1, \Pi_1, z_0^1, \Delta_1)$ and $A_2 = (\Sigma, Q_2, q_0^2, \Pi_2, z_0^2, \Delta_2)$ be automata that recognize L_1 and L_2 respectively. We assume that Q_1 and Q_2 are disjoint, and Π_1 and Π_2 are disjoint.

1) $L_1 \cup L_2$ is recognized by $A = (\Sigma, Q, q_0, \Pi, z_0, \Delta)$ where $Q = Q_1 \cup Q_2 \cup \{q_0\}$, $\Pi = \Pi_1 \cup \Pi_2 \cup \{z_0\}$ and $\Delta = \Delta_1 \cup \Delta_2 \cup \{q_0(x, z) \to q_0^1(x, z), q_0(x, z) \to q_0^2(x, z)\}$.

2) $L_1 \cap L_2$ is recognized by $A = (\Sigma, Q, q_0, \Pi, z_0, \Delta)$ where $Q = Q_1 \times Q_2$, $q_0 = (q_0^1, q_0^2)$, $\Pi = \Pi_1 \times \Pi_2$, $z_0 = (z_0^1, z_0^2)$, and Δ is the following set of transitions:

- $(q^1, q^2)(f(x_1, \ldots, x_n), z) \rightarrow$
  $$f((q_1^1, q_1^2)(x_1, (e_1^1, e_1^2)(z)), \ldots, (q_n^1, q_n^2)(x_n, (e_n^1, e_n^2)(z)))$$
  if $f \in \Sigma_c$, $q^1(f(x_1, \ldots, x_n), z) \rightarrow f(q_1^1(x_1, e_1^1(z)), \ldots, q_n^1(x_n, e_n^1(z))) \in \Delta_1$
  and $q^2(f(x_1, \ldots, x_n), z) \rightarrow f(q_1^2(x_1, e_1^2(z)), \ldots, q_n^2(x_n, e_n^2(z))) \in \Delta_2$.

- $(q^1, q^2)(f(x_1, \ldots, x_n), (e^1, e^2)(z)) \rightarrow f((q_1^1, q_1^2)(x_1, z), \ldots, (q_n^1, q_n^2)(x_n, z))$
  if $f \in \Sigma_r$, $q^1(f(x_1, \ldots, x_n), e^1(z)) \rightarrow f(q_1^1(x_1, z), \ldots, q_n^1(x_n, z)) \in \Delta_1$ and
  $q^2(f(x_1, \ldots, x_n), e^2(z)) \rightarrow f(q_1^2(x_1, z), \ldots, q_n^2(x_n, z)) \in \Delta_2$.

- $(q^1, q^2)(f(x_1, \ldots, x_n), z_0) \rightarrow f((q_1^1, q_1^2)(x_1, z_0), \ldots, (q_n^1, q_n^2)(x_n, z_0))$
  if $f \in \Sigma_r$, $q^1(f(x_1, \ldots, x_n), z_0^1) \rightarrow f(q_1^1(x_1, z_0^1), \ldots, q_n^1(x_n, z_0^1)) \in \Delta_1$ and
  $q^2(f(x_1, \ldots, x_n), z_0^2) \rightarrow f(q_1^2(x_1, z_0^2), \ldots, q_n^2(x_n, z_0^2)) \in \Delta_2$.

- $(q^1, q^2)(f(x_1, \ldots, x_n), z) \rightarrow f((q_1^1, q_1^2)(x_1, z), \ldots, (q_n^1, q_n^2)(x_n, z))$
  if $f \in \Sigma_l$, $q^1(f(x_1, \ldots, x_n), z) \rightarrow f(q_1^1(x_1, z), \ldots, q_n^1(x_n, z)) \in \Delta_1$ and
  $q^2(f(x_1, \ldots, x_n), z) \rightarrow f(q_1^2(x_1, z), \ldots, q_n^2(x_n, z)) \in \Delta_2$.

- $(q^1, q)(x, z) \rightarrow (q_1^1, q)(x, z)$ if $q \in Q_2$ and $q^1(x, z) \rightarrow q_1^1(x, z) \in \Delta_1$.

- $(q, q^2)(x, z) \rightarrow (q, q_1^2)(x, z)$ if $q \in Q_1$ and $q^2(x, z) \rightarrow q_1^2(x, z) \in \Delta_2$.

Note that we crucially use the fact that A_1 and A_2 being VPTA's over the same pushdown alphabet, they synchronize on the push and pop operations on the stack.

3) VPTA's are particular Guessarian's pushdown tree automata [6], which have been proved to be equivalent to context-free languages (i.e. generated by context-free grammars). Therefore emptiness and membership are decidable.

Remark 4. : VPTL's are different from languages accepted by NP-NTA's [1], even if they have the same closure and decidability properties. Indeed, NP-NTA's deal with binary nested trees (sort of DAG's), which are necessarily infinite (all branches are infinite). Moreover, statuses call, return, local, are not attached to symbols in Σ, they are attached to nodes, i.e. positions.

3   Visibly Context-Free Term Rewrite Systems

Definition 5. *A rewrite system R is* growing *[8] if for every $l \rightarrow r \in R$, each variable occurring both in l and in r occurs at depth 0 or 1 in l.*
A rewrite system R is context-free *if for every $l \rightarrow r \in R$, $l = f(x_1, \ldots, x_n)$ where $x_1, \ldots, x_n$ are distinct variables.*
A symbol is reducible *if it occurs at the top of at least one rewrite rule. So, the set of reducible symbols is $RED(R) = \{f \in \Sigma \mid \exists l \rightarrow r \in R, l(\epsilon) = f\}$.*

Note that context-free is a restriction stronger than growing. However, even if R is context free, joinability is undecidable, and in general the set of descendants $R^*(\{t\})$ is not a VPTL (otherwise emptiness of VPTL's would be undecidable). This is why the stronger restriction *visibly context-free* is introduced in the following.

Proposition 6. *Joinability in context-free rewrite systems is undecidable.*

Proof. Let $(u_1, v_1), \ldots, (u_m, v_m)$ be an instance of PCP (Post Correspondence Problem). Let $R = \{f(x) \rightarrow u_i(f(i(x))) \mid i \in \{1, \ldots, m\}\} \cup \{g(x) \rightarrow v_i(g(i(x))) \mid i \in \{1, \ldots, m\}\} \cup \{f(x) \rightarrow s(x), g(x) \rightarrow s(x)\}$.
R is context-free. However

$$\exists t \mid f(a) \rightarrow_R^* t \,{}_R^*\!\!\leftarrow g(a) \iff R^*(f(a)) \cap R^*(g(a)) \neq \emptyset \iff$$
$$\exists i_1, \ldots, i_k, j_1, \ldots, j_{k'} \mid u_{i_1} \ldots u_{i_k} s\, i_k \ldots i_1 = v_{j_1} \ldots v_{j_{k'}} s\, j_{k'} \ldots j_1 \iff$$
$$k = k' \wedge i_1 = j_1, \ldots i_k = j_k \wedge u_{i_1} \ldots u_{i_k} = v_{i_1} \ldots v_{i_k} \iff \text{ this PCP instance}$$
has at least one solution.

Given a pushdown alphabet Σ and a term t, if we try to reduce $q(t, z_0)$ with transitions of a VPTA over Σ, for each $p \in Pos(t)$ the height of the current stack obtained when reducing at position p depends only on call and return symbols within t, and does not depend on q.

Definition 7. *We define the weight $w(f)$ of $f \in \Sigma \cup Var$ by:*
- $w(f) = 1$ *if* $f \in \Sigma_c$,
- $w(f) = -1$ *if* $f \in \Sigma_r$,
- $w(f) = 0$ *if* $f \in \Sigma_l$ *or f is a variable.*

The height of stack is the mapping $h : Pos(t) \rightarrow Z$ defined inductively by:
- $h(\epsilon) = w(t(\epsilon))$,
- $\forall p \in PosNonVar(t), \forall i \in \{1, \ldots, ar(t(p))\}, h(p.i) = h(p) + w(t(p.i))$.

Definition 8. *The linear context-free rewrite system R is* visibly *over the pushdown alphabet $\Sigma = \Sigma_c \cup \Sigma_r \cup \Sigma_l$ if*
- $RED(R) \subseteq \Sigma_l$
- $\forall l \rightarrow r \in R, Var(l) = Var(r)$ *and* $\forall p \in PosNonVar(r) :$
  - $h(p) \geq 0$
  - $\forall i \in \{1, \ldots, ar(t(p))\}(t(p.i) \in Var \implies (h(p) = 0 \wedge \forall p' < p, h(p') > 0))$

VCF-TRS *means Visibly Context-Free Term Rewrite System.*

Consequently, if $l \rightarrow r \in R$, then $l(\epsilon) \in \Sigma_l$, and
- r is a variable
- or r is shallow[1] and $r(\epsilon) \in \Sigma_l$
- or $r(\epsilon) \in \Sigma_c$ and every position just above a variable is the corresponding return (it pops from the stack the symbol pushed by $r(\epsilon)$).

Example 3. $R = \{f(x) \rightarrow f(f(x))$ is not visibly context-free, because $f \in RED(R) \subseteq \Sigma_l$ and for Positions $p = 1$, $p' = \epsilon$ in the right-hand-side, p is just above a variable whereas $p' < p \wedge \neg(h(p') > 0)$. Intuitively, in the right-hand-side, to distinguish the language generated by reducing the inner f from the one generated by the outer f, we need the stack. But the stack is not used since every symbol is local.

---
[1] Every variable occurs at depth 1.

Now let $c \in \Sigma_c$ and $s \in \Sigma_r$. $R' = \{f(x) \to c(f(f(f(s(x)))))\}$ is visibly context-free.

$$R'' = \{\ f \quad \to \quad c \quad \}$$

$$
\begin{array}{ccc}
\diagup\ \backslash & & \diagup\ \backslash \\
x \quad y & f & f \\
& \diagup\ \backslash \quad \diagup\ \backslash & \\
s \quad a & b \quad u & \\
\vert & \vert & \\
x & y &
\end{array}
$$

is visibly-context free with $\Sigma_c = \{c\}$, $\Sigma_r = \{s, a, b, u\}$, $\Sigma_l = \{f\}$.
The TRS given in Example 4 (page 260) is visibly context-free.

Definition 9. *Given a rewrite system R and a set of ground terms E, the set of* descendants *of E by R is $R^*(E) = \{t' \in T_\Sigma \mid \exists t \in E, t \to_R^* t'\}$.*

Theorem 10. *Let R be a linear visibly context-free rewrite system and E be a visibly pushdown tree language over the same pushdown alphabet Σ. Then $R^*(E)$ is a also a visibly pushdown tree language over Σ.*

Theorem 10 comes from the algorithm presented in the following section, which is proved to be terminating, complete, and sound.

Corollary 11. *Reachability and joinability are decidable for linear visibly context-free rewrite systems.*

Consequently, and according to the proof of Proposition 6, the PCP instances such that R is visibly context-free form a decidable sub-class of PCP.

Theorem 12. *It is decidable whether two linear terms with disjoint variables are unifiable modulo a confluent linear VCF-TRS.*

Proof. Let S be the set of all ground substitutions.
Since t and t' have disjoint variables and R is confluent, t and t' are R-unifiable iff there exists $\theta, \theta' \in S$ s.t. $\theta t \to_R^* u \,{}^*_R\!\leftarrow \theta' t'$, which is equivalent to

$$R^*(\{\sigma t \mid \sigma \in S\}) \cap R^*(\{\sigma' t' \mid \sigma' \in S\}) \neq \emptyset$$

Since t and t' are linear, $\{\sigma t \mid \sigma \in S\}$ and $\{\sigma' t' \mid \sigma' \in S\}$ are regular languages, and from Theorem 2 are also VPTL's. From Theorem 10, their descendants are also VPTL's. Then we can compute their intersection and check the emptiness.

3.1   Algorithm for Computing Descendants

The algorithm is illustrated by Example 4 (see below).

The algorithm starts with an automaton A_E that recognizes E, and achieves overlap steps. An overlap step overlaps a rewrite rule of R with a transition of Δ, and adds new states and new transitions into the automaton. If a transition existed already, it is not added.

Let $l \to r \in R$. Since R is supposed to be linear visible context-free, l has the form $l = f(x_1, \ldots, x_n)$ where $f \in \Sigma_l$ (because f is reducible). If Δ contains a transition like $q(f(x_1, \ldots, x_n), z) \to f(q_1(x_1, z), \ldots, q_n(x_n, z))$, a term of the form $C[\sigma l]$ may be recognized by the automaton. In order to recognize $C[\sigma r]$ as well, the algorithms adds states and transitions so that $q(r, z) \to_\Delta^* \theta r$ where $\theta = (x_1/q_1(x_1, z), \ldots, x_n/q_n(x_n, z))$. To do it, we introduce states q^p for each $p \in PosNonVar(r) \backslash \{\epsilon\}$. If $l \to r$ causes several overlap steps, we re-use the same states q^p (otherwise, the algorithm would not terminate). Thanks to the stack and the restrictions on R, it does not make a confusion, i.e. the algorithm is sound. However, if r contains call and return symbols, we use new stack symbols for each overlap step (otherwise the algorithm would not be sound).

To each transition is associated a unique identifier (i, p) where $i \in \mathbb{N}$ and p is a position. Intuitively, transition (i, p) has been created by the ith overlap step, and allows to recognize the symbol $r(p)$ for some $l \to r \in R$. By convention, the transitions of the initial automaton A_E have identifiers of the form $(0, p)$ (and in this case, p's are chosen arbitrarily).
We will write $(i, p) \oplus (l \to r)$ to denote the overlap step between the transition (i, p) and the rewrite rule $l \to r$.

The Overlap Step $(x, u) \oplus (l_j \to r_j)$. Let A be the current automaton, and suppose that i_{max} overlap steps have already been done. Let $i = i_{max} + 1$. Suppose there are $l_j \to r_j \in R$ and a transition in Δ of the form $q(l_j, z) \to \theta l_j$ identified by (x, u).

In order to know which stack symbols should be popped by return symbols, we first define a mapping $stack : Pos(r_j) \to T_{\{e_i^k | k \in \{1, \ldots, armax(\Sigma)\}\} \cup \{z_0\}}$, in an inductive way ($armax(\Sigma)$ is the maximum arity of symbols in Σ). Intuitively, $stack(p)$ is the stack obtained when starting with the initial stack z_0 and reading r_j until position p (just before reading the symbol that occurs at position p). For a stack s, $head(s)$ denotes the top symbol of s, and $tail(s)$ is the stack obtained by popping the head of s.

$$stack(\epsilon) = z_0$$

$$stack(p.k) = \begin{vmatrix} stack(p) & \text{if } r_j(p) \in \Sigma_l \\ e_i^k(stack(p)) & \text{if } r_j(p) \in \Sigma_c \\ tail(stack(p)) & \text{if } r_j(p) \in \Sigma_r \end{vmatrix}$$

In the transitions below, each symbol of the form q_j^y is a state that encodes position y of r_j, except for border positions of r_j, i.e. when $y \in \{\epsilon\} \cup PosVar(r_j)$. In this case we use the states coming from transition (x, u), hence:

- $q_j^\epsilon = q$
- $\forall p.k \in PosVar(r_j)$, $q_j^{p.k} = (\theta(r_j(p.k)))(\epsilon)$.

For each $p \in PosNonVar(r_j)$, we add into Δ the following transition (except if it is already in Δ) identified by (i, p):

- if $r_j(p) \in \Sigma_l$: $q_j^p(r_j(p)(x_1, \ldots, x_n), z) \to r_j(p)(q_j^{p.1}(x_1, z), \ldots, q_j^{p.n}(x_n, z))$
- if $r_j(p) \in \Sigma_c$:
$$q_j^p(r_j(p)(x_1, \ldots, x_n), z) \to r_j(p)(q_j^{p.1}(x_1, e_i^1(z)), \ldots, q_j^{p.n}(x_n, e_i^n(z)))$$

- if $r_j(p) \in \Sigma_r$ (let $e_i^k = head(stack(p))$) : $q_j^p(r_j(p))(x_1, \ldots, x_n), e_i^k(z)) \rightarrow$
$r_j(p)(q_j^{p.1}(x_1, z), \ldots, q_j^{p.n}(x_n, z))$
- however, if $r_j \in Var$, we add : $q(r_j, z) \rightarrow \theta r_j$ (identified by (i, ϵ)).

Note that states do not depend on the current overlap step i, whereas stack symbols do. States depend only on the rewrite rule number j.

Definition 13. *Let Q_{sat} denote the set of states, and Δ_{sat} denote the set of transitions, saturated by overlap steps (all overlap steps have been achieved).*

Example 4. Let $\Sigma_c = \{c, u\}$, $\Sigma_r = \{g, s, w\}$, $\Sigma_l = \{f, h, a\}$.

$$R = \{ \, f \; \xrightarrow{1} \; c, \quad h \xrightarrow{2} u \} \quad E = \{ \, f \, \} \text{ then } R^*(E) = \{ \quad c^n \quad | \, n \in \mathbb{N} \}$$

with the tree structures:

f with children x, y; c with child f (f with children g, h; g with child x; h with child s; s with child y); h with children x, h (h with child w; w with child x); u with child h.

$E = \{ f \}$ with children a, a.

$R^*(E) = \{ c^n \}$ with f having children g^n and $(u^i h\, w^i s)^n$ with children a and a.

c^n means $c(c(\cdots (c$ where c occurs n times, and
$(u^i h\, w^i s)^n$ means $u^{i_1}(h(w^{i_1}(s(\cdots(u^{i_n}(h(w^{i_n}(s(a)))))))))$ for any $i_1, \ldots, i_n \in \mathbb{N}$.
with $s(a)$ having child a.

We start with the following transitions which recognize E :
$$(0, \epsilon) : \; q_0^\epsilon(f(x, y), z) \rightarrow f(q_0^1(x, z), q_0^1(y, z))$$
$$(0, 1) : \; q_0^1(a, z) \rightarrow a$$

The algorithm computes the overlaps steps and adds new transitions. Note that once the first overlap step for one particular rewrite rule has been processed, the other overlap steps for this rule add fewer transitions since some of the generated transitions already exist.

- Overlap step $(0, \epsilon) \oplus rule1$
$$(1, \epsilon) : \; q_0^\epsilon(c(x), z) \rightarrow c(q_1^1(x, e_1^1(z)))$$
$$(1, 1) : \; q_1^1(f(x, y), z) \rightarrow f(q_1^{1.1}(x, z), q_1^{1.2}(y, z))$$
$$(1, 1.1) : \; q_1^{1.1}(g(x), e_1^1(z)) \rightarrow g(q_0^1(x, z))$$
$$(1, 1.2) : \; q_1^{1.2}(h(x), z) \rightarrow h(q_1^{1.2.1}(x, z))$$
$$(1, 1.2.1) : \; q_1^{1.2.1}(s(x), e_1^1(z)) \rightarrow s(q_0^1(x, z))$$

- Overlap step $(1, 1) \oplus rule1$
$$(2, \epsilon) : \; q_1^1(c(x), z) \rightarrow c(q_1^1(x, e_2^1(z)))$$
$$(2, 1.1) : \; q_1^{1.1}(g(x), e_2^1(z)) \rightarrow g(q_1^{1.1}(x, z))$$
$$(2, 1.2.1) : \; q_1^{1.2.1}(s(x), e_2^1(z)) \rightarrow s(q_1^{1.2}(x, z))$$

- Overlap step $(1, 1.2) \oplus rule2$
$$(3, \epsilon) : \; q_1^{1.2}(u(x), z) \rightarrow u(q_2^1(x, e_3^1(z)))$$
$$(3, 1) : \; q_2^1(h(x), z) \rightarrow h(q_2^{1.1}(x, z))$$
$$(3, 1.1) : \; q_2^{1.1}(w(x), e_3^1(z)) \rightarrow w(q_1^{1.2.1}(x, z))$$

- Overlap step $(3,1) \oplus rule2$

$$(4, \epsilon): \quad q_2^1(u(x), z) \rightarrow u(q_2^1(x, e_4^1(z)))$$
$$(4, 1.1): \quad q_2^{1.1}(w(x), e_4^1(z)) \rightarrow w(q_2^{1.1}(x, z))$$

For readability, we omit parentheses for unary symbols. Consider the term $ccf(gga, uhwshsa)$, also denoted $ccf(\alpha, \beta\gamma)$ where $\alpha = gga$, $\beta = uhws$, and $\gamma = hsa$. This term is in $R^*(E)$, and is recognized in the following way:

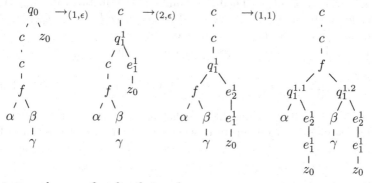

Now, let us replace α, β, γ by their values:

$q_1^{1.1}(\alpha, e_2^1 e_1^1(z_0)) = q_1^{1.1}(gg(a), e_2^1 e_1^1(z_0)) \rightarrow_{(2,1.1)} g(q_1^{1.1}(g(a), e_1^1(z_0))) \rightarrow_{(1,1.1)}$
$gg(q_0^1(a, z_0)) \rightarrow_{(0,1)} gg(a) = \alpha$

On the other hand,

$q_1^{1.2}(\beta\gamma, e_2^1 e_1^1(z_0)) = q_1^{1.2}(uhws\gamma, e_2^1 e_1^1(z_0)) \rightarrow_{(3,\epsilon)} u(q_2^1(hws\gamma, e_3^1 e_2^1 e_1^1(z_0))) \rightarrow_{(3,1)}$
$uh(q_2^{1.1}(ws\gamma, e_3^1 e_2^1 e_1^1(z_0))) \rightarrow_{(3,1.1)} uhw(q_1^{1.2.1}(s\gamma, e_2^1 e_1^1(z_0))) \rightarrow_{(2,1.2.1)}$
$uhws(q_1^{1.2}(\gamma, e_1^1(z_0))) = \beta(q_1^{1.2}(hs(a), e_1^1(z_0))) \rightarrow_{(1,1.2)}$
$\beta h(q_1^{1.2.1}(s(a), e_1^1(z_0))) \rightarrow_{(1,1.2.1)} \beta hs(q_0^1(a, z_0)) \rightarrow_{(0,1)} \beta hsa = \beta\gamma$

Note that although a is local (then does not check the stack top), the stack is necessarily empty when a is recognized, which ensures that there are as many c occurrences as g occurrences. This is due to the fact that the transitions deal with the outermost c and the innermost g as particular cases.

A consequence of Example 4 is:

Proposition 14. *Regular languages are not closed under rewriting by linear VCF-TRS.*

3.2   Termination

Although each overlap step uses new stack symbols, the algorithm terminates. It comes from the fact that when computing an overlap step $(x, u) \oplus (l_j \rightarrow r_j)$, transition (x, u) necessarily deals with a reducible symbol of Σ, which is local.

Proposition 15. *Q_{sat} and Δ_{sat} are finite.*

Proof. Let $A_E = (\Sigma, Q_E, q_0, \Pi_E, z_0, \Delta_E)$ be the initial automaton, i.e. an automaton that recognizes the initial language E. ¿From the algorithm

$$Q_{sat} = Q_E \cup \{q_j^p \mid l_j \rightarrow r_j \in R, p \in PosNonVar(r_j) \backslash \{\epsilon\}\}$$

Then Q_{sat} is finite.

In the following, for any finite set S, $|S|$ will denote the number of elements of S. Let $f \in RED(R)$. Since $RED(R) \subseteq \Sigma_l$, every transition in Δ_{sat} that uses f is of the form:

$$s(f(x_1, \ldots, x_n), z) \rightarrow f(s_1(x_1, z), \ldots, s_n(x_n, z))$$

where $s, s_1, \ldots, s_n \in Q_{sat}$. Then the number of transitions in Δ_{sat} that uses a reducible symbol is less than or equal to $x = |RED(R)| \times |Q_{sat}|^{armax(\Sigma)+1}$ where $armax(\Sigma)$ is the maximum arity of symbols in Σ.

Then the number of overlap steps is less than or equal to $y = x \times |R|$. Therefore

$$|\Delta_{sat}| \leq |\Delta_E| + y \times Max(\{|PosNonVar(r_j)| \mid l_j \rightarrow r_j \in R\} \cup \{1\})$$

Note that $\cdots \cup \{1\}$ comes from the fact that in an overlap step, a collapsing rule generates one new empty transition, whereas the number of positions of its rhs is 0.

3.3   Completeness

Lemma 16. *Let $l \rightarrow r \in R$, $q \in Q_{sat}$, s be a stack, and σ be a substitution. If $q(l, s) \rightarrow_{\Delta_{sat}} \sigma l$, then $q(r, s) \rightarrow^*_{\Delta_{sat}} \sigma r$.*

Proof. According to the form of transitions, σ is necessarily of the form $\sigma = (x_1/q_1(x_1, s), \ldots, x_n/q_n(x_n, s))$.

By hypothesis $q(l, s) \rightarrow_{(i,j)} \sigma l$. Then Transition $(i, j) = (q(l, z) \rightarrow \theta l)$ where z is a variable and $\theta = (x_1/q_1(x_1, z), \ldots, x_n/q_n(x_n, z))$.

The overlap step $(i, j) \oplus (l \rightarrow r)$ has been computed within Δ_{sat}, then $q(r, z) \rightarrow^*_{\Delta_{sat}} \theta r$. By instantiating z by s, we get $q(r, s) \rightarrow^*_{\Delta_{sat}} \sigma r$.

Lemma 17. *Let $t \in T_\Sigma$ and $l \rightarrow r \in R$. Recall that q_0 is the initial state and z_0 is the initial stack. If $q_0(t, z_0) \rightarrow^*_{\Delta_{sat}} t$ and $t \rightarrow_{[p, l \rightarrow r, \gamma]} t'$, then $q_0(t', z_0) \rightarrow^*_{\Delta_{sat}} t'$.*

Proof. From the hypotheses, $t|_p = \gamma l$ and

$$q_0(t, z_0) \rightarrow^*_{\Delta_{sat}} t[p \leftarrow q(\gamma l, s)] \rightarrow_{\Delta_{sat}} t[p \leftarrow \theta l] \rightarrow^*_{\Delta_{sat}} t[p \leftarrow \gamma l] = t$$

where $\theta = (x_1/q_1(\gamma x_1, s), \ldots, x_n/q_n(\gamma x_n, s))$.

Then $q(l, s) \rightarrow_{\Delta_{sat}} \sigma l$ where $\sigma = (x_1/q_1(x_1, s), \ldots, x_n/q_n(x_n, s))$. ¿From the previous lemma, $q(r, s) \rightarrow^*_{\Delta_{sat}} \sigma r$, then $\gamma q(r, s) = q(\gamma r, s) \rightarrow^*_{\Delta_{sat}} \gamma \sigma r = \theta r$.

Therefore

$$q_0(t', z_0) = q_0(t[p \leftarrow \gamma r], z_0) \rightarrow^*_{\Delta_{sat}} t[p \leftarrow q(\gamma r, s)] \rightarrow^*_{\Delta_{sat}} t[p \leftarrow \theta r] \rightarrow^*_{\Delta_{sat}} t[p \leftarrow \gamma r] = t'$$

Proposition 18. *If t is recognized by the saturated automaton, and $t \rightarrow^*_R t'$, then t' is also recognized by the saturated automaton.*

Proof. From the previous lemma, and by induction on the length of $t \rightarrow^*_R t'$.

3.4   Soundness

Proving soundness is more difficult, and needs to take into account all the restrictions.

Definition 19. *A transition in Δ_{sat} identified by (i, p) is a base-transition if $i \neq 0$ and $p = \epsilon$.*
In other words, a base-transition is a transition created by an overlap step and that recognizes the top symbol $r(\epsilon)$ for some $l \to r \in R$.

Definition 20. *If the transition identified by (i', p') has been added into Δ_{sat} by the overlap step $(i, p) \oplus l \to r$, we write $parent(i', p') = (i, p) \oplus l \to r$.*

The following lemma means that if a base transition is used, then an instance of the right-hand-side of some rewrite rule is recognized.

Lemma 21. *If $q_0(t, z_0) \to^*_{\Delta_{sat}} \to_{[p, (x', y')]} t' \to^*_{\Delta_{sat}} t$ such that (x', y') is a base-transition (let $parent(x', y') = (x, y) \oplus l_k \to r_k$) and no base-transition is used in $t' \to^*_{\Delta_{sat}} t$, then there is a substitution σ such that $t|_p = \sigma(r_k)$.*

Proof.   - If r_k is a variable, necessarily $\exists \sigma \mid t|_p = \sigma(r_k)$.
  - if r_k is of the form $f(x_1, \ldots, x_n)$, rewriting by (x', y') generates $f(\ldots)$, then $t|_p(\epsilon) = f$. Consequently t_p is an instance of r_k.
  - Otherwise, rewriting by (x', y') generates $r_k(\epsilon)(q_k^1(\ldots), \ldots, q_k^n(\ldots))$. According to the form of the transitions added by the algorithm, rewriting (in one step) any state q_j^u generates $r_j(u)$, except if a base-transition is used. Since no base-transition is used within $t' \to^*_{\Delta_{sat}} t$, then each $q_k^i(\ldots)$ generates an instance of $r_k|_i$, therefore the sub-derivation $\to_{[p, (x', y')]} t' \to^*_{\Delta_{sat}} t$ generates an instance of r_k. Thus $t|_p$ is an instance of r_k.

The following lemma means (loosely) that if the right-hand-side of some rewrite rule is recognized using a base-transition (which is a transition added by the algorithm), then the corresponding left-hand-side is also recognized. The idea is: if a right-hand-side is not recognized by the initial automaton, but is recognized using some transitions added by the algorithm, then it should be a descendant of a term (the corresponding lhs) recognized by older transitions.

Lemma 22. *Let $l \to r \in R$, and we write $Var(r) = \{x_1, \ldots, x_n\}$. Let s be a stack, $q, q_1, \ldots, q_n \in Q_{sat}$, $\sigma = (x_1/q_1(x_1, s), \ldots, x_n/q_n(x_n, s))$, and (i, ϵ) be a base-transition in Δ_{sat} such that $parent(i, \epsilon) = (j, u) \oplus l \to r$.*
If $q(r, s) \to_{[(i, \epsilon)]} t' \to^*_{\Delta_{sat}} \sigma r$ and no base-transition is used within $t' \to^*_{\Delta_{sat}} \sigma r$, then $q(l, s) \to_{[(j, u)]} \sigma l$ and $j < i$.

Proof. Since R is visibly context-free:

  - If r is shallow or is a variable, then $r(\epsilon) \in Var \cup \Sigma_l$. So, Transition (i, ϵ) does not modify the stack, and variables of r occurs at depth at most 1. Therefore $t' = \sigma(r(\epsilon)(r|_1, \ldots, r|_k))$. ¿From the algorithm, $(j, u) = (q(l, z) \to \theta l)$ where $\theta = (x_1/q_1(x_1, z), \ldots, x_n/q_n(x_n, z))$, and $j < i$. By instantiating z by s we get $q(l, s) \to_{[(j, u)]} \sigma l$.

- Otherwise, $r(\epsilon) \in \Sigma_c$ and for every $p \in PosNonVar(r)$ located just above a variable, $r(p)$ is the corresponding return. Since each overlap step uses new stack symbols, rewrite steps within $t' \to^*_{\Delta_{sat}} \sigma r$ or at such positions p use transitions also created by the overlap step $(j, u) \oplus l \to r$ (i.e. transitions identified by $(i, \ldots)$). ¿From the algorithm, $(j, u) = (q(l, z) \to \theta l)$ where $\theta = (x_1/q_1(x_1, z), \ldots, x_n/q_n(x_n, z))$, and $j < i$. By instantiating z by s we get $q(l, s) \to_{[(j,u)]} \sigma l$.

Definition 23. *Let t be a ground term. A successful derivation for t is a derivation D that allows to recognizes t, i.e. of the form*

$$D = q_0(t, z_0) \to_{[(i_1, p_1)]} \cdots \to_{[(i_k, p_k)]} t$$

The composed length of D is $|D| = i_1 + \cdots + i_k$.
The term recognized by D is $term(D) = t$.

Terms recognized by successful derivations are descendants indeed.

Proposition 24. *For every successful derivation D in the saturated automaton, $term(D) \in R^*(E)$.*

Proof. By strong induction on $|D|$.

If D uses only transitions of the initial automaton A_E (that recognizes E), the property trivially holds. Otherwise D uses at least one transition created by an overlap step. Consider the first step of D that uses a transition (say (i_l, p_l)) created by an overlap step:

$$D = q_0(t, z_0) \to^*_{A_E} t_1 \to_{[(i_l, p_l)]} \to^*_{\Delta_{sat}} t$$

t_1 does not contains states added by the algorithm, i.e. states of the form q_j^p. But the transitions created by an overlap step that are not base-transitions are of the form $q_j^p(\ldots) \to \ldots$. Therefore (i_l, p_l) is necessarily a base-transition.

Thus D contains at least one base-transition. Now consider the last step of D that uses a base transition (say (i, p')):

$$D = q_0(t, z_0) \to^*_{\Delta_{sat}} t'' \to_{[p, (i, p')]} t' \to^*_{\Delta_{sat}} t$$

No base-transition is used within $t' \to^*_{\Delta_{sat}} t$. Then we have the derivation:

$$E = t''|_p = q(t|_p, s) \to_{[\epsilon, (i, p')]} u \to^*_{\Delta_{sat}} t|_p$$

and no base-transition is used within $u \to^*_{\Delta_{sat}} t|_p$.

Let $parent(i, p') = (j, p'') \oplus l_k \to r_k$. Then $j < i$. From Lemma 21, $\exists \sigma \mid t|_p = \sigma r_k$, then

$$E = q(\sigma r_k, s) \to_{[\epsilon, (i, p')]} u \to^*_{\Delta_{sat}} \sigma r_k$$

From the form of transitions, and since r_k is linear, we can deduce from E:

$$q(r_k, s) \to_{[\epsilon, (i, p')]} u \to^*_{\Delta_{sat}} \theta r_k \quad \text{and} \quad \sigma \theta r_k \to^*_{\Delta_{sat}} \sigma r_k$$

where $Var(r_k) = \{x_1, \ldots, x_n\}$ and $\theta = (x_1/q_1(x_1, s), \ldots, x_n/q_n(x_n, s))$, because the stack is not modified since $\forall p \in PosVar(r_k)$, $w(p) = 0$.

From Lemma 22, $q(l_k, s) \to_{[(j, p'')]} \theta l_k$. Then we have the derivation:

$$G = q(\sigma l_k, s) \to_{[(j, p'')]} \sigma \theta l_k \to^*_{\Delta_{sat}} \sigma l_k$$

$|G| < |E|$ since $j < i$.

Consider D again. $t''|_p = q(t|_p, s)$ and σl_k is a ground term without states. Therefore we have the derivation:

$$H = q_0(t[p \leftarrow \sigma l_k], z_0) \rightarrow^*_{\Delta_{sat}} t''[p \leftarrow q(\sigma l_k, s)] \rightarrow^*_{\Delta_{sat}} t[p \leftarrow \sigma l_k]$$

H is a successful derivation and $|H| < |D|$. By induction hypothesis $t[p \leftarrow \sigma l_k] \in R^*(E)$. Since $t[p \leftarrow \sigma l_k] \rightarrow_R t[p \leftarrow \sigma r_k] = t$, we have $t \in R^*(E)$.

4 Conclusion

A question arises: are visibly pushdown tree languages closed under complementation? This property holds for visibly pushdown string languages [2]. When dealing with trees, it seems to hold as well. However, it is difficult to prove it, since our automata work top-down, and top-down automata cannot be determinized, unlike bottom-up automata. Moreover, the stack is duplicated by n-ary symbols, which is a major difference with respect to strings.

On the other hand, the algorithm for computing descendants could be extended to allow reducible symbols that are call or return.

Thanks to expressivity and properties, we hope that visibly pushdown tree languages, as well as visibly context-free rewrite systems, could be used in other domains as decision procedures.

References

1. Alur, R., Chaudhuri, S., Madhusudan, P.: Languages of Nested Trees. In: Ball, T., Jones, R.B. (eds.) CAV 2006. LNCS, vol. 4144, Springer, Heidelberg (2006)
2. Alur, R., Madhusudan, P.: Visibly Pushdown Languages. In: Proc. 36th ACM Symposium on Theory of Computing (STOC'04), pp. 202–211. ACM Press, New York (2004)
3. Comon, H., Dauchet, M., Gilleron, R., Lugiez, D., Tison, S., Tommasi, M.: Tree Automata Techniques and Applications (TATA), http://www.grappa.univ-lille3.fr/tata
4. Genet, T., Klay, F.: Rewriting for cryptographic protocol verification. In: McAllester, D. (ed.) CADE 2000. LNCS, vol. 1831, Springer, Heidelberg (2000) (extended version in Technical Report RR-3921, Inria 2000)
5. Gouranton, V., Réty, P., Seidl, H.: Synchronized Tree Languages Revisited and New Applications. In: Honsell, F., Miculan, M. (eds.) ETAPS 2001 and FOSSACS 2001. LNCS, vol. 2030, Springer, Heidelberg (2001)
6. Guessarian, I.: Pushdown Tree Automata. Mathematical Systems Theory 4(16), 237–263 (1983)
7. Hermann, M., Galbavý, R.: Unification of Infinite Sets of Terms Schematized by Primal Grammars. Theoretical Computer Science, 176 (1997)
8. Jacquemard, F.: Decidable approximations of term rewrite systems. In: Ganzinger, H. (ed.) RTA 1996. LNCS, vol. 1103, pp. 362–376. Springer, Heidelberg (1996)
9. Limet, S., Réty, P.: A New Result about the Decidability of the Existential One-Step Rewriting Theory. In: Narendran, P., Rusinowitch, M. (eds.) RTA 1999. LNCS, vol. 1631, Springer, Heidelberg (1999)

10. Limet, S., Salzer, G.: Proving properties of term rewrite systems via logic programs. In: van Oostrom, V. (ed.) RTA 2004. LNCS, vol. 3091, pp. 170–184. Springer, Heidelberg (2004)
11. Limet, S., Salzer, G.: Manipulating tree tuple languages by transforming logic programs. In: Dahn, I., Vigneron, L. (eds.) Electronic Notes in Theoretical Computer Science, vol. 86, Elsevier, Amsterdam (2003)
12. Lugiez, D., Schnoebelen, P.: The Regular Viewpoint on PA-Processes. Theoretical Computer Science (2000)
13. Nagaya, T., Toyama, Y.: Decidability for Left-Linear Growing Term Rewriting Systems. In: Narendran, P., Rusinowitch, M. (eds.) RTA 1999. LNCS, vol. 1631, Springer, Heidelberg (1999)
14. Raoult, J.C.: Rational Tree Relations. Bulletin of the Belgian Mathematical Society Simon Stevin 4, 149–176 (1997)

Proving Termination Using Recursive
Path Orders and SAT Solving*

Peter Schneider-Kamp[1], René Thiemann[1], Elena Annov[2],
Michael Codish[2], and Jürgen Giesl[1]

[1] LuFG Informatik 2, RWTH Aachen, Germany
{psk,thiemann,giesl}@informatik.rwth-aachen.de
[2] Department of Computer Science, Ben-Gurion University, Israel
{annov,mcodish}@cs.bgu.ac.il

Abstract. We introduce a propositional encoding of the recursive path
order with status (RPO). RPO is a combination of a multiset path order
and a lexicographic path order which considers permutations of the arguments in the lexicographic comparison. Our encoding allows us to apply
SAT solvers in order to determine whether a given term rewrite system
is RPO-terminating. Furthermore, to apply RPO within the dependency
pair framework, we combined our novel encoding for RPO with an existing encoding for argument filters. We implemented our contributions in
the termination prover AProVE. Our experiments show that due to our
encoding, combining termination provers with SAT solvers improves the
performance of RPO-implementations by orders of magnitude.

1 Introduction

Since the past year, several papers have illustrated the huge potential in applying
SAT solvers for various types of termination problems for term rewrite systems
(TRSs). The key idea is classic: the specific termination problem for a TRS $\mathcal{R}$ is
encoded to a propositional formula φ which is satisfiable if and only if $\mathcal{R}$ has the
desired termination property. Satisfiability of φ is tested using a state-of-the-art
SAT solver and the termination proof for $\mathcal{R}$ is reconstructed from a satisfying
assignment of φ. However, in order to obtain significant speedups, it is crucial
to base the approach on polynomial encodings which are also small in practice.

The first such attempt addresses LPO-termination [16]. This work is based
on BDDs and does not yield competitive results. A significant improvement is
described in [3] and further extended in [4,23] for argument filters as used in
the popular dependency pair framework [1,10] for termination of TRSs. Both [3]
and [4,23] describe extremely fast SAT-based implementations. Successful SAT
encodings of other termination techniques are presented in [8,9,14,24]. A common
theme in all of these works is to represent (finite domain) integer variables as
binary numbers in bit representation and to encode arithmetic constraints as
Boolean functions on these representations.

---

* Supported by the Deutsche Forschungsgemeinschaft DFG under grant GI 274/5-1.

B. Konev and F. Wolter (Eds.): FroCos 2007, LNAI 4720, pp. 267–282, 2007.

This paper introduces the first SAT-based encoding for recursive path orders. The main new and interesting contributions are (1) the encoding for the lexicographic comparison w.r.t. permutations, (2) the encoding for the multiset extension of the base order, and (3) the combination of the encoding for precedences and argument filters in order to use RPO with dependency pairs.

Our encoding of RPO is implemented in the termination prover AProVE [11]. The combination of a termination prover with a SAT solver yields a surprisingly fast implementation of RPO. All 865 TRSs in the *Termination Problem Data Base (TPDB)* [21] are analyzed in about 100 seconds for the case of strict precedences. Allowing non-strict precedences takes about 3 times longer. Moreover, power increases considerably compared to the implementation of LPO described in [4]: 27 additional termination proofs are obtained. The TPDB is the collection of examples used in the annual *International Termination Competition* [19].

After the necessary preliminaries on RPO in Sect. 2, Sect. 3 shows how to encode both multiset comparisons and lexicographic comparisons w.r.t. permutations, and how to combine them into a single class of orders. Sect. 4 combines these encodings with the concept of argument filters. In Sect. 5 we describe the implementation of our results and provide extensive experimental evidence indicating speedups in orders of magnitude. We conclude in Sect. 6.

2   Preliminaries

The classical approach to prove termination of a TRS $\mathcal{R}$ is to find a *reduction order* $\succ$ which orients all rules $\ell \to r$ in $\mathcal{R}$ (i.e., $\ell \succ r$). A reduction order is an order which is well founded, monotonic, and stable (closed under contexts and substitutions). In practice, most reduction orders amenable to automation are *simplification orders* [6]. We refer to [2] for further details on term rewriting.

Three of the most prominent simplification orders are the lexicographic path order (LPO) [15], the multiset path order (MPO) [6], and the recursive path order (RPO) [18] which combines the lexicographic and multiset path order allowing also permutations in the lexicographic comparison. This section introduces their definitions using a formulation that is suitable for the subsequent SAT encoding.

We assume an algebra of terms constructed over sets of function symbols $\mathcal{F}$ and variables $\mathcal{V}$. For a quasi-order $\succsim$ (i.e., a transitive and reflexive relation), we define $s \succ t$ iff $s \succsim t$ and $t \not\succsim s$ and we define $s \sim t$ iff both $s \succsim t$ and $t \succsim s$. Path orders are defined in terms of lexicographic and multiset extensions of a base order (on terms). We often denote tuples of terms as $\bar{s} = \langle s_1, \ldots s_n \rangle$, etc.

Definition 1 (lexicographic extension). *Let $\succsim$ be a quasi-order. The lexicographic extensions of $\succ$, $\sim$, and $\succsim$ are defined on sequences of terms:*

- $\langle s_1, \ldots, s_n \rangle \sim^{lex} \langle t_1, \ldots, t_m \rangle$ *if and only if* $n = m$ *and* $s_i \sim t_i$ *for all* $1 \leq i \leq n$
- $\langle s_1, \ldots, s_n \rangle \succ^{lex} \langle t_1, \ldots, t_m \rangle$ *if and only if (a)* $m = 0$ *and* $n > 0$; *or (b)* $s_1 \succ t_1$; *or (c)* $s_1 \sim t_1$ *and* $\langle s_2, \ldots, s_n \rangle \succ^{lex} \langle t_2, \ldots, t_m \rangle$.
- $\succsim^{lex} = \sim^{lex} \cup \succ^{lex}$

So for tuples of numbers $\bar{s} = \langle 3, 3, 4, 0 \rangle$ and $\bar{t} = \langle 3, 2, 5, 6 \rangle$, we have $\bar{s} >^{lex} \bar{t}$ as $s_1 = t_1$ and $s_2 > t_2$ (where $>$ is the usual order on numbers).

The multiset extension of an order $\succ$ is defined as follows: $\bar{s} \succ^{mul} \bar{t}$ holds if $\bar{t}$ is obtained by replacing at least one element of $\bar{s}$ by a finite number of (strictly) smaller elements. However, the order of the elements in $\bar{s}$ and $\bar{t}$ is irrelevant. For example, let $\bar{s} = \langle 3, 3, 4, 0 \rangle$ and $\bar{t} = \langle 4, 3, 2, 1, 1 \rangle$. We have $\bar{s} >^{mul} \bar{t}$ because $s_1 = 3$ is replaced by the smaller elements $t_3 = 2$, $t_4 = 1$, $t_5 = 1$ and $s_4 = 0$ is replaced by zero smaller elements. So each element in $\bar{t}$ is "covered" by some element in $\bar{s}$. Such a cover is either by a larger s_i (then s_i may cover several t_j) or by an equal s_i (then one s_i covers one t_j). In this paper we formalize the multiset extension by a *multiset cover* which is a pair of mappings (γ, ε). Intuitively, γ expresses which elements of $\bar{s}$ cover which elements in $\bar{t}$ and ε expresses for which s_i this cover is by means of equal terms and for which by means of greater terms. This formalization facilitates encodings to propositional logic.

So in the example above, we have $\gamma(1) = 3$, $\gamma(2) = 2$ (since t_1 is covered by s_3 and t_2 is covered by s_2), and $\gamma(3) = \gamma(4) = \gamma(5) = 1$ (since t_3, t_4, and t_5 are all covered by s_1). Moreover, $\varepsilon(2) = \varepsilon(3) = true$ (since s_2 and s_3 are replaced by equal components), whereas $\varepsilon(1) = \varepsilon(4) = false$ (since s_1 and s_4 are replaced by (possibly zero) smaller components). Of course, in general multiset covers are not unique. For example, t_2 could also be covered by s_1 instead of s_2.

Definition 2 (multiset cover). *Let $\bar{s} = \langle s_1, \ldots s_n \rangle$ and $\bar{t} = \langle t_1, \ldots t_m \rangle$ be tuples of terms. A multiset cover (γ, ε) is a pair of mappings $\gamma : \{1, \ldots, m\} \to \{1, \ldots, n\}$ and $\varepsilon : \{1, \ldots, n\} \to \{false, true\}$ such that for each $1 \leq i \leq n$, if $\varepsilon(i)$ (indicating equality) then $\{j \mid \gamma(j) = i\}$ is a singleton set.*

For $\bar{s} = \langle s_1, \ldots s_n \rangle$ and $\bar{t} = \langle t_1, \ldots t_m \rangle$ we define that $\bar{s} \succsim^{mul} \bar{t}$ if there exists a multiset cover (γ, ε) such that $\gamma(j) = i$ implies that either: $\varepsilon(i) = true$ and $s_i \sim t_j$, or $\varepsilon(i) = false$ and $s_i \succ t_j$.

Definition 3 (multiset extension). *Let $\succsim$ be a quasi-order on terms. The multiset extensions of $\succsim$, $\succ$, and $\sim$ are defined on tuples of terms:*

- $\langle s_1, \ldots, s_n \rangle \succsim^{mul} \langle t_1, \ldots, t_m \rangle$ *if and only if there exists a multiset cover (γ, ε) such that for all i, j, $\gamma(j) = i \Rightarrow$ (if $\varepsilon(i)$ then $s_i \sim t_j$ else $s_i \succ t_j$).*
- $\langle s_1, \ldots, s_n \rangle \succ^{mul} \langle t_1, \ldots, t_m \rangle$ *if and only if $\langle s_1, \ldots, s_n \rangle \succsim^{mul} \langle t_1, \ldots, t_m \rangle$ and for some i, $\neg\varepsilon(i)$, i.e., some s_i is not used for equality but rather replaced by zero or more smaller arguments t_j.*
- $\langle s_1, \ldots, s_n \rangle \sim^{mul} \langle t_1, \ldots, t_m \rangle$ *if and only if $\langle s_1, \ldots, s_n \rangle \succsim^{mul} \langle t_1, \ldots, t_m \rangle$, $n = m$, and for all i, $\varepsilon(i)$, i.e., all s_i are used to cover some t_j by equality.*

Let $\geq_{\mathcal{F}}$ denote a quasi-order (a so-called *precedence*) on the set of function symbols $\mathcal{F}$ and let $>_{\mathcal{F}} = (\geq_{\mathcal{F}} \setminus \leq_{\mathcal{F}})$ and $\approx_{\mathcal{F}} = (\geq_{\mathcal{F}} \cap \leq_{\mathcal{F}})$. Then $\geq_{\mathcal{F}}$ induces corresponding lexicographic and multiset path orders on terms.

Definition 4 (lexicographic and multiset path orders). *For a precedence $\geq_{\mathcal{F}}$ and $\rho \in \{lpo, mpo\}$ we define the relations $\succ_\rho$ and $\sim_\rho$ on terms. We use the notation $\bar{s} = \langle s_1, \ldots s_n \rangle$ and $\bar{t} = \langle t_1, \ldots t_m \rangle$.*

- $s \succ_\rho t$ iff $s = f(\bar{s})$ and one of the following holds:
  - (1) $s_i \succ_\rho t$ or $s_i \sim_\rho t$ for some $1 \leq i \leq n$; or
  - (2) $t = g(\bar{t})$ and $s \succ_\rho t_j$ for all $1 \leq j \leq m$ and either:
    - (i) $f >_\mathcal{F} g$ or (ii) $f \approx_\mathcal{F} g$ and $\bar{s} \succ_\rho^{ext} \bar{t}$;
- $s \sim_\rho t$ iff (a) $s = t$; or (b) $s = f(\bar{s})$, $t = g(\bar{t})$, $f \approx_\mathcal{F} g$, and $\bar{s} \sim_\rho^{ext} \bar{t}$;

where $\succ_\rho^{ext}$ and $\sim_\rho^{ext}$ are the lexicographic or multiset extensions of $\succ_\rho$ and $\sim_\rho$ for the respective cases when $\rho = lpo$ and $\rho = mpo$.

Example 1. Consider the following three TRSs for adding numbers:

(a) $\left\{\; \mathsf{add}(0,y) \to y \;,\quad \mathsf{add}(\mathsf{s}(x),y) \to \mathsf{add}(x,\mathsf{s}(y)) \;\right\}$

(b) $\left\{\; \mathsf{add}(x,0) \to x \;,\quad \mathsf{add}(x,\mathsf{s}(y)) \to \mathsf{s}(\mathsf{add}(y,x)) \;\right\}$

(c) $\left\{\; \mathsf{add}(x,0) \to x \;,\quad \mathsf{add}(x,\mathsf{s}(y)) \to \mathsf{add}(\mathsf{s}(x),y) \;\right\}$

Example (a) is LPO-terminating for the precedence $\mathsf{add} >_\mathcal{F} \mathsf{s}$, but not MPO-terminating for any precedence. Example (b) is MPO-terminating for $\mathsf{add} >_\mathcal{F} \mathsf{s}$, but not LPO-terminating for any precedence as the second rule swaps x and y. Example (c) is neither LPO- nor MPO-terminating. However, termination could be proved using a path order where lexicographic comparison proceeds from right to left instead of left to right. The following definitions extend this observation to arbitrary permutations of the order in which we compare arguments.

As remarked before, the RPO combines such an extension of the LPO with MPO. This combination is facilitated by a *status function* which indicates for each function symbol if its arguments are to be compared based on a multiset extension or based on a lexicographic extension using some permutation μ.

Definition 5 (status function). *A status function σ maps each symbol $f \in \mathcal{F}$ of arity n either to the symbol $\mathtt{mul}$ or to a permutation μ_f on $\{1, \ldots, n\}$.*

Definition 6 (recursive path order with status). *For a precedence $\geq_\mathcal{F}$ and status function σ we define the relations $\succ_{rpo}$ and $\sim_{rpo}$ on terms. We use the notation $\bar{s} = \langle s_1, \ldots s_n \rangle$ and $\bar{t} = \langle t_1, \ldots t_m \rangle$.*

- $s \succ_{rpo} t$ iff $s = f(\bar{s})$ and one of the following holds:
  - (1) $s_i \succ_{rpo} t$ or $s_i \sim_{rpo} t$ for some $1 \leq i \leq n$; or
  - (2) $t = g(\bar{t})$ and $s \succ_{rpo} t_j$ for all $1 \leq j \leq m$ and either:
    - (i) $f >_\mathcal{F} g$ or (ii) $f \approx_\mathcal{F} g$ and $\bar{s} \succ_{rpo}^{f,g} \bar{t}$;
- $s \sim_{rpo} t$ iff (a) $s = t$; or (b) $s = f(\bar{s})$, $t = g(\bar{t})$, $f \approx_\mathcal{F} g$, and $\bar{s} \sim_{rpo}^{f,g} \bar{t}$;

where $\succ_{rpo}^{f,g}$ and $\sim_{rpo}^{f,g}$ are the tuple extensions of $\succ_{rpo}$ and $\sim_{rpo}$ defined by:

- $\langle s_1, \ldots s_n \rangle \succ_{rpo}^{f,g} \langle t_1, \ldots t_m \rangle$ iff one of the following holds:
  - (1) σ maps f and g to permutations μ_f and μ_g; and
    $$\mu_f \langle s_1, \ldots, s_n \rangle \succ_{rpo}^{lex} \mu_g \langle t_1, \ldots, t_m \rangle;$$
  - (2) σ maps f and g to $\mathtt{mul}$; and $\langle s_1, \ldots s_n \rangle \succ_{rpo}^{mul} \langle t_1, \ldots t_m \rangle$.
- $\langle s_1, \ldots s_n \rangle \sim_{rpo}^{f,g} \langle t_1, \ldots t_m \rangle$ iff one of the following holds:

(1) σ maps f and g to μ_f and μ_g; and $\mu_f \langle s_1, \ldots, s_n \rangle \sim_{rpo}^{lex} \mu_g \langle t_1, \ldots, t_m \rangle$;

(2) σ maps f and g to mul; and $\langle s_1, \ldots s_n \rangle \sim_{rpo}^{mul} \langle t_1, \ldots t_m \rangle$.

Def. 6 can be specialized to capture the previous path orders by taking specific forms of status functions: LPO when σ maps all symbols to the identity permutation; lexicographic path order w.r.t. permutation (LPOS) when σ maps all symbols to some permutation; MPO when σ maps all symbols to mul.

The RPO termination problem is to determine for a given TRS if there exists a precedence and a status function such that the system is RPO-terminating. There are two variants of the problem: "strict-" and "quasi-RPO termination" depending on if the precedence $\geq_{\mathcal{F}}$ is strict or not (i.e., on whether $f \approx_{\mathcal{F}} g$ can hold for $f \neq g$). The corresponding decision problems, strict- and quasi-RPO termination, are decidable and NP complete [5]. In this paper we address the implementation of decision procedures for RPO termination problems by encoding them into corresponding SAT problems.

3 Encoding RPO Problems

We introduce an encoding τ which maps constraints of the form $s \succ_{rpo} t$ to propositional statements about the status and the precedence of the symbols in the terms s and t. A satisfying assignment for the encoding of such a constraint indicates a precedence and a status function such that the constraint holds.

The first part of the encoding is straightforward and similar to the one in [3,4]. All "missing" cases (e.g., $\tau(x \succ_{rpo} t)$ for variables x) are defined to be *false*.

$$\tau(f(\bar{s}) \succ_{rpo} t) = \bigvee_{i=1}^{n} (\tau(s_i \succ_{rpo} t) \vee \tau(s_i \sim_{rpo} t)) \quad \vee \quad \tau_2(f(\bar{s}) \succ_{rpo} t) \tag{1}$$

$$\tau_2(f(\bar{s}) \succ_{rpo} g(\bar{t})) = \bigwedge_{j=1}^{m} \tau(f(\bar{s}) \succ_{rpo} t_j) \wedge \left(\begin{array}{c} (f >_{\mathcal{F}} g) \vee \\ ((f \approx_{\mathcal{F}} g) \wedge \tau(\bar{s} \succ_{rpo}^{f,g} \bar{t})) \end{array} \right) \tag{2}$$

$$\tau(s \sim_{rpo} s) = true \tag{3}$$

$$\tau(f(\bar{s}) \sim_{rpo} g(\bar{t})) = (f \approx_{\mathcal{F}} g) \wedge \tau(\bar{s} \sim_{rpo}^{f,g} \bar{t}) \tag{4}$$

The propositional encoding of the "partial order constraints" of the form $f >_{\mathcal{F}} g$ and $f \approx_{\mathcal{F}} g$ is performed following the approach applied in [3,4]. The basic idea is to interpret the symbols in $\mathcal{F}$ as indices in a partial order taking finite domain values from the set $\{0, \ldots, m-1\}$ where m is the number of symbols in $\mathcal{F}$. Each symbol $f \in \mathcal{F}$ is then represented using $\lceil \log_2 m \rceil$ propositional variables and the constraints are encoded as integer constraints on the binary representations.

In Sect. 3.1 and 3.2. we encode lexicographic comparisons w.r.t. permutations and multiset comparison. Then in Sect. 3.3 we combine them into $\succ_{rpo}^{f,g}$ and $\sim_{rpo}^{f,g}$.

3.1 Encoding Lexicographic Comparisons w.r.t. Permutation

For lexicographic comparisons with permutations, we associate with each symbol $f \in \mathcal{F}$ (of arity n) a permutation μ_f encoded through n^2 propositional variables

$f_{i,k}$ with $i, k \in \{1, \ldots, n\}$. Here, $f_{i,k}$ is *true* iff $\mu_f(i) = k$ (i.e., the i-th argument of $f(s_1, \ldots, s_n)$ is considered at k-th position when comparing lexicographically). To ease presentation, we define that $f_{i,k}$ is *false* for $k > n$.

For the encoding to be correct, we impose constraints on the variables $f_{i,k}$ to ensure that they indeed correspond to a permutation on $\{1, \ldots, n\}$. So for each $i \in \{1, \ldots, n\}$ there must be exactly one $k \in \{1, \ldots, n\}$ and for each $k \in \{1, \ldots, n\}$ there must be exactly one $i \in \{1, \ldots, n\}$ such that $f_{i,k}$ is *true*.

We denote by $one(b_1, \ldots, b_n)$ the constraint expressing that exactly one of the bits $b_1, \ldots, b_n$ is *true*. Then our encoding includes a formula of the form

$$\bigwedge_{f/n \in \mathcal{F}} \left(\bigwedge_{i=1}^{n} one(f_{i,1}, \ldots, f_{i,n}) \quad \wedge \quad \bigwedge_{k=1}^{n} one(f_{1,k}, \ldots, f_{n,k}) \right) \tag{5}$$

We apply a linear encoding to propositional logic for constraints of the form $one(b_1, \ldots, b_n)$ which introduces $\approx 2n$ fresh Boolean variables which we denote here as $one(b_i, \ldots, b_n)$ (expressing that one of the variables $b_i, \ldots, b_n$ is *true*) and $zero(b_i, \ldots, b_n)$ (expressing that all of the variables $b_i, \ldots, b_n$ are *false*) for $1 < i \leq n$. The encoding applies a ternary propositional connective $x \rightarrow y \,;\, z$ (denoting if-then-else) equivalent to $(x \rightarrow y) \wedge (\neg x \rightarrow z)$:

$$\bigwedge_{1 \leq i \leq n} \left(\begin{array}{c} \left(one(b_i, \ldots, b_n) \leftrightarrow \left(\begin{array}{c} (b_i \rightarrow zero(b_{i+1}, \ldots, b_n) \\ ;\ one(b_{i+1}, \ldots, b_n) \end{array} \right) \right) \\ \wedge\, (zero(b_i, \ldots, b_n) \leftrightarrow \neg b_i \wedge zero(b_{i+1}, \ldots, b_n)) \end{array} \right)$$

where $one(b_{n+1}, \ldots, b_n) = \textit{false}$ and $zero(b_{n+1}, \ldots, b_n) = \textit{true}$. This encoding introduces $\approx 2n$ conjuncts each involving a formula with at most 4 Boolean variables. So the encoding is more concise than the more straightforward one which introduces a quadratic number of conjuncts $\neg b_i \vee \neg b_j$ for all $1 \leq i < j \leq n$.

Now consider the encoding of $\bar{s} \sim_{rpo}^{f,g} \bar{t}$ and $\bar{s} \succ_{rpo}^{f,g} \bar{t}$ for the case where the arguments of f and g are compared lexicographically (thus, we use the notation $\sim_{lex}^{f,g}$ and $\succ_{lex}^{f,g}$). Like in Def. 6, let $\bar{s} = \langle s_1, \ldots, s_n \rangle$ and $\bar{t} = \langle t_1, \ldots, t_m \rangle$. Now equality constraints of the form $\bar{s} \sim_{lex}^{f,g} \bar{t}$ are encoded by stating that for all k, the arguments s_i and t_j used at the k-th position in the comparison (as denoted by $f_{i,k}$ and and $g_{j,k}$) must be equal. This implies that $\bar{s} \sim_{lex}^{f,g} \bar{t}$ only holds if $n = m$.

$$\tau(\bar{s} \sim_{lex}^{f,g} \bar{t}) = (n = m) \wedge \left(\bigwedge_{k=1}^{n} \bigwedge_{i=1}^{n} \bigwedge_{j=1}^{m} f_{i,k} \wedge g_{j,k} \rightarrow \tau(s_i \sim_{rpo} t_j) \right) \tag{6}$$

To encode $\bar{s} \succ_{lex}^{f,g} \bar{t}$, we define auxiliary relations $\succ_{lex}^{f,g,k}$, where $k \in \mathbb{N}$ denotes that the k-th component of $\bar{s}$ and $\bar{t}$ is currently being compared. Thus $\succ_{lex}^{f,g} = \succ_{lex}^{f,g,1}$, since the comparison starts with the first component. For any k, there are three cases to consider when encoding $\bar{s} \succ_{lex}^{f,g,k} \bar{t}$. If there is no s_i that can be used for the k-th comparison (i.e., $k > n$), then we encode to *false*. If there is such an s_i but no such t_j (i.e., $m < k \leq n$), then we encode to *true*. If there are both an s_i and a t_j used for the k-th comparison (i.e., $f_{i,k}$ and $g_{j,k}$ hold), then we encode to a disjunction that either s_i is greater than t_j, or s_i is equal to t_j, and we continue the encoding at position $k + 1$. Since exactly one $f_{i,k}$ is *true*, the disjunction and conjunction over all $f_{i,k}$ (with $i \in \{1, \ldots, n\}$) coincide (similar for $g_{j,k}$). Here, we use a disjunction of conjunctions, as this will be more convenient in Sect. 4.

$$\tau(\bar{s} \succ_{lex}^{f,g,k} \bar{t}) = \begin{cases} false & \text{if } k > n \\ true & \text{if } m < k \leq n \\ \bigvee_{i=1}^{n} \Big(f_{i,k} \wedge \Big(\bigwedge_{j=1}^{m} g_{j,k} \to & \text{otherwise} \\ \quad (\tau(s_i \succ_{rpo} t_j) \vee (\tau(s_i \sim_{rpo} t_j) \wedge \tau(\bar{s} \succ_{lex}^{f,g,k+1} \bar{t}))) \Big) \Big) \end{cases} \tag{7}$$

Example 2. Consider again the TRS of Ex. 1(c):

$$\{ \ \mathsf{add}(x,0) \to x \ , \ \ \mathsf{add}(x,\mathsf{s}(y)) \to \mathsf{add}(\mathsf{s}(x),y) \ \}$$

In the encoding of the constraints for the second rule, we have to encode the comparison $\langle x, \mathsf{s}(y) \rangle \succ_{lex}^{add,add,1} \langle \mathsf{s}(x), y \rangle$, which yields:

$$\Big(add_{1,1} \wedge \Big(add_{1,1} \to \big(\tau(x \succ_{rpo} \mathsf{s}(x)) \vee (\tau(x \sim_{rpo} \mathsf{s}(x)) \wedge \tau(\langle x, \mathsf{s}(y) \rangle \succ_{lex}^{add,add,2} \langle \mathsf{s}(x), y \rangle)) \big) \Big)$$
$$\wedge \Big(add_{2,1} \to \big(\tau(x \succ_{rpo} y) \vee (\tau(x \sim_{rpo} y) \wedge \tau(\langle x, \mathsf{s}(y) \rangle \succ_{lex}^{add,add,2} \langle \mathsf{s}(x), y \rangle)) \big) \Big) \Big)$$
$$\vee \Big(add_{2,1} \wedge \Big(add_{1,1} \to \big(\tau(\mathsf{s}(y) \succ_{rpo} \mathsf{s}(x)) \vee (\tau(\mathsf{s}(y) \sim_{rpo} \mathsf{s}(x)) \wedge \tau(\langle x, \mathsf{s}(y) \rangle \succ_{lex}^{add,add,2} \langle \mathsf{s}(x), y \rangle)) \big) \Big)$$
$$\wedge \Big(add_{2,1} \to \big(\tau(\mathsf{s}(y) \succ_{rpo} y) \vee (\tau(\mathsf{s}(y) \sim_{rpo} y) \wedge \tau(\langle x, \mathsf{s}(y) \rangle \succ_{lex}^{add,add,2} \langle \mathsf{s}(x), y \rangle)) \big) \Big) \Big)$$

Seeing that $\tau(x \succ_{rpo} \mathsf{s}(x)) = \tau(x \sim_{rpo} \mathsf{s}(x)) = \tau(x \succ_{rpo} y) = \tau(x \sim_{rpo} y) = \tau(\mathsf{s}(y) \succ_{rpo} \mathsf{s}(x)) = \tau(\mathsf{s}(y) \sim_{rpo} \mathsf{s}(x)) = false$ and $\tau(\mathsf{s}(y) \succ_{rpo} y) = true$, the above formula can be simplified to $add_{2,1} \wedge \neg add_{1,1}$. Together with the constraint (5) which ensures that the variables $add_{i,k}$ specify a valid permutation μ_{add}, this implies that $add_{1,2}$ and $\neg add_{2,2}$ must be *true*. And indeed, for the permutation $\mu_{\mathsf{add}} = \langle 2,1 \rangle$ the tuple $\mu_{\mathsf{add}}(\langle x, \mathsf{s}(y) \rangle) = \langle \mathsf{s}(y), x \rangle$ is greater than the tuple $\mu_{\mathsf{add}}(\langle \mathsf{s}(x), y \rangle) = \langle y, \mathsf{s}(x) \rangle$.

3.2 Encoding Multiset Comparisons

For multiset comparisons, we associate $\bar{s}$ and $\bar{t}$ with a multiset cover (γ, ε) encoded by $n * m$ propositional variables $\gamma_{i,j}$ and n variables ε_i. Here, $\gamma_{i,j}$ is *true* iff $\gamma(j) = i$ (s_i covers t_j) and ε_i is *true* iff $\varepsilon(i) = true$ (s_i is used for equality).

For the encoding to be correct, we again have to impose constraints on these variables to ensure that (γ, ε) indeed forms a multiset cover. So for each $j \in \{1, \ldots, m\}$ there must be exactly one $i \in \{1, \ldots, n\}$ such that $\gamma_{i,j}$ is *true*, and for each $i \in \{1, \ldots, n\}$, if ε_i is *true* then there must be exactly one $j \in \{1, \ldots, m\}$ such that $\gamma_{i,j}$ is *true*. Thus, our encoding includes the following formula:

$$\bigwedge_{j=1}^{m} one(\gamma_{1,j}, \ldots, \gamma_{n,j}) \quad \wedge \quad \bigwedge_{i=1}^{n} (\varepsilon_i \to one(\gamma_{i,1}, \ldots, \gamma_{i,m})) \tag{8}$$

Now we encode $\bar{s} \succ_{rpo}^{f,g} \bar{t}$ for the case where f and g have multiset status. To have an analogous notation to the case of lexicographic comparisons, we use the notation $\succ_{mul}^{f,g}$ instead of $\succ_{rpo}^{mul}$. This will also be convenient later in Sect. 4. The encoding of $\succsim_{mul}^{f,g}$, $\succ_{mul}^{f,g}$, and $\sim_{mul}^{f,g}$ is similar to Def. 3. To encode $\bar{s} \succsim_{mul}^{f,g} \bar{t}$, one has to require that if $\gamma_{i,j}$ and ε_i are *true*, $s_i \sim_{rpo} t_j$ holds, and else, if $\gamma_{i,j}$ is *true* and ε_i is not, $s_i \succ_{rpo} t_j$ holds. For $\succ_{mul}^{f,g}$, we must have at least one s_i that is not used for equality, and for $\sim_{mul}^{f,g}$, all s_i must be used for equality.

$$\tau(\bar{s} \succsim_{mul}^{f,g} \bar{t}) = \bigwedge_{i=1}^{n} \bigwedge_{j=1}^{m} \left(\gamma_{i,j} \to ((\varepsilon_i \to \tau(s_i \sim_{rpo} t_j)) \land (\neg \varepsilon_i \to \tau(s_i \succ_{rpo} t_j)))) \right) \tag{9}$$

$$\tau(\bar{s} \succ_{mul}^{f,g} \bar{t}) = \tau(\bar{s} \succsim_{mul}^{f,g} \bar{t}) \land \neg \bigwedge_{i=1}^{n} \varepsilon_i \tag{10}$$

$$\tau(\bar{s} \sim_{mul}^{f,g} \bar{t}) = \tau(\bar{s} \succsim_{mul}^{f,g} \bar{t}) \land \bigwedge_{i=1}^{n} \varepsilon_i \tag{11}$$

Example 3. Consider again the rules for the TRS from Ex. 1(b):

$$\{ \quad \mathsf{add}(x,0) \to x \; , \quad \mathsf{add}(x,\mathsf{s}(y)) \to \mathsf{s}(\mathsf{add}(y,x)) \quad \}.$$

In the encoding of the constraints for the second rule, we have to encode the comparison $\langle x, \mathsf{s}(y) \rangle \succ_{mul}^{f,g} \langle y, x \rangle$, which yields:

$$\left(\gamma_{1,1} \to \left((\varepsilon_1 \to \tau(x \sim_{rpo} y)) \land (\neg \varepsilon_1 \to \tau(x \succ_{rpo} y)) \right) \right)$$
$$\land \left(\gamma_{1,2} \to \left((\varepsilon_1 \to \tau(x \sim_{rpo} x)) \land (\neg \varepsilon_1 \to \tau(x \succ_{rpo} x)) \right) \right)$$

$$\land \left(\gamma_{2,1} \to \left((\varepsilon_2 \to \tau(\mathsf{s}(y) \sim_{rpo} y)) \land (\neg \varepsilon_2 \to \tau(\mathsf{s}(y) \succ_{rpo} y)) \right) \right)$$
$$\land \left(\gamma_{2,2} \to \left((\varepsilon_2 \to \tau(\mathsf{s}(y) \sim_{rpo} x)) \land (\neg \varepsilon_2 \to \tau(\mathsf{s}(y) \succ_{rpo} x)) \right) \right)$$

Seeing that $\tau(x \sim_{rpo} y) = \tau(x \succ_{rpo} y) = \tau(x \succ_{rpo} x) = \tau(\mathsf{s}(y) \sim_{rpo} y) = \tau(\mathsf{s}(y) \sim_{rpo} x) = \tau(\mathsf{s}(y) \succ_{rpo} x) = \textit{false}$ and $\tau(x \sim_{rpo} x) = \tau(\mathsf{s}(y) \succ_{rpo} y) = \textit{true}$, the above formula can be simplified to $\neg \gamma_{1,1} \land (\neg \gamma_{1,2} \lor \varepsilon_1) \land (\neg \gamma_{2,1} \lor \neg \varepsilon_2) \land \neg \gamma_{2,2}$. Together with the constraint (8) which ensures that the variables $\gamma_{i,j}$ and ε_i specify a valid multiset cover (γ, ε), this implies that $\gamma_{2,1}$, $\neg \varepsilon_2$, $\gamma_{1,2}$, and ε_1 must hold. And indeed, for the multiset cover (γ, ε) with $\gamma(1) = 2$, $\gamma(2) = 1$, $\varepsilon(1) = \textit{true}$, and $\varepsilon(2) = \textit{false}$, the tuple $\langle x, \mathsf{s}(y) \rangle$ is greater than $\langle y, x \rangle$.

3.3   Combining Lexicographic and Multiset Comparisons

We have shown how to encode lexicographic and multiset comparisons. In order to combine $\succ_{lex}^{f,g}$ and $\succ_{mul}^{f,g}$ into $\succ_{rpo}^{f,g}$ as well as $\sim_{lex}^{f,g}$ and $\sim_{mul}^{f,g}$ into $\sim_{rpo}^{f,g}$, we introduce for each symbol $f \in \mathcal{F}$ a variable m_f, which is *true* iff the arguments of f are to be compared as multisets (i.e., the status function maps f to *mul*).

$$\tau(\bar{s} \succ_{rpo}^{f,g} \bar{t}) = \left(m_f \land m_g \land \tau(\bar{s} \succ_{mul}^{f,g} \bar{t}) \right) \lor \left(\neg m_f \land \neg m_g \land \tau(\bar{s} \succ_{lex}^{f,g,1} \bar{t}) \right) \tag{12}$$

$$\tau(\bar{s} \sim_{rpo}^{f,g} \bar{t}) = \left(m_f \land m_g \land \tau(\bar{s} \sim_{mul}^{f,g} \bar{t}) \right) \lor \left(\neg m_f \land \neg m_g \land \tau(\bar{s} \sim_{lex}^{f,g} \bar{t}) \right) \tag{13}$$

Similar to Def. 6, the above encoding function τ can be specialized to other standard path orderings: lexicographic path order w.r.t. permutation (LPOS) when m_f is set to *false* for all $f \in \mathcal{F}$; LPO when additionally $f_{i,k}$ is set to *true* iff $i = k$; MPO when m_f is set to *true* for all $f \in \mathcal{F}$.

We conclude this section with an approximation of the size of the propositional formula obtained when encoding $s \succ_{rpo} t$ where $s = f(s_1, \ldots, s_n)$ and

$t = g(t_1, \ldots, t_m)$ with the total size of terms s and t being k. A single step of unfolding Def. 6 results in a formula containing at least n copies of t (with all its subterms) and m copies of s (with all its subterms) occurring in constraints of the form $s' \succ_{rpo} t'$. Hence, without memoing, the final encoding is clearly exponential in k. To obtain a polynomial encoding, we introduce sharing of common subformulas in the propositional formula. The approach is similar to that proposed by Tseitin to obtain a linear CNF transformation of Boolean formulas [22]. If $\tau(s' \succ_{rpo} t')$ occurs in the encoding $\tau(s \succ_{rpo} t)$, then we do not immediately perform the encoding of $s' \succ_{rpo} t'$ as well. Instead, we introduce a fresh Boolean variable of the form $X_{s' \succ_{rpo} t'}$, and encode also the meaning of such fresh variables. The encoding of $X_{s' \succ_{rpo} t'}$ is of the form $X_{s' \succ_{rpo} t'} \leftrightarrow \tau(s' \succ_{rpo} t')$. Again, when constructing $\tau(s' \succ_{rpo} t')$, all subformulas $\tau(s'' \succ_{rpo} t'')$ encountered are replaced by Boolean variables $X_{s'' \succ_{rpo} t''}$. In total, there are at most $\mathcal{O}(k^2)$ fresh Boolean variables to encode. As the encodings of multiset comparisons and lexicographic comparisons are both of size $\mathcal{O}(k^3)$, the size of the overall encoding is in $\mathcal{O}(k^5)$. Thus, the size of the encoding is indeed polynomial.[3]

4 RPO and Dependency Pairs

One of the most powerful and popular techniques for proving termination of term rewriting is the *dependency pair* (DP) method [1,10]. This method has proven highly successful for systems which are not simply terminating, i.e., where termination cannot be shown directly using simplification orders such as LPO, MPO, and RPO. Instead it is the combination of the simplification order, in our case RPO, with the DP method which significantly increases termination proving power. A main advantage of the DP method is that it permits the use of orders that are not monotonic and thus allows the application of *argument filters*.

An argument filter is a function which specifies for every function symbol f, which parts of a term $f(\ldots)$ may be eliminated before comparing terms with the underlying simplification order. More formally (we adopt notation of [17]):

Definition 7 (argument filter). *An argument filter π maps every n-ary function symbol to an argument position $i \in \{1, \ldots, n\}$ or to a (possibly empty) list $[i_1, \ldots, i_p]$ with $1 \leq i_1 < \cdots < i_p \leq n$. An argument filter π induces a mapping from terms to terms:*

$$\pi(t) = \begin{cases} t & \text{if } t \text{ is a variable} \\ \pi(t_i) & \text{if } t = f(t_1, \ldots, t_n) \text{ and } \pi(f) = i \\ f(\pi(t_{i_1}), \ldots, \pi(t_{i_p})) & \text{if } t = f(t_1, \ldots, t_n) \text{ and } \pi(f) = [i_1, \ldots, i_p] \end{cases}$$

For a relation $\succ$ on terms, let $\succ^\pi$ be the relation where $s \succ^\pi t$ holds if and only if $\pi(s) \succ \pi(t)$. An argument filter with $\pi(f) = i$ is called collapsing on f.

---

[3] A finer analysis shows that not all multiset and lexicographic comparisons are large. For example, for $s = f(a_1, \ldots, a_n)$ and $t = g(b_1, \ldots, b_n)$ with constants a_i and b_j, there is one comparison of two n-tuples with encoding size $\mathcal{O}(n^3)$, but the other $n^2 + 2n$ comparisons only need size $\mathcal{O}(n)$ each. In fact, one can show that the size of the overall encoding is in $\mathcal{O}(k^3)$.

Example 4. Consider the following rewrite rule (which will later turn out to be a dependency pair when proving the termination of Ex. 5):

$$\mathsf{ADD}'(x, \mathsf{s}(y), z) \to \mathsf{ADD}'(y, x, \mathsf{s}(z))$$

The rule cannot be oriented by RPO. Lexicographic comparison fails as the first two arguments are swapped. Multiset comparison is prevented by the third argument ($\mathsf{s}(z)$ cannot be covered). But an argument filter $\pi(\mathsf{ADD}') = \{1, 2\}$, which eliminates the third argument of ADD', enables the multiset comparison.

While very powerful in the context of the DP method, argument filters also present a severe bottleneck for automation, as the search space for argument filters is enormous (exponential in the arities of the function symbols). A SAT encoding for the LPO with argument filters is presented in [4] where the combined constraints on the argument filter and on the precedence of the LPO (which influence each other) are encoded as a single SAT problem.

This paper applies a similar strategy to combine RPO with argument filters. The combined search for an argument filter π, a precedence $>_{\mathcal{F}}$, and a status function σ are encoded into a single propositional formula. This formula is satisfiable iff there is an argument filter and an RPO which orient a set of inequalities. Each model of the encoding indicates such an argument filter and RPO.

4.1   Dependency Pairs and Argument Filters

We provide here a simplified presentation of the DP method and refer to [1,10] for further details. For a TRS $\mathcal{R}$ over the symbols $\mathcal{F}$, the *defined* symbols $\mathcal{D}_{\mathcal{R}} \subseteq \mathcal{F}$ consist of all root symbols of left-hand sides of $\mathcal{R}$. The signature $\mathcal{F}$ is extended by a fresh *tuple symbol* F for each defined symbol $f \in \mathcal{D}_{\mathcal{R}}$. Then for each rule $f(s_1, \ldots, s_n) \to r$ in $\mathcal{R}$ and each subterm $g(t_1, \ldots, t_m)$ of r with $g \in \mathcal{D}_{\mathcal{R}}$, $F(s_1, \ldots, s_n) \to G(t_1, \ldots, t_m)$ is a *dependency pair*, intuitively indicating that a function call to f may lead to a function call to g. The set of dependency pairs of $\mathcal{R}$ is denoted $DP(\mathcal{R})$. So in Ex. 1(b), add is the only defined symbol and there is one dependency pair: $\mathsf{ADD}(x, s(y)) \to \mathsf{ADD}(y, x)$.

The main result of the DP method states that a TRS $\mathcal{R}$ is terminating iff there is no infinite $\mathcal{R}$-chain of its dependency pairs $\mathcal{P} = DP(\mathcal{R})$. This means that there is no infinite sequence of dependency pairs $s_1 \to t_1, s_2 \to t_2, \ldots$ from $\mathcal{P}$ such that for all i there is a substitution σ_i where $t_i \sigma_i$ is terminating w.r.t. $\mathcal{R}$ and $t_i \sigma_i \to_{\mathcal{R}}^* s_{i+1} \sigma_{i+1}$. Termination proofs in the DP method are stated in terms of *DP problems* which are pairs of the form $(\mathcal{P}, \mathcal{R})$ where $\mathcal{P}$ is a set of dependency pairs and $\mathcal{R}$ a TRS. Such a pair is read as posing the question: "Is there an infinite $\mathcal{R}$-chain of dependency pairs from $\mathcal{P}$?" Hence, termination of $\mathcal{R}$ is stated as the initial DP problem $(\mathcal{P}, \mathcal{R})$ with $\mathcal{P} = DP(\mathcal{R})$.

Starting from the initial DP problem, termination proofs repeatedly restrict $(\mathcal{P}, \mathcal{R})$ to obtain a smaller DP problem $(\mathcal{P}', \mathcal{R})$ with $\mathcal{P}' \subset \mathcal{P}$ while maintaining a soundness property to guarantee that there is an infinite $\mathcal{R}$-chain of pairs from $\mathcal{P}'$ whenever there is an infinite $\mathcal{R}$-chain of pairs from $\mathcal{P}$. Thus, if one reaches the DP problem $(\varnothing, \mathcal{R})$, then termination is proved.

One of the main techniques to restrict DP problems involves the notion of a *reduction pair* $(\succsim, \succ)$ where $\succsim$ is reflexive, transitive, monotonic, and stable and $\succ$ is a stable well-founded order compatible with $\succsim$ (i.e., $\succsim \circ \succ \subseteq \succ$ or $\succ \circ \succsim \subseteq \succ$). But $\succ$ need not be monotonic. Given a DP problem $(\mathcal{P}, \mathcal{R})$ and a reduction pair $(\succsim, \succ)$, the technique requires that (a) the dependency pairs in $\mathcal{P}$ are weakly or strictly decreasing and, (b) all rules in $\mathcal{R}$ are weakly decreasing. Then it is sound to obtain $\mathcal{P}'$ by removing all strictly decreasing dependency pairs from $\mathcal{P}$. It is possible to further strengthen the approach [12,13] by introducing a notion of *usable rules* and considering these in (b) instead of all rules. Arts and Giesl show in [1] that if $(\succsim, \succ)$ is a reduction pair and π is an argument filter, then $(\succsim^\pi, \succ^\pi)$ is also a reduction pair. In particular, we focus on reduction pairs of this form to prove termination of TRS where the direct application of RPO fails.

Example 5. Building on the rule from Ex. 4, consider the TRS (on the left) for addition using an accumulator and its three dependency pairs (on the right):

$$\mathsf{add}(x, y) \rightarrow \mathsf{add}'(x, y, 0) \qquad\qquad \mathsf{ADD}(x, y) \rightarrow \mathsf{ADD}'(x, y, 0)$$
$$\mathsf{add}'(0, 0, z) \rightarrow z$$
$$\mathsf{add}'(\mathsf{s}(x), y, z) \rightarrow \mathsf{add}'(x, y, \mathsf{s}(z)) \qquad \mathsf{ADD}'(\mathsf{s}(x), y, z) \rightarrow \mathsf{ADD}'(x, y, \mathsf{s}(z))$$
$$\mathsf{add}'(x, \mathsf{s}(y), z) \rightarrow \mathsf{add}'(y, x, \mathsf{s}(z)) \qquad \mathsf{ADD}'(x, \mathsf{s}(y), z) \rightarrow \mathsf{ADD}'(y, x, \mathsf{s}(z))$$

To orient the DPs we use $(\succsim^\pi_{rpo}, \succ^\pi_{rpo})$ where $\pi(\mathsf{ADD}) = \pi(\mathsf{ADD}') = [1, 2]$, $\pi(\mathsf{s}) = [1]$, and where $\succsim_{rpo}$ and $\succ_{rpo}$ are induced by the precedence $\mathsf{ADD} >_{\mathcal{F}} \mathsf{ADD}'$ and the status function σ that maps ADD and ADD' to mul. Since the problematic third accumulator argument (in the last two DPs) is filtered away, all three DPs are strictly decreasing and can be removed, as there are no usable rules. This results in the DP problem $(\varnothing, \mathcal{R})$ which proves termination for the TRS.

4.2   Encoding RPO with Argument Filters

To encode argument filters, each n-ary function symbol $f \in \mathcal{F}$ is associated with n propositional variables $f_1, \ldots, f_n$, and another variable $list_f$. Here, f_i is *true* iff $i \in \pi(f)$ or $i = \pi(f)$, and $list_f$ is *true* iff π is not collapsing on f. To ensure that these $n+1$ propositional variables indeed correspond to an argument filter, we impose the following constraints which express that if π collapses f then it is replaced by exactly one of its subterms:

$$\neg list_f \rightarrow one(f_1, \ldots, f_n).$$

To encode the combination of RPO with argument filters, consider again the equations (1) - (4). Each reference to a subterm must now be "wrapped" by the question: "has this subterm been filtered by π?" In the following, similar to the encoding of Sect. 3, all "missing" cases are defined to be *false*. Equations (1') - (3') enhance Equations (1) - (3). Equations (4a') and (4b') enhance Equation (4) in the cases when one of the terms is a variable x and (4c') considers the other case and examines whether the filter collapses the root symbols or not.

$$\tau(f(\bar{s}) \succ_{rpo}^{\pi} t) = \bigvee_{i=1}^{n} \left(f_i \wedge \left(\begin{array}{c} \tau(s_i \succ_{rpo}^{\pi} t) \ \vee \\ (list_f \wedge \tau(s_i \sim_{rpo}^{\pi} t)) \end{array} \right) \right) \ \vee \ \tau_2(f(\bar{s}) \succ_{rpo}^{\pi} t) \tag{1'}$$

$$\tau_2(f(\bar{s}) \succ_{rpo}^{\pi} g(\bar{t})) = \bigwedge_{j=1}^{m} \left(g_j \rightarrow \tau(f(\bar{s}) \succ_{rpo}^{\pi} t_j) \right) \ \wedge \tag{2'}$$

$$\left(list_g \rightarrow \left(list_f \wedge \left((f >_{\mathcal{F}} g) \vee ((f \approx_{\mathcal{F}} g) \wedge \tau(\bar{s} \succ_{rpo}^{f,g,\pi} \bar{t})) \right) \right) \right)$$

$$\tau(s \sim_{rpo}^{\pi} s) = true \tag{3'}$$

$$\tau(f(\bar{s}) \sim_{rpo}^{\pi} x) = (\neg list_f \wedge \bigwedge_{i=1}^{n} \left(f_i \rightarrow \tau(s_i \sim_{rpo}^{\pi} x) \right) \quad \text{for variables } x \tag{4a'}$$

$$\tau(x \sim_{rpo}^{\pi} g(\bar{t})) = (\neg list_g \wedge \bigwedge_{j=1}^{m} \left(g_j \rightarrow \tau(x \sim_{rpo}^{\pi} t_j) \right) \quad \text{for variables } x \tag{4b'}$$

$$\tau(f(\bar{s}) \sim_{rpo}^{\pi} g(\bar{t})) = \left(\neg list_f \rightarrow \bigwedge_{i=1}^{n} \left(f_i \rightarrow \tau(s_i \sim_{rpo}^{\pi} g(\bar{t})) \right) \right) \ \wedge \tag{4c'}$$

$$\left((list_f \wedge \neg list_g) \rightarrow \bigwedge_{j=1}^{m} \left(g_j \rightarrow \tau(f(\bar{s}) \sim_{rpo}^{\pi} t_j) \right) \right) \ \wedge$$

$$\left((list_f \wedge list_g) \rightarrow \left((f \approx_{\mathcal{F}} g) \wedge \tau(\bar{s} \sim_{rpo}^{f,g,\pi} \bar{t}) \right) \right)$$

For the lexicographic comparison with permutations, we enhance Formula (5) to specify the relation between filters and permutations. Only non-filtered arguments are permuted. Moreover, for an n-ary symbol f with $\ell < n$ non-filtered arguments, the permutation should map all ℓ non-filtered arguments to positions from $\{1, \ldots, \ell\}$. Formula (5a') states that if some argument of f is considered at the k-th position (i.e., some $f_{i,k}$ is *true*), then there is exactly one such argument. Formula (5b') specifies that filtered arguments may not be used in the permutation. So if the i-th argument of f is filtered (i.e., f_i is *false*), then the permutation variables $f_{i,k}$ (for $1 \leq k \leq n$) are also *false*. Formula (5c') states that if the i-th argument of f is not filtered (i.e., f_i is *true*), then the i-th argument of f is considered at exactly one position in the permutation. Finally, Formula (5d') expresses that all ℓ non-filtered arguments are permuted "to the left", i.e., to positions from $\{1, \ldots, \ell\}$. Hence, if an argument is mapped to position k, then some argument is also mapped to position $k - 1$.

$$\bigwedge_{k=1}^{n} \left(\bigvee_{i=1}^{n} f_{i,k} \rightarrow one(f_{1,k}, \ldots, f_{n,k}) \right) \tag{5a'} \qquad \bigwedge_{i=1}^{n} \left(\neg f_i \rightarrow \bigwedge_{k=1}^{n} \neg f_{i,k} \right) \tag{5b'}$$

$$\bigwedge_{i=1}^{n} (f_i \rightarrow one(f_{i,1}, \ldots, f_{i,n})) \tag{5c'} \qquad \bigwedge_{k=2}^{n} \left(\bigvee_{i=1}^{n} f_{i,k} \rightarrow \bigvee_{i=1}^{n} f_{i,k-1} \right) \tag{5d'}$$

For the encoding of $f(\bar{s}) \sim_{rpo}^{f,g,\pi} g(\bar{t})$ and $f(\bar{s}) \succ_{rpo}^{f,g,\pi} g(\bar{t})$ when the arguments of f and g are compared lexicographically, we use the notation $\sim_{lex}^{f,g,\pi}$ and $\succ_{lex}^{f,g,\pi}$. For an equality constraint of the form $\bar{s} \sim_{lex}^{f,g,\pi} \bar{t}$ we enhance Equation (6). There must be a one-to-one correspondence between the non-filtered arguments of $\bar{s}$ and of $\bar{t}$ via the permutations for f and for g. To express this, we use a constraint of the form $eq\_arity(f,g)$ in Equation (6′) which states that the number of non-filtered arguments of f and of g are the same. It corresponds to the constraint $(n = m)$ in Equation (6) and is encoded as

$$eq\_arity(f, g) = \bigwedge_{k=1}^{\max(n,m)} \left(\bigvee_{i=1}^{n} f_{i,k} \leftrightarrow \bigvee_{j=1}^{m} g_{j,k} \right)$$

$$\tau(\bar{s} \sim_{lex}^{f,g,\pi} \bar{t}) = eq\_arity(f, g) \wedge \bigwedge_{k=1}^{n} \bigwedge_{i=1}^{n} \bigwedge_{j=1}^{m} \left(f_{i,k} \wedge g_{j,k} \rightarrow \tau(s_i \sim_{rpo}^{\pi} t_j) \right) \tag{6′}$$

Next we enhance Equation (7) to define $\succ_{rpo}^{f,g,\pi} = \succ_{rpo}^{f,g,1,\pi}$. For $m < k \leq n$ we now require that f considers an argument at the k-th position. The remaining cases are structurally identical to the corresponding cases of Equation (7).

$$\tau(\bar{s} \succ_{lex}^{f,g,k,\pi} \bar{t}) = \begin{cases} false & \text{if } k > n \\ \bigvee_{i=1}^{n} f_{i,k} & \text{if } m < k \leq n \\ \bigvee_{i=1}^{n} \left(f_{i,k} \wedge \left(\bigwedge_{j=1}^{m} g_{j,k} \rightarrow & \text{otherwise} \\ \quad (\tau(s_i \succ_{rpo}^{\pi} t_j) \vee (\tau(s_i \sim_{rpo}^{\pi} t_j) \wedge \tau(\bar{s} \succ_{lex}^{f,g,k+1,\pi} \bar{t}))) \right) \right) \end{cases} \tag{7′}$$

For the multiset comparison, we enhance Formula (8) such that the multiset cover only considers non-filtered arguments of $f(\bar{s})$ and $g(\bar{t})$. Formula (8a′) states that if the j-th argument of g is not filtered (i.e., g_j is *true*), then there must be exactly one argument of f that covers it. Formula (8b′) states that if the i-th argument of f is filtered (i.e., f_i is *false*), then it cannot cover any arguments of g. Formula (8c′) specifies that if the j-th argument of g is filtered (i.e., g_j is *false*), then there is no argument of f that covers it. Finally, Formula (8d′) is taken straight from the original Formula (8).

$$\bigwedge_{j=1}^{m} (g_j \rightarrow one(\gamma_{1,j}, \dots, \gamma_{n,j})) \tag{8a′}$$

$$\bigwedge_{i=1}^{n} \left(\neg f_i \rightarrow \neg \bigvee_{j=1}^{m} \gamma_{i,j} \right) \tag{8b′}$$

$$\bigwedge_{j=1}^{m} \left(\neg g_j \rightarrow \neg \bigvee_{i=1}^{n} \gamma_{i,j} \right) \tag{8c′}$$

$$\bigwedge_{i=1}^{n} \left(\varepsilon_i \rightarrow one(\gamma_{i,1}, \dots, \gamma_{i,m}) \right) \tag{8d′}$$

Now we define $\tau(\bar{s} \succsim_{mul}^{f,g,\pi} \bar{t}) = \tau(\bar{s} \succsim_{mul}^{f,g} \bar{t})$. For the encoding of $\succ_{mul}^{f,g,\pi}$ and $\sim_{mul}^{f,g,\pi}$, we restrict Equations (10) and (11) to arguments that are not filtered:

$$\tau(\bar{s} \succ_{mul}^{f,g,\pi} \bar{t}) = \tau(\bar{s} \succsim_{mul}^{f,g} \bar{t}) \wedge \neg \bigwedge_{i=1}^{n} (f_i \rightarrow \varepsilon_i) \tag{10′}$$

$$\tau(\bar{s} \sim_{mul}^{f,g,\pi} \bar{t}) = \tau(\bar{s} \succsim_{mul}^{f,g} \bar{t}) \wedge \bigwedge_{i=1}^{n} (f_i \rightarrow \varepsilon_i) \tag{11′}$$

Finally, for the combination of lexicographic and multiset comparisons, we simply change the equations (12) and (13) to use $\succ_{mul}^{f,g,\pi}$ instead of $\succ_{mul}^{f,g}$ etc.:

$$\tau(\bar{s} \succ_{rpo}^{f,g,\pi} \bar{t}) = \left(m_f \wedge m_g \wedge \tau(\bar{s} \succ_{mul}^{f,g,\pi} \bar{t}) \right) \vee \left(\neg m_f \wedge \neg m_g \wedge \tau(\bar{s} \succ_{lex}^{f,g,1,\pi} \bar{t}) \right) \tag{12′}$$

$$\tau(\bar{s} \sim_{rpo}^{f,g,\pi} \bar{t}) = \left(m_f \wedge m_g \wedge \tau(\bar{s} \sim_{mul}^{f,g,\pi} \bar{t}) \right) \vee \left(\neg m_f \wedge \neg m_g \wedge \tau(\bar{s} \sim_{lex}^{f,g,\pi} \bar{t}) \right) \tag{13′}$$

Example 6. We solved the inequality $\mathsf{ADD}'(x, \mathsf{s}(y), z) \succsim_{(\sim)} \mathsf{ADD}'(y, x, \mathsf{s}(z))$ in Ex. 5 by the argument filter $\pi(\mathsf{ADD}') = [1, 2]$ and RPO. To find such argument filters and the status and precedence of the RPO, such inequalities are now encoded into propositional formulas. Indeed, the formula resulting from our inequality is satisfiable by the corresponding setting of the propositional variables (i.e., $m_{\mathsf{ADD}'} = list_{\mathsf{ADD}'} = \mathsf{ADD}'_1 = \mathsf{ADD}'_2 = true$ and $\mathsf{ADD}'_3 = false$). So we use a multiset comparison for the filtered tuples $\langle x, \mathsf{s}(y) \rangle$ and $\langle y, x \rangle$. Hence, as in Ex. 3 we set $\gamma_{1,2} = \varepsilon_1 = \gamma_{2,1} = true$ and $\varepsilon_2 = false$.

In recent refinements of the DP method [12], the choice of the argument filter π also influences the set of usable rules which contribute to the inequalities that have to be oriented. We showed in [4] how to extend the encoding of LPO and argument filters in order to take this refinement into account as well. In a similar way, this refinement can also be integrated into our encoding of RPO and argument filters. Finally, similar to Sect. 3.3 one can easily show that the size of our encoding is again polynomial.

5   Implementation and Experiments

We implemented the encoding of RPO (also in combination with argument filters) in the termination analyzer AProVE [11], using the SAT4J solver [20]. (We also tried other SAT solvers like MiniSAT [7] and obtained similar results.) The encoding can also be restricted to instances of RPO like LPO or MPO.

We tested the implementation on all 865 TRSs from the TPDB [21]. The experiments were run on a 2.2 GHz AMD Athlon 64 with a time-out of 60 seconds (as in the *International Termination Competition* [19]). For each encoding we give the number of TRSs which could be proved terminating (with the number of time-outs in brackets) and the analysis time (in seconds) for the full collection.

The first two rows compare our new SAT-based approach for direct application of path orders to the previous dedicated solvers for path orders in AProVE 1.2 which did not use SAT solving. The last two rows give a similar comparison for path orders within the DP framework. The columns contain the data for LPO with strict and non-strict precedence (denoted *lpo/qlpo*), for LPO with status (*lpos/qlpos*), for MPO (*mpo/qmpo*), and for RPO with status (*rpo/qrpo*).

	Solver	lpo	qlpo	lpos	qlpos	mpo	qmpo	rpo	qrpo
1	SAT-based (direct)	123 (0) 31.0	127 (0) 44.7	141 (0) 26.1	155 (0) 40.6	92 (0) 49.4	98 (0) 74.2	146 (0) 50.0	162 (0) 85.3
2	dedicated (direct)	123 (5) 334.4	127(16) 1426.3	141 (6) 460.4	154(45) 3291.7	92 (7) 653.2	98(31) 2669.1	145(10) 908.6	158 (65) 4708.2
3	SAT-based (arg. filt.)	357 (0) 79.3	389 (0) 199.6	362 (0) 69.0	395 (2) 261.1	369 (0) 110.9	408 (1) 267.8	375 (0) 108.8	416 (2) 331.4
4	dedicated (arg. filt.)	350(55) 4039.6	374(79) 5469.4	355(57) 4522.8	380(92) 6476.5	359(69) 5169.7	391(82) 5839.5	364(74) 5536.6	394(102) 7186.1

The table shows that with our new SAT encoding, performance improves by orders of magnitude over existing solvers both for direct analysis with path orders and for the combination of path orders and argument filters in the DP framework. Note that without a time-out, this effect would be aggravated. By using SAT, the number of time-outs reduces dramatically from up to 102 to at most 2. The two remaining SAT examples with time-out have function symbols of high arity and can only be shown terminating by further sophisticated termination techniques in addition to RPO. Apart from these two, there are only 15 examples that take longer than two seconds and only 3 of these take longer than 10 seconds. The table also shows that the use of RPO instead of LPO increases power substantially, while in the SAT-based setting, runtimes increase only mildly.

6   Conclusion

In [4] we demonstrated the power of propositional encoding and application of SAT solving to LPO termination analysis. This paper extends this approach to the more powerful class of recursive path orders. The main new challenges were the encoding of multiset comparisons and of lexicographic comparisons w.r.t. permutations as well as the combination with argument filters.

We solved this problem by a novel SAT encoding which combines all of the constraints originating from these notions into a single search process. Through implementation and experimentation we showed that our encoding leads to speedups in orders of magnitude over existing termination tools as well as increased termination proving power. To experiment with our SAT-based implementation and for further details on our experiments please visit our evaluation web site at http://aprove.informatik.rwth-aachen.de/eval/SATRPO/.

References

1. Arts, T., Giesl, J.: Termination of term rewriting using dependency pairs. Theoretical Computer Science 236, 133–178 (2000)
2. Baader, F., Nipkow, T.: Term Rewriting and All That. Cambridge University Press, Cambridge (1998)
3. Codish, M., Lagoon, V., Stuckey, P.J.: Solving partial order constraints for LPO termination. In: Pfenning, F. (ed.) RTA 2006. LNCS, vol. 4098, pp. 4–18. Springer, Heidelberg (2006)
4. Codish, M., Schneider-Kamp, P., Lagoon, V., Thiemann, R., Giesl, J.: SAT solving for argument filterings. In: Hermann, M., Voronkov, A. (eds.) LPAR 2006. LNCS (LNAI), vol. 4246, pp. 30–44. Springer, Heidelberg (2006)
5. Comon, H., Treinen, R.: Ordering constraints on trees. In: Tison, S. (ed.) CAAP 1994. LNCS, vol. 787, pp. 1–14. Springer, Heidelberg (1994)
6. Dershowitz, N.: Orderings for term-rewriting systems. Theoretical Computer Science 17, 279–301 (1982)
7. Eén, N., Sörensson, N.: An Extensible SAT-solver. In: Giunchiglia, E., Tacchella, A. (eds.) SAT 2003. LNCS, vol. 2919, pp. 502–518. Springer, Heidelberg (2004)
8. Endrullis, J., Waldmann, J., Zantema, H.: Matrix interpretations for proving termination of term rewriting. In: Furbach, U., Shankar, N. (eds.) IJCAR 2006. LNCS (LNAI), vol. 4130, pp. 574–588. Springer, Heidelberg (2006)

9. Fuhs, C., Giesl, J., Middeldorp, A., Schneider-Kamp, P., Thiemann, R., Zankl, H.: SAT solving for termination analysis with polynomial interpretations. In: Marques-Silva, J., Sakallah, K.A. (eds.) SAT 2007. LNCS, vol. 4501, pp. 340–354. Springer, Heidelberg (2007)

10. Giesl, J., Thiemann, R., Schneider-Kamp, P.: The dependency pair framework: Combining techniques for automated termination proofs. In: Baader, F., Voronkov, A. (eds.) LPAR 2004. LNCS (LNAI), vol. 3452, pp. 301–331. Springer, Heidelberg (2005)

11. Giesl, J., Schneider-Kamp, P., Thiemann, R.: AProVE 1.2: Automatic termination proofs in the dependency pair framework. In: Furbach, U., Shankar, N. (eds.) IJCAR 2006. LNCS (LNAI), vol. 4130, pp. 281–286. Springer, Heidelberg (2006)

12. Giesl, J., Thiemann, R., Schneider-Kamp, P., Falke, S.: Mechanizing and improving dependency pairs. Journal of Automated Reasoning 37(3), 155–203 (2006)

13. Hirokawa, N., Middeldorp, A.: Tyrolean termination tool: Techniques and features. Information and Computation 205(4), 474–511 (2007)

14. Hofbauer, D., Waldmann, J.: Termination of string rewriting with matrix interpretations. In: Pfenning, F. (ed.) RTA 2006. LNCS, vol. 4098, pp. 328–342. Springer, Heidelberg (2006)

15. Kamin, S., Lévy, J.J.: Two generalizations of the recursive path ordering. Unpublished Manuscript, University of Illinois, IL, USA (1980)

16. Kurihara, M., Kondo, H.: Efficient BDD encodings for partial order constraints with application to expert systems in software verification. In: Orchard, B., Yang, C., Ali, M. (eds.) IEA/AIE 2004. LNCS (LNAI), vol. 3029, pp. 827–837. Springer, Heidelberg (2004)

17. Kusakari, K., Nakamura, M., Toyama, Y.: Argument filtering transformation. In: Nadathur, G. (ed.) PPDP 1999. LNCS, vol. 1702, pp. 47–61. Springer, Heidelberg (1999)

18. Lescanne, P.: Computer experiments with the REVE term rewriting system generator. In: Demers, A., Teitelbaum, T. (eds.) POPL 1983, pp. 99–108 (1983)

19. Marché, C., Zantema, H.: The termination competition. In: Baader, F. (ed.) Proc. RTA 2007. LNCS, vol. 4533, pp. 303–313. Springer, Heidelberg (2007)

20. SAT4J satisfiability library for Java, http://www.sat4j.org

21. The termination problem data base, http://www.lri.fr/~marche/tpdb/

22. Tseitin, G.: On the complexity of derivation in propositional calculus. In: Studies in Constructive Mathematics and Mathematical Logic, pp. 115–125 (1968)

23. Zankl, H., Hirokawa, N., Middeldorp, A.: Constraints for argument filterings. In: van Leeuwen, J., Italiano, G.F., van der Hoek, W., Meinel, C., Sack, H., Plášil, F. (eds.) SOFSEM 2007. LNCS, vol. 4362, pp. 579–590. Springer, Heidelberg (2007)

24. Zankl, H., Middeldorp, A.: Satisfying KBO constraints. In: Baader, F. (ed.) RTA 2007. LNCS, vol. 4533, pp. 389–403. Springer, Heidelberg (2007)

Author Index

Lecture Notes in Artificial Intelligence (LNAI)

Vol. 4434: G. Lakemeyer, E. Sklar, D.G. Sorrenti, T. Takahashi (Eds.), RoboCup 2006: Robot Soccer World Cup X. XIII, 566 pages. 2007.

Vol. 4429: R. Lu, J.H. Siekmann, C. Ullrich (Eds.), Cognitive Systems. X, 161 pages. 2007.

Vol. 4428: S. Edelkamp, A. Lomuscio (Eds.), Model Checking and Artificial Intelligence. IX, 185 pages. 2007.

Vol. 4426: Z.-H. Zhou, H. Li, Q. Yang (Eds.), Advances in Knowledge Discovery and Data Mining. XXV, 1161 pages. 2007.

Vol. 4411: R.H. Bordini, M. Dastani, J. Dix, A.E.F. Seghrouchni (Eds.), Programming Multi-Agent Systems. XIV, 249 pages. 2007.

Vol. 4410: A. Branco (Ed.), Anaphora: Analysis, Algorithms and Applications. X, 191 pages. 2007.

Vol. 4399: T. Kovacs, X. Llorà, K. Takadama, P.L. Lanzi, W. Stolzmann, S.W. Wilson (Eds.), Learning Classifier Systems. XII, 345 pages. 2007.

Vol. 4390: S.O. Kuznetsov, S. Schmidt (Eds.), Formal Concept Analysis. X, 329 pages. 2007.

Vol. 4389: D. Weyns, H.V.D. Parunak, F. Michel (Eds.), Environments for Multi-Agent Systems III. X, 273 pages. 2007.

Vol. 4386: P. Noriega, J. Vázquez-Salceda, G. Boella, O. Boissier, V. Dignum, N. Fornara, E. Matson (Eds.), Coordination, Organizations, Institutions, and Norms in Agent Systems II. XI, 373 pages. 2007.

Vol. 4384: T. Washio, K. Satoh, H. Takeda, A. Inokuchi (Eds.), New Frontiers in Artificial Intelligence. IX, 401 pages. 2007.

Vol. 4371: K. Inoue, K. Satoh, F. Toni (Eds.), Computational Logic in Multi-Agent Systems. X, 315 pages. 2007.

Vol. 4369: M. Umeda, A. Wolf, O. Bartenstein, U. Geske, D. Seipel, O. Takata (Eds.), Declarative Programming for Knowledge Management. X, 229 pages. 2006.

Vol. 4343: C. Müller (Ed.), Speaker Classification. X, 355 pages. 2007.

Vol. 4342: H. de Swart, E. Orłowska, G. Schmidt, M. Roubens (Eds.), Theory and Applications of Relational Structures as Knowledge Instruments II. X, 373 pages. 2006.

Vol. 4335: S.A. Brueckner, S. Hassas, M. Jelasity, D. Yamins (Eds.), Engineering Self-Organising Systems. XII, 212 pages. 2007.

Vol. 4334: B. Beckert, R. Hähnle, P.H. Schmitt (Eds.), Verification of Object-Oriented Software. XXIX, 658 pages. 2007.

Vol. 4333: U. Reimer, D. Karagiannis (Eds.), Practical Aspects of Knowledge Management. XII, 338 pages. 2006.

Vol. 4327: M. Baldoni, U. Endriss (Eds.), Declarative Agent Languages and Technologies IV. VIII, 257 pages. 2006.

Vol. 4314: C. Freksa, M. Kohlhase, K. Schill (Eds.), KI 2006: Advances in Artificial Intelligence. XII, 458 pages. 2007.

Vol. 4304: A. Sattar, B.-h. Kang (Eds.), AI 2006: Advances in Artificial Intelligence. XXVII, 1303 pages. 2006.

Vol. 4303: A. Hoffmann, B.-h. Kang, D. Richards, S. Tsumoto (Eds.), Advances in Knowledge Acquisition and Management. XI, 259 pages. 2006.

Vol. 4293: A. Gelbukh, C.A. Reyes-Garcia (Eds.), MICAI 2006: Advances in Artificial Intelligence. XXVIII, 1232 pages. 2006.

Vol. 4289: M. Ackermann, B. Berendt, M. Grobelnik, A. Hotho, D. Mladenič, G. Semeraro, M. Spiliopoulou, G. Stumme, V. Svátek, M. van Someren (Eds.), Semantics, Web and Mining. X, 197 pages. 2006.

Vol. 4285: Y. Matsumoto, R.W. Sproat, K.-F. Wong, M. Zhang (Eds.), Computer Processing of Oriental Languages. XVII, 544 pages. 2006.

Vol. 4274: Q. Huo, B. Ma, E.-S. Chng, H. Li (Eds.), Chinese Spoken Language Processing. XXIV, 805 pages. 2006.

Vol. 4265: L. Todorovski, N. Lavrač, K.P. Jantke (Eds.), Discovery Science. XIV, 384 pages. 2006.

Vol. 4264: J.L. Balcázar, P.M. Long, F. Stephan (Eds.), Algorithmic Learning Theory. XIII, 393 pages. 2006.

Vol. 4259: S. Greco, Y. Hata, S. Hirano, M. Inuiguchi, S. Miyamoto, H.S. Nguyen, R. Słowiński (Eds.), Rough Sets and Current Trends in Computing. XXII, 951 pages. 2006.

Vol. 4253: B. Gabrys, R.J. Howlett, L.C. Jain (Eds.), Knowledge-Based Intelligent Information and Engineering Systems, Part III. XXXII, 1301 pages. 2006.

Vol. 4252: B. Gabrys, R.J. Howlett, L.C. Jain (Eds.), Knowledge-Based Intelligent Information and Engineering Systems, Part II. XXXIII, 1335 pages. 2006.

Vol. 4251: B. Gabrys, R.J. Howlett, L.C. Jain (Eds.), Knowledge-Based Intelligent Information and Engineering Systems, Part I. LXVI, 1297 pages. 2006.

Vol. 4248: S. Staab, V. Svátek (Eds.), Managing Knowledge in a World of Networks. XIV, 400 pages. 2006.

Vol. 4246: M. Hermann, A. Voronkov (Eds.), Logic for Programming, Artificial Intelligence, and Reasoning. XIII, 588 pages. 2006.

Vol. 4223: L. Wang, L. Jiao, G. Shi, X. Li, J. Liu (Eds.), Fuzzy Systems and Knowledge Discovery. XXVIII, 1335 pages. 2006.

Vol. 4213: J. Fürnkranz, T. Scheffer, M. Spiliopoulou (Eds.), Knowledge Discovery in Databases: PKDD 2006. XXII, 660 pages. 2006.

Vol. 4212: J. Fürnkranz, T. Scheffer, M. Spiliopoulou (Eds.), Machine Learning: ECML 2006. XXIII, 851 pages. 2006.

Vol. 4211: P. Vogt, Y. Sugita, E. Tuci, C.L. Nehaniv (Eds.), Symbol Grounding and Beyond. VIII, 237 pages. 2006.

Vol. 4203: F. Esposito, Z.W. Raś, D. Malerba, G. Semeraro (Eds.), Foundations of Intelligent Systems. XVIII, 767 pages. 2006.

Vol. 4201: Y. Sakakibara, S. Kobayashi, K. Sato, T. Nishino, E. Tomita (Eds.), Grammatical Inference: Algorithms and Applications. XII, 359 pages. 2006.